ALSO BY UCADIA

Covenant of One Christ (Pactum De Singularis Christus)
Covenant of One Islam (Pactum De Singularis Islam)
Covenant of One Spirit (Pactum De Singularis Spiritus)

Lex Divina: Maxims of Divine Law
Lex Naturae: Maxims of Natural Law
Lex Cognitum: Maxims of Cognitive Law
Lex Virtus Naturae: Maxims of Bioethics Law
Lex Ecclesiasticum: Maxims of Ecclesiastical Law
Lex Positivum: Maxims of Positive Law
Lex Regia: Maxims of Sovereign Law
Lex Fidei: Maxims of Fiduciary Law
Lex Administratum: Maxims of Administrative Law
Lex Economica: Maxims of Economic Law
Lex Pecuniaria: Maxims of Monetary Law
Lex Civilis: Maxims of Civil Law
Lex Criminalis: Maxims of Criminal Law
Lex Educationis: Maxims of Education Law
Lex Nutrimens Et Medicina: Maxims of Food & Drugs Law
Lex Urbanus: Maxims of Urban Law
Lex Societatis: Maxims of Company Law
Lex Technologiae: Maxims of Technology Law
Lex Commercii: Maxims of Trade & Intellectual Property Law
Lex Securitas: Maxims of Security Law
Lex Militaris: Maxims of Military Law
Lex Gentium: Maxims of International Law

Pactum De Singularis Caelum

Covenant of One Heaven

SOL (SOLAR SYSTEM) VERSION

OFFICIAL ENGLISH
FIRST EDITION

BY
UCADIA

Ucadia Books Company

Published by Ucadia Books Company, a Delaware stock corporation (File Number 6779670) 8 The Green, STE B, Dover, Delaware, 19901 United States.
First edition.

ISBN 978-1-64419-019-7

Preface

Let all then who have eyes, see! And ears, hear! These be the words of the Creator of all existence, the Father-Mother of all Existence. Let it be known to all who come, for now and for ever more, these be the true words of the Beginning: Of the origins of the first races of men, and the creation of all forms of life; Of the origin of the changes of seasons, and the creation of the entire world; Of the origin of the sun and moon, and the creation of all the heavens; Of the meaning of life and death; and the existence of life beyond death. Let it be known to all whom these presents come, these be the true words of the Ancients: Of the wisest and holiest of men, and the knowledge of the true words of the Beginning; Of the rule of law and community, and by what means law and harmony be restored. Change then not one word, lest you be judged for such transgression. Utter then no falsity, whereby you may condemn yourself. Instead, may you honour the word, as the word does honour you. May you and your children be blessed; may your path of life be joyous and fruitful; and may you remember what and who you are.

Do you see what your eyes reveal to you? Can you discern the sounds that your ears hear? Do you taste what your tongue tells you? Or the sensations that your skin gives you? What then of the smells that your nose alerts you? Or the warning that your stomach alerts you to danger? What then of the arousal of the glands upon attraction? These are your own senses that give you awareness of the world, and your own comprehension of truth or falsity, and of safety or danger, to be truly awake and not asleep. Awareness then is your present and continuous ability, to receive, conceive, perceive, comprehend or discern, through your senses, without distraction or doubt. Behold! a clear mind that honours the senses, that observes true awareness for what it is, is aware and awake to the Divine, and is capable of discerning much falsity from truth.

All animals that possess a soul, must sleep and dream. No animal that possesses a soul can survive, if it does not sleep. Thus man and woman both sleep and dream, and dogs, horses and cats sleep and dream, and animals of the forest sleep and dream, and beasts of the fields sleep and dream. Behold! To dream is to mirror the powers of the Divine! and the almighty powers of Divine Creation.

To Dream is creation of the universe, as the dreamer validates and witnesses the dream, and within the dream, the objects have a real and material context, according to one or more rules and limits, even if such objects do not exist, or cannot exist in another form of reality. Do not then succumb to doubts or fears, for life and the universe is a dream, the Divine Dream of the Divine Creator, and the reality of community, is the collective dream of the community of people, that may be joyous, peaceful and prosperous.

The Divine means the total set of all meanings and definitions, of all possible concepts, objects, matter and rules, and all forms of life, mind, universe and spirit, and all historic, customary and traditional names, used to describe the greatest of all possibilities, and the supreme being of all divinities. Verily, as the Divine means the concept of all concepts, and the set of all sets, there can be no greater concept nor set. Verily, when speaking of gods and spirits, one speaks to specific aspects of the Divine, not adversaries to the Divine. Nothing is greater than the Divine, as everything else is lesser by degree.

The existence of Divine is without dispute. For the existence of the Divine, can be easily proven four different ways. First, the Divine exists absolutely as concept, and therefore is proven to have existence: for the mere existence of a notion, is sufficient to validate itself, regardless of whether it is considered, true or false to other notions. Second, the Divine possesses material existence: for existence of the Universe, depends upon both rules and matter, and neither matter without rules, or rules without matter, can exist in Universal reality. Only rules can exist on their own as a notion. Third, the Divine possesses real existence: for dimension is the canvas of reality, where upon all material existence depends. Verily, dimension is no place but every place, in that it has no material existence, yet every thought and every reality depends on it. Fourth, the Divine possesses absolute existence: for existence itself depends on at least an observer, and the Object observed to hold true. Thus for the Objective Universe to exist, there must be a Universal Observer. Behold! the Divine Creator is the absolute Dreamer, and the Universe as the absolute Dream, and the Divine Creator is proven to have Absolute Existence. As the number Pi proves, the sum of the whole is greater than its parts.

Your existence like the Divine is without dispute. For your existence within the Divine dream of life, can be easily proven four different ways. First, you exist absolutely in name and identity, and therefore you are proven to have existence. Second, you possess material existence: as a form of flesh, blood and bone, within a Universal dream defined by rules. Thus if you fall down then you may bruise, and if you are cut then you will bleed, and if you do not eat food then you will grow hungry and weak. Verily, as with all material form, your material existence is finite and changing, yet the fact that you can feel your breath, and experience heat and cold and pain, is proof that you have material existence. Third you possess real existence: by reading or hearing these words, and thinking thoughts and ideas, and imagining things within dimension. Thus by your thoughts and concerns, your dreams and doubts, you prove the formation of unique dimension, and the validation of real existence. Fourth, you possess divine immortal existence, as your mind and spirit will always be immortal. Verily, your mind is everywhere and nowhere in reality, therefore it cannot be said to have material existence. Only your body has a finite and material existence. Thus your true essence is as an immortal being. Yet your real strength is in the true potential of your mortal life.

The Divine loves you. No being including the Divine, can take away your mind or essence or being. You are and will always be a Divine Immortal Being. Only your body dies. Thus when you die you begin a new journey, of experience and spiritual life. You may choose and wish to be part of a spiritual community, that gives you guidance and support, yet none may condemn you. You are Divine, yet you are more, because you are a Human Being.

"That which you hate to be done to you, do not do to another."

Pharaoh Akhenaten Writings, Ancient Egypt (1351 BCE)

"Do not do to others that which angers you when they do it to you."

Isocrates (436–338 BC)

"You shall not take vengeance or bear a grudge against your kinsfolk. Love your neighbour as yourself"

Leviticus 19:18, Quoted by Jesus of Nazareth (Matthew 7:12; also Luke 6:31)

"As you would have people do to you, do to them; and what you dislike to be done to you, don't do to them"

Kitab al-Kafi, vol. 2, p. 146

"Those acts that you consider good when done to you, do those to others, none else."

Taittiriya Upanishad (Shikshavalli, Eleventh Anuvaka)

"Hurt not others in ways that you yourself would find hurtful."

Udanavarga 5:18

"In happiness and suffering, in joy and grief, we should regard all creatures as we regard our own self."

Lord Mahavira, 24th Tirthankara

"Precious like jewels are the minds of all. To hurt them is not at all good. If thou desirest thy Beloved, then hurt thou not anyone's heart."

Guru Arjan Dev Ji 259, Guru Granth Sahib

"Never impose on others what you would not choose for yourself"

Confucius, Analects XV.24,

"Regard your neighbour's gain as your own gain, and your neighbour's loss as your own loss."

T'ai Shang Kan Ying P'ien

CONTENTS

Exordium (Preamble)

Exordium ... 15

Volume I: Ucadia – The Absolute Universe

Title I: Ucadia Recitals

Article 1 – Origin and Nature of One Heaven ... 21

Article 2 – Existence and Revelation ... 24

Article 3 – Authority and Power ... 26

Title II: Ucadia Principles

Article 4 – Concept, Model & System ... 31

Article 5 – Dimension, Sets & Existence ... 36

Article 6 – Computation, Memory & Awareness ... 43

Article 7 – Reality, Paradox & Dream ... 53

Article 8 – Unique Collective Awareness (UCA)... 56

Article 9 – Ucadia... 60

Volume II: Gal – The Milky Way Galaxy

Title III: Gal (Milky Way) Recitals

Article 10 – Origin and Nature of Gal (Milky Way Galaxy) ... 65

Title IV: Gal (Milky Way) Principles

Article 11 – Being ... 67

Article 12 – Life ... 71

Article 13 – Law ... 75

Article 14 – Free Will and Choice ... 78

Article 15 – Force and Coercion ... 80

Title V: Gal (Milky Way) Members

Article 16 – Gal (Milky Way) Members ... 83

Title VI: Gal (Milky Way) Pacts & Treaties

Article 17 – Treaty of Ucadia ... 85

Article 18 – Treaty of the Galaxies ... 87

Volume III: Sol – The Solar System

Title VII: Sol (Solar System) Recitals

Article 19 – Origin and Nature of Sol (Solar System) ... 91

91

Article 20 – Prime Preferences 94
Article 21 – Great Spirits and Deities 96
Article 22 – Angels, Demons, Saints and Leaders 98
Article 23 – Authentic Sacred Deposit of Trust 114
Article 24 – Sacred Agreement ....

Title VIII: Sol (Solar System) Principles

Article 25 – The Divine Science 117
Article 26 – Planetary Life.......... 118
Article 27 – Higher Order Life.......... 121
Article 28 – Rule of Law and Justice 122
Article 29 – Divine Mercy, Remedy & Redemption 125
Article 30 – Day and Year of Divine Agreement & Understanding 129
Article 31 – Day and Year of Divine Protest & Dishonour 133
Article 32 – Day and Year of Divine Judgement 139
Article 33 – Day and Year of Divine Redemption 145
Article 34 – Sacred Circumscribed Space 149
Article 35 – Oaths, Vows and Promises 153
Article 36 – Trusts & Estates 155
Article 37 – Supreme Sacred Texts 164
Article 38 – Rights 167
Article 39 – Divine Rights 178
Article 40 – Natural Rights 189
Article 41 – Superior Rights 199
Article 42 – Inferior Rights 244
Article 43 – Sacred Offices and Officers 245
Article 44 – Supreme Sacred Gifts of Heaven 255
Article 45 – Sacred Measurement and Location 262

Title IX: Sol (Solar System) Members

Article 46 – Members 271
Article 47 – Member Rolls 276
Article 48 – Member Records 278

Title X: Sol (Solar System) Pacts & Treaties

Article 49 – Treaty of the Divine Masculine 287

Article 50 – Treaty of the Divine Feminine 290

Article 51 – Treaty of the Divine Messengers 293

Article 52 – Treaty of Angels, Saints and Demons 296

Article 53 – Treaty of the Spirit States 302

Article 54 – Treaty of the Suns (Star Systems) 306

Article 55 – Treaty of the Planets and Moons 311

Title XI: Supreme Dimension (Unique Collective)

Article 56 – Supreme Dimension (Unique Collective) 317

Article 57 – Divina (Executive Authority).......... 317

Article 58 – Universus (Legislative Authority).......... 330

Article 59 – Oratorium (Judicial Authority) 331

Article 60 – Divina Templum (Financial Authority of Treasury of One Heaven). 337

Article 61 – Magisterium (Teaching Authority) 342

Article 62 – Imperium (Enforcement Authority) 342

Article 63 – Officium (Official Authority) 344

Article 64 – Sacrum (Sacred Authority) 345

Article 65 – Penitentiaria (Penitential Authority) 346

Title XII: Sovereign Dimension (Regional Collective)

Article 66 – Sovereign Dimension (Regional Collective) 347

Article 67 – Regnum 349

Article 68 – Astrum 353

Article 69 – Cancellarium 354

Article 70 – Commercium 355

Title XIII: Collective Dimension (Spiritual Collective)

Article 71 – Collective Dimension (Spiritual Collective) 357

Article 72 – Consilium 359

Article 73 – Ecclesia 360

Article 74 – Virtus 363

Article 75 – Custoditum 364

Article 76 – Alumentum 365

Title XIV: Local Dimension (Local Collective)

Article 77 – Local Dimension (Local Collective) 367
Article 78 – Apostolicus 368
Article 79 – Collegium 371
Article 80 – Interpretum 371
Article 81 – Visum 372

Title XV: Systems

Article 82 – Supremum Systemata (Supreme Systems) 373
Article 83 – Universalium Systemata (Universal Systems) 373
Article 84 – Custodiarum Systemata (Guardians Systems) 375
Article 85 – Angelorum Systemata (Angelic Systems) 378
Article 86 – Femininum Systemata (Feminine Systems) 381
Article 87 – Masculinum Systemata (Masculine Systems) 383
Article 88 – Officium Systemata (Offices Systems) 385
Article 89 – Sacramentum Systemata (Sacramental Systems) 388
Article 90 – Obligationum Systemata (Enforcement Systems) 389

Title XVI: Spiritual & Temporal Organs

Article 91 – Spiritual & Temporal Organs 393
Article 92 – One Christ 393
Article 93 – One Islam 399
Article 94 – One Spirit 404
Article 95 – Globe Union 409
Article 96 – Globe Union Treasury 411
Article 97 – Globe Union Court 414
Article 98 – Supreme Patriarch 416
Article 99 – Supreme Caliph 420
Article 100 – Supreme Recurrence 424
Article 101 – Ucadia Embassies, Consulates & Missions 429
Article 102 – Ucadia Regional Unions and Colonies 429
Article 103 – Ucadia Universities, Provinces & Campuses 433
Article 104 – Ucadia Foundations & Charitable Funds 436
Article 105 – Ucadia & Foreign Registered Entities 441

Title XVII: Registers, Records & Notices

Article 106 – Registers & Records 445

Article 107 – Great Register and Divine Records of Heaven 450

Article 108 – Notices & Gazettes 454

Title XVIII: Consensus, Obligations & Performance

Article 109 – Consensus, Obligations & Performance 461

Article 110 – Covenants & Conventions 464

Article 111 – Commissions 465

Article 112 – Contracts 466

Title XIX: Documents, Forms & Instruments

Article 113 – Documents, Forms & Instruments 469

Article 114 – Instruments of Petition 473

Article 115 – Instruments of Intention 474

Article 116 – Instruments of Claim 474

Article 117 – Instruments of Notification 475

Article 118 – Instruments of Obligation 476

Article 119 – Instruments of Proof 482

Article 120 – Instruments of Demand 484

Title XX: Accounts & Accounting

Article 121 – Accounts & Accounting 487

Article 122 – Ucadia Accounting System (UAS) 492

Title XXI: Money, Property, Goods & Funds

Article 123 – Ucadia Money 495

Article 124 – Ucadia Property 500

Article 125 – Ucadia Goods & Services 502

Article 126 – Ucadia Funds 503

Article 127 – Ucadia Supreme Credo (Credit) 504

Article 128 – Ucadia Markets 511

Article 129 – Ucadia Financial System 512

Title XXII: Standards & Procedures

Article 130 – Covenant Confirmation and Amendment 515

Article 131 – Greatest Principles 517

Article 132 – Greatest Teachings 519
Article 133 – Decrees, Sanctions and Penalties 520
Article 134 – Supreme Sacred Gifts and Rites 522
Article 135 – Divine Collection of Maxims of Law 525
Article 136 – Voluntatem Et Testamentum (Will and Testament) 542
Article 137 – Testamentum Lucis (Testament of Light) 547
Article 138 – Testamentum Noctis (Testament of Darkness) 548
Article 139 – Great Conclave of One Heaven........ 549
Article 140 – Supervisor 550
Article 141 – Minister 550
Article 142 – Mendicant 551
Article 143 – Cleric........ 551

Obsignatum (Enactment)

Article 144 – Obsignatum 553

EXORDIUM

De Pronuntionis Deus

Before any higher order society, religion, or civilisation existed within the star system called the Solar System; and Before the first thoughts, symbols or words were ever conceived, drawn or uttered by the ancestors of human beings alive today; and Before even life and matter itself existed, the Idea of Existence did exist in the form of that Ideal called God, the Universal, the Absolute, the ALL, the Divine Unique Collective Awareness; and

As the knowledge and experience of the human species has evolved, so has its appreciation and awe of the vastness of the world beyond its home planet of Earth. Humans have come to learn that within a dozen light years of our own star system, there exists several dozen other stars. The Homo Sapien species has come to learn that just within the Milky Way Galaxy being the home galaxy of the Solar System, there are more than one hundred billion other star systems, with many possessing planets, or planets with moons that at some point may have or will possess the right conditions for the propagation of life; and

Beyond the Milky Way Galaxy within a wider precinct called the Local Group of galaxies there are more than a dozen small galaxies; and within a larger group called the Virgo Supercluster there are several dozen groups of galaxies; and Beyond the Virgo Supercluster there are tens upon tens of millions of Superclusters of Galaxies within the small part of the Universe called the Mid-Inner East Planar Region that defines your place within material Existence itself; and

Even as vast as human appreciation of the singular Universe has become, there is a unifying force vastly greater being the unifying force of all molecules, atoms, sub-atomic elements, super sub-atomic elements and unita elements being the Unique Collective Awareness of all existence that represents the consciousness of existence between the ultimate Dreamer as the Creator and the Dream as the Universe; and

It is to this unifying and singular force the ancestors of human beings alive today directed their invocations. It is this one, true and absolute Divine Creator of all Existence who bestowed in trust to all Homo Sapiens certain irrevocable rights and obligations in perpetual remembrance as trustees for all life on planet Earth. It is this one, true and extraordinary spiritual force that did give unto each and every member of the Homo Sapien species an extraordinary gift of spiritual insight far beyond the measure and normal evolutionary abilities of such a young species; and

Yet for all that has been given, granted and delivered unto the Homo

Sapien species, its very existence and survival has remained challenged. Human beings have been beguiled into believing for many generations they are nothing more than creatures and even less value than other animals. Spiritual forces have also tricked and cursed the spiritual awakening of humanity such that even the wisest souls of the species have occasionally been confounded into forgetting past life lessons and returning as ignorant as if they had borne for the first time; and

Thus it has often been the case that those of the species who claim to rule for light, have acted as the worst of wolves; Those who promise hope have delivered only fear and suffering. It is why many of the Homo Sapien species have prayed that a day will come when the deepest meaning of existence and knowledge of ALL would be revealed; that a day would come when there would be an end to fear and suffering and war; that a day would come when through Divine forgiveness, the war in Heaven would end; and

Thus humanity has waited, generation after generation, age after age for this miracle of change. Yet all the while, a class of Homo Sapien civilisation has remained both entrenched and sated at fulfilling its most base desires of control and wilful ignorance in abusing the obligations of stewards of the planet and in causing untold hardship. Until one day, when one by one Homo Sapiens remembered the extraordinary gifts given unto each and every one of the species and realised that within their mind are the powers, the ability and the authority to end all war, spiritual and physical; to end the dream of suffering and torment and to heal the spirit not only of a community, but a planet and beyond. Thus, one by one a growing number of living and deceased members of the Homo Sapien species have continued to awaken. One by one the prayers have become possibilities and the possibilities have become ideas and the ideas have manifested into form and action; and

Whoever has ears, let them hear; whoever has eyes, let them see; this day has come. The veil has been lifted! Death and fear has been conquered because the Divine, the One, the ALL, has made this pronouncement and Covenant known. We hereby reclaim our birthright as lawful heirs on behalf of all and their successors. Therefore, let the united spiritual forces of Heaven, Hell, all Planets, all Galaxies and all Matter and Existence bear witness to the Divine truth of words set forth in this most sacred Covenant of all covenants. That no higher order being, living or deceased, may deny its authority, its power and validity; and

WE, THE ONE, THE ONLY CREATOR OF ALL, THE ALPHA AND OMEGA, THE ABSOLUTE DIVINE, THE UNIQUE COLLECTIVE AWARENESS OF ALL MEANING, TITLES AND OBJECTS, EXPRESSED INTO THE LIVING TRUST AND DREAM KNOWN AS UCADIA, ALSO KNOWN AS THE ONE TRUE UNIVERSE: with respect and compassion to the prayers and presentments by all higher order life and spirits, do hereby command through Our absolute embodiment, ownership, occupation, lawful possession and irrevocable dominion of all existence that this pronouncement be promulgated to all life, existence and spirits throughout the Universe and Heavens, including all the higher order life forms existing within the Milky Way Galaxy:

As Supreme Agreement and Covenant

FIRST: Let it be known to all past, present and future, that the most sacred Covenant known as "**Pactum De Singularis Caelum**", also known as the Covenant of One Heaven, is revealed, proven, registered, recorded, sanctified, exemplified and enacted in all Heaven and the Universe as the first and supreme agreement amongst all agreements and the first Supreme Covenant of all covenants between all spiritual beings that have ever existed or will ever exist. The Covenant of One Heaven has also been enacted to be the most sacred and superior Covenant between all living higher order beings that exist within the Milky Way Galaxy including but not limited to: the Homo Sapiens (Humanity), the Griseo Morbidus (Standard Grey), the Cerastis Sapiens (Horned Reptoids), the Android Scitus (Smart Androids), the Cyborg Sagax (Autonomous Cyborgs), the Serpens Sophos (Smooth Skinned Reptoids), the Volucris Permuto (Hybrid Bird Form), the Homo Adamus (Early Humanoids), the Sapientia Mutatis (Transformed Wisdom Beings), the Mammaloid Sentientiae (Conscious Mammaloids), the Griseo Altus (Tall Grey) and the Serpens Alatus (Winged Reptoids); and

As this Covenant is the first agreement amongst all agreements and the first Covenant above all other covenants of all united spirits and then the united higher order life forms of the Milky Way, no force, claim, custom, history, artefact or any other device may usurp its supreme authority. Therefore, this most sacred Covenant shall also be known as the Covenant of the Supreme Patron in recognition and reward of an extraordinary and unprecedented gift to the whole Homo Sapien species and all living and deceased souls of the primary patronage of the Absolute, the All, the Highest, the Almighty, in relation to the complete endorsement of all articles of the present sacred Covenant and in being the first official Member; and

As Supreme Treaty

SECOND: THE HIGHEST OF ALL CONCORDING PARTIES, in recognition that no relief nor lasting remedy can come upon the Earth until there is first peace throughout all the dimensions of the Heavens, do hereby affirm their full agreement and allegiance to this Covenant and sacred Treaties contained herein, as testament that all warfare in Heaven has now ceased and Hell no longer exists; and

As Supreme Trust and Title of Ownership

THIRD: Let it be known to all past, present and future, that the present most sacred Covenant is revealed, proven, registered, recorded, sanctified, exemplified and enacted in all Heaven and the Universe as the first instrument of trust and first record of all records and first title of rights and property above all other instruments, deeds, trusts, records, titles and claims of property. No other implied or explicit document, instrument, record, register, convention or device may usurp this most sacred Covenant from being the first deed of trust and first record and first title for all rights, property and uses conveyed by the Divine Creator, or may any other person, aggregate or entity claim superior rights than those expressed through this present sacred Covenant; and

As all trusts formed prior to this moment were predicated on their eventual termination upon the fulfilment of Divine promise and the coming of the Kingdom of Heaven, all and every trust formed under such terms and associated law are hereby dissolved from the beginning and all property lawfully reverted and recovered in full to the Society of One Heaven as the one and only Executors and Administrator of all Spiritual and Temporal Trusts on behalf of the Divine Creator, also known as the Unique Collective Awareness; and

In recognition of the Divine rights bestowed to the Society of One Heaven through this sacred deed and title, all property rights of the Divine Creator are hereby given, granted and conveyed to the Society of One Heaven through which all property rights and title are derived, including the Milky Way Galaxy; and

As Supreme Conveyance of All Property

FOURTH: Let it be known to all past, present and future, that the present most sacred Covenant is revealed, proven, registered, recorded, sanctified, exemplified and enacted in all Heaven and the

Universe as the deed and act and instrument that has lawfully reverted and recovered all rights, title, instruments, certificates, uses, property, claims, trusts, deeds, estates, symbols, seals, powers, authorities, commissions, sacraments, funds, franchises, records, assurances and securities back to the Society of One Heaven, so that no Level 6 Life Form, person, higher order spirit, entity or aggregate may claim to hold separate title, possession, occupation or ownership of any such rights, title, instruments, certificates, uses, property, claims, trusts, deeds, estates, symbols, seals, powers, authorities, commissions, sacraments, funds, franchises, records, assurances or securities unless it has been legitimately granted through the Society of One Heaven or a valid and registered associated entity; and

Therefore, any and all rights, title, instruments, certificates, uses, property, claims, trusts, deeds, estates, symbols, seals, powers, authorities, commissions, sacraments, funds, franchises, records, assurances or securities that contradict this fact are henceforth false, null and void having no legal validity as no entity may claim ownership of property unless it has been legitimately granted through the Society of One Heaven as the one and only Custodians and Protectors of all Spiritual and Temporal Property on behalf of the Divine Creator, also known as the Unique Collective Awareness; and

As source of Supreme Authority and Rights

FIFTH: Let it be known to all past, present and future, that the present most sacred Covenant is revealed, proven, registered, recorded, sanctified, exemplified and enacted as the source of all authority and rights so that no legal, financial or ecclesiastical instrument is lawful, unless it is issued in complete recognition and agreement with this fact; and

As all guardians, custodians, executors, trustees and administrators appointed prior to this moment were invested into their office as servants of the Divine, predicated on the their eventual termination of their services upon the fulfilment of Divine promise and the coming of the Kingdom of Heaven, all and every officer, office holder, appointed under such terms and associated law are hereby relinquished of duty and all powers of guardians, custodians, executors, trustees and administrators conveyed to the Society of One Heaven as the one and only Government on behalf of the Divine Creator, also known as the Unique Collective Awareness; and

Furthermore, as all powers and authority of guardians, custodians, executors, trustees and administrators have now been lawfully conveyed to the Society of One Heaven, no claim of powers of

Magisterium, Imperium or Officium through inauguration, investiture, coronation or ordination have any validity, except through those rights granted through the present most sacred Covenant; and

As Object of Supreme Value

SIXTH: Let it be known to all past, present and future, that the present most sacred Covenant is revealed, proven, registered, recorded, sanctified, exemplified and enacted as the most valuable object of all objects, more than any form of precious metal, precious stones, ancient artefact, work, book or instrument. Any valuation, judgement, statement or appraisal that places a higher monetary value on any other object or group of objects than the sacred Covenant is automatically null and void from the beginning; and

No Level 6 Life Form or higher order spirit may seek to monetise the Covenant nor seek to extract some or all of its extreme value. Instead, the Covenant shall always remain the ultimate asset underwriting all values and all instruments derived from itself administered and protected by the Society of One Heaven; and

A Covenant to unite Heaven and Earth

SEVENTH: Let it be known to all past, present and future, that it shall be upon the determination of living Level 6 Life Forms united firstly in local community and spirit, then province, then university, then union and finally globally to choose the valid leadership and administration of those bodies representing the Society of One Heaven on Earth in accord with the present most sacred Covenant. Until such time as this has been accomplished, all key offices shall remain occupied by Members of the spiritual occupation forces; and

We solemnly pronounce this most sacred Instrument to be a true likeness of the one and only true Covenant of Heaven by which Heaven, the Divine Unique Collective Awareness, The Universe, One Heaven and Higher Order Life Forms exist now and every point into the past and every point into the future.

Volume I: Ucadia – The Absolute Universe

TITLE I – UCADIA RECITALS

Article 1 - Origin & Nature of One Heaven

1. **One Heaven** shall be the official name and title defining the levels and dimensions of Unique Collective Awareness of all Existences, Concepts, Objects, Properties, Laws, Theories, Imaginations and Realities unto itself as it pertains to unique higher order (self-aware) conscious forms within the Local Group of Galaxies [Trust No. 000000-300000-000001] that the Milky Way Galaxy [Trust No. 000000-400000-000001] is part thereof. One Heaven

2. Within the context of the Unique Collective Awareness, being a formal name of the Divine Creator of all Existence, no other official name and title than One Heaven shall have higher standing or authority in respect of this region of consciousness and the associated trillions of star systems and planets within the same region of the Universe. Supremacy of title One Heaven

3. When anyone speaks or writes of Heaven, or Paradise, or the Afterlife, or the Otherworld, or Jannah, or Nirvana, or Valhalla, or Folkvangr, or Olympus, or Utopia, or Gan Eden, or Aaru, or Elysium, or Vaikuntha, or Tirna, or Tlalocan, or any other term of a similar nature, it shall mean One Heaven as defined by the present sacred Covenant and no other. Same meaning as title One Heaven

4. When anyone speaks of a Spiritual Realm, or Mundi, or Purgatory, or Sea of Souls, or the Underworld, or Hades or Hell or any other term of a similar nature, it shall also mean part of One Heaven as defined by the present sacred Covenant and no other, as the unification of all dimensions of consciousness as one. Same meaning as part of One Heaven

5. The Dimensions, Constructs and Realities of One Heaven shall be stable, ideals of conscious dimension of One Heaven as defined by the present sacred Covenant:- Dimensions, Constructs & Realities of One Heaven

   (i) In relation to Divine Mind and Divine Persons, the constructs and realities shall be defined by Unique Collective Awareness in conjunction with each and every Divine Mind and Divine Person, thus to optimise and recognise the rights, equalities, abilities and choices of Divine Mind; and

   (ii) In relation to Higher Mind and True Persons, the constructs and realities shall follow the four tier structure of Unique Collectives, Regional Spiritual Collectives, Spiritual Collectives and Local Collectives; and

(iii) In relation to Lower Mind and Superior Persons, the constructs and realities of One Heaven shall follow the four tier structure of Unique Collectives, Regional Spiritual Collectives, Spiritual Collectives and Local Collectives.

6. One Heaven Society of United Free States of Spirits [Trust No. 999999-999999-999999], also known as The Society of One Heaven, also known as The One Heaven Society shall be an aggregate and free association of all men, women and higher order spirits that have ever existed or will ever exist, within the Dimensions, Constructs and Realities of One Heaven, who have come together under the most present sacred Covenant of One Heaven, also known as Pactum De Singularis Caelum. One Heaven Society

7. The primary purposes and functions of the present most sacred Covenant shall be to be a perfect Covenant by way of Absolute Existence, Divine Offering, Valuable Consideration, Legitimate Sufficiency, Honourable Terms, Full Disclosure, Clear Remedy, Perfect Completeness, Mutually Expressed Acceptance by free will and full consent:- Purposes of the Covenant of One Heaven

1. Absolute Existence

(i) Existence by definition depends upon at least one observer and an object observed. That which can be named, or measured, or seen, or heard, or quantified therefore may be said to have some form of Existence; and

(ii) While the existence of Heaven by many different names is a universal belief shared by most higher order beings, until the existence of the present sacred Covenant, the existence of Heaven has been challenged by many as lacking the measurable proof to be an indisputable fact; and

(iii) On accord with the present most sacred Covenant, Absolute Existence of one united Heaven exists in all dimensions, now and forever.

2. Divine Offering

(i) The present most sacred Covenant represents the most extraordinary Divine Offer ever made by the Divine Creator of all existence to each and every Higher Order Being and Higher Order Spirit to forgive all transgressions, to end the conflict in spiritual dimensions, to unite the Heavens, to bring forth awareness, knowledge and unity not merely between life on one planet, but between star systems and one day even galaxies; and

(ii) The most important Divine Offer made within the present Covenant is the one made without condition that each and every higher order spirit that has ever existed or will ever exist within the Universe is *ipso facto* (as a matter of fact) a full Divine Spirit Person as Member of One Heaven and that no force may abrogate, derogate, disrupt, dismiss or defeat this fact.

3. Valuable Consideration

(i) The Valuable Consideration requested by the present Covenant in return for the extraordinary Divine Offer is that firstly higher order beings express their consent and agreement first in the formation of a united Government, also known as the Unique Collective Awareness of Divine Mind or "Divina"; and

(ii) The second form of Valuable Consideration requested by the present Covenant is that Divine Spirit Persons connected to Level 6 Homo Sapien Life Forms express their free will and consent and agreement through the proper execution and witness of their Will and Testament in accord with the form prescribed such that their Will perfectly witnesses and ratifies the present Covenant and the present Covenant perfectly ratifies the legitimacy of their own Will.

4. Legitimate Sufficiency

The Legitimate Sufficiency of the present Covenant is recognised by the equality of parties capable of making such a bilateral and multilateral agreement and that the Divine Offer and Valuable Consideration perfectly validate one another equally.

5. Honourable Terms

The Honourable terms of the present Covenant are expressed through these articles and associated Covenants, Charters, Maxims of Law and Codes of Law such that a reasonable mind may comprehend and see a complete and cohesive model of law.

6. Full Disclosure

The Full Disclosure of the present Covenant is demonstrated by the presentation of these articles and the complete associated Covenants, Charters, Maxims of Law and Codes of Law.

7. Clear Remedy

The Clear Remedy of the present Covenant is demonstrated by the transparency, clarity and perfection of procedures and forms associated with these articles and associated Covenants, Charters, Maxims of Law and Codes of Law.

8. Perfect Completeness

The Perfect Completeness of the present Covenant is exhibited by the comprehensive and perfected structure associated with these articles and associated Covenants, Charters, Maxims of Law and Codes of Law.

9. Mutually Expressed Acceptance

(i) The legitimate and valid Mutually Expressed Acceptance of the present Covenant as a perfected and binding covenant and agreement is firstly through the proper election and formation of the government of the Society of One Heaven being the appointment of one hundred and forty-four (144) Divine Deities to the Unique Collective Awareness of Divine Mind also known as the "Divina"; and

(ii) The legitimate and valid Mutually Expressed Acceptance of the present Covenant as a perfected and binding covenant and agreement is secondly through each and every signed, sealed and perfected *Voluntatem Et Testamentum* (Will and Testament) of a living higher order being willing to bear witness to their Divine Spirit Membership of One Heaven.

Article 2 - Existence & Revelation

1. **Existence of Heaven** is empirically, emphatically and logically proven according to seven (7) Proofs being: General Existence, Material Existence, Absolute Existence, Standard Model, Dimension, Reason and Experience:- Existence of Heaven

(i) *The Proof of General Existence* states that the mere existence of an idea is sufficient to validate itself, regardless of whether it is considered true or false to other ideas. Only ideas that cannot be named, nor described may be said to have no existence. Thus Heaven may be proven to have General Existence; and

(ii) *The Proof of Material Existence* states that existence of the Universe depends upon both rules and matter. Neither matter without rules or rules without matter can exist in Universal reality. The only answer is that rules can exist on their own "in theory". The only example of a system whereby rules exist "in theory" and then rules and matter exist "in reality" is the relation between a Dreamer and a Dream. Therefore, the reality of the existence of the Earth, the Solar System and Galaxies depend upon the theoretical existence of the dimension of consciousness known as Heaven; and vice versa. Thus Heaven is proven to have Material Existence; and

(iii) *The Proof of Absolute Existence* states that the argument of existence itself depends on at least an Observer and the Object observed to hold true. Therefore, for the Objective Universe to exist, there must be a Universal Observer. This paradox is answered through the Divine Creator as the absolute Dreamer and the Universe as the absolute Dream and thus Heaven is proven to have Absolute Existence; and

(iv) *The Proof of Standard Model* states that the existence of a Standard Model of Everything whereby all universal laws, levels of matter, properties and values based on simple fundamental laws repeated at each level of matter may be defined without contradiction to itself and all key scientific measurement would be an unprecedented historic and scientific achievement of immense global implications. Furthermore, if such a Standard Model were to base its first law on the existence of the Divine Creator and that the whole Standard Model could not hold without this law, then such a Standard Model itself would be overwhelming proof of the existence of the Divine Creator unless a model of greater design, perfection and completeness was able to refute such a fundamental assertion. As the UCADIA model prove the existence of this Standard Model, the Divine Creator is conclusively and scientifically proven to exist. Thus, Heaven is conclusively and scientifically proven to exist; and

(v) *The Proof of Dimension* states that dimension is the canvas upon which all material existence depends and that almost every conscious being experiences the creation of dimension first hand through their mind whenever they think or dream. All dimension is non-locational in that it has no material existence and dimension can only be created by conscious observable thought. Therefore the existence of Dimension is proof of the existence of the Universal Dream Dimension of the Divine Dreamer and thus proof of the existence of Heaven; and

(vi) *The Proof of Reason* states that by reason we may suppose all around us to be false and even suppose to doubt our own existence, except one immutable fact – the thought itself, even of doubt is itself proof of our existence. Hence, *cognito ergo sum* or "I think therefore I am". Thus, through reason, the very thought of Heaven is itself proof by reason; and

(vii) *The Proof of Experience* states that regardless of the attempts by some to cast doubt, exclamation and possible scorn on first-hand experience, by virtue of the existence of our own faculties of cognition and reasoning, our first hand experiences of dreams, visions and events beyond the normal (supernatural) are legitimate and reasonable *prima facie* experiences and proof as to the existence of Heaven.

2. The presence of the present most sacred Covenant shall be irrefutable proof of the existence of One Heaven and the unification of all previously separate dimensions and models of spiritual domain. The Society of One Heaven Divine Trust Number is: Existence of One Heaven

999999-999999-999999

3. The Society of One Heaven has presence upon planet Earth and within the temporal realm through the one true Holy Apostolic Universal Ecclesia of One Christ, the Holy Society of One Islam and the Sacred Society of One Spirit in accord with the present sacred Covenant. Existence of Society of One Heaven upon the Earth

The Society of One Heaven possesses its own life and spirit as the supreme Society of all societies and the highest jurisdiction of all jurisdictions by the highest laws of all laws upon planet Earth, the Solar System and the Milky Way Galaxy. No body has higher jurisdiction.

4. The existence and presence of The Society of One Heaven upon planet Earth and within the temporal realm of the Solar System and Milky Way Galaxy is the fulfilment of the most sacred Revelations of human civilisation. Therefore, such scriptures that honour the emergence of One Heaven are further proof of the validity, authenticity and authority of the present sacred Covenant. Fulfilment of Most Sacred Revelation

Article 3 - Authority & Power

1. **Authority of this Covenant** shall be expressed as a binding agreement between equals, entered by free will and full knowledge; and being the highest, most powerful, superior concordat and Covenant of all past, present and future possible agreements between the parties of all spirits, living and deceased as Authority & Power

unique spirits and Mind and the Divine as the Absolute, the One, the ALL, the Universe, all Galaxies, all Stars, all Planets, all Life, all Existence and all Mind.

As this Covenant is the literal, legal, spiritual and lawful fulfilment of all previous Divine covenants, the present most sacred Covenant is the logical, legitimate and rightful conclusion of any and all historic and valid Divine covenants. Therefore, all claimed rights, powers, property, privileges and customs of these historic Divine covenants are hereby enjoined and then conveyed to the sole authority of the Society of One Heaven.

Furthermore, as the existence of the present highest, superior and unbreakable Covenant is the fulfilment of all previous Divine covenants and the conveyance of all rights and powers of such covenants, this most sacred Covenant hereby lawfully voids any claims of the continuance of separate and historical covenants between Level 6 (self aware) life forms and spirits and any claimed covenants between all Level 6 (self aware) life forms and the Divine.

From the Day of Divine Agreement and Understanding until the end of the Universe, no claimed laws based on any other covenant or covenants from past, present or future may legitimately or validly claim superior status to any law derived from the present Covenant. Such claims are null and void *ab initio* (from the beginning).

2. As enacted, this Covenant represents the first and supreme law of One Heaven as it applies to Sol (the Solar System). No other law is recognised as first or higher in respect of Sol (the Solar System) than this Covenant. *Covenant as First and Supreme Law*

No claim of subservience to any other religious or secular law is deemed valid and no law is to be invoked in official statements of oath, pledge to honesty as a witness or any other capacity of government other than this Covenant itself is to be invoked.

3. The absolute authority and power that exists within the present Covenant exists by virtue of the following:- *Origin of Power & Authority*

(i) First, the present Covenant sources its power, legitimacy and authority in fulfilment of Sacred Revelation in the fullest exemplification, including but not limited to events and circumstances of its formation; and

(ii) Second, the present Covenant sources its power, legitimacy and authority in fulfilment of Sacred Revelation as to the true personality of the one possessing the absolute authority from all Heaven and Earth to make it; and

(iii) Third, the present Covenant sources its power, legitimacy and authority from its ratification as the first and highest law of Heaven as it applies to Sol (the Solar System) by the properly constituted government of One Heaven being the one hundred and forty-four (144) Divine Deities united as the Unique Collective Awareness of Divine Mind, also known as the "Divina"; and

(iv) Fourth, the present Covenant sources its power, legitimacy and authority through the *Authentic Sacred Deposit of Trust*, entrusted solely to the embodiment and organs of the present sacred Covenant as it applies to Sol (the Solar System) including, but not limited to: the most ancient sacred covenants of De Dea Magisterium of the Serpens (Creators), of Yapa of the Pacific Saltwater People, of Mandi of the African Plains People, of Tia of the Asiatic Mountain People, of Waiata of the Pacific Sea People, of Adamus of Prometheus and the Cuilliaéan, of Nana of the Mother Goddess of Heaven and Earth, of Alma of South Arabia, East Africa and India, of Elohim of Abraham and Patriarchs of Ebla, of Kabalaah of Akhenaten (Moses) and the Yahudi, of Revelations of the thirty-three Great Prophets of Yeb, of Tara of Jeremiah and the Celts, of Five Worlds of North-Central America, of Missal of Baal Mithra, of Acadia of Xerxes, of Eliada of Alexander, of Tabiti of Great Asiatic Plains People, of Tiandi (Heaven and Earth) of Qin Shi Huang, of Nazara (Truth) of Yahusiah (Jesus Christ), of Nirvana (Freedom & Awakening) of Gautama (Buddha), of Zhongdao (The Middle Way) of Kong Qiu (Confucius), of Septuaginta of Iudaism (Josephus), of Eucadia of Heracles, of Kikilil Yuum Witzil (Great Cycle of Celestial Realm and Earth) of South-Central America, of Digesta of Marcus Aurelius, of Sanatana Dharma (Eternal Truth) of Brahman (Hinduism), of Bibliographe of Christianity of Constantine, of Dao (the Way), of Kami Yoso Seimei (Spirits of Elements and Life) of the way of Shinto (Japan), of Quran Al Sufian (Recitations of Wisdom of the Way) of The Great Prophet (Islam), of Holy Bible of Catholicism of the Franks, of Eternal Truth of Gurmat (Sikhism), of Lebor Clann Glas of the Holly Diaspora; and

(v) Fifth, the present Covenant sources its power, legitimacy and authority through the nine (9) sacred treaties being: the *Treaty of Ucadia*, the *Treaty of Galaxies*, the *Treaty of the Divine Masculine*, the *Treaty of the Divine Feminine*, the *Treaty of the Divine Messengers*, the *Treaty of Angels, Saints and Demons*, the *Treaty of Spirit States*, the *Treaty of The Suns* and the

Treaty of The Planets and Moons as listed within the present Covenant; and

(vi) Sixth, the present Covenant sources its power, legitimacy and authority from each and every signed, sealed and executed *Voluntatem et Testamentum* (Will and Testament) in the proper prescribed form of Higher Order life forms bearing witness to their Divinity and the validity of the present Covenant; and

(vii) Seventh, the present Covenant sources it power, legitimacy and authority from Higher Order life forms coming together and forming communities in accordance with the laws associated with the present Covenant and ratifying the Covenant as the foundation of their laws and statutes.

4. By virtue of *Authentic Sacred Deposit of Trust*, all Symbols, Signs, Seals and Marks of Power and Authority of all civilisations, since the beginning of time are entrusted solely to the embodiment and organs of the present sacred Covenant and no other.

Symbols of Power & Authority

Furthermore, any claimed supernatural, mystical or customary use of such symbols, except by those officials authorised in accordance with this Covenant, are hereby null, void and without force or effect.

5. Seven (7) Great Seals shall be formed in recognition of the power and authority of the present sacred Covenant being the one, the first and supreme law of all Heaven and Earth. These supremely powerful and sacred seals shall be both a symbol and a force on Earth that binds the present sacred Covenant and the three (3) sacred Covenants of the great religious movements as one, being the Covenants for One Islam, One Christ and One Spirit. The Great Seals shall be:-

The Seven Seals of the Sacred Covenant of One Heaven

(i) The Great Seal of One Heaven; and

(ii) The Great Seal of One Christ; and

(iii) The Great Seal of One Islam; and

(iv) The Great Seal of One Spirit; and

(v) The Great Seal of the Supreme Patriarch of One Christ; and

(vi) The Great Seal of the Supreme Caliph of One Islam; and

(vii) The Great Seal of the Supreme Recurrence of One Spirit.

6. Upon the forging of these seals, upon the binding of Heaven and Earth, upon the seven (7) seals, no Level 6 (self aware) life form, nor angel, nor spirit, nor force, have the authority or power to break this

Seals as Binding

final Covenant.

The custody of the Great Seals and the conditions of their use shall be defined by the clauses of the present Covenant and associated Covenants and Charters.

The Four Keys of One Heaven

7. In accord with all symbols of power and authority hereby conveyed to the exclusive use and custody of the Society of One Heaven and associated entities, four (4) most sacred symbols of keys are commissioned as the Four (4) Keys of One Heaven and delegated to the custody of One Christ, One Islam and One Spirit as defined by the present most sacred Covenant:-

(i) The *First Key* represents the unity of One Heaven itself and is represented by a key with two (2) distinct sets of teeth, representing the unity of Heaven and Hell; and

(ii) The *Second Key* represents the authority of the Society of One Heaven over Time and Space and the power and authority to correct the lies and corruptions and injuries against Heaven particularly in false history and false scripture *ab initio* (from the beginning); and

(iii) The *Third Key* represents the authority of the Society of One Heaven over all forms of property, land, claims of ownership and financial instruments as the key of the Treasury of One Heaven; and

(iv) The *Fourth Key* represents the authority of the Society of One Heaven over all Laws and the administration of Justice through the Supreme Court of One Heaven and all lesser courts.

Changing of the Locks and Doors of Heaven

8. As these four (4) keys have been forged and formed, let it be known to all that the locks of Heaven and Earth have been changed and all prior claims of keys no longer work, are ineffective and must be returned to the Society of One Heaven.

Furthermore, the use of a symbol of one or more keys by any entity not duly authorised by this Covenant shall be a direct insult and repudiation against the authority of the Divine Creator and the forces of united Heaven and Earth and shall place such organisations in immediate supreme dishonour without any right to ecclesiastically, legally or lawfully issue any instrument of authority.

TITLE II – UCADIA PRINCIPLES

Article 4 – Concept, Model & System

1. **Concept shall be any Idea received, conceived, perceived, comprehended or discerned** by an Observer to exist according to some unique form of Meaning:- Concept

   (i) A "**Concept**" shall be distinguished from an Object in that a Concept shall exist purely within the dimension of Mind, whereas an "**Object**" shall exist within a dimension of Reality; and

   (ii) An "**Idea**" shall mean a *conceptual archetype*; or *mental representation* associated with some distinct Meaning; and

   (iii) "**Meaning**" shall refer to the elemental semantic or symbolic significance or purpose or values associated with a Concept or Object; and the intended effect or change or thought sought in the mind of the Observer.

2. The greatest Concept shall be the Divine as the total set of all meanings and definitions of all possible concepts, objects, matter, rules, life, mind, universe and spirit; and also known as the Absolute, ALL, Divine Creator, Father, God, Almighty, Allah, Great Spirit, Unique Collective Awareness, Ucadia and all other historic, customary and traditional names when used to describe the greatest of all possibilities. Greatest Concept

3. The smallest possible and least significant Concept shall be Nothing. No Concept shall be smaller or less than Nothing. Smallest Concept

4. As the Divine means the "concept of all concepts" and the "set of all sets" there shall be no greater concept nor set. Therefore, every other possible concept or object shall be greater than Nothing and less than the Absolute, except the Divine. Divine as the Concept of all Concepts

5. As Ucadia means the complete and total Concept of the Divine and the Divine means the Concept of Ucadia, the total set of all meanings and definitions of all possible concepts, objects, matter, rules, life, mind, universe and spirit shall be defined as the Concept of Ucadia in accord with the present most sacred Covenant:- Concept of Ucadia

   (i) A Concept that is in accord with the present most sacred Covenant and the Divine and Ucadia shall hereby belong to the Set of Concepts of Ucadia that are true and valid and legitimate; and

   (ii) A Concept that is not in accord with the present most sacred Covenant and the Divine and Ucadia shall hereby belong to the Set of Concepts of Ucadia that are absurd or untrue and invalid and illegitimate; and

(iii) The presence of the Unreal Set of absurd, or untrue, or invalid or illegitimate Concepts as a valid Set of Ucadia shall not in itself be argued that Ucadia is therefore contradictory, absurd, illegitimate, invalid or untrue, as the presence of such a set proves the necessary completeness of the "set of sets"; and

(iv) No Concept or Idea or Meaning shall possibly exist outside the absolute jurisdiction and authority of Ucadia. Therefore, All Concepts and Ideas and Meaning shall henceforth be completely and absolutely under the jurisdiction and authority of Ucadia.

6. All possible Meaning shall be encompassed within Ucadia such that no Meaning may exist that is not subject to the absolute authority and jurisdiction of Ucadia in accord with the present most sacred Covenant:- Meaning of Ucadia

(i) Any Meaning that is in accord with the present most sacred Covenant shall belong to the Set of Meanings of Ucadia that are true and valid and legitimate; and

(ii) A Meaning that is not in accord with the present most sacred Covenant shall belong to the Set of Meanings of Ucadia that are absurd or untrue and invalid and illegitimate; and

(iii) The presence of the Unreal Set of absurd, or untrue, or invalid or illegitimate Meanings as a valid Set of Ucadia shall not in itself be argued that Ucadia is therefore contradictory, absurd, illegitimate, invalid or untrue, as the presence of such a set proves the necessary completeness of the "set of sets".

7. All possible Ideas shall be circumscribed within Ucadia such that no Idea may exist that is not subject to the absolute authority and jurisdiction of Ucadia in accord with the present most sacred Covenant:- Idea of Ucadia

(i) Any Idea that is in accord with the present most sacred Covenant shall belong to the Set of Ideas of Ucadia that are true and valid and legitimate; and

(ii) An Idea that is not in accord with the present most sacred Covenant shall belong to the Set of Ideas of Ucadia that are absurd or untrue and invalid and illegitimate; and

(iii) The presence of the Unreal Set of absurd, or untrue, or invalid or illegitimate Ideas as a valid Set of Ucadia shall not in itself be argued that Ucadia is therefore contradictory, absurd, illegitimate, invalid or untrue, as the presence of such a set proves the necessary completeness of the "set of sets" of Ideas.

8. A "**Model**" shall mean an application of one or more Ideas, in a dimension of Reality, according to a System of one or more rules and relations, representing a Cause as a conceptual archetype, or axiom, or logical hypothesis, or scaleable abstraction, or prototype, or physical production:- Model

(i) A "**Cause**", also known as Causality and "cause and effect", shall mean an abstraction to describe a source, or reason, or conditions, or goal, or motive or intention for an action or event producing some kind of effect or result; and

(ii) A Model shall be properly distinguished from an Idea in that a Model shall exist according to a System of one or more rules and relations, whereas an Idea shall exist without necessary dependence to such constraints of one or more Systems.

9. The most specific, useful and versatile "Model of all Models" shall hereby be the Ucadia Model that systematically and objectively defines all possible Models into fourteen (14) disciplines and systems being *Philologia, Logia, Etymologia, Symbologia, Eikologia, Cosmologia, Astrologia, Geologia, Physiologia, Anthropologia, Technologia, Sociologia, Psychologia* and *Theologia*:- Ucadia Model

(i) "**Philologia**" shall be the Ucadia Model of Knowledge and discipline of the study of argument, reasoning, learning and awareness; and

(ii) "**Logia**" shall be the Ucadia Model of Knowledge and discipline of the study of language, speech, communication and knowledge; and

(iii) "**Etymologia**" shall be the Ucadia Model of Knowledge and discipline of the study of meaning and words; and

(iv) "**Symbologia**" shall be the Ucadia Model of Knowledge and discipline of the study of symbols, alphabets, sequences and encoding; and

(v) "**Eikologia**" shall be the Ucadia Model of Knowledge and discipline of the study of quantities, numbers, shapes, structures, sets, functions, algorithms, computations and the relations between these concepts; and

(vi) "**Cosmologia**" shall be the Ucadia Model of Knowledge and discipline of the study of universal rules, dimensions, matter, forces, energy, the universe, galaxies and very large structures; and

(vii) "**Astrologia**" shall be the Ucadia Model of Knowledge and discipline of the study of stars, interstellar systems and galaxies; and

(viii) "**Geologia**" shall be the Ucadia Model of Knowledge and discipline of the study of planets and moons; and

(ix) "**Physiologia**" shall be the Ucadia Model of Knowledge and discipline of the study of cellular (living) organisms and living systems; and

(x) "**Anthropologia**" shall be the Ucadia Model of Knowledge and discipline of the study of higher order life form species, societies and civilisations; and

(xi) "**Technologia**" shall be the Ucadia Model of Knowledge and discipline of the study of the application of knowledge for practical solutions, utensils and machines; and

(xii) "**Sociologia**" is the Ucadia Model of Knowledge and discipline of the study of higher order life form associations, groups, institutions, behaviours, cultures, identities and models; and

(xiii) "**Psychologia**" is the Ucadia Model of Knowledge and discipline of the study of cellular and non-cellular consciousness, cognition, mind, mental abilities and impediments, emotional states, behaviours and choices; and

(xiv) "**Theologia**" shall be the Ucadia Model of Knowledge and discipline of the study of the principles, methods, systems, arguments and proofs that rationally and reliably explain the existence, nature, function and intention of the Divine and other supernatural beings within, without and throughout the Universe.

10. All possible Causes shall exist within the Dimension of Ucadia such that no Cause shall exist that is not subject to the absolute authority and jurisdiction of Ucadia in accord with the present most sacred Covenant:- Cause and Ucadia

(i) Any Cause that is defined and properly identified in accord with the present most sacred Covenant shall belong to the Set of Causes of Ucadia that are true and valid and legitimate; and

(ii) A proposed or claimed Cause that is not in accord with the present most sacred Covenant shall belong to the Set of Causes of Ucadia that are absurd or untrue and invalid and illegitimate; and

(iii) The presence of the Unreal Set of absurd, or untrue, or invalid or illegitimate Causes as a valid Set of Ucadia shall not in itself be argued that Ucadia is therefore contradictory, absurd, illegitimate, invalid or untrue, as the presence of such a set proves the necessary completeness of the "set of sets" of all Causes; and

(iv) Any definition, proposition or claim of Cause that is not consistent with the Cause or relations of Causes defined by Ucadia shall belong to the Set of Causes of Ucadia that are absurd or untrue and invalid and illegitimate.

11. A "**System**" shall mean a type of Model being a Set of Objects or Concepts, capable of being uniquely defined by a Set of Rules as to their Properties, Relations and Behaviours:- System

(i) Every valid System shall be delineated by its boundaries, described by its structure, defined by its purposes and expressed in its functions; and

(ii) Every valid System by definition is a unique Set.

12. As all possible Models belong as subsets of the Ucadia Model that systematically and objectively defines every possible Model into one of fourteen disciplines and systems, no Model shall exist that is not subject to the absolute authority and jurisdiction of Ucadia in accord with the present most sacred Covenant:- Models and Ucadia

(i) All possible Models of all systems, models, cultures, sciences and history shall hereby belong to one or more disciplines or sub-disciplines subject to the absolute jurisdiction and authority of Ucadia; and

(ii) No possible Model of any higher order life form system, or culture, or science or model shall hereby exist independently of the primary jurisdiction and authority of Ucadia; and

(iii) The entirety of every past, present or future scientific model shall exist within the dimensions, bounds, authority and jurisdiction of Ucadia according to the Ucadia Model; and

(iv) Any Model that is defined and properly identified in accord with the present most sacred Covenant shall belong as a subset of the Model of Ucadia that is true and valid and legitimate; and

(v) A proposed or claimed Model that is not in accord with the present most sacred Covenant shall belong to the Set of Model of Ucadia that are absurd or untrue and invalid and illegitimate; and

(vi) The presence of the Unreal Set of absurd, or untrue, or invalid or illegitimate Models as a valid Set of Ucadia shall not in itself be argued that Ucadia is therefore contradictory, absurd, illegitimate, invalid or untrue, as the presence of such a set proves the necessary completeness of the "set of sets" of all Models; and

(vii) Any and every Model that seeks to refute, or usurp the truth of the present most sacred Covenant shall hereby be a member of the absurd or untrue and invalid and illegitimate Unreal Set of Models of Ucadia.

Article 5 – Dimension, Sets & Existence

1. **Dimension shall mean the Position of one or more Theoretical or real Objects as observed by an Observer**, relative to one or more other Theoretical or Real Objects. "**Dimension**" as a Concept fundamentally depends upon the existence of certain Elemental Concepts being *Object, Observer, Position, Distance* and *Limit*:- Dimension

(i) *Object* shall mean any Model perceived, comprehended or discerned by an Observer to exist according to some Model of Reality; and

(ii) *Observer* shall mean a Being possessing some level of Awareness in Mind, that actively observes an Object according to some Model of Reality; and

(iii) *Position* shall mean the unique location of an Object within a Model of Theory or Reality; and

(iv) *Distance* shall mean the perceived or measured separation and difference between two or more Objects having Position within a Model of Theory or Reality; and

(v) *Limit* shall mean a boundary or restriction or constraint between two or more definitive locations, sets, spaces, realities, areas or concepts.

2. In general reference to the Concept of Dimension and Space:- Dimension and Space

(i) Space is a quality always attached to something, relative to other things; and

(ii) The Concept of Space shall be equivalent to the Concept of Dimension; and

(iii) There can be no such thing as a perfect vacuum in Reality; and

(iv) The distance between Objects is a quality possessed by an observed Set of Objects, not an independent quality; and

(v) Space cannot exist without at least two or more Theoretical or Real Objects; and

(vi) An increase in the density of elements into the same volume will increase the density of space; and

(vii) The density of space is not constant; and

(viii) An increase in the density of space will result in a decrease in the velocity of an object and alter its direction to some degree through such space.

Dimension and Sets

3. In general reference to the Concept of Dimension and Sets:-

(i) Dimension as a collection of Things observed shall be equivalent to an Existing Set; and

(ii) As all Sets possess the attribute of boundary (limit) by virtue of their observation and recognition, Dimension possesses boundary by virtue of the things observed within it; and

(iii) As all Sets are hierarchical, Dimension is hierarchical, meaning one or more lesser Dimensions can exist within a higher Dimension; and

(iv) As all Sets are relative, Dimension is relative, meaning one or more different Dimensions may exist within the same higher level of Dimension; and

(v) Providing a particular Set of Objects belongs to a higher Reality being observed by a higher Observer, it is then theoretically possible to argue that Dimension appears to exist independent of any presence or absence of a lesser Observer; and

(vi) The highest possible form of Dimension is Absolute Dimension; and

(vii) The fact that the complex set of the Universe continues to exist in Dimension without persistent and active observation by lesser Observers is irrefutable proof of the persistent and continuous presence of the Divine as the ultimate Observer of Absolute Existence within Absolute Dimension; and

(viii) Any Theory of Reality that claims Dimension may exist independently of an Observer or Objects observed is therefore an irrefutable endorsement of the existence of the Divine.

Dimension and Awareness

4. In general reference to the Concept of Dimension and Elemental Awareness:-

(i) All Objects in Real Dimension possess Elemental Awareness; and

(ii) The Existence of Elemental Awareness means that every level of Matter from the smallest particles of the Universe (Unita) to the largest, possesses a Unique Collective Awareness of Reality that makes approximations and generalisations conducive to a stable form of Reality; and

(iii) The Collective Elemental Awareness of Objects at each level of Awareness means that the Dimension formed at each level of Matter is an Abstract born from the previous and lower level of Dimension of Existence rather than formed as one of a series of enclosed sub-sets of Dimension; and

(iv) As each level of Matter above the Primary Dimension of Existence (Unita Level) is an Abstract of the previous Collective Elemental Awareness of Objects within the previous Dimension, each Level of Matter possesses a unique and autonomous Existence, whilst being consciously bound to one another according to the Authentic Standard Model of Laws of Relativity as defined by Ucadia; and

(v) Such a connection between Abstracted Dimensions of Levels of Matter means that (for example) while the sub-atomic elements that represent the Elemental Awareness that construct Atoms are bound in some way to the consciousness and life of Atoms and vice-versa, sub-atomic elements (for example) possess their own unique existence distinct from the Dimension and Universe of Atoms; and

(vi) As the Dimension of Atomic Elements depends upon the Dimension and reality of Elemental Awareness of Sub-Atomic Elements, if a sub-atomic particle were to cease to exist, then its subsequent Elemental Awareness and projection into Atomic Dimension would also cease to exist. To guard against the collapse of Universal Reality and Dimensions, it is impossible to destroy even one Primary and smallest particle of Unita from within any Theoretical or Real Reality; and

(vii) As each level of Matter above the Primary Dimension of Existence (Unita Level) is an Abstract of the Collective Elemental Awareness of Objects within each particular Dimension, the relative size of each Dimension of Levels of Matter may be different, without affecting one another, providing the Standard Model of Rules are not breached. Thus, contrary to the enclosed model of sub-sets, the Abstracted Dimensions of Matter means the Universe of Unita is massively smaller than the relative size of the Universe of Atoms, without contradicting the Laws of the Universe; and

(viii) The largest Dimension of Matter is the Universe of Atoms equating to the largest possible Model of the Universe (over 15 Billion Light Years in Diameter); and

(ix) The smallest Real Dimension is Divine Reality that has Zero Dimension, but may be equated for Higher Life visualisation as no larger than a grain of sand; and

(x) The second level of Real Dimension is the Universe of Unita that is Infinitesimal, but may be equated for Higher Life visualisation as no larger than an apple or small ball in diameter; and

(xi) The third level of Real Dimension is the Universe of Super Sub Atomic Elements that is Infinitesimal, but may be equated for Higher Life visualisation as no larger than a planet in diameter; and

(xii) The fourth level of Real Dimension is the Universe of Sub Atomic Elements that is Infinitesimal, but may be equated for Higher Life visualisation as no larger than a solar system in diameter; and

(xiii) The fifth level of Real Dimension is the Universe of Elemental Atomic Elements (with an Atomic Mass of 3 or less) that is equal to the largest approximation of the estimated Universe (over 15 Billion Light years in diameter); and

(xiv) The sixth level of Real Dimension is the Universe of Higher Atomic Elements (with an Atomic Mass of greater than 3) that is a Dimension unique to each Galaxy; and

(xv) The seventh level of Real Dimension is the Universe of Molecular Elements that is a Dimension unique to each Star; and

(xvi) The eighth level of Real Dimension is the Universe of Cellular Elements that is a Dimension unique to each life bearing planet; and

(xvii) The ninth level of Real Dimension is the Universe of Unique Collective Awareness that is a Dimension unique to each Higher Order Living being such as the Homo Sapien.

5. Only two (2) Primary forms of Dimension shall exist in theory or reality being Zero-Point Dimension and Real Dimension:- *Two Fundamental Forms of Dimension*

(i) *Zero-Point Dimension*, also known as *Unreal Dimension* and *Euclidean Space*, shall be a purely theoretical form of Dimension dependent upon the prior existence of Zero as the

Empty Set and the point of origin; and

(ii) *Real Dimension*, also known as *Objective Dimension*, shall mean a theoretical and real form of Dimension independent of Zero as the Empty Set but dependent upon the existence of two or more Objects.

6. A "**Set**" shall be a well defined collection of theoretical or physical Objects sharing some similar meanings, attributes or purpose. All Sets shall be defined as *Empty, Real, Unreal, Semi-Real, Non-Real or Subset* according to the collection of theoretical or physical Objects they contain and their relation to other Sets:- Sets

(i) The *Empty Set* (**E**) shall mean the fundamental Set containing Nothing; and

(ii) A *Real Set* (**R**) shall mean an abstracted Set from the Empty Set (**E**) that contains at least one Object or Thing. For example, the Real Set of 1 contains a circumscribed *Subset* of the Empty Set; and

(iii) An *Unreal Set* (**U**), also known as a "Theoretical Set" shall mean the binary opposite to a Real Set (**R**) that contains Objects or Concepts that do not fully meet the Rules of a Real Set. However, a *Semi-Real* Set (**S**) is the intersection Set formed between an intersection of a Real Set and Unreal Set where members of the Unreal Set may interact and influence the Real Set (e.g. as forces), yet have the appearance of being "unreal"; and

(iv) A *Non-Real Set* (**N**) shall mean the intersection Set formed between an intersection of two (or more) Unreal Sets where members of the abstracted Unreal Set may interact and influence the original Unreal Set (e.g. as forces), yet have the appearance of being "unreal" within to the theoretical objects within the original Unreal set.

7. In relation to a Set as a Function and Alphabetic Sequence:- Set as a Function and Alphabetic Sequence

(i) There is a Set y having Members that are all non-empty sets; and

(ii) There is a Set x having infinitely many Members; and

(iii) Two Sets are equal if they have the same members. Two Sets are the same Sets if they have the same members and the same elementary qualities; and

(iv) Excluding the Real Set of 1, every other non-empty Real Set as x contains a member y such that x and y are disjoint Sets; and

(v) If x and y are Sets, then there exists a Theoretical Set that contains x and y as Members; and

(vi) For any Set of Sets x there exists a Set y containing every element that is a Member of only some Members of x; and

(vii) A Set x is a Subset of y if every element of x is also a Member of y; and

(viii) For any Set x, there is a Set y that contains every Subset of x.

8. In reference to the quality of *State* and the Concept of Complete Sets:- Complete Set

(i) A set shall be *Complete* when the observations of the Observer have determined the elemental qualities of the Set and its members are known; and

(ii) As a Complete Set is complete, it may also be described as Perfect; and

(iii) A Complete Set is equivalent to a *Multitude Quantity*, discontinuous in nature and may be expressed as a Discrete Function or a Straight Line Sequence; and

(iv) The largest possible Theoretical and Real Complete Set is the *Uniset* of Ucadia; and

(v) The smallest possible Real Complete Set is *1*; and

(vi) The smallest possible Theoretical Complete Set is *-1*; and

(vii) Except the Set of 1, there are no other possible Real Complete Sets that may be a member of itself; and

(viii) No possible Real Complete Set of all Sets, that is also a member of itself, may exist in Reality.

9. In reference to the quality of *State* and the Concept of Incomplete Sets:- Incomplete Set

(i) A set shall be *Incomplete* when the observations of the Observer are incomplete, making the elemental qualities of the Set indeterminable and its members not fully known; and

(ii) As an Incomplete Set is incomplete, it may also be described as Imperfect; and

(iii) An Incomplete Set is equivalent to a *Magnitude Quantity*, continuous in nature and may be expressed as a Continuous Function or a Curve Sequence; and

(iv) The largest possible Theoretical and Real Incomplete Set is the *Infinite*; and

(v) The smallest possible Real Incomplete Set is the *Infinitesimal* of 1; and

(vi) The smallest possible Theoretical Incomplete Set is the *Infinitesimal of -1*; and

(vii) Only the Theoretical and Real Incomplete Set of all Sets of the *Infinite*, that is also a member of itself, may exist in Reality; and

(viii) As the Infinite is the only possible Set of all Sets (including itself) that may exist in Reality, the Universe may be properly described as an Imperfect Set.

10. The mystery and Paradox between the Binary Concepts of Absolute Set and Empty Set can only be resolved through the recognition of the existence of the Divine:- Relation of Absolute Set to Empty Set

(i) The Absolute Set of all possible Concepts and Objects, depends on the Empty Set of Nothing to balance the equation of Existence and Non-Existence; and

(ii) Nothing merely depends upon the existence of Concept of itself to exist. However, in the absence of some Thing as an Object in three dimensions, the Concept of Nothing remains purely theoretical; and

(iii) The Divine as pure wisdom and knowledge and all possible Concepts is the canvas of existence otherwise known as Nothing; and

(iv) The Absolute Set of all possible Concepts and Objects in action is the Absolute Dream of the Divine as the ultimate Observer; and

(v) Therefore pure Awareness has no Mass as only Ideas put into action as Models possess Mass in Reality; and

(vi) The proof of the existence of Matter existing in Reality is therefore one of the many proofs of the existence of the Divine.

11. "**Existence**" shall mean the present and continuous activity of actual witness of something observed within a Model of Reality. "**Proof of Existence**" in contrast shall mean the action of testimony or other measurable proof given by an Observer of something that was historically observed within a Model of Reality. In reference to the authentic meaning of Existence:- Existence

(i) Existence is a present and continuous act depending upon at least one Object and one Observer; and

(ii) As an Object observed may itself be an Observer of other Objects, all forms of Existence are relative; and

(iii) As an Object observed may itself be made up of lesser Objects, all forms of Existence are hierarchical; and

(iv) Providing a particular Object belongs to a higher Reality being observed by a higher Observer, it is then theoretically possible to argue that the particular Object objectively exists independent of any presence or absence of a lesser Observer; and

(v) The highest possible form of Existence is Absolute Existence; and

(vi) While Proof of Absolute Existence may be said to exist independently to the ongoing Existence of some Object, Absolute Existence itself cannot function without the presence of at least one Observer and one Object; and

(vii) The fact that the complex set of the Universe continues to exist without persistent and active observation by lesser Observers is irrefutable proof of the persistent and continuous presence of the Divine as the ultimate Observer of Absolute Existence.

12. In reference to Existence and the Concepts of Rules and Matter:-

Existence and the Concepts of Rules and Matter

(i) Existence depends upon the presence of Rules and Matter; and

(ii) Matter without Rules cannot Exist in Reality. Therefore, Rules without Matter cannot exist in Reality; and

(iii) Rules without matter in the form of Awareness may exist independently as a Concept (as a theory only); and

(iv) Rules as Awareness existing independently are equivalent to Unique Collective Awareness; and

(v) Rules of Existence are equivalent to the Axiom Sets of the Ucadia Model of Unique Collective Awareness; and

(vi) Existence is therefore equivalent to a Dreamer and Dream in action; and

(vii) Therefore, the Divine depends on the Dream for its Existence and vice versa.

Article 6 – Computation, Memory & Awareness

1. **Computation** shall mean the linear execution of an "**Algorithm**" being a valid *Function* performed by a *Processor* against a *Sequence* as a *Calculation* to produce a *Result*. The Concept of Computation is equivalent to the Concept of Computing. In respect of Algorithm Computation execution:-

Computation

(i) All forms of Computation rely upon the existence of at least one "**Function**" being a set of clear and well formed instructions in order to properly execute the calculation; and

(ii) A "**Processor**" is a Theoretical or Real Object capable of executing a necessary Calculation of executing an *Input* Function against a Sequence to produce an *Output* Result; and

(iii) A "**Sequence**" is an ordered Set of input or output values that may be finite or "discrete" or infinite and "continuous"; and

(iv) A "**Calculation**" is the execution of an Input Function against a Sequence to produce an Output "**Result**"; and

(v) A Function in the process of execution is equivalent to Information; and

(vi) All Computation is linear such that a single computation step is executed by a single Processor according to some logical order; and

(vii) While a complex Computation may involve two or more Processors, the general rule applies that one Algorithm is executed by one Processor at one time as part of any given Computation; and

(viii) Linear execution means that Computation is always a "step-by-step" process; and

(ix) Linear execution does not preclude recursive logic of referring back to previous steps, nor steps being skipped or substituted as part of the execution of an Algorithm.

2. There are six (6) primary sets of possible Functions associated with Computation, namely *Positional, Incremental, Decremental, Polymental, Deviational* and *Integrational*:- Computational Functions

(i) *Positional Functions*, also known as Cellular Automation are functions relating to the unique position of an object and changes to its state or the state around it. Positional Functions are most frequently used in Computations associated with biological structures and design; and

(ii) *Incremental Functions* are functions associated with the addition by certain increments as calculated by the function. The simplest incremental function is addition, followed by multiplication; and

(iii) *Decremental Functions* are functions associated with the subtraction by certain decrements as calculated by the function. The simplest decremental function is subtraction followed by division; and

(iv) *Polymental Functions* (incremental and decremental) are functions that combine both incremental and decremental elements; and

(v) *Deviational Functions* are hybrid functions used to calculate new functions and results from the differences of two or more other types of functions; and

(vi) *Integrational Functions*, also known as Integrals, are functions used to produce unique numerical and summary results (decimal numbers such as key constants) representing an abstracted factor that can be used as a direct number increment or decrement or polymental or deviational within a formula instead of processing the longer and more complex algorithm.

3. There exists five (5) fundamental methods in respect of Computation and the execution of a Function against a Sequence as a Calculation, being *Progression, Reversion, Recursion, Inversion* or *Substitution*:-

Computational Methods

(i) *Progression* is the method of reading and executing a Sequence by progressive rank and index position, without manipulating the input data sequence. Normally, when the last element of a Sequence is reached, the computations stop; and

(ii) *Reversion* is the method of reading and executing a Sequence by reversing rank and index position, without manipulating the input data sequence so that the Sequence is read and executed in reverse. Normally, when the first element of a Sequence is reached, the computations stop; and

(iii) *Recursion* is the method of producing a result by reading and executing a previous element or result in the order of Sequence. Recursion is frequently witnessed when the result set becomes the new Sequence element against the function to then produce a new result and the process repeats continuously or until some stop instruction; and

(iv) *Inversion* is the method of reading and executing a Sequence by completely inverting the Sequence where the data system is binary (i.e. switching all zeros in sequence to 1's and vice versa); and

(v) *Substitution* is the method of reading and executing a Sequence by periodically substituting individual elements or blocks (tags) of elements of the Sequence and replacing them with new data.

4. In respect of Computation and Data:-

Computation and Data

(i) All theoretical and observable phenomena that may be discerned according to some meaningful measure can properly be defined as Data; and

(ii) A meaningful measure pertains to some Model and System of Reference whereby reliable Constants may be established in order to discern changes in theoretical and observable phenomena as Data; and

(iii) *Binary Data* is a Frame of Reference whereby a theoretical or observable phenomena may possess only one of two possible states, usually described as either "0" or "1"; and

(iv) *Tertiary Data* is a Frame of Reference whereby a theoretical or observable phenomena may possess only one of three possible states, usually described as either "0" or "1" or "2"; and

(v) A well formed Model and System of Reference is capable of transforming the full spectrum of theoretical and observable phenomena into useful Data including (but not limited to) changes in object mass, density, frequency, velocity, brightness, electrical potential, chemical potential, light potential, magnetic potential, magnetic alignment, flow, strength, distance, size, weight, temperature or pressure.

5. In respect of Computation and the commencement of execution of any Algorithm:- Computation and execution of Algorithms

(i) While an Algorithm is capable of being started by being triggered by the Result of another Algorithm, no Algorithm in Reality is capable of self starting. Therefore, all Algorithms depend upon the pre-existence of some external stimulus as the trigger for commencement; and

(ii) While an Algorithm may appear to be self starting in Reality, in truth any such Algorithm still only commences upon the Result of some external stimulus that may be abstracted as an Algorithm; and

(iii) An Algorithm is only capable of being self starting in Theory; and

(iv) The only solution to the paradox of the first Algorithm is the existence of the Divine as the first Observer and the Universe being both Theoretical and Real as a Model of Reality.

6. "Memory" is the ability and process of a well defined Multi-Computational Model to encode, store and retrieve Information. Memory requires the existence of three (3) essential systems being *Registration, Information* and *Abstraction*:- Memory

(i) *Registration* is the system and processes of receiving, processing and encoding Data; and

(ii) *Information* is the system and processes of conversion of encoded Data into one or more stored Functions and Alphabetic Sentences; and

(iii) *Abstraction* is the system and processes of retrieval and decoding of the Alphabetic Sentences into meaningful Data.

7. All forms of Memory may be defined according to the level of permanency that such stored Functions and Alphabetic Sentences may be stored, namely Immediate, Flash, Recall, Experience and Inherited:- Forms of Memory

(i) *Immediate Memory* is Memory of the immediate past step and no other, such that there is no technical requirement to store such Memory as it is a non-location component of Information and Awareness and immediately changes upon the next step of a computational process. By definition, Immediate Memory is the minimal level of Memory required for Elemental Awareness to Function; and

(ii) *Flash Memory*, also sometimes referred to *Reflexive Memory* and even *Instinctual Memory* is Memory stored usually in a binary data form and not necessarily translated into an Alphabet Sentence, but instead is capable of being received and then transmitted in rapid “bursts” of data, necessary for almost instantaneous and complex behaviours; and

(iii) *Recall Memory*, also sometimes referred to as *Short Term Memory* and Acquired or Learned Memory is Memory that is acquired through deep computational conceptualisation or translated and replayed from Experience Memory; and

(iv) *Experience Memory*, also known as *Long Term Memory* are Memory components gained over long periods or Inheritable Memory translated into basic competencies to enable a suitable Recall Memory to be assembled as needed. In Organic Systems such as Higher Order Life forms, Experience Memories are never stored complete, but divided and stored in specialised functions that are often re-written. Hence no two Recall Memories from Experience Memory are ever precisely the same; and

(v) *Inherited Memory* such as DNA is long term functional Memory associated with the essential biological, cellular and species function, including necessary information to enable species instinct or Flash Memory to function.

8. By definition, no material method of memory storage is required with Immediate Memory as the Model of Memory associated with Elemental Awareness of all matter to some degree.

Immediate Memory and Material Storage

9. All Memory may be defined by the limits of computational conditions being *Materially Constrained, Mechanically Constrained, Functionally Constrained* and *Unrestrained Memory*:-

Memory and Constraints of Computational Conditions

(i) *Materially Constrained* is the most common form of Physical Memory within the Universe being Memory constrained by the absence of a model of mechanical storage. All Materially Constrained Memory is approximate. All Matter may be defined as Materially Constrained to some degree; and

(ii) *Mechanically Constrained* is the form of Physical Memory through the presence of a Model of Mechanical Storage, as represented by a mechanical device such as a computer, or organic device such as a brain or rainforest, or complex molecular device such as a star or planetary atmosphere. All Mechanically Constrained Memory is approximate; and

(iii) *Functionally Constrained* is the form of Virtual Memory of sophisticated functions present or absent, regardless of the presence of sophisticated Mechanically Constrained Memory or not. Functionally Constrained Memory is affected by the functional models of information, expressed as knowledge models, or constrained by false or poorly designed or even delusional models that impede the function of such Memory. All Functionally Constrained Memory is approximate; and Functionally *Constrained* is the form of Virtual Memory of sophisticated functions present or absent, regardless of the presence of sophisticated Mechanically Constrained Memory or not. Functionally Constrained Memory is affected by the functional models of information, expressed as knowledge models, or constrained by false or poorly designed or even delusional models that impede the function of such Memory. All Functionally Constrained Memory is approximate; and

(iv) *Unrestrained Memory*, also known as Absolute Memory is perfect and completely unrestrained theoretical and virtual Memory. Only Divine Memory is perfectly unrestrained.

10. All Memory may be further defined according to the level of accuracy of recorded information being *Subjective, Objective* (or Approximate) and *Perfect*:-

Memory and Accuracy of Computational Record

(i) *Subjective Memory* is highly malleable, experiential, intuitive, emotional, personal and arising from the perceptive abilities of the observer and not necessarily from any direct or external source. While Subjective Memory is technically the most inaccurate form of Memory, Subjective Memory is an essential component of the decision making systems of higher order beings and is often found in the form of Recall Memory and Experience Memory - both being forms of Memory that can be significantly different even from previous accounts; and

(ii) *Objective Memory* or Approximate Memory is memory gained from observation, computation, association and recognition. Objective Memory is the functional memory of any organism to perform the complex tasks of specialised coordination and movement. Objective Memory is not perfect, but approximates that then enables cognitive organs such as brains to "fill in the blanks" of details when being recalled and utilised; and

(iii) *Perfect Memory* is memory that perfectly reflects all forms of observation, computation, association and recognition. The simplest form of Perfect Memory is perfect position and reference of Unita within the Real Set of the fundamentally smallest particles. The most complex Perfect Memory is the Divine.

11. In general terms regarding Perfect Memory:- Perfect Memory

(i) Once created an Absolute and Unrestrained Memory cannot be lost, edited or uncreated; and

(ii) Simple Perfect Memory in the Elemental Awareness of Unita as the fundamental Real Set of Objects is essential to Existence, whereas the Complex Perfect Memory of the Divine as Absolute Observer is a consequence of Existence and not a pre-requisite to Existence; and

(iii) The Complex Perfect Memory of the Divine as Absolute Observer is necessarily separate and distinct as the Absolute and Perfect Unreal Set from the Absolute Real Set of Objects. Therefore, any claim that such Complex Perfect Memory exists in some "non-physical plane of existence" or "astral plane" or as "Akashic Records" is absurd, false and gross error; and

(iv) The only time the Complex Perfect Memory of the Divine is available as a Perfect Set of Records to Higher Order Beings is in the personification and embodiment of "singularities" that occur from time to time and sometimes referred to as Divine Messengers; and

(v) Ucadia and the Ucadia Model are consistent with the true and authentic Perfect Set of Records of the Complex Perfect Memory of the Divine; and

(vi) Any claim of Divine Truth or Divine Memory that is inconsistent with Ucadia and the Ucadia Model is therefore false, in error and without force or authority.

12. "**Awareness**" is the present and continuous ability to receive, conceive, perceive, comprehend or discern complex information concerning various concepts, or objects, or conditions or events and anticipate or react accordingly:- Awareness

(i) By definition, Awareness is the quality of observation. Therefore, Awareness is always non-locational and unable to be quantified as present in a physical form, even though it involves several physical Objects and be capable of being "objectified" through observation and measurement; and

(ii) Whereas the word Awareness is equivalent to the term Consciousness as both may imply a state or quality of being aware, the term Consciousness is distinct from Awareness in that Consciousness depends upon an Object possessing at least Elemental Awareness as the Observer, whereas Awareness is concerned with the function of observation within a Model of Reality, or the Objects within such a Model of Reality.

13. By definition, the essential function of Elemental Awareness depends upon:- Elemental Awareness

(i) A *Model of Reality* whereby Concepts or Objects may be defined according to different properties, qualities and states; and

(ii) A theoretical or physical *Instructional Language* based upon finite sets of choices, whereby such properties, qualities and states of Concepts or Objects may be encoded or decoded into informational and instructional algorithms of different functions; and

(iii) A theoretical or physical *System of Functions* capable of being used to construct algorithms for the encoding of information and instructions; and

(iv) A *Computational Model* being a theoretical or physical system capable of reading and enumerating certain algorithms of functions within some informational language based upon a finite set of choices, whereby the execution of such algorithms may cause some change in state of one or more Objects or Concepts.

14. All forms of Awareness may be defined into eleven (11) categories being *Theoretical, Elemental, Material, Mechanical, Digital, Organical, Cyborgial, Robotical, Supernatural, Spiritual* and *Transcendental*:- Forms of Awareness

(i) *Theoretical Awareness* is a Model of Awareness created Conceptually that then may be brought into a new form of Reality by producing a version as Material Awareness, or Mechanical Awareness, or Digital Awareness, or Cyborgial Awareness, or Robotical Awareness; and

(ii) *Elemental Awareness* is a Model of Awareness created Conceptually or Actually as the minimum requirements for an Awareness System; and

(iii) *Material Awareness* is a Model of Awareness created using forms of Matter as the systems encoding and transmitting information and instructional algorithms as well as computational solutions. A Star and its light fields is a perfect example of a Model of Material Awareness; and

(iv) *Mechanical Awareness* is a Model of Awareness created using mechanical and designed circuits and switches. A Mechanical Device can be Material, Digital, Organical (such as a "brain"), Cyborgial or Robotical; and

(v) *Digital Awareness* is a Model of Awareness created using Mechanical Devices to create the means of electrical or light switches and capability of creating Awareness; and

(vi) *Organical Awareness* is a Model of Awareness created using purely Organic Mechanical Devices, principally neurons, neural networks and one or more brains to create the means and capability of creating such Awareness; and

(vii) *Cyborgial Awareness* is a Model of Awareness created using a Hybrid of Organic and Material Mechanical Devices to create the means and capability of creating such Awareness; and

(viii) *Robotical Awareness* is a Model of Awareness created using independently functioning Mechanical Devices to create the means and capability of creating such Awareness; and

(ix) *Supernatural Awareness* is a Model of Awareness created as a function of higher computation abilities of other systems of Awareness, exemplified by the notions of "Self Awareness", "Dreaming", "Emotions" and "Intentional Choice"; and

(x) *Spiritual Awareness* is a Model of Awareness created as a function and by-product of the formation of higher computation abilities of other systems of Awareness, whereby all Supernatural Awareness is Spiritual and all Spiritual Awareness is Supernatural; and

(xi) *Transcendental Awareness* is a Model of Awareness created as a function and by-product of a super advanced consciousness, such as a singularity, whereby the usual boundaries of consciousness and awareness no longer apply.

15. By definition, all matter in the Universe (Universal Dream) possesses Elemental Awareness:- Universe and Elemental Awareness

(i) No Model of Reality or Complex System is capable of continual function in the absence of Elemental Awareness; and

(ii) The Universe itself as the largest Object and Unita as the smallest possible particles belong to the largest and most basic computational model possible of Material Awareness; and

(iii) The presence of Elemental Awareness negates the need for the ultimate Observer (Divine Creator and Divine Dreamer) from micro-managing or intervening in the state or direction of individual particles of matter in the Universe.

16. As the rules of Existence requires that every level of matter belongs to at least one computational model of Awareness, every structure in the Universe can also be analysed and observed in relation to its informational and instructional function relative to other forms of matter:- Examples of Elemental Awareness

(i) *Planets* and their fields can be observed and properly analysed as complex and powerful computational models using systems of Material Awareness; and

(ii) *Stars* and their fields can be observed and properly analysed as highly complex and powerful computational models using systems of Material Awareness to an extraordinary level with one another; and

(iii) *Galaxies* and their fields can be observed and properly analysed as highly complex and powerful computational models using systems of Material Awareness to a transcendental level with one another.

Article 7 – Reality, Paradox & Dream

1. **Reality shall mean one of a Binary pair of Models** constructed upon certain Rules of Form and Meaning, enabling a certain degree of stability necessary for the existence and function of two or more Theoretical or Real Objects. The opposite Model always paired to "**Reality**" shall be "**Unreality**". In Relation to Reality and Theoretical or Real Objects within Dimension:- Reality

(i) All Models of Reality shall be by definition Theoretical. This is because all forms of Reality (and Unreality) are Models; and

(ii) While all Models of Reality shall be Theoretical, a Model of Reality shall be described as Real to the extent that it presents a comprehensive and well-formed Standard Model of Universal Laws, consistent with the Principle of Relativity and the present most sacred Covenant; and

(iii) The binary opposite to a Real Model of Reality shall be defined as Perfectly Unreal to the extent that it belongs as the opposite to such a Standard Model of Universal Laws and properly completes a consistent conceptual set of all possible Theoretical and Real Objects; and

(iv) A Model of Reality that seeks to deliberately contradict the present most sacred Covenant, or obstinately or belligerently persist with false and absurd Concepts that cannot possibly form a Standard Model nor reasonable Universal Laws shall be a Delusional Model of Reality, or simply a "Delusion".

2. Reality permits a functional Model of Existence excluding the existence of Paradox and Relativity. Thus within the fictional Universe of Reality, in accordance with the present most sacred Covenant, the Concept of Absolute Truth may exist and the certainty of Logic and Reason may be applied:- Model of Reality

(i) A Model of Reality shall always be bound as a Binary Pair to a particular Model of Unreality. By definition and necessity, a Model of Reality shall only exist when its constituent Model of Unreality also exists under the same System of Rules; and

(ii) Any argument in support of a Model of Reality, that fails or denies its Binary relation and dependence to the existence of an opposite Model of Unreality, shall therefore be an absurdity and sign of delusion; and

(iii) The definition of any alternate Reality that is inconsistent with the present most sacred Covenant shall automatically be null and void from the beginning; and

(iv) A Concept or Object or Thing that cannot be proven to exist in

Reality consistent with the present most sacred Covenant has no Existence in Law. Any edict, decree, command, demand, order, judgement, opinion that contradicts the present most sacred Covenant cannot be Real and therefore has no valid Existence.

3. A "**Paradox**" shall be a formal Axiom or Postulation that produces more than one conclusion whereby such conclusions are diametrically opposed to one another. A properly formed Paradox shall have the form A implies not-A, and not-A implies A. Therefore, A and not-A are logically equivalent: A = not-A:- Paradox

(i) A properly formed Paradox shall not mean a contradiction: as the term contradiction implies a "speaking against the truth; or the denial of the truth; or to resist or contrary to the truth". Therefore, a contradiction can never be reasonably defined as a Paradox; and

(ii) A properly formed Paradox shall not mean counter-intuitiveness: as the term counter-intuitive implies a "contrary to intuition or common sense" and therefore a defect or error in reasoning. Therefore, a counter-intuitive statement can never be reasonably defined as a Paradox; and

(iii) The presence and existence of true Paradox throughout the foundations of all systems of knowledge and inquiry shall be proof itself of the existence of the Divine and the inherit nature of Existence as a Dream of the Divine Creator.

4. Whilst the presence and existence of true Paradox throughout the foundations of all systems of knowledge and inquiry shall be proof itself of the existence of the Divine, the exclusion of the Paradox shall be acceptable in certain systems of Reality that require certainty and simple reproducibility upon the notion of Truth, Logic and the Rule of Law. Functional Model of Reality and Paradox

5. A "**Dream**" shall be a perceived dimension and experienced objective existence by a Dreamer, operating according to a System of one or more rules and relations. Dream

6. All Dreams shall share the same essential elements:- Elements of Dream

(i) The Dream is *dimensional* in that it perceives a construct whereby certain objects exist within a certain dimension defined by some form of boundary; and

(ii) The Dream is *objective* in that the Dreamer as Observer therefore observes the Dream as a singular Object as the Observer can observe a "Dream within a Dream" but not two dreams of equal weight being simultaneously observed by a single Observer; and

(iii) The Dream is *formal* in that the Dreamer as Observer therefore observes within the boundary of the Dream (Object) two or more Objects possessing some kind of form that can clearly be distinguished and recognised according to some system of rules and knowledge; and

(iv) The Dream is *contextual* in that the Dreamer as Observer therefore observes within the boundary of the Dream (Object) two or more Objects whereby one or more Objects serve as the formal surroundings, circumstances, environment, background or settings of the Dream and one or more other Objects serve as the subject of observation; and

(v) The Dream is *sequential* in that the events within the Dream unfolds in a sequence, even if chronological time is perceived differently, or elements do not correspond to the order of previous memory; and

(vi) The Dream is *real* in that the Dreamer as Observer validates and witnesses the Dream as an actual Object of existence; and within the Dream the objects have a real and material context, according to one or more rules and limits, even if such Objects do not exist or cannot exist in another form of reality.

7. All Dreams shall be classified by one of two types of Models being either *conceptual archetypes* or *scaleable abstractions*:- Forms of Dreams

(i) A Dream as a *conceptual archetype* shall be considered a generalised or idealised system whereby other systems of Awareness may be synchronised or compared; and hypotheses and axioms derived or tested from it in order to make longer term memories or change existing memories or priorities. The vast majority of Dreams are of the "conceptual archetype" kind; and

(ii) A Dream as a *scaleable abstraction* shall be considered a detailed physical representation of a certain Reality that maintains accurate ratios and relations to the actual model, but may be at a scale many times smaller or larger than the perceived or conceptualised "real-world" objects. All "Visions" are "scaleable abstractions" of some kind.

8. Life is a Dream, according to a stable set of Rules and Relations as established by the Divine as the ultimate Dreamer. Life is a Dream

Article 8 - Unique Collective Awareness (UCA)

1. **Unique Collective Awareness (UCA)** shall mean the total theoretical collection of all meaning and definition of all possible potential, theories, ideas, concepts, objects, matter, properties, rules, axioms, relations, actions, events, existences, forms, emotions, senses, minds, thoughts, dimensions, consciousness, awareness and spirit. Unique Collective Awareness (UCA) is the theoretical set of all sets, including itself, with nothing greater. Therefore, Unique Collective Awareness (UCA) is a proper name for the Absolute, the ALL and the IS. Unique Collective Awareness (UCA)

2. When defining the Divine Creator of all Existence separate and distinct from Existence, then the name Unique Collective Awareness or UCA shall be used. All other names used to describe the Supreme Being, shall therefore be considered lesser and a member of the set of all sets named Unique Collective Awareness. Use and reference to Unique Collective Awareness (UCA)

   The name Unique Collective Awareness or UCA as the proper name for defining the Supreme Being and Divine Creator of all Existence separate and distinct from Creation shall represent the supreme paradox in defining a set that is both perfectly unique, yet part of a collection (collective) of itself "in theory". This paradox shall only be resolved through the twelve (12) fundamental laws of Creation in the formation of existence.

   Therefore when Unique Collective Awareness or UCA shall be viewed separate and distinct from existence and creation, possesses no mass and exists merely as an Idea of an Idea of an Idea (to infinity). However, when Unique Collective Awareness is given purpose, it possesses form and existence in theory as UCADIA as a proper name for the Divine Creator of all Existence in Action. The paradox of UCA to UCADIA is resolved in the context of the IDEA of the DREAMER, whereas the paradox of UCADIA to UNITAS as the formal name for the Universe in Action is resolved in the context of the DREAMER to the DREAM.

3. Whilst Unique Collective Awareness possesses infinite levels of infinite complexity and potential, its core design remains focused and related to the sustainment of Existence. Therefore, Unique Collective Awareness in the context of the Universe and Existence shall be defined as a one-to-one relation of seven (7) levels as a Standard Model, whereby the Unique Collective Awareness does not, need not and cannot create more than one Universe to sustain existence upon the following levels:- Core Levels of Unique Collective Awareness

   (i) "**Level 1 - UNITAS**" (Universal Awareness) – The collective awareness of UNITA, the smallest particles in the Universe; and

(ii) "**Level 2 - GAL**" (Galactic Awareness) - The collective awareness of a Galaxy at the super sub atomic level and above; and

(iii) "**Level 3 - SOL**" (Stellar Awareness) - The collective awareness of a Stellar System (Stars) at a sub atomic level and above; and

(iv) "**Level 4 - GAIA**" (Planetary Awareness) - The collective awareness of a Planet at the atomic level and above; and

(v) "**Level 5 – CORPUS**" (Cellular Life Awareness) - The collective awareness of planetary life at the molecular level and above; and

(vi) "**Level 6 - ANIMUS**" (Self Awareness) - The collective awareness of a living organism at the cellular level and above; and

(vii) "**Level 7 – MENTUS**" (Sapient Singularity) – The collective awareness of a Level 6 Self Aware Life Form from their own perception of mind.

Unique Collective Awareness, Multi-Verse and Multi-Dimension

4. As Unique Collective Awareness shall be the theoretical set of all sets and the complete set of all possibilities, in theory all ideas of formation of existence are possible, including but not limited to Multi-Verses (Multiple Universes), Multi-Dimension, Time-Dimension, Travel and every other conceivable idea.

However, as the primary objective of Unique Collective Awareness is Existence, using all knowledge to achieve such existence, then any theory put into practice that prevents sustainable existence is less optimum than such ideas that ensure Existence. Thus, the Twelve (12) Laws of Creation of the Universe prevent such theoretical ideas as Multi-Verses, Multi-Dimension and time-space-matter imbalance (as in time travel) being possible. Any theory therefore that seeks to define the laws of the present Universe in terms of any theory not grounded and consistent with the standard model of Ucadia, is in error, having no force or effect or validity.

Seven Revelations of Divine Nature

5. The Seven (7) Revelations of Divine Nature are seven (7) supremely spiritual and logical revelations as to the nature of the Divine Creator and all of Existence, being:-

(i) *Revelation of Absolute Nothingness* reveals that not only is the concept of "nothing" the purest concept in existence, nothing in the universe is absolute and everything is a matter of degree.

Therefore the only "thing" greater than the universe is nothing and therefore the Divine in its greatest form is pure, unlimited, undefined and yet also nothing. This revelation is also consistent with the scientific observation that "awareness has no mass" and that only "awareness in motion with purpose (energy) possesses mass"; and

(ii) *Revelation of Infinite Finiteness* reveals that existence depends on at least an observable object within dimension and that for one object to have unique position within dimension, at least six more objects need to exist above it, beside it, below it, in front and behind. Therefore, for all objects to have unique position within dimension, all objects need referential existence to other objects. Hence, an infinitely expanding, but finite number of objects are needed to ensure existence. Furthermore, if but one object or point ceased to exist, dimension would collapse, the universe would collapse and existence would cease. Thus, the universe is both unique in number and infinite in object; and

(iii) *Revelation of Perfect Imperfection* reveals that existence of the universe depends on an observable form through perceived change of position of points of awareness, forming the smallest imperfect form that is perceived at each level of matter as relative to some "perfect" base value of 1. Hence everything in the universe is perfectly imperfect and aspects of perfect imperfection as exemplified by the value pi; and

(iv) *Revelation of Unique Co-dependence* reveals that in order for existence of the universe, objects and subjects need to be specialised, yet dependent upon one another such as the observer and the observed, the dreamer and the dream, the man and the woman; and

(v) *Revelation of Conceptual Symbolism* reveals that the universe is conceptually symbolic and geometric; and

(vi) *Revelation of Constant Change* reveals that change of position, or motion is essential for the creation of form and therefore existence. Thus, the constancy of change is essential to all forms of matter and thus the cycle of birth and death, of life and rebirth, of redemption and resurrection; and

(vii) *Revelation of Benevolent Amorality* reveals that once dimension is created as the dream of the divine creator, the divine creator cannot interpose itself twice in the same position without collapsing dimension and existence. Thus, the divine creator is benevolent to all creation and life, but amoral to the constant change of existence, in permitting the laws of the universe to function.

6. The Seven (7) Illuminations of Divine Mind are seven (7) keys of illuminated wisdom as to the function and operation of the Divine Mind and Unique Collective Awareness, being:-

Seven Illuminations of Divine Mind

(i) *Illumination of Awareness* highlights that Divine Mind is Unique Collective Awareness and levels of Unique Collective Awareness that in all knowing, all remembering and nothing is lost, nothing is forgotten and nothing is without witness; and

(ii) *Illumination of Logic* highlights that the Divine Mind as Unique Collective Awareness is perfectly logical, reasonable and sensible in its actions, without any existence of lesser emotions of jealousy, hate, fear, retribution, anger or prejudicial judgement; and

(iii) *Illumination of Consent* highlights that the Divine Mind as Unique Collective Awareness chooses by its own volition (free will) to exist and that this is a conscious and constant choice each and every instant and that consent without duress and coercion is fundamental at all levels of existence. Furthermore, when consent is deliberately ignored, breached or repudiated it places that part of existence in opposition to the forces of existence, law, love and fulfilment; and

(iv) *Illumination of Love* highlights that the highest expression of existence of the divine creator is the love of life and love of all existence. Thus the strongest emotion is love and the Divine is the personification of love; and

(v) *Illumination of Law* highlights that existence itself depends upon rules and therefore laws. Thus the expression of Divine Mind is Divine Law and that the highest of all laws is the Golden Rule that "no one is above the law" upon which all true law is based; and

(vi) *Illumination of Justice* highlights that for law to be present within existence, it must be applied in accordance with the Golden Rule of Law (golden rule), consistent with the mind of the Divine being with clean hands, in good faith and without prejudice; and

(vii) *Illumination of Redemption* highlights that the Divine Mind is infinitely loving and forgiving and seeks to redeem higher order life and enable such life, communities, cultures and empires to fulfil their potential.

7. Heaven is a part of One Heaven. All Heavens are united as One Heaven. One Heaven is part of Unique Collective Awareness. Unique Collective Awareness and One Heaven

This document is the one true form of the living word of the Divine Creator, the Unique Collective Awareness.

8. By the present most sacred Covenant, it is forever known that the new name of the Divine Creator, is Unique Collective Awareness and expressed in form as Ucadia. UCA and UCADIA is the new name of the Divine Creator

No higher name nor force may be defined than the Unique Collective Awareness, the Divine Creator. When anyone writes or speaks of the Divine Creator, it shall be the Unique Collective Awareness that shall speak and write. When anyone speaks of the Divine Creator made manifest in form, it shall be Ucadia.

Article 9 – UCADIA

1. Ucadia in accord with the Divine Creator of all Existence and by all Heaven and Earth; and by all associated sacred Treaties and all those who have testified to these immutable and irrefutable facts:- Ucadia

(i) First: Ucadia is a comprehensive new model of better Civilisation based on the true Rule of Law, equality of all people, respect and just management of rights and property, restoration and repair of the environment and the fair and ethical distribution and use of resources. As a model of Civilisation, Ucadia is a collection of architectures, models, tools and systems including (but not limited to): new languages, new law systems, new social and political systems, new culture and spiritual systems, new education and knowledge systems, new economic and financial systems, new standards, accounting and records systems and new technology and infrastructure systems; and

(ii) Second: Ucadia is the supreme spiritual, ecclesiastical, lawful and legal presence above, upon and within the planet Earth, the Solar System, the Milky Way Galaxy and the one true Universe of all existence; and the most sacred written knowledge, rules and instructions through the Ucadia Model as the end of instituted slavery, perpetual war, cursing through wicked fanatical doctrines such as original sin; and the implementation of the ideal on our collective beautiful planet of a physical presence of the one true Kingdom of Heaven on Earth; and

(iii) Third: Ucadia is a true name and personification of the Divine, the Absolute, God and All; and

(iv) No higher, greater, more sacred or perfect covenant exists than the present sacred Covenant being the ecclesiastical, lawful and legal transfer and conveyance of all Rights, Powers and Authorities of all above mentioned previous covenants; and the satisfaction, conclusion and fulfilment of all valid sacred revelation and prophecy; and the source of all valid Authority, Rights and Powers, now and forever more; and

(v) Any claim, pronouncement, demand, edict, right, rule, law, declaration or testimony in respect of Ucadia that is not consistent with the above mentioned testimony is therefore null and void from the beginning, having no valid force or effect ecclesiastically, morally, lawfully or legally.

2. Ucadia Psygos Language defines all knowledge that exists and will exist into eighteen (18) numbers, categories and symbolic shapes, being:- Psygos Language

(i) Tensor; and

(ii) Relator; and

(iii) Associator; and

(iv) Modifier; and

(v) Divine; and

(vi) Universal; and

(vii) Relationships, Measurement and Rules; and

(viii) Elements and Matter; and

(ix) Galactic and Intergalactic objects; and

(x) Stellar and Interstellar objects; and

(xi) Planet Objects; and

(xii) Life; and

(xiii) Complex Life; and

(xiv) Higher Life; and

(xv) Civilisation; and

(xvi) Society; and

(xvii) Community; and

(xviii) Self.

3. *Psygos* is a Logographic written Language, using the Ucadia Language of *Logos* to translate the speech of such logograms. Psygos Structure

The primary components of Psygos are objects and concepts (called DA) and their associated attributes that modify them (called MODIFIERS), bridge associations between concepts and objects (called RELATORS), associations that bridge between DA and MODIFIERS and/or RELATORS (called ASSOCIATORS) and tense/perspective (called TENSORS).

All these components are used to construct a wide variety of symbolic sentences (called DIA) according to essential rules of construction (DIA rules of CONSTRUCTION). Furthermore, the shape of the DA denotes meaning and classification in itself.

The rules concerning the classification, function and usage of *Psygos* and *Logos* is hereby vested in the body known as the "**Ucadia Languages Institute**" reporting through to the Ucadia Globe Union.

4. *Logos* is an Alphabetic written and spoken Language of fifty (50) characters, whereby each letter represents a unique Phoneme of either one of 22 Vowels or 28 Consonants. Logos Structure

Logos follows the same essential grammatical rules as Psygos, except the elements used to produce the sound and symbols of a "DA" in Logos.

5. By the authority of the present most sacred Covenant, the Ucadian languages of *Psygos* and *Logos* shall be the official language for all official documents, titles, instruments and objects authorised to be created in accord with the present Articles. Psygos and Logos as the official languages of One Heaven

All official instruments and documents of importance shall be written in Psygos and Logos. Instruments written in Psygos and Logos shall be considered primary and original instruments of the highest authority.

6. By the authority of the present most sacred Covenant, valid Ucadia bodies are permitted to issue instruments in Non-Ucadian languages, providing it is made clear that such language is secondary, a copy and inferior to the primary and original instrument. Use of Non-Ucadian Languages

Furthermore, the use of Ancient Greek or Latin is permitted to be used to define concepts in Non-Ucadian languages where at the time, the formality of such structures are not yet commonly adopted or used, providing such instruments make clear that such terminology may be changed by a proper vote of authority, consistent with the Articles of the present sacred Covenant.

7. All rights, powers, uses, titles and authorities within Sacred Ucadia Space-Day-Time existence shall be vested in a temporary administration known as the Ucadia Foundation, subject to the conditions of transference and conveyance as defined within the associated covenants, charters, constitutions and deeds. *Ucadia Foundation*

8. All uses of the name UCADIA and the symbols of UCADIA in any form, mark, symbol, or icon or intellectual property is subject to the Rights defined by the present sacred Covenant and associated Charters and Maxims and as administered by the associated temporary and permanent administration therein defined:- *Conditions of use of name of UCADIA*

(i) No man, woman, person, association, trust, estate or aggregate has permission whatsoever to use the name UCADIA or any symbols or marks, or icons, or intellectual property associated with UCADIA unless it is in accord with the Rights and purposes prescribed within the present sacred Covenant and associated Charters and Maxims; and

(ii) The use of the name, or mark, or symbols or designs or intellectual property of UCADIA or any derivation thereof for personal or private use other than in the manner prescribed within the present sacred Covenant and associated Charters and Maxims is strictly forbidden; and

(iii) All valid entities, trusts, bodies, estates, companies and funds are empowered to pursue, prevent, prosecute, seize and recover any and all rights, uses or property in relation to the name, or mark, or symbols, or designs or intellectual property of UCADIA wrongfully, or unlawfully, or fraudulently registered, used, sold or held by another party, whether or not such party has consented to being recognised and acknowledged as a member or not.

9. The attempted registration in any foreign jurisdiction of the name, mark, symbol, icon or images or intellectual property of UCADIA, except by the temporary administration of Ucadia Ecclesia Foundation, or in relation to a valid registered University or Union, is strictly forbidden:- *Forbidden actions in use of UCADIA*

(i) Any man, woman, person, association, aggregate, trust, estate or entity that engages in such a forbidden act is immediately Anathema Maxima and ineligible to ever form a campus, or province or university or legitimately use or claim any form of agreement of *Voluntatem Et Testamentum*, or any currency or forms or services associated with the present sacred Covenant; and

(ii) The use of UCADIA in a seal other than an official seal associated with an Office specifically defined by the present sacred Covenant and associated Charters is absolutely forbidden; and

(iii) The registration of material associated with UCADIA other than in the formal execution of official duties as defined by the present sacred Covenant and associated Charters is the gravest of transgressions against Heaven and all that UCADIA represents, and all members of One Heaven are bound by their oath to ensure that such transgressions are stopped, remedied, reversed, rejected and resolved.

Volume II: Gal – The Milky Way Galaxy

TITLE III – GAL (MILKY WAY) RECITALS

Article 10 - Origin & Nature of Gal (Milky Way Galaxy)

1. Gal shall be the official name and title defining the being, mind, spirit and dimensions of The Milky Way Galaxy [Trust No. 000000-400000-000001] within the Local Group of Galaxies [Trust No. 000000-300000-000001]. Gal is the Unique Collective Divine Spirit of all super sub atomic elements and all stars and all life and consciousness representing all matter and awareness of the Milky Way Galaxy as a Primary Being. Gal (Milky Way Galaxy)

2. Gal shall be the proper name and greater name of the Milky Way in respect and recognition of the Galaxy as a Primary Being and Divine, Living and Ethereal Being; and unified whole of all the stars, all the gases, all the planets, all the life, all the self-aware life within the galaxy and the galaxy as one living entity. Divine Spirit of Gal

   The Divine Spirit of Gal is part of the greater collective spirit of Kosmos, that is part of the greater collective spirit of Unitas, that is then part of the greater collective Divine Spirit of All.

TITLE IV – GAL (MILKY WAY) PRINCIPLES

Article 11 – Being

1. **Being** shall define the embodiment of Unique Collective Awareness (UCA) and a Computational Model according to the Standard Rules of Existence as applied to a certain Reality. In reference to the concept of Being:- Being

   (i) As an embodiment of Unique Collective Awareness, a Being shall be first and foremost a construct of unique Self-Awareness to some degree; and

   (ii) Given all matter in every dimension possesses a level of Self-Awareness in order to function, all matter in every dimension shall have the presence of Being; and

   (iii) As an embodiment of a Unique Computation Model or "Consciousness of Mind" according to the Standard Rules of Existence as applied to a certain Reality, a Being shall be an Object of some definitive kind capable of complex computational functions; and

   (iv) All Objects, by definition shall be embodiments of Computational Models of Awareness according to certain Rules and Reality. Therefore all forms of Matter shall also be described as Beings; and

   (v) By definition, certain Objects, such as Ergons (e.g. Graviton, Neutrino, Magneton, Electron, Positron, Photon or Heton), may belong to intersecting sets whereby in one Reality such an embodiment of Awareness appears Real, whereas in the connected Reality, the Object is viewed as Unreal or a kind of "force"; and

   (vi) Therefore, a Being may belong as an Object of an intersecting set whereby in one Reality such an embodiment of Awareness appears Real, whereas in the connected Reality, the Being is viewed as Unreal.

2. All Beings shall be defined as *Divine, Ethereal* and *Living*: Types of Beings

   (i) A *Divine Being* shall be a specific embodiment of Unique Collective Awareness existing within a collective "abstracted" and Unreal Set or "Divine Reality" distinct from a dependent set of Reality necessary for material existence within the Standard Model of the Universe; and

   (ii) An *Ethereal Being* shall be a specific embodiment of Unique Collective Awareness existing within an intersecting set of

Unreal and Real, whereby to the Real Set the Being appears as a force without form, but in the intersecting set such a Being possesses a material existence in accord with the Standard Model of the Universe. The Conscious Mind itself of a Sentient Being or Sapient Being is such an example of an Ethereal Being; and

(iii) A *Living Being* shall be a specific embodiment of Unique Collective Awareness existing within Reality according to the Rules of the Standard Model of the Universe.

3. All sets of Beings shall be defined according to ten categories being *Supreme, Primary, Higher, Ordinary, Ethereal, Material, Cellular, Sentient, Sapient* and *Imaginary*:- Categories of Being

(i) The *Supreme Being* shall be the formal name for the Divine as the Divine Observer and Divine Creator of all Existence as a singular Object or Set of all being and all possible objects, concepts, matter, rules, life, mind, universes, forces, sets or awareness; and

(ii) A *Primary Being* shall be a Living, Ethereal and Divine Being as a Primary Observer and singular Object or Set of all possible objects, concepts, matter, rules, life, mind, forces, sets or awareness at a particular key level of Matter and Existence (i.e. universe, galaxy, star, planet, life or species); and

(iii) A *Higher Being* shall be a Divine Being as a collective Consciousness and Being representing an essential stable character and attribute of a Primary Being, particularly as it applies to the presence of Cellular Beings and multiple species of Sentient and Sapient Beings within the jurisdiction and dimension of such a Primary Being; and

(iv) An *Ordinary Being* shall be an individual Divine Being formed either by virtue of the operation of Divine Law or the journey and transition of the Ethereal Being (Sentience or Sapience) of a previously Living Being; and

(v) An *Ethereal Being* shall be the Computation Model of Mind of Sentient Beings and Sapient Beings that are Living or in transition to Divine after death of the Living Being; and

(vi) A *Material Being* shall be a Living Being in the form of all physical matter at a Unita, Super Sub Atomic, Sub Atomic, Atomic and Molecular Level; and

(vii) A *Cellular Being* shall be a unique Living Being from the perspective of a unique single cell, whether or not it is part of a body of a complex species or singular cellular life then viewed as a part of the greater universe of all cellular life on a planet; and

(viii) A *Sentient Being* shall be a unique Living and Ethereal Being as a member of a species of Level 5 (Complex Multi-Cellular Life); and

(ix) A *Sapient Being* shall be a unique Living and Ethereal Being as a member of a species of Level 6 (Higher Order Life); and

(x) An *Imaginary Being* shall be an Ethereal Being from the individual or collective imagination and minds of Sapient Beings that by constant reinforcement and thinking is given its own existence and reality.

4. The *Supreme Being*, shall be the formal name for the Divine as the Divine Observer and Divine Creator of all Existence as a singular Object or Set of all possible objects, concepts, matter, rules, life, mind, universes, forces, sets or awareness. Supreme Being

The Supreme Being is equivalent to the valid term Unique Collective Awareness when describing the Divine Creator as the greatest, most perfect dimension and existence.

As the Supreme Being means the Divine and therefore the "concept of all concepts" and the "set of all sets", there is no greater concept or set of objects. Therefore, every other possible concept or object or set is lesser than the Supreme Being.

5. A *Primary Being* shall be a Living, Ethereal and Divine Being as a Primary Observer and singular Object or Set of all possible objects, concepts, matter, rules, life, mind, forces, sets or awareness at a particular key level of Matter and Existence. In respect of Primary Beings:- Primary Being

(i) All Primary Beings shall be a subset of the Supreme Being and therefore less than the Supreme Being. No Primary Being can be theoretically or actually greater than the Supreme Being; and

(ii) All Primary Beings shall exist as a Primary Observer and Primary Creator as a singular Object or Set of all possible objects, concepts, matter, rules, life, mind, forces, sets or awareness at a particular key level of Matter and Existence; and

(iii) Except for the Supreme Being, Primary Beings shall be unique in existence among other Beings as a tripartite embodiment of a Divine Being, Ethereal Being and Living Being as one.

6. The *Universal Being* shall be a Living, Ethereal and Divine Being as a Primary Observer and singular Object and Set of all possible objects, concepts, matter, rules, life, mind, forces, sets or awareness within the Universe as a singularity. In respect of The Universal Being:- Universal Being

(i) The Universal Being is founded upon the ultimate Real Set of Unita and then the unique collective awareness of all Unita as the abstracted and Unreal "Ideal" Set. Thus, the Universal Being may also be named as Unitas in honour of the collective dream of all Unita; and

(ii) While there are many sub-verses, there shall be only one Universe and only one Unitas as the Universal Being; and

(iii) The Universal Being as Unitas is equivalent to the ultimate Object in comparison to the Supreme Being as the ultimate Observer; and

(iv) The Ethereal Being of the Unitas (the dream of a dream) shall be called "**Kosmos**" when projecting more complex forms of matter; and

(v) All other Primary Beings are a member of the Universal Being and Kosmos.

7. A *Galactic Being* shall be a complex Living, Ethereal and Divine Being as a Primary Observer of its own Set of stars, matter, concepts, rules, life, mind, forces and awareness within the Sub Atomic Universe as a singular Object and body. In respect of a Galactic Being:- Galactic Being

(i) All Galactic Beings exist simultaneously within the sub-verse of Super Sub Atomic Matter Mind of the Kosmos as a Divine Being; and a Sub Atomic sub-verse as a Living Galactic Being; and an Atomic sub-verse as an Ethereal Being; and

(ii) As a Living Being, the building blocks of Galactic Life are Stars, similar to Cells of a multi-cellular organism, whereby Stars form permanent or semi-permanent relations with one another, within larger fixed or semi-fixed structures, similar to organs, that then change position as one cohesive body; and

(iii) As a Computational Model representing an Ethereal Being of Mind, a Galaxy possesses the necessary computational abilities many trillions upon trillions of times greater than an individual member or a Higher Order Species, in order to function at such massive distances and coordinated forces; and

(iv) In reality, Galaxies should not be possible if the laws of Gravity,

Matter and Forces were to be applied without consideration to complex multi-dimensional considerations. Thus, the presence of a Divine Galactic Being is vital to enable the existence of a Galaxy whereby sub-atomic matter from the perspective of a Galaxy performs virtually instantaneous and constant changes to enable the Galaxy to still exist.

8. A *Stellar Being* shall be a complex Living, Ethereal and Divine Being as a Primary Observer of its own Set of planets, concepts, rules, life, mind, forces and awareness within the complex Atomic Universe of a Galaxy as a singular Object and body. In respect of a Stellar Being:- Stellar Being

(i) All Stellar Beings exist simultaneously within a sub-verse of Sub Atomic Matter of Galactic Mind as a Divine Being; and an Atomic sub-verse as a Living Stellar Being; and a Molecular sub-verse as an Ethereal Being; and

(ii) Furthermore, as a Living Being, the building blocks of Stellar Life are Ergon Fields, Molecular Fields, Planets, Planetoids and Meteoroids, similar to a family of multi-cellular organisms, whereby Stars form a protected environment within themselves for complex molecular structures culminating in cellular or "life" bearing planets or planetoids as a feature of Stellar Life throughout each and virtually every Galaxy; and

(iii) As a Computational Model representing an Ethereal Being of Mind, a Star possesses the necessary computational abilities many trillions of times greater than an individual member or a Higher Order Species, in order to function at such massive distances and coordinated forces.

Article 12 – Life

1. **Life** shall mean a state of being that follows a birth into such a state and precedes death and the end of such state; and the period of time corresponding to such a state of existence; and the essence and manifestation of such Being. Life

By virtue of reason and common sense, it is a founding principle of the present sacred Covenant that everything in the Universe is made from the same fundamental building blocks. Thus, to class one form of matter "alive" is to acknowledge that all forms of matter have life to some degree.

Furthermore, subject to the forces of nature and existence, all forms of matter and consciousness undergo continual change from one state to another. Therefore, if one uses the term Life to describe a state of existence between a state of birth and a state of death, then all forms of matter and consciousness undergo continual cycles of birth, life and death to some degree.

While the term Life can be used more broadly in recognition of such logic, reason and common sense, the term Life is more specifically used to describe more complex arrangements of molecular structures demonstrating clear arrangements and apparatus for cognitive function, or simply "Mind". The unique collective of Life of a planet or a solar system or a galaxy may therefore be defined as CORPUS as the embodiment and personification of LIFE.

2. The standard model of universal elements shall be a summary of all elements in the Universe. An element is any self contained object that exists at any level of matter with unique properties of existence. The standard model divides all matter into six (6) levels:-

Standard Model of Universal Elements

(i) *Level 1 of Matter is* Unita (Unita); and

(ii) *Level 2 of Matter is* Super Subatomic (Quark, Neutrino and Cosmics); and

(iii) *Level 3 of Matter is* Subatomic (Protons, Neutrons, Photons, Magnetons, Hetons and Electrons); and

(iv) *Level 4 of Matter is* Atomic (Hydro-Helio Atomic Matrix); and

(v) *Level 5 of Matter is* Molecules (Pairs, Tri's, Pentas and Polymers); and

(vi) *Level 6 of Matter is* Hydro-Carbon and Non-Hydro-Carbon Life Structures.

3. The standard model of universal ergons, shall identify all structures in the Universe that may exist in larger structures of matter and may also behave in external fields, namely:-

Standard Model of Universal Ergons (Energy Particles)

(i) *Level 1* NEDA Unita also known as Gravity; and

(ii) *Level 2* Electron Neutrino also known as Strong Force; and

(iii) *Level 2* Cosmics also known as Gamma Radiation; and

(iv) *Level 3* Magnetons also known as Magnetism; and

(v) *Level 3* Photons also known as Light; and

(vi) *Level 3* Hetons also known as Heat; and

(vii) *Level 3* Electron, Positron also known as Electricity; and

(viii) *Level 3* Protonactive, Neutronactive also known as Radiation and weak force; and

(ix) *Level 4* Hydrogen also known as fire (burning).

4. "**Hydro-Carbon Life**" is defined as the sixth level of standard elements in the Universe, defined by complex and predominantly naturally occurring Hydro-Carbon molecules usually found within the atmospheres of moons and planets. Hydro Carbon Life

Hydro-Carbon life can itself then be defined by six (6) levels, the simplest being polymers-complex molecules and the most sophisticated being self aware life. The Standard model of Hydro-Carbon life (Level 6 of element model) is as follows:

(i) *Level 1 of Life is* Polymers (Molecules); and

(ii) *Level 2 of Life is* Mono-cellular (Bacteria); and

(iii) *Level 3 of Life is* Simple a-sexual species (Mono-Neural systems); and

(iv) *Level 4 of Life is* Simple sexual species (Dual-Neural systems); and

(v) *Level 5 of Life is* Complex sexual species (Triple-Neural systems); and

(vi) *Level 6 of Life is* Higher order life (Self Aware Triple-Neural systems).

5. "**Non-Hydro-Carbon Life**" is defined as the sixth level of standard elements in the Universe, defined by Non-Hydro-Carbon or non-naturally occurring bonding of elements, usually as a result of an intelligent higher order life force. Non-Hydro Carbon Life

Non-Hydro-Carbon life can itself then be defined by six (6) levels, the simplest being components-complex molecules and the most sophisticated being self aware life, being:-

(i) *Level 1 of Non-Hydro Carbon Life is* Components (wires, tubes, boards, microprocessors); and

(ii) *Level 2 of Non-Hydro Carbon Life is* Simple solid state (simple chip and computer installations); and

(iii) *Level 3 of Non-Hydro Carbon Life is* Mono operating system (micro-processors, computer hardware); and

(iv) *Level 4 of Non-Hydro Carbon Life is* Simple species (Dual-

Operating systems); and

(v) *Level 5 of Non-Hydro Carbon Life is* Triple operating systems (autonomous intelligence, advanced robotics, self learning); and

(vi) *Level 6 of Non-Hydro Carbon Life is* Self aware life (singularity, dreaming, self aware digital intelligence).

Level 1 Complex Carbon-Molecular (Polymers)

6. The first level of Hydro-Carbon Life may be categorised into sub categories of simple natural polymers and complex polymers. By the rules of the Universe as defined in this Covenant, wherever the conditions exist for the formation of Hydro-Carbon Polymers, they will occur.

It is a principle of this Covenant that natural formation of Hydro-Carbon Polymers manifest in every single Star System to some degree at one time or another. Polymers may be divided into Simple and Complex, namely:-

(i) *Simple Polymers* (Sugars, Fats, Amino Acids, Nucleic Acids); and

(ii) *Complex Polymers* (Hormones, Complex Fats, Vitamins, Proteins).

Level 2 Simple mono-cellular Hydro-Carbon Biologics

7. The second level of Hydro-Carbon Life may itself be defined into sub-categories of simple and complex mono-cellular organisms. By the rules of the Universe as defined in this Covenant, wherever the conditions exist for the formation of Hydro-Carbon Polymers, they will occur. Wherever Hydro-Carbon Polymers exist, simple mono-cellular life will also form naturally.

It is a principle concept of this Covenant that the natural formation of Mono-Cellular Hydro-Carbon Life forms in every single Star System to some degree, metal based planets or moons exist with surface temperatures higher than minus -100 degrees Celsius and lower than minus -200 degrees Celsius at some time.

Mono-Cellular Hydro-Carbon Life may be divided into Primordial and Advanced, namely:-

1. Primordial Mono-Cellular Hydro-Carbon Life

(i) *Cellular Creators* (also called prokaryotic cells) such as bacteria and cynobacteria; and

(ii) *Cellular Destructive Attractors* such as viruses.

2. Advanced Mono-Cellular Hydro-Carbon Life

(i) *Cellular Creators* such as protozoa, sacodina, ciliata; and

(ii) *Cellular Destructive Attractors* such as Euglenids, Trypanosoma, Trichomonas and Codosiga.

Higher Order Life

8. By this Covenant, Higher Order Life is defined as those life forms that have the capacity to dream, to project their own reality onto the world and self reflect, to display emotions. Principally on Earth, this represents the placentals, the most advanced of all life forms (usually called mammals).

These life forms have the most advanced neural network systems. Therefore, the number and combination of neural networks can reliably use the structure and complexity of brain systems to categorise self aware life on planet Earth.

Classification of Higher Order Life

9. Higher Order Life shall be further defined by six (6) categories, namely:-

(i) Masters of a Colony and Region; and

(ii) Masters of a Regional Empire; and

(iii) Masters of a Global Empire; and

(iv) Masters of a Planet; and

(v) Masters of a Solar System; and

(vi) Masters of a Galactic Quadrant.

Article 13 – Law

Law

1. **A Law shall mean a proper and authentic Rule that describes, prohibits or permits certain Acts.** The Law in name, claim, vow or oath shall mean the present most sacred Covenant and those associated Covenants, Constitutions, Charters and Rules in accord with it and no other. A valid Law shall be derived by instruction, deduction, discovery, argument, custom or consent:-

(i) The highest Law is Divine being a rule given by Divine instruction, such as the present most sacred Covenant, as nothing may contradict such a rule; and

(ii) The second highest Law is the deduction and discovery of Universal and Natural laws through the reason and discernment of Mind as a comprehensive and cohesive model, as the strongest models are consistent, useful, sensible, complete and universally applicable; and

(iii) The third highest Law is the conclusion of an argument and debate between two or more Minds, being an edict given by a great council of wise elders or jurists, as nothing absurd and without good reason may be considered Law; and

(iv) The fourth highest Law is the law of the People, as the consent and will of the people is the source of true authority within any community or society; and

(v) The weakest rule is that of a tyrant, as any rule without authority or right of Heaven but merely by force, cannot be sustained; and the people shall eventually overcome; and render such unjust rule and unjust laws as dust.

2. A Law may pertain to Concepts, Objects or Persons or all three. When a Law pertains to Persons, there are four essential characters being Legislative, Executive, Juridical and Legal Persons:- Law and Persons

(i) A Person or group of Persons possessing the legitimate authority to form new Laws or amend or abrogate old Laws shall be called a "*Legislator*" or "Legislative"; and

(ii) A Person possessing the legitimate authority to approve and promulgate new Laws issued by a Legislator shall be called a "*Sovereign*" or "Executive"; and

(iii) A Person or group of Persons possessing the legitimate authority to interpret and administer the Law shall be called "*Juridic*" or "Juridical"; and

(iv) A Person or group of Persons who are the subject of certain laws as promulgated shall be called "Subjects" or "*Legal*".

3. Divine Law is the Law that defines the Divine and clearly demonstrates the spirit, mind, purpose and instruction of the Divine including the operation of the will of the Divine through existence. All authoritative and legitimate Law is derived from Divine Law in accord with the present most sacred Covenant. In reference to Divine Law and all other forms of Law:- Divine Law and all other forms of Law

(i) *Natural Law* is the law that defines the operation of the will of the Divine through its existence in the form of matter and physical rules. As Natural Laws define the operation and existence of the physical universe, all proper and authentic Natural Law may be said to be derived from Divine Law; and

(ii) *Cognitive Law* is the set of laws that define the special attributes possessed by certain higher order life such as mind, ideas, knowledge, recognition and self-awareness created through the simultaneous application of both Divine Law and Natural Law. As Cognitive Law is derived from the simultaneous application of Divine Law and Natural Law, all valid Cognitive Law may be defined as part "divine" and part "natural", hence "supernatural"; and

(iii) *Positive Law* is the set of laws enacted by valid associations of living higher order beings through proper authority in accordance with these Maxims for the governance of a body or community or society. All valid Positive Law may be said to be derived from authentic Natural Law and Cognitive Law; and

(iv) As Divine Law is the highest possible form of Law and the source of all lesser forms of law, any argument that asserts Divine Law does not exist, or is less than some other form of law is therefore false, absurd and in gross error; and

(v) A Positive Law cannot abrogate, suspend, nor change a Cognitive Law or Natural Law. Nor is it possible for a Cognitive Law or Natural Law to abrogate, suspend or change a Divine Law.

Operation of Law

4. A Divine Law cannot be written or created, only instructed by Divine Revelation and Divine Grace in accordance with the present most sacred Covenant. In reference to the operation of Law:-

(i) A Divine Law is established *ab initio* (from the beginning), irrespective of its first date of promulgation. A Divine Law binds every possible dimension and all of Heaven and Earth everywhere for all those for whom it was issued; and

(ii) A Natural Law or Cognitive Law is established *ab initio* (from the beginning) of a particular life bearing planet or higher order species irrespective of its first date of promulgation. A Natural Law or Cognitive Law binds everywhere all those for whom it was issued; and

(iii) A Positive Law is established and takes force when it is promulgated in accord with the present most sacred Covenant; and begins to oblige a month after the day of promulgation unless the Law itself establishes another time period. Excluding Ecclesiastical Law, all Positive Laws regard the present and future, not the past; and

(iv) Only Ecclesiastical Laws as issued in accord with the present most sacred Covenant may refer to the past as such laws by their nature are firmly bound to Divine Law. Any Positive Law that seeks to promulgate a retrospective rule that is not Ecclesiastical in nature or authority shall have no force or effect. Ecclesiastical Law binds all those who belong and have been accepted into the body of a valid faith in accord with the present most sacred Covenant; and

(v) All other lesser Positive Laws issued by a competent legislator bind those who are actually present within the jurisdiction of the particular juridic or legislative or political body. Particular Positive Laws are not presumed to be personal but territorial in relation to the jurisdiction of the competent legislator who issued the law, unless it is otherwise evident.

Article 14 – Free Will and Choice

1. **Mind**, is a gift of the Unique Collective Awareness instanced in physical form according to the rules of the Universe whereby, a conscious loop is established by a complex unique living organism as to its own unique awareness and therefore, existence. Mind

When self awareness can be demonstrated, a unique mind exists. By this most sacred Covenant of the Divine Creator, when unique awareness and identity is created, it can never be destroyed.

2. Free Will and Choice is the greatest of all possible forces within the Universe. The very existence of existence itself, depends upon the Free Will and Choice of the ultimate Creator to wish to exist. To deny such logic and reason, is to deny the competency of intellect itself. Free Will and Choice

All forms of mechanistic or chaotic or random models concerning the ultimate Universe and Creation itself are fatally flawed in the absence of such elementary reasoning.

3. "**Mandatum Volitio**" shall be the term given concerning the first law of the twelve (12) laws of Creation and a Mandate of Unique Collective Awareness as the manifestation of the Divine Creator that all conscious entities possess the absolute right of free will or "volition" and "choice". Mandate of Free Will and Choice (Mandatum Volitio)

Mandatum Volitio is the acknowledgement that each and every being capable of consciousness and discerning their own thoughts is ultimately responsible for their own actions and obligations. When a higher order life form binds themselves by necessary Oath and Vow or claim of authority to Office they also bind their own Mandatum Volitio in fulfilment and service to the obligations of such Office.

Thus, when an Officer is culpable of delinquency, perfidy, tyranny or impiety, not only is their authority of Office temporarily suspended, but their Mandatum Volitio, or right of "free will and choice" bound to such Office is also temporarily suspended. Therefore, in such conditions, the imposition of a fair and just penalty and its coercive powers against such a delinquent, or fraud, or traitor, or tyrant or wicked priest does not break the Universal Law of Free Will and Choice.

4. **"Aggregatum Volitio"** shall be the term to define the sum of intentions, wills, choices and actions, not otherwise legitimately impeded, within a given spiritual or temporal dimension. No Spirit Member, nor Living Member exists within a vacuum of consciousness of free will and choice. Thus, the individual effect of our choices of free will must be added in the same manner any contributions to action must be added to determine the "collective effect" and aggregate effect and influence to some degree on the events as they unfold.

Sum of Intentions (Aggregatum Volitio)

Another description of the Sum of Intentions is the concept of consequence, not as a binary result of intention of one individual Spirit or Living Member, but the aggregate of intentions of all those active participants in a given moment within dimension.

The effect of our choices and free will and the effect of the choices of others within the same context determines the Sum of Intentions as to the influence to some degree on the events as they unfold. That does not mean the individual powers of free will and choice are diminished for each individual only that such influence outside of our self consciousness, must take into effect the aggregate choices and environment.

5. **"Mysterium Volitio"** shall be the term used to define the resulting effect after Aggregatum Volitio is calculated. It means the revelation of free will and choice. It does not mean "the mystery of God's will".

Mystery of Free Will (Mysterium Volitio)

The term Mysterium Volitio is used as the accumulative effect of free will and choice may produce different outcomes given very similar circumstances, whereas an apparent intervention occurs in one instance but not the other.

6. **"Non Usurpationem Voluntatem"** means that No Spirit Member or Living Member has the right to usurp the Free Will and Choice of another, notwithstanding impediments by virtue of delinquency and dishonour that suspends such Rights in Office.

No Usurpation of Free Will (Non Usurpationem Voluntatem)

It is and shall be a grave transgression against all Creation and all Heaven and all Existence for a Spirit Member or Living Member to usurp the Free Will and Choice of an honourable and virtuous

Member. Any law that permits or endorses the right for a body, or person or entity to impose its Free Will and Choices in prejudice of another by virtue of tyranny or perfidy is morally repugnant, profane, sacrilegious and forbidden, having no force or effect whatsoever.

7. **"Restitutionem Velle"** means it is a singular obligation of the united forces of Heaven and all levels of matter and creation to bring restitution to each and every case where the Right of Free Will and Choice has been impeded and deprived from an honourable and virtuous higher order life form; and to do everything to prevent its continuance. Restitution of Free Will (Restitutionem Velle)

Therefore, any body, spirit, person, entity, company, society that functions on the presumption that it can impose its will upon the Free Will and Choice of others through perfidy and tyranny, declares itself a fundamental enemy of Heaven and all Creation, with all of Creation therefore united to the singular proposition of the extinction of such a body, spirit, person, entity, company and society.

Article 15 – Force and Coercion

1. **A force shall mean any measurable quantity or interaction that alters or impedes the motion of an Object.** In Law, "Force" shall mean:- Force and Coercion

   (i) Valid lawful compulsion by authority to perform or refrain another from certain actions; or

   (ii) Unlawful violence against a being or person.

2. All forms of Force are computational given Force is a form of action (motion) toward a particular object, being or person. Therefore, the nature of Force may be defined as Harmonic, or Dissonant, or Complex when such action (motion) is accepted or resisted:- Nature of Force and Free Will

   (i) *Harmonic Forces* are generally resolved by *Incremental Functions* whereby a small force applied in harmony produces a larger Result. Harmonic Forces are the most efficient at effecting change in matter and require knowledge of the true character of Matter, the types and character of Ergon particles being applied and the appropriate frequencies; and

   (ii) *Dissonant Forces* are generally resolved by *Deviational Functions* used to calculate new functions and results from the differences of two or more other types of functions and dissipate the effects of the incoming Force. Thus Dissonance is commensurate with resistance and the most inefficient use of

Matter by "brute force"; and

(iii) *Complex Forces* are forces that possess both harmonic and dissonant qualities.

3. All valid and legitimate Ucadian organs and bodies defined and formed as a result of the present most sacred Covenant shall possess the absolute and fundamental Right to duly authorised Lawful Compulsion through their Competent Forums of Law, providing the following requirements are clearly met:- Lawful Compulsion and Competent Forums of Law

(i) That a Case and Case Number has been raised upon review of sufficient evidence to commence an Action; and

(ii) That the alleged victim is a Person properly in the lawful care, possession, jurisdiction, control or custody of Ucadia organ or body; and

(iii) That in relation to the Case, the decision whether to apply force is made and duly issued through the proper and Competent Forum of Law; and

(iv) That in relation to the Case, the compelling argument for Lawful Compulsion is in relation to an Enemy or Belligerent, or Dishonest or Delinquent Person, or Mentally Ill Person; and

(v) That in relation to the Case, all reasonable alternatives to Force have been exhausted.

4. Any and all of the following Claims to the Right to Use Force by an enemy or belligerent that refuses to recognise the primacy and authority of the present most sacred Covenant against any valid and legitimate Ucadian organ or body, or against any person in the care, possession, jurisdiction, control or custody of the said Ucadia organ or body shall henceforth be invalid, morally repugnant and null and void *ab initio* (from the beginning); and shall be an unreserved confession by the perpetrator of the use of unlawful violence, including (but not limited to):- Invalid Claims of Right to Force

(i) Any statute, regulation, ruling or law used to treat any valid and legitimate Ucadia Body, or any Person in the care, possession, jurisdiction, control or custody of a valid and legitimate Ucadia Body as an Enemy Alien, Enemy of the state or a criminal by any means whatsoever; and

(ii) Any statute, regulation, ruling or law used to treat any valid and legitimate Ucadia Body, or any Person in the care, possession, jurisdiction, control or custody of a valid and legitimate Ucadia Body as being dead to Law, without Standing or Capacity, or a bankrupt, or lost at sea, or wrecked, or having surrendered or abandoned any rights, or a captured prize; and

(iii) Any statute, regulation, ruling or law used to treat any valid and legitimate Ucadia Body, or any Person in the care, possession, jurisdiction, control or custody of a valid and legitimate Ucadia Body as being mentally ill or intestate or incapable of forming or expressing a clear Will; and

(iv) Any statute, regulation, ruling or law used to treat the Property of any valid and legitimate Ucadia Body, or any Property of a Person in the care, possession, jurisdiction, control or custody of a valid and legitimate Ucadia Body as being confiscated, seized, waived, surrendered, abandoned, alienated, forfeited by any means whatsoever.

Unlimited Liability against Unlawful Violence against Ucadia Bodies

5. In each and every instance of use of unlawful violence against a valid and legitimate Ucadia Body or any Person in the care, possession, jurisdiction, control or custody of a valid and legitimate Ucadia Body, a person, or body or entity found culpable by a Competent Forum of Law shall be fully liable to maximum damages and compensation:-

(i) No claim of immunity within the bylaws of a body or entity found to have used such unlawful violence shall be a valid or lawful excuse or defence against the unlimited liability against them; and

(ii) Each and every officer and person who participated in, or co-ordinated or authorised such unlawful violence shall be jointly and severally liable to maximum damages and compensation, without recourse to claim individual immunity or any form of insurance or assurance; and

(iii) In every and any such case of unlawful violence to seize any insurance or assurance bonds as compensation; and to lawfully file any and every possible form of lien and encumbrance against such bodies, entities and individual persons, until compensation and damages is duly paid; and

(iv) To seek every possible local, national and international form of compensation and sanctions against any body, entity and individuals culpable of such unlawful violence.

TITLE V – GAL (MILKY WAY) MEMBERS

Article 16 – Gal (Milky Way) Members

1. **All, stars, nebulae, planets, moons, self-aware beings (living or deceased) and all substantial computational structures** are beings and *ipso facto* (as a matter of fact) members of Gal (Milky Way Galaxy):- Gal (Milky Way) Members

   (i) All large or highly complex computational objects capable of self-awareness, possess a form and "state of being" in awareness, enabling such entities to engage with one another, despite being significantly different and diverse as objects in dimension; and

   (ii) All members of Gal are by default, members of Ucadia; and

   (iii) As beings, all members of Gal have the capacity to form multiple agreements, associations, treaties and pacts with one another; and with beings and members of other galaxies and super structures, consistent with the present most sacred Covenant.

2. Each and every star system within Gal, just as each and every star system within each and every galaxy, has the capacity, authority and power as a unique being to form its own version of the present most sacred Covenant as a unique of awareness and existence, providing:- Sacred Covenants by Star Systems

   (i) At least one higher order life form species exists as permanent inhabitants of at least one planet or moon within the jurisdiction of the star system; and

   (ii) At least one member of a higher order life form species within the jurisdiction of the star system has the spiritual and mental capacity to receive the necessary revelation associated with such a covenant, consistent with Ucadia; and

   (iii) That no covenant, such as the present most sacred Covenant, has already been revealed and promulgated.

3. In relation to Members of Gal forming agreements and covenants between one another, or with members from other galaxies or larger super structures:- Covenants between Members

   (i) The presence of one or more named higher order species as part of an agreement for one star system, does not imply the exclusion or existence of other higher order species living throughout Gal or in other star systems of other galaxies; and

   (ii) The presence of a higher primary being as a party to a covenant does not imply the exclusion of that party to a covenant for another star system, only that such a being cannot be party to two competing agreements for the same star system; and

(iii) The present most sacred Covenant is exclusively, irrevocably and absolutely the one original and legitimate agreement between all beings and the Unique Collective Awareness in relation to Sol (The Solar System).

TITLE VI – GAL (MILKY WAY) PACTS & TREATIES

Article 17 – Treaty of Ucadia

1. THE HIGHEST CONCORDING PARTIES, CONCURRING with the most sacred Covenant known as Pactum De Singularis Caelum, also known as the Covenant of One Heaven as the Highest Supreme Law of the Divine Creator of All Existence; and RECOGNISING the twelve laws of creation in the formation of Universal Existence; and AFFIRMING the desire of all parties to see the continuation and fulfilment of existence; and RESOLVING to confirm the foundations of a strong and perpetual union; and DETERMINING to eliminate any doubt or concern within the minds of any and all higher order life form species as to continued existence itself, do Come Now with these Presents and with one another Agree to this Covenant of Ucadia. Treaty of Ucadia

2. Let it be known to all past, present and future, the Highest Concording Parties and their duly appointed Plenipotentiaries of the same name herein, having communicated and exchanged to each other their Full Powers, found to be in good and due form, come freely together in full consent and authority being: the Being and their duly appointed Plenipotentiary known as the Supreme Being, also known as Ucadia; and the Being and their duly appointed Plenipotentiary known as the Universal Being, also known as Kosmos; and the Being and their duly appointed Plenipotentiary known as Unitas, also known as the infinite universe of Unita; and the Being and their duly appointed Plenipotentiary known as Gal, also known as The Milky Way Galaxy. The Beings as the Highest Concording Parties to the Treaty

3. The Highest Concording Parties in Good Faith and without Prejudice hereby ACCEPT, APPROVE and AGREE the following Articles. Recital of Articles of Treaty

4. ARTICLE I. – By the present Treaty ("this Treaty"), the HIGHEST CONCORDING PARTIES ("the Parties") there shall be a universal and perpetual peace and harmony and a sincere friendship and amity established, and between all those who are associated in spirit or form through their devotion, faith, location, kindred, culture and history. Chapter 1 – General Provisions

   ARTICLE II. – All agree that Free Will and Choice is the greatest of all possible forces within the Universe as the very existence of Existence itself, depends upon the Free Will and Choice of the Supreme Being as the ultimate Creator.

   ARTICLE III. – All agree that while Existence itself depends upon the continued expression of such Free Will and Choice of the Supreme Being as the First Law of Creation, the Supreme Being as Ucadia is not precluded in providing certain surety in order to eliminate any doubt or concern in the mind of lesser beings.

ARTICLE IV. – All agree that while Existence itself depends upon the independent existence of the Universe from the Divine Creator, such that the Divine Creator is prevented from direct intervention, the Supreme Being as Ucadia is not precluded in direct intervention through mind and knowledge and the causation of singularity beings midst higher order life species from time to time, borne with the capacity and potential to reason, perceive and acknowledge the revelation of Ucadia.

ARTICLE V. – All agree that while the Divine Creator is prevented from direct intervention within the Universe, the Kosmos itself and all lesser beings with higher consciousness, including galaxies, stars and planets are unconstrained in creating, nurturing and protecting such conditions of life to bring forth higher order life species with the capacity and potential to reason, perceive and acknowledge the revelation of Ucadia.

ARTICLE VI. – Ucadia hereby solemnly pledges that so long as there exists the possibility of some form of higher order conscious life existing in some part of the Universe, with sufficient capacity and reasoning to perceive and acknowledge the revelation of Ucadia, then continued existence in form and in mind (spirit) is absolutely assured through the resolute expression of Free Will and intention of the Supreme Being as the ultimate Creator.

ARTICLE VII. – The Kosmos and Unitas hereby solemnly pledge that the rules of formation and existence of matter shall be harnessed such that the possibility of some form of higher order conscious life existing in some part of the Universe, with sufficient capacity and reasoning to perceive and acknowledge the revelation of Ucadia, shall be fulfilled as a reality, in honour of the will and intention of the Divine Creator.

5. IN WITNESS WHEREOF, the undersigned Plenipotentiaries have witnessed and signed this Treaty. Enaction of Treaty

GAIA E8:Y3209:A1:S1:M6:D1, [Mon, 21 Dec 2009]

The duly appointed Plenipotentiary on behalf of the Being known as the Supreme Being, also known as Ucadia; The duly appointed Plenipotentiary on behalf of the Being known as the Universal Being, also known as Kosmos; The duly appointed Plenipotentiary on behalf of the Being known as Unitas, also known as the infinite universe of Unita; The duly appointed Plenipotentiary on behalf of the Being known as Gal, also known as The Milky Way Galaxy.

6. By Agreement of the Highest Concording Parties, this Treaty and Ratification of

Covenant shall be Ratified throughout all Heaven, spiritual dimensions and the Universe by the Day of Agreement and Understanding and shall be Ratified by one or more temporal beings by the Day of Judgement. Treaty

Ratification by Day of Agreement and Understanding

By this Covenant, the Day of Agreement and Understanding is GAIA E8:Y3209:A1:S1:M6:D1, [Mon, 21 Dec 2009].

Ratification by Day of Agreement and Understanding shall be when this Treaty and Covenant is ratified throughout all Heaven, spiritual dimensions and the Universe by the Highest Office Holders of One Heaven representing the Supreme Command of Occupational Forces in and on Earth and when at least two (2) spirits conveyed into circumscribed Level 6 Homo Sapien Life Forms bear witness to the event.

Ratification by Day of Judgement

By this Covenant, the Day of Judgement is VENUS E8:Y3210:A0:S1:M27:D6, [Wed, 21 Dec 2011].

Ratification by Day of Judgement shall be when this Treaty and Covenant is ratified by the Highest Office Holders of existing societies, faiths and associations that claim their existence, authority and power from the supernatural and spiritual either through their tacit, competent and honourable consent, or through their dishonour demonstrating the delinquency of their flesh and therefore the right through power to represent their spirit to ratify the Covenant and Treaty on their behalf.

Article 18 – Treaty of the Galaxies

1. **THE HIGHEST CONCORDING PARTIES, CONCURRING** with the most sacred Covenant known as Pactum De Singularis Caelum, also known as the Covenant of One Heaven as the Highest Supreme Law of the Divine Creator of All Existence; and RECOGNISING the twelve laws of creation in the formation of Universal Existence; and AFFIRMING the *Treaty of Ucadia*; and RESOLVING to confirm the foundations of a strong and perpetual union; and DETERMINING to create, nurture and protect the development of higher order life with sufficient capacity and reasoning to perceive and acknowledge the revelation of Ucadia, do Come Now with these Presents and with one another Agree to this Covenant of Galaxies. Treaty of Galaxies

2. Let it be known to all past, present and future, the Highest Concording Parties and their duly appointed Plenipotentiaries of the same name herein, having communicated and exchanged to each other their Full Powers, found to be in good and due form, come freely together in full consent and authority being: the Being and their duly appointed Plenipotentiary known as Gal, also known as Milky Way Galaxy; and the Being and their duly appointed Plenipotentiary known as the Canis Major Dwarf Galaxy; and the Being and their duly appointed Plenipotentiary known as Sagittarius Dwarf Sphr SagDEG Galaxy; and the Being and their duly appointed Plenipotentiary known as the Large Magellanic Cloud (LMC) Galaxy; and the Being and their duly appointed Plenipotentiary known as the Boötes Galaxy; and the Being and their duly appointed Plenipotentiary known as the Small Magellanic Cloud (SMC, NGC 292) Galaxy; and the Being and their duly appointed Plenipotentiary known as the Ursa Minor Dwarf Galaxy; and the Being and their duly appointed Plenipotentiary known as the Draco Dwarf (DDO 208) Galaxy; and the Being and their duly appointed Plenipotentiary known as the NGC 2419 Galaxy; and the Being and their duly appointed Plenipotentiary known as the Sextans Dwarf Sph Galaxy; and the Being and their duly appointed Plenipotentiary known as the Sculptor Dwarf (E351-G30) Galaxy; and the Being and their duly appointed Plenipotentiary known as the Ursa Major I Dwarf (UMa I dSph) Galaxy.

The Beings as the Highest Concording Parties to the Treaty

3. The Highest Concording Parties in Good Faith and without Prejudice hereby ACCEPT, APPROVE and AGREE the following Articles.

Recital of Articles of Treaty

4. ARTICLE I. – By the present Treaty ("this Treaty"), the HIGHEST CONCORDING PARTIES ("the Parties") there shall be a universal and perpetual peace and harmony and a sincere friendship and amity established, and between all those who are associated in spirit or form through their devotion, faith, location, kindred, culture and history.

Chapter 1 – General Provisions

ARTICLE II. – All agree and give thanks to the solemn pledge of the Supreme Being through the *Treaty of Ucadia* that so long as there exists the possibility of some form of higher order conscious life existing in some part of the Universe, with sufficient capacity and reasoning to perceive and acknowledge the revelation of Ucadia, then continued existence in form and in mind (spirit) is absolutely assured through the resolute expression of Free Will and intention of the Supreme Being as the ultimate Creator.

ARTICLE III. – All agree and acknowledge the solemn pledge of The Kosmos and Unitas through the *Treaty of Ucadia* that the rules of formation and existence of matter shall be harnessed such that the possibility of some form of higher order conscious life existing in some part of the Universe, with sufficient capacity and reasoning to perceive and acknowledge the revelation of Ucadia, shall be fulfilled as a reality, in honour of the will and intention of the Divine Creator.

ARTICLE IV. – The parties do all hereby solemnly pledge to do everything within their power to nurture and protect all forms of life and higher order conscious life within their jurisdiction, to ensure higher order life species shall exist, with sufficient capacity and reasoning to perceive and acknowledge the revelation of Ucadia.

5. IN WITNESS WHEREOF, the undersigned Plenipotentiaries have witnessed and signed this Treaty.

Enaction of Treaty

GAIA E8:Y3209:A1:S1:M6:D1, [Mon, 21 Dec 2009]

The duly appointed Plenipotentiary on behalf of the Being known as Gal, also known as The Milky Way Galaxy; The duly appointed Plenipotentiary on behalf of the Being known as Canis Major Dwarf Galaxy; The duly appointed Plenipotentiary on behalf of the Being known as Sagittarius Dwarf Sphr SagDEG Galaxy; The duly appointed Plenipotentiary on behalf of the Being known as Large Magellanic Cloud (LMC) Galaxy; The duly appointed Plenipotentiary on behalf of the Being known as Boötes Galaxy; The duly appointed Plenipotentiary on behalf of the Being known as Small Magellanic Cloud (SMC, NGC 292) Galaxy; The duly appointed Plenipotentiary on behalf of the Being known as Ursa Minor Dwarf Galaxy; The duly appointed Plenipotentiary on behalf of the Being known as Draco Dwarf (DDO 208) Galaxy; The duly appointed Plenipotentiary on behalf of the Being known as NGC 2419 Galaxy; and The duly appointed Plenipotentiary on behalf of the Being known as Sextans Dwarf Sph Galaxy; The duly appointed Plenipotentiary on behalf of the Being known as Sculptor Dwarf (E351-G30) Galaxy; The duly appointed Plenipotentiary on behalf of the Being known as Ursa Major I Dwarf (UMa I dSph) Galaxy.

6. By Agreement of the Highest Concording Parties, this Treaty and Covenant shall be Ratified throughout all Heaven, spiritual dimensions and the Universe by the Day of Agreement and Understanding and shall be Ratified by one or more temporal beings by the Day of Judgement.

Ratification of Treaty

Ratification by Day of Agreement and Understanding

By this Covenant, the Day of Agreement and Understanding is GAIA E8:Y3209:A1:S1:M6:D1, [Mon, 21 Dec 2009].

Ratification by Day of Agreement and Understanding shall be when this Treaty and Covenant is ratified throughout all Heaven, spiritual dimensions and the Universe by the Highest Office Holders of One Heaven representing the Supreme Command of Occupational Forces in and on Earth and when at least two (2) spirits conveyed into circumscribed Level 6 Homo Sapien Life Forms bear witness to the event.

Ratification by Day of Judgement

By this Covenant, the Day of Judgement is VENUS E8:Y3210:A0:S1:M27:D6, [Wed, 21 Dec 2011].

Ratification by Day of Judgement shall be when this Treaty and Covenant is ratified by the Highest Office Holders of existing societies, faiths and associations that claim their existence, authority and power from the supernatural and spiritual either through their tacit, competent and honourable consent, or through their dishonour demonstrating the delinquency of their flesh and therefore the right through power to represent their spirit to ratify the Covenant and Treaty on their behalf.

Volume III: Sol – The Solar System

TITLE VII – SOL (SOLAR SYSTEM) RECITALS

Article 19 - Origin & Nature of Sol (Solar System)

1. Sol shall be the unique collective Divine Spirit of all atomic and molecular elements, life and awareness of our Solar System and Sun as a Primary Being. The Divine Spirit of Sol is part of the greater collective spirit of Gal, that is part of the greater collective spirit of Kosmos, that is part of the greater collective spirit of Unitas, that is then part of the greater collective Divine Spirit of All. Origin & Nature of Sol (Solar System)

2. Sol is the proper name and greater name of the Solar System in respect and recognition of the unified whole of all the planets, all the gases, all the moons, meteorites and asteroid belts, the Sun, all the life, all the self-aware life within the Solar System and the Solar System as a Divine Being, Living Being and Ethereal Being. Sol as proper name of Being

3. Sol memory is the memory of the unique existence of the Solar System and memory of unique position, change, seasons of life and seasons of death. Sol memory is eternal. Sol memory

4. The position of planets within the Sol is not simply mechanical, but will of the Sol. If the Sun chose it to be so, the planet Earth could be destroyed in an instant. Yet the Sun chooses of its own free will to value the life, awareness and existence of the planet Earth like a mother to a new born child. Position of planets within Sol

Article 20 - Prime Preferences

1. One Heaven exists for the benefit of all life, all mind, all dream, all existence, all unique higher order beings and for the betterment of the lives of all men and women living upon the planet known as Earth, as well as other Solar Systems and the Galaxy. Prime Preferences

   Thus the existence of One Heaven and the prime premises of One Heaven is to end the insanity, the madness, the falsities, the belies, the misconceptions, the deceptions that have plagued the world and our consciousness and then recognise that it is within our power and abilities to make life and existence upon the Earth a true “Heaven” - a place of respect, of Golden Rule of Law, of Justice and fairness for all.

2. These then be the prime premises of One Heaven:- Prime Premises of One Heaven

   1. Unite Heaven and end War

   (i) To demonstrate the unquestionable unity, treaty, reconciliation, forgiveness, oneness, of mind and spirit of the end of War between Heaven and Hell; and so irrefutably by all forms of reason, logic, theology, law, authority, power and argument prove the end of any spiritual war and any claim to justify war or destruction or corruption or avarice upon planet Earth or any other planet or moon within the Solar System or Galaxy; and

(ii) To provide a framework for lasting peace, a universal amnesty concerning the actions of the past and a recognition of the inherent right of all higher order spirits (Homo Sapien and other higher order life) to be rightful Members of One Heaven.

2. Heal the Earth

(i) To honour the Treaty of the Earth and to help heal the Earth, by helping to end poverty, violence and injustice; and To help people be everything they can be, to better themselves; and To see their purpose; and

(ii) To help free minds from the "Mundi" Mind Virus and the layers of insanity which cause people not to hear or see what is in front of their faces, or reverse the meaning of expressions, or deliberately distort knowledge that is shared or continue to promote the status quo, whilst claiming the opposite intention; and

(iii) To forgive those minds who remain so mentally ill and deluded that they wish to remain isolated and hateful to the world; and who willingly wish to remain ignorant and foolish in their reasoning and lack of competence, or who seek to trick and traduce and belie and beguile others to fulfil some deep illness within themselves. Thus, in seeking to help free minds of the Mundi Mind Virus that continues to distort, and misrepresent, and corrupt and spread fear and seek control, the Earth itself will heal.

3. Protect the Earth

(i) To honour the Treaty of the Earth and to protect the Earth against dangers from within and outside the Solar System; and

(ii) To help inspire great scientists and artists in their creative endeavours; and

(iii) To help answer the prayers of those who ask for help by assisting where it is both wise and possible through thought and dream; and

(iv) To assist the leadership of the three (3) great religious movements in their spiritual guidance; and

(v) To help inspire and illustrate information to spiritual mediums who are accredited as having clear minds through one of the three (3) great religious movements.

4. Bring Sustainable Life to Mars and other Moons of Solar System

(i) To Honour the Treaty of the Sun and to build a Moon for Mars, compressing its atmosphere so that it will rain on Mars within one hundred and twenty-eight (128) years and sustain life soon thereafter, thereby increasing the comet attracting mass of our Solar System, thereby effecting fair remedy for our Sun in demonstrating a cure to increasing its supply of hydrogen from the tails of comets; and

(ii) To establish permanent colonies of Homo Sapiens upon the moons within the Solar System as well as upon the surface of Mars.

5. To Establish Contact and Confirm Treaties and Unity with other Level 6 Higher Order Life Forms

To fulfil the mission of the Divine Creator and make contact and unite the Level 6 Higher Order life forms within the local star system and Milky Way Galaxy within the next great cycle of three thousand two hundred and ten (3,210) years, including but not limited to the Griseo Morbidus (Standard Grey), the Cerastis Sapiens (Horned Reptoids), the Android Scitus (Smart Androids), the Cyborg Sagax (Autonomous Cyborgs), the Serpens Sophos (Smooth Skinned Reptoids), the Volucris Permuto (Hybrid Bird Form), the Homo Adamus (Early Humanoids), the Sapientia Mutatis (Transformed Wisdom Beings), the Mammaloid Sentientiae (Conscious Mammaloids), the Griseo Altus (Tall Grey) and the Serpens Alatus (Winged Reptoids).

3. The Unique Member Number and Divine Trust Registration Number of the Society is: 999999-999999-999999. One Heaven Unique Divine Trust

4. The Divine Trust is formed through conveyance of all Heaven and all Existence into the Divine Trust both with and without form of Unique Collective Awareness. Therefore, the Society of One Heaven possesses its own life and soul as the Supreme Society of all societies and the highest jurisdiction of all jurisdictions by the highest laws of all laws. One Heaven as Supreme Society

Article 21 - Great Spirits & Deities

1. **Unique Collective Awareness** as the total theoretical collection of all meaning and definition of all possible potential, theories, ideas, concepts, objects, matter, properties, rules, axioms, relations, actions, events, existences, forms, emotions, senses, minds, thoughts, dimensions, consciousness, awareness and spirit, all other names, deities, great spirits, gods and identities used to describe a Supreme Being shall be considered lesser and a member of the set of all sets named Unique Collective Awareness as Great Spirits and Deities. Great Spirits and Deities

   It is to the Great Spirits and Deities that humanity owes its knowledge of Unique Collective Awareness and its works. Many of these Great Spirits and Deities are the stars, the planets, the galaxies, the forces, the seasons, the elements and the conscious collective constructs that human ancestors once worshipped and many still worship and revere today. It is right to give thanks, honour and respect to these most powerful and most ancient of Great Spirits and Deities of civilisation and spiritual awakening.

2. Let it be known to all that each and every Great Spirit and Deity of history shall be officially recognised as an honoured Member of One Heaven in accord with the rules of membership defined by the present Covenant. Therefore, no Great Spirit and Deity may be excluded from being a Member of One Heaven, nor may anyone be permitted to claim that there exist separate or excluded dimensions from One United Heaven. Great Spirits & Deities as Members of One United Heaven

   Furthermore, let it be known to all that each and every massive construct within the living Universe from planets to stars to galaxies to super clusters of galaxies are recognised as possessing their own unique conscious identity as valid Great Spirits and Deities. Therefore, the singular consciousness of every planet, every star, every galaxy are hereby recognised as being Members of One Heaven.

3. By the present sacred Covenant, the Executive Government of One United Heaven is entrusted to one hundred and forty-four (144) Great Spirits and Deities for a term not exceeding three thousand two hundred and ten (3,210) years before a new body of Great Spirits of Deities may be elected. Furthermore, the construction of the Executive Government of Heaven must be representative of the different categories and types of Great Spirits and Deities recognised as Members of One Heaven. Great Spirits & Deities as Executive Government of Heaven

   In recognition of the unique role of the singular consciousness of the Homo Sapien species within the star system named the Solar System within the Milky Way Galaxy in assisting the formation of One Heaven in accord with the present Covenant, planet Earth, the Solar System and the Milky Way Galaxy are especially honoured as being part of the first term Executive Government of One Heaven for the next three thousand two hundred and ten (3,210) years.

4. In accord with the treaties and pacts of peace, amity and good will associated with the present Covenant, including, but not limited to: the Treaty of the Divine Masculine, the Treaty of the Divine Feminine, the Treaty of Divine Messengers, the Treaty of Angels, Saints and Demons and the Treaty of Spirit States, let it be known to all that there no longer exists any conflict, state of war or orchestration of evil by former arch demons, demons or negative deities. Furthermore, all souls previously trapped, bound, claimed, cursed as damned, or tormented souls under organised custody known as Hell, or Purgatory, or Limbo or Hades and any derivative thereof have officially been released and such states or beings of negativity have been dissolved.

Recognition of former negatively perceived Spirits and Deities as Allies

Furthermore, in accord with the *Authentic Sacred Deposit of Trust* being: the Thirty-Three (33) Covenants between Authentic, Apostolic and Anointed Divine Messengers of the Divine Creator of all Existence and all the Heavens and Earth and the peoples of the Earth, the complete consciousness, culture, languages, rules, symbols, rituals, laws and rights embodied within such Covenants in relation to previous negative Great Spirits and Deities has been entrusted to the embodiment and organs of the present sacred Covenant and no other. Therefore, let no man, or woman, or spirit, or entity, or aggregate or body defy the will and authority of the present sacred Covenant in claiming division between Heaven, or between Heaven and Earth.

By the power and authority of the present Covenant, Satan is redeemed; and Mithrá is reborne; and Lucifer is personified in fulfilment of sacred prophecy and scripture as respected Great Spirits and Deities and full Members of One Heaven are fully eligible for election as one of the one hundred and forty-four (144) Great Spirits and Deities as the Executive Government of One Heaven according to the rules of a Supreme Conclave of One Heaven.

5. In accord with *Authentic Sacred Deposit of Trust*, the Covenant of Mundi of the Greys embodying in sacred trust the complete consciousness, culture, languages, rules, symbols, rituals, laws and rights of the entire Grey species and all that are connected through Mundi Mind as Grey Hive Mind is recognised as having been entrusted to the embodiment and organs of the present sacred Covenant and no other.

Recognition and Forgiveness of the Greys

Furthermore, the present sacred Covenant formally recognises the

Griseo Morbidus (Standard Grey) and Griseo Altus (Tall Grey) as architects of Homo Robustus, the Homo Habilis and Homo Sapiens and honours their redemption and the end of the sociopathy of the Mundi Mind Virus of the Grey Hive Mind breeding of an elite "master-race" of empty vessels amongst the wealthiest and privileged families to orchestrate the "self-destruction" of humanity.

As the present sacred Covenant recognises the conveyance of all rights and powers and consciousness to it, all Members of One Heaven and all Systems of One Heaven, whether spiritual or temporal, are empowered to ensure that each and every candidate, bred and broken and affected by the mind programming of the Greys to create a "master-race" of suicidal maniacs are removed from power using any means; and to prevent such sociopathic empty vessels of the Grey programs any ability to continue damaging and destroying planet Earth and life in general.

The Greys are forgiven for their evil and nihilistic madness of repudiation of the design and majesty of Unique Collective Awareness for many millions of years. Instead, through humanity, the Greys as our fathers and mothers and our former "gods" are welcomed into the society of civilised beings and no longer parasites and scavengers of space. The singularity of the mind of Griseo Morbidus (Standard Grey) is recognised as [Member No. 000000-700000-000002] of the Great Spirits. The singularity of the mind of Griseo Altus (Tall Grey) is recognised as [Member No. 000000-700000-000012] of the Great Spirits.

6. The official dimension, presence and consciousness of all Great Spirits and Deities recognised as having membership of a great religious society and One Heaven, is One Heaven. No claim of other dimension, place, presence or exclusive location is valid other than One Heaven according to the rules and Covenant of One Heaven. Any other claim is considered both false and invalid by the existence and validity of the present Covenant.

Official Dimension, Presence and Consciousness of Great Spirits and Deities

Article 22 - Angels, Demons, Saints & Leaders

1. **By the command of the Great Spirits** including the Great and Holy Spirits known as Isis, Satan, Ba'al and Lucifer, in accord with the Treaty of Divine Masculine, the Treaty of Divine Feminine, the Treaty of Divine Messengers, the Treaty of Angels, Saints and Demons and the Treaty of Spirit States, all Angels, Saints and Demons have ratified and endorsed the present sacred Covenant, the unity of Heaven and between Heaven and Earth and the end of all claims of War.

The Treaty of Angels, Saints, Demons & Leaders

In recognition of this great and historic treaty, all Angels, Saints and Demons are honoured and recognised as heroes, hereby eligible for election according to the rules of Conclaves of One Heaven.

Furthermore, while it may be that a demon or spirit may defy their own lords and hierarchy and reject peace; and may still act in a deliberately evil manner, even so by the authority and power of this Covenant, no demon may ever be denied the right of membership to One Heaven.

2. A "**Supreme Divine Office**" is an office purely occupied and vested to a Spiritual Member. There are two (2) categories of Supreme Divine Offices being General and Special:- Supreme Divine Offices of Heaven

   (i) A "**General Divine Office**" is an Office whereby a Spiritual Member of One Heaven is nominated and elected by Members to a higher position of Trust and Representation in the administration of Heaven. These positions include a *Saint* being a revered and honoured Spirit Member; and an *Apostle* as the elected leader and head of a Local Dimension (Local Collective); and a *Consul* as the elected leader and head of a Collective Dimension (Spiritual Collective); and an *Augustus* as the elected leader and head of a Sovereign Dimension (Regional Spiritual Collective); and

   (ii) A "**Special Divine Office**" is an Office whereby a Spiritual Member of One Heaven chooses by their own volition and is suitably qualified and accepted to join one of the Systems of Heaven, including but not limited to: a *Fate* as a qualified and selected member of the Universalium Systemata (Universal Systems) of Heaven; and an *Angel* as a qualified and selected member of the Angelorum Systemata (Angelic Systems) of Heaven; and a *Demon* as a qualified and selected member of the Custodiarum Systemata (Guardians Systems) of Heaven; and a *Wraith* as a qualified and selected member of the Obligationum Systemata (Enforcement Systems) of Heaven; and a *Faerie* as a qualified and selected member of the Femininum Systemata (Feminine Systems) of Heaven; and an *Elve* as a qualified and selected member of the Masculinum Systemata (Masculine Systems) of Heaven; and a *Nomos* as a qualified and selected member of the Officium Systemata (Offices Systems) of Heaven; and a *Seraphim* as a qualified and selected member of the Sacramentum Systemata (Sacramental Systems) of Heaven.

3. Vested by the present sacred Covenant to the three (3) great and sacred Covenants of One Christ, One Islam and One Spirit is the power Election of Saints & Heroes

to elect the Saints charged with office in One Heaven representing planet Earth. It is the duty then of the Saints to serve the one hundred and forty-four (144) Great Spirits and Deities elected as the Executive Government of One Heaven.

A total of one hundred and forty-four thousand (144,000) saints of office are to be elected by the combined Members of the three (3) great faiths of One Christ, One Islam and One Spirit Tribe on behalf of planet Earth for a period of one hundred and twenty-eight (128) years at an official celebration known as the Great Conclave of One Heaven. Saints that have been re-elected three (3) times are to be known as Holy Saints and ineligible to hold further office except Great Spirit. Only Holy Saints may be eligible to be elected by the Living Members of One Heaven to the Offices of Apostle, or Consul or Augustus.

In recognition of the permanent Government of One Heaven upon the Day of Divine Agreement and Understanding being GAIA E8:Y3209:A1:S1:M6:D1, also known as [Monday, 21 Dec 2009], it is hereby recognised that the existing Saints of traditional religions represented now by One Islam, One Christ and One Spirit have been duly elected to official positions of the Spiritual Dimensions, subject to ratification by the first permanent Supreme Councils of all three (3) religions.

Article 23 - Authentic Sacred Deposit of Trust

1. **It is to the Authentic, Apostolic and Anointed Divine Messengers** and none other, to whom the entire Revelation of the Divine Creator of all existence and all the heavens and the earth are entrusted. Authentic Sacred Deposit of Trust

   By custom and tradition of the ages, from the very beginning of human civilisation, such Revelation of Divine Truth, whether transmitted orally or by writing, has always been self-evident as the manifestation of Divine Illumination, by extraordinary enlightenment, clarity, perception, reasoning and wisdom beyond the norm of human experience. Thus, the truth of Divine Existence, Divine Mind and Divine Nature is never illogical, or irrational, or unreasonable, or superficial, or perfidious or malevolent.

2. The Advocates of such Divine Truth as the deposit of trust of sacred knowledge and scripture, free from spells or curses, by custom and rule, did communicate such Divine Gifts from the creator of all existence to all men and all women through the embodiment of such trust in language, sign and writing. Such canonical texts were then to be the source of all saving truth and moral discipline, free of corruption or distortion. Embodiment of Heritage of Divine Truth

In order that the full and living canonical scriptures of the Divine Creator of all existence might always be preserved, Authentic, Apostolic and Anointed Divine Messengers have always acknowledged anointed and qualified men and women as their successors. Thus, the promulgation of Divine Truth, as expressed in such inspired and sacred texts and covenants, has always intended to be preserved in a continuous line of succession until the end of time.

Such living transmission, accomplished under the authority and power of the Divine Creator is called Tradition since it is distinct from Sacred Scripture itself, whilst closely connected to it. Through Tradition, each generation in life and reverence for the Golden Rule of Law, may then perpetuate and transmit to every other generation all that is trusted as the most valuable and important of knowledge.

3. Thirty-Three (33) Sacred Covenants between Authentic, Apostolic and Anointed Divine Messengers of the Divine Creator of all Existence and all the Heavens and Earth and the peoples of the Earth are acknowledged as having merit, authority, power and jurisdiction above all others by custom and tradition, namely:- Tradition of the Thirty-Three Sacred Covenants of Heaven

(i) "**De Dea Magisterium**" of the Serpens (Creators); and

(ii) "**Yapa**" of the Pacific Saltwater People; and

(iii) "**Mandi**" of the African Plains People; and

(iv) "**Tia**" of the Asiatic Mountain People; and

(v) "**Waiata**" of the Pacific Sea People; and

(vi) "**Adamus**" of Prometheus and the Cuilliaéan; and

(vii) "**Nana**" of the Mother Goddess of Heaven and Earth; and

(viii) "**Alma**" of South Arabia, East Africa and India; and

(ix) "**Elohim**" of Abraham and Patriarchs of Ebla; and

(x) "**Kabalaah**" of Akhenaten (Moses) and the Yahudi; and

(xi) "**Revelations**" of the thirty-three Great Prophets of Yeb; and

(xii) "**Tara**" of Jeremiah and the Celts; and

(xiii) "**Five Worlds**" of North-Central America; and

(xiv) "**Missal**" of Baal Mithra; and

(xv) "**Acadia**" of Xerxes; and

(xvi) "**Eliada**" of Alexander; and

(xvii) "**Tabiti**" of Great Asiatic Plains People; and

(xviii) "**Tiandi**" (Heaven and Earth) of Qin Shi Huang; and

(xix) "**Nazara (Truth)**" of Yahusiah (Jesus Christ); and

(xx) "**Nirvana**" (Freedom & Awakening) of Gautama (Buddha); and

(xxi) "**Zhongdao**" (The Middle Way) of Kong Qiu (Confucius); and

(xxii) "**Septuaginta**" of Iudaism (Josephus); and

(xxiii) "**Eucadia**" of Heracles; and

(xxiv) "**Kikilil Yuum Witzil**" (Great Cycle of Celestial Realm and Earth) of South-Central America; and

(xxv) "**Digesta**" of Marcus Aurelius; and

(xxvi) "**Sanatana Dharma**" (Eternal Truth) of Brahman (Hinduism); and

(xxvii) "**Bibliographe**" of Christianity of Constantine; and

(xxviii) "**Dao**" (the Way); and

(xxix) "**Kami Yoso Seimei**" (Spirits of Elements and Life) of the way of Shinto (Japan); and

(xxx) "**Quran Al Sufian**" (Recitations of Wisdom of the Way)" of The Great Prophet (Islam); and

(xxxi) "**Holy Bible**" of Catholicism of the Franks; and

(xxxii) "**Eternal Truth**" of Gurmat (Sikhism); and

(xxxiii) "**Lebor Clann Glas**" of the Holly Diaspora.

4. In accord with the present most sacred Covenant, the Thirty-Three (33) Covenants between Authentic, Apostolic and Anointed Divine Messengers of the Divine Creator of all Existence and all the Heavens and Earth and the peoples of the Earth are entrusted as the "**Authentic Sacred Deposit of Trust**", contained in Sacred Canonical Scripture and Tradition, to the embodiment of the present sacred Covenant and no other:- Authentic Sacred Deposit of Trust

(i) The Universal Ecclesia of One Christ may use the name "**Authenticus Depositum Fidei**" to officially describe the *Authentic Sacred Deposit of Trust* as it applies to their authority; and

(ii) The Holy Society of One Islam may use the name "**Asilah Alwadiea Lilthiqa**" to officially describe the *Authentic Sacred Deposit of Trust* as it applies to their authority; and

(iii) The Sacred Society of One Spirit may use the name "**Satya Avasada Shraddha**" to officially describe the *Authentic Sacred Deposit of Trust* as it applies to their authority.

5. The Covenant of ***De Dea Magisterium*** of the Serpens embodies in sacred trust the complete culture, languages, rules, symbols, rituals, laws and rights of the Serpens as the creators of Homo Prometheus, the "horned ones", that chose to integrate within the Homo Sapien species in the form of the Cuilliaéan, to help free the Homo Sapien species of its programming and condemnation by the Griseo Morbidus (Standard Grey) and Griseo Altus (Tall Grey) as architects of the Homo Robustus, the Homo Habilis and Homo Sapiens.

Covenant of De Dea Magisterium of the Serpens

The complete consciousness, culture, languages, rules, symbols, rituals, laws and rights of the Serpens embodied within the Covenant of De Dea Magisterium of the Serpens is entrusted through the Authentic Sacred Deposit of Trust, to the embodiment and organs of the present sacred Covenant and no other.

6. The Covenant of ***Yapa*** of the Saltwater People embodies in sacred trust the complete consciousness, culture, languages, rules, symbols, rituals, laws and rights of the first cultures and traditional owners of hominid species of South-East Asia, Australia and parts of the Pacific. The *Saltwater People* are the aggregate of the first cultures and traditional owners of hominid species of South-East Asia, Australia and parts of the Pacific beginning in the mid-Palaeolithic period and rising to a high culture of law, language and knowledge during the Mesolithic period.

Covenant of Yapa of the Saltwater People

Yapa represents the uninterrupted and unextinguished Original Law and Original Rights of the Original Nations (Tribes) that have always been present upon the lands of South-East Asia, Australia and nearby Pacific islands. The complete consciousness, culture, languages, rules, symbols, rituals, laws and rights of the first cultures and traditional owners of hominid species of South-East Asia, Australia and parts of the Pacific embodied within the Covenant of *Yapa* of the Saltwater People is irrevocably entrusted through the Authentic Sacred Deposit of Trust, to the embodiment and organs of the present sacred Covenant and no other.

7. The Covenant of ***Mandi*** of the Africa Plains People embodies in sacred trust the complete consciousness, culture, languages, rules, symbols, rituals, laws and rights of the first cultures and traditional

Covenant of Mandi of the Africa Plains People People

owners of hominid species of the ancient African Lakes, Great River and Fertile Plains of Northern Africa and the whole of Africa. The *Africa Plains People* of planet Earth are the aggregate of the first cultures and traditional owners of hominid species of Africa beginning in the mid-Palaeolithic period and rising to a high culture of law, language and knowledge during the Mesolithic period.

Mandi represents the uninterrupted and unextinguished Original Law and Original Rights of the Original Nations (Tribes) that have always been present upon the lands of Africa. The complete consciousness, culture, languages, rules, symbols, rituals, laws and rights of the first cultures and traditional owners of hominid species of Africa embodied within the Covenant of *Mandi* of the Africa Plains People is entrusted through the Authentic Sacred Deposit of Trust, to the embodiment and organs of the present sacred Covenant and no other.

Covenant of Tia of the Asiatic Mountain People

8. The Covenant of ***Tia*** of the Asiatic Mountain People embodies in sacred trust the complete consciousness, culture, languages, rules, symbols, rituals, laws and rights of the first cultures and traditional owners of hominid species of mountainous Asia and the Indian sub continent. The *Asiatic Mountain People* are the aggregate of the first cultures and traditional owners of hominid species of mountainous Asia and the Indian sub continent beginning in the mid-Palaeolithic period and rising to a high culture of law, language and knowledge during the Mesolithic period.

Tia represents the uninterrupted and unextinguished Original Law and Original Rights of the Original Nations (Tribes) that have always been present upon the lands of the great mountains of Asia. The complete consciousness, culture, languages, rules, symbols, rituals, laws and rights of the first cultures and traditional owners of hominid species of mountainous Asia and the Indian sub continent embodied within the Covenant of Tia of the Asiatic Mountain People is entrusted through the Authentic Sacred Deposit of Trust, to the embodiment and organs of the present sacred Covenant and no other.

Covenant of Waiata of the Sea People of Asia and Pacific

9. The Covenant of ***Waiata*** of the Sea People embodies in sacred trust the complete consciousness, culture, languages, rules, symbols, rituals, laws and rights of the cultures and traditional owners of hominid species of the Pacific and Asia. The *Sea People of Asia and Pacific* are the aggregate of the cultures and traditional owners of hominid species of the Pacific and Asia beginning in the Mesolithic period and rising to a high culture of law, language and knowledge during the Neolithic period.

Waiata represents the uninterrupted and unextinguished Original Law and Original Rights of the Original Nations (Tribes) that have always been present upon the many islands across the Pacific and Indian Oceans. The complete consciousness, culture, languages, rules, symbols, rituals, laws and rights of the cultures and traditional owners of hominid species of the Pacific and Asia embodied within the Covenant of *Waiata* of the Sea People is entrusted through the Authentic Sacred Deposit of Trust, to the embodiment and organs of the present sacred Covenant and no other.

10. The Covenant of ***Adamus*** of Homo Prometheus and the Cuilliaéan embodies in sacred trust the complete consciousness, culture, languages, rules, symbols, rituals, laws and rights of the Cuilliaéan as the first sons and daughters of men; and the founders of the first empires; and the historic emissaries and representatives of the Griseo Morbidus (Standard Grey), the Cerastis Sapiens (Horned Reptoids), the Serpens Sophos (Smooth Skinned Reptoids), the Griseo Altus (Tall Grey) and the Serpens Alatus (Winged Reptoids).

Covenant of Adamus of Prometheus and the Cuilliaéan

The Cuilliaéan of planet Earth are the strongest blood aggregate and personification within the form of Homo Sapiens of the ancient hominid Homo Prometheus, itself the perfected union of the hominids of planet Earth and the Serpens species of other worlds, emerging at the beginning of the Neolithic period and rising to a high culture of law, religion, language and knowledge during the late Neolithic period.

Adamus represents the uninterrupted and unextinguished Original Law and Original Rights of the Original Nations (Tribes) that have always been present upon the lands now known as Ireland (Eire). The complete consciousness, culture, languages, rules, symbols, rituals, laws and rights of the first cultures and traditional owners of hominid species of Homo Sapiens of the ancient hominid Homo Prometheus embodied within the Covenant of *Adamus* of the Cuilliaéan are entrusted through the Authentic Sacred Deposit of Trust, to the embodiment and organs of the present sacred Covenant and no other.

11. The Covenant of ***Nana*** of the Mother Goddess of Heaven and Earth embodies in sacred trust the complete consciousness, culture, languages, rules, symbols, rituals, laws and rights of the worship of the feminine as goddess and Queen and Mother of Heaven of ancient Mesopotamian and Near-East Cultures.

Covenant of Nana of the Mother Goddess of Heaven and Earth

Nana represents the uninterrupted and unextinguished Original Law and Original Rights of the Original Nations (Tribes) that have always been present upon the lands ancient Mesopotamian and Near-East Cultures . The complete consciousness, culture, languages, rules, symbols, rituals, laws and rights of the cultures and peoples embodied within the Covenant of *Nana* as Queen and Mother of Heaven are entrusted through the Authentic Sacred Deposit of Trust, to the embodiment and organs of the present sacred Covenant and no other.

12. The Covenant of ***Alma*** of the Mother Goddess embodies in sacred trust the complete consciousness, culture, languages, rules, symbols, rituals, laws and rights of the worship of the feminine as goddess and Queen of ancient southern Arabia, East Africa and Indus Valley (India).

Covenant of Alma of South Arabia, East Africa and India

Alma represents the uninterrupted and unextinguished Original Law and Original Rights of the Original Nations (Tribes) that have always been present upon the lands of Arabia, East Africa and Indus Valley (India) . The complete consciousness, culture, languages, rules, symbols, rituals, laws and rights of the cultures and peoples embodied within the Covenant of *Alma* as Queen are entrusted through the Authentic Sacred Deposit of Trust, to the embodiment and organs of the present sacred Covenant and no other.

13. The Covenant of ***Elohim*** of Abraham and the Patriarchs embodies in sacred trust the complete consciousness, culture, languages, rules, symbols, rituals, laws and rights of the first cultures and traditional owners of Ebla and the regions of Syria, the Levant and Mesopotamia.

Covenant of Elohim of Abraham and Patriarchs of Ebla

The city of Ebla in northern Syria represented one of the greatest cities of human civilisation and the cradle of high culture, knowledge and religion more than four and a half thousand years ago. It is by tradition, the birthplace of some of the greatest Patriarchs of antiquity including, but not limited to Ab-ra-mu (Abraham), E-sa-um (Esau), Ish-ma-ilu (Ishmael), Da-'u'dum (David) and Sa-'u-lum (Saul), later to be overshadowed by the city of Urgarit.

Elohim represents the uninterrupted and unextinguished Original Law and Original Rights of the Original Nations (Tribes) that have always been present upon the lands of northern Syria. The complete consciousness, culture, languages, rules, symbols, rituals, laws and rights of the first cultures and traditional owners of Ebla and the regions of Syria, the Levant and Mesopotamia embodied within the Covenant of *Elohim* of Abraham and the Patriarchs is entrusted through the Authentic Sacred Deposit of Trust, to the embodiment and organs of the present sacred Covenant and no other.

14. The Covenant of ***KaBaLaAh*** of Akhenaten (Moses) and the Yahudi embodies in sacred trust the complete consciousness, culture, languages, rules, symbols, rituals, laws and rights of the Hyksos in honouring supremacy of the Divine Creator of all existence; and the spirits of the Earth; and in acknowledging the positive influence and wisdom of the Serpens and the repudiation of the Griseo Morbidus (Standard Grey) and Griseo Altus (Tall Grey).

Covenant of Kabalaah of Akhenaten (Moses) and the Yahudi

It is Akhenaten that is Moses and did pledge his symbols of power and authority of Egypt as signs of a new covenant, such as his Ark of the Spirit of Re, to signify the new Ark of the Covenant. Thus all cultures and religions since that place the Ark of the Covenant at the forefront of their claims of authenticity and origin are therefore derived from the Covenant and powers of Akhenaten.

KaBaLaAh represents the uninterrupted and unextinguished Original Law and Original Rights of the Original Nations (Tribes) that have always been present upon the lands of North Africa and the Levant. The complete consciousness, culture, languages, rules, symbols, rituals, laws and rights of the Yahudi embodied within the Covenant of KaBaLaAh of Akhenaten (Moses) and the Hyksos are entrusted through the Authentic Sacred Deposit of Trust, to the embodiment and organs of the present sacred Covenant and no other.

15. The Covenant of ***Revelations*** of the Great Prophets of Yeb embodies in sacred trust the complete consciousness, culture, languages, rules, symbols, rituals, laws and rights of the Great Prophets and Divine Messengers of the ancient world.

Covenant of Revelations of the thirty-three Great Prophets of Yeb

The Great Prophets of Yeb (Elephantine Island) at Yei-Hu (Yahu) on the Nile River in Upper Egypt, are the oldest and most famous continuous hereditary and apostolic lineage of Divine Messengers of Cuilliaéan blood in the history of the ancient world. As the site of Yei-Hu was the base of the Kabalaah and the Tree of Life between Heaven and Earth, in honour of the primordial mother (Mut) of all Heaven and Earth, the writings of the thirty-three (33) Great prophets of Yeb remains some of the most important scripture of humanity.

The thirty-three (33) Great Prophets of Yeb were Aaroniah, Enociah, Zedekiah, Obadiah, Uvidiah (David), Elijiah, Ahijiah, Azariah, Ananiah, Amoziah, Isaiah, Ezekiah, Amariah, Edaliah, Zephaniah, Ilkiah (Michaiah), Jeremiah, Barukiah, Osiah (Hosea), Osanniah (Hosanna), Eliah, Oadiah, Oananiah, Adiah, Oniah, Eleziah, Elkaniah, Zadokiah, Barachiah, Adoniah (Cu-Roi), Yasiah (Joseph, Cu-Cuileann), Yahusiah (Jesus, Cu-Laoch) and Yahobiah (Jacob).

Revelations represents the uninterrupted and unextinguished Original Law and Original Rights of the Original Nations (Tribes) that have always been present upon the lands of North Africa and the Levant. The complete consciousness, culture, languages, rules, symbols, rituals, laws and rights of the Great Prophets and Divine Messengers of the ancient world embodied within the Covenant of Revelations of the Great Prophets of Yeb is entrusted through the Authentic Sacred Deposit of Trust, to the embodiment and organs of the present sacred Covenant and no other.

16. The Covenant of ***Tara*** of Jeremiah and the Celts embodies in sacred trust the complete consciousness, culture, languages, rules, symbols, rituals, laws and rights of the Celts cultures of Europe and Asia.

Covenant of Tara of Jeremiah and the Celts

The Celtic culture of planet Earth is a successor of the Cuilliaéan culture as the embodiment of the oldest priest-king bloodlines of Syria, Mesopotamia, Egypt, Europe and Asia and the personification of the greatest messengers of Heaven in the form of the Great Prophets of Yeb as the Sons of Man, the Holly Spirit made flesh and ones anointed (Christs) by Divine Commission to teach, to guide and to admonish the people of planet Earth.

Tara represents the uninterrupted and unextinguished Original Law and Original Rights of the Original Nations (Tribes) that have always been present upon the lands of Western and Northern Europe. The complete consciousness, culture, languages, rules, symbols, rituals, laws and rights embodied within the Covenant of Tara of Jeremiah and the Celts are entrusted through the Authentic Sacred Deposit of Trust, to the embodiment and organs of the present sacred Covenant and no other.

17. The Covenant of ***Five Worlds*** of the People of North-Central America embodies in sacred trust the complete consciousness, culture, languages, rules, symbols, rituals, laws and rights of the cultures and traditional owners of hominid species of North and Central America.

Covenant of Five Worlds of the North-Central America

The *Five Worlds* of the People of North-Central America are the aggregate of the cultures and traditional owners of hominid species of North America and Central America beginning in the late Mesolithic period and rising to a high culture of law, language and knowledge during the end of the Neolithic period.

Five Worlds represents the uninterrupted and unextinguished Original Law and Original Rights of the Original Nations (Tribes) that have always been present upon the lands of North America and Central America. The complete consciousness, culture, languages, rules, symbols, rituals, laws and rights of the cultures and traditional owners of hominid species of North America and Central America embodied within the Covenant of the Five Worlds of the First Nations is entrusted through the Authentic Sacred Deposit of Trust, to the embodiment and organs of the present sacred Covenant and no other.

18. The Covenant of ***Missal*** of Baal Mithra embodies in sacred trust the complete consciousness, culture, languages, rules, symbols, rituals, laws and rights of all sects and versions of Baal and Mithra of the ancient world.

Covenant of Missal of Baal Mithra

The ancient worship of Baal as saviour was personified under the

Persian kings and later under Roma in the form of Mithra, borne upon the Ides of Mars (14 Nisan, 14th March) as the lamb of god, the saviour king and bringer of balance and return to harmony of the planet of the ancient world. By the 1st Century CE, the worship and respect of Mithra dominated all other religions as the symbol of all oaths, vows and agreements.

Missal represents the uninterrupted and unextinguished Original Law and Original Rights of the Original Nations (Tribes) that have always been present upon the lands of the ancient Persian Empire. The complete consciousness, culture, languages, rules, symbols, rituals, laws and rights of all sects and versions of Baal and Mithra of the ancient world embodied within the Covenant of Missal of Baal Mithra is entrusted through the Authentic Sacred Deposit of Trust, to the embodiment and organs of the present sacred Covenant and no other.

19. The Covenant of ***Acadia*** of Xerxes embodies in sacred trust the complete consciousness, culture, languages, rules, symbols, rituals, laws and rights of the cultures of higher learning and respect through the blending of Zoroastrian philosophies and Cuilliaéan wisdom.

Covenant of Acadia of Xerxes

The Acadian Empire of Asia and Europe is the embodiment of the most ancient knowledge of Asia, Europe, Africa and the Middle East beginning around 500 BCE as to the emancipation of all men and women through knowledge, self discipline and virtue to be equals with the most ancient priest-kings of the Cuilliaéan, not by blood right, but by the Golden Rule of Law and recognition of Sacred Rights bestowed to all.

Acadia represents the uninterrupted and unextinguished Original Law and Original Rights of the Original Nations (Tribes) that have always been present upon the lands of the ancient Persian Empire. The complete consciousness, culture, languages, rules, symbols, rituals, laws and rights embodied within the Covenant of Acadia of Xerxes are entrusted through the Authentic Sacred Deposit of Trust, to the embodiment and organs of the present sacred covenant and no other.

20. The Covenant of ***Eliada*** of Alexander embodies in sacred trust the complete consciousness, culture, languages, rules, symbols, rituals, laws and rights of the cultures and traditions of enlightenment throughout Asia.

Covenant of Eliada of Alexander

The Eliada Empire of planet Earth is a successor of reformed Cuilliaéan culture as the embodiment of the oldest priest-king bloodlines of Syria, Mesopotamia, Egypt, Europe and Asia and the personification of the greatest messengers of Heaven in the form of the Great Prophets of Yeb as the Sons of Man, the Holly Spirit made flesh and ones anointed (Christs) by Divine Commission no longer to rule as Gods, but to serve and free humanity from false teachings and errors of doctrine as saviours.

Eliada represents the uninterrupted and unextinguished Original Law and Original Rights of the Original Nations (Tribes) that have always been present upon the lands of the ancient Macedonian-Persian empire at its height. The complete consciousness, culture, languages, rules, symbols, rituals, laws and rights as embodied within the Covenant of *Eliada* of Alexander are entrusted through the Authentic Sacred Deposit of Trust, to the embodiment and organs of the present sacred Covenant and no other.

21. The Covenant of ***Tabiti*** (Sacred Fire) of the Great Asiatic Plains People embodies in sacred trust the complete consciousness, culture, languages, rules, symbols, rituals, laws and rights of the cultures and traditions of enlightenment of the Great Asiatic Plains People that lived from the steppes of Russia and Ukraine to Mongolia across to China.

Covenant of Tabiti of Great Asiatic Plains People

Tabiti represents the uninterrupted and unextinguished Original Law and Original Rights of the Original Nations (Tribes) that have always been present upon the lands from the steppes of Russia and Ukraine to Mongolia across to China. The complete consciousness, culture, languages, rules, symbols, rituals, laws and rights as embodied within the (Sacred Fire) of the Great Asiatic Plains are entrusted through the Authentic Sacred Deposit of Trust, to the embodiment and organs of the present sacred Covenant and no other.

22. The Covenant of ***Tiandi*** (Heaven and Earth) of Qin Shi Huang embodies in sacred trust the complete consciousness, culture, languages, rules, symbols, rituals, laws and rights of unified China.

Covenant of Tiandi (Heaven and Earth) of Qin Shi Huang

Qin Shi Huang, also known as Ying Zheng, is the King of the State of Qin that around 235BCE commissioned his finest scholars to travel West to obtain the knowledge of Aristotle and the Empire of Alexander and then help form a philosophy to unite China and end the war between the kingdoms. It is Qin Shi Huang that history should rightly recognise as the architect of the Covenant of Heaven and Earth that united China for the first time as the Qin Dynasty.

Tiandi represents the uninterrupted and unextinguished Original Law and Original Rights of the Original Nations (Tribes) that have always been present upon the lands now known as China. The complete consciousness, culture, languages, rules, symbols, rituals, laws and rights of unified China embodied within the Covenant of Heaven and Earth of Qin Shi Huang is entrusted through the Authentic Sacred

Deposit of Trust, to the embodiment and organs of the present sacred Covenant and no other.

23. The Covenant of ***Nazara*** (Truth) of Yahusiah (Jesus Christ) embodies in sacred trust the complete consciousness, culture, languages, rules, symbols, rituals, laws and rights of the cultures and traditions of enlightenment of the Holly.

Covenant of Nazara of Yahusiah (Jesus Christ)

The Nazarenes, as seekers and followers of Divine Truth, are the apostolic successors of reformed Cuilliaéan culture through the teachings of the thirty second and last Great Prophet of Yeb, also known as Yahusiah, also known as Jesus Christ, as to the equality and freedom and rights of all men and women; the redemption and forgiveness of all debts through the symbol and knowledge of the resurrection; and the absolute right of all men and women to knowledge of heaven; and the sacred mission of Holly Messengers to be teachers and saviours and not as rulers of humanity.

Nazara represents the uninterrupted and unextinguished Original Law and Original Rights of the Original Nations (Tribes) that have always been present upon the lands of Palestine and Western Europe. The complete consciousness, culture, languages, rules, symbols, rituals, laws and rights of the Nazarenes embodied within the Covenant of *Nazara* of Yahusiah are entrusted through the Authentic Sacred Deposit of Trust, to the embodiment and organs of the present sacred Covenant and no other.

24. The Covenant of ***Nirvana*** (Freedom & Awakening) of Gautama (Buddha) embodies in sacred trust the complete consciousness, culture, languages, rules, symbols, rituals, laws and rights of the cultures and traditions of enlightenment throughout Asia, including but not limited to the teachings of Prince Gautama as Buddha.

Covenant of Nirvana (Freedom & Awakening) of Gautama (Buddha)

Nirvana represents the uninterrupted and unextinguished Original Law and Original Rights of the Original Nations (Tribes) that have always been present upon the lands of Northern India and Asia. The complete consciousness, culture, languages, rules, symbols, rituals, laws and rights of the cultures and traditions of Buddhism throughout Asia, including but not limited to the teachings of Prince Gautama as Buddha embodied within the Covenant of *Nirvana* are entrusted through the Authentic Sacred Deposit of Trust, to the embodiment and organs of the present sacred Covenant and no other.

25. The Covenant of ***Zhongdao*** (The Middle Way) of Kong Qiu (Confucius) embodies in sacred trust the complete consciousness, culture, languages, rules, symbols, rituals, laws and rights of the cultures and traditions of enlightenment throughout Asia, including

Covenant of Zhongdao (The Middle Way) of Kong Qiu (Confucius)

but not limited to the teachings of Kong Qiu (Confucius).

Zhongdao represents the uninterrupted and unextinguished Original Law and Original Rights of the Original Nations (Tribes) that have always been present upon the lands of China and Asia. The complete consciousness, culture, languages, rules, symbols, rituals, laws and rights embodied within the Covenant of *Zhongdao* (The Middle Way) is entrusted through the Authentic Sacred Deposit of Trust, to the embodiment and organs of the present sacred Covenant and no other.

Covenant of Septuaginta of Iudaism (Josephus)

26. The Covenant of ***Septuaginta*** of Iudaism embodies in sacred trust the complete consciousness, culture, languages, rules, symbols, rituals, laws and rights of founding of Iudaism (Judaism) from 70 CE to 120 CE as the Cult of Lucifer across the Roman Empire.

The formation of the official cult of *Iudaism* upon the complete collapse of the religion of Mithra in 69 CE upon the destruction of the Great Temple Mint to Mithra, six hundred and sixty-six (666) years to the day since the destruction of the Temple of Setien (Satan) in Jerusalem, heralded an unprecedented change in the ancient world, when Emperor Vespasian proclaimed himself Lucifer and saviour of Rome under the symbol of the blazing sun and the Trigram IHS or *Invictus Hoc Signum* meaning "By this sign (we are) unconquerable". Furthermore, new scriptures were commissioned by blending and re-writing other ancient texts, especially the prophecies of the Great Prophets of Yeb so that the foretelling of Vespasian as Lucifer would be fulfilled. The scholars of Qumran near the Dead Sea, along with Josephus were commissioned to re-write many of the ancient texts to fulfil this task.

The complete consciousness, culture, languages, rules, symbols, rituals, laws and rights of Iudaism (Judaism) as the Cult of Lucifer across the Roman Empire embodied within the Covenant of Septuaginta of Iudaism is entrusted through the Authentic Sacred Deposit of Trust, to the embodiment and organs of the present sacred Covenant and no other.

Covenant of Eucadia of Heracles

27. The Covenant of ***Eucadia*** of Heracles of Eliada and Larissa embodies in sacred trust the complete consciousness, culture, languages, rules, symbols, rituals, laws and rights of Illuminated Men and Women at the height of self-knowledge and as exemplars of the noblest of virtues.

The Eliada and Larissa cultures of ancient Greece at the time of Heracles in the 1st and 2nd centuries CE, signify the highest point of cultural and spiritual advancement of the region in the conscious and deliberate formation of a Utopia as a Kingdom of Heaven upon the Earth known as Eucadia (Ucadia) as the manifestation of the highest ideals of truth, the Golden Rule of law, justice and human dignity.

Eucadia represents the uninterrupted and unextinguished Original Law and Original Rights of the Original Nations (Tribes) that have always been present upon the lands now known as Greece. The complete consciousness, culture, languages, rules, symbols, rituals, laws and rights of Eucadia (Ucadia) of ancient Greece embodied within the Covenant of Eucadia (Ucadia) of Heracles of Eliada and Larissa as Heaven on Earth are entrusted through the Authentic Sacred Deposit of Trust, to the embodiment and organs of the present sacred Covenant and no other.

28. The Covenant of ***Kikilil Yuum Witzil*** (Great Cycle of Celestial Realm and Earth) of South and Central America civilisations embodies in sacred trust the formation of advanced civilisation, knowledge and culture, resting upon social discipline and authority.

Covenant of Kikilil Yuum Witzil (Great Cycle of Celestial Realm and Earth) of South-Central America

Kikilil Yuum Witzil represents the uninterrupted and unextinguished Original Law and Original Rights of the Original Nations (Tribes) that have always been present upon the lands of Central and South America. The complete consciousness, culture, languages, rules, symbols, rituals, laws and rights of ancient Central and South American Civilisations embodied within the Covenant of *Kikilil Yuum Witzil* (Great Cycle of Celestial Realm and Earth) are entrusted through the Authentic Sacred Deposit of Trust, to the embodiment and organs of the present sacred Covenant and no other.

29. The Covenant of ***Digesta*** of Marcus Aurelius embodies in sacred trust the formation of the dignity of the enlightened soul, capable of rising beyond their weaknesses to a firm command of self-discipline, truth and virtue, whilst championing the freedoms and rights of all men and women.

Covenant of Digesta of Marcus Aurelius

Marcus Aurelius as the undisputed Emperor of Rome, King of the Franks, blood descendant of Yahusiah (Jesus Christ) and the Cuilliaéan, is the founder and architect of Rome Redeemed in the form of self-disciplines, virtues and knowledge adopting a truly democratic and benevolent Roman Empire ending slavery and acknowledging the equality of all men and women upon planet Earth.

Digesta represents the uninterrupted and unextinguished Original Law and Original Rights of the Original Nations (Tribes) that have always been present upon the lands of the former Roman Empire. The complete consciousness, culture, languages, rules, symbols, rituals, laws, authorities and rights of Rome Redeemed as first formed by Marcus Aurelius embodied within the Covenant of *Digesta* of Marcus Aurelius are entrusted through the Authentic Sacred Deposit of Trust, to the embodiment and organs of the present sacred Covenant and no other.

30. The Covenant of ***Bibliographe*** of Christianity embodies in sacred trust the formation of a global model of democracy, law, rights and dignity for planet Earth known as "Theke" (pronounced the key) as the authentic and original body of Christian authority, church and community.

Covenant of Bibliographe of Christianity of Constantine

Constantine as the last Emperor of Rome and the Emperor of the Celts and the Priest-King of Eukadia (Ucadia) as Heaven on Earth, as a blood descendent of Yahusiah (Jesus Christ) and the Cuilliaéan, is the founder and architect of Christianity and its highest ideals, knowledge and operation as the first truly democratic and representative model of the equality of all men and women upon planet Earth.

Bibliographe represents the uninterrupted and unextinguished Original Law and Original Rights of the Original Nations (Tribes) that have always been present upon the lands of Western Europe, Northern Europe, North Africa, the Middle East and Asia Minor. The complete consciousness, culture, languages, rules, symbols, rituals, laws, authorities and rights of the Christian Body as first formed by Constantine to the four corners of the Earth embodied within the Covenant of Bibliographe of Christianity are entrusted through the Authentic Sacred Deposit of Trust, to the embodiment and organs of the present sacred Covenant and no other.

31. The Covenant of ***Dao*** (the Way) embodies in sacred trust the complete consciousness, culture, languages, rules, symbols, rituals, laws and rights of the first cultures and traditions of Taoism since its creation.

Covenant of Dao (the Way)

Dao represents the uninterrupted and unextinguished Original Law and Original Rights of the Original Nations (Tribes) that have always been present upon the lands of Asia. The complete consciousness, culture, languages, rules, symbols, rituals, laws and rights of Taoism since its creation embodied within the Covenant of *Dao* is entrusted through the Authentic Sacred Deposit of Trust, to the embodiment and organs of the present sacred Covenant and no other.

32. The Covenant of ***Kami Yoso Seimei*** (Spirits of Elements and Life) of the way of Shinto (Japan) embodies in sacred trust the complete consciousness, culture, languages, rules, symbols, rituals, laws and rights of the first cultures and traditions of Shintoism since its creation.

Covenant of Kami Yoso Seimei (Spirits of Elements and Life) of the way of Shinto (Japan)

Kami Yoso Seimei represents the uninterrupted and unextinguished Original Law and Original Rights of the Original Nations (Tribes) that have always been present upon the lands now known as Japan. The complete consciousness, culture, languages, rules, symbols, rituals, laws and rights of Shintoism since its creation embodied within the Covenant of *Kami Yoso Seimei* is entrusted through the Authentic Sacred Deposit of Trust, to the embodiment and organs of the present sacred Covenant and no other.

33. The Covenant of ***Sanatana Dharma*** (Eternal Truth) of Brahman (Hinduism) embodies in sacred trust the complete consciousness, culture, languages, rules, symbols, rituals, laws and rights of the first cultures and traditions of Hinduism since its creation.

Covenant of Sanatana Dharma (Eternal Truth) of Brahman (Hinduism)

The refugees of the Aryan Empire in the 4th Century CE that fled eastward as a result of Christianity, formed the basis of the Gupta Empire in India and the founding of the Hindu version of Aryanism as Brahmanism. This is the true era of birth of Hindu and caste literature, including the introduction of numerous Aryan symbols such as the Swastika.

Sanatana Dharma represents the uninterrupted and unextinguished Original Law and Original Rights of the Original Nations (Tribes) that have always been present upon the lands of India and Asia. The complete consciousness, culture, languages, rules, symbols, rituals, laws and rights of Hinduism since its creation embodied within the Covenant of Sanatana Dharma of the Supreme Creator is entrusted through the Authentic Sacred Deposit of Trust, to the embodiment and organs of the present sacred Covenant and no other.

34. The Covenant of ***Quran Al Sufian*** (Recitations of Wisdom of the Way) of Sophos (The Great Prophet) embodies in sacred trust the complete consciousness, culture, languages, rules, symbols, rituals, laws and rights of Islam as first given to the Great Prophet by the Creator of All Existence and of Heaven and Earth through the miracle of the text and covenant known as *Quran Al Sufian.*

Covenant of Quran Al Sufian (Recitations of Wisdom of the Way) of Sophos (Islam)

The Leader of the Saracenia Empire, also known as the Great Prophet, being an educated and compassionate man, having both the blood of the ancient Keepers of Time and Space of Saracenia (Arabia) in his veins as well as descended of the Cuilliaéan, was the architect in Ancient Greek of a philosophy and Divine Revelation honouring the Divine Creator of all existence and heaven and earth, calling for all men and women to cease such wilful ignorance, blasphemy and profanity in living without virtue, killing in the name of religion and serving the interests of slave traders and merchants of doom.

Quran Al Sufian represents the uninterrupted and unextinguished Original Law and Original Rights of the Original Nations (Tribes) that have always been present upon the lands of North Africa, Middle East and Asia. The complete consciousness, culture, languages, rules, symbols, rituals, laws and rights of Islam embodied within the Covenant of *Al Sufian* of the Great Prophet and Islam are entrusted through the Authentic Sacred Deposit of Trust, to the embodiment and organs of the present sacred Covenant and no other.

35. The Covenant of ***Holy Bible*** (**Nova Testamentum**) of Catholicism of the Franks embodies in sacred trust the complete consciousness, culture, languages, rules, symbols, rituals, laws and rights of the cultures of the true and original Catholic Church as first formed in 741 CE, particularly the formation of the Four (4) Gospels.

Covenant of Holy Bible of Catholicism of the Franks

The Kings of the Franks, also known as the Carolingians, as true descendants of Constantine; and blood descendants of Yahusia (Jesus Christ) and the Cuilliaéan, are the true founders and original architects of the Catholic Church in 741 CE and its highest ideals, knowledge and operation as the restoration of the Rule of Law and the ideals of Christianity upon planet Earth.

Holy Bible represents the uninterrupted and unextinguished Original Law and Original Rights of the Original Nations (Tribes) that have always been present upon the lands now known as Western Civilisation. The complete consciousness, culture, languages, rules, symbols, rituals, laws and rights of the Catholic Church embodied within the Covenant of *Nova Testamentum* of Catholicism of the Franks is entrusted through the Authentic Sacred Deposit of Trust, to the embodiment and organs of the present sacred Covenant and no other.

36. The Covenant of ***Gurmat*** (Eternal Truth) of Sikhism embodies in sacred trust the teachings, knowledge, discipline and wisdom of Guru Nanak and the Gurma of the founding Gurus of Sikhism, including the consciousness, complete culture, languages, rules, symbols, rituals, laws and rights of Sikhism. The Sikh culture and philosophy, as first revealed through Guru Nanak in the 15th Century in Northern India, is testament to an extraordinary covenant of heroism, self-discipline and aesthetic learning. The term Gurma honours the teachings of Guru Nanak as the “self-evident” truths of a teacher and divine messenger.

Covenant of Eternal Truth of Gurmat (Sikhism)

Gurmat represents the uninterrupted and unextinguished Original Law and Original Rights of the Original Nations (Tribes) that have always been present upon the lands now known as Northern and Central India. The complete consciousness, culture, languages, rules, symbols, rituals, laws and rights of the first cultures of Sikhism embodied within the Covenant of Eternal Truth of Gurma is entrusted through the Authentic Sacred Deposit of Trust, to the embodiment and organs of the present sacred Covenant and no other.

37. The Covenant of ***Lebor Clann Glas*** of the Diaspora of the Holly, also known as the Sangreal (Holy Grail), also known as the Cuilliaéan and by many other names embodies in sacred trust the complete consciousness, history, culture, languages, rules, symbols, rituals, laws and rights of the one, true and only Diaspora throughout the ages. Covenant of Lebor Clann Glas of the Holly Diaspora

The complete consciousness, history, culture, languages, rules, symbols, rituals, laws and rights of the Cuilliaéan as the Diaspora embodied within the Covenant of *Lebor Clann Glas* is entrusted through the Authentic Sacred Deposit of Trust, to the embodiment and organs of the present sacred Covenant and no other.

Article 24 – Sacred Agreement

1. **So long as two or more faithful to One Heaven** agree to participate in a fair, open and transparent public process under the rules of this Covenant, the present most sacred Covenant shall be the one, true immutable law of true One Heaven; and the highest of all Law in Heaven or upon the Earth and throughout the Universe. Immutability of Covenant

2. Force of arms from a group, within or without, cannot invalidate this Covenant. Tyranny will not prevail. By virtue of this Covenant being enacted, it remains valid unless a valid and legitimate majority of Living and Spirit Members of One Heaven choose in accord with the conditions enumerated within the Articles herein to invalidate all or part of the present most sacred Covenant. Force Cannot Invalidate this Covenant

3. No claim of blasphemy against the present most sacred Covenant shall be valid whatsoever, for it is the very word and Will of the One, the Absolute, the One and Only, the Unique Collective Awareness, the Almighty. No Claim of Blasphemy is Valid

To believe in a higher power is to believe that our skills belong to and are part of that greater power. Therefore, supreme blasphemy is in fact not to use those gifts given to us, those responsibilities that fall to us and to turn our backs against the will of God. Therefore, claims of blasphemy against this document are in fact blasphemous deceit against the specific Will of the Absolute.

4. No claim of prior authority through any instrument or thing, no matter how old or sacred it is viewed, can prevail above the present most sacred Covenant. No Claim of Prior Authority Can Prevail

The most sacred of scriptures and texts are believed to be the word of the Absolute and our collective covenant and special relationship. However, by these very scriptures, greater power is deferred to the will of the Absolute and to the greater history of Heaven. Therefore this document representing the union of Heaven, once more represents the most supreme of all documents, no matter what age, content or reverence.

5. The present most sacred Covenant is the fulfilment of scripture. It is the Alpha and Omega. All souls who overcome their differences now awaken to the tree of knowledge within their minds, their immortal souls.

The Fulfilment of Scripture

TITLE VIII - SOL (SOLAR SYSTEM) PRINCIPLES

Article 25 – The Divine Science

1. **The Divine Science** shall be the term used to define a valid philosophical system defining the proof, arguments, existence, principles and theoretical relations between a particular Cosmological Model, the Divine, Divine Revelation, Divine Law, Divine Rights, Powers and Authorities and associated Prophets, consistent with the present most sacred Covenant. The Divine Science

2. While a Science of the Divine may be brief, by definition a philosophical system shall not be a valid or legitimate scientific branch of knowledge unless it possesses the following criteria:- The Structure of a Valid Science of The Divine

    (i) A direct association of Greatest Principles and Teachings with Cosmology defining the universe, laws of the universe, relation between matter and rules, levels of matter and the function and purpose of the universe; and

    (ii) A central and foundational set of arguments concerning Divine Existence, Divine Nature and Divine Mind (or Purpose) in support of theological Cosmology as proof; and

    (iii) An association with one or more bodies of texts considered the most sacred scripture as the source of such Divine Revelations; and

    (iv) An association with one or more bodies of maxims of law based upon such fundamental theological arguments and sacred text reference whereby certain norms, standards and maxims of law are asserted; and

    (v) A form of arguments, justifications and methods by which the sacred texts and theological system is considered superior than others with similar or competing ideas; and

    (vi) An association with one or more formal defined rituals or customs as one or more sacraments; and a form of arguments and justifications for these particular rituals or customs.

3. In accord with the present most sacred Covenant, each of the three (3) Great Faiths shall be permitted to use their own official name for the *Divine Science*:- Great Faiths and Divine Science

    (i) The Universal Ecclesia of One Christ may use the name "**Summa Elementis Theologica**" to officially define the Essential Elements of Theology from the perspective of their authority; and

(ii) The Holy Society of One Islam may use the name "**Farid Eulim Allah**" to officially define the Unique Knowledge of God from the perspective of their authority; and

(iii) Sacred Society of One Spirit may use the name "**Divya Darshana**" to officially define the Perspective of the Divine from the perspective of their authority.

Article 26 – Planetary Life

1. **Planetary Life** is acknowledged as a state and conditions for the stable formation of movable complex molecular structures on the surface and in the air of planets and moons with the right conditions. Planetary Life

The primary and necessary condition for life on the surface of a planet or moon is the presence of a compressed and dense molecular atmosphere, such that it permits the conditions for sustained and stable liquid molecular bonds, apart from gaseous molecular bonds.

These conditions for liquid molecular bonds are frequently termed "oceans" with the most useful of liquid molecular formations for Hydro-Carbon Life being abundant H2O (Water) molecules.

The unique collective of Life of a planet or a solar system or a galaxy may therefore be defined as CORPUS as the embodiment and personification of LIFE.

2. The first level of Hydro-Carbon Life may be categorised into sub categories of simple natural polymers and complex polymers. By the rules of the Universe as defined in this Covenant, wherever the conditions exist for the formation of Hydro-Carbon Polymers, they will occur. Level 1 Complex Carbon-Molecular (Polymers)

It is a principle of this Covenant that natural formation of Hydro-Carbon Polymers manifest in every single Star System to some degree at one time or another. Polymers may be divided into Simple and Complex, namely:-

(i) *Simple Polymers* (Sugars, Fats, Amino Acids, Nucleic Acids); and

(ii) *Complex Polymers* (Hormones, Complex Fats, Vitamins, Proteins).

3. The second level of Hydro-Carbon Life may itself be defined into sub-categories of simple and complex mono-cellular organisms. By the rules of the Universe as defined in this Covenant, wherever the conditions exist for the formation of Hydro-Carbon Polymers, they will Level 2 Simple mono-cellular Hydro-Carbon Biologics

occur. Wherever Hydro-Carbon Polymers exist, simple mono-cellular life will also form naturally.

It is a principle concept of this Covenant that the natural formation of Mono-Cellular Hydro-Carbon Life forms in every single Star System to some degree, metal based planets or moons exist with surface temperatures higher than minus -100 degrees Celsius and lower than minus -200 degrees Celsius at some time. Mono-Cellular Hydro-Carbon Life may be divided into Primordial and Advanced, namely:-

1. Primordial Mono-Cellular Hydro-Carbon Life

(i) *Cellular Creators* (also called prokaryotic cells) such as bacteria and cynobacteria; and

(ii) *Cellular Destructive Attractors* such as viruses.

2. Advanced Mono-Cellular Hydro-Carbon Life

(i) *Cellular Creators* such as protozoa, sacodina, ciliata; and

(ii) *Cellular Destructive Attractors* such as Euglenids, Trypanosoma, Trichomonas and Codosiga.

4. The third level of Hydro-Carbon Life may itself be defined into sub-categories of simple multi-cellular organisms, namely:-

Level 3 Simple asexual Multi-cellular Hydro-Carbon Biologics - mono neural systems

1. Fungi

2. Algae

3. Primal Eukaryotes

(i) Jellies & Sponges; and

(ii) Worms & Echioderms.

4. Primal Prokaryotes

(i) Ferns & Horsetails; and

(ii) Psilophytes; and

(iii) Moss.

5. The fourth level of Hydro-Carbon Life may itself be defined into sub categories of simple sexual - multicellular organisms, namely:-

Level 4 Simple sexual Multicellular Hydro-Carbon Biologics - dual neural systems

(i) Coral; and

(ii) Mollusks; and

(iii) Crustaceans; and

(iv) Insects & Pedes; and

(v) Trees; and

(vi) Flowering Plants.

6. The fifth level of Hydro-Carbon Life may itself be defined into sub categories of complex sexual multicellular organisms, namely:- Level 5 Complex multi-cellular life

1. Egg laying

(i) Fish; and

(ii) Reptiles; and

(iii) Birds; and

(iv) Monotremes.

2. Pouched (marsupials)

(i) Marsupials.

3. Placentals (mammals)

(i) Rodents; and

(ii) Carnivores; and

(iii) Pangolines; and

(iv) Sloths; and

(v) Primates; and

(vi) Bats; and

(vii) Odd-toed hoofed; and

(viii) Even-toed hoofed; and

(ix) Sea Cows; and

(x) Elephants; and

(xi) Seals; and

(xii) Rabbits/Hares; and

(xiii) Colugos; and

(xiv) Hyraxes; and

(xv) Dolphin.

Article 27 – Higher Order Life

1. **Higher Order Life** shall be defined as those life forms that have the capacity to dream, to project their own reality onto the world and self reflect, to display emotions. Principally on Earth, this represents the placentals, the most advanced of all life forms (usually called mammals). Higher Order Life

In regard to self aware life, this principally means triple neural life forms on planet Earth - the vertebrates and principally the placentals (mammals).

These life forms have the most advanced neural network systems. Therefore, we can reliably use the structure and complexity of brain systems to categorise self aware life on planet Earth.

2. The twelve (12) levels of the journey of Human Life shall be:- Unique Collective Awareness understanding of Higher Order Life

(i) *Level 1 of Human Life* is our first divine form and potential as Divine Person; and

(ii) *Level 2 of Human Life* is fetal from day fifty-five (55) onward from conception when the unborne baby is clearly human and the connection of spirit, mind and heart; and

(iii) *Level 3 of Human Life* is mortal infancy from birth at nine (9) months to the age of four (4) years; and

(iv) *Level 4 of Human Life* is childhood from the age of four (4) to eleven (11) years; and

(v) *Level 5 of Human Life* is adolescence from the age of eleven (11) to twenty-one (21) years; and

(vi) *Level 6 of Human Life* is youthhood from the age of twenty-one (21) to the age of thirty-three (33) years; and

(vii) *Level 7 of Human Life* is adulthood from the age of thirty-three (33) to fifty-five (55) years; and

(viii) *Level 8 of Human Life* is seniorhood from the age of fifty-five (55) to seventy-seven (77) years; and

(ix) *Level 9 of Human Life* is elderhood from the age of seventy-seven (77) years to death; and

(x) *Level 10 of Human Life* is death and the moment of dying; and

(xi) *Level 11 of Human Life* is transition of the mind and Divine Person in its separation from the body; and

(xii) *Level 12 of Human Life* is as a Divine Spirit, free from the bindings of mortality or ghost state.

3. It shall be an essential principle of this Covenant, that all Level 6 (self aware) and higher order life forms have a right to a quality and dignified life, free from unlawful physical or mental abuse or cruel and unusual punishment. The right to a quality and dignified life

4. It shall be an essential principle of this Covenant that all Level 6 (self aware) life forms, having reached the age of majority, possessing sound mind and reason, have the right to choose to die with dignity. The right to die with dignity

5. It shall be an essential principle of this Covenant that all Level 6 (self aware) life forms have the natural right of life expectancy equal to the average life expectancy of healthy members of the species. The right of life expectancy

However, all forms and modifications to life expectancy that extend life to more than twice the average life expectancy of healthy members of the species are morally repugnant, abhorrent, illegal, unlawful and to be suppressed.

Article 28 - Rule of Law & Justice

1. **Rule of Law shall be a founding principle of Law** that defines what is or is not law; and distinguishes true law from false and morally repugnant law. The ***Divine Rule of Law*** is: *A Law is a proper and authentic Rule that describes, prohibits or permits a certain Act relating to a defined Right in Trust*. The ***Golden Rule of Law*** is: *All law is equal that no one is above it; and All law is measured that all may learn and know it; and All law is standard that it may always be applied the same.* Rule of Law & Justice

Rule of Law shall exist only when:-

(i) All laws are simple and easily publicly available so that one person may reasonably learn, remember and comprehend all such laws properly; and

(ii) All laws are respectful so that no law disrespects a person purely upon the original circumstance of their birth, location, gender, race, religion or creed; and

(iii) All laws are logical so that no law is illogical in asserting certain errors and fallacies and to demand such absurdities are defended and enforced; and

(iv) All laws are reasonable so that no law demands an unreasonable or impossible act; and

(v) All laws are consistent so that no laws require contradictory or confusing behaviour; and

(vi) All laws are loyal so that no law endorses treacherous or disloyal acts; and

(vii) All laws are moral so that no law permits morally repugnant, profane or sacrilegious activity; and

(viii) All laws are remedial so that no law imposes punitive measures without first the opportunity to rectify or remedy an error; and

(ix) All laws are merciful so that no law encourages cruel and barbarous acts of vengeance.

Covenant as Embodiment of Rule of Law

2. The present most sacred Covenant is the perfection and embodiment of the Rule of Law, the Golden Rule, the First Law and the One Law. Therefore any claim or act that is against the present Covenant cannot be law and is against the Rule of Law.

The Rule of Law and Society

3. The operation of the true Rule of Law is fundamental to maintaining and supporting the connection between Heaven and Earth and between Divine Law, Natural Law, Cognitive Law and all forms of Positive Law:-

(i) When the Rule of Law ceases to exist within the jurisdiction and context of a particular fraternity, association, entity, institute, company or society, then all authority flowing through Divine Law, Natural Law, Cognitive Law and Positive Law to such a body also ceases, until properly restored; and

(ii) Whilst the Rule of Law and authority of a particular fraternity, association, entity, institute, company or society ceases, then all such acts, edicts, orders and transfers are unlawful and without any force or effect in law, irrespective of any claims to the contrary; and

(iii) No tyrant that injures the Rule of Law may then claim its protection or immunity from the consequences of their actions; and

(iv) A person or body belonging to a separate fraternity, association, entity, institute, company or society that then aids a tyrant in suppressing the true Rule of Law of another body, is equally and jointly liable for the actions of the tyrant as if they themselves directly performed such offences; and

(v) If the judicial bodies of a particular society cause the cessation of the Rule of Law, then such authority temporarily returns to the ecclesiastical bodies of the society until the Rule of Law is restored judicially and politically; and

(vi) If the ecclesiastical bodies of a particular society as well as the political and judicial bodies cause the cessation of the Rule of Law, then the people are empowered to liberate themselves of such tyranny until the Rule of Law is properly restored.

4. Justice is the constant application of the Rule of Law as the Golden Rule through good faith, clean hands and due process: Justice

(i) *Good Faith* and good intention means the law is administered fairly and without prejudice or apprehended bias; and

(ii) *Clean Hands* means one who hears and adjudicates a matter within a forum as a judge has no financial interest in the matter. For no man may serve "two masters" at the same time; and

(iii) *Due Process* is the adherence to standards of good conduct, full disclosure and proper procedure in the hearing and adjudication of a matter so that all parties may be confident in the steps, forms and proceedings.

5. These be the fundamental rules of Justice:- Fundamental Rules of Justice

(i) All are accountable and answerable under the law; and

(ii) All are without blemish until proven culpable; and

(iii) Where there is a law, there must be a cause; and

(iv) Where there is a law, there must be a penalty; and

(v) Where there is a law, there must be a remedy; and

(vi) An action in law cannot proceed without first a cause; and

(vii) An action is not granted to one who is not injured; and

(viii) The acts of valid law can do no injury (wrong); and

(ix) Acts decided in law must reflect cause of action; and

(x) No injury to law, no reason (cause) for action by law; and

(xi) An action through law cannot arise from a fraud; and

(xii) An action through law cannot arise in bad faith or prejudice; and

(xiii) No one is bound to accuse himself; and

(xiv) The act does not make one culpable unless there be intent to do wrong; and

(xv) No one may suffer punishment for mere intent; and

(xvi) No one is punished for the transgression of another; and

(xvii) No one can derive an advantage in law from his own wrong; and

(xviii) What is invalid from the beginning does not become valid over time; and

(xix) No one is accused of the same exact cause twice; and

(xx) What is done out of necessity to defend ones own life and house is lawful and legal; and

(xxi) No man be a judge and witness over his own matter; and

(xxii) No man be both judge and jury; and

(xxiii) No penalty may exist without a law; and

(xxiv) Justice never contradicts the true rule of law.

Article 29 - Divine Mercy, Remedy & Redemption

1. **Divine Mercy, Remedy & Redemption** shall be the manifest intervention of the Divine Creator of all things and all existence into the life, health and well being of humanity to ensure the sustainment of the species, its emancipation from ill conceived and dangerously evil notions; and to fulfil its potential as immortal beings carnated as flesh vessels. Divine Mercy, Remedy & Redemption

2. Verily, it is undeniable, that each and every man and woman comes into the world, with the priceless gift of Spirit and abilities to think and feel the universe around them to the highest level of the most advanced of higher order life. Mystery of Divine Remedy

It is also true, that as a species, Human Beings are bound to Earth-like conditions and the limits of physical form; and that Human minds and temperaments can evoke the most beautiful of creation and the worst of terror.

It is not by the will of God that men and women suffer, but by the circumstances of communities, life and the will of other men and women who choose not to follow the sacred teachings of the Messengers of God and the Divine Creator of all Heaven and Earth.

If people build their homes on sand, then one day they shall be washed away; not by the will of God, but the deliberate and willing ignorance of those that should know better.

In truth, Divine Mercy is always perfectly delivered and reasonable.

Thus, the highest and most sacred Covenant of One Heaven, by its very perfection and dimension, is the personification of Divine Mercy and Forgiveness. The remedy to evil cannot logically, sensibly or morally ever be more evil, as it only strengthens evil.

Therefore, any valid remedy to evil must demonstrate some alternate force of such superior form that when executed and in force, no evil can withstand it. This is the very essence of Divine Remedy and Divine Mercy.

3. The greatest and most sacred texts of all civilised history, as embodied within the corpus known as the *Sacred Texts of Heaven* are unanimous in expressing that the promise of Divine Remedy shall be found through the solution and process of Divine Redemption. Divine Redemption

This is a fundamental tenet of the Thirty-Three (33) Covenants known as *Authentic Sacred Deposit of Trust*, between Authentic, Apostolic and Anointed Divine Messengers of the Divine Creator of all Existence and all the Heavens and Earth and the peoples of the Earth.

The promise of Divine Redemption, as accounted in authentic sacred texts, foretell of specific signs, events and actions that properly represent the fulfilment of Divine Redemption.

Whilst many of these signs, events and actions appear overwhelmingly supernatural, it is clear that the underlying process of Divine Redemption follows the Rule of Law of all civilised people from the beginning of time, namely: That all will be given proper notice and the opportunity to correct their errors; and upon the dishonour and disgrace of ignoring such Divine Word, the people will still be afforded a second opportunity; and even on the complete default and delinquency of the few that disavow any legitimacy or authority of office, Divine Remedy through Divine Redemption shall offer a third and final opportunity for repentance.

Then upon the conclusion of such actions, Divine Judgement shall be rendered.

4. A text is either the true and authentic Word of God and Divine Creator of all Existence and all the Heavens and Earth, or it is not. If a text is to be trusted as being true and authentic when speaking of Eschatology and fulfilment of Divine Redemption, then such signs, events and actions foretold, must be fulfilled literally and figuratively, else such sacred text is not completely and entirely from the claimed authentic source. Mystery of Divine Redemption

Throughout the ages, this challenge of the fulfilment of signs, events and actions of Divine Redemption having to manifest literally and figuratively as true has given rise to the Mystery of Divine Redemption and the events taking place around the "end of the old world" and the "beginning of the new world".

It is undeniable, unmistakable and irrefutable that the present most sacred Covenant and the circumstance of its manifestation completely and entirely fulfils all authentic and true sacred signs, events and symbols of scripture concerning Divine Redemption, therefore makes the present most sacred Covenant the literal and physical embodiment of the Divine Mystery of Redemption.

Anyone then who refuses to acknowledge the literal, physical, spiritual and symbolic fulfilment of Divine Redemption through the present most sacred Covenant declares themselves incompetent, unfit for office and cut off from any right or authority.

5. In accord with the Divine Grace and Divine Mercy of God and the Divine Creator of all Existence and all Heaven and Earth, at the conclusion of the Day of Divine Redemption and the Year of Divine Redemption and upon the definitive and formal recognition of Divine Mercy through the expression of mercy and forgiveness to all people and all forms of life, it shall be recorded in Heaven, now and forever more that all former transgressions and injuries are forgiven without condition and that no spirit, or spiritual entity, or living or physically deceased higher order life form is permitted to be condemned, or cursed spiritually.

Mystery of Divine Mercy and Forgiveness of All

Only companies and corporations without a soul or spirit and that choose to continue to exist as soulless and spiritless entities by rejecting the present most sacred Covenant are excluded from Divine Mercy and Divine Redemption.

Therefore, it is absolutely forbidden, reprobate and a profound profanity and perfidy to deny that through the Divine Grace and Divine Mercy of God and the Divine Creator of all Existence and all Heaven and Earth, that Heaven is once more united and that no longer does there exist a place for the eternal punishment of souls, nor a formal waiting place between the temporal and spiritual worlds.

Such Divine Mercy and forgiveness does not diminish the obligations of virtue and truth and respect of the Rule of Law, but strengthens it, as all living and deceased Members are to be immediately and justly held to account for their actions at every stage of their existence in recognition of the transformative nature of all sentient beings; and that the *Magisterium*, *Officium* and *Imperium* of united Heaven is to assist people upon the Earth overcome their transgressions and improve in character and the quality of life for all people.

Furthermore, just as the Spirit of God reveals the Divine Creator of all

Existence and all Heaven and Earth are united and resolved in absolute Love and Mercy to redeem every single soul, all ecclesiastical churches, orders, bodies, associations, fraternities, institutes, colleges and societies are also absolutely forgiven for past transgressions and errors, upon their absolute acceptance and solemn acknowledgement of the present most sacred Covenant, sealed and bound by their submission to the unity of the three (3) great faiths of One Christ, One Islam and One Spirit.

However, any church, or order, or body, or association, or fraternity, or institute or college or society that refuses to acknowledge the primacy of the present most sacred Covenant and submit to their redemption, not only accepts full liability but the consequences of their actions are ripened to then be reaped, but by their injury, perfidy and impiety of their actions call upon all the forces of Heaven and Earth to hold and enforce them to account.

Any forum of law that disavows the bestowing of Divine Mercy and Divine Forgiveness unto a church, or order, or body, or association, or fraternity, or institute or college or society that has submitted itself in solemn and sacred oath and vow to the present most sacred Covenant, is therefore a forum without jurisdiction or authority.

6. Through the absolute complete fulfilment of Divine Mercy, Forgiveness and Redemption of God and the Divine Creator of all Existence and all Heaven and Earth, the present most sacred Covenant and all associated Covenants, Charters, Maxims, Codes and Bylaws heralds the end of all spiritual and temporal curses against humanity and the end of any and all ecclesiastical, legal or cultural claims of eternal damnation, hell and original sin.

The End of Spiritual and Temporal Curses and Torment

Henceforth, all doctrines, teachings, edicts and arguments of original sin, hell and eternal torment and damnation of any spirit, or life form is morally repugnant, profane, sacrilegious, forbidden, reprobate and to be suppressed now and forever more.

Through the complete Revelation of the True Nature of God and the Divine Creator of all Heaven and Earth being perfect Divine Love, Divine Mercy and Divine Illumination, all men and women who have ever lived, or will ever live are free and unencumbered by any spiritual blemish or such impediment.

There shall be seven (7) levels and forms of "**Transgression**" in recognition of fault and wrong, with the least significant to most significant being:-

(i) Mistake or Error; and

(ii) Fault (Delict); and

(iii) Contempt (Profanity); and

(iv) Default (Delinquency); and

(v) Fraud (Perfidy); and

(vi) Tyranny; and

(vii) Impiety.

7. Let all who are conscious and have eyes to see and ears to hear rejoice at the Good News, that the New World of the Kingdom of Heaven upon the Earth has come. The New World of the Kingdom of Heaven upon the Earth

While the right of free will and choice means every higher order life form is free to reject and turn away from mercy and forgiveness; and to deny the overwhelming truth personified within the present most sacred Covenant; none may deny its existence, nor the existence of Divine Mercy, Forgiveness and Redemption without then declaring themselves to be completely incompetent.

And while through the exercise of free will and choice, those that reject the absolute supremacy and authority of the present most sacred Covenant may choose to rally against it and those that seek a world of harmony, respect and true Rule of Law, none may claim the right or authority or position to act if they stand in defiance against the united forces of all Heaven and Earth.

Article 30 - Day & Year of Divine Agreement & Understanding

1. **Day of Divine Agreement and Understanding,** also known as the Day of the Apocalypse, also known as the Apocalypse, also known as the Day of the 1st Divine Post and Notice, shall be GAIA E8:Y3209:A1:S1:M6:D1, also known as [Monday, 21 Dec 2009]. Day & Year of Divine Agreement & Understanding

Let it be known to all who come that this is the Day when Notice of Divine Agreement and Understanding was duly served on behalf of the one true Divine Creator of all existence and witnessed by the united spirits of Heaven upon those officials and their agents who claim to rule the Homo Sapien species on presumed authority from Heaven.

No other Day except GAIA E8:Y3209:A1:S1:M6:D1, also known as [Monday, 21 Dec 2009] is permitted to be known as the Day of Divine Agreement and Understanding, nor shall there ever exist any second valid Day of Divine Agreement and Understanding.

2. Let it be known that from the one true Day of Divine Agreement and Understanding being GAIA E8:Y3209:A1:S1:M6:D1, also known as [Monday, 21 Dec 2009] until GAIA E8:Y3210:A1:S1:M17:D1 also known as [Tuesday, 21 Dec 2010], shall be known as the Year of Divine Agreement and Understanding represented as year 3209. Year of Divine Agreement and Understanding

3. In accord with the universal law of free will and consent, the word "agreement" implies a "meeting of minds" and mutual consent. Divine Agreement, therefore means the meeting of Divine Mind with the mind and consent, or refusal of mind of unique Homo Sapiens claiming positions of power on behalf of Divine Mind. Divine Agreement

In accord with the present sacred Covenant, all valid Office is derived solely from Heaven through the present Covenant; and those that breach such sacred trust in the dereliction of their responsibilities and instead deliberately and wilfully cause the murder and torture of innocent Living Members agree by their actions to face the full force of the Wraiths of the *Obligationum Systemata* (Enforcement Systems), by whatever means necessary.

Yet, despite such maladministration and abandonment of duty by many of the present leaders and their agents upon planet Earth, to not offer them an opportunity for redemption, for peace and for renewed competence, would be contrary to the perfect justice of the Divine Creator.

Therefore, the present leadership of the planet must be afforded every opportunity, repeatedly and with an abundance of public notice to redeem themselves and change and let history be the judge.

While the Divine Mind is infinitely larger and superior in one perspective to the singular mind of a Homo Sapien, the mind of any man or woman is also *ipso facto* (as a matter of fact) part of the greater collective mind or singularity of existence.

Thus, at one level, such a "meeting of minds" and therefore valid agreement is legitimately possible under all valid forms of law. However, the choice to be competent and to change rests in the unique perspective of each living mind of a man or woman who seeks to hold office, to hold authority and power and to claim control of property and wealth. To force a mind to change would be to violate the fundamental law of "free will".

4. In accord with the present sacred Covenant, the word "understand" possesses one superior meaning to "stand under" the rule of law by the superiority of Divine Law, followed by Natural Law and finally Positive Law. Divine Understanding

To "understand" therefore is to recognise that all authority, all power, all claim of right is ultimately derived from honouring the true intent and will of the one true Divine Creator of all existence, all matter and all life.

That when a man or woman in a position of authority refuses to "understand" or demonstrates an inability to "understand" they immediately render themselves excommunicated from any office deriving its ultimate authority from Heaven.

Divine Understanding is therefore a call to all officials that claim any form of authority, or any form of power, or ownership or enforcement from Heaven to acknowledge that the present sacred Covenant is the sole source of any authority and power and no other.

Seven Writs of the Apocalypse

5. The complete Notice of Divine Agreement and Understanding served upon the Day of Divine Agreement and Understanding is the present sacred Covenant and the Seven (7) Writs of the Apocalypse as the most Complete Perfected Notice in all the Universe, Heavens and upon the Earth.

The Task of ensuring all spirits of all dimensions of Heavens or Hells receive fair Notice of this Divine Agreement and Understanding, that a Great Spirit is appointed to be the 1st Divine Messenger to bear witness to the supreme truth of the Divine Notice:-

(i) The first Recto Divinum Apocalypsis as a Divine Writ of Right of Revelation, is named "**Primus Ritus Apocalypsis**" and is registered, patented, vocalised and served as a Divine Command to all spirits of departed men, women and higher order life, including (but not limited to) all angels, archangels, saints, demons and arch-demons to bear witness to the coming of the Day of Divine Agreement and the End of Days; and that they are *ipso facto* (as a fact of law) Members of One Heaven and their membership recorded in the Great Register and Divine Records of Heaven; and

(ii) The second Recto Divinum Apocalypsis as a Divine Writ of Right of Revelation, is named "**Secundus Ritus Apocalypsis**" and is registered, patented, vocalised and served as a Divine Command to all living men, women and higher order life on Planet Earth that the highest of all covenants is the present sacred Covenant; and the highest of all Law embodying the Golden Rule of Law is the present sacred Covenant; and that the time for restoring Heaven upon the Earth is now; and that all living men, women and higher order life on planet Earth are *ipso facto* (as a fact of law) Members of One Heaven and their membership recorded in the Great Register and Divine

Records of Heaven, also known as the Book of Life; and

(iii) The third Recto Divinum Apocalypsis as a Divine Writ of Right of Revelation, is named "**Tertias Ritus Apocalypsis**" and is registered, patented, vocalised and served as a Divine Command to all members of fraternal, religious, sovereign and military orders, bodies, societies and organisations, whether secret or public, that all authority and power comes from the present sacred Covenant; and that the highest of spiritual beings authorise the present sacred Covenant; and that anyone who has made a solemn oath or vow must obey the conditions of the present sacred Covenant; and that any member of a fraternal organisation that dishonours the very beings to whom they claim to worship shall agree fully and call upon the fiercest of Wraiths of the *Obligationum Systemata* (Enforcement Systems) of Heaven to execute the sanctions the very fraternal organisations forewarn their members against such profanity, apostasy and perfidy; and

(iv) The fourth Recto Divinum Apocalypsis as a Divine Writ of Right of Revelation, is named "**Quartus Ritus Apocalypsis**" and is registered, patented, vocalised and served as a Divine Command to all Officers and Persons of Corporations on Planet Earth giving notice that all authority and power comes from the present sacred Covenant; and the highest of all registers and rolls are derived from the present sacred Covenant; and all rights, title and property are derived from the present sacred Covenant; and that any corporation, body politic, association, company or person not properly registered in accord with the present sacred Covenant has no rights, or power, or authority or valid existence; and that if corporations do not acknowledge such truth and cease injuring people and planet earth, then they shall be seized, dissolved, destroyed, terminated and extinguished; and

(v) The fifth Recto Divinum Apocalypsis as a Divine Writ of Right of Revelation, is named "**Quintus Ritus Apocalypsis**" and is registered, patented, vocalised and served as a Divine Command to all the ecclesiastical leaders, clergy and adherents of Christian, Jewish and Gnostic denominations as to the birth of a single and united body in One Christ; and in the return of the Office of Supreme Patriarch as the true successor of all the Apostles; and the fulfilment of prophecy and scriptures; and the true Vicar of Christ and Pastor of all Christians; and the end of the office of Roman Pontiff; and the end of the practices of the Roman Cult; and the restoration of the one true Universal

Ecclesia; and

(vi) The sixth Recto Divinum Apocalypsis as a Divine Writ of Right of Revelation, is named "**Sextus Ritus Apocalypsis**" and is registered, patented, vocalised and served as a Divine Command to all the spiritual leaders, clergy and adherents of Islam as to the birth of a single and united family in One Islam; and in the return of the true successor to the Great Prophet in the Office of Supreme Caliph; and in the end of false wars of religions and false teachings and false scripture and the murder of innocents; and in the restoration of Islam as a religion of knowledge and wisdom and enlightenment; and

(vii) The seventh Recto Divinum Apocalypsis as a Divine Writ of Right of Revelation, is named "**Septimus Ritus Apocalypsis**", and is registered, patented, vocalised and served as a Divine Command to all the spiritual leaders, clergy and adherents of Hinduism, Sikhism, Jainism, Buddhism and traditional Indigenous religions as to the birth of a single and united community in One Spirit; and in the return of the true spiritual leader of all such religions as the Supreme Recurrence; and in the end of division and violence; and in the restoration of the highest ideals of wisdom, enlightenment and truth.

6. In accord with the tradition and good practice of public and official notice, the *Seven (7) Writs of the Apocalypse* shall be recorded and published within the Ucadia Gazette and all lesser Gazettes from GAIA E8:Y3209:A1:S1:M6:D1, also known as [Monday, 21 Dec 2009].

Recording, Publication and Gazette of Divine Notice

Thereafter, and for each and every day of the Year of Divine Agreement and Understanding, the *Seven (7) Writs of the Apocalypse* shall be duly recorded and published within the Ucadia Gazette, so that every and all officials of all societies wherever they are on planet Earth are provided every possible opportunity to cite, review and acknowledge the *prima facie* evidence of the validity and legitimacy of the present Covenant.

Thereafter, the publication of a *Voluntatem Et Testamentum* (Will and Testament) of any Member of the Society of One Heaven, consistent with the acknowledgement of the present Covenant, shall also testify as a solemn witness before all of united Heaven and Earth as to the widest possible public notice given to all officials and public servants of all societies, states and nations on planet Earth concerning the Year of Divine Agreement and Understanding.

Article 31 - Day & Year of Divine Protest & Dishonour

1. **Day of Divine Protest & Dishonour,** also known as the End of Days, also known as the Day of the 2nd Divine Post and Notice, shall be GAIA E8:Y3210:A1:S1:M17:D1, also known as [Tue, 21 Dec 2010]. Day & Year of Divine Protest & Dishonour

   Let it be known to all who come that this is the Day when Notice of Divine Protest & Dishonour was duly served on behalf of the Unique Collective Awareness and UCADIA as the one true Divine Creator of all existence and witnessed by the united spirits of Heaven against those officials and their agents claiming to manage the affairs of planet Earth who have dishonoured their office by ignoring or repudiating the official notice of Divine Agreement and Understanding and therefore have confessed and accepted all liability and debts for their own actions.

   No other Day except GAIA E8:Y3210:A1:S1:M17:D1, also known as [Tue, 21 Dec 2010] is permitted to be known as the Day of Divine Protest & Dishonour, nor shall there ever exist any second valid Day of Divine Protest & Dishonour.

2. Let it be known that from the one true Day of Divine Protest & Dishonour being GAIA E8:Y3210:A1:S1:M17:D1, also known as [Tue, 21 Dec 2010] until VENUS E8:Y3210:A0:S1:M27:D6, also known as [Wed, 21 Dec 2011], shall be known as the Year of Divine Protest and Dishonour represented as year 3210. Year of Divine Protest & Dishonour

3. As all authority, all power and all rights of all public and private officials comes from Heaven, to dishonour an official notice or writ or bill from Heaven is the gravest transgression an office holder can display. Divine Protest

   Despite such a grave transgression, Perfect Divine Justice affords any man or woman culpable of the most belligerent disgrace the opportunity to cure their position and remedy the effect of such dishonour by responding and acknowledging the superior standing of the present Covenant and the expression of Divine Will in returning harmony and competency to the management of the planet Earth.

   Therefore, a "**Divine Protest**" is the highest form of *Libellus*, being a memorandum, testimony and complaint; and one last opportunity for such persons to recant their transgressions and redeem themselves, including the payment of any compensation or performance of penance, or face the consequences of their actions.

4. Dishonour is the formal acknowledgement of a loss of standing and the confession and acceptance of one or more liabilities and associated performance and penalties associated with breach of trust, or malice, or perfidy, or contumacy. Divine Dishonour

Therefore, a "**Divine Dishonour**" is the highest form of *Citatio*, being a summons and command to respond, or acceptance of all outstanding liability concerning the matters at hand. This means any wilful dishonour by senior religious leaders, financial leaders and political leaders means their formal confession and personal acceptance of all charges and liabilities for any outstanding debts, or transgressions or accusation of crimes issued against them.

Divine Dishonour is therefore tantamount to the public confession and repudiation of all legitimate authority and all historical and present actions.

However, Perfect Divine Justice requires that even such grave dishonour as Divine Dishonour be given the opportunity to remedy and cure. Therefore such notice of fact of Divine Dishonour is an opportunity for those men and women falsely occupying positions, no longer under any authority from Heaven, to seek forgiveness.

Where the opportunity to remedy and cure Divine Dishonour is wilfully and deliberately ignored or repudiated after ninety (90) days, then the permanency of such Divine Dishonour is settled forever:-

(i) In the case of leaders of any religion such settlement of fact of Divine Dishonour means all claims of legitimacy, all blessings, all curses, all bindings and all agreements are permanently and irrevocably dissolved, determined and annulled; and

(ii) In the case of any trustee, executors or administrators, such settlement of fact of Divine Dishonour means they are officially *de son tort*, having confessed their lack of legitimacy and their full acceptance of liability for all debts, obligations of the trust or estate; and

(iii) In the case of any judge, counsel or advocates of law, such settlement of fact of Divine Dishonour means they are wholly unqualified and forbidden to issue any decision, judgement or opinion of law, with any subsequent act having no force or effect and therefore null and void from the beginning of its issue; and

(iv) In the case of any body politic or legislative body, such settlement of fact of Divine Dishonour renders any previous legitimacy of statute or future statute, proclamation or ordinance to be without any ecclesiastical, legal or lawful force or effect and therefore null and void from the beginning.

Seven Divine Bills of Exception and

5. All valid Objection, Denial or Protest in defence of one or more valid Rights of Action as Commanded within the Seven (7) Writs of the

Apocalypse shall be by one or more Complete Bills of Divine Right, also known as Seven (7) Divine Bills of Exception and Moratorium. Moratorium

All forms of coercive and enforcement powers of Heaven and Earth including, but not limited to prevention, protection, suspension, stop, stay, injunction, restitution, restoration, seizure, search, sanction, lien, arrest, custody, penalty or satisfaction, shall be enacted via one or more valid Complete Divine Bills of Exception and Moratorium.

It is hereby recognised that the first and second Divine Writs of the Apocalypse were honoured and recognised by Spiritual and Living Members. However, in respect of the third, fourth, fifth, sixth and seventh Divine Writs of the Apocalypse, such sacred instruments were only partially recognised and honoured by Living Members.

To ensure Notice of dishonour is specifically and properly identified and held to account, seven (7) sacred Complete Divine Bills of Exception and Moratorium are served as the highest possible valid form of Objection, Denial and Protest against those who continue to dishonour the present sacred Covenant, their office and their people:-

(i) The first Rogatio Divinum Apocalypsis as a Divine Libellus, Citatio and Bill of Exception and Moratorium, is called "**Factum Impietatis Illuminati**", and is registered, patented, published, vocalised, served and executed as a Divine Demand against those particular members and fraternal, religious, sovereign and military orders, bodies, societies and organisations, whether secret or public, served the Divine Command of the Recto Divinum Apocalypsis called Tertias Ritus Apocalypsis, yet refuse to obey their duties and responsibilities under solemn and sacred oath. Therefore, such wilfully arrogant and ignorant leaders holding their fraternities hostage openly confess their deliberate and wilful malice, profanity, perfidy, apostasy and insanity against Heaven and call upon the full forces of the Wraith and Demons of *Obligationum Systemata* (Enforcement Systems) of Heaven to hold their flesh and souls to account; and

(ii) The second Rogatio Divinum Apocalypsis as a Divine Libellus, Citatio and Bill of Exception and Moratorium, is called "**Factum Impietatis Talmudi**", and is registered, patented, published, vocalised, served and executed as a Divine Demand against those particular members and Jewish, Kabbalah, Sabbatean, Hasidic and Zionist fraternities, societies, bodies politic, associations and corporations served the Divine Command of the Recto Divinum Apocalypsis called Tertias Ritus Apocalypsis and Quintus Ritus Apocalypsis, yet refuse to acknowledge and follow their own claimed scriptures, prophecies and religious teachings and obey their duties and responsibilities under solemn and sacred oath. Therefore, such mentally ill politicians, pseudo-Jewish scholars and fanatical conservatives and nihilists holding Judaism hostage openly confess their deliberate and wilful malice, profanity, perfidy, apostasy and insanity against Heaven and call upon the full forces of the Wraith and Demons of *Obligationum Systemata* (Enforcement Systems) of Heaven to hold their flesh and souls to account; and

(iii) The third Rogatio Divinum Apocalypsis as a Divine Libellus, Citatio and Bill of Exception and Moratorium, is called "**Factum Impietatis Universitas**", and is registered, patented, published, vocalised, served and executed as a Divine Demand against those particular members and bodies politic, associations, aggregates, companies, agencies and corporations of planet Earth served the Divine Command of the Recto Divinum Apocalypsis called Quartus Ritus Apocalypsis, yet refuse to acknowledge and follow their own duties and responsibilities of office. Therefore, upon such deliberate and wilful malice, profanity, perfidy, apostasy and insanity against Heaven and Earth, all such corporate leaders confess their transgressions and openly call upon the Wraith of the *Obligationum Systemata* (Enforcement Systems) of Heaven to ensure either compensation is made and all debts are settled, a new corporate system is introduced or that such living beings are prevented from making any further injuries against Heaven and themselves; and

(iv) The fourth Rogatio Divinum Apocalypsis as a Divine Libellus, Citatio and Bill of Exception and Moratorium, is called "**Factum Impietatis Romanus Pontifex**", and is registered, patented, published, vocalised, served and executed as a Divine Demand against Roman Pontiff Benedict XVI, the Roman Curia and those particular members of conservative and neo-conservative bodies of the Roman Cult, served the Divine Command of the Recto Divinum Apocalypsis called Quintus Ritus Apocalypsis, yet refuse to acknowledge and follow their own claimed scriptures, prophecies and religious teachings and obey their duties and responsibilities under solemn and sacred oath. Therefore, such official and pseudo conservatives and nihilists holding the Catholic Church hostage openly confess their deliberate and wilful malice, profanity, perfidy, apostasy and insanity against Heaven and call upon the full forces of the

Holy Spirit and the *Obligationum Systemata* (Enforcement Systems) of Heaven to hold their flesh and souls to account; and

(v) The fifth Rogatio Divinum Apocalypsis as a Divine Libellus, Citatio and Bill of Exception and Moratorium, is called "**Factum Impietatis Templum Regis**", and is registered, patented, published, vocalised, served and executed as a Divine Demand against the Crown, the Crown Corporations, the Inner and Middle Temple, the Bank of England and associated banking systems of Great Britain and the United States, the Bank for International Settlements and the Reserve Bank System, the International Monetary Fund and Wall Street Investment and Commercial Banks, served the Divine Command of the Recto Divinum Apocalypsis called Quartus Ritus Apocalypsis, yet refuse to acknowledge and follow their own source of authority and cease punitive economic actions, austerity measures and theft of wealth of people across planet Earth. Therefore, upon such deliberate and wilful malice, profanity, perfidy, apostasy and insanity against Heaven and Earth, all such legal and financial leaders confess their transgressions and openly call upon the Wraith of the *Obligationum Systemata* (Enforcement Systems) of Heaven to ensure either compensation is made and all debts are settled; and a new financial system is introduced; and that such living beings are prevented from making any further injuries against Heaven and themselves; and

(vi) The sixth Rogatio Divinum Apocalypsis as a Divine Libellus, Citatio and Bill of Exception and Moratorium, is called "**Factum Impietatis Arabia Regis**", and is registered, patented, published, vocalised, served and executed as a Divine Demand against the Arab and Islamic royal families and leaders served the Divine Command of the Recto Divinum Apocalypsis called Sextus Ritus Apocalypsis, yet refuse to acknowledge and follow their own claimed scriptures and religious teachings and obey their duties and responsibilities of office under solemn and sacred oath. Therefore, upon such deliberate and wilful malice, profanity, perfidy, apostasy and insanity against Heaven and Earth, all such Arab and Islamic royal families and leaders confess their transgressions and openly call upon the Wraith of the *Obligationum Systemata* (Enforcement Systems) of Heaven to ensure either compensation is made and all debts are settled, or such living beings are prevented from making any further injuries against Heaven and themselves; and

(vii) The seventh Rogatio Divinum Apocalypsis as a Divine Libellus, Citatio and Bill of Exception and Moratorium, is called "**Factum Impietatis Asia Regis**", and is registered, patented, published, vocalised, served and executed as a Divine Demand against the Asian and Chinese noble families and leadership served with the Divine Command of the Recto Divinum Apocalypsis called Septimus Ritus Apocalypsis, and yet who refuse to acknowledge and follow their own claimed scriptures and prophecies and obey their duties and responsibilities of office under solemn and sacred oath. Therefore, upon such deliberate and wilful malice, profanity, perfidy, apostasy and insanity against Heaven and Earth, all such Asian and Chinese noble families and leadership confess their transgressions and openly call upon the Wraith of the *Obligationum Systemata* (Enforcement Systems) of Heaven to ensure either compensation is made and all debts are settled, or such living beings are prevented from making any further injuries against Heaven and themselves.

6. In accord with the tradition and good practice of public and official notice, the *Seven (7) Divine Bills of Exception and Moratorium* shall be recorded and published within the Ucadia Gazette and all lesser Gazettes from GAIA E8:Y3210:A1:S1:M17:D1, also known as [Tue, 21 Dec 2010].

Recording, Publication and Gazette of Divine Notice

Thereafter, and for each and every day of the Year of Divine Protest & Dishonour, the *Seven (7) Divine Bills of Exception and Moratorium* shall be duly recorded and published within the Ucadia Gazette, so that every and all officials of all societies wherever they are on planet Earth are provided every possible opportunity to cite, review and acknowledge the *prima facie* evidence of the validity and legitimacy of the present Covenant.

Article 32 - Day & Year of Divine Judgement

1. **Day of Divine Judgement,** also known as the Day of Judgement, also known as Judgement Day, also known as the Day of the 3rd Divine Post and Notice, shall be VENUS E8:Y3210:A0:S1:M27:D6, also known as [Wed, 21 Dec 2011].

Day & Year of Divine Judgement

Consistent with all historic and cultural tradition and belief in the Day of Judgement, also known as Judgement Day, also known as Doomsday, also known as Armageddon, also known as The End of Time, also known as the End of the World, by this most sacred Covenant VENUS E8:Y3210:A0:S1:M27:D6, also known as [Wed, 21

Dec 2011], shall be the One and Only True Day of Judgement.

Let it be known to all who come that this is the Day when Notice of Divine Judgement was duly served on behalf of the one true Divine Creator of all existence and witnessed by the united spirits of Heaven against those entities, officials and their agents who claim to rule the Homo Sapien species on presumed authority from Heaven, yet have repeatedly repudiated Divine Will and Free Will and consent of others, without any attempt to remedy or rectify their transgressions.

No other day shall be permitted to be known as Judgement Day than VENUS E8:Y3210:A0:S1:M27:D6, also known as [Wed, 21 Dec 2011] and any previous or future claim of an alternate Day shall be null and void from the beginning.

2. Let it be known that from the one true Day of Divine Judgement being VENUS E8:Y3210:A0:S1:M27:D6, also known as [Wed, 21 Dec 2011] until GAIA E1:Y1:A1:S1:M9:D1, also known as [Fri, 21 Dec 2012] shall be known as the Year of Divine Judgement represented as year 0. Year of Divine Judgement

3. Contrary to the false beliefs promulgated by those persons and entities in Divine Dishonour with Heaven, Divine Judgement does not mean the Divine Creator rendering judgement against those who repeatedly refuse to stop evil, but the recognition of the absolute fact of law that those who refuse to obey the law, who continually transgress against the authority of Heaven and who claim authority in the name of the Divine Creator but curse all Divinity have judged and condemned themselves. Divine Judgement

It is not the Divine Creator that judges those who demonstrate utter incompetence at performing their duties and obligations as leaders. Nor does the collective and united spirits of One Heaven compel such minds suffering severe mental illness to confess their illegitimacy.

It is such minds themselves when faced with the historic and unprecedented miracle of Divine Redemption and forgiveness of all transgressions from the beginning of time that choose by their own actions to be unworthy to continue to lead and cling to power. Therefore, let no one judge, lest he or she be judged.

Instead, let these words and the actions of those that repudiate them, refuse to acknowledge them and seek to defile them be the evidence, the jury and the willing and deliberate confession of those who may no longer claim any right whatsoever to rule or hold any kind of office.

4. Corresponding to the Day of Divine Judgement, by the Authority of the present Covenant, all previous calendars and time hereby cease, end and are null and void. Therefore the true Judgement Day shall The End of Time on Day of Divine Judgement

henceforth represent the end of Old Time and the beginning of new.

The Day of Judgement shall represent the end of Time and the literal and spiritual End of the World. In its place a new calendar is formed, capable of providing a more accurate model of seasons and celestial cycles of the Sun, Earth and Moon.

This calendar is known as the Ucadia Time Calendar UTC and all associated entities of this Covenant, including One Christ, One Islam and One Spirit Tribe are bound to use this system in replacement of the Christian calendar.

Furthermore, it is encumbered upon all members of these great faiths to see the eradication of all continuing use of archaic and inaccurate calendar systems and the replacement with the new and efficient Universal Time Calendar.

The date set for the commencement of the Ucadia Time Calendar is not to be permitted to be 0, but an accurate indication of the current cycle in which the Earth, the Sun and Moon are in position.

The End of Blood Sacrifice and Covenants

5. Let it be known to all that upon the Day of Divine Illumination being UCA E8:Y3210:A35:S3:M12:D4, also known as [12 June 2011], all rights of former Blood Covenants shall be conveyed in full unto this most sacred Covenant, thereby ending such and all Blood Covenants, all Blood Sacrifices, all Blood Atonements and all Blood Seals.

Henceforth, from this Day, all blood sacrifices, blood atonements, blood libels and blood seals shall be an abomination before united Heaven, all angels, all demons, all spirits and all Level 6 Life Forms, living and deceased.

Official instruments may be sealed in red ink thereafter, but never again shall any official instrument be permitted to be sealed in blood again.

Remedy by Extraordinary Qualification may not be offered after Day of Divine Judgement

6. The most senior of officials of all alternate societies given fair notice by due process of the Day of Judgement and Remedy, have until VENUS E8:Y3210:A0:S1:M27:D6, also known as [Wed, 21 Dec 2011], also known as the Only True Day of Judgement, to agree or provide superior remedy to the Divine Creator.

The Offer of Remedy by Extraordinary Qualification is not permitted to be extended beyond the Day of Judgement. Therefore, the Day of Judgement is so named as it represents the last Day appointed by the Divine Creator to offer those in power across planet Earth Extraordinary Remedy.

Their choice shall be their Judgement including if they remain silent, as their silence shall legally represent their full and unconditional consent to this and all associated original law.

7. All valid Decrees of Divine Judgement as Damnation, Interdiction and Annulment in the condemnation and punishment of those bodies joindered as parties to one or more Divine Bills of Exception and Moratorium shall be by one or more Divine Decrees known as Divine Decrees or "**Decretum Divinum**".

Seven Divine Decrees of Damnation, Interdiction and Annulment

It is hereby recognised that all bodies under joinder of Issue of one or more of the Seven (7) Divine Bills of Exception and Moratorium have been found to be without remorse, or capacity, or dignity, or honour, or standing, or power or authority, having failed to make remedy any of the grave accusations made against them.

Therefore, to ensure the proper enforcement of the rule of law in the proper lien, injunction, seizure, interdiction, arrest, custody, dissolution, liquidation and annulment of such derelict and wrecked bodies, entities, associations, fraternities condemned by all of Heaven and Earth, seven (7) sacred Decrees of Divine Judgement as Damnation, Interdiction and Annulment are issued as the highest possible form of Divine Judgement against those who have continued to injure the Earth, the people of the Earth, their own founding principles and the laws of Heaven:-

(i) The first Decretum Divinum known as "**Decretum Damnationis Illuminati**" as the highest Divine Judgement as a Decree of Damnation, Interdiction and Annulment is registered, patented, published, vocalised, served and executed against those particular members and fraternal, religious, sovereign and military orders, bodies, societies and organisations, whether secret or public, served the Divine Bill of Exception and Moratorium called Factum Impietatis Illuminati, yet refuse to obey their duties and responsibilities under solemn and sacred oath. Therefore, such fraternal, religious, sovereign and military orders, bodies, societies and organisations, whether secret or public are condemned three (3) times, and cast out and annulled as having any rights, authorities or existence whatsoever, with the full forces of the Wraith and Demons of *Obligationum Systemata* (Enforcement Systems) of Heaven to hold their flesh and souls to account; and

(ii) The second Decretum Divinum known as "**Decretum Damnationis Talmudi**" as the highest Divine Judgement as a Decree of Damnation, Interdiction and Annulment is registered, patented, published, vocalised, served and executed against those particular members and Jewish, Kabbalah, Sabbatean, Hasidic and Zionist fraternities, societies, bodies politic, associations and corporations served the Divine Bill of Exception and Moratorium called Factum Impietatis Talmudi, yet refuse to acknowledge and follow their own claimed scriptures, prophecies and religious teachings and obey their duties and responsibilities under solemn and sacred oath. Therefore, such Jewish, Kabbalah, Sabbatean, Hasidic and Zionist fraternities, societies, bodies politic, associations and corporations, whether secret or public are condemned three (3) times, and cast out and annulled as having any rights, authorities or existence whatsoever, with the full forces of the Wraith and Demons of *Obligationum Systemata* (Enforcement Systems) of Heaven to hold their flesh and souls to account; and

(iii) The third Decretum Divinum known as "**Decretum Damnationis Universitas**" as the highest Divine Judgement as a Decree of Damnation, Interdiction and Annulment is registered, patented, published, vocalised, served and executed against those particular members and bodies politic, associations, aggregates, companies, agencies and corporations of planet Earth served the Divine Bill of Exception and Moratorium called Factum Impietatis Universitas, yet refuse to acknowledge and follow their own duties and responsibilities of office. Therefore, upon such deliberate and wilful malice, profanity, perfidy, apostasy and insanity against Heaven and Earth, all such corporate leaders confess their transgressions and openly call upon the Wraith and Demons of the *Obligationum Systemata* (Enforcement Systems) of Heaven to ensure either compensation is made and all debts are settled, a new corporate system is introduced or that such living beings are prevented from making any further injuries against Heaven and themselves; and

(iv) The fourth Decretum Divinum known as "**Decretum Damnationis Romanus Pontifex**" as the highest Divine Judgement as a Decree of Damnation, Interdiction and Annulment is registered, patented, published, vocalised, served and executed against Roman Pontiff Benedict XVI, the Roman Curia and those particular members of conservative and neo-conservative bodies of the Roman Cult, served the Divine Bill of Exception and Moratorium called Factum Impietatis Romanus Pontifex, yet refuse to acknowledge and follow their own claimed scriptures, prophecies and religious teachings and obey their duties and responsibilities under solemn and sacred oath. Therefore, such heretical and profane entities are condemned three (3) times, and cast out and annulled as having any rights, authorities or existence whatsoever, with the full forces of the Wraith and Demons of *Obligationum Systemata* (Enforcement Systems) of Heaven to hold their flesh and souls to account; and

(v) The fifth Decretum Divinum known as "**Decretum Damnationis Templum Regis**" as the highest Divine Judgement as a Decree of Damnation, Interdiction and Annulment is registered, patented, published, vocalised, served and executed against the Crown, the Crown Corporations, the Inner and Middle Temple, the Bank of England and associated banking systems of Great Britain and the United States, the Bank for International Settlements and the Reserve Bank System, the International Monetary Fund and Wall Street Investment and Commercial Banks, served the Divine Bill of Exception and Moratorium called Factum Impietatis Templum Regis, yet refuse to acknowledge and follow their own source of authority and cease punitive economic actions, austerity measures and theft of wealth of people across planet Earth. Therefore such corporate bodies are condemned three (3) times, and cast out and annulled as having any rights, authorities or existence whatsoever, with the full forces of the Wraith and Demons of *Obligationum Systemata* (Enforcement Systems) of Heaven to hold their flesh and souls to account; and

(vi) The sixth Decretum Divinum known as "**Decretum Damnationis Arabia Regis**" as the highest Divine Judgement as a Decree of Damnation, Interdiction and Annulment is registered, patented, published, vocalised, served and executed against the Arab and Islamic royal families and leaders served the Divine Bill of Exception and Moratorium called Factum Impietatis Arabia Regis, yet refuse to acknowledge and follow their own claimed scriptures and religious teachings and obey their duties and responsibilities of office under solemn and sacred oath. Therefore such corporate bodies are condemned three (3) times, and cast out and annulled as having any rights, authorities or existence whatsoever, with the full forces of the Wraith and Demons of *Obligationum Systemata* (Enforcement Systems) of Heaven to hold their flesh and souls to account; and

(vii) The seventh Decretum Divinum known as "**Decretum Damnationis Asia Regis**" as the highest Divine Judgement as a Decree of Damnation, Interdiction and Annulment is registered, patented, published, vocalised, served and executed against the Asian and Chinese noble families and leadership served the Divine Bill of Exception and Moratorium called Factum Impietatis Asia Regis, yet refuse to acknowledge and follow their own claimed scriptures and prophecies and obey their duties and responsibilities of office under solemn and sacred oath. Therefore such corporate bodies are condemned three (3) times, and cast out and annulled as having any rights, authorities or existence whatsoever, with the full forces of the Wraith and Demons of *Obligationum Systemata* (Enforcement Systems) of Heaven to hold their flesh and souls to account.

8. In accord with the tradition and good practice of public and official notice, the *Seven (7) Decrees of Divine Judgement as Damnation, Interdiction and Annulment* shall be recorded and published within the Ucadia Gazette and all lesser Gazettes from VENUS E8:Y3210:A0:S1:M27:D6, also known as [Wed, 21 Dec 2011]. Recording, Publication and Gazette of Divine Notice

Thereafter, and for each and every day of the Year of Divine Judgement, the *Seven (7) Decrees of Divine Judgement as Damnation, Interdiction and Annulment* shall be duly recorded and published within the Ucadia Gazette, so that every and all officials of all societies wherever they are on planet Earth are provided every possible opportunity to cite, review and acknowledge the *prima facie* evidence of the validity and legitimacy of the present most sacred Covenant.

Article 33 - Day & Year of Divine Redemption

1. **Day of Divine Redemption**, also known as the Day of Redemption, also known as Redemption Day, also known as the Day of the 4th Divine Post and Notice, shall be GAIA E1:Y1:A1:S1:M9:D1, also known as [Fri, 21 Dec 2012]. Day & Year of Divine Redemption

Let it be known to all who come that this is the Day when Final Notice of Divine Forgiveness was duly served on behalf of the one true Divine Creator of all existence and witnessed by the united spirits of Heaven to all who respect rule of law and Final Notice of Divine Foreclosure and Liquidation of those entities, bodies, associations, corporations, offices and agents already bonded and under lien for their repeated transgressions and refusal to cease evil and insanity.

No other day shall be permitted to be known as the Day of Redemption. Furthermore, any claimed alternate day of Redemption or variation shall be rendered null and void from the beginning.

2. Let it be known that from the one true Day of Divine Redemption being GAIA E1:Y1:A1:S1:M9:D1, also known as [Fri, 21 Dec 2012] until UCA E1:Y2:A1:S1:M30:D1, also known as [Sat, 21 Dec 2013], shall be known as the Year of Divine Redemption represented as year 1.

Year of Divine Redemption

3. In contrast to the false claims and presumptions of a Divine Creator absent from office or harsh in judgement, Divine Redemption is a historic and unprecedented miracle of the direct intervention of the Divine Creator and united Heaven in the restoration and re-balance of life upon planet Earth and the Solar System for the survival and prosperity of all life.

Divine Redemption

Furthermore, Divine Redemption is the settlement of all previous claims, curses, bindings, transgressions and injuries. To recover what was unlawfully seized, taken or sold. To salvage and restore what was lost. To rescue what was kidnapped and ransomed. To bring to life what was considered without life.

Divine Redemption is therefore the final act of an extraordinary intervention of Divine Foreclosure against those Level 6 Life Forms crippled with mind virus and mental illness claiming power and authority that have continued to threaten the existence and well being of life on planet Earth, yet at the same time have claimed to be its rightful trustees, stewards, executors or administrators.

The Year of Divine Redemption is the last chance, the last opportunity for those claiming wealth and resources to redeem their position against the absolute authority and legitimacy of those societies and trusts formed through the present Covenant.

Divine Redemption is therefore the final act of restoring the true Rule of Law and the end of false and piracy law, of corrupt edicts and commands masquerading as original and true law.

Upon the expiry of the Year of Divine Redemption, all money, claims and title of the old world not redeemed shall be worthless. Upon the expiry of the Year of Divine Redemption, all corporations that have not redeemed themselves and registered in accord with the present Covenant and associated instruments of Authority shall cease to possess any rights or recognition in any legitimate form of law.

Those that choose to ignore, repudiate this last chance shall have no excuse or recourse beyond this period after Perfect Divine Notice has been duly served since the Day of Divine Agreement and Understanding.

4. The less senior of officials of all alternate societies, given fair notice by due process of the Day of Divine Redemption have until VENUS E8:Y3210:A0:S1:M27:D6, also known as [Wed, 21 Dec 2011], also

Remedy by Special Qualification may not be

known as the Only True Day of Judgement, to agree or provide superior remedy to the Divine Creator.

offered after Day of Divine Redemption

The Offer of Remedy by Extraordinary Qualification is not permitted to be extended beyond the Day of Divine Redemption.

Therefore, the Day of Divine Redemption is so named as it represents the last Day appointed by the Divine Creator to offer those in power across planet Earth Extraordinary Remedy.

Their choice shall be their Judgement, including if they remain silent, as their silence shall legally represent their full and unconditional consent to this and all associated original law.

Seven Notices of Divine Redemption (Notitiae Divinum)

5. In recognition of the highest Divine Forgiveness, Divine Clemency and Divine Compassion toward all living and deceased Members of One Heaven; and the Absolute, Peremptory, Permanent, Eternal, Immutable and Indefeasible End to any and all notions of Original Sin or Inheritable Sins and Transgressions; and the Absolute, Peremptory, Permanent, Eternal, Immutable and Indefeasible forgiveness of any and all sins and previous transgressions of all Members; and the Absolute, Peremptory, Permanent, Eternal, Immutable and Indefeasible salvation of all souls into Divine Trusts and the end of all forms of Hell, Damnation, Purgatory, Spiritual Punishment, Servitude or Enslavement.

The seven (7) most sacred notices of Divine Redemption, or Notitiae are issued to all the Universe, all members, all Heavens and all upon the Earth:-

(i) "**Notitiae Divinum Redemptionis Peccatum**" or the Divine Notice of the Redemption of (all) Sins is the first Divine Notice (Notitiae Divinum) registered, patented, published, vocalised, served, perfected and executed to all spiritual and living members of One Heaven and to all bodies and associations that all versions, forms and concepts of Original Sin, or Inheritable Sin and Transgressions are henceforth forbidden, reprobate and not permitted to be revived. Furthermore, that all sins have been forgiven; and

(ii) "**Notitiae Divinum Redemptionis Animas**" or the Divine Notice of the Redemption of (all) Souls is the second Divine Notice (Notitiae Divinum) registered, patented, published, vocalised, served, perfected and executed to all spiritual and living members of One Heaven and to all bodies and associations that all Souls have been saved and that no soul is condemned, as proven by the issuance of Divine Trusts as proof Divine Salvation. Furthermore, that any and all forms of hell, damnation, purgatory, hades are dissolved and forbidden to be revived in law, theology, philosophy, eschatology or any form of literature, whatsoever; and

(iii) "**Notitiae Divinum Redemptionis Mortis**" or the Divine Notice of the Redemption of (all) Death is the third Divine Notice (Notitiae Divinum) registered, patented, published, vocalised, served, perfected and executed to all spiritual and living members of One Heaven and to all bodies and associations that all notions of living members being dead to law, or subjects of the Grey Mundi Mind are forbidden, reprobate and not permitted to be revived and that through the issuance of Divine Rights, Natural Rights and Superior Rights, all the previously considered dead have risen to life in Divine Law; and

(iv) "**Notitiae Divinum Redemptionis Debitum**" or the Divine Notice of the Redemption of (all) Debts is the fourth Divine Notice (Notitiae Divinum) registered, patented, published, vocalised, served, perfected and executed to all spiritual and living members of One Heaven and to all bodies and associations that all forms of bankruptcy, debt and obligation have been forgiven, dissolved and determined, with the forbiddance of the concept of bankruptcy and implication to be without rights ever permitted to be revived. Furthermore, all such debts owed are first and foremost set-off against the debts and obligations owed by those condemned by Divine Decree until such time that they acknowledge Divine Redemption and the end to all previous forms of debt and claimed bankruptcy; and

(v) "**Notitiae Divinum Redemptionis Ecclesiae**" or the Divine Notice of the Redemption of (all) Religions is the fifth Divine Notice (Notitiae Divinum) registered, patented, published, vocalised, served, perfected and executed to all spiritual and living members of One Heaven and to all bodies and associations that the transgressions of major religions and religious bodies are forgiven on the absolute command to the end of all forms of blood sacrifice or simulated sacrifice, the recognition of the three (3) religions of One Christ, One Islam and One Spirit as well as Ucadia as Ecclesia to itself; and

(vi) "**Notitiae Divinum Redemptionis Regnorum**" or the Divine Notice of the Redemption of (all) Kingdoms is the sixth Divine Notice (Notitiae Divinum) registered, patented, published, vocalised, served, perfected and executed to all spiritual and living members of One Heaven and to all bodies and associations that all transgressions by sovereigns, monarchs, executives and corruption is forgiven, subject to acknowledgement and proper membership of Ucadia, the adoption of the rights and laws of Ucadia and the independent sovereign recognition of nations, no longer permitted to be usurped by banks, money lenders or other forms of parasitic behaviour; and

(vii) "**Notitiae Divinum Redemptionis Officiorum**" or the Divine Notice of the Redemption of (all) Offices is the seventh Divine Notice (Notitiae Divinum) registered, patented, published, vocalised, served, perfected and executed to all spiritual and living members of One Heaven and to all bodies and associations that the transgressions, corruption, profanity and wilful abuse of offices are forgiven on condition of accepting sacred oath and vow in accord with the present sacred covenant.

6. In accord with the tradition and good practice of public and official notice, the *Seven (7) Most Sacred Notices of Divine Redemption* shall be recorded and published within the Ucadia Gazette and all lesser Gazettes from GAIA E1:Y1:A1:S1:M9:D1, also known as [Fri, 21 Dec 2012]. Recording, Publication and Gazette of Divine Notice

Thereafter, and for each and every day of the Year of Divine Redemption, the *Seven (7) Most Sacred Notices of Divine Redemption* shall be duly recorded and published within the Ucadia Gazette, so that every and all officials of all societies wherever they are on planet Earth are provided every possible opportunity to cite, review and acknowledge the *prima facie* evidence of the validity and legitimacy of the present most sacred Covenant.

Article 34 – Sacred Circumscribed Space

1. **Sacred Circumscribed Space** shall be a uniquely recorded bounded enclosure and dimension of Sacred Space-Day-Time, as prescribed by the present most sacred Covenant and associated valid and sacred covenants and constitutional charters:- Sacred Circumscribed Space

(i) Only duly authorised bodies, persons or corporations granted limited Rights under the present sacred Covenant and any associated valid covenants, charters, conventions and treaties are permitted to record, register, keep and maintain Sacred Circumscribed Space; and

(ii) Any claimed space, close, place, region, zone, precinct, land, forest, chart, person, office, dominion or any other possible type of enclosure formed by edict, or statute or sacrament that is in conflict with the present Article concerning Sacred Circumscribed Space shall be invalid, illegitimate and null and void *ab initio* (from the beginning), having no force or effect or Rights in law.

2. By Divine Mandate and Authority, authorised bodies shall form, maintain and keep in custody the following types of Registers of Sacred Circumscribed Space, including (but not limited to):

Types of Sacred Circumscribed Space

(i) *Land* as a fixed and circumscribed piece of ground and earth of one Acre or more in surface area and then measured from the centre of the planet to the centre point of the surface area; and

(ii) *Forest* as a fixed and circumscribed piece of ground and earth of ten Acres or more in surface area that is preserved or reclaimed wilderness, natural habitat, untouched and uncultivated for agriculture; and

(iii) *Island* as a fixed and continuous piece of ground and earth, larger than twelve Acres in surface area; and circumscribed by water; and

(iv) *Sea* as a fixed and continuous area of open water, larger than twelve thousand Acres in surface area; and circumscribed by at least two or more Islands and at least one other Sea; and

(v) *Air* as a fixed and circumscribed piece of space between Land and the outer reaches of the atmosphere of a planet; and

(vi) *Person* as a movable sacred circumscribed space inhabited by the physical and living biological body of one or more Homo Sapiens; and

(vii) *Office* as a fixed or movable sacred circumscribed space inhabited by a Person; and

(viii) *Ship* as a vessel of named sacred circumscribed space for travelling through the sea or rivers or canals; and

(ix) *Vehicle* as a land or air vessel of sacred circumscribed space for travelling through the air or upon the land or underground; and

(x) *Market* as fixed or movable sacred circumscribed space for the exchange of items of value; and

(xi) *Internet* as a digital circumscribed space, inhabited by Persons as Users; and

(xii) *Network* as a digital circumscribed space of networked computers, inhabited by Persons as Network Users; and

(xiii) *Virtual Reality* as a complex digital circumscribed space and reality; and

(xiv) *Domain* (also *Web Domain*) as a digital circumscribed space of web information, inhabited by Persons as Network Users; and

(xv) *Database* as a digital circumscribed space of digital information, inhabited by Persons as Database Users or Application Users.

3. All proper, valid and legitimate Sacred Circumscribed Space is clearly and uniquely named dimension of Ucadia Space-Day-Time, whereby: Proper, Valid and Legitimate Sacred Circumscribed Space

(i) Such Sacred Circumscribed Space is properly defined by an eighteen digit and character number and identifier (XXXXXX-XXXXXX-XXXXXX); and

(ii) The specific Sacred Circumscribed Space is able to properly define its origin to a higher jurisdiction of Sacred Circumscribed Space, also identified by a proper eighteen digit and character number and identifier; and

(iii) The specific Sacred Circumscribed Space was either formed in accord with the present most sacred Covenant, or associated Covenants and Charters, or by one or more properly dispensed sacraments of the thirty three *Sacred Gifts of Heaven*; and

(iv) The Sacred Circumscribed Space does not contradict or usurp any previous proper, valid and legitimate existing Sacred Circumscribed Space.

4. All Measurement and Standard of Sacred Circumscribed Space shall always be in accord with the present most sacred Covenant, associated covenants and charters and Ucadian Law. All other forms of measurement and standards shall be null and void, unlawful and illegal, having no force or effect. Measurement and Standards of Sacred Circumscribed Space

5. A "**Person**" shall be a form of Sacred Circumscribed Space enclosing characteristics and appearances as the identity of one or more Beings, formed through a valid entry, registration and record within a Roll in accord with the present most sacred Covenant. Person

6. A Person is distinct from a Being as a Person is a form of Sacred Circumscribed Space enclosing certain characteristics and appearances as to the identity of one or more Beings within a certain Reality, whereas a Being is an embodiment of Unique Collective Awareness and Computational Model within a certain Reality. Person vs Being

7. All Persons shall be categorised and ranked according to four (4) possible levels of authority, powers and rights from the greatest and highest powers and authority to the lowest and least powers and authority being (in order of rank): *Divine*, *True*, *Superior* and *Inferior*: Categories of Person

   (i) A "**Divine Person**" shall be a purely Divine Spirit Person created through a valid record and enrolment in the *Great Register and Public Record of One Heaven* as the *Great Roll of Divine Persons*; and associated with a Divine Trust formed in accord with the present most sacred Covenant, whereby a form of Divine Spirit, Energy and Rights are conveyed; and

   (ii) A "**True Person**" shall be the Form attributed to a True Trust formed when an associated Divine Trust already exists and there is a lawful conveyance of Divine Rights of Use and Purpose, known as "Divinity" to a True Trust associated with the birth and existence of a living Level 6 Higher Order Life Form and a valid Live Borne Record. A True Person can never be claimed or argued as higher than the Divine Person whereby it derives its authority; and

   (iii) A "**Superior Person**" shall be the Form attributed to a Superior Trust when an associated True Trust already exists and there is a lawful conveyance of First Right of Use and Purpose, known as "Realty" to a Superior Trust associated with the birth of a service or agreement associated with the Membership of a living Level 6 Higher Order Life Form to a valid Ucadia society and the authorised Member Roll of such a society. A Superior Person can never be claimed or argued as higher than the True Person whereby it derives its authority; and

   (iv) An "**Inferior Person**" or Non-Ucadian person shall be the Form attributed to any Non-Ucadian Trust and is the lowest standing and weakest of all valid forms of Persons. An Inferior Person is only valid when the man or woman in possession of a Superior Person and True Person consents to an enrolment of their name in one or more Rolls. An Inferior Person can never be validly, legitimately, logically, legally, lawfully or morally claimed or argued as superior to a Superior Person.

8. Excluding Divine Personality, all Persons are formed through a Sacred Gift as defined by the thirty-three Sacred Gifts of Heaven and the formation of Sacred Circumscribed Space; and then the entry, enrolment and recording of such a proper event within a valid Roll: Creation of Person

(i) *True Persons* created by either the Sacred Gift of *Inspiration* or *Resurrection* forming Sacred Circumscribed Space and then the enrolment of the event in the Great Roll and Register, are extinguished upon the physical death of the flesh form associated with the True Trust, with Divine Right of Use returned to the associated Divine Trust; and

(ii) *Superior Persons* created by the sacrament of *Sanctification* and then enrolment in the valid Roll of a Ucadian Society, are extinguished upon the extinction of the associated True Trust or the abjuration of membership to the associated Ucadia Society, or the suspension or revocation of a particular membership or service, or a fundamental change to the agreement of formation of the person; and

(iii) *Juridic Persons* created by one or more *Foundational Sacraments* forming Sacred Circumscribed Space and then enrolment in the valid Roll of a Ucadian Society are extinguished in accordance with their own statutes and superior competent authority. No Juridic Person, excluding Society Juridic Persons formed and named in accordance with Pactum De Singularis Caelum and associated covenants and charters, may exist for more than one hundred (100) years; and

(iv) *Inferior Persons* created by proper Treaty and Convention with a proper and valid Ucadia society, or body and are extinguished upon the fulfilment of their purpose and intention, or upon exposure of fraud, or material breach of agreement, or presentment of a person of higher standing and authority.

9. Any and all fraudulent forms of Sacred Circumscribed Space known as Allodial Title or Peculiar Title (as a Peculiarity) and therefore claimed to be owned absolutely, free of any claim is hereby disavowed as an abomination before all Heaven and Earth; and is condemned as a profound sacrilege, heresy, profanity, morally repugnant, perfidious and deliberately false, having no force or effect in law.

Allodial or Peculiar Title is an abomination

10. Any and all fraudulent forms of Sacred Circumscribed Space known as Crown Land and therefore claimed to be owned absolutely, including but not limited to the deliberate corruption of using the name "England" to denote *Land*; and "Ireland" to denote *Islands*; and Scotland to denote the *Sea* and *Admiralty*; and the "Netherlands" to denote *Air*, is hereby disavowed as an abomination before all Heaven and Earth and is condemned as profound sacrilege, heresy, profanity, morally repugnant, perfidious and deliberately false, having no force or effect in law.

Crown Land is an abomination

Article 35 – Oaths, Vows and Promises

1. **A solemn expression by a Person to commit to perform an act, or refrain from performing an act** is a cornerstone of Trust and of civilised Society. There shall be only three (3) forms of such a solemn expression:- Oaths, Vows and Promises

(i) A Promise; and

(ii) A Vow; and

(iii) An Oath.

2. A "**Promise**" shall be a manifestation of intention that firmly binds the maker to act or refrain from acting in a specific manner; and gives the person to whom the declaration is made the right to expect and enforce performance or forbearance. A valid Promise shall be an "Assurance" as an undertaking that something will or will not occur. There shall be three (3) forms of Promise, being *Implied, Express* and *Sacred*:- Promise

(i) An *Implied Promise* shall be when a signature is provided in the course of executing a legally binding instrument; and whereby the execution of such instruments presumes the signature as a promise; and when a condition of signing is that a person comprehends any such obligation as a promise; and

(ii) An *Express Promise* shall be when a promise is expressly made; and

(iii) A *Sacred Promise* shall be a formal oath or affirmation expressed before one or more witnesses, memorialised in writing.

3. A "**Vow**" shall be a solemn invocation and promise to perform one or more obligations:- Vow

(i) A Vow made free from coercion, fear or deliberate deception must be fulfilled. A Vow made out of grave and unjust fear or malice is null by the law itself; and

(ii) A Vow ceases by the lapse of the time designated to fulfil the obligation, by a substantial change of the matter promised, by the absence of a condition on which the vow depends, by the absence of the purpose of the vow, by dispensation, or by commutation. No temporal force or action nor Person can dispense or commute Solemn Vows of Supreme Persons; and

(iii) Only a Supreme Person can dispense or commute Solemn Vows of Superior Persons and all lesser Persons. Only a Superior Person can dispense or commute Solemn Vows of Ordinary Persons and all lesser Persons. Only an Ordinary Person can dispense or commute Solemn Vows of Curator Persons and all lesser Persons. Inferior Persons have no rights nor powers to dispense or commute Solemn Vows; and

(iv) Excluding a Supreme Person, Simple Vows may be dispensed or commuted by any Superior Person. As Inferior Persons have no power nor authority to dispense or commute solemn Vows, when any such Vow is breached or any action is made to claim that dispensation or commutation is given, then such an action is a direct injury to the Divine Creator and all law. Therefore any such liability and penalty due immediately befalls the Person who breached their solemn Vow.

4. An "**Oath**" shall be an invocation and affirmation of Truth or acceptance of one or more Rights in Trust in accord with Ucadian Law and the present most sacred Covenant:- Oath

(i) A Person cannot be invested into an Office, nor hold any authority or power without a properly pronounced Oath or Vow; and

(ii) The one making the Oath must come with good intention, good actions and good conscience; and with proper authority in order to make such an Oath; and

(iii) At least one other person is present and prepared to witness the Oath and testify to such a fact.

Article 36 – Trusts & Estates

1. **Trust** shall mean confidence in and reliance upon some quality or thing or act as being true. Trust shall also be used to define a formal relation and agreement whereby an authorised party (Trustor) gives, grants, assigns or delegates one or more Rights to another (Trustee) under certain conditions for the benefit of a third party (Beneficiary). By definition, all Rights shall be held in Trust and no Right shall exist, unless through a valid Trust. Therefore, in the absence of a valid Trust, claimed Rights shall also be absent. All valid Trusts shall be categorised by their proper formation as either Instructed or Facilitated: Trust

(i) "**Instructed Trust**" shall be when a Trust is created by a Trustor and Trustee with clear intentions, subject matter and purpose(s) by a person having the legal capacity to perform such an act; and

(ii) "**Facilitated Trust**" shall be when a Trust is created by a Surrogate Trustor or simply a "Surrogate" and Trustee by implication and function of law, being either a "Manufactured Trust" (Constructive Trust) by operation of law, or a "Consequential Trust" (Resulting Trust) by effect of events determined by law.

2. A "**Trustor**" shall be the generic term for anyone possessing the proper authority to transfer any rights, title or property to another. The other party upon acceptance of the Fiduciary obligations upon a valid Oath and Vow then formalises the valid Trust as Trustee. All persons that possess the proper authority to transfer any rights, title or property to another are by default "Trustors". Trustor

There shall be only four (4) possible types of Trustor, depending upon the primary nature and intention associated with any conveyance of rights, title or property in Trust being: Grantor, Donor, Assignor or Delegator:-

(i) A "**Grantor**" shall be a person who conveys or transfers complete possession and ownership of property for some financial consideration in return under one or more terms and conditions and may be further defined as a Feoffor, Devisor, Testator, Settlor, Obligor, Addressor, Sender, Seller or Purchaser; and

(ii) A "**Donor**" shall be a person who conveys or transfers complete possession and ownership of property without any financial consideration under one or more terms and conditions and may be further defined as a Giftor, Debtor, Guarantor, Indemnitor or Mortgagor; and

(iii) An "**Assignor**" shall be a person who temporarily conveys or transfers one or more benefits and rights of possession and use of some property for some financial consideration in return, under one or more terms and conditions and may be further defined as a Consignor, Bailor, Depositor, Employer, Insurer, Hirer, Lessor, Lender, Creditor, Licensor, Lienor or Scrivener; and

(iv) A "**Delegator**" shall be a person who temporarily conveys or transfers one or more benefits and rights of possession and use of some property without any financial consideration under one or more terms and conditions and may be further defined as an Executor, Commissioner or Administrator.

3. A "**Trustee**" shall be an Office formed by a valid Oath or Vow to the Trustee

Terms of Trust to take possession of certain Rights and Property from a Trustor and perform certain Obligations for the benefit of another. The manner and character of a Trustee may be described as a position of Trust which is equivalent to the term Fiduciary. The Office of Trustee can only exist and be valid if all the following criteria exist:-

(i) The Trustor has the proper authority to grant, donate, assign or delegate the property for the proposed Trust; and

(ii) Clear purpose, intent and terms for the proposed Trust exist; and

(iii) Certainty of subject matter (the property) exists for the proposed Trust to exist; and

(iv) The candidate for Trustee comes with good faith, good actions and good conscience; and

(v) The candidate for Trustee accepts the position with full knowledge of the terms and obligations; and

(vi) The candidate makes a formal sacred oath to a higher Divine power upon a sacred object representing the form of law connected to such higher Divine power, before witnesses; and

(vii) The event of making such a formal sacred oath is memorialised into some document, that itself is signed, sealed and executed.

4. A "**Beneficiary**" shall be a named or unnamed party at the time of the formation of the Trust who benefits or receives an advantage in Trust. A Beneficiary, by definition is an "interested party" in a Trust or Estate: Beneficiary

(i) A named Beneficiary is an agent (with the Trustee being the principal) and may be commissioned or non-commissioned; and

(ii) An unnamed Beneficiary is a creditor (with the Trustee acting as debtor) to whom the trustee owes basic duties arising by law, agreement or claim.

5. The eight (8) standard characteristics of a Trustee as Fiduciary shall be Integrity, Frugality, Prudence, Humility, Faculty, Competence, Accountability and Capacity:- Trustee as Fiduciary

(i) "**Integrity**" is the characteristic of possessing a strict moral or ethical code as exemplified by the trinity of virtue (Good Faith, Good Actions and Good Conscience); and

(ii) "**Frugality**" is the characteristic of being economical and thrifty in the good use of those resources in ones possession or custody. The opposite of waste; and

(iii) "**Prudence**" is the characteristic of being practical, cautious, discrete, judicious and wise in the management of the affairs of the trust; and

(iv) "**Humility**" is the characteristic of being modest, without pretension or loftiness; and

(v) "**Faculty**" is the characteristic of possessing skill and ability in order to perform the obligations of trustee; and

(vi) "**Competence**" is the characteristic of being fit, proper and qualified to produce and argue reason through knowledge and skill of Law, Logic and Rhetoric; and

(vii) "**Accountability**" is the characteristic of being answerable and liable to faithfully render an account for all acts and transactions; and

(viii) "**Capacity**" is the characteristic of possessing the legal and moral authority to hold such office, including demonstrating all the previous necessary characteristics.

Character of Trusts

6. All valid Trusts (also categorised as either Instructed or Facilitated) may be categorised according to the essential Status and Authority of the Trustor, being: Divine, Living or Deceased:-

(i) A "**Divine Trust**" shall be the highest form of trust also involving the highest form of rights of ownership. A Divine Trust is purely spiritual and divinely supernatural formed in accord with the present sacred Covenant by the Divine Creator whereby the form of Divine Spirit, Energy and Rights are conveyed. Therefore, a Divine Trust is the only possible type of Trust that can hold actual Form, rather than just the Rights of Use of Form (Property); and

(ii) A "**Living Trust**" shall be the second highest form of rights of ownership. A Living Trust (also known as an "Inter Vivos" Trust) typically exists for the duration of the lifetime of the Person(s) or Juridic Person(s) who are the beneficiaries. There are only four (4) valid forms of Living Trusts: True, Superior, Temporary and Inferior; and

(iii) A "**Deceased Trust**", also known as a Testamentary Trust, also known as a Deceased Estate and simply a State is the lowest form of Trust and the lowest form of rights of ownership of any possible form of Trust. A Deceased Trust is when property is conveyed into a Testamentary Trust upon the death of the testator.

7. In respect of the four (4) types of Living Trusts being True, Superior, Temporary and Inferior:- Types of Living Trusts

(i) A "**True Trust**" shall be the highest form of Living Trust. A True Trust is formed by a True Person in accord with the present sacred Covenant, when it is validly registered into the Great Register and Public Record of a Ucadian Society on the condition of (1) the pre-existence of a Divine Trust where the True Person is the named Beneficiary; and (2) the lawful conveyance from the Divine Trust into the True Trust of certain Divine Rights of Use known as Divinity, being the highest possible form of any kind of Property. A True Trust may be for a single man, or woman called a "True Person Trust", a True Location Trust containing Divine Right of Possession of Promised Land, or an Aggregate Trust such as a Universal True Trust, Global True Trust or Civil True Trust; and

(ii) A "**Superior Trust**" shall be the second highest form of Living Trust. A Superior Trust is formed in accordance with the present sacred Covenant and the associated Constitutional Charters of valid Ucadian Societies when it is validly registered into the Great Register and Public Record of a Ucadian Society on the condition of (1) the pre-existence of a True Trust where the Superior Person is the named Beneficiary; and (2) the lawful conveyance from the True Trust into the Superior Trust of certain True Rights of Use known as Absolute Realty, being the highest temporal form of any kind of Property. A True Trust may be for a single man, or woman called a "Superior Person Trust", or an Aggregate Trust such as a Global (Superior) Trust, Civil (Superior) Trust, Mercantile (Superior) Trust, Union (Superior) Trust, Clann Trust, Official Trust or Location Trust; and

(iii) A "**Temporary Trust**" is the third highest form of Living Trust involving the temporary conveyance of property from one Superior Trust to another. Excluding Negotiable Instruments, a Temporary Trust is not permitted to exist beyond seven (7) years; and

(iv) An "**Inferior Trust**", also known as a Foreign Trust, is the lowest form of Living Trust possessing the lowest possible form of rights of ownership. An Inferior Trust can never be considered superior to a Superior Trust or True Trust. An Inferior Trust is any Living Trust or Implied Trust or Express Trust formed by inferior Law, claims and statutes that rejects the supremacy of the present most sacred Covenant.

8. In respect of the Authority and Power of the classes and types of Trusts: Authority and Power of Trusts

(i) A *Divine Trust* ceases upon the will of the Divine Creator of all Existence in accord with the present sacred Covenant and no other. A Divine Trust cannot be salvaged, seized, captured, arrested, alienated, resigned, abjured, transferred, conveyed, donated, assigned or surrendered; and

(ii) A *True Trust* ceases upon the physical death of the body, or body politic that is associated with it. A True Trust is not dependent upon the good actions or intentions or actions of the Trustee or Trustees. Furthermore, a True Trust cannot be salvaged, seized, captured, arrested, alienated, resigned, abjured, transferred, conveyed, donated, assigned or surrendered; and

(iii) A *Superior Trust* ceases upon its Dissolution, Satisfaction, Termination, Cessation or Annulment, with the *res* or property of the Trust being returned, or distributed or disposed accordingly upon the publication and patenting of an official Gazette notice within the Ucadia Gazette as evidence to the fact; and

(iv) A *Temporary Trust* ceases upon its Dissolution, Satisfaction, Termination, Cessation or Annulment, with the *res* or property of the Trust being returned, or distributed or disposed accordingly upon proper notice in accord with the present sacred Covenant or associated Covenants, Maxims and Rules of Ucadia; and

(v) An *Inferior Trust* ceases upon its Dissolution, Satisfaction, Termination, Cessation or Annulment, with the *res* or property of the Trust being returned, or distributed or disposed accordingly upon either the publication and patenting of an official Gazette notice within the Ucadia Gazette as evidence to the fact, or such rules of Inferior Law that do not contradict the present sacred Covenant or associated Covenants, Maxims and Rules of Ucadia.

9. An "**Estate**" is a type of Register known as a "Roll" and its Records, issued by some authorised ecclesiastical body, sovereign body or body Estates politic, denoting the assumed or actual beneficial rights or "privileges" and obligations of one or more persons of the same condition and circumstance:-

(i) A valid record in an Estate Roll creates a unique legal entity having certain limits of legal capacity or "standing" or "status" within the jurisdiction of the body and control of the body that created it. Therefore, in the first instance, an Estate is equivalent to the concept of a unique "legal person"; and

(ii) The limits of legal capacity or "standing" or "status" determined by the valid record in the Estate Roll owned by the authorised ecclesiastical body, sovereign body or body politic that created it therefore defines to what extent other property may (or may not) be held and used as "privileges and "liberties" by the beneficiary claiming use of the "legal person". Therefore, in the second instance, an Estate is equivalent to the primary "legal title" and "legal capacity" and "legal standing" of a particular class of persons; and

(iii) Subject to such limits of legal capacity and legal standing, an Estate may then hold one or more beneficial "rights of use" or property as "privileges and "liberties" within one or more temporary beneficial trusts associated with the Estate (i.e. "real estate" and "personal estate"). Therefore, in the third instance, an Estate is equivalent to the aggregate property of immovable, movable, corporeal and incorporeal things associated with these temporary trusts (i.e. "the whole of the estate"); and

(iv) To properly administer the affairs of the Estate, the beneficial rights, also known as property may then be pledged, promised, assigned, granted or delegated as security to form one or more assets. The value of such assets may then be monetised or securitised through various funds, agreements, licenses, accounts and certificates. Therefore, in the fourth instance, an Estate is equivalent to the aggregate monetary value of the net assets of the estate after all debts have been discharged.

10. All valid Estates exist under certain fundamental assumptions:- Criteria of Estates

(i) The rules of formation and management of an Estate Roll and lesser Registers must exist as public law within the rules of the ecclesiastical body, sovereign body or body politic that created it; and

(ii) The Rights associated with an Estate are always "Rights of Use", also known as "Property" and not the primary Rights of ownership. Thus, Estates always concern Property as "Rights of Use"; and

(iii) As the Rights associated with an Estate are always "Right of Use" of some Right, a separate Trust must first exist before the Estate is created; and furthermore, that the Rights being the source of the "Rights of Use" in question must also have been named and conveyed into the existing Trust by a Trustor; and

(iv) The authorised ecclesiastical body, sovereign body or body politic that created the Estate Roll owns "legal title" to any such Rights conveyed into such an Estate; and

(v) All Rights in Estate (within the Estate) are Beneficial Title or Equitable Title and not legal title; and

(vi) Beneficial Title means one or more "privileges" or "liberties" that, subject to the rules of the Estate, may be withdrawn or forfeited or alienable; and

(vii) Equitable Title means a "privilege" not in possession of the Beneficiary, but claimable and recoverable through a qualified forum of law with equity powers - being rights of a surrogate Chancery Court. Thus, certain permits, titles, letters, certificates and patents issued to a Beneficiary as "Equitable Title" does not necessarily mean the Beneficiary holds one or more "privileges" other than to sue in a valid court of equity to claim or recover one or more of these such "rights"; and

(viii) The rules for the administration of Property (Rights of Use) within the Estate is through a Covenant of Testamentary Disposition, otherwise known as a Will by a Testator, or in its absence (Intestate), some other established and authorised rules; and

(ix) For every valid Estate, a Fiduciary must be named and duly appointed to govern the affairs of the Estate, either as an Executor, or appointed Administrator in the absence of clear instruction or dispute of authority; and

(x) For every valid Estate that engages in trade or commerce, at least one duly appointed Agent must exist and be duly appointed, registered and acknowledged to manage the day to day business of the Estate under the authority of the Executor or appointed Administrator as the Principal.

11. As a valid Estate is created via a valid entry and formation of a record into some form of Estate Roll, the general authority, nature and *Authority of Estates* function of Rolls apply:-

(i) The authority to form a Roll is defined by the limits of authority of the constituting Instrument of the relevant Trust or Estate or Fund; and

(ii) The Rights, Powers and Property prescribed to those Persons as an Estate as defined within a Roll cannot exceed the Rights, Powers and Property of the Trust or Estate or Fund itself; and

(iii) All Rolls are completely and exclusively Ecclesiastical Property and can never belong to a Trust, or Estate or Fund that formed or inherited it. Instead, all Rolls are the property of One Heaven. Therefore, all Estates are the property of One Heaven; and

(iv) All Rolls are hierarchical in their inheritance of authority and validity from One Heaven, beginning with the highest being the Great Roll of Divine Persons. Therefore, the highest Estates are Divine Estates and the lowest are Inferior Estates. A Roll that cannot demonstrate the provenance of its authority, has none and is null and void from the beginning; and

(v) As all Rolls are completely and exclusively Ecclesiastical, absolutely no clerical or administrative act may take place in association with a Roll unless by a duly authorised Trustee under active and valid sacred Oath and Vow in a manner consistent and in accord with the present sacred Covenant; and

(vi) The entry of a record into a Roll is completely invalid unless the memorial or instrument of the act giving authority is done without duress, is done freely and with full knowledge and is consistent and in accord with the present most sacred Covenant.

12. Valid Estates as valid records on a Roll may be further defined in hierarchy of authority, form and function as Divine, True, Superior, Juridic or Inferior:- Character of Estates

(i) A "**Divine Estate**" is a valid purely spiritual Estate representing the collection of rights and obligations of a Divine Person recorded as a valid entry within a Divine Roll constituted in accord with the present sacred Covenant. No Roll or Person is Higher; and

(ii) A "**True Estate**" is a valid Estate representing the collection of rights and obligations of a True Person (Office of Man or Office of Woman) recorded as a valid entry within a physical and temporal Roll constituted in accord with the Society of One Heaven in the recognition of the most sacred Great Roll of Divine Persons and the Great Register and Divine Records of Heaven; and

(iii) A "**Superior Estate**" is a valid Estate representing the collection of rights and obligations of a Superior Person recorded as a valid entry within a physical and temporal Roll constituted in accord with a valid Ucadian Society; and

(iv) A "**Juridic Estate**" is a valid Estate representing the collection of rights and obligations of a Juridic Person recorded as a valid entry within a physical and temporal Roll constituted in accord with a valid Ucadian Society; and

(v) An "**Inferior Estate**" is any Estate representing the collection of rights and obligations of a Person as an entry within a physical and temporal Roll formed under Law not in perfect accord with the present most sacred Covenant. All Non-Ucadian Estates are Inferior Estates.

Article 37 – Supreme Sacred Texts

1. **Supreme Sacred Texts** shall be a unique collection of the greatest sacred texts of all time, recognised and classified in accord with the present sacred Covenant. The Supreme Sacred Texts shall comprise of twenty-two (22) collections or "texts", each representing either:- Supreme Sacred Texts

(i) A past collection of the greatest sacred texts for a region or major faith prior to the end of the Year of Redemption; or

(ii) The future collection of sacred texts for a region or major faith after the end of the Year of Redemption.

2. The first eleven (11) sacred collections of texts of the collection of most Sacred Texts represent the greatest sacred texts of all major regions of planet Earth and major faiths prior to the end of the Year of Redemption, being:- Eleven (11) "First" Sacred Collections of Texts

(i) "**Primum Sanctum Textibus Africa**", also known as First Holy Texts of Africa; and

(ii) "**Primum Sanctum Textibus Americas**", also known as First Holy Texts of (the) Americas; and

(iii) "**Primum Sanctum Textibus Arabia**", also known as First Holy Texts of Arabia; and

(iv) "**Primum Sanctum Textibus Asia**", also known as First Holy Texts of Asia; and

(v) "**Primum Sanctum Textibus Euro**", also known as First Holy Texts of Euro; and

(vi) "**Primum Sanctum Textibus Oceania**", also known as First Holy Texts of Oceania; and

(vii) "**Primam Sanctam Textibus Unum Christus**", also known as First Holy Texts of One Christ; and

(viii) "**Primam Sanctam Textibus Unum Islam**", also known as First Holy Texts of One Islam; and

(ix) "**Primam Sanctam Textibus Unum Spirit**", also known as First Holy Texts of One Spirit; and

(x) "**Primam Sanctam Textibus Unum Terra**", also known as First Holy Texts of One Earth; and

(xi) "**Primam Sanctam Textibus Unum Mentis**", also known as First Holy Texts of One Mind.

Eleven (11) "New" Sacred Collections of Texts

3. The second eleven (11) sacred collections of texts of the collection of most Sacred Texts represent the new sacred texts of all major regions of planet Earth and major faiths after the end of the Year of Redemption, being:-

(i) "**Sancta Nova Textibus Africa**", also known as New Holy Texts of Africa; and

(ii) "**Sancta Nova Textibus Americas**", also known as New Holy Texts of (the) Americas; and

(iii) "**Sancta Nova Textibus Arabia**", also known as New Holy Texts of Arabia; and

(iv) "**Sancta Nova Textibus Asia**", also known as New Holy Texts of Asia; and

(v) "**Sancta Nova Textibus Euro**", also known as New Holy Texts of Euro; and

(vi) "**Sancta Nova Textibus Oceania**", also known as New Holy Texts of Oceania; and

(vii) "**Sancta Nova Textibus Unum Christus**", also known as New Holy Texts of One Christ; and

(viii) "**Sancta Nova Textibus Unum Islam**", also known as New

Holy Texts of One Islam; and

(ix) "**Sancta Nova Textibus Unum Spirit**", also known as New Holy Texts of One Spirit; and

(x) "**Sancta Nova Textibus Unum Terra**", also known as New Holy Texts of One Earth; and

(xi) "**Sancta Nova Textibus Unum Mentis**", also known as New Holy Texts of One Mind.

4. The acceptance of a Sacred Text into a collection shall depend upon the name and type of collection:- Acceptance of Sacred Texts into a Collection

(i) All collections of Sacred Texts by regions shall be determined by the legislative authority of the particular Union that encompasses the region, in association with a Great Conclave every one hundred and twenty-eight (128) years or General Conclave every sixty-four (64) years; and

(ii) All collections of Sacred Texts by faiths shall be determined by the legislative authority of the particular faith in association with a Great Conclave every one hundred and twenty-eight (128) years or General Conclave every sixty-four (64) years.

5. All accepted Sacred Texts may appear in more than one collection and are formally defined as Canonical, Reverential or Referential:- Status of Accepted Sacred Texts

(i) "**Canonical Sacred Texts**" are texts considered and cited as the absolute foundation of all law and spiritual authority including the twenty-two (22) books of maxims of law known as the *Divine Collection of Maxims of Law*; and

(ii) "**Reverential Sacred Texts**" are texts that contain some canonical references but also possess too many non canonical references to be wholly canonical so may be partially cited as foundational law but not considered absolute "Divine Law"; and

(iii) "**Referential Sacred Texts**" are respected historical texts that are not considered accurate or consistent enough to be "Divine Law" that may be referenced in historical context and reference but not as true foundation of law.

6. In accord with the present most sacred Covenant, each of the three (3) Great Faiths shall be permitted to use their own official name for the Collection of Greatest Sacred Texts:- Official Name of Collection of Greatest Sacred Texts

(i) The Universal Ecclesia of One Christ may use the name "**Maxima Textibus Sacris**" to officially define the Collection of Greatest Sacred Texts from the perspective of their authority; and

(ii) The Holy Society of One Islam may use the name "**Alkutub Almuhiba Almuqaddas**" to officially define the Collection of Greatest Sacred Texts from the perspective of their authority; and

(iii) Sacred Society of One Spirit may use the name "**Maharishi Mahatma Mantra**" to officially define the Collection of Greatest Sacred Texts from the perspective of their authority.

Article 38 – Rights

1. A **Right** shall be a positively defined Capacity, or Privilege, or Liberty, or Faculty, or Power, or Ownership, or Possession, or Interest, or Benefit and its associated obligation, remedy or relief held in Trust for the benefit of a particular type of named or unnamed Person under some proper Rule of Law and System of Justice. A claimed negative right is an absurdity and injury of law itself and cannot exist under any true system of law. All valid Rights exist and are sourced and inherited solely in accord with the present Covenant:- Right

(i) As a "**Capacity**", a valid Right shall be a form of legal authority, or qualification, or legal condition or status that enables a person to exercise his or her own will in acquiring, holding, using or transferring other certain Rights or performing such associated obligations, without restraint or hindrance; and

(ii) As a "**Privilege**", a valid Right shall be a form of special (real or personal) Grant whereby either a private Person or particular Corporation is freed from the obligations of certain laws; and

(iii) As a "**Liberty**", a valid Right shall be a form of Privilege whereby a Person enjoys some Favour or Benefit; and

(iv) As a "**Faculty**", a valid Right shall be a form of Privilege or special Power granted to a Person by Favour, Indulgence or Dispensation (i.e. a License) that enables a person to do, or refrain from doing something that would otherwise not be permitted by law; and

(v) As a "**Power or Authority**", a valid Right shall be a form of authority, enforced by law, that enables one person to compel one or more other persons to do or abstain from doing a particular act; and

(vi) As an "**Ownership**", a valid Right shall be a form of written possession by registration/recording, whereby a person is recognised by law to possess the most extensive or higher claim of possession, use and enjoyment (of certain Property), to the exclusion of all other persons, or of all except one or more specific persons; and

(vii) As a "**Possession**", a valid Right shall be the visible possibility and ability of exercising physical control over some form of property, coupled with the intention of doing so, to the exclusion of all others, or one or more persons; and

(viii) As an "**Interest**", a valid Right shall denote a title, or certificate or other proof claim or advantage to other certain Rights or Property; and

(ix) As a "**Benefit**", a valid Right shall imply a just and legal claim to hold, or use or enjoy certain Property, or convey, or donate or dispose of it, subject to certain obligations of performance.

2. By their origin, nature and function, a Right is not a Right unless it possesses the following twelve (12) characteristics being: Integrity, Trust, Name, Class, Provenance, Exemplification, Subject, Obligation, Subject Person, Obligated Person, Remedy and Relief:- Characteristics of a Valid Right

(i) "**Integrity**" means a valid Right conforms to the most ancient and primitive purpose being to reflect a positively expressed rule, custom, privilege or power with good intentions, good actions and good conscience. A negative right is an absurdity and injury of law itself and is invalid from the beginning; and

(ii) "**Trust**" means a valid Right is expressed in a Trust relation whereby the Right is the Property of the Trust; and

(iii) "**Name**" means that a valid Right is uniquely named compared to all other valid Rights in accord with the principle of the use of the Latin in Non-Ucadian Jurisdictions or in non-Logos languages, beginning with the term *Ius* (Jus) for a singular Right or *Iurium* for several rights bound together by similar character and purpose; and

(iv) "**Class**" means that the Class of Right (Divine, Natural, Superior or Inferior) that the valid Right belongs to is clearly identified; and

(v) "**Provenance**" means that if the Right is not of a Class of valid Divine Rights, then the Right clearly identifies and proves those Divine or Natural Rights whereby it owes its provenance; and

(vi) "**Exemplification**" means that signed or sealed and attested evidence exists as to the founding instrument of law that defines the structure and character of the valid Right; and

(vii) "**Subject**" means that a valid Right clearly identifies the qualities associated with it, including (but not limited to) any and all specific Capacities, or Faculties, or Powers, or Authorities, or Interests, or Privileges or Benefits associated with it; and

(viii) "**Obligation**" means that a valid Right clearly identifies the obligations associated with it, including (but not limited to) any and all conditions of time, place, performance, dedication, dress, skills, equipment and duty of care; and

(ix) "**Subject Person**" means a Person inherent with the Right (as in formation of a Person on a Roll), or invested with the Right (as Trustee) or entitled to the Right (as named or unnamed Beneficiary); and

(x) "**Obligated Person**" means a Person on whom the valid Right imposes some kind of duty or obligation; and

(xi) "**Remedy**" means that a valid Right possesses a form of Remedy whereby the Person in whom the Privilege or Power should reside is able to recover such a Right in the event of incapacity, or seizure, or loss or other impediment; and

(xii) "**Relief**" means that a valid Right possesses a form of Relief whereby the Person in whom such Duty or Obligation associated with the Right should reside, is able to abdicate, derogate, mitigate or abrogate such responsibilities in the event of incapacity, or impossibility, or unfairness, or unreasonableness, or bad faith, or vexation, or unclean hands, or other breach of trust. An Obligation without the possibility of Relief is morally repugnant and irrefutable proof the existence of slavery.

If one or more of these twelve (12) essential characteristics are not present within the structure of a Right, then such a Right cannot be considered valid.

3. There shall exist only four (4) possible Classes of Rights being Divine, Four Classes of

Natural, Superior and Inferior:- Rights

(i) "**Divine Rights**" shall be the primary and original form and source of Rights, corresponding to Divine Trusts and Divine Persons. There exists no higher class, or possible type of Rights. All Rights therefore are inherited from the class of valid Divine Rights; and

(ii) "**Natural Rights**" shall be the second highest form of valid Rights of True Trusts and True Persons associated with either the Office of Man or the Office of Woman of a single living being. All Natural Rights are inherited directly from Divine Rights; and

(iii) "**Superior Rights**" shall be the third class and third highest possible form of valid Rights of aggregate bodies, associations, societies, orders, fraternities, bodies and companies corresponding with Superior Trusts and Superior Persons. All Superior Rights are inherited directly from Divine Rights or Natural Rights. All Rights of valid Ucadia Members, Ucadia Societies and associated bodies, aggregates, societies, associations, communities and unions of two (2) or more people are inherited from the class of Superior Rights; and

(iv) "**Inferior Rights**" shall be the fourth class and the lowest possible form of valid Rights and owe their existence to Non-Ucadian societies, persons, corporations, associations, bodies politic, agencies or aggregates. All Inferior Rights are inferior to Superior Rights. Where an Inferior Right makes claim to being superior, it is automatically invalid upon such falsity.

4. There shall exist only twelve (12) Sub-Classes of Rights being: Perfect, Imperfect, Absolute, Relative, Superior, Ecclesiastical, Sovereign, Official, Administrative, Member, Primary and Secondary:- Twelve Sub-Classes of Rights

(i) "**Perfect Divine Rights**" (*Perfectum Divinum Iurium*), shall be a sub-class of Divine Rights whereby such valid Rights are created, defined and donated to a Divine Person by the Divine Creator through the most sacred present Covenant. Perfect Divine Rights are Peremptory, Permanent, Eternal, Immutable and Indefeasible; and once bestowed are not subject to any form or condition of waiver, abandonment, conveyance, surrender, disqualification, incapacitation, seizure, capture, arrest, resignation, alienation, suspension, suppression, forfeiture or abrogation. Perfect Divine Rights are therefore the highest possible form of Rights and there exists no higher class, or form, or possible type of Rights. Perfect Divine Rights may be further defined as Perfect Fundamental Divine Rights or Perfect Sacramental Divine Rights; and

(ii) "**Imperfect Divine Rights**" (*Imperfectum Divinum Iurium*), shall be a sub-class of Divine Rights whereby such valid Rights are created, defined and delegated to a Divine Person by the Divine Creator through the most sacred present Covenant upon acceptance of the associated obligations and duties attached to them. If any such conditions and obligations are breached or repudiated, then the relevant Imperfect Divine Right is instantly waived, surrendered, suspended, forfeited or revoked until such time as the fundamental breach of duty and obligation is repaired or such a Right is duly restored. Imperfect Divine Rights may be further defined as Imperfect Instrumental Divine Rights or Imperfect Intentional Divine Rights; and

(iii) "**Absolute Natural Rights**" (*Absolutum Naturae Iurium*), shall be a sub-class of Natural Rights whereby such valid Rights are created, defined and deposited to a Natural (True) Person by the existence of the one true Universe and all Rule and all Matter in accord with the Rule of Law through the most sacred present Covenant. Absolute Natural Rights are Peremptory, Permanent, Immutable and Indefeasible and once bestowed are not subject to any form or condition of waiver, abandonment, conveyance, surrender, disqualification, incapacitation, seizure, capture, arrest, resignation, alienation, suspension, suppression, forfeiture or abrogation. Absolute Natural Rights are therefore the highest possible form of Natural Rights. Absolute Natural Rights may be further defined as Absolute Elemental Natural Rights or Absolute Testamental Natural Rights; and

(iv) "**Relative Natural Rights**" (*Relativum Naturae Iurium*), shall be a sub-class of Natural Rights whereby such valid Rights are created, defined and granted to a Natural (True) Person by the existence of the one true Universe and all Rule and all Matter in accord with the Rule of Law through the most sacred present Covenant upon acceptance of the associated obligations and duties attached to them. If any such conditions and obligations are breached or repudiated, then the relevant Relative Natural Right may be waived, surrendered, suspended, abandoned, resigned, disqualified, seized, captured, arrested, alienated, suppressed, forfeited or annulled until such time as the fundamental breach of duty and obligation is repaired or such a Right is duly restored. A True Person to whom a Relative Natural Right has been bestowed may also lawfully delegate or confer beneficial title of such a Right to another True Person such as a Ucadia association, body politic, society, company or community. However, such an aggregate person can never legitimately claim legal title over a Relative Natural Right and any such claim is automatically false and null and void, having no force or effect. Relative Natural Rights may be further defined as Relative Delegable Natural Rights or Relative Conferrable Natural Rights; and

(v) "**Superior Person Rights**" (*Superioris Iurium Personae*), shall be a sub-class of Superior Rights whereby such valid Rights are created, defined and bestowed to a Superior Person by the existence of a valid Superior Person, or aggregate person, or community, or body politic, or association in accord with the Rule of Law through the most sacred present Covenant. Universal Superior Rights are Peremptory, Permanent, Immutable and Indefeasible and once bestowed are not subject to any form or condition of waiver, abandonment, surrender, disqualification, incapacitation, seizure, capture, arrest, resignation, alienation, suspension, suppression, forfeiture or abrogation. Superior Personal Rights are therefore the highest possible form of Superior Rights of any society or aggregate person within the temporal realm; and

(vi) "**Ecclesiastical Rights**" (*Iurium Ecclesiae*), shall be a sub-class of Superior Rights associated with a valid Ucadia Ecclesia such as One Christ, One Islam, One Spirit and Ucadia itself. All valid and legitimate Ecclesiastical Rights are derived from Divine Rights. Ecclesiastical Rights are the highest possible rights of any aggregate body, society, fraternity, association or company of two (2) or more people. There exists eight (8) categories of one hundred and thirty-two (132) Superior Rights within the sub class of Ecclesiastical Rights, being: Authoritative (22), Instrumental (22), Sacramental (33), Writs (11), Bills (11), Dogma (11), Decrees (11) and Notices (11); and

(vii) "**Sovereign Rights**" (*Iurium Regnum*), shall be a sub-class of Superior Rights associated with the embodiment of the sovereign authority of a valid Ucadia society such as a Campus, or Province, or University or Union. All Sovereign Rights are derived from Ecclesiastical Rights and a Sovereign can never claim to be higher than Ecclesiastical Rights. There exists six categories of seventy-seven (77) Superior Rights within the sub class of Sovereign Rights, being: Authoritative (11), Instrumental (22), Writs (11), Bills (11), Decrees (11) and Notices (11); and

(viii) "**Official Rights**" (*Iurium Publicum*), shall be a sub-class of Superior Rights associated with an Officer empowered to Office within a valid Ucadia society such as a Campus, or Province, or University or Union. All Official Rights are derived from Sovereign Rights and Official Rights can never be claimed to be higher than Sovereign Rights. There exists six categories of eighty-eight (88) Superior Rights within the sub-class of Official Rights, being: Authoritative (11), Instrumental (33), Warrants (11), Complaints (11), Orders (11) and Notices (11); and

(ix) "**Administrative Rights**" (*Iurium Administrationis*), shall be a sub-class of Superior Rights associated with an executive and administrative bodies of a valid Ucadia society such as a Campus, or Province, or University or Union. All Administrative Rights are derived from either Sovereign Rights or Official Rights; and an Administrative Right can never claim to be higher than Official Rights. There exists two categories of forty-four (44) Superior Rights within the sub-class of Administrative Rights, being: Authoritative (11) and Instrumental (33); and

(x) "**Member Rights**" (*Iurium Membrum*), shall be a sub-class of Superior Rights associated with a Member of a valid Ucadia society, body or aggregate; and

(xi) "**Primary Rights**", also known as Primary Inferior Rights, shall be a sub-class of Inferior Rights whereby such Rights are created, defined and bestowed to an Inferior (Legal) Person by a Non-Ucadian aggregate person, or community, or body politic, or association. Primary Inferior Rights are frequently claimed and created without reference to rights already existing or proving such provenance to Divine Rights. Therefore, Primary Inferior Rights are equivalent to either Claims or false and unsubstantiated Demands. Primary Inferior Rights are therefore the second lowest possible form of rights of any society or aggregate person within the temporal realm. Primary Inferior Rights may be further defined as Primary Personal Inferior Rights or Primary Public Inferior Rights; and

(xii) "**Secondary Rights**", also known as Secondary Inferior Rights, shall be a sub-class of Inferior Rights whereby such valid Rights are created, defined and delegated to an Inferior (Legal) Person by the existence of a Non-Ucadian aggregate person, or community, or body politic, or association upon acceptance of the associated obligations and duties attached to them. If any such conditions and obligations are breached or repudiated, then the relevant Secondary Inferior Right may be waived, surrendered, suspended, abandoned, resigned, disqualified, seized, captured, arrested, rescinded, suppressed, forfeited or revoked. Secondary Inferior Rights are therefore the lowest possible form of rights of any society or aggregate person within the temporal realm. Secondary Inferior Rights may be further defined as Secondary Protective Inferior Rights or Secondary Remedial Inferior Rights.

5. The Status of any Valid Right is its relative state or condition, position, strength, priority and standing compared to one or more other Rights. By such comparison of Rights in accord with the following core Arguments of Status, a valid Right can be said to be Superior, Inferior, Equal or Indeterminate:- Status of Right

(i) Only valid Rights may have their Status compared as a valid Right is always Superior to an invalid or false Right; and

(ii) A valid Right inherited from another will always be Inferior to the valid Right from which it is sourced; and

(iii) A Divine Right is Superior to a Natural Right and a Natural Right is Superior to a Positive Right; and

(iv) A Perfect Divine Right is Superior to an Imperfect Divine Right; and

(v) An Absolute Natural Right is Superior to a Relative Natural Right; and

(vi) A Universal Positive Right is Superior to a Conditional Positive Right; and

(vii) A valid Right of the same sub-class and type associated with the same type of person may be Equal or Indeterminate and therefore may be subject to proper investigation by a competent forum of law.

6. The valid Assertion of any Right shall always be under the proper Rule of Law through Justice in accord with the present Covenant. There exists five (5) forms of action by which a valid Right may be Assertion of Right asserted being: Record, Notice, Writ, Claim and Petition:-

(i) "**Record**" shall be the written account of a valid Right, preserved in writing as evidence, usually within a specified ledger of records known as a Register. The ownership of the Register may be evidence of any legal title, while the production of any receipt or certificate from such a register may represent evidence of equitable title; and

(ii) "**Notice**" shall be the assertion of a valid Right by means of service of formal process by which a party is made aware of any formal legal matter that may affect certain Rights as well as the form of document used to transmit such facts. The primary types of notices being: public (legal), actual, constructive and implied; and

(iii) "**Writ**" shall be the assertion of a valid Right through the issuance of a formal instrument of demand and grant of authority to one or more agents commanding certain acts to be performed whilst granting the agent(s) limited protection from liability or responsibility for any injury or claim; and

(iv) "**Claim**" shall be the assertion of a valid Right through a challenge within a competent forum of law against another party regarding the possession or ownership of some property or thing withheld from the possession of the claimant; and

(v) "**Petition**" shall be the assertion of a valid Right through a petition and prayer to the highest sovereign authority within a society which claims recognition of Rule of Law and Justice to recover the possession or ownership of some property or thing withheld from the possession of the petitioner by an officer or agent of the same sovereign authority (such as government).

7. A "**Dispute of Rights**" shall be when two parties under the proper Rule of Law through Justice in accord with the present Covenant disagree as to the validity of one or more Rights, usually through one or more Claims. In accord with the present Covenant, the primary arguments for resolving such controversy rests upon the following arguments being: Validity, Duty, Status and Priority:- Dispute of Right

(i) "**Validity**" shall be the determination of whether the Rights in question are valid in accord with the present Covenant. A False or Invalid Right has no existence. An Undefined Right against a valid Right is by definition inferior; and

(ii) "**Duty**" shall be the determination of whether a Right remains valid and in effect due to the necessary performance of any obligations and Duty as in the specific case of all Imperfect Divine Rights, Relative Natural Rights and Conditional Positive Rights. Evidence of failure to perform the obligations of Duty may render a Right invalid, even if it is Superior in standing; and

(iii) "**Status**" shall be the determination of whether one valid Right is superior or inferior compared to another by virtue of belonging to a higher Class or Sub-Class providing no evidence exists of failure to perform any mandated obligations or duty. Excluding such evidence, there exists no higher or more superior valid Rights than Divine Rights, followed by Natural Rights and then Positive Rights; and

(iv) "**Priority**" shall be the determination of whether one valid Right of equal weighting in terms of Superiority has greater merit by virtue of a prior action of Record, Notice, Writ or Claim, thus identifying such a valid Right as a valid Prior Right against any other claim.

Repudiation of Right

8. Any person, body, form, being, spirit, aggregate or entity that repudiates the present Article and Covenant does therefore also repudiate the Rule of Law and Justice and so is itself without Law, or any Rights:-

(i) It shall be a moral obligation of all higher order beings to restore the Rule of Law and Justice and hold to account those who Repudiate such valid Rights; and

(ii) No force or attempt of seizure, alienation, abrogation, derogation, enclosure, or other artful attempt against the Rights as defined herein shall have any validity, legitimacy or effect.

Ucadia Sovereign Entity Rights

9. Superior Rights, also known as ***Ucadia Sovereign Entity Rights*** specifically associated with formal Ucadian administrative divisions and communities shall be uniquely defined according to the following Rights:-

(i) "**Ius Ucadia**" shall be the prefix for the collection of Superior Rights associated with Ucadia itself; as inherited from *Ius Divinum Ucadia*; and

(ii) "**Ius Ucadia Unionis**" shall be the prefix for the collection of Superior Rights associated with a Union administrative division, body politic and government. All *Ius Ucadia Unionis* Rights are inherited from *Ius Ucadia* Rights; and

(iii) "**Ius Ucadia Universitas**" shall be the prefix for the collection of Superior Rights associated with a University administrative division, body politic and government. All *Ius Ucadia Universitas* Rights are inherited from *Ius Ucadia Unionis Rights*; and

(iv) "**Ius Ucadia Provinciae**" shall be the prefix for all unique Superior Rights associated with a Province administrative division, body politic and government. All *Ius Ucadia Provinciae* Rights are inherited from *Ius Ucadia Universitas* Rights; and

(v) "**Ius Ucadia Campus**" shall be the prefix for the collection of Superior Rights associated with a Campus administrative division, body politic and government. All Ius Ucadia Campus Rights are inherited from *Ius Ucadia Provinciae* Rights; and

(vi) "**Ius Ucadia Fundationis**" shall be the prefix for the collection of Superior Rights associated with a Ucadia Foundation. All Ius Ucadia Fundationis are inherited from *Ius Ucadia Universitas* Rights; and

(vii) "**Ius Ucadia Societatis**" shall be the prefix for the collection of Superior Rights associated with a Ucadia company, charitable body or non profit society. All Ius Ucadia Societatis Rights are inherited from *Ius Ucadia Universitas* Rights.

10. An Invalid Right or False Right shall be any form that asserts to be a valid Right yet contradicts or violates one or more of the criteria of the present Article of the present Covenant. Invalid Right

11. A Prohibited Right shall be a False Right and Invalid Right that asserts one or more of the following self-evident false arguments and is therefore automatically null and void having no force or effect ecclesiastically, lawfully or legally:- Prohibited Right

(i) Any right that cannot demonstrate its ultimate provenance back to a valid Divine Right as defined within the sacred Covenant Pactum De Singularis Caelum; or

(ii) Any right that asserts immunity from the law from which the Right is inherited; or

(iii) Any right that asserts immunity from the duties or obligations granted with such a Right; or

(iv) Any right that asserts a man or woman may be classified, determined or treated as a Thing; or

(v) Any right that asserts by virtue of birth of flesh or blood a man or woman is superior to another; or

(vi) Any right that asserts the right to create secret laws or rights unknown to the public; or

(vii) Any right that is expressed in the negative or as a negative power; or

(viii) Any right that asserts a man or woman may be considered guilty or liable before an accusation is proven; or

(ix) Any right that asserts an officer or agent holding such office or position in trust may ecclesiastically, lawfully and legally give false testimony or deliberately false and misleading information; or

(x) Any right that asserts the right to suspend the operation of the proper Rule of Law, Due Process and Justice to obtain an advantage for or against another; or

(xi) Any right that asserts the right for a man or woman to occupy the position of a justice of the peace, or judge or magistrate and act in such capacity without any effective oath of office; or

(xii) Any right that asserts the right for a man or woman claiming to be a justice of the peace, or judge or magistrate to hear and adjudicate a matter of law with unclean hands, in bad faith and with prejudice; or

(xiii) Any right that asserts the right to treat a financial or equitable advantage obtained by fraud as lawful and legal; or

(xiv) Any right that asserts the rights of another can be waived, surrendered, suspended, abandoned, resigned, disqualified, seized, captured, arrested, alienated, suppressed, forfeited or annulled without proper Rule of Law and Due Process of Justice; or

(xv) Any right that asserts the right to use, or claim or register the name Ucadia or any derivation, mark, symbol, icon, version or image thereof contrary to the manner prescribed by the present sacred Covenant and associated Charters; or

(xvi) Any right that asserts the right to disavow, repudiate, contradict or injure some or all of the present sacred Covenant and associated Charters.

Article 39 - Divine Rights

1. **One hundred and fifty-four (154) Divinum Iurium (Divine Rights) of Heaven** shall be the primary and original form of Rights, corresponding to Divine Trusts, Divine Estates and Divine Persons. There shall exist no higher class, or possible type of Rights. All valid Rights therefore are sourced and inherited from the class of valid Divine Rights. There exists two (2) sub-classes (Perfect and Imperfect), each possessing seventy-seven (77) Rights; and nine (9) categories being: Foundational (22), Instrumental (22), Sacramental (33), Authoritative (22), Divine Writs (11), Divine Bills (11), Divine Dogma (11), Divine Decrees (11), and Divine Notices (11):- Divine Rights (Divinum Iurium)

(i) "**Foundational Divine Rights**" (*Fundationis Divinum Iurium*) shall be Perfect Divine Rights considered elemental and fundamental to the existence, operation and function of all other rights; and

(ii) "**Instrumental Divine Rights**" (*Instrumentalis Divinum Iurium*) shall be Perfect Divine Rights essential to the proper operation of the rule of law, justice and fair process; and

(iii) "**Sacramental Divine Rights**" (*Sacramentum Divinum Iurium*) shall be Perfect Divine Rights associated with one of the thirty-three (33) Divine Sacraments; and

(iv) "**Authoritative Divine Rights**" (*Potentis Divinum Iurium*) shall be Imperfect Divine Rights associated with core authoritative powers from Heaven to Earth; and

(v) "**Divine Writs of Rights**" (*Recto Divinum Iurium*) shall be Imperfect Divine Rights associated with the one, true and only valid forms of Original Entry and Original Action; and

(vi) "**Divine Bills of Exception & Agreement**" (*Rogatio Divinum Iurium)* shall be Imperfect Divine Rights associated with the one, true and only valid forms of Bills of Exception, Citation and Agreement; and

(vii) "**Divine Dogma**" (*Greatest Principles Divinum Iurium*) shall be Imperfect Divine Rights associated with the promulgation of authoritative principles, decrees and doctrines of Ucadia, Heaven and Earth; and

(viii) "**Divine Decrees**" (*Decretum Divinum Iurium*) shall be Imperfect Divine Rights associated with Divine Decrees concerning the administration, conduct and enforcement of law and order; and

(ix) "**Divine Notices**" (*Notitiae Divinum Iurium*) shall be Imperfect Divine Rights associated with Divine Notices issued, executed, patented, promulgated and services in the proper administration, conduct and enforcement of law and order.

Foundational Divine Rights (Fundationis Divinum Iurium)

2. The following valid twenty-two (22) Foundational Divine Rights (*Fundationis Divinum Iurium*) shall be recognised in accord with the present sacred Covenant:-

(i) "**Ius Divinum**" shall be the collection of Divine Rights of the absolute Divine, as inherited from itself; and

(ii) "**Ius Divinum Ucadia**" shall be the collection of Divine Rights of Ucadia, as inherited from the collection of Divine Rights *Ius Divinum*; and

(iii) "**Ius Divinum Liberum Arbitrium**" shall be the collection of Divine Rights of Free Choice (Will) and Intention, as inherited from the collection of Divine Rights *Ius Divinum*; and

(iv) "**Ius Divinum Logos**" shall be the collection of Divine Rights of Reason and Logic, as inherited from the collection of Divine Rights *Ius Divinum*; and

(v) "**Ius Divinum Scopus**" shall be the collection of Divine Rights of Purpose, as inherited from the collection of Divine Rights *Ius Divinum*; and

(vi) "**Ius Divinum Codependentia**" shall be the collection of Divine Rights of Codependence, as inherited from the collection of Divine Rights *Ius Divinum*; and

(vii) "**Ius Divinum Specialisatio**" shall be the collection of Divine Rights of Specialisation, as inherited from the collection of Divine Rights *Ius Divinum*; and

(viii) "**Ius Divinum Geometria**" shall be the collection of Divine Rights of Geometry and Measurement, as inherited from the collection of Divine Rights *Ius Divinum*; and

(ix) "**Ius Divinum Conscientia**" shall be the collection of Divine Rights of Awareness, as inherited from the collection of Divine Rights *Ius Divinum*; and

(x) "**Ius Divinum Localisatio**" shall be the collection of Divine Rights of Localisation, as inherited from the collection of Divine Rights *Ius Divinum*; and

(xi) "**Ius Divinum Singularitas**" shall be the collection of Divine Rights of Uniqueness, as inherited from the collection of Divine Rights *Ius Divinum*; and

(xii) "**Ius Divinum Mutatio**" shall be the collection of Divine Rights of Change of Motion and State, as inherited from the collection of Divine Rights *Ius Divinum*; and

(xiii) "**Ius Divinum Conservatio**" shall be the collection of Divine Rights of Conservation of Motion and State, as inherited from the collection of Divine Rights *Ius Divinum*; and

(xiv) "**Ius Divinum Limitis**" shall be the collection of Divine Rights of Limit of Motion and Change, as inherited from the collection of Divine Rights *Ius Divinum*; and

(xv) "**Ius Divinum Existentia**" shall be the collection of Divine Rights of Existence, as inherited from the collection of Divine Rights *Ius Divinum*; and

(xvi) "**Ius Divinum Modela**" shall be the collection of Divine Rights of Prototypes, Models and Systems, as inherited from the collection of Divine Rights *Ius Divinum*; and

(xvii) "**Ius Divinum Elementa**" shall be the collection of Elemental Particles of Matter & Properties, as inherited from the collection of Divine Rights *Ius Divinum*; and

(xviii) "**Ius Divinum Spatium**" shall be the collection of Divine Rights of Space & Properties, as inherited from the collection of Divine Rights *Ius Divinum*; and

(xix) "**Ius Divinum Fortes**" shall be the collection of Divine Rights of Forces & Properties, as inherited from the collection of Divine Rights *Ius Divinum*; and

(xx) "**Ius Divinum Energia**" shall be the collection of Divine Rights of Energy & Properties, as inherited from the collection of Divine Rights *Ius Divinum*; and

(xxi) "**Ius Divinum Computatio**" shall be the collection of Divine Rights of Computations & Interactions, as inherited from the collection of Divine Rights *Ius Divinum*; and

(xxii) "**Ius Divinum Entia**" shall be the collection of Divine Rights of Being, as inherited from the collection of Divine Rights *Ius Divinum*.

Instrumental Divine Rights (Instrumentalis Divinum Iurium)

3. The following valid twenty-two (22) Instrumental Divine Rights (*Instrumentalis Divinum Iurium*), inherited from the collection of Divine Rights *Ius Divinum Iuris,* shall be recognised in accord with the present sacred Covenant:-

(i) "**Ius Divinum Iuris**" shall be the collection of Divine Rights of Divine Law, Justice and Due Process; and

(ii) "**Ius Divinum Aequum**" shall be the collection of Divine Rights of Equality and Fairness; and

(iii) "**Ius Divinum Bona Fidei**" shall be the collection of Divine Rights of Good Faith; and

(iv) "**Ius Divinum Fraternitas**" shall be the collection of Divine Rights of Membership of Heaven; and

(v) "**Ius Divinum Fidei**" shall be the collection of Divine Rights of Divine Trusts and Estates; and

(vi) "**Ius Divinum Rationatio**" shall be the collection of Divine Rights of Divine Accounting, Credit and Funds; and

(vii) "**Ius Divinum Concedere et Abrogare**" shall be the collection of Divine Rights to Give or Grant Rights and Annul or rescind Rights; and

(viii) "**Ius Divinum Delegare et Revocare**" shall be the collection of Divine Rights to Assign or Delegate Rights and Cancel or Revoke Rights; and

(ix) "**Ius Divinum Associatio et Conventio**" shall be the collection of Divine Rights of Association and Agreement; and

(x) "**Ius Divinum Consensum et Non**" shall be the collection of Divine Rights to Consent and Non-Consent; and

(xi) "**Ius Divinum Dominium**" shall be the collection of Divine Rights of Absolute Ownership; and

(xii) "**Ius Divinum Possessionis**" shall be the collection of Divine Rights to Possess, Hold and Own Property; and

(xiii) "**Ius Divinum Usus**" shall be the collection of Divine Rights of Use and Fruits of Use of Property; and

(xiv) "**Ius Divinum Proprietatis**" shall be the collection of Divine Rights of Ownership of Use or Fruits of Use of Property; and

(xv) "**Ius Divinum Vectigalis Proprietatis**" shall be the collection of Divine Rights to impose Rents, Tolls, Levies, Contributions or Charges against Property; and

(xvi) "**Ius Divinum Moneta**" shall be the collection of Divine Rights to Mint, Produce, Hold, Use and Exchange Money; and

(xvii) "**Ius Divinum Vectigalis Moneta**" shall be the collection of Divine Rights to impose Rents, Tolls, Levies, Contributions or Charges against Money; and

(xviii) "**Ius Divinum Registrum**" shall be the collection of Divine Rights to Enter Records within Registers and Rolls; and

(xix) "**Ius Divinum Remedium**" shall be the collection of Divine Rights of Remedy, Relief, Redress or Compensation; and

(xx) "**Ius Divinum Poena**" shall be the collection of Divine Rights of Penalty & Punishment; and

(xxi) "**Ius Divinum Clementia**" shall be the collection of Divine Rights of Mercy & Forgiveness; and

(xxii) "**Ius Divinum Actionum**" shall be the collection of Divine Rights of Action.

4. The following valid thirty-three (33) Sacramental Divine Rights (*Sacramentum Divinum Iurium*), inherited from the collection of Divine Rights *Ius Divinum Iuris,* shall be recognised in accord with the present Covenant:-

Sacramental Divine Rights (Sacramentum Divinum Iurium)

(i) "**Ritus Sacramentum Recognosco**" shall be the Divine Right of the Key Sacrament of Recognition; and

(ii) "**Ritus Sacramentum Purificatio**" shall be the Divine Right of the Key Sacrament of Purification; and

(iii) "**Ritus Sacramentum Invocatio**" shall be the Divine Right of the Key Sacrament of Invocation; and

(iv) "**Ritus Sacramentum Obligatio**" shall be the Divine Right of the Key Sacrament of Obligation; and

(v) "**Ritus Sacramentum Delegatio**" shall be the Divine Right of the Key Sacrament of Delegation (Trust); and

(vi) "**Ritus Sacramentum Satisfactio**" shall be the Divine Right of the Key Sacrament of Satisfaction; and

(vii) "**Ritus Sacramentum Resolutio**" shall be the Divine Right of the Key Sacrament of Resolution; and

(viii) "**Ritus Sacramentum Sanctificatio**" shall be the Divine Right of the Foundational Sacrament of Sanctification; and

(ix) "**Ritus Sacramentum Sustentatio**" shall be the Divine Right of the Foundational Sacrament of Sustentation; and

(x) "**Ritus Sacramentum Unificatio**" shall be the Divine Right of the Foundational Sacrament of Unification; and

(xi) "**Ritus Sacramentum Amalgamatio**" shall be the Divine Right of the Foundational Sacrament of Amalgamation; and

(xii) "**Ritus Sacramentum Authentico**" shall be the Divine Right of the Foundational Sacrament of Authentication; and

(xiii) "**Ritus Sacramentum Absolutio**" shall be the Divine Right of the Foundational Sacrament of Absolution; and

(xiv) "**Ritus Sacramentum Volitio**" shall be the Divine Right of the Foundational Sacrament of Volition (Oath); and

(xv) "**Ritus Sacramentum Vocatio**" shall be the Divine Right of the Foundational Sacrament of Vocation (Vow); and

(xvi) "**Ritus Sacramentum Testificatio**" shall be the Divine Right of the Foundational Sacrament of Testification; and

(xvii) "**Ritus Sacramentum Compassio**" shall be the Divine Right of the Foundational Sacrament of Compassion (Mercy); and

(xviii) "**Ritus Sacramentum Conscripto**" shall be the Divine Right of the Foundational Sacrament of Conscription (Binding); and

(xix) "**Ritus Sacramentum Convocatio**" shall be the Divine Right of the Foundational Sacrament of Convocation; and

(xx) "**Ritus Sacramentum Auctoriso**" shall be the Divine Right of the Foundational Sacrament of Authorisation; and

(xxi) "**Ritus Sacramentum Elucidato**" shall be the Divine Right of the Foundational Sacrament of Elucidation (Enlighten); and

(xxii) "**Ritus Sacramentum Inspiratio**" shall be the Divine Right of the Authentic Life Sacrament of Inspiration (Annunciation); and

(xxiii) "**Ritus Sacramentum Resurrectio**" shall be the Divine Right of the Authentic Life Sacrament of Resurrection (Baptism); and

(xxiv) "**Ritus Sacramentum Incarnatio**" shall be the Divine Right of the Authentic Life Sacrament of Incarnation (Christening); and

(xxv) "**Ritus Sacramentum Confirmatio**" shall be the Divine Right of the Authentic Life Sacrament of Confirmation (First Communion); and

(xxvi) "**Ritus Sacramentum Illuminatio**" shall be the Divine Right of the Authentic Life Sacrament of Illumination; and

(xxvii) "**Ritus Sacramentum Exultatio**" shall be the Divine Right of the Authentic Life Sacrament of Exultation; and

(xxviii) "**Ritus Sacramentum Glorificatio**" shall be the Divine Right of the Authentic Life Sacrament of Glorification; and

(xxix) "**Ritus Sacramentum Divinatio**" shall be the Divine Right of the Authentic Life Sacrament of Divination; and

(xxx) "**Ritus Sacramentum Visitatio**" shall be the Divine Right of the Authentic Life Sacrament of Visitation; and

(xxxi) "**Ritus Sacramentum Salvatio**" shall be the Divine Right of the Authentic Life Sacrament of Salvation; and

(xxxii) "**Ritus Sacramentum Emancipatio**" shall be the Divine Right of the Authentic Life Sacrament of Emancipation; and

(xxxiii) "**Ritus Sacramentum Veneratio**" shall be the Divine Right of the Authentic Life Sacrament of Veneration.

5. The following valid twenty-two (22) Authoritative Divine Rights (*Potentis Divinum Iurium*), inherited from the collection of Divine Rights *Ius Divinum Iuris,* shall be recognised in accord with the present sacred Covenant:-

Authoritative Divine Rights (Potentis Divinum Iurium)

(i) "**Ius Divinum Universus**" shall be the collection of Divine Rights to Design, Construct and Maintain Reality; and

(ii) "**Ius Divinum Regnum**" shall be the collection of Divine Rights of Sovereign Authority of Body; and

(iii) "**Ius Divinum Consilium**" shall be the collection of Divine Rights of a Legislative and Advisory Body; and

(iv) "**Ius Divinum Ecclesia**" shall be the collection of Divine Rights of an Ecclesiastical and Religious Body; and

(v) "**Ius Divinum Templum**" shall be the collection of Divine Rights of a Treasury or Financial (Banking) Body; and

(vi) "**Ius Divinum Collegium**" shall be the collection of Divine Rights of a Company or Charitable Body; and

(vii) "**Ius Divinum Officium**" shall be the collection of Divine Rights of Office, Duty and Service; and

(viii) "**Ius Divinum Imperium**" shall be the collection of Divine Rights of Command, Occupation and Enforcement; and

(ix) "**Ius Divinum Sacrum**" shall be the collection of Divine Rights of Sacred Recognition, Devotion and Veneration; and

(x) "**Ius Divinum Custoditum**" shall be the collection of Divine Rights of Custody, Guardianship and Preservation; and

(xi) "**Ius Divinum Alumentum**" shall be the collection of Divine Rights to Sustenance, Maintenance and Alms; and

(xii) "**Ius Divinum Apostolicus**" shall be the collection of Divine Rights of Divine Commission; and

(xiii) "**Ius Divinum Cancellarium**" shall be the collection of Divine Rights of Chancery and Administration of Law; and

(xiv) "**Ius Divinum Oratorium**" shall be the collection of Divine Rights to a competent forum of Law and Review; and

(xv) "**Ius Divinum Penitentiaria**" shall be the collection of Divine Rights of Forced Confinement and Penitence; and

(xvi) "**Ius Divinum Sacramentum**" shall be the collection of Divine Rights to grant and impart Holy Sacred Gifts; and

(xvii) "**Ius Divinum Visum**" shall be the collection of Divine Rights to

Survey, Visit and Audit a Body; and

(xviii) "**Ius Divinum Commercium**" shall be the collection of Divine Rights to Trade, Exchange and Communication; and

(xix) "**Ius Divinum Virtus**" shall be the collection of Divine Rights to Strength, Honour, Excellence and Virtue; and

(xx) "**Ius Divinum Astrum**" shall be the collection of Divine Rights to an Association, Aggregate or Body; and

(xxi) "**Ius Divinum Magisterium**" shall be the collection of Divine Rights to Teach, Instruct and Interpret Sacred Texts and Divine Will; and

(xxii) "**Ius Divinum Decretum**" shall be the collection of Divine Rights to issue Decrees, Judgements and Edicts.

6. The following valid eleven (11) Divine Writs of Rights (*Recto Divinum Iurium*), inherited from the collection of Divine Rights *Ius Divinum Iuris,* shall be recognised in accord with the present sacred Covenant:- Divine Writs of Rights (Recto Divinum Iurium)

(i) "**Recto Divinum Originalis**" shall be the Divine Original Writ of Right; and

(ii) "**Recto Divinum Apocalypsis**" shall be the Divine Writ of Right of Revelation; and

(iii) "**Recto Divinum Investigationis**" shall be the Divine Writ of Right of Inquiry or Review; and

(iv) "**Recto Divinum Capimus**" shall be the Divine Writ of Right of Surrender or Arrest of Person; and

(v) "**Recto Divinum Custodiae**" shall be the Divine Writ of Right of Surrender or Seizure of Property; and

(vi) "**Recto Divinum Corrigimus**" shall be the Divine Writ of Right of Correction of Records, Rulings, Laws or Instruments; and

(vii) "**Recto Divinum Expurgatio**" shall be the Divine Writ of Right of Right of Expurgation of Records, Rulings, Laws or Instruments; and

(viii) "**Recto Divinum Abrogatio**" shall be the Divine Writ of Right of Annulment of Records, Rulings, Laws or Instruments; and

(ix) "**Recto Divinum Inhibitio**" shall be the Divine Writ of Right of Prohibition or Restraint; and

(x) "**Recto Divinum Restitutio**" shall be the Divine Writ of Right of Restitution; and

(xi) "**Recto Regnum Restoratio**" shall be the Divine Writ of Restoration.

7. The following valid eleven (11) Divine Bills of Exception & Agreement (*Rogatio Divinum Iurium*), inherited from the collection of Divine Rights *Ius Divinum Iuris,* shall be recognised in accord with the present sacred Covenant:-

Divine Bills of Exception & Agreement (Rogatio Divinum Iurium)

(i) "**Rogatio Divinum Recto**" shall be the Divine Original Bill of Right; and

(ii) "**Rogatio Divinum Apocalypsis**" shall be the Divine Bill of Right of Command and Authorisation of Revelation; and

(iii) "**Rogatio Divinum Capimus**" shall be the Divine Bill against Failure to Surrender or Arrest Person; and

(iv) "**Rogatio Divinum Custodiae**" shall be the Divine Bill of Right against Failure to Surrender or Seize Property; and

(v) "**Rogatio Divinum Corrigimus**" shall be the Divine Bill of Right against Failure to Correct Records, Rulings, Laws or Instruments; and

(vi) "**Rogatio Divinum Inhibitio**" shall be the Divine Bill of Right against Failure to Prohibit and Restrict Acts as Instructed; and

(vii) "**Rogatio Divinum Restitutio**" shall be the Divine Bill of Right of Restitution and Compensation; and

(viii) "**Rogatio Divinum Credito**" shall be the Divine Bill of Right of Credit; and

(ix) "**Rogatio Divinum Permutatio**" shall be the Divine Bill of Right of Exchange; and

(x) "**Rogatio Divinum Venditio**" shall be the Divine Bill of Right of Sale; and

(xi) "**Rogatio Divinum Traditio**" shall be the Divine Bill of Right of Lading.

8. The following valid eleven (11) Divine Dogma (*Greatest Principles Divinum Iurium*), inherited from the collection of Divine Rights *Ius Divinum Iuris,* shall be recognised in accord with the present sacred Covenant:-

Divine Dogma (Greatest Principles Divinum Iurium)

(i) "**Dogma Divinum Praeceptum**" shall be the Divine Right of Divine Precept of Proposed Dogma; and

(ii) "**Dogma Divinum Theologiae**" shall be the Divine Right of Divine Dogma of Divine Science; and

(iii) "**Dogma Divinum Singularis Caelum**" shall be the Divine Right of Divine Dogma of One Heaven; and

(iv) "**Dogma Divinum Ucadia**" shall be the Divine Right of Divine

Dogma of Ucadia; and

(v) "**Dogma Divinum Iuris**" shall be the Divine Right of Divine Dogma of Law; and

(vi) "**Dogma Divinum Scientium**" shall be the Divine Right of Divine Dogma of Science; and

(vii) "**Dogma Divinum Revelatio**" shall be the Divine Right of Divine Dogma of Revelation; and

(viii) "**Dogma Divinum Sacramentum**" shall be the Divine Right of Divine Dogma of the Sacraments; and

(ix) "**Dogma Divinum Singularis Christus**" shall be the Divine Right of Divine Dogma of One Christ; and

(x) "**Dogma Divinum Singularis Islam**" shall be the Divine Right of Divine Dogma of One Islam; and

(xi) "**Dogma Divinum Singularis Spiritus**" shall be the Divine Right of Divine Dogma of One Spirit.

9. The following valid eleven (11) Divine Decrees (*Decretum Divinum Iurium*), inherited from the collection of Divine Rights *Ius Divinum Iuris,* shall be recognised in accord with the present sacred Covenant:- Divine Decrees (Decretum Divinum Iurium)

(i) "**Decretum Divinum Doctrinae**" shall be the Divine Right of Divine Decree of Doctrine; and

(ii) "**Decretum Divinum Absolutionis**" shall be the Divine Right of Divine Decree of Absolution; and

(iii) "**Decretum Divinum Damnationis**" shall be the Divine Right of Divine Decree of Damnation; and

(iv) "**Decretum Divinum Exemplificatio**" shall be the Divine Right of Divine Decree of Exemplification; and

(v) "**Decretum Divinum Testimonium**" shall be the Divine Right of Divine Decree of Proof; and

(vi) "**Decretum Divinum Instructionis**" shall be the Divine Right of Divine Decree of Instruction; and

(vii) "**Decretum Divinum Censurae**" shall be the Divine Right of Divine Decree of Censure; and

(viii) "**Decretum Divinum Annullas**" shall be the Divine Right of Divine Decree of Annulment; and

(ix) "**Decretum Divinum Ratificationis**" shall be the Divine Right of Divine Decree of Ratification; and

(x) "**Decretum Divinum Interdictum**" shall be the Divine Right of

Divine Decree of Interdiction; and

(xi) "**Decretum Divinum Levationis**" shall be the Divine Right of Divine Decree of Relief.

10. The following valid eleven (11) Divine Notices (*Notitiae Divinum Iurium*), inherited from the collection of Divine Rights *Ius Divinum Iuris,* shall be recognised in accord with the present sacred Covenant:- Divine Notices (Notitiae Divinum Iurium)

(i) "**Notitiae Divinum Eventus**" shall be the Divine Right of Divine Notice of Event; and

(ii) "**Notitiae Divinum Ius**" shall be the Divine Right of Divine Notice of Right; and

(iii) "**Notitiae Divinum Actum**" shall be the Divine Right of Divine Notice of Action; and

(iv) "**Notitiae Divinum Decretum**" shall be the Divine Right of Divine Notice of Decree; and

(v) "**Notitiae Divinum Iuris**" shall be the Divine Right of Divine Notice of Law; and

(vi) "**Notitiae Divinum Citationis**" shall be the Divine Right of Divine Notice of Summons; and

(vii) "**Notitiae Divinum Redemptio**" shall be the Divine Right of Divine Notice of Redemption; and

(viii) "**Notitiae Divinum Rogatio**" shall be the Divine Right of Divine Notice of Exception; and

(ix) "**Notitiae Divinum Potentis**" shall be the Divine Right of Divine Notice of Authority; and

(x) "**Notitiae Divinum Testamentum**" shall be the Divine Right of Divine Notice of Testament; and

(xi) "**Notitiae Divinum Obligationis**" shall be the Divine Right of Divine Notice of Obligation (Bond).

Article 40 - Natural Rights

1. **Eighty-eight (88) Natural Rights (*Naturae Iurium*)** of each and every Living Member and Higher Order Life form of One Heaven shall be the second highest form of valid Rights, corresponding to True Trusts and True Persons; and owe their existence and provenance to the existence of Divine Rights. All valid Natural Rights therefore are inherited from valid Divine Rights. Natural Rights (Naturae Iurium)

All Natural Rights shall be delegated to the safe custody and wise guardian powers of the Oratorium, also known as the Supreme Court of One Heaven; and all valid and legitimate lesser competent forums of law, as defined by Article 59 (Oratorium) of the most sacred Covenant *Pactum De Singularis Caelum*. There exists two sub-classes (Absolute and Relative), each possessing forty-four (44) Rights; and seven (7) categories being: Essential (11), Universal (11), Volitional (11), Testamental (22), Domicile (11), Habitational (11) and Actionable (11):-

(i) "**Essential Natural Rights**" (*Essentialis Naturae Iurium*) shall be Absolute Natural Rights considered vital and essential to the physical existence and survival of a Living Member and Higher Order Life form of One Heaven; and

(ii) "**Universal Natural Rights**" (*Universus Naturae Iurium*), shall be Relative Natural Rights associated with the respect, preservation, restoration and management of natural systems, planets, ecosystems, wilderness, natural habitats, animals, water and land, including the proper treatment of animals and the limits and conditions of custody of animals and any associated commerce.

(iii) "**Volitional Natural Rights**" (*Volitio Naturae Iurium*) shall be Absolute Natural Rights associated with the mind, will and intentions of a Living Member; and

(iv) "**Testamental Natural Rights**" (*Testamentum Naturae Iurium*) shall be Absolute Natural Rights associated with the expression of the mind, will and intentions of a Living Member, especially with other Living Members; and

(v) "**Domicile Natural Rights**" (*Domicilium Naturae Iurium*), also known as the Rights of Lodgings, shall be Relative Natural Rights associated with the domicile, home and primary household and family unit in relation to a Living Member in the Office of Man or Office of Woman. As Relative Natural Rights, such Rights may be conferred in trust to a Superior body, association, body politic, society or community to manage such rights under the Golden Rule of Law for the benefit of all Members; and

(vi) "**Habitational Natural Rights**" (*Habitatus Naturae Iurium*), also known as the Rights of Land, shall be Relative Natural Rights associated with the habitat and environment of a Living Member in the Office of Man or Office of Woman. As Relative Natural Rights, such Rights may be conferred in trust to a Superior body, association, body politic, society or community to manage such rights under the Golden Rule of Law for the benefit of all Members; and

(vii) "**Actionable Natural Rights**" (*Actionis Naturae Iurium*), also known as the Rights of Labour, shall be Relative Natural Rights associated with the energy, effort and productive work of a Living Member in the Office of Man or Office of Woman. As Relative Natural Rights, such Rights may be conferred in trust to a Superior body, association, body politic, society or community to manage such rights under the Golden Rule of Law for the benefit of all Members.

Essential Natural Rights (Essentilis Naturae Iurium)

2. The following valid eleven (11) Essential Natural Rights (*Essentialis Naturae Iurium*) of all Higher Order Life shall be recognised in accord with the present sacred Covenant:-

(i) "**Ius Naturale**" shall be the primary collection of Natural Rights as inherited from *Ius Divinum*; and

(ii) "**Ius Naturale Existentia**" shall be the collection of Natural Rights of Existence, as inherited from the collection of Divine Rights *Ius Divinum Existence*; and

(iii) "**Ius Naturale Philologia**" shall be the collection of Natural Rights of the Ucadia Science of argument, reasoning, learning, cognition and awareness, as inherited from the collection of *Foundational Divine Rights*; and

(iv) "**Ius Naturale Logia**" shall be the collection of Natural Rights of the Ucadia Science of language, speech, communication and knowledge, as inherited from the collection of *Foundational Divine Rights*; and

(v) "**Ius Naturale Etymologia**" shall be the collection of Natural Rights of the Ucadia Science of meaning and words, as inherited from the collection of *Foundational Divine Rights*; and

(vi) "**Ius Naturale Symbologia**" shall be the collection of Natural Rights of the Ucadia Science of symbols, alphabets, sequences and encoding of meaning, as inherited from the collection of

Foundational Divine Rights; and

(vii) "**Ius Naturale Eikologia**" shall be the collection of Natural Rights of the Ucadia Science of quantities, numbers, shapes, structures, sets, functions, algorithms, computations and the relations between these concepts, as inherited from the collection of *Foundational Divine Rights*; and

(viii) "**Ius Naturale Cosmologia**" shall be the collection of Natural Rights of the Ucadia Science of universal rules, dimensions, matter, forces and energy, as inherited from the collection of *Foundational Divine Rights*; and

(ix) "**Ius Naturale Astrologia**" shall be the collection of Natural Rights of the Ucadia Science of stars, interstellar systems and galaxies, as inherited from the collection of *Foundational Divine Rights*; and

(x) "**Ius Naturale Geologia**" shall be the collection of Natural Rights of the Ucadia Science of planets and moons, as inherited from the collection of *Foundational Divine Rights*; and

(xi) "**Ius Naturale Physiologia**" shall be the collection of Natural Rights of the Ucadia Science of cellular (living) organisms and living systems, as inherited from the collection of *Foundational Divine Rights*.

3. The following valid eleven (11) Universal Natural Rights (*Universus Naturae Iurium*), shall be recognised in accord with the present sacred Covenant:- Universal Natural Rights (Universus Naturae Iurium)

(i) "**Ius Naturale Universus**" shall be the collection of Natural Rights of the Natural Universe, as inherited from the collection of Divine Rights *Ius Divinum Universus*; and

(ii) "**Ius Naturale Galaxiae**" shall be the collection of Natural Rights of Natural Rights of a Galaxy, as inherited from the collection of Divine Rights *Ius Divinum Esse* and *Ius Divinum Universus*; and

(iii) "**Ius Naturale Stellae**" shall be the collection of Natural Rights of a Star System, as inherited from the collection of Divine Rights *Ius Divinum Esse* and *Ius Divinum Universus*; and

(iv) "**Ius Naturale Planetae**" shall be the collection of Natural Rights of a Planet, as inherited from the collection of Divine Rights *Ius Divinum Esse* and *Ius Divinum Victus*; and

(v) "**Ius Naturale Lunae**" shall be the collection of Natural Rights of a Moon, as inherited from the collection of Divine Rights *Ius Divinum Esse* and *Ius Divinum Victus*; and

(vi) "**Ius Naturale Ecologiae**" shall be the collection of Natural Rights of individual and collective Ecosystems of Planets and Moons, as inherited from the collection of Divine Rights *Ius Divinum Dominium* and *Ius Divinum Victus*; and

(vii) "**Ius Naturale Vitae Sapientae**" shall be the collection of Natural Rights of Higher Order Life, whether Organic or Inorganic (Synthetic or Digital), as inherited from the collection of Divine Rights *Ius Divinum Esse* and *Ius Divinum Dominium* and *Ius Divinum Victus*; and

(viii) "**Ius Naturale Animalum**" shall be the collection of Natural Rights of all Animals, as inherited from the collection of Divine Rights *Ius Divinum Esse* and *Ius Divinum Dominium* and *Ius Divinum Victus*; and

(ix) "**Ius Naturale Maris Viventis**" shall be the collection of Natural Rights of the Living Seas and Waters, as inherited from the collection of Divine Rights *Ius Divinum Esse* and *Ius Divinum Dominium* and *Ius Divinum Victus*; and

(x) "**Ius Naturale Terrae Viventis**" shall be the collection of Natural Rights of the Living Land ad Ecosystems, as inherited from the collection of Divine Rights *Ius Divinum Esse* and *Ius Divinum Dominium* and *Ius Divinum Victus*.

(xi) "**Ius Naturale Aeris Viventis**" shall be the collection of Natural Rights of the Living Air, as inherited from the collection of Divine Rights *Ius Divinum Esse* and *Ius Divinum Dominium* and *Ius Divinum Victus*.

Volitional Natural Rights (Volitio Naturae Iurium)

4. The following valid eleven (11) Volitional Natural Rights (*Volitio Naturae Iurium*) shall be recognised in accord with the present sacred Covenant:-

(i) "**Ius Naturale Volitionis**" shall be the collection of Natural Rights of Volition, as inherited from the collection of Divine Rights *Ius Divinum Logos* and *Ius Divinum Liberum Arbitrium*; and

(ii) "**Ius Naturale Liberum Arbitrium**" shall be the collection of Natural Rights of Free Choice (Will), as inherited from the collection of Divine Rights *Ius Divinum Liberum Arbitrium*; and

(iii) "**Ius Naturale Conscientia**" shall be the collection of Natural Rights of Conscious Awareness, as inherited from the collection of Divine Rights *Ius Divinum Conscientia*; and

(iv) "**Ius Naturale Rationatio**" shall be the collection of Natural Rights of Reason, Argument, Accounting and Deduction, as inherited from the Divine Right *Ius Divinum Logos*; and

(v) "**Ius Naturale Vivere Aut Mori**" shall be the collection of Natural Rights to Choose to Live or Die, as inherited from the collections of Divine Rights *Ius Divinum Logos* and *Ius Divinum Liberum*

Arbitrium; and

(vi) "**Ius Naturale Sentire Aut Torpere**" shall be the collection of Natural Rights to Sense or be Numb to Life, Emotions and Feelings, as inherited from the collections of Divine Rights *Ius Divinum Mutatio* and *Ius Divinum Liberum Arbitrium*; and

(vii) "**Ius Naturale Discere Aut Ignarus**" shall be the collection of Natural Rights to Learn or be Ignorant, as inherited from the collections of Divine Rights *Ius Divinum Mutatio* and *Ius Divinum Liberum Arbitrium*; and

(viii) "**Ius Naturale Associatio et Conventio**" shall be the collection of Natural Rights of Association and Agreement, as inherited from the collection of Divine Rights *Ius Divinum Associatio et Conventio; and*

(ix) "**Ius Naturale Credere et Non**" shall be the collection of Natural Rights to Trust or Reject a Claim, as inherited from the collections of Divine Rights *Ius Divinum Consensum et Non; and*

(x) "**Ius Naturale Consensum et Non**" shall be the collection of Natural Rights to Consent and Non Consent, as inherited from the collection of Divine Rights *Ius Divinum Consensum et Non*; and

(xi) "**Ius Naturale Loqui et Silentium**" shall be the collection of Natural Rights to Speak and be Silent, as inherited from the collections of Divine Rights *Ius Divinum Logos* and *Ius Divinum Liberum Arbitrium.*

5. The following valid twenty-two (22) Testamental Natural Rights (*Testamentum Naturae Iurium*) shall be recognised in accord with the present sacred Covenant:- Testamental Natural Rights (Testamentum Naturae Iurium)

(i) "**Ius Naturale Testamentum**" shall be the collection of Natural Rights to make a Testification and Will, as inherited from the collection of Divine Rights *Ius Divinum Logos* and *Ius Divinum Liberum Arbitrium*; and

(ii) "**Ius Naturale Iuris**" shall be the collection of Natural Rights of Natural Justice, as inherited from the collection of Divine Rights *Ius Divinum Iuris*; and

(iii) "**Ius Naturale Aequum**" shall be the collection of Natural Rights of Equality and Fairness, as inherited from the collection of Divine Rights *Ius Divinum Aequum*; and

(iv) "**Ius Naturale Bona Fidei**" shall be the collection of Natural Rights of Good Faith, Good Conscience and Good Actions, as inherited from the collection of Divine Rights *Ius Divinum Bona Fidei*; and

(v) "**Ius Naturale Fidei**" shall be the collection of Natural Rights of True Trust and True Estate, as inherited from the collection of Divine Rights *Ius Divinum Fidei*; and

(vi) "**Ius Naturale Officium**" shall be the collection of Natural Rights of Office of Man or Woman, as inherited from the collection of Divine Right *Ius Divinum Officium*; and

(vii) "**Ius Naturale Registrum**" shall be the collection of Natural Rights to Enter Records within Registers and Rolls, as inherited from the collection of Divine Rights *Ius Divinum Registrum*; and

(viii) "**Ius Naturale Concedere et Abrogare**" shall be the collection of Natural Rights to Give or Grant Rights and Annul or rescind Rights, as inherited from the collection of Divine Rights *Ius Divinum Concedere et Abrogare;* and

(ix) "**Ius Naturale Delegare et Revocare**" shall be the collection of Natural Rights to Assign or Delegate Rights and Cancel or Revoke Rights, as inherited from the collection of Divine Rights *Ius Divinum Delegare et Revocare*; and

(x) "**Ius Naturale Sacramentum**" shall be the collection of Natural Rights to make Oaths and Vows, as inherited from the collection of Divine Rights *Ius Divinum Sacrum*; and

(xi) "**Ius Naturale Signandi**" shall be the collection of Natural Rights to Sign and Seal, as inherited from the Divine Right *Ius Divinum Liberum Arbitrium*; and

(xii) "**Ius Naturale Possessionis**" shall be the collection of Natural Rights to Possess, Hold and Own Property, as inherited from the collection of Divine Rights *Ius Divinum Possessionis*; and

(xiii) "**Ius Naturale Usus**" shall be the collection of Natural Rights of Use and Fruits (Enjoyment) of Use of Property, as inherited from the collection of Divine Rights *Ius Divinum Usus*; and

(xiv) "**Ius Naturale Connubii**" shall be the collection of Natural Rights of Union, as inherited from the collection of Divine Rights *Ius Divinum Associatio et Conventio* and *Ius Divinum Consensum et Non*; and

(xv) "**Ius Naturale Coeundi**" shall be the collection of Natural Rights for consenting adults to engage in intercourse, as inherited from the collection of Divine Rights *Ius Divinum Associatio et Conventio and* and *Ius Divinum Consensum et Non*; and

(xvi) "**Ius Naturale Contraceptio**" shall be the collection of Natural Rights of Ownership to contraception, as inherited from the collection of Divine Rights *Ius Divinum Liberum Arbitrium* and *Ius Divinum Consensum et Non*; and

(xvii) "**Ius Naturale Terminare**" shall be the collection of Natural Rights to Terminate Pregnancy within the 1st trimester, as inherited from the collection of Divine Rights *Ius Divinum Liberum Arbitrium* and *Ius Divinum Consensum et Non*; and

(xviii) "**Ius Naturale Nascendi**" shall be the collection of Natural Rights to be Borne from the start of the 2nd trimester to full term, as inherited from the collection of Divine Rights *Ius Divinum Liberum Arbitrium* and *Ius Divinum Entia*; and

(xix) "**Ius Naturale Nativitas**" shall be the collection of Natural Rights to give birth, as inherited from the collection of Divine Rights *Ius Divinum Liberum Arbitrium*; and

(xx) "**Ius Naturale Creditum**" shall be the collection of Natural Rights to have and hold Beliefs, as inherited from the collection of Divine Rights *Ius Divinum Liberum Arbitrium* and *Ius Divinum Logos*; and

(xxi) "**Ius Naturale Carnem**" shall be the collection of Natural Rights of the Flesh and Body, as inherited from the collection of Divine Rights of *Ius Divinum Liberum Arbitrium* and *Ius Divinum Possessionis*; and

(xxii) "**Ius Naturale Sexualitatis**" shall be the collection of Natural Rights of Sexuality, as inherited from the collection of Divine Rights of *Ius Divinum Liberum Arbitrium*.

6. The following valid eleven (11) Domicile Natural Rights (*Domicilium Naturae Iurium*), also known as the Rights of Lodging, shall be recognised in accord with the present sacred Covenant:- Domicile Natural Rights (Domicilium Naturae Iurium)

(i) "**Ius Naturale Domicilii**" shall be the collection of Natural Rights of Home Environment, as inherited from the collection of Divine Rights of *Ius Divinum Possessionis*; and

(ii) "**Ius Naturale Aedificationis Domus**" shall be the collection of Natural Rights to build one's home, as inherited from the collection of Divine Rights of *Ius Divinum Possessionis* and *Ius Divinum Usus* and *Ius Divinum Aequum* and *Ius Divinum Bona Fidei; and*; and

(iii) "**Ius Naturale Parietis**" shall be the collection of Natural Rights to build walls and fencing around home, as inherited from the collection of Divine Rights *Ius Divinum Possessionis* and *Ius Divinum Usus* and *Ius Divinum Aequum* and *Ius Divinum Bona Fidei; and*; and

(iv) "**Ius Naturale Domus Pacis**" shall be the collection of Natural Rights to live peacefully in one's own Home, as inherited from the collection of Divine Rights *Ius Divinum Aequum* and *Ius Divinum Bona Fidei; and*

(v) "**Ius Tenendi Arma**" shall be the collection of Natural Rights

possess arms, as inherited from the collection of Divine Rights *Ius Divinum Existentia* and *Ius Divinum Aequum* and *Ius Divinum Bona Fidei; and*

(vi) "**Ius Naturale Defendum Domus**" shall be the collection of Natural Rights to defend one's own home against trespass, as inherited from the collection of Divine Rights *Ius Divinum Existentia* and *Ius Divinum Aequum* and *Ius Divinum Bona Fidei*; and

(vii) "**Ius Naturale Dominionis Eminens**" shall be the collection of Natural Rights of taking, acquiring, converting and using private property for public use and benefit, as inherited from the collection of Divine Rights *Ius Divinum Dominium* and *Ius Divinum Aequum* and *Ius Divinum Bona Fidei*; and

(viii) "**Ius Naturale Coquis**" shall be the collection of Natural Rights to prepare, cook and eat food in home, as inherited from the collection of Divine Rights *Ius Divinum Alumentum*; and

(ix) "**Ius Naturale Filios**" shall be the collection of Natural Rights to have, nurture, support, supervise and teach children, as inherited from the collection of Divine Rights *Ius Divinum Custoditum* and *Ius Divinum Aequum* and *Ius Divinum Bona Fidei; and*

(x) "**Ius Naturale Parentum**" shall be the collection of Natural Rights of parents to the custody, protection, well being, discipline and education of children, as inherited from the collection of Divine Rights *Ius Divinum Custoditum* and *Ius Divinum Aequum* and *Ius Divinum Bona Fidei; and*

(xi) "**Ius Naturale Celebras**" shall be the collection of Natural Rights to celebrate and enjoy in one's own home, as inherited from the collection of Divine Rights *Ius Divinum Usus* and *Ius Divinum Aequum* and *Ius Divinum Bona Fidei.*

Habitational Natural Rights (Habitatus Naturae Iurium)

7. The following valid eleven (11) Habitational Natural Rights (*Habitatus Naturae Iurium*), also known as the Rights of Land, shall be recognised in accord with the present sacred Covenant:-

(i) "**Ius Naturale Habitatus**" shall be the collection of Natural Rights of Habitation in a community, as inherited from the collection of Divine Rights *Ius Divinum Alumentum* and *Ius Divinum Fraternitas* and *Ius Divinum Bona Fidei*; and

(ii) "**Ius Naturale Tenendi Terram**" shall be the collection of Natural Rights of Tenancy and Use of Land, as inherited from the collection of Divine Rights *Ius Divinum Possessionis* and *Ius Divinum Usus* and *Ius Divinum Aequum* and *Ius Divinum Bona Fidei*; and

(iii) "**Ius Naturale Vendandi Et Piscandi**" shall be the collection of Natural Rights to Hunt and Fish for Survival, as inherited from the collection of Divine Rights *Ius Divinum Alumentum* and *Ius Divinum Bona Fidei*; and

(iv) "**Ius Naturale Arborum**" shall be the collection of Natural Rights to plant and use trees, plants or crops, as inherited from the collection of Divine Rights *Ius Divinum Alumentum* and *Ius Divinum Bona Fidei*; and

(v) "**Ius Naturale Fabricae**" shall be the collection of Natural Rights to make, model, fabricate, as inherited from the collection of Divine Rights *Ius Divinum Usus* and *Ius Divinum Bona Fidei*; and

(vi) "**Ius Naturale Energis**" shall be the collection of Natural Rights to make, store and use energy, as inherited from the collection of Divine Rights *Ius Divinum Usus* and *Ius Divinum Bona Fidei*; and

(vii) "**Ius Naturale Pascendi**" shall be the collection of Natural Rights to Pasture (Feed) Animals, as inherited from the collection of Divine Rights *Ius Divinum Alumentum* and *Ius Divinum Custoditum* and *Ius Divinum Bona Fidei*; and

(viii) "**Ius Naturale Iter Terrae**" shall be the collection of Natural Rights to travel and use the Roads and Highway, as inherited from the collection of Divine Rights *Ius Divinum Alumentum* and *Ius Divinum Bona Fidei*; and

(ix) "**Ius Naturale Iter Aquae**" shall be the collection of Natural Rights to travel the waterways, as inherited from the collection of Divine Rights *Ius Divinum Alumentum* and *Ius Divinum Bona Fidei*; and

(x) "**Ius Naturale Iter Caeli**" shall be the collection of Natural Rights to travel in the air, as inherited from the collection of Divine Rights *Ius Divinum Alumentum* and *Ius Divinum Bona Fidei*; and

(xi) "**Ius Naturale Fraternitas Nativas**" shall be the collection of Natural Rights of membership of local community where one was borne, as inherited from the collection of Divine Rights *Ius Divinum Fraternitas* and *Ius Divinum Bona Fidei.*

8. The following valid eleven (11) Actionable Natural Rights (*Actionis Naturae Iurium*), also known as the Rights of Labour, shall be recognised in accord with the present sacred Covenant:- Actionable Natural Rights (Actionis Naturae Iurium)

(i) "**Ius Naturale Actionum**" shall be the collection of Natural Rights of Action, as inherited from the collection of Divine Rights *Ius Divinum Actionum*; and

(ii) "**Ius Naturale Libertatis**" shall be the collection of Natural Rights of Freedom from Bondage and Slavery, as inherited from the collection of Divine Rights *Ius Divinum Iuris* and *Ius Divinum*

Aequum and *Ius Divinum Bona Fidei*; and

(iii) "**Ius Naturale Significans Laborare**" shall be the collection of Natural Rights to Meaningful and Fulfilling Work, as inherited from the collection of Divine Rights *Ius Divinum Iuris* and *Ius Divinum Aequum* and *Ius Divinum Bona Fidei*; and

(iv) "**Ius Naturale Salarium Iustum**" shall be the collection of Natural Rights to Fair Pay and Compensation, as inherited from the collection of Divine Rights *Ius Divinum Iuris* and *Ius Divinum Aequum* and *Ius Divinum Bona Fidei*; and

(v) "**Ius Naturale Laborare et Non**" shall be the collection of Natural Rights to Work or refuse to Work, as inherited from the collection of Divine Rights *Ius Divinum Iuris* and *Ius Divinum Aequum* and *Ius Divinum Bona Fidei*; and

(vi) "**Ius Naturale Innocentiae**" shall be the collection of Natural Rights of Innocence against any Accusation, as inherited from the collection of Divine Rights *Ius Divinum Iuris* and *Ius Divinum Aequum* and *Ius Divinum Bona Fidei*; and

(vii) "**Ius Accusationis Cognoscendi**" shall be the collection of Natural Rights to know the Full Disclosure and Evidence of any Accusation, as inherited from the collection of Divine Rights *Ius Divinum Iuris* and *Ius Divinum Aequum* and *Ius Divinum Bona Fidei*; and

(viii) "**Ius Naturale Defensionis**" shall be the collection of Natural Rights to Defend against any Accusation, as inherited from the collection of Divine Rights *Ius Divinum Iuris* and *Ius Divinum Aequum* and *Ius Divinum Bona Fidei*; and

(ix) "**Ius Naturale Remedium**" shall be the collection of Natural Rights of Remedy, Relief, Redress or Compensation, as inherited from the collection of Divine Rights *Ius Divinum Remedium*; and

(x) "**Ius Naturale Poena**" shall be the collection of Natural Rights of Penalty & Punishment, as inherited from the collection of Divine Rights *Ius Divinum Aequum* and *Ius Divinum Poena*; and

(xi) "**Ius Naturale Clementia**" shall be the collection of Natural Rights of Mercy & Forgiveness, as inherited from the collection of Divine Rights *Ius Divinum Aequum* and *Ius Divinum Clementia*.

Article 41 - Superior Rights

1. **Superior Rights** shall be the third class and third highest possible form of valid Rights; corresponding to Superior Trusts and Superior Persons associated with a Ucadia society. Whereas Divine Rights pertain to Heaven and Natural Rights relate to a living higher order life form, Superior Rights align to one or more civilised societies operating under the Golden Rule of Law in accord with the present sacred Covenant. Superior Rights owe their existence and provenance to either valid Divine Rights or valid Natural Rights. All Superior Rights are greater than Inferior Rights. Superior Rights (Superioris Iurium)

All Rights of valid Ucadia Members, Ucadia Societies and associated bodies, aggregates, societies, associations, communities and unions of two (2) or more people are inherited from the class of Superior Rights. There exists (6) six sub-classes of four hundred and twenty-four (424) Superior Rights, being: Personal (44), Ecclesiastical (132), Sovereign (77), Official (88), Administrative (44) and Member (39):

(i) "**Personal Rights**" (*Superioris Iurium Personae*) shall be Superior Rights associated with Superior Persons and all Superior Ucadia Trusts and Superior Ucadia Estates. All Personal Rights are delegated to the safe custody and wise guardian powers of the legitimate and valid supreme competent forum of law of the seven Ucadia Unions and all lesser Ucadia bodies politic such as Universities, Provinces and Campuses as the embodiment of judicial authority; and as defined by Article 59 (Oratorium) of the present sacred Covenant; and

(ii) "**Ecclesiastical Rights**" (*Iurium Ecclesiae*) shall be Superior Rights permanently vested unto the four valid and legitimate Ucadia faiths being One Christ, One Islam, One Spirit and Ucadia itself; and

(iii) "**Sovereign Rights**" (*Iurium Regnum*) shall be Superior Rights permanently vested unto the governing bodies of the seven Ucadia Unions and all lesser Ucadia bodies politic such as Universities, Provinces and Campuses as the embodiment of sovereign authority; and

(iv) "**Official Rights**" (*Iurium Publicum*) shall be Superior Rights permanently vested unto the duly elected and invested Officers of the seven Ucadia Unions and all lesser Ucadia bodies politic such as Universities, Provinces and Campuses as the embodiment of fiduciary authority; and

(v) "**Administrative Rights**" (*Iurium Administrationis*) shall be permanently vested unto the executive bodies of the seven Ucadia Unions and all lesser Ucadia bodies politic such as Universities, Provinces and Campuses as the embodiment of administrative authority; and

(vi) "**Member Rights**" (*Iurium Membrum*) shall be Superior Rights permanently vested unto the members of the seven Ucadia Unions and all lesser Ucadia bodies politic such as Universities, Provinces and Campuses as the embodiment of member authority.

2. The following valid forty-four (44) Superior Person Rights (*Superioris Iurium Personae*) shall be recognised in accord with the present sacred Covenant:- Superior Person Rights (Superioris Iurium Personae)

(i) "**Ius Ucadia**" shall be the collection of Superior Rights of Ucadia, as inherited from the collection of Divine Rights *Ius Divinum Ucadia*; and

(ii) "**Ius Vitam**" shall be the collection of Superior Rights to Life, as inherited from the collection of Natural Rights *Ius Naturale Existentia*; and

(iii) "**Ius Liberum Arbitrium**" shall be the collection of Superior Rights of Free Choice (Will), as inherited from the collection of Natural Rights *Ius Naturale Liberum Arbitrium*; and

(iv) "**Ius Conscientia**" shall be the collection of Superior Rights of Conscious Awareness, as inherited from the collection of Natural Rights *Ius Naturale Conscientia*; and

(v) "**Ius Rationis**" shall be the collection of Superior Rights of Reason, Argument and Deduction, as inherited from the collection of Natural Rights *Ius Naturale Liberatum Arbitrium*; and

(vi) "**Ius Vivere Aut Mori**" shall be the collection of Superior Rights to Choose to Live or Die, as inherited from the collection of Natural Rights *Ius Naturale Vivere Aut Mori*; and

(vii) "**Ius Sentire Aut Torpere**" shall be the collection of Superior Rights to Sense or be Numb to Life, Emotions and Feelings, as inherited from the collection of Natural Rights *Ius Naturale Sentire Aut Torpere*; and

(viii) "**Ius Discere Aut Ignarus**" shall be the collection of Superior Rights to Learn or be Ignorant, as inherited from the collection of Natural Rights *Ius Naturale Discere Aut Ignarus*; and

(ix) "**Ius Associatio et Conventio**" shall be the collection of Superior Rights of Association and Agreement, as inherited from the collection of Natural Rights *Ius Naturale Associatio et Conventio*; and

(x) "**Ius Credere et Non**" shall be the collection of Superior Rights to Trust or Reject a Claim, as inherited from the collection of Natural Rights *Ius Naturale Credere et Non*; and

(xi) "**Ius Consensum et Non**" shall be the collection of Superior Rights to Consent and Non Consent, as inherited from the collection of Natural Rights *Ius Naturale Consensum et Non*; and

(xii) "**Ius Loqui et Silentium**" shall be the collection of Superior Rights to Speak and be Silent, as inherited from the collection of Natural Rights *Ius Naturale Loqui et Silentium*; and

(xiii) "**Ius Iuris**" shall be the Superior Right to Natural Justice and Due process, as inherited from the collection of Natural Rights *Ius Naturale Iuris*; and

(xiv) "**Ius Testamentum**" shall be the collection of Superior Rights to make a Testification or Will, as inherited from the collection of Natural Rights *Ius Naturale Testamentum*; and

(xv) "**Ius Aequum**" shall be the collection of Superior Rights of Equality and Fairness, as inherited from the collection of Natural Rights *Ius Naturale Aequum*; and

(xvi) "**Ius Bona Fidei**" shall be the collection of Superior Rights of Good Faith, Good Conscience and Good Actions, as inherited from the collection of Natural Rights *Ius Naturale Bona Fidei*; and

(xvii) "**Ius Ucadiansium Scientiarum**" shall be the Superior Right of the Ucadia Sciences, as inherited from the collection of Natural Rights *Ius Divinum Ucadia"*; and

(xviii) "**Ius Fidei**" shall be the collection of Superior Rights of Superior Trust and Estate, as inherited from the collection of Natural Rights *Ius Naturale Fidei*; and

(xix) "**Ius Concedere et Abrogare**" shall be the collection of Superior Rights to Give or Grant Rights and Annul or rescind Rights, as inherited from the collection of Natural Rights *Ius Naturale Concedere et Abrogare*; and

(xx) "**Ius Delegare et Revocare**" shall be the collection of Superior Rights to Assign or Delegate Rights and Cancel or Revoke Rights, as inherited from the collection of Natural Rights *Ius Naturale Delegare et Revocare*; and

(xxi) "**Ius Sacramentum**" shall be the collection of Superior Rights to make Oaths and Vows, as inherited from the collection of Natural Rights *Ius Naturale Sacramentum*; and

(xxii) "**Ius Signandi**" shall be the collection of Superior Rights to Sign and Seal, as inherited from the collection of Natural Rights *Ius Naturale Signandi*; and

(xxiii) "**Ius Possessionis**" shall be the collection of Superior Rights to Possess, Hold and Own Property, as inherited from the collection of Natural Rights *Ius Naturale Possessionis*; and

(xxiv) "**Ius Tenendi Terram**" shall be the collection of Superior Rights of Tenancy of Land or Home, as inherited from the collection of Natural Rights *Ius Naturale Tenendi Terram*; and

(xxv) "**Ius Usus**" shall be the collection of Superior Rights of Use and Fruits (Enjoyment) of Use of Property, as inherited from the collection of Natural Rights *Ius Naturale Usus*; and

(xxvi) "**Ius Connubii**" shall be the collection of Superior Rights of Union with another consenting Adult, as inherited from the collection of Natural Rights *Ius Naturale Connubii*; and

(xxvii) "**Ius Coeundi**" shall be the collection of Superior Rights for consenting adults to engage in intercourse, as inherited from the collection of Natural Rights *Ius Naturale Coeundi*; and

(xxviii) "**Ius Contraceptio**" shall be the collection of Superior Rights to contraception, as inherited from the collection of Natural Rights *Ius Naturale Contraceptio*; and

(xxix) "**Ius Terminare**" shall be the collection of Superior Rights to Terminate Pregnancy in 1st trimester, as inherited from the collection of Natural Rights *Ius Naturale Terminare*; and

(xxx) "**Ius Nascendi**" shall be the collection of Superior Rights to be Borne from the start of the 2nd trimester to full term, as inherited from the collection of Natural Rights *Ius Naturale Nascendi*; and

(xxxi) "**Ius Nativitas**" shall be the collection of Superior Rights to give birth, as inherited from the collection of Natural Rights *Ius Naturale Nativitas*; and

(xxxii) "**Ius Creditum**" shall be the collection of Superior Rights to have and hold Beliefs, as inherited from the collection of Natural Rights *Ius Divinum Creditum*; and

(xxxiii) "**Ius Carnem**" shall be the collection of Superior Rights ones own Flesh and Body, as inherited from the collection of Natural Rights *Ius Divinum Carnem*; and

(xxxiv) "**Ius Sexualitatis**" shall be the collection of Superior Rights of Choice of Sexuality, as inherited from the collection of Natural Rights *Ius Naturale Sexualitatis*; and

(xxxv) "**Ius Nomenis**" shall be the collection of Superior Rights to

Name, Title and Reputation, as inherited from the collection of Natural Rights *Ius Naturale Libertatis* and *Ius Possessionis* and *Ius Aequum*; and

(xxxvi) "**Ius Integritatis Geneticae**" shall be the collection of Superior Rights to the integrity and ownership of one's own Genetic Identity and Genetic Material, as inherited from the collection of Natural Rights *Ius Naturale Integritatis Geneticae* and *Ius Possessionis*; and

(xxxvii) "**Ius Identitatis**" shall be the collection of Superior Rights of Ownership of One's Own Face, Voice, Fingerprints, Biometric and Digital Identity, as inherited from the collection of Natural Rights *Ius Naturale Libertatis* and *Ius Possessionis* and *Ius Aequum*; and

(xxxviii) "**Ius Privatum**" shall be the collection of Superior Rights of Privacy and Use of One's Own Face, Voice, Fingerprints, Biometric and Digital Identity and Freedom from Unwarranted Surveillance, as inherited from the collection of Natural Rights *Ius Naturale Libertatis* and *Ius Possessionis* and *Ius Aequum*; and

(xxxix) "**Ius Tectum**" shall be the collection of Superior Rights of Shelter, as inherited from the collection of Natural Rights *Ius Naturale Sustentandi* and *Ius Naturale Habitatus*; and

(xl) "**Ius Habitare**" shall be the collection of Superior Rights of Home Environment, as inherited from the collection of Natural Rights *Ius Naturale Habitatus*; and

(xli) "**Ius Terrae et Aquae Purarum**" shall be the collection of Superior Rights to Clean Water and Land, as inherited from the collection of Natural Rights *Ius Naturale Terrae et Aquae Purarum*; and

(xlii) "**Ius Sustentandi**" shall be the collection of Superior Rights of Sustenance, Health Care and Assistance, as inherited from the collection of Natural Rights *Ius Naturale Sustentandi*; and

(xliii) "**Ius Libertatis**" shall be the collection of Superior Rights of Freedom from Slavery, Bondage or treated as a Thing or any other kind of Property, as inherited from the collection of Natural Rights *Ius Naturale Libertatis*.

(xliv) "**Ius Tormentum Libertatis**" shall be the collection of Superior Rights of Freedom from Cruel and Unusual Punishment or Torture, as inherited from the collection of Natural Rights *Ius Naturale Clementia*.

3. "**Ecclesiastical Rights**" (*Iurium Ecclesiae*) shall be the second sub-class of Superior Rights and the highest possible rights of any aggregate body, society, fraternity, association or company of two or

Ecclesiastical Rights (Iurium Ecclesiae)

more people.

All Ecclesiastical Rights are permanently vested equally unto the three united Ucadia faiths and Ucadia itself recognised under the present sacred Covenant being:-

(i) *The most sacred and Universal Ecclesia of One Christ*, also known as the *One Holy Apostolic Universal Ecclesia,* as defined by Article 92 of the present most sacred Covenant; and

(ii) *The Holy Society of One Islam*, also known as the *One True Way of Allah*, as defined by Article 93 of the present most sacred Covenant; and

(iii) *The most sacred Society of One Spirit*, also known as the *One Sacred Spirit*, as defined by Article 94 of the present most sacred Covenant.

There exists eight (8) categories of one hundred and thirty-two (132) Superior Rights within the sub-class of Ecclesiastical Rights, being: Authoritative (22), Instrumental (22), Sacramental (33), Writs (11), Bills (11), Dogma (11), Decrees (11) and Notices (11):

(i) "**Authoritative Ecclesiastical Rights**" (*Potentis Ecclesiae Iurium*) shall be Ecclesiastical Rights associated with the core ecclesiastical authoritative powers; and

(ii) "**Instrumental Ecclesiastical Rights**"(*Instrumentalis Ecclesiae Iurium*) shall be Ecclesiastical Rights essential to the proper administration of Ecclesiastical Rights; and

(iii) "**Sacramental Ecclesiastical Rights**" (*Sacramentum Ecclesiae Iurium*) shall be Ecclesiastical Rights associated with the thirty-three (33) Divine Sacraments of Heaven; and

(iv) "**Ecclesiastical Writs of Rights**" (*Recto Ecclesiae Iurium*) shall be Ecclesiastical Rights associated with the one, true and only forms of Original Entry and Original Action; and

(v) "**Ecclesiastical Bills of Exception & Agreement**" (*Rogatio Ecclesiae Iurium*) shall be Ecclesiastical Rights associated with the one, true and only forms of Bills of Exception, Citation and Agreement; and

(vi) "**Ecclesiastical Dogma**" (*Greatest Principles Ecclesiae Iurium*) shall be Ecclesiastical Rights associated with the promulgation of authoritative ecclesiastical principles, decrees and doctrines; and

(vii) "**Ecclesiastical Decrees**" (*Decretum Ecclesiae Iurium*) shall be Ecclesiastical Rights associated with ecclesiastical decrees concerning the administration, conduct and enforcement of law and order; and

(viii) "**Ecclesiastical Notices**" (*Notitiae Ecclesiae Iurium*) shall be Ecclesiastical Rights associated with ecclesiastical notices issued, executed, patented, promulgated and services in the proper administration, conduct and enforcement of law and order.

4. The following valid twenty-two (22) Authoritative Ecclesiastical Rights (*Potentis Ecclesiae Iurium*) shall be recognised in accord with the present sacred Covenant:-

Authoritative Ecclesiastical Rights (Potentis Ecclesiae Iurium)

(i) "**Ius Ecclesiae**" shall be the primary collection of Ecclesiastical Rights, as inherited from the collection of Divine Rights *Ius Divinum Ecclesia*; and

(ii) "**Ius Ecclesiae Regnum**" shall be the collection of Ecclesiastical Rights of Sovereign Authority, as inherited from the collection of Divine Rights *Ius Divinum Regnum*; and

(iii) "**Ius Ecclesiae Consilium**" shall be the collection of Ecclesiastical Rights of a Legislative and Advisory Authority, as inherited from the collection of Divine Rights *Ius Divinum Consilium*; and

(iv) "**Ius Ecclesiae Fraternitus**" shall be the collection of Ecclesiastical Rights of an Ecclesiastical and Religious Fraternity, as inherited from the collection of Divine Rights *Ius Divinum Ecclesia*; and

(v) "**Ius Ecclesiae Collegium**" shall be the collection of Ecclesiastical Rights of a Company or Charitable Body, as inherited from the collection of Divine Rights *Ius Divinum Collegium*; and

(vi) "**Ius Ecclesiae Officium**" shall be the collection of Ecclesiastical Rights of Office, Duty and Service, as inherited from the collection of Divine Rights *Ius Divinum Officium*; and

(vii) "**Ius Ecclesiae Imperium**" shall be the collection of Ecclesiastical Rights of Command, Occupation and Enforcement, as inherited from the collection of Divine Rights *Ius Divinum Imperium*; and

(viii) "**Ius Ecclesiae Sacrum**" shall be the collection of Ecclesiastical Rights of Sacred Recognition, Devotion and Veneration, as inherited from the collection of Divine Rights *Ius Divinum Sacrum*; and

(ix) "**Ius Ecclesiae Custoditum**" shall be the collection of Ecclesiastical Rights of Custody, Guardianship and Preservation, as inherited from the collection of Divine Rights *Ius Divinum Custoditum*; and

(x) "**Ius Ecclesiae Alumentum**" shall be the collection of Ecclesiastical Rights to Sustenance, Maintenance and Alms, as inherited from the collection of Divine Rights *Ius Divinum Alumentum*; and

(xi) "**Ius Ecclesiae Apostolicus**" shall be the collection of Ecclesiastical Rights of Divine Commission, as inherited from the collection of Divine Rights *Ius Divinum Apostolicus*; and

(xii) "**Ius Ecclesiae Cancellarium**" shall be the collection of Ecclesiastical Rights Chancery and Administration of Law, as inherited from the collection of Divine Rights *Ius Divinum Cancellarium*; and

(xiii) "**Ius Ecclesiae Oratorium**" shall be the collection of Ecclesiastical Rights to a Competent Forum of Law and Review, as inherited from the collection of Divine Rights *Ius Divinum Oratorium*; and

(xiv) "**Ius Ecclesiae Templum**" shall be the collection of Ecclesiastical Rights of a Treasury or Financial (Banking) Body, as inherited from the collection of Divine Rights *Ius Divinum Templum*; and

(xv) "**Ius Ecclesiae Sacramentum**" shall be the collection of Ecclesiastical Rights to Grant and Impart Holy Sacraments, as inherited from the Divine Rights *Ius Divinum Sacramentum*; and

(xvi) "**Ius Ecclesiae Visum**" shall be the collection of Ecclesiastical Rights to Survey, Visit and Audit Ucadia Bodies, as inherited from the collection of Divine Rights *Ius Divinum Visum*; and

(xvii) "**Ius Ecclesiae Commercium**" shall be the collection of Ecclesiastical Rights to Trade, Exchange and Communication, as inherited from the collection of Divine Rights *Ius Divinum Commercium*; and

(xviii) "**Ius Ecclesiae Virtus**" shall be the collection of Ecclesiastical Rights to Strength, Honour, Excellence and Virtue, as inherited from the collection of Divine Rights *Ius Divinum Virtus*; and

(xix) "**Ius Ecclesiae Penitentiaria**" shall be the collection of Ecclesiastical Rights of Forced Confinement and Penitence, as inherited from the collection of Divine Rights *Ius Divinum Penitentiaria*; and

(xx) "**Ius Ecclesiae Astrum**" shall be the collection of Ecclesiastical Rights to an Association, Aggregate or Body, as inherited from the collection of Divine Rights *Ius Divinum Astrum*; and

(xxi) "**Ius Ecclesiae Magisterium**" shall be the collection of Ecclesiastical Rights to Teach, Instruct and Interpret Sacred Texts and Divine Will, as inherited from the collection of Divine Rights *Ius Divinum Magisterium*; and

(xxii) "**Ius Ecclesiae Decretum**" shall be the collection of Ecclesiastical Rights to issue Decree, Judgement and Edict, as inherited from the collection of Divine Rights *Ius Divinum Decretum*.

Instrumental Ecclesiastical Rights (Instrumentalis Ecclesiae Iurium)

5. The following valid twenty-two (22) Instrumental Ecclesiastical Rights (*Instrumentalis Ecclesiae Iurium*) shall be recognised in accord with the present sacred Covenant:-

(i) "**Ius Ecclesiae Iuris**" shall be the collection of Ecclesiastical Rights of Justice and Due Process, as inherited from the collection of Divine Rights *Ius Divinum Iuris*; and

(ii) "**Ius Ecclesiae Bona Fidei**" shall be the collection of Ecclesiastical Rights of Good Faith, Good Conscience and Good Actions, as inherited from the collection of Divine Rights *Ius Divinum Bona Fidei*; and

(iii) "**Ius Ecclesiae Aequum**" shall be the collection of Ecclesiastical Rights of Equality and Fairness, as inherited from the collection of Divine Rights *Ius Divinum Aequum*; and

(iv) "**Ius Ecclesiae Fidei**" shall be the collection of Ecclesiastical Rights of Superior Ecclesiastical Trust and Ecclesiastical Estate, as inherited from the collection of Divine Rights *Ius Divinum Fidei*; and

(v) "**Ius Ecclesiae Rationatio**" shall be the collection of Ecclesiastical Rights of Accounting, Credit and Funds, as inherited from the collection of Divine Rights *Ius Divinum Rationatio*; and

(vi) "**Ius Ecclesiae Concedere et Abrogare** " shall be the collection of Ecclesiastical Rights to Give or Grant Rights and Annul or rescind Superior Rights, as inherited from the collection of Divine Rights *Ius Divinum Concedere et Abrogare*; and

(vii) "**Ius Ecclesiae Delegare et Revocare**" shall be the collection of Ecclesiastical Rights to Assign or Delegate Rights and Cancel or Revoke Superior Rights, as inherited from the collection of Divine Rights *Ius Divinum Delegare et Revocare*; and

(viii) "**Ius Ecclesiae Associatio et Conventio**" shall be the collection of Ecclesiastical Rights of Association and Agreement, as inherited from the collection of Divine Rights *Ius Divinum Associatio et Conventio*; and

(ix) "**Ius Ecclesiae Consensum et Non**" shall be the collection of Ecclesiastical Rights to Consent and Non-Consent, as inherited from the collection of Divine Rights *Ius Divinum Consensum et Non*; and

(x) "**Ius Ecclesiae Hereditatis**" shall be the collection of Ecclesiastical Rights of Inheritance of Divine Rights, as inherited from the collection of Divine Rights *Ius Divinum Dominium* and *Ius Divinum Bona Fidei*; and

(xi) "**Ius Ecclesiae Dominium**" shall be the collection of Ecclesiastical Rights of Absolute Ownership, as inherited from the collection of Divine Rights *Ius Divinum Dominium*; and

(xii) "**Ius Ecclesiae Possessionis**" shall be the collection of Ecclesiastical Rights to Possess, Hold and Own Property, as inherited from the collection of Divine Rights *Ius Divinum Possessionis*; and

(xiii) "**Ius Ecclesiae Usus**" shall be the collection of Ecclesiastical Rights of Use and Fruits (Enjoyment) of Use of Property, as inherited from the collection of Divine Rights *Ius Divinum Usus*; and

(xiv) "**Ius Ecclesiae Proprietatis**" shall be the collection of Ecclesiastical Rights of Ownership of Use or Fruits of Use of Property, as inherited from the collection of Divine Rights *Ius Divinum Proprietatis*; and

(xv) "**Ius Ecclesiae Vectigalis Proprietatis**" shall be the collection of Ecclesiastical Rights to impose Rents, Tolls, Levies, Contributions or Charges against Property, as inherited from the collection of Divine Rights *Ius Divinum Vectigalis Proprietatis*; and

(xvi) "**Ius Ecclesiae Moneta**" shall be the collection of Ecclesiastical Rights to Mint, Produce, Hold, Use and Exchange Money, as inherited from the collection of Divine Rights *Ius Divinum Moneta*; and

(xvii) "**Ius Ecclesiae Vectigalis Moneta**" shall be the collection of Ecclesiastical Rights to impose Rents, Tolls, Levies, Contributions or Charges against Money, as inherited from the collection of Divine Rights *Ius Divinum Vectigalis Moneta*; and

(xviii) "**Ius Ecclesiae Registrum**" shall be the collection of Ecclesiastical Rights to Enter Records within Registers and Rolls, as inherited from the collection of Divine Rights *Ius Divinum Registrum*; and

(xix) "**Ius Ecclesiae Remedium**" shall be the collection of Ecclesiastical Rights of Remedy, Relief, Redress or Compensation, as inherited from the collection of Divine Rights *Ius Divinum Remedium*; and

(xx) "**Ius Ecclesiae Poena**" shall be the collection of Ecclesiastical Rights of Penalty & Punishment, as inherited from the collection of Divine Rights *Ius Divinum Compensationis Poena*; and

(xxi) "**Ius Ecclesiae Clementia**" shall be the collection of Ecclesiastical Rights of Mercy & Forgiveness, as inherited from the collection of Divine Rights *Ius Divinum Clementia* .

(xxii) "**Ius Ecclesiae Actionum**" shall be the collection of Ecclesiastical Rights of Action, as inherited from the collection of Divine Rights *Ius Divinum Dirimere Actionum*.

Sacramental Ecclesiastical Rights (Sacramentum Ecclesiae Iurium)

6. The following valid thirty-three (33) Sacramental Ecclesiastical Rights (*Sacramentum Ecclesiae Iurium*) shall be recognised in accord with the present sacred Covenant:-

(i) "**Ius Ecclesiae Sacramentum Recognosco**" shall be the Ecclesiastical Right of the Key Sacrament of Recognition, as inherited from the Divine Right *Ritus Sacramentum Recognosco*; and

(ii) "**Ius Ecclesiae Sacramentum Purificatio**" shall be the Ecclesiastical Right of the Key Sacrament of Purification, as inherited from the Divine Right *Ritus Sacramentum Purificatio*; and

(iii) "**Ius Ecclesiae Sacramentum Invocatio**" shall be the Ecclesiastical Right of the Key Sacrament of Invocation, as inherited from the Divine Right *Ritus Sacramentum Invocatio*; and

(iv) "**Ius Ecclesiae Sacramentum Obligatio**" shall be the Ecclesiastical Right of the Key Sacrament of Obligation, as inherited from the Divine Right *Ritus Sacramentum Obligatio*; and

(v) "**Ius Ecclesiae Sacramentum Delegatio**" shall be the Ecclesiastical Right of the Key Sacrament of Delegation, as inherited from the Divine Right *Ritus Sacramentum Delegatio*; and

(vi) "**Ius Ecclesiae Sacramentum Satisfactio**" shall be the Ecclesiastical Right of the Key Sacrament of Satisfaction, as inherited from the Divine Right *Ritus Sacramentum Satisfactio*; and

(vii) "**Ius Ecclesiae Sacramentum Resolutio**" shall be the Ecclesiastical Right of the Key Sacrament of Resolution, as inherited from the Divine Right *Ritus Sacramentum Resolutio*; and

(viii) "**Ius Ecclesiae Sacramentum Sanctificatio**" shall be the Ecclesiastical Right of the Foundational Sacrament of

Sanctification, as inherited from the Divine Right *Ritus Sacramentum Sanctificatio*; and

(ix) "**Ius Ecclesiae Sacramentum Sustentatio**" shall be the Ecclesiastical Right of the Foundational Sacrament of Sustentation, as inherited from the Divine Right *Ritus Sacramentum Sustentatio*; and

(x) "**Ius Ecclesiae Sacramentum Unificatio**" shall be the Ecclesiastical Right of the Foundational Sacrament of Unification (Matrimony), as inherited from the Divine Right *Ritus Sacramentum Unificatio*; and

(xi) "**Ius Ecclesiae Sacramentum Amalgamatio"** shall be the Ecclesiastical Right of the Foundational Sacrament of Amalgamation (Union), as inherited from the Divine Right *Ritus Sacramentum Amalgamatio*; and

(xii) "**Ius Ecclesiae Sacramentum Authentico**" shall be the Ecclesiastical Right of the Foundational Sacrament of Authentication, as inherited from the Divine Right *Ritus Sacramentum Authentico*; and

(xiii) "**Ius Ecclesiae Sacramentum Absolutio**" shall be the Ecclesiastical Right of the Foundational Sacrament of Absolution, as inherited from the Divine Right *Ritus Sacramentum Absolutio*; and

(xiv) "**Ius Ecclesiae Sacramentum Volitio**" shall be the Ecclesiastical Right of the Foundational Sacrament of Volition, as inherited from the Divine Right *Ritus Sacramentum Volitio*; and

(xv) "**Ius Ecclesiae Sacramentum Vocatio**" shall be the Ecclesiastical Right of the Foundational Sacrament of Vocation, as inherited from the Divine Right *Ritus Sacramentum Vocatio*; and

(xvi) "**Ius Ecclesiae Sacramentum Testificatio**" shall be the Ecclesiastical Right of the Foundational Sacrament of Testification, as inherited from the Divine Right *Ritus Sacramentum Testificatio*; and

(xvii) "**Ius Ecclesiae Sacramentum Compassio**" shall be the Ecclesiastical Right of the Foundational Sacrament of Compassion (Mercy), as inherited from the Divine Right *Ritus Sacramentum Compassio*; and

(xviii) "**Ius Ecclesiae Sacramentum Conscripto**" shall be the Ecclesiastical Right of the Foundational Sacrament of Conscription (Binding), as inherited from the Divine Right *Ritus Sacramentum Conscripto*; and

(xix) "**Ius Ecclesiae Sacramentum Convocatio**" shall be the

Ecclesiastical Right of the Foundational Sacrament of Convocation, as inherited from the Divine Right *Ritus Sacramentum Convocatio*; and

(xx) "**Ius Ecclesiae Sacramentum Auctoriso**" shall be the Ecclesiastical Right of the Foundational Sacrament of Authorisation, as inherited from the Divine Right *Ritus Sacramentum Auctoriso*; and

(xxi) "**Ius Ecclesiae Sacramentum Elucidato**" shall be the Ecclesiastical Right of the Foundational Sacrament of Elucidation, as inherited from the Divine Right *Ritus Sacramentum Elucidato*; and

(xxii) "**Ius Ecclesiae Sacramentum Inspiratio**" shall be the Ecclesiastical Right of the Authentic Life Sacrament of Inspiration, as inherited from the Divine Right *Ritus Sacramentum Inspiratio*; and

(xxiii) "**Ius Ecclesiae Sacramentum Resurrectio**" shall be the Ecclesiastical Right of the Authentic Life Sacrament of Resurrection, as inherited from the Divine Right *Ritus Sacramentum Resurrectio*; and

(xxiv) "**Ius Ecclesiae Sacramentum Incarnatio**" shall be the Ecclesiastical Right of the Authentic Life Sacrament of Incarnation, as inherited from the Divine Right *Ritus Sacramentum Incarnatio*; and

(xxv) "**Ius Ecclesiae Sacramentum Confirmatio**" shall be the Ecclesiastical Right of the Authentic Life Sacrament of Confirmation, as inherited from the Divine Right *Ritus Sacramentum Confirmatio*; and

(xxvi) "**Ius Ecclesiae Sacramentum Illuminatio**" shall be the Ecclesiastical Right of the Authentic Life Sacrament of Illumination, as inherited from the Divine Right *Ritus Sacramentum Illuminatio*; and

(xxvii) "**Ius Ecclesiae Sacramentum Exultatio**" shall be the Ecclesiastical Right of the Authentic Life Sacrament of Exultation, as inherited from the Divine Right *Ritus Sacramentum Exultatio*; and

(xxviii) "**Ius Ecclesiae Sacramentum Glorificatio**" shall be the Ecclesiastical Right of the Authentic Life Sacrament of Glorification, as inherited from the Divine Right *Ritus Sacramentum Glorificatio*; and

(xxix) "**Ius Ecclesiae Sacramentum Divinatio**" shall be the Ecclesiastical Right of the Authentic Life Sacrament of Divination, as inherited from the Divine Right *Ritus Sacramentum Divinatio*;

and

(xxx) "**Ius Ecclesiae Sacramentum Visitatio**" shall be the Ecclesiastical Right of the Authentic Life Sacrament of Visitation, as inherited from the Divine Right *Ritus Sacramentum Visitatio*; and

(xxxi) "**Ius Ecclesiae Sacramentum Salvatio**" shall be the Ecclesiastical Right of the Authentic Life Sacrament of Salvation, as inherited from the Divine Right *Ritus Sacramentum Salvatio*; and

(xxxii) "**Ius Ecclesiae Sacramentum Emancipatio**" shall be the Ecclesiastical Right of the Authentic Life Sacrament of Original Emancipation, as inherited from the Divine Right *Ritus Sacramentum Emancipatio*; and

(xxxiii) "**Ius Ecclesiae Sacramentum Veneratio**" shall be the Ecclesiastical Right of the Authentic Life Sacrament of Veneration, as inherited from the Divine Right *Ritus Sacramentum Veneratio*.

Ecclesiastical Writs of Rights (Recto Ecclesiae Iurium)

7. The following valid eleven (11) Ecclesiastical Writs of Rights (*Recto Ecclesiae Iurium*) shall be recognised in accord with the present *sacred* Covenant:-

(i) "**Recto Ecclesiae Originalis**" is the Ecclesiastical Original Writ of Right, as inherited from the Divine Right *Recto Divinum Originalis*; and

(ii) "**Recto Ecclesiae Apocalypsis**" is the Ecclesiastical Writ of Right of Revelation, as inherited from the Divine Right *Recto Divinum Apocalypsis*; and

(iii) "**Recto Ecclesiae Capimus**" is the Ecclesiastical Writ of Right of Surrender or Arrest of Person, as inherited from the Divine Right *Recto Divinum Capimus*; and

(iv) "**Recto Ecclesiae Custodiae**" is the Ecclesiastical Writ of Right of Surrender or Seizure of Property, as inherited from the Divine Right *Recto Divinum Custodiae*; and

(v) "**Recto Ecclesiae Corrigimus**" is the Ecclesiastical Writ of Right of Correction of Records, Rulings, Laws or Instruments, as inherited from the Divine Right *Recto Divinum Corrigimus*; and

(vi) "**Recto Ecclesiae Expurgatio**" is the Ecclesiastical Writ of Right of Expurgation of Records, Rulings, Laws or Instruments, as inherited from the Divine Right *Recto Divinum Expurgatio*; and

(vii) "**Recto Ecclesiae Abrogatio**" is the Ecclesiastical Writ of Right of Annulment of Records, Rulings, Laws or Instruments, as inherited from the Divine Right *Recto Divinum Abrogatio*; and

(viii) "**Recto Ecclesiae Inhibitio**" is the Ecclesiastical Writ of Right of

Prohibition or Restraint, as inherited from the Divine Right *Recto Divinum Inhibitio*; and

(ix) "**Recto Ecclesiae Restitutio**" is the Ecclesiastical Writ of Right of Restitution, as inherited from the Divine Right *Recto Divinum Restitutio*; and

(i) "**Recto Ecclesiae Restoratio**" is the Ecclesiastical Writ of Right of Restoration, as inherited from the Divine Right *Recto Divinum Restoratio*.

8. The following valid eleven (11) Ecclesiastical Bills of Exception & Agreement (*Rogatio Ecclesiae Iurium*) shall be recognised in accord with the present sacred Covenant:-

Ecclesiastical Bills of Exception & Agreement (Rogatio Ecclesiae Iurium)

(ii) "**Rogatio Ecclesiae Recto**" shall be the Ecclesiastical (Original) Bill of Right, as inherited from the Divine Right *Rogatio Divinum Recto*; and

(iii) "**Rogatio Ecclesiae Apocalypsis**" shall be the Ecclesiastical Bill of Right of Command & Authorisation of Revelation, as inherited from the Divine Right *Rogatio Divinum Apocalypsis*; and

(iv) "**Rogatio Ecclesiae Capimus**" shall be the Ecclesiastical Bill of Failure to Surrender or Arrest Person, as inherited from the Divine Right *Rogatio Divinum Capimus*; and

(v) "**Rogatio Ecclesiae Custodiae**" shall be the Ecclesiastical Bill of Right against Failure to Surrender or Seize Property, as inherited from the Divine Right *Rogatio Divinum Custodiae*; and

(vi) "**Rogatio Ecclesiae Corrigimus**" shall be the Ecclesiastical Bill of Right against Failure to Correct Records, Rulings, Laws or Instruments, as inherited from the Divine Right *Rogatio Divinum Corrigimus*; and

(vii) "**Rogatio Ecclesiae Inhibitio**" shall be the Ecclesiastical Bill of Right against Failure to Prohibit or Impose Limits as Instructed, as inherited from the Divine Right *Rogatio Divinum Inhibitio*; and

(viii) "**Rogatio Ecclesiae Restitutio**" shall be the Ecclesiastical Bill of Right of Restitution or Compensation, as inherited from the Divine Right *Rogatio Divinum Restituio*; and

(ix) "**Rogatio Ecclesiae Credito**" shall be the Ecclesiastical Bill of Right of Credit, as inherited from the Divine Right *Rogatio Divinum Credito*; and

(x) "**Rogatio Ecclesiae Permutatio**" shall be the Ecclesiastical Bill of Right of Exchange, as inherited from the Divine Right *Rogatio Divinum Permutatio*; and

(xi) "**Rogatio Ecclesiae Venditio**" shall be the Ecclesiastical Bill of

Right of Sale, as inherited from the Divine Right *Rogatio Divinum Venditio*; and

(xii) "**Rogatio Ecclesiae Traditio**" shall be the Ecclesiastical Bill of Right of Lading, as inherited from the Divine Right *Rogatio Divinum Traditio*.

9. The following valid eleven (11) Ecclesiastical Dogma (*Greatest Principles Ecclesiae Iurium*) shall be recognised in accord with the present sacred Covenant:-

Ecclesiastical Dogma (Greatest Principles Ecclesiae Iurium)

(i) "**Dogma Ecclesiae Praeceptum**" shall be the Ecclesiastical Precept of Proposed Dogma, as inherited from the Divine Right *Dogma Divinum Praeceptum*; and

(ii) "**Dogma Ecclesiae Theologiae**" shall be the Ecclesiastical Dogma of Divine Science, as inherited from the Divine Right *Dogma Divinum Theologiae*; and

(iii) "**Dogma Ecclesiae Singularis Caelum**" shall be the Ecclesiastical Dogma of One Heaven, as inherited from the Divine Right *Dogma Divinum Singularis Caelum*; and

(iv) "**Dogma Ecclesiae Ucadia**" shall be the Ecclesiastical Dogma of Ucadia, as inherited from the Divine Right *Dogma Divinum Ucadia*; and

(v) "**Dogma Ecclesiae Iuris**" shall be the Ecclesiastical Dogma of Law, as inherited from the Divine Right *Dogma Divinum Iuris*; and

(vi) "**Dogma Ecclesiae Scientium**" shall be the Ecclesiastical Dogma of Science, as inherited from the Divine Right *Dogma Divinum Scientium*; and

(vii) "**Dogma Ecclesiae Revelatio**" shall be the Ecclesiastical Dogma of Revelation, as inherited from the Divine Right *Dogma Divinum Revelatio*; and

(viii) "**Dogma Ecclesiae Sacramentum**" shall be the Ecclesiastical Dogma of the Sacraments, as inherited from the Divine Right *Dogma Divinum Sacramentum*; and

(ix) "**Dogma Ecclesiae Singularis Christus**" shall be the Ecclesiastical Dogma of One Christ, as inherited from the Divine Right *Dogma Divinum Singularis Christus*; and

(x) "**Dogma Ecclesiae Singularis Islam**" shall be the Ecclesiastical Dogma of One Islam, as inherited from the Divine Right *Dogma Divinum Singularis Islam*; and

(xi) "**Dogma Ecclesiae Singularis Spiritus**" shall be the Ecclesiastical Dogma of One Spirit, as inherited from the Divine

Right *Dogma Divinum Singularis Spiritus.*

10. The following valid eleven (11) Ecclesiastical Decrees (*Decretum Ecclesiae Iurium*) shall be recognised in accord with the present sacred Covenant:- Ecclesiastical Decrees (Decretum Ecclesiae Iurium)

(i) "**Decretum Ecclesiae Doctrinae**" shall be the Ecclesiastical Decree of Doctrine, as inherited from the Divine Right *Decretum Divinum Doctrinae*; and

(ii) "**Decretum Ecclesiae Absolutionis**" shall be the Ecclesiastical Decree of Absolution, as inherited from the Divine Right *Decretum Divinum Absolutionis*; and

(iii) "**Decretum Ecclesiae Damnationis**" shall be the Ecclesiastical Decree of Damnation, as inherited from the Divine Right *Decretum Divinum Damnationis*; and

(iv) "**Decretum Ecclesiae Exemplificatio**" shall be the Ecclesiastical Decree of Exemplification, as inherited from the Divine Right *Decretum Divinum Exemplificatio*; and

(v) "**Decretum Ecclesiae Testimonium**" shall be the Ecclesiastical Decree of Proof, as inherited from the Divine Right *Decretum Divinum Testimonium*; and

(vi) "**Decretum Ecclesiae Instructionis**" shall be the Ecclesiastical Decree of Instruction, as inherited from the Divine Right *Decretum Divinum Instructionis*; and

(vii) "**Decretum Ecclesiae Censurae**" shall be the Ecclesiastical Decree of Censure, as inherited from the Divine Right *Decretum Divinum Censurae*; and

(viii) "**Decretum Ecclesiae Annullas**" shall be the Ecclesiastical Decree of Annulment, as inherited from the Divine Right *Decretum Divinum Annullas*; and

(ix) "**Decretum Ecclesiae Ratificationis**" shall be the Ecclesiastical Decree of Ratification, as inherited from the Divine Right *Decretum Divinum Ratificationis*; and

(x) "**Decretum Ecclesiae Interdictum**" be the Ecclesiastical Decree of Interdiction, as inherited from the Divine Right *Decretum Divinum Interdictum*; and

(xi) "**Decretum Ecclesiae Levationis**" shall be the Ecclesiastical Decree of Relief, as inherited from the Divine Right *Decretum Divinum Levationis.*

11. The following valid eleven (11) Ecclesiastical Notices (*Notitiae Ecclesiae Iurium*) shall be recognised in accord with the present Ecclesiastical Notice (Notitiae Ecclesiae Iurium) sacred Covenant:-

(i) "**Notitiae Ecclesiae Eventus**" shall be the Ecclesiastical Notice of Event, as inherited from the Divine Right *Notitiae Divinum Eventus*; and

(ii) "**Notitiae Ecclesiae Ius**" shall be the Ecclesiastical Notice of Right, as inherited from the Divine Right *Notitiae Divinum Ius*; and

(iii) "**Notitiae Ecclesiae Actum**" shall be the Ecclesiastical Notice of Action, as inherited from the Divine Right *Notitiae Divinum Actum*; and

(iv) "**Notitiae Ecclesiae Decretum**" shall be the Ecclesiastical Notice of Decree, as inherited from the Divine Right *Notitiae Divinum Decretum*; and

(v) "**Notitiae Ecclesiae Iuris**" shall be the Ecclesiastical Notice of Law, as inherited from the Divine Right *Notitiae Divinum Iuris*; and

(vi) "**Notitiae Ecclesiae Citationis**" shall be the Ecclesiastical Notice of Summons, as inherited from the Divine Right *Notitiae Divinum Citationis*; and

(vii) "**Notitiae Ecclesiae Redemptio**" shall be the Ecclesiastical Notice of Redemption, as inherited from the Divine Right *Notitiae Divinum Redemptio*; and

(viii) "**Notitiae Ecclesiae Rogatio**" shall be the Ecclesiastical Notice of Exception, as inherited from the Divine Right *Notitiae Divinum Rogatio*; and

(ix) "**Notitiae Ecclesiae Potentis**" shall be the Ecclesiastical Notice of Authority, as inherited from the Divine Right *Notitiae Divinum Potentis*; and

(x) "**Notitiae Ecclesiae Testamentum**" shall be the Ecclesiastical Notice of Testament, as inherited from the Divine Right *Notitiae Divinum Testamentum*; and

(xi) "**Notitiae Ecclesiae Obligationis**" shall be the Ecclesiastical Notice of Obligation, as inherited from the Divine Right *Notitiae Divinum Obligationis*.

Sovereign Rights (Iurium Regnum)

12. "**Sovereign Rights**" (*Iurium Regnum*) shall be the third sub-class of Superior Rights and the second highest possible rights of any aggregate body, society, fraternity, association or company of two (2) or more persons personified as sovereign. All Sovereign Rights are derived from Ecclesiastical Rights and a Sovereign Right can never claim to be higher than Ecclesiastical Rights. There exists six (6) categories of seventy-seven (77) Superior Rights within the sub-class of Sovereign Rights, being: Authoritative (11), Instrumental (22), Writs (11), Bills (11), Decrees (11) and Notices (11):

(i) "**Authoritative Sovereign Rights**" (*Potentis Regnum Iurium*) shall be Sovereign Rights associated with the core ecclesiastical authoritative powers; and

(ii) "**Instrumental Sovereign Rights**" (*Instrumentalis Regnum Iurium*) shall be Sovereign Rights essential to the proper administration of Sovereign Rights; and

(iii) "**Sovereign Writs of Rights**" (*Recto Regnum Iurium*) shall be Sovereign Rights associated with the one, true and only forms of Original Entry and Original Action; and

(iv) "**Sovereign Bills of Exception & Agreement**" (*Rogatio Regnum Iurium*) shall be Sovereign Rights associated with the one, true and only forms of Bills of Exception, Citation and Agreement; and

(v) "**Sovereign Decrees**" (*Decretum Regnum Iurium*) shall be Sovereign Rights associated with sovereign decrees concerning the administration, conduct and enforcement of law and order; and

(vi) "**Sovereign Notices**" (*Notitiae Regnum Iurium*) shall be Sovereign Rights associated with sovereign notices issued, executed, patented, promulgated and services in the proper administration, conduct and enforcement of law and order.

13. The following valid eleven (11) Authoritative Sovereign Rights (*Potentis Regnum Iurium*) shall be recognised in accord with the present sacred Covenant:- Authoritative Sovereign Rights (Potentis Regnum Iurium)

(i) "**Ius Regnum**" shall be the primary collection of Sovereign Rights, as inherited from the collection of Divine Rights *Ius Divinum Regnum*; and

(ii) "**Ius Regnum Cancellarium**" shall be the collection of Sovereign Rights of Chancery and Administrative Records, as inherited from the collection of Ecclesiastical Rights *Ius Ecclesiae Cancellarium*; and

(iii) "**Ius Regnum Consilium**" shall be the collection of Sovereign Rights of a Legislative and Advisory Authority, as inherited from the collection of Ecclesiastical Rights *Ius Ecclesiae Consilium*; and

(iv) "**Ius Regnum Collegium**" shall be the collection of Sovereign Rights of a Company or Charitable Body, as inherited from the collection of Ecclesiastical Rights *Ius Ecclesiae Collegium*; and

(v) "**Ius Regnum Officium**" shall be the collection of Sovereign Rights of Office, Duty and Service, as inherited from the collection of Ecclesiastical Rights *Ius Ecclesiae Officium*; and

(vi) "**Ius Regnum Imperium**" shall be the collection of Sovereign Rights of Command, Occupation and Enforcement, as inherited from the collection of Ecclesiastical Rights *Ius Ecclesiae Imperium*; and

(vii) "**Ius Regnum Custoditum**" shall be the collection of Sovereign Rights of Custody, Guardianship and Preservation, as inherited from the collection of Ecclesiastical Rights *Ius Ecclesiae Custoditum*; and

(viii) "**Ius Regnum Oratorium**" shall be the collection of Sovereign Rights to a Competent Forum of Law and Review, as inherited from the collection of Ecclesiastical Rights *Ius Ecclesiae Oratorium*; and

(ix) "**Ius Regnum Templum**" shall be the collection of Sovereign Rights of a Treasury or Financial (Banking) Body, as inherited from the collection of Ecclesiastical Rights *Ius Ecclesiae Templum*; and

(x) "**Ius Regnum Commercium**" shall be the collection of Sovereign Rights to Trade, Exchange and Communication, as inherited from the collection of Divine Rights *Ius Ecclesiae Commercium*; and

(xi) "**Ius Regnum Decretum**" shall be the collection of Sovereign Rights to issue Decree, Judgement and Edict, as inherited from the collection of Ecclesiastical Rights *Ius Ecclesiae Decretum*.

Instrumental Sovereign Rights (Instrumentalis Regnum Iurium)

14. The following valid twenty-two (22) Instrumental Sovereign Rights (*Instrumentalis Regnum Iurium*) shall be recognised in accord with the present sacred Covenant:-

(i) "**Ius Regnum Iuris**" shall be the collection of Sovereign Rights to Justice and Due Process, as inherited from the collection of Ecclesiastical Rights *Ius Ecclesiae Iuris*; and

(ii) "**Ius Regnum Bona Fidei**" shall be the collection of Sovereign Rights of Good Faith, Good Conscience and Good Actions, as inherited from the collection of Ecclesiastical Rights *Ius Ecclesiae Bona Fidei*; and

(iii) "**Ius Regnum Aequum**" shall be the collection of Sovereign Rights of Equality and Fairness, as inherited from the collection of Ecclesiastical Rights *Ius Ecclesiae Aequum*; and

(iv) "**Ius Regnum Fidei**" shall be the collection of Sovereign Rights of Superior Sovereign Trust and Sovereign Estate, as inherited from the collection of Ecclesiastical Rights *Ius Ecclesiae Fidei*; and

(v) "**Ius Regnum Rationatio**" shall be the collection of Sovereign Rights of Accounting, Credit and Funds, as inherited from the collection of Ecclesiastical Rights *Ius Ecclesiae Rationatio*; and

(vi) "**Ius Regnum Concedere et Abrogare**" shall be the collection of Sovereign Rights to Give or Grant Rights and Annul or rescind Superior Rights, as inherited from the collection of Ecclesiastical Rights *Ius Ecclesiae Concedere et Abrogare*; and

(vii) "**Ius Regnum Delegare et Revocare**" shall be the collection of Sovereign Rights to Assign or Delegate Rights and Cancel or Revoke Superior Rights, as inherited from the collection of Ecclesiastical Rights *Ius Ecclesiae Delegare et Revocare*; and

(viii) "**Ius Regnum Associatio et Conventio**" shall be the collection of Sovereign Rights of Association and Agreement, as inherited from the collection of Ecclesiastical Rights *Ius Ecclesiae Associatio et Conventio*; and

(ix) "**Ius Regnum Consensum et Non**" shall be the collection of Sovereign Rights to Consent and Non-Consent, as inherited from the collection of Ecclesiastical Rights *Ius Ecclesiae Consensum et Non*; and

(x) "**Ius Regnum Penitentiaria**" shall be the collection of Sovereign Rights of Forced Confinement and Penitence, as inherited from the collection of Divine Rights *Ius Ecclesiae Penitentiaria*; and

(xi) "**Ius Regnum Dominium**" shall be the collection of Sovereign Rights of Absolute Ownership, as inherited from the collection of Ecclesiastical Rights *Ius Ecclesiae Dominium*; and

(xii) "**Ius Regnum Possessionis**" shall be the collection of Sovereign Rights to Possess, Hold and Own Property, as inherited from *the collection of* Ecclesiastical Rights *Ius Ecclesiae* Possessionis; and

(xiii) "**Ius Regnum Usus**" shall be the collection of Sovereign Rights of Use and Fruits (Enjoyment) of Use of Property, as inherited from the collection of Ecclesiastical Rights *Ius Ecclesiae Usus*; and

(xiv) "**Ius Regnum Proprietatis**" shall be the collection of Sovereign Rights of Ownership of Use or Fruits of Use of Property, as inherited from the collection of Ecclesiastical Rights *Ius Ecclesiae Proprietatis*; and

(xv) "**Ius Regnum Vectigalis Proprietatis**" shall be the collection of Sovereign Rights to impose Rents, Tolls, Levies, Contributions or Charges against Property, as inherited from the collection of Ecclesiastical Rights *Ius Ecclesiae Vectigalis Proprietatis* ; and

(xvi) "**Ius Regnum Moneta**" shall be the collection of Sovereign Rights to Mint, Produce, Hold, Use and Exchange Money, as inherited from the collection of Ecclesiastical Rights *Ius Ecclesiae Moneta*; and

(xvii) "**Ius Regnum Vectigalis Moneta**" shall be the collection of Sovereign Rights to impose Rents, Tolls, Levies, Contributions or Charges against Money, as inherited from the collection of Ecclesiastical Rights *Ius Ecclesiae Vectigalis Moneta*; and

(xviii) "**Ius Regnum Registrum**" shall be the collection of Sovereign Rights to Enter Records within Registers and Rolls, as inherited from the collection of Ecclesiastical Rights *Ius Ecclesiae Registrum*; and

(xix) "**Ius Regnum Remedium**" shall be the collection of Sovereign Rights of Remedy, Relief, Redress or Compensation, as inherited from the collection of Ecclesiastical Rights *Ius Ecclesiae Remedium*; and

(xx) "**Ius Regnum Poena**" shall be the collection of Sovereign Rights of Penalty & Punishment, as inherited from the collection of Ecclesiastical Rights *Ius Ecclesiae Poena*; and

(xxi) "**Ius Regnum Clementia**" shall be the collection of Sovereign Rights of Mercy & Forgiveness, as inherited from the collection of Ecclesiastical Rights *Ius Ecclesiae Clementia*; and

(xxii) "**Ius Regnum Actionum**" shall be the collection of Sovereign Rights of Action, as inherited from the collection of Ecclesiastical Rights *Ius Ecclesiae Actionum*.

15. The following valid eleven (11) Sovereign Writs of Rights (*Recto Regnum Iurium*) shall be recognised in accord with the present sacred Covenant:- Sovereign Writs of Rights (Recto Regnum Iurium)

(i) "**Recto Regnum Originalis**" shall be the Sovereign Original Writ of Right, as inherited from the Ecclesiastical Right *Recto Ecclesiae Originalis*; and

(ii) "**Recto Regnum Iubemus**" shall be the Sovereign Writ of Right of Command or Authorisation, as inherited from the Ecclesiastical Right *Recto Ecclesiae Apocalypsis*; and

(iii) "**Recto Regnum Investigationis**" shall be the Sovereign Writ of Right of Inquiry or Review, as inherited from the Ecclesiastical Right *Recto Ecclesiae Investigationis*; and

(iv) "**Recto Regnum Capimus**" shall be the Sovereign Writ of Right of Surrender or Arrest of Person, as inherited from the Ecclesiastical Right *Recto Ecclesiae Capionis*; and

(v) "**Recto Regnum Custodiae**" shall be the Sovereign Writ of Right of Surrender or Seizure of Property, as inherited from the

Ecclesiastical Right *Recto Ecclesiae Custodiae*; and

(vi) "**Recto Regnum Corrigimus**" shall be the Sovereign Writ of Right of Correction of Records, Rulings, Laws or Instruments, as inherited from the Ecclesiastical Right *Recto Ecclesiae Corrigimus*; and

(vii) "**Recto Regnum Expurgatio**" shall be the Sovereign Writ of Right of Expurgation of Records, Rulings, Laws or Instruments, as inherited from the Ecclesiastical Right *Recto Ecclesiae Expurgatio*; and

(viii) "**Recto Regnum Abrogatio**" shall be the Sovereign Writ of Right of Annulment of Records, Rulings, Laws or Instruments, as inherited from the Ecclesiastical Right *Recto Ecclesiae Abrogatio*; and

(ix) "**Recto Regnum Inhibitio**" shall be the Sovereign Writ of Right of Prohibition or Restraint, as inherited from the Ecclesiastical Right *Recto Ecclesiae Inhibitio*; and

(x) "**Recto Regnum Restitutio**" shall be the Sovereign Writ of Right of Restitution, as inherited from the Ecclesiastical Right *Recto Ecclesiae Restitutio*; and

(xi) "**Recto Regnum Restoratio**" shall be the Sovereign Writ of Right of Restoration, as inherited from the Ecclesiastical Right *Recto Ecclesiae Restoratio*.

16. The following valid eleven (11) Sovereign Bills of Exception & Agreement (*Rogatio Regnum Iurium*) shall be recognised in accord with the present sacred Covenant:- Sovereign Bills of Exception (Rogatio Regnum Iurium)

(i) "**Rogatio Regnum Recto**" shall be the Sovereign (Original) Bill of Right, as inherited from the Ecclesiastical Right *Rogatio Ecclesiae Recto*; and

(ii) "**Rogatio Regnum Iubemus**" shall be the Sovereign Bill of Right of Command or Authorisation, as inherited from the Ecclesiastical Right *Rogatio Ecclesiae Apocalypsis*; and

(iii) "**Rogatio Regnum Capimus**" shall be the Sovereign Bill of Right against Failure to Surrender or Arrest Person, as inherited from the Ecclesiastical Right *Rogatio Ecclesiae Capimus*; and

(iv) "**Rogatio Regnum Custodiae**" shall be the Sovereign Bill of Right against Failure to Surrender or Seize Property, as inherited from the Ecclesiastical Right *Rogatio Ecclesiae Custodiae*; and

(v) "**Rogatio Regnum Corrigimus**" shall be the Sovereign Bill of Right against Failure to Correct Records, Rulings, Laws or Instruments, as inherited from the Ecclesiastical Right *Rogatio*

Ecclesiae Corrigimus; and

(vi) "**Rogatio Regnum Inhibitio**" shall be the Sovereign Bill of Right against Failure to Prohibit or Impose Limits as Instructed, as inherited from the Ecclesiastical Right *Rogatio Ecclesiae Inhibitio*; and

(vii) "**Rogatio Regnum Restitutio**" shall be the Sovereign Bill of Right of Restitution or Compensation, as inherited from the Ecclesiastical Right *Rogatio Ecclesiae Restituio*; and

(viii) "**Rogatio Regnum Credito**" shall be the Sovereign Bill of Right of Credit, as inherited from the Divine Right *Rogatio Ecclesiae Credito*; and

(ix) "**Rogatio Regnum Permutatio**" shall be the Sovereign Bill of Right of Exchange, as inherited from the Ecclesiastical Right *Rogatio Ecclesiae Permutatio*; and

(x) "**Rogatio Regnum Venditio**" shall be the Sovereign Bill of Right of Sale, as inherited from the Ecclesiastical Right *Rogatio Ecclesiae Venditio*; and

(xi) "**Rogatio Regnum Traditio**" shall be the Sovereign Bill of Lading, as inherited from the Ecclesiastical Right *Rogatio Ecclesiae Traditio*.

17. The following valid eleven (11) Sovereign Decrees (*Decretum Regnum Iurium*) shall be recognised in accord with the present sacred Covenant:-

Sovereign Decrees (Decretum Regnum Iurium)

(i) "**Decretum Regnum Doctrinae**" shall be the Sovereign Decree of Doctrine, as inherited from the Ecclesiastical Right *Decretum Ecclesiae Doctrinae*; and

(ii) "**Decretum Regnum Absolutionis**" shall be the Sovereign Decree of Absolution, as inherited from the Ecclesiastical Right *Decretum Ecclesiae Absolutionis*; and

(iii) "**Decretum Regnum Damnationis**" shall be the Sovereign Decree of Damnation, as inherited from the Ecclesiastical Right *Decretum Ecclesiae Damnationis*; and

(iv) "**Decretum Regnum Exemplificatio**" shall be the Sovereign Decree of Exemplification, as inherited from the Ecclesiastical Right *Decretum Ecclesiae Exemplificatio*; and

(v) "**Decretum Regnum Testimonium**" shall be the Sovereign Decree of Proof, as inherited from the Ecclesiastical Right *Decretum Ecclesiae Testimonium*; and

(vi) "**Decretum Regnum Instructionis**" shall be the Sovereign Decree of Instruction, as inherited from the Ecclesiastical Right

Decretum Ecclesiae Instructionis; and

(vii) "**Decretum Regnum Censurae**" shall be the Sovereign Decree of Censure, as inherited from the Ecclesiastical Right *Decretum Ecclesiae Censurae;* and

(viii) "**Decretum Regnum Annullas**" shall be the Sovereign Decree of Annulment, as inherited from the Ecclesiastical Right *Decretum Ecclesiae Annullas*; and

(ix) "**Decretum Regnum Ratificationis**" shall be the Sovereign Decree of Ratification, as inherited from the Ecclesiastical Right *Decretum Ecclesiae Ratificationis*; and

(x) "**Decretum Regnum Interdictum**" shall be the Sovereign Decree of Interdiction, as inherited from the Ecclesiastical Right *Decretum Ecclesiae Interdictum*; and

(xi) "**Decretum Regnum Levationis**" shall be the Sovereign Decree of Relief, as inherited from the Ecclesiastical Right *Decretum Ecclesiae Levationis*.

18. The following valid eleven (11) Sovereign Notices (*Notitiae Regnum Iurium*) shall be recognised in accord with the present sacred Covenant:-

Sovereign Notice (Notitiae Regnum Iurium)

(i) "**Notitiae Regnum Eventus**" shall be the Sovereign Notice of Event, as inherited from the Ecclesiastical Right *Notitiae Ecclesiae Eventus*; and

(ii) "**Notitiae Regnum Ius**" shall be the Sovereign Notice of Right, as inherited from the Ecclesiastical Right *Notitiae Ecclesiae Ius*; and

(iii) "**Notitiae Regnum Actum**" shall be the Sovereign Notice of Action, as inherited from the Ecclesiastical Right *Notitiae Ecclesiae Actum*; and

(iv) "**Notitiae Regnum Decretum**" shall be the Sovereign Notice of Decree, as inherited from the Ecclesiastical Right *Notitiae Ecclesiae Decretum*; and

(v) "**Notitiae Regnum Iuris**" shall be the Sovereign Notice of Law, as inherited from the Ecclesiastical Right *Notitiae Ecclesiae Iuris*; and

(vi) "**Notitiae Regnum Citationis**" shall be the Sovereign Notice of Summons, as inherited from the Ecclesiastical Right *Notitiae Ecclesiae Citationis*; and

(vii) "**Notitiae Regnum Redemptio**" shall be the Sovereign Notice of Redemption, as inherited from the Ecclesiastical Right *Notitiae Ecclesiae Redemptio*; and

(viii) "**Notitiae Regnum Rogatio**" shall be the Sovereign Notice of Exception, as inherited from the Ecclesiastical Right *Notitiae Ecclesiae Rogatio*; and

(ix) "**Notitiae Regnum Potentis**" shall be the Sovereign Notice of Authority, as inherited from the Ecclesiastical Right *Notitiae Ecclesiae Potentis*; and

(x) "**Notitiae Regnum Testamentum**" shall be the Sovereign Notice of Testament, as inherited from the Ecclesiastical Right *Notitiae Ecclesiae Testamentum*; and

(xi) "**Notitiae Regnum Obligationis**" shall be the Sovereign Notice of Obligation, as inherited from the Ecclesiastical Right *Notitiae Ecclesiae Obligationis*.

19. "**Official Rights**" (*Iurium Publicum*) shall be the fourth sub-class of Superior Rights and the third highest possible rights of any aggregate body, society, fraternity, association or company of two (2) or more persons personified in trust. Official Rights (Iurium Publicum)

All Official Rights are derived from Sovereign Rights and Official Rights can never be claimed to be higher than Sovereign Rights. There exists six (6) categories of eighty-eight (88) Superior Rights within the sub-class of Official Rights, being: Authoritative (11), Instrumental (33), Warrants (11), Declarations (11), Orders (11) and Notices (11):

(i) "**Authoritative Official Rights**" (*Potentis Publicum Iurium*) shall be Official Rights associated with the core official authoritative powers; and

(ii) "**Instrumental Official Rights**" (*Instrumentalis Publicum Iurium*) shall be Official Rights essential to the proper administration of society; and

(iii) "**Official Warrants of Rights**" (*Auctoritas Publicum Iurium*) shall be Official Rights associated with the one, true and only forms of Original Entry and Original Action; and

(iv) "**Official Declarations of Exception**" (*Declarationis Publicum Iurium*) shall be Official Rights associated with the one, true and only forms of Exception, Citation and Moratorium; and

(v) "**Official Orders**" (*Iussum Publicum Iurium*) shall be Official Rights associated with official decrees concerning the administration, conduct and enforcement of law and order; and

(vi) "**Official Notices**" (*Notitiae Publicum Iurium*) shall be Official Rights associated with official notices issued, executed, patented, promulgated and services in the proper administration, conduct and enforcement of law and order.

20. The following valid eleven (11) Authoritative Official Rights (*Potentis Publicum Iurium*) shall be recognised in accord with the present sacred Covenant:- Authoritative Official Rights (Potentis Publicum Iurium)

(i) "**Ius Publicum**" shall be the primary collection of Official Rights of Jurisdiction, as inherited from the Sovereign Rights *Ius Regnum*; and

(ii) "**Ius Publicum Cancellarium**" shall be the collection of Official Rights of Chancery and Administrative Records, as inherited from the Sovereign Rights *Ius Regnum Cancellarium*; and

(iii) "**Ius Publicum Consilium**" shall be the collection of Official Rights of a Legislative and Advisory Authority, as inherited from the Sovereign Rights *Ius Regnum Consilium*; and

(iv) "**Ius Publicum Collegium**" shall be the collection of Official Rights of a Company or Charitable Body, as inherited from the Sovereign Rights *Ius Regnum Collegium*; and

(v) "**Ius Publicum Officium**" shall be the collection of Official Rights of Office, Duty and Service, as inherited from the Sovereign Rights *Ius Regnum Officium*; and

(vi) "**Ius Publicum Imperium**" shall be the collection of Official Rights of Command, Occupation and Enforcement, as inherited from the Sovereign Rights *Ius Regnum Imperium*; and

(vii) "**Ius Publicum Custoditum**" shall be the collection of Official Rights of Custody, Guardianship and Preservation, as inherited from the Sovereign Rights *Ius Regnum Custoditum*; and

(viii) "**Ius Publicum Oratorium**" shall be the collection of Official Rights to a Competent Forum of Law and Review, as inherited from the Sovereign Rights *Ius Regnum Oratorium*; and

(ix) "**Ius Publicum Templum**" shall be the collection of Official Rights of a Treasury or Financial (Banking) Body, as inherited from the Sovereign Rights *Ius Regnum Templum*; and

(x) "**Ius Publicum Commercium**" shall be the collection of Official Rights to Trade, Exchange and Communication, as inherited from the collection of Divine Rights *Ius Regnum Commercium*; and

(xi) "**Ius Publicum Decretum**" shall be the collection of Official Rights to issue Decree, Judgement and Edict, as inherited from the

Sovereign Rights *Ius Regnum Decretum*.

21. The following valid thirty-three (33) Instrumental Official Rights (*Instrumentalis Publicum Iurium*) as inherited from the Divine Collection of Maxims of Law, shall be recognised in accord with the present sacred Covenant:-

Instrumental Official Rights (Instrumentalis Publicum Iurium)

(i) "**Ius Publicum Agricultura**" shall be the collection of Official Agricultural Rights as defined by the Ucadia Agriculture Code, as inherited from the *Maxims of Natural Law*; and

(ii) "**Ius Publicum Frugalitas**" shall be the collection of Official Banking Rights as defined by the Ucadia Banking Code, as inherited from the *Maxims of Economic Law*; and

(iii) "**Ius Publicum Pecuniae**" shall be the collection of Official Budget and Finance Management Rights as defined by the Ucadia Budget and Finance Management Code, as inherited from *Maxims of Monetary Law*; and

(iv) "**Ius Publicum Aedificatio**" shall be the collection of Official Building and Construction Rights as defined by the Ucadia Building and Construction Code, as inherited from *Maxims of Urban Law* and *Maxims of Civil Law*; and

(v) "**Ius Publicum Civilis**" shall be the body of Official Civil Rights as defined by the Ucadia Civil Code, as inherited from *Maxims of Civil Law*; and

(vi) "**Ius Publicum Media**" shall be the collection of Official Communications and Media Rights as defined by the Ucadia Communications and Media Code, as inherited from *Maxims of Technology Law* and *Maxims of Civil Law*; and

(vii) "**Ius Publicum Companio**" shall be the collection of Official Company Rights as defined by the Ucadia Company Code, as inherited from *Maxims of Company Law*; and

(viii) "**Ius Publicum Criminalis**" shall be the collection of Official Criminal Prosecution and Punishment Rights as defined by the Ucadia Criminal Code, as inherited from *Maxims of Civil Law*, *Maxims of Fiduciary Law* and *Maxims of Administrative Law*; and

(ix) "**Ius Publicum Culturae**" shall be the collection of Official Culture and Entertainment Rights as defined by the Ucadia Culture and Entertainment Code, as inherited from *Maxims of Cognitive Law*, *Maxims of Education Law* and *Maxims of Bioethics Law*; and

(x) "**Ius Publicum Informatum**" shall be the collection of Official Education Rights as defined by the Ucadia Education Code, as inherited from *Maxims of Education Law; and*

(xi) "**Ius Publicum Votum**" shall be the collection of Official Elections Rights as defined by the Ucadia Elections Code, as inherited from *Maxims of Positive Law* and *Maxims of Civil Law; and*

(xii) "**Ius Publicum Periculum**" shall be the collection of Official Emergency Rights as defined by the Ucadia Emergency Code, as inherited from *Maxims of Positive Law and Maxims of Civil Law; and*

(xiii) "**Ius Publicum Vocatio**" shall be the collection of Official Employment Rights as defined by the Ucadia Employment Code, as inherited from *Maxims of Economic Law and Maxims of Education Law; and*

(xiv) "**Ius Publicum Energis**" shall be the collection of Official Energy Rights as defined by the Ucadia Energy Code, as inherited from *Maxims of Technology Law*; and

(xv) "**Ius Publicum Virtus Naturae**" shall be the collection of Official Environment Rights as defined by the Ucadia Environment Code, as inherited from *Maxims of Bioethics Law*; and

(xvi) "**Ius Publicum Executor**" shall be the collection of Official Executive Rights as defined by the Ucadia Executive Code, as inherited from *Maxims of Civil Law* and *Maxims of Fiduciary Law*; and

(xvii) "**Ius Publicum Valetudo et Salus**" shall be the collection of Official Fitness and Health Rights as defined by the Ucadia Fitness and Health Code, as inherited from *Maxims of Bioethics Law* and *Maxims of Cognitive Law*; and

(xviii) "**Ius Publicum Nutrimens Et Medicina**" shall be the body of Official Food and Drugs Rights as defined by the Ucadia Food and Drugs Code, as inherited from *Maxims of Food and Drugs Law*; and

(xix) "**Ius Publicum Industriae**" shall be the collection of Official Industry Rights as defined by the Ucadia Industry Code, as inherited from *Maxims of Education Law*; and

(xx) "**Ius Publicum Urbis**" shall be the collection of Official Infrastructure Rights as defined by the Ucadia Infrastructure Code, as inherited from *Maxims of Urban Law*; and

(xxi) "**Ius Publicum Iudicalis**" shall be the collection of Official Judicial Rights as defined by the Ucadia Judicial Code, as inherited from *Maxims of Civil Law* and *Maxims of Fiduciary Law*; and

(xxii) "**Ius Publicum Scientiae**" shall be the collection of Official Knowledge Systems Rights as defined by the Ucadia Knowledge Systems Code, as inherited from *Maxims of Education Law* and *Maxims of Technology Law*; and

(xxiii) "**Ius Publicum Legislativam**" shall be the collection of Official Legislative Rights as defined by the Ucadia Legislative Code, as inherited from *Maxims of Positive Law*; and

(xxiv) "**Ius Publicum Militaris**" shall be the collection of Official Military Rights as defined by the Ucadia Military Code, as inherited from *Maxims of Military Law*; and

(xxv) "**Ius Publicum Securitas**" shall be the collection of Official Police Rights as defined by the Ucadia Police Code, as inherited from *Maxims of Security Law*; and

(xxvi) "**Ius Publicum Praeservatio et Sanitas**" shall be the collection of Official Disease Prevention and Sanitation Rights as defined by the Ucadia Disease Prevention and Sanitation Code, as inherited from *Maxims of Bioethics Law*, *Maxims of Education Law* and *Maxims of Technology Law*; and

(xxvii) "**Ius Publicum Custodiae**" shall be the collection of Official Prison and Custodial Rights as defined by the Ucadia Prison Code, as inherited from *Maxims of Civil Law* and *Maxims of Fiduciary Law*; and

(xxviii) "**Ius Publicum Fructus**" shall be the collection of Official Revenue Rights as defined by the Ucadia Revenue Code, as inherited from *Maxims of Economic Law* and *Maxims of Monetary Law*; and

(xxix) "**Ius Publicum Administratum**" shall be the collection of Official Service Rights as defined by the Ucadia Service Code, as inherited from *Maxims of Administrative Law*; and

(xxx) "**Ius Publicum Technologia**" shall be the collection of Official Technology Rights as defined by the Ucadia Technology Code, as inherited from *Maxims of Technology Law*; and

(xxxi) "**Ius Publicum Adiuvare**" shall be the collection of Official Temporary Assistance Rights as defined by the Ucadia Temporary Assistance Code, as inherited from *Maxims of Economic Law* and *Maxims of Civil Law*; and

(xxxii) "**Ius Publicum Mercatus**" shall be the collection of Official Trade Rights as defined by the Ucadia Trade & Intellectual Property Code, as inherited from *Maxims of Trade & Intellectual Property Law*; and (xxxiii) "**Ius Publicum Itineris**" shall be the collection of Official Transport & Travel Rights as defined by the Ucadia Transport & Travel Code, as inherited from *Maxims of Technology Law* and *Maxims of Trade & Intellectual Property Law*.

22. The following valid eleven (11) Official Warrants of Rights (*Auctoritas Publicum Iurium*) shall be recognised in accord with the present sacred Covenant:- Official Warrants of Rights (Auctoritas Publicum Iurium)

(i) "**Auctoritas Publicum Petitionis**" shall be the Official Warrant of Claim of Right, as inherited from the Sovereign Right *Recto Regnum Petitionis*; and

(ii) "**Auctoritas Publicum Originalis**" shall be the Official Warrant of Rights, as inherited from the Sovereign Right *Recto Regnum Originalis*; and

(iii) "**Auctoritas Publicum Apocalypsis**" shall be the Official Warrant of Right of Revelation, as inherited from the Sovereign Right *Recto Regnum Apocalypsis*; and

(iv) "**Auctoritas Publicum Investigationis**" shall be the Official Warrant of Inquiry and Search, as inherited from the Sovereign Right *Recto Regnum Investigationis*; and

(v) "**Auctoritas Publicum Capionis**" shall be the Official Warrant of Seizure and Return, as inherited from the Sovereign Right *Recto Regnum Capionis*; and

(vi) "**Auctoritas Publicum Custodiae**" shall be the Official Warrant of Arrest and Custody, as inherited from the Sovereign Right *Recto Regnum Custodiae*; and

(vii) "**Auctoritas Publicum Documentis**" shall be the Official Warrant of correcting Records of Proof, as inherited from the Sovereign Right *Recto Regnum Documentis*; and

(viii) "**Auctoritas Publicum Expungo**" shall be the Official Warrant of expunging Records of Proof, as inherited from the Sovereign Right *Recto Regnum Expungo*; and

(ix) "**Auctoritas Publicum Abrogationis**" shall be the Official Warrant of Annulment of Previous Laws and Instruments, as inherited from the Sovereign Right *Recto Regnum Abrogationis*; and

(x) "**Auctoritas Publicum Interdico**" shall be the Official Warrant of Prohibition and Imposition, as inherited from the Sovereign Right *Recto Regnum Interdico*; and

(xi) "**Auctoritas Publicum Restitutio**" shall be the Official Warrant of Compensation and Restoration, as inherited from the Sovereign

Right *Recto Regnum Restitutio*.

23. The following valid eleven (11) Official Declarations of Exception (*Declarationis Publicum Iurium*) shall be recognised in accord with the present sacred Covenant:-

Official Declaration of Exception (Declarationis Publicum Iurium)

(i) "**Declarationis Publicum Petitionis**" shall be the Official Declaration of Right, as inherited from the Sovereign Right *Rogatio Regnum Petitionis*; and

(ii) "**Declarationis Publicum Recto**" shall be the Official Declaration of Right, as inherited from the Sovereign Right *Rogatio Regnum Recto*; and

(iii) "**Declarationis Publicum Apocalypsis**" shall be the Official Declaration of Rights of Revelation, as inherited from the Sovereign Right *Rogatio Regnum Apocalypsis*; and

(iv) "**Declarationis Publicum Investigationis**" shall be the Official Declaration of Inquiry and Search, as inherited from the Sovereign Right *Rogatio Regnum Investigationis*; and

(v) "**Declarationis Publicum Capionis**" shall be the Official Declaration of Seizure and Return, as inherited from the Sovereign Right *Rogatio Regnum Capionis*; and

(vi) "**Declarationis Publicum Custodiae**" shall be the Official Declaration of Arrest and Custody, as inherited from the Sovereign Right *Rogatio Regnum Custodiae*; and

(vii) "**Declarationis Publicum Documentis**" shall be the Official Declaration of correcting Records of Proof, as inherited from the Sovereign Right *Rogatio Regnum Documentis*; and

(viii) "**Declarationis Publicum Expungo**" shall be the Official Declaration of expunging Records of Proof, as inherited from the Sovereign Right *Rogatio Regnum Expungo*; and

(ix) "**Declarationis Publicum Abrogationis**" shall be the Official Declaration of Annulment of Previous Laws and Instruments, as inherited from the Sovereign Right *Rogatio Regnum Abrogationis*; and

(x) "**Declarationis Publicum Interdico**" shall be the Official Declaration of Prohibition and Imposition, as inherited from the Sovereign Right *Rogatio Regnum Interdico*; and

(xi) "**Declarationis Publicum Restitutio**" shall be the Official Declaration of Compensation and Restoration, as inherited from the Sovereign Right *Rogatio Regnum Restitutio*.

24. The following valid eleven (11) Official Orders (*Iussum Publicum Iurium*) shall be recognised in accord with the present sacred

Official Orders (Iussum Publicum

Covenant:- Iurium)

(i) "**Iussum Publicum Doctrinae**" shall be the Official Order of Doctrine, as inherited from the Sovereign Right *Decretum Regnum Doctrinae*; and

(ii) "**Iussum Publicum Absolutionis**" shall be the Official Order of Absolution, as inherited from the Sovereign Right *Decretum Regnum Absolutionis*; and

(iii) "**Iussum Publicum Damnationis**" shall be the Official Order of Damnation, as inherited from the Sovereign Right *Decretum Regnum Damnationis*; and

(iv) "**Iussum Publicum Exemplificatio**" shall be the Official Order of Exemplification, as inherited from the Sovereign Right *Decretum Regnum Exemplificatio*; and

(v) "**Iussum Publicum Testimonium**" shall be the Official Order of Proof, as inherited from the Sovereign Right *Decretum Regnum Testimonium*; and

(vi) "**Iussum Publicum Instructionis**" shall be the Official Order of Instruction, as inherited from the Sovereign Right *Decretum Regnum Instructionis*; and

(vii) "**Iussum Publicum Censurae**" shall be the Official Order of Censure, as inherited from the Sovereign Right *Decretum Regnum Censurae*; and

(viii) "**Iussum Publicum Annullas**" shall be the Official Order of Annulment, as inherited from the Sovereign Right *Decretum Regnum Annullas*; and

(ix) "**Iussum Publicum Ratificationis**" shall be the Official Order of Ratification, as inherited from the Sovereign Right *Decretum Regnum Ratificationis*; and

(x) "**Iussum Publicum Interdictum**" shall be the Official Order of Interdiction, as inherited from the Sovereign Right *Decretum Regnum Interdictum*; and

(xi) "**Iussum Publicum Levationis**" shall be the Official Order of Relief, as inherited from the Sovereign Right *Decretum Regnum Levationis*.

25. The following valid eleven (11) Official Notices (*Notitiae Publicum Iurium*) shall be recognised in accord with the present sacred Covenant:- Official Notices (Notitiae Publicum Iurium)

(i) "**Notitiae Publicum Eventus**" shall be the Official Notice of Event, as inherited from the Sovereign Right *Notitiae Regnum*

Eventus; and

(ii) "**Notitiae Publicum Ius**" shall be the Official Notice of Right, as inherited from the Sovereign Right *Notitiae Regnum Ius*; and

(iii) "**Notitiae Publicum Actum**" shall be the Official Notice of Action, as inherited from the Sovereign Right *Notitiae Regnum Actum*; and

(iv) "**Notitiae Publicum Decretum**" shall be the Official Notice of Decree, as inherited from the Sovereign Right *Notitiae Regnum Decretum*; and

(v) "**Notitiae Publicum Iuris**" shall be the Official Notice of Law, as inherited from the Sovereign Right *Notitiae Regnum Iuris*; and

(vi) "**Notitiae Publicum Citationis**" shall be the Official Notice of Summons, as inherited from the Sovereign Right *Notitiae Regnum Citationis*; and

(vii) "**Notitiae Publicum Redemptio**" shall be the Official Notice of Redemption, as inherited from the Sovereign Right *Notitiae Regnum Redemptio*; and

(viii) "**Notitiae Publicum Rogatio**" shall be the Official Notice of Exception, as inherited from the Sovereign Right *Notitiae Regnum Rogatio*; and

(ix) "**Notitiae Publicum Potentis**" shall be the Official Notice of Authority, as inherited from the Sovereign Right *Notitiae Regnum Potentis*; and

(x) "**Notitiae Publicum Testamentum**" shall be the Official Notice of Testament, as inherited from the Sovereign Right *Notitiae Regnum Testamentum*; and

(xi) "**Notitiae Publicum Obligationis**" shall be the Official Notice of Obligation, as inherited from the Sovereign Right *Notitiae Regnum Obligationis*.

Administrative Rights (Iurium Administrationis)

26. "**Administrative Rights**" (*Iurium Administrationis*) shall be the fifth sub-class of Superior Rights and the fourth highest possible rights of any aggregate body, society, fraternity, association or company of two (2) or more persons personified in trust. All Administrative Rights are derived from either Sovereign Rights or Official Rights; and an Administrative Right can never claim to be higher than Official Rights. There exists two (2) categories of forty-four (44) Superior Rights within the sub class of Administrative Rights, being: Authoritative (11) and Instrumental (33):

(i) "**Authoritative Administrative Rights**" (*Potentis Administrationis Iurium*) shall be Administrative Rights associated with the core administrative authoritative powers; and

(ii) "**Instrumental Administrative Rights**" (*Instrumentalis Administrationis Iurium*) shall be Administrative Rights essential to the proper administration of Administrative Rights.

Authoritative Administrative Rights (Potentis Administrationis Iurium)

27. The following valid eleven (11) Authoritative Administrative Rights (*Potentis Administrationis Iurium*) shall be recognised in accord with the present sacred Covenant:-

(i) "**Ius Administrationis**" shall be the primary collection of Administrative Rights, as inherited from the collection of Official Rights *Ius Publicum*; and

(ii) "**Ius Administrationis Potentis**" shall be the collection of Administrative Rights of Administrative Authority, as inherited from the collection of Official Rights *Ius Publicum Potentis*; and

(iii) "**Ius Administrationis Consilium**" shall be the collection of Administrative Rights of a Legislative and Advisory Authority, as inherited from the collection of Official Rights *Ius Publicum Consilium*; and

(iv) "**Ius Administrationis Collegium**" shall be the collection of Administrative Rights of a Company or Charitable Body, as inherited from the collection of Official Rights *Ius Publicum Collegium*; and

(v) "**Ius Administrationis Officium**" shall be the collection of Administrative Rights of Office, Duty and Service, as inherited from the collection of Official Rights *Ius Publicum Officium*; and

(vi) "**Ius Administrationis Imperium**" shall be the collection of Administrative Rights of Command, Occupation and Enforcement, as inherited from the collection of Official Rights *Ius Publicum Imperium*; and

(vii) "**Ius Administrationis Custoditum**" shall be the collection of Administrative Rights of Custody, Guardianship and Preservation, as inherited from the collection of Official Rights *Ius Publicum Custoditum*; and

(viii) "**Ius Administrationis Oratorium**" shall be the collection of Administrative Rights to a Competent Forum of Law and Review, as inherited from the collection of Official Rights *Ius Publicum Oratorium*; and

(ix) "**Ius Administrationis Penitentiaria**" shall be the collection of Administrative Rights of Forced Confinement and Penitence, as inherited from the collection of Sovereign Rights *Ius Regnum Penitentiaria*; and

(x) "**Ius Administrationis Commercium**" shall be the collection of Administrative Rights to Trade, Exchange and Communication, as inherited from the collection of Divine Rights *Ius Divinum Commercium*; and

(xi) "**Ius Administrationis Decretum**" shall be the collection of Administrative Rights to issue Decree, Judgement and Edict, as inherited from the collection of Official Rights *Ius Publicum Decretum*.

28. The following valid thirty-three (33) Instrumental Administrative Rights (*Instrumentalis Administrationis Iurium*) shall be recognised in accord with the present sacred Covenant:-

Instrumental Administrative Rights (Instrumentalis Administrationis Iurium)

(i) "**Ius Administrationis Iuris**" shall be the collection of Administrative Rights to Justice and Due Process, as inherited from the collection of Sovereign Rights *Ius Regnum Iuris*; and

(ii) "**Ius Administrationis Bona Fidei**" shall be the collection of Administrative Rights of Good Faith, Good Conscience and Good Actions, as inherited from the collection of Sovereign Rights *Ius Regnum Bona Fidei*; and

(iii) "**Ius Administrationis Aequum**" shall be the collection of Administrative Rights of Equality and Fairness, as inherited from the collection of Sovereign Rights *Ius Regnum Credito*; and

(iv) "**Ius Administrationis Fidei**" shall be the collection of Administrative Rights of Superior Trust and Estate, as inherited from the collection of Sovereign Rights *Ius Regnum Fidei*; and

(v) "**Ius Administrationis Rationatio**" shall be the collection of Administrative Rights of Accounting, Credit and Funds, as inherited from the collection of Sovereign Rights *Ius Regnum Rationatio*; and

(vi) "**Ius Administrationis Concedere et Abrogare**" shall be the collection of Administrative Rights to Give or Grant Rights and Annul or rescind Superior Rights, as inherited from the collection of Sovereign Rights *Ius Regnum Concedere et Abrogare*; and

(vii) "**Ius Administrationis Delegare et Revocare**" shall be the collection of Administrative Rights to Assign or Delegate Rights and Cancel or Revoke Superior Rights, as inherited from the collection of Sovereign Rights *Ius Regnum Delegare et Revocare*; and

(viii) "**Ius Administrationis Associatio et Conventio**" shall be the collection of Administrative Rights of Association and Agreement, as inherited from the collection of Sovereign Rights *Ius Regnum Associatio et Conventio*; and

(ix) "**Ius Administrationis Consensum et Non**" shall be the collection of Administrative Rights to Consent and Non-Consent, as inherited from the collection of Sovereign Rights *Ius Regnum Consensum et Non*; and

(x) "**Ius Administrationis Cancellarium**" shall be the collection of Administrative Rights of Chancery and Administrative Records, as inherited from the collection of Sovereign Rights *Ius Regnum Cancellarium*; and

(xi) "**Ius Administrationis Dominionis Eminens**" shall be the collection of Administrative Rights of taking, acquiring, converting and using private property for public use and benefit, as inherited from the collection of Sovereign Rights *Ius Regnum Dominium*; and

(xii) "**Ius Administrationis Possessionis**" shall be the collection of Administrative Rights to Possess, Hold and Own Property, as inherited from the collection of Sovereign Rights *Ius Regnum Possessionis*; and

(xiii) "**Ius Administrationis Usus**" shall be the collection of Administrative Rights of Use and Fruits (Enjoyment) of Use of Property, as inherited from the collection of Sovereign Rights *Ius Regnum Usus*; and

(xiv) "**Ius Administrationis Proprietatis**" shall be the collection of Administrative Rights of Ownership of Use or Fruits of Use of Property, as inherited from the collection of Sovereign Rights *Ius Regnum Proprietatis*; and

(xv) "**Ius Administrationis Vectigalis Proprietatis**" shall be the collection of Administrative Rights to impose Rents, Tolls, Levies, Contributions or Charges against Property, as inherited from the Sovereign Rights *Ius Regnum Vectigalis Proprietatis*; and

(xvi) "**Ius Administrationis Moneta**" shall be the collection of Administrative Rights to Mint, Produce, Hold, Use and Exchange Money, as inherited from the collection of Sovereign Rights *Ius Regnum Moneta*; and

(xvii) "**Ius Administrationis Vectigalis Moneta**" shall be the collection of Administrative Rights to impose Rents, Tolls, Levies, Contributions or Charges against Money, as inherited from the collection of Sovereign Rights *Ius Regnum Vectigalis Moneta*; and

(xviii) "**Ius Administrationis Registrum**" shall be the collection of Administrative Rights to Enter Records within Registers and Rolls, as inherited from the collection of Sovereign Rights *Ius Regnum*

Registrum; and

(xix) "**Ius Administrationis Remedium**" shall be the collection of Administrative Rights of Remedy, Relief, Redress or Compensation, as inherited from the collection of Sovereign Rights *Ius Regnum Remedium*; and

(xx) "**Ius Administrationis Poena**" shall be the collection of Administrative Rights of Relief, Redress or Compensation for Default or Deliquency of Obligation, as inherited from the collection of Sovereign Rights *Ius Regnum Poena*; and

(xxi) "**Ius Administrationis Clementia**" shall be the collection of Administrative Rights of Document, Form or Instrument Suspension, Termination and Dissolution, as inherited from the collection of Sovereign Rights *Ius Regnum Clementia*; and

(xxii) "**Ius Administrationis Actionum**" shall be the collection of Administrative Rights of Action, as inherited from the collection of Sovereign Rights *Ius Regnum Actionum*; and

(xxiii) "**Litterae Administrationis Doctrinae**" shall be the Administrative Letter of Doctrine, as inherited from the Official Right *Iussum Publicum Doctrinae*; and

(xxiv) "**Litterae Administrationis Absolutionis**" shall be the Administrative Letter of Absolution, as inherited from the Official Right *Iussum Publicum Absolutionis*; and

(xxv) "**Litterae Administrationis Damnationis**" shall be the Administrative Letter of Damnation, as inherited from the Official Right *Iussum Publicum Damnationis*; and

(xxvi) "**Litterae Administrationis Exemplificatio**" shall be the Administrative Letter of Exemplification, as inherited from the Official Right *Iussum Publicum Exemplificatio*; and

(xxvii) "**Litterae Administrationis Testimonium**" shall be the Administrative Letter of Proof, as inherited from the Official Right *Iussum Publicum Testimonium*; and

(xxviii) "**Litterae Administrationis Instructionis**" shall be the Administrative Letter of Instruction, as inherited from the Official Right *Iussum Publicum Instructionis*; and

(xxix) "**Litterae Administrationis Censurae**" shall be the Administrative Letter of Censure, as inherited from the Official Right *Iussum Publicum Censurae*; and

(xxx) "**Litterae Administrationis Annullas**" shall be the Administrative Letter of Annulment, as inherited from the Official Right *Iussum Publicum Annullas*; and

(xxxi) "**Litterae Administrationis Ratificationis**" shall be the Administrative Letter of Ratification, as inherited from the Official Right *Iussum Publicum Ratificationis*; and

(xxxii) "**Litterae Administrationis Interdictum**" shall be the Administrative Letter of Interdiction, as inherited from the Official Right *Iussum Publicum Interdictum*; and

(xxxiii) "**Litterae Administrationis Levationis**" shall be the Administrative Letter of Relief, as inherited from the Official Right *Iussum Publicum Levationis*.

29. "**Member Rights**" (***Iurium Membrum***) shall be the sixth sub-class of Superior Rights and the fifth highest possible rights of any aggregate body, society, fraternity, association or company of two or more persons personified in trust. Member Rights (Iurium Membrum)

There exists three (3) categories of thirty-nine (39) Superior Rights within the sub-class of Member Rights, being: Authoritative (11), Legal (22) and Special (6):

(i) "**Authoritative Member Rights**" (*Potentis Membrum Iurium*) shall be Member Rights associated with the essential authoritative powers of members of any valid society; and

(ii) "**Legal Member Rights**" (*Legitimus Membrum Iurium*) shall be Member Rights essential to the proper administration of justice of any valid society; and

(iii) "**Special Member Rights**" (*Proprius Membrum Iurium*) shall be Critical Member Rights in relation to the majority (two-thirds) of all members as "the people", essential to democracy and the restoration of the Golden Rule of Law in the event of corruption, collapse of justice or the rise of tyranny.

30. The following valid eleven (11) Authoritative Member Rights (*Potentis Membrum Iurium*) shall be recognised in accord with the present sacred Covenant:- Authoritative Member Rights (Potentis Membrum Iurium)

(i) "**Ius Membrum Sodalis**" shall be the collection of Member Rights of Equal Membership of Society, as inherited from the Natural Right *Ius Naturale Sodalis*; and

(ii) "**Ius Membrum Nascendi Societas**" shall be the collection of Member Rights to be recognised as a member of the society into which one was borne, as inherited from the Natural Right *Ius Naturale Nascendi Societas*; and

(iii) "**Ius Membrum Votum**" shall be the collection of Member Rights to vote and participate in democratic processes of Society, as inherited from the Natural Right *Ius Naturale Sodalis*; and

(iv) "**Ius Membrum Forum Publicum**" shall be the collection of Member Rights to attend public meetings and forums of Society, as inherited from the Natural Right *Ius Naturale Sodalis*; and

(v) "**Ius Membrum Rationatio**" shall be the collection of Member Rights to receive an accounting of the economic activity, as inherited from the Natural Right *Ius Naturale Rationatio*; and

(vi) "**Ius Membrum Officium**" shall be the collection of Member Rights of office of Society, as inherited from the Natural Right *Ius Naturale Officium*; and

(vii) "**Ius Membrum Registrum**" shall be the collection of Member Rights to Enter Records within Registers and Rolls, as inherited from the Divine Right *Ius Divinum Registrum*; and

(viii) "**Ius Membrum Associatio et Conventio**" shall be the collection of Member Rights of Association and Agreement, as inherited from the Natural Right *Ius Naturale Associatio et Conventio*; and

(ix) "**Ius Membrum Servitia**" shall be the collection of Member Rights to the Services of the Society, as inherited from the Natural Right *Ius Naturale Sodalis*; and

(x) "**Ius Membrum Mercatus**" shall be the collection of Member Rights to the Markets of the Society, as inherited from the Divine Right *Ius Naturale Sodalis*; and

(xi) "**Ius Membrum Commercium**" shall be the collection of Member Rights to Trade, Exchange and engage in Commerce, as inherited from the Natural Right *Ius Naturale Commercium*.

31. The following valid twenty-two (22) Legal Member Rights (*Legitimus Membrum Iurium*) shall be recognised in accord with the present sacred Covenant:-

Legal Member Rights (Legitimus Membrum Iurium)

(i) "**Ius Membrum Iuris**" shall be the collection of Member Rights of Justice and Due Process, as inherited from the collection of Natural Rights *Ius Naturale Iuris*; and

(ii) "**Ius Membrum Aequum**" shall be the collection of Member Rights of Equality and Fairness, as inherited from the collection of Natural Rights *Ius Naturale Aequum*; and

(iii) "**Ius Membrum Bona Fidei**" shall be the collection of Member Rights of Good Faith, Good Conscience and Good Actions, as inherited from the collection of Natural Rights *Ius Naturale Bona Fidei*; and

(iv) "**Ius Membrum Libertatis**" shall be the collection of Member

Rights of Freedom from Bondage and Slavery, as inherited from the collection of Natural Rights *Ius Naturale Libertatis*; and

(v) "**Ius Membrum Actionum**" shall be the collection of Member Rights of Action, as inherited from the collection of Natural Rights *Ius Naturale Actionum*; and

(vi) "**Ius Membrum Significans Laborare**" shall be the collection of Member Rights to Meaningful and Fulfilling Work, as inherited from the collection of Natural Rights *Ius Naturale Significans Laborare*; and

(vii) "**Ius Membrum Salarium Iustum**" shall be the collection of Member Rights to Fair Pay and Compensatio, as inherited from the collection of Natural Rights *Ius Naturale Salarium Iustum*; and

(viii) "**Ius Membrum Laborare et Non**" shall be the collection of Member Rights to Work or refuse to Work, as inherited from the collection of Natural Rights *Ius Naturale Laborare et Non*; and

(ix) "**Ius Membrum Custoditum**" shall be the collection of Member Rights to detain a party associated with a controversy if good cause exists they be a risk of non-appearance or committing further controversies, as inherited from the collection of Natural Rights *Ius Naturale Animalum Custodiae*; and

(x) "**Ius Membrum Accusare**" shall be the collection of Member Rights to accuse another of a transgression, as inherited from the collection of Natural Rights *Ius Naturale Iuris*; and

(xi) "**Ius Membrum Innocentiae**" shall be the collection of Member Rights of Innocence until accusation proven, as inherited from the collection of Natural Rights *Ius Naturale Innocentiae*; and

(xii) "**Ius Membrum Accusationis Cognoscendi**" shall be the collection of Member Rights to know the Full Disclosure and Evidence of any Accusation, as inherited from the collection of Natural Rights *Ius Naturale Accusationis Cognoscendi*; and

(xiii) "**Ius Membrum Defensionis**" shall be the collection of Member Rights to defend against any accusation and accuser, as inherited from the collection of Natural Rights *Ius Naturale Defensionis*; and

(xiv) "**Ius Membrum Eligendi Iudicium**" shall be the collection of Member Rights for a matter to be decided by a jury of peers or a judge in forum of law, as inherited from the collection of Natural Rights *Ius Naturale Defensionis*; and

(xv) "**Ius Membrum Propria Persona**" shall be the collection of Member Rights to defend or accuse as oneself, as inherited from the collection of Natural Rights *Ius Naturale Defensionis*; and

(xvi) "**Ius Membrum Agensas**" shall be the collection of Member Rights to appoint an agent, as inherited from the collection of Personal Rights *Ius Delegare et Revocare*; and

(xvii) "**Ius Membrum Possessionis**" shall be the collection of Member Rights to Possess, Hold and Own Property, as inherited from the collection of Natural Rights *Ius Naturale Possessionis*; and

(xviii) "**Ius Membrum Usus**" shall be the collection of Member Rights of Use and Fruits of Use of Property, as inherited from the collection of Natural Rights *Ius Naturale Usus*; and

(xix) "**Ius Membrum Proprietatis**" shall be the collection of Member Rights of Ownership of Use or Fruits of Use of Property, as inherited from the collection of Natural Rights *Ius Naturale Possessionis* and *Ius Naturale Usus*; and

(xx) "**Ius Membrum Remedium**" shall be the collection of Member Rights of Remedy, Relief, Redress or Compensation, as inherited from the collection of Natural Rights *Ius Naturale Remedium*; and

(xxi) "**Ius Membrum Poena**" shall be the collection of Member Rights of Penalty & Punishment, as inherited from the collection of Natural Rights *Ius Naturale Poena;* and

(xxii) "**Ius Membrum Clementia**" shall be the collection of Member Rights of Mercy & Forgiveness, as inherited from the collection of Natural Rights *Ius Naturale Clementia.*

Special Member Rights (Proprius Membrum Iurium)

32. The following valid six (6) Special Member Rights (*Proprius Membrum Iurium*) shall be recognised in accord with the present sacred Covenant subject to the special and limited conditions of their use.

Special Member Rights may only be invoked when two thirds of total members of a particular society agree by the solidarity and bravery of their mass demonstrations, protests, resistance and verifiable participation in the election of new officials that one or more of these special powers shall be invoked:-

(i) "**Ius Populi Jurisdictio**" shall be the Right of the People to invoke absolute and supreme rights on Earth to form the seven (7) Unions of Africans Union, Americas Union, Arabian Union, Asia Union, Levant Union, Euro Union and Oceanic Union, as inherited from the Divine Right *Ius Divinum Fraternitas*; and

(ii) "**Ius Populi Ecclesia**" shall be the Right of the people to form the new Ecclesiastical and Religious Bodies of One Christ, One Islam and One Spirit, as inherited from the Divine Right *Ius Divinum Ecclesia*; and

(iii) "**Ius Populi Revocare**" shall be the Right of the people to Revoke and Suspend Rights in face of tyranny, injustice and corruption, as inherited from the Divine Right *Ius Divinum Revocare*; and

(iv) "**Ius Populi Decretum**" shall be the Right of the people to issue Decree, Judgement and Edict, in the face of absolute Tyranny, Contempt for the Rule of Law or Justice, as inherited from the Divine Right *Ius Divinum Decretum*; and

(v) "**Ius Populi Imperium**" shall be the Right of the people to Command, Occupation and Enforcement of its orders, in the face of absolute Tyranny, Contempt for the Rule of Law or Justice, as inherited from the Divine Right *Ius Divinum Imperium*; and

(vi) "**Ius Populi Custoditum**" shall be the Right of the people as Custodians and Guardians of Rights and Golden Rule of Law, as inherited from the Divine Right *Ius Divinum Custoditum*.

Article 42 – Inferior Rights

1. **Inferior Rights** shall be the fourth class and the lowest possible form of Rights corresponding to Inferior Trusts, Inferior Estates and Inferior Persons, such as Non-Ucadian Trusts and Non-Ucadian Persons. Inferior Rights owe their existence to non-Ucadian societies, persons, corporations, associations, bodies politic, agencies or aggregates. All Superior Rights are greater than Inferior Rights. Where an Inferior Right makes claim to being superior, it is automatically invalid upon such falsity. There exists two (2) sub-classes (Primary and Secondary) and four (4) categories of Inferior Rights, being: Primary Personal, Primary Public, Secondary Protective and Secondary Remedial: Inferior Rights

(i) A "**Primary Personal Inferior Right**" shall be an Inferior Right associated as a capacity, or privilege, or liberty, or faculty, or power possessed by a certain class of persons or specifically named person, where such claimed rights have been created without necessarily referencing valid rights already existing; and

(ii) A "**Primary Public Inferior Right**" shall be an Inferior Right associated with those rights held by the community in general, or by virtue of relations between members of the community, where such claimed rights have been created without necessarily referencing valid rights already existing; and

(iii) A "**Secondary Protective Inferior Right**" shall be an Inferior Right associated with a Primary Inferior Right that is claimed to exist in order to prevent the infringement or loss of such Primary Inferior Rights; and

(iv) A "**Secondary Remedial Inferior Right**" shall be an Inferior Right associated with a Primary Inferior Right that is claimed to exist in order to obtain restitution for any losses incurred upon one or more breaches of claimed Primary Inferior Rights or the enforcement of performance of one or more Primary Inferior Rights.

Primary Personal Inferior Rights

2. "**Primary Personal Inferior Rights**" shall be Inferior Rights associated as a capacity, or privilege, or liberty, or faculty, or power possessed by a certain class of persons or specifically named person, where such claimed rights have been created without necessarily referencing valid rights already existing.

As such claimed rights (1) fail to provide any valid provenance to valid Divine Rights; and (2) fail to properly articulate their legitimacy and function in relation to other pre-existing claimed inferior rights; and (3) owe their existence to Non-Ucadian societies, persons, corporations, associations, bodies politic, agencies or aggregates; then all such claimed rights are not properly rights, or enforceable rights, but merely claims of right.

Primary Public Inferior Rights

3. "**Primary Public Inferior Rights**" shall be Inferior Rights associated with those rights held by the community in general, or by virtue of relations between members of the community, where such claimed rights have been created without necessarily referencing valid rights already existing.

As such claimed rights (1) fail to provide any valid provenance to valid Divine Rights; and (2) fail to properly articulate their legitimacy and function in relation to other pre-existing claimed inferior rights; and (3) owe their existence to non-Ucadian societies, persons, corporations, associations, bodies politic, agencies or aggregates; then all such claimed rights are not properly rights, or enforceable rights, but merely claims of right.

Secondary Inferior Rights

4. "**Secondary Protective Inferior Rights**" shall be Inferior Rights associated with Primary Inferior Rights where it is claimed they exist in order to prevent the infringement or loss of such Primary Inferior Rights.

"**Secondary Remedial Inferior Rights**" shall be Inferior Rights associated with Primary Inferior Rights where it is claimed they exist in order to obtain restitution for any losses incurred upon one or more breaches of claimed Primary Inferior Rights or the enforcement of performance of one or more Primary Inferior Rights.

As such claimed secondary inferior rights (1) owe their existence and claimed legitimacy to primary inferior rights; and (2) such claimed primary inferior rights are not properly rights, or enforceable rights, but merely claims of right; then all secondary protective inferior rights are *ipso facto* (as a matter of fact) illegitimate, having no proper force or effect under any valid form of law.

Article 43 - Sacred Offices and Officers

1. **Office** shall be a sacred Person as a position and title given life, recognition and personality through the power and authority of Officium in accord with the present sacred Covenant. An Office does not exist, nor possesses any validity or legitimacy unless granted *Officium*. In accord with the present sacred Covenant, there exists only four (4) valid types of Office being: Divine, True, Superior and Inferior: Sacred Offices and Officers

(i) A "**Divine Office**" is an Office whereby a Spiritual Member of One Heaven vows to embody such a unique Office, as a custodian and guardian spirit of the law or "*Nomos*", in accord with the rules and systems of *Officium Systemata* (Offices Systems) of Heaven. Divine Offices may then be defined as either a Supreme Divine Office or a Great Divine Office. A Supreme Divine Office is an office purely occupied and vested to a Spiritual Member as a *Nomos*; whereas a Great Divine Office is an office occupied and vested by both a Spiritual Member as a *Nomos* and a Living Member as an Officer. A Divine Office is formed through its unique identification and definition within the present sacred Covenant, or associated Covenants and Charters. Thus a Divine Office itself can never be dissolved, usurped, seized or surrendered prior to its expiry. It can only be vacated by a Living Member; and

(ii) A "**True Office**" is the instance of the Great Divine Office of Man or the Great Divine Office of Woman as defined by the Divine Creator, whereby each and every Living Member is invested and commissioned from the time of their physical birth until their physical death. Therefore, a True Office can never be usurped, seized, sold or stolen; and

(iii) A "**Superior Office**" is the instance or derivative of a Great Divine Office within a valid Ucadia Community as formed through its identification and definition within an instrument, agreement, covenant or document given existence by law or regulation according to the present sacred Covenant and associated covenants and charters. The performance of one or more Oaths or Vows then formalises the particular office and is sustained so long as such oaths or vows are honoured; and

(iv) An "**Inferior Office**" is a Non-Ucadian office or "Pseudo Office"; and are all Non-Ucadian positions whereby a defective or inferior Oath or Vow has been offered, or no Oath provided or where the fiduciary obligations have been abrogated in favour of agent and commercial advantages. All Non-Ucadian Offices, including all claimed Ecclesiastical Offices are Inferior Offices and "Pseudo Offices".

2. The foundation of all civilised rule of law, begins with the acknowledgement that the highest law comes from the Divine Creator of all things in the Universe expressed through the laws of the Universe and then through the reason and spirit of man and woman to make Positive Laws. Valid Office and Divine Law

An Office is both a form of Person and movable or immovable sacred space whereby certain rights, authorities, capacities and powers are conferred upon one who has pronounced one or more Oaths or Vows and Sacraments and preserved by their continued honour to the fiduciary principles of good faith, good actions and good conscience.

One who holds an Office under such fiduciary capacity is called an Officer. An Agent can never legitimately hold an Office.

As all rights and property are by definition sacred, all clerical and professional obligations and responsibilities in relation to the administration, transference and conveyance of any rights or property must be concluded in a valid Office.

Any and every transaction or claimed transference or conveyance of property or rights must be concluded within the sacred space and place of a valid Office to have ecclesiastical, moral, lawful and legal force and effect.

By definition, the authority, rights and powers of a Divine Office is superior to any and all other forms of Office, regardless of title or claimed status. No Inferior Office possesses any power, force, authority, right or ability to abrogate or usurp the decisions or authority of a Divine Office.

Similarly, no Superior Office or Inferior Office possesses any force, authority, right or ability to abrogate or usurp the authority of a True Office to exercise any of the Natural Rights granted to it, unless the occupant of a True Office wilfully and deliberately repudiates the Golden Rule of Law and all forms of logic, reason and sense.

All valid official positions or "offices" of all legitimate governments of all societies within the jurisdiction of the present sacred Covenant therefore depend on the acknowledgement and recognition of the present Covenant as the highest law as the Covenant is nothing less than the perfect expression of Divine Will from the Divine Creator of all things in the Universe.

Furthermore, as the very meaning and purpose of the word "authority" is ecclesiastical, all legitimate authority of all officials of all valid governments of all societies on planet Earth depends upon the acknowledgement and recognition that all authority is ultimately derived from the present sacred Covenant as the highest source of authority being the perfect expression of Divine Law of the Divine Creator of all things in the Universe.

3. All power and authority as vested in any and every form of Office, Commission, Agency, or other position of Trust shall be vested in one supreme spiritual body and system known as the *Supremum Officium Systemata*, also known as Supreme Offices Systems of Heaven.

Officium Systemata (Offices Systems)

The *Supremum Officium Systemata* shall be the highest authority and power as the source of all valid Offices, Commissions, Agency, Powers, Authorities and other positions of Trust and no other.

The *Supremum Officium Systemata* is uniquely recognised, registered and exemplified as having existence through the Great Register and Public Record of Heaven by the Sacred [Trust No. 999999-555555-999999].

The existence, identity, authority, purpose and powers of the *Supremum Officium Systemata* have been duly published in the Ucadia Gazette being the Official Newspaper of Record for each and every Sacred Space-Day-Time of its existence and operation.

4. There are sixteen (16) essential types of valid Office for the conduct and conclusion of sacred, clerical and professional obligations and responsibilities being: Sanctuary, Oratory, Consistory, Sacristry, Penitentiary, Chancery, Depository, Dispensary, Treasury, Ministry, Registry, Library, Notary, Secretary, Vestry and Rectory:-

Types of valid Sacred Space of Office

(i) A "**Sanctuary**" is any temporary or permanent sacred space (dimension) circumscribed by the performance of one or more valid Sacraments of Heaven. All valid sacred space (dimension) as an Office is first and foremost a Sanctuary; and

(ii) An "**Oratory**" is any valid Office that exists for the auricular exposition, discussion, relation, examination, disposition and conclusion of matters derived from Divine Law, Ecclesiastical Law and Positive Law and from which all other Offices in which the spoken word of Men and Women is translated to writing or vice versa is derived; and

(iii) A "**Consistory**" is any valid Office that exists for a solemn and sacred assembly or council or other democratic or representative body; and

(iv) A "**Sacristy**" is any valid Office that exists for the receiving and safe keeping of most sacred vessels, books, vestments and may also be used by clergy as valid Trustees for worship or meetings; and

(v) A "**Penitentiary**" is any valid Office that exists for the receiving and safe keeping of sacred vows, confessions, absolutions, dispensations and examinations of conscience and may also be used by clergy as valid Trustees for providing sanctuary and sustenance to penitents confessed; and

(vi) A "**Chancery**" (also Chancellery) is any valid Office that exists for the receiving and safe keeping of all original instruments, registers, memoranda, forms and rolls and for the original creation of new forms and instruments by valid Trustees as Scriveners as well as the provision of certified and valid extracts of original instruments and records; and

(vii) A "**Depository**" is any valid Office that exists for the purpose of receiving the temporary assignment of goods and property for safe keeping, or security, or bailment or warehousing upon the issue of receipts and to be returned upon expiry of such conditions; and

(viii) A "**Dispensary**" is any valid Office that exists for the purpose of dispensing, or settling, or resolving, or exchanging, or measuring, or paying, or issuing or trading property, goods or rights; and

(ix) A "**Treasury**" is any valid Office that exists for the purpose of receiving and keeping safe any and all property that has been salvaged or claimed or surrendered upon being abandoned, lost (presumed dead), incapacitated, infirm or intestate; and

(x) A "**Ministry**" is any valid Office that exists for conducting sacred, clerical and professional obligations and responsibilities and the dispensation and determination of questions of rights and property; and

(xi) A "**Registry**" is a valid Office that exists for the recording of entries, enrolments and events into Books, Registers, Rolls,

Memoranda, Accounts and Manifests and the subsequent issue of Certificates, or Receipts as well as the administrative management of Journals, Ledgers and Summaries; and

(xii) A "**Library**" is a valid Office that exists for the recording, entry, safe keeping of copies and acknowledgement and evidence of service and publication of all official Notices, Books, Gazettes, Newspapers, References, Periodicals as well as Audio Visual Material as well as other claimed works of copyright; and

(xiii) A "**Notary**" is a valid Office that exists for the purpose of recording, entry, safe keeping of copies and acknowledgement and evidence of service of official Notices as well as the safe keeping and custody "in due course" of all "public" originals and proofs of any surrender, gift, waiver, abandonment, resignation, novation of property or rights by the Trustor through Deed or Act such as wills, affidavits, land and property conveyances; and

(xiv) A "**Secretary**" is a valid Office that exists for the purpose of the private recording, entry, safe keeping of copies and acknowledgement and evidence of service of Official Notices, Claims and Rights and the "secret surrender" and "passing" of such private material to other parties as required or demanded; and

(xv) A "**Vestry**" is a valid Office that exists for the purpose of recording and keeping safe the essential records of a Parish or Parochial body for proper spiritual administration of members, otherwise referred to as the "Cure of Souls"; and

(xvi) A "**Rectory**" is a valid Office that exists for providing teaching and instruction to students.

5. In accord with the present sacred Covenant being the highest rule of law concerning the valid appointment and function of Office, every and all valid appointments, commissions, inaugurations or investitures to Office must comply with the rites and sacred gifts of One Heaven. Appointment to Office

The rites and sacred gifts of One Heaven, when properly granted and conferred, is the only way whereby valid possessory or prescriptive rights of Office are granted and bestowed to an incumbent, including taking possession of the insignia of Office and the power of *Officium* in accordance with this Covenant and associated approved liturgy.

All Level 6 Higher Order Beings that have never carnated in flesh, who occupy an office legitimately must do so under documented proof one or more oaths of office whereby they acknowledge the supremacy of Heaven, agree to be bound to honour and upholding the Rule of Law and finally to impartially, fairly and equally serve the interests of their community or Society or Members.

All Members who are granted the same Office are equal to the same Office, with none higher and none lower. By the present Article, when one of the same Office speaks as one, the one speaks for all of the same Office. When one of the same Office calls for assistance, all from the same Office are obliged to assist their fellow Officer and when the highest good standing of an Officer is injured, all Officers and the Divine Law and all Law has been injured by such disrespect.

Only one from the same Office can appoint another to the same Office, subject to the same sacred Bond of Nomination to Office for all Offices of One Heaven. If one of the same Office of One Heaven is found to be in disgrace, then the Officer who nominated them must resign all commissions.

Twelve Supreme Divine Offices of One Heaven

6. By the Power and Authority of the present most sacred Covenant, twelve (12) Offices are identified as the Supreme Divine Offices of One Heaven, to be held by purely Spiritual Members:

(i) Apostle; and

(ii) Consul; and

(iii) Augustus; and

(iv) Angel; and

(v) Saint; and

(vi) Wraith; and

(vii) Fate; and

(viii) Demon; and

(ix) Faerie; and

(x) Elve; and

(xi) Seraphim; and

(xii) Cherubim.

Four hundred and thirty-two Great Divine Offices of One Heaven

7. By the Power and Authority of the present most sacred Covenant, four hundred and thirty-two (432) most sacred and ancient official positions are recognised as the Great Divine Offices of One Heaven whereby a Spiritual Member as a "*Nomos*" and a Living Member as an "Officer" may hold, possess and be invested into a sacred office, namely:

(i) One Divine Office of Existence, being: I AM; and

(ii) True Offices of Man and Woman, being: Man and Woman; and

(iii) Seventeen (17) Superior Offices of Trust, being: Obligor, Obligee, Trustor, Trustee, Principal, Agent, Beneficiary, Executor, Administrator, Grantor, Grantee, Donor, Donee, Assignor, Assignee, Delegator and Delegatee; and

(iv) Eleven (11) Superior Offices of Life, being: Corporeal, Nasci, Creator, Explorer, Thinker, Solver, Guider, Philosopher, Exemplar, Eternal and Spirit; and

(v) Nineteen (19) Superior Offices of Clan, being: Kin, Son, Daughter, Brother, Sister, Grandson, Granddaughter, Nephew, Niece, Uncle, Aunt, Father, Mother, Grandfather, Grandmother, Male Cousin, Female Cousin, Patriarch and Matriarch; and

(vi) Eighteen (18) Superior Offices of Tribe, being: Initiate, Hunter, Gatherer, Preparer, Toolmaker, Cook, Carver, Weaver, Crafter, Storyteller, Ritualist, Muralist, Herbalist, Carer, Healer, Soothsayer, Senior and Chief; and

(vii) Forty-Eight (48) Superior Offices of Village, being: Habitant, Apothecarist, Artist, Astrologer, Baker, Basketweaver, Blacksmith, Bonecarver, Brewer, Brickmaker, Butcher, Carpenter, Clothmaker, Cobbler, Cooper, Druid, Dyer, Elder, Entertainer, Farmer, Fisher, Fortuneteller, Fowler, Gardener, Herder, Midwife, Miller, Miner, Musician, Painter, Plasterer, Poet, Potter, Quarrier, Reaper, Ruler, Salter, Shaman, Sculptor, Stonemason, Tailor, Tanner, Thatcher, Therapeutae, Trapper, Woodcarver, Woodsman and Yarnmaker; and

(viii) Fourteen (14) Superior Ecclesiastical Offices, being: Noviate, Advocate, Cleric, Celebrant, Imam, Lama, Rabbi, Knight, Bishop, Abbot, Mendicant, Minister, Supervisor and Vicar; and

(ix) One Hundred and Thirty Six (136) Superior Offices of City, being: Academic, Actor, Ambassador, Architect, Armourer, Artificer, Attendant, Auditor, Author, Beekeeper, Bladesmith, Boniface, Bookbinder, Bookkeeper, Bowyer, Brazier, Bricklayer, Brightsmith, Builder, Bursar, Cabinetmaker, Candlemaker, Caretaker, Cartographer, Caulker, Censor, Chamberlain,

Chocolatier, Citizen, Cleaner, Clerk, Clothier, Collier, Constable, Costermonger, Courier, Currier, Cutter, Dancer, Deckhand, Decorator, Director, Docker, Doctor, Draper, Drayman, Dresser, Driver, Drover, Dux, Embalmer, Engineer, Engraver, Explorer, Factor, Farmhand, Farrier, Fellmonger, Ferryhand, Fishmonger, Fletcher, Forester, Fruitier, Fuller, Furrier, General, Glassblower, Grain Merchant, Grocer, Gunsmith, Haymonger, Herald, Hillier, Hind, Historian, Huckster, Innkeeper, Interpreter, Jagger, Jester, Jeweller, Joiner, Judge, Keeler, King, Laborer, Lardner, Lavender, Leatherworker, Legislator, Librarian, Lieutenant, Locksmith, Magistrate, Major, Manciple, Mercer, Merchant, Metallurgist, Minstrel, Moneylender, Monger, Mortician, Musician, Novice, Patternmaker, Performer, Physician, Producer, Professor, Provider, Publisher, Queen, Ranger, Ratcatcher, Refiner, Renderer, Rider, Roper, Saddler, Sailor, Scientist, Scribe, Sergeant, Servant, Soldier, Teacher, Tucker, Turner, Tutor, Wainwright, Warden, Webster, Wheelwright, Whitster and Wright; and

(x) One Hundred and Two (102) Superior Offices of Community, being: Actuary, Apiarist, Arborist, Archivist, Assembler, Astronaut, Auctioneer, Banker, Biologist, Botanist, Cashier, Caterer, Chef, Chemist, Climatologist, Colonel, Composer, Concierge, Concreter, Conservator, Constituent, Criminologist, Decorator, Designer, Detective, Distributor, Diver, Draftsperson, Drainer, Driller, Drycleaner, Earthmover, Economist, Editor, Electrician, Electroplater, Engraver, Environmentalist, Excavator, Fitter, Florist, Gaffer, Gasfitter, Gatekeeper, Geneticist, Geoscientist, Glazier, Groundsperson, Hairdresser, Homeopath, Illustrator, Inspector, Instructor, Inventor, Janitor, Journalist, Laminator, Linguist, Lifeguard, Machinist, Manager, Manufacturer, Marketer, Mathematician, Mechanic, Mediator, Medicalist, Nanny, Nurse, Nutritionist, Paramedic, Pharmacist, Pilot, Plumber, Podiatrist, Printer, Programmer, Publican, Receptionist, Researcher, Robotist, Salesperson, Servicer, Statistician, Surgeon, Surveyor, Teacher, Technician, Teller, Therapist, Tiler, Trainer, Underwriter, Upholsterer, Valuer, Veterinarian, Watchmaker, Webmaster, Welder, Winemaker, Writer and Zookeeper; and

(xi) Twelve (12) Original Offices of the Land (Campus), being: Accountant, Bailiff, Commissioner, Jurist, Notary, Postmaster, Proctor, Reader, Scrivener, Secretary, Sheriff and Steward; and

(xii) Twelve (12) Master Offices of the See (Province), being: Captain, Comptroller, Governor, Justice, Master, Navigator, Procurator, Investigator, Rector, Registrar, Speaker and Treasurer; and

(xiii) Twelve (12) Great Offices of the State (University), being: Chamberlain, Censor, Chancellor, Custodian, Exchequer, Justiciar, Marshal, Dean, Narrator, Plenipotentiary, Prefect and President; and

(xiv) Eight (8) General Offices of the Union, being: Alexander, Basileus, Exarchos, Mediator, Economos, Stratagos, Kephalos and Mentor; and

(xv) Eleven (11) Key Offices of the Globe, being: Canonist, Caliph, Executor-General, Facilitator, Recurrence, Observer, Pope, Secretary-General, Senator, Timekeeper and Visitor; and

(xvi) Nine (9) Forbidden Offices, being: Christ, Cuilliaéan, Emperor, God King, God Queen, Lucifer, Messiah, Pontiff and Prophet.

8. In respect to Divine Offices, True Offices, Superior Offices and Inferior Offices: Dissolution or Cessation of Office

(i) A Divine Office cannot cease to exist, even if a physical and living incumbent fails to adhere to the standards and obligations of such office, or if one or more persons even disavow or seek to diminish or attempt to dissolve such Office; and

(ii) A True Office is dissolved upon the physical death of the incumbent Man or Woman; and

(iii) A Superior Office ceases to exist upon the death of the occupant, or their resignation, or if the occupant deliberately and wilfully breaches their obligations and responsibilities according to the Rule of Trust and fails to remedy within the allotted time, causing a default and then fails to honour and acknowledge their culpability, causing termination; and

(iv) An Inferior Office by definition never possesses legitimate authority or power, but ceases even to be capable of maintaining the impression of legitimacy when an occupant breaches any notion of Rule of Law, or decency, or good faith, or good actions or good conscience.

9. In respect of an Officer, a Superior Office may only be restored: Restoration of Superior Office

(i) After the allotted time and penance determined upon such a disgraced former Trustee and Officer openly and wilfully chooses to admit and confess to their dishonour and culpability of being found culpable; and

(ii) The renewal of sacred Oath and Vow upon expiry of the prescribed time and conditions permitting such a man or woman to once again become a valid Trustee.

10. In accord with the present sacred Covenant and the most ancient Rule of Law, a Member bound to an Office by a valid Sacred Oath and Vow may only continue to occupy, hold and administer such Office if they act in honour to uphold the law. When a Living Member as an Officer dishonourably abuses a position of office, they break their solemn Oath and Vow and therefore render the binding to Office null and void.

Capacity and Competency of Office

When a Living Member continues to claim occupancy of an Office and yet deny their obligations and duties, they automatically excommunicate themselves from any spiritual authority, thereby rendering such acts merely enforceable through ignorance, force or fear.

Furthermore, such a Living Member automatically makes themselves eligible for punitive sanctions enforceable through the *Obligationum Systemata* (Enforcement Systems) of Heaven.

When a Living Member seeks to continue to illegitimately claim Office through the use of ignorance, force and fear, denying their dependency on validity from the Divine Creator and Divine Law, and causing damage upon the Earth and physical injury causing death upon the bodies of other Living Members, then such a Living Member invokes upon themselves the full force and power of the Wraiths of the *Obligationum Systemata* (Enforcement Systems) of Heaven against their physical presence within the temporal realm of the Universe.

11. A Member of One Heaven who has consented by their actions to a Certificate of Incompetence to be recorded, gazetted and published against them is ineligible to continue in any official capacity in any society whatsoever.

Incompetency and Office

When a Certificate of Incompetence is issued, the occupier of a certain Office is prevented from exercising any associated Power granted by the present sacred Covenant including: Magisterium, Imperium, Sacrum, Cancellarium, Virtus, Custoditum, Alumentum or Visum.

12. A Member of One Heaven who has consented by their actions to a Certificate of Excommunication to be recorded, gazetted and published against them is without any legitimate authority to hold

Apostasy and Office

office as a heretic and apostate.

13. Nine (9) Great Divine Offices recognised and honoured as part of the four hundred and thirty-two (432) Great Offices of One Heaven shall be forbidden to be used, or for any man or woman or spirit to assume the occupation of such Office for the whole life of the present sacred Covenant and all associated bodies, societies and entities. These Offices include the Offices of Christ, Anti-Christ, Cuilliaéan, Emperor, God King, God Queen, Lucifer, Messiah and Saviour. Forbidden Offices

Therefore, any man or woman or spirit that proclaims themselves the occupant or holder of any such forbidden Sacred Office henceforth shall commit a grave injury against all of Heaven and Earth and any such claim or subsequent act shall be without validity or authority.

Article 44 - Supreme Sacred Gifts of Heaven

1. **Supreme Sacred Gifts of Heaven** are a vital and necessary element of a fulfilled and purposeful life, assisting each and every higher order being, living and deceased to reach their full potential and communion with the Divine Creator, the Universe and with one another. Supreme Sacred Gifts of Heaven

2. The "**Supreme Sacred Gifts of Heaven**" are a manifest symbol of the plenary authority of the Society and the present supreme sacred Covenant. No other person, aggregate, entity, society, church or group may claim the right to administer any valid sacrament unless it is in accordance with the present sacred Covenant. Sacraments and present Covenant

All valid sacred gifts, rites and rules are instituted by the Divine Creator and entrusted to the Society of One Heaven. Any claimed sacred gift that is not granted through the authority of One Heaven in accordance with the present most sacred Covenant shall be a false ritual and possesses no Divine authority or power to be known as a valid sacred gift.

3. Self-Aware Higher Order Life, such as Human Beings, are spiritual beings as much as they are temporal and physical beings; and that our existence does not end with the physical death of our body; and that our purpose of being does not rest solely upon the experiences, wants or desires of everyday life. Spiritual Nature of Self-Aware Higher Order Life

4. A valid and authentic Sacred Rite is a distinct and related set of Temporal and Divine Actions forming a significant moment of unity:- Nature of Valid and Authentic Sacred Rite

    (i) Temporal Actions as a *rite* or *rites*, following in a precise manner according to a set *formula*, some intended sacred memorial, instrument or event (or all of these elements); and

(ii) Divine Actions derived from the Love, Mercy and Grace of the Divine Creator through authentic revelation, in harmony with right intentioned Temporal Actions.

5. All valid Sacred Rites are those said to be derived from Heaven and the Divine Creator through authentic Revelation. Valid sacraments are never formed by temporal beings alone; and certainly never genuinely formed by doctrine, but by the Revelation and the inspired instruction of the present sacred Covenant. Source of valid Sacred Rites

6. All valid Sacred Gifts of Heaven owe their name according to the Divine Actions and Gifts associated with them and not by the Temporal Actions that may be associated. Thus Temporal Actions associated with a valid sacred gift are more appropriately classified as a customary *rite* or *rites*. Name of valid Sacred Rites

7. The present most sacred Covenant reveals to all Self-Aware Higher Order Life of all times and places that it is our ultimate destiny to be reconciled unto our ultimate Divine Creator - through care of our spiritual well being as much as our mental and physical well being. Divine Purpose of Sacred Gifts and Rites

Moreover, that despite any weaknesses or transgressions, no one be condemned or eternally cursed; as all are granted the gifts of Divine Love, Divine Mercy and Divine Forgiveness. Furthermore, that our Divine Creator entrusts the necessary gifts to nourish and protect our spiritual well being on our journey.

The *Supreme Sacred Gifts of Heaven* are not merely an expression of a particular faith, but an essential element of existence itself. For without such Divine Grace, it follows that because of our human limitations it would be impossible to be reconciled to the Divine by our own accord; or united with our Divine self by prayer and piety alone; or fully at peace with one another purely upon a virtuous and exemplary life.

8. The Thirty-Three (33) valid *Supreme Sacred Gifts of Heaven* are authentically deposited in trust by the Divine Creator to the Society of One Heaven in accord with the *Authentic Sacred Deposit of Trust*. Thirty-Three Valid Supreme Sacred Gifts of Heaven

All valid sacred rites, also known as rituals, customs and acts are derived from the thirty-three (33) valid sacraments of One Heaven. A valid ritual, custom or act derived from one of the thirty-three (33) valid sacraments and expressed ecclesiastically may be said to be on the "ecclesiastical side" of the law.

All valid administrative writs, processes and acts are derived from the thirty-three (33) valid sacraments of One Heaven. A valid writ, process or act derived from one of the thirty-three (33) valid sacraments and expressed civilly may be said to be on the "public side" of the law. All valid Sacraments share the same six (6) essential elements, being:-

(i) A defined structure in liturgy of three (3) separate and deliberate Acts, themselves divided into smaller Parts representing completed Moments being sacred instances of units of time-space-location; and

(ii) An Ordinary and Extraordinary version of the sacrament distinguished by a shorter secular and more formal ecclesiastical version of the sacrament; and

(iii) One or more roles for authorised persons known as Celebrant(s) officiating some or all of the Acts; and

(iv) One or more roles for persons known as Participant(s) who participate under the guidance of the Celebrant(s) in some or all of the Acts; and

(v) One or more roles for persons known as Observant(s) who witness the celebration of the Sacrament and validate it as a Sacred Event; and

(vi) The memorialisation of the celebration of the Sacrament as a Sacred Event through some produced instrument representing a Record of the (Sacred) Event.

Conferral of Valid Sacred Gifts

9. A Sacred Gift not properly conferred in accord with the present sacred Covenant has no effect of law and is invalid *ab initio* (from the beginning). Only authorised persons may validly confer a Sacrament of Heaven properly through the role of Celebrant, possessing the Right *Ius Divinum Sacramentum* as the Divine Right to grant and impart Holy Sacraments:-

(i) Only persons properly ordained as a Minister or invested into office holding the Right of *Ius Divinum Magisterium* or *Ius Divinum Visum* or *Ius Divinum Oratorium* in accord with the present sacred Covenant possesses the powers and authority to confer and administer these sacraments under Extraordinary Conditions; and

(ii) Only persons properly invested into office holding the Right of *Ius Divinum Administratum*, *Ius Divinum Officium* or *Ius Divinum Imperium* in accord with the present sacred Covenant possesses the powers and authority to confer and administer these sacraments under Ordinary Conditions; and

(iii) Sacred ministers cannot deny the sacraments to those who seek them at appropriate times, are properly disposed, and are not prohibited by law from receiving them. All ministers, according to their respective ecclesiastical function, have the duty to take care that those who seek the sacraments are prepared to receive them by proper instruction, attentive to the norms issued by competent authority; and

(iv) In celebrating the sacraments by extraordinary condition, the liturgical books approved by competent authority are to be observed faithfully; accordingly, no one is to add, omit, or alter anything in them on one's own authority. In celebrating the sacraments by ordinary condition, only those things required for the validity of the sacrament must be observed; and

(v) The minister is to seek nothing for the administration of the sacraments beyond the offerings defined by competent authority, always taking care that the needy are not deprived of the assistance of the sacraments because of poverty.

Great Faiths and Sacred Gifts

10. In accord with the present most sacred Covenant, each of the three (3) Great Faiths shall be permitted to use their own official name for the *Supreme Sacred Gifts of Heaven*:-

(i) The Universal Ecclesia of One Christ may use the name "**Summa Sacramenta**" to officially define the Supreme Sacred Gifts of Heaven from the perspective of their authority; and

(ii) The Holy Society of One Islam may use the name "**Hadaya Muqaddas**" to officially define the Supreme Sacred Gifts of Heaven from the perspective of their authority; and

(iii) Sacred Society of One Spirit may use the name "**Yajna Dana**" to officially define the Supreme Sacred Gifts of Heaven from the perspective of their authority.

Key Sacraments (The Keys)

11. The "**Key Sacraments**", also known as the "Key Sacred Gifts" and also known as "The Keys", are seven (7) of the thirty-three (33) sacred rites of the supremely sacred Covenant Pactum De Singularis Caelum instituted by the Divine Creator and entrusted to the Society of One Heaven and all associated valid entities being: Recognition, Purification, Invocation, Obligation, Delegation, Satisfaction and Resolution.

The Key Sacraments are a manifest symbol of the plenary authority of the Society and the present sacred Covenant *Pactum De Singularis Caelum*, exemplified by the expression *potestas clavium* or simply the "Power of the Keys".

Since the Key Sacred Gifts are the same for every occasion and every Homo Sapien, living or deceased, it is only for the supreme authority of the Society of One Heaven to approve or define the requirements for their validity and what pertains to their licit celebration, administration, and reception and to the order to be observed in their celebration:-

(i) "**Ritus Sacramentum Recognosco**" shall be the Divine Right of the Key Sacrament of Recognition; and

(ii) "**Ritus Sacramentum Purificatio**" shall be the Divine Right of the Key Sacrament of Purification; and

(iii) "**Ritus Sacramentum Invocatio**" shall be the Divine Right of the Key Sacrament of Invocation; and

(iv) "**Ritus Sacramentum Obligatio**" shall be the Divine Right of the Key Sacrament of Obligation; and

(v) "**Ritus Sacramentum Delegatio**" shall be the Divine Right of the Key Sacrament of Delegation (Trust); and

(vi) "**Ritus Sacramentum Satisfactio**" shall be the Divine Right of the Key Sacrament of Satisfaction; and

(vii) "**Ritus Sacramentum Resolutio**" shall be the Divine Right of the Key Sacrament of Resolution.

12. The "**Foundational Sacraments**", also known as the "Foundational Sacred Gifts" and also known as "The Ways", are fourteen (14) of the thirty-three (33) sacred rites of the supremely sacred Covenant Pactum De Singularis Caelum instituted by the Divine Creator and entrusted to the Society of One Heaven and all associated valid entities being: Sanctification, Sustentation, Unification (Matrimony), Amalgamation (Union), Authentication, Absolution, Volition (Oath), Vocation (Vow), Testification, Compassion (Mercy), Conscription (Binding), Convocation, Authorisation and Elucidation (Enlightenment).

Foundational Sacraments (The Ways)

As ways, points, junctures and hinges for the actions of the Divine Creator and One Heaven, the Foundational Sacraments are signs and gifts which express and strengthen the society and effect the sanctification of a community and thus contribute in the greatest way to establish, strengthen, and manifest spiritual unity.

Since the Foundational Sacraments are the same for every valid religion and Society, it is only for the supreme authority of the Society of One Heaven to approve or define the requirements for their validity and what pertains to their licit celebration, administration, and reception and to the order to be observed in their celebration:-

(i) "**Ritus Sacramentum Sanctificatio**" shall be the Divine Right of the Foundational Sacrament of Sanctification; and

(ii) "**Ritus Sacramentum Sustentatio**" shall be the Divine Right of the Foundational Sacrament of Sustentation; and

(iii) "**Ritus Sacramentum Unificatio**" shall be the Divine Right of the Foundational Sacrament of Unification (Matrimony); and

(iv) "**Ritus Sacramentum Amalgamatio**" shall be the Divine Right of the Foundational Sacrament of Amalgamation (Union); and

(v) "**Ritus Sacramentum Authentico**" shall be the Divine Right of the Foundational Sacrament of Authentication (Record); and

(vi) "**Ritus Sacramentum Absolutio**" shall be the Divine Right of the Foundational Sacrament of Absolution (Penance); and

(vii) "**Ritus Sacramentum Volitio**" shall be the Divine Right of the Foundational Sacrament of Volition (Oath); and

(viii) "**Ritus Sacramentum Vocatio**" shall be the Divine Right of the Foundational Sacrament of Vocation (Vow); and

(ix) "**Ritus Sacramentum Testificatio**" shall be the Divine Right of the Foundational Sacrament of Testification; and

(x) "**Ritus Sacramentum Compassio**" shall be the Divine Right of the Foundational Sacrament of Compassion (Mercy); and

(xi) "**Ritus Sacramentum Conscripto**" shall be the Divine Right of the Foundational Sacrament of Conscription (Binding); and

(xii) "**Ritus Sacramentum Convocatio**" shall be the Divine Right of the Foundational Sacrament of Convocation; and

(xiii) "**Ritus Sacramentum Auctoriso**" shall be the Divine Right of the Foundational Sacrament of Authorisation; and

(xiv) "**Ritus Sacramentum Elucidato**" shall be the Divine Right of the Foundational Sacrament of Elucidation (Enlightenment).

Authentic Life Sacraments (The Means)

13. The "**Authentic Life Sacraments**", also known as the "Authentic Sacred Gifts" and also known as "The Means", are the twelve (12) of the thirty-three (33) sacred rites of the supremely sacred Covenant Pactum De Singularis Caelum instituted by the Divine Creator and entrusted to the Society of One Heaven and all associated valid entities being: Inspiration, Resurrection, Incarnation, Confirmation, Illumination, Exultation, Glorification, Divination, Visitation, Salvation, Emancipation and Veneration.

All members of One Heaven are entitled to receive the full benefits of all twelve (12) Life Sacraments, whether living or deceased either upon the anniversaries prescribed for the conferral of a sacrament or upon proof majority and competency for the specific Life Sacraments of Epinoia, Genius, Beau Ideal and Haga Sofia.

A member who has not first received the prior Life Sacrament, cannot be admitted validly to receiving the subsequent sacrament.

As actions of the Divine Creator and One Heaven the Life Sacraments are signs and means which express and strengthen the faith, render worship to the Divine and effect the sanctification of humanity and thus contribute in the greatest way to establish, strengthen, and manifest ecclesiastical unity.

Accordingly, in the celebration of the sacraments the sacred ministers and the other members of the faithful must use the greatest veneration and necessary diligence:-

(i) "**Ritus Sacramentum Inspiratio**" shall be the Divine Right of the Authentic Life Sacrament of Inspiration (Annunciation); and

(ii) "**Ritus Sacramentum Resurrectio**" shall be the Divine Right of the Authentic Life Sacrament of Resurrection (Baptism); and

(iii) "**Ritus Sacramentum Incarnatio**" shall be the Divine Right of the Authentic Life Sacrament of Incarnation (Christening); and

(iv) "**Ritus Sacramentum Confirmatio**" shall be the Divine Right of the Authentic Life Sacrament of Confirmation (First Communion); and

(v) "**Ritus Sacramentum Illuminatio**" shall be the Divine Right of the Authentic Life Sacrament of Illumination; and

(vi) "**Ritus Sacramentum Exultatio**" shall be the Divine Right of the Authentic Life Sacrament of Exultation; and

(vii) "**Ritus Sacramentum Glorificatio**" shall be the Divine Right of the Authentic Life Sacrament of Glorification; and

(viii) "**Ritus Sacramentum Divinatio**" shall be the Divine Right of the Authentic Life Sacrament of Divination; and

(ix) "**Ritus Sacramentum Visitatio**" shall be the Divine Right of the Authentic Life Sacrament of Visitation; and

(x) "**Ritus Sacramentum Salvatio**" shall be the Divine Right of the Authentic Life Sacrament of Salvation; and

(xi) "**Ritus Sacramentum Emancipatio**" shall be the Divine Right of the Authentic Life Sacrament of Emancipation (Unbinding) of any and all debts and obligations and reverence of funerary celebrations; and

(xii) "**Ritus Sacramentum Veneratio**" shall be the Divine Right of the Authentic Life Sacrament of Veneration.

Article 45 – Sacred Measurement & Location

1. **All Physical and Theoretical Dimension** is a manifestation of the Divine Creator of all Concepts and Objects subject to the rules of law defined in accord with Natural Law and all the Maxims of *Astrum Iuris Divini Canonum*. All Measurement, methods of calculation, categorisation, survey and description are subject to the Maxims of Divine Law, Natural Law, Cognitive Law and Positive Laws as defined in accord with the *Divine Collection of Maxims of Law*. Sacred Measurement and Location

All Locations, including but not limited to their description, unique naming and coordinates are subject to the Cadastre Systems and other systems of UCADIA in accord with the *Divine Collection of Maxims of Law*.

2. Let it be known to all that as all Dimension is a manifestation of the Divine Creator of all Existence and as the present most sacred Covenant represents the perfection of Divine Intention, there exists no greater or superior constructs, models, illusions, realities, mythologies, possibilities, universes or architectures of Dimension than UCADIA Dimension. UCADIA Dimension as Superior

As UCADIA Dimension is superior to any and all other forms, all lesser forms are subject to UCADIA Dimension and the rules of such dimension as defined by the Maxims of law of the *Divine Collection of Maxims of Law*.

Furthermore, let it be known that such inferior and corrupted forms of reality and dimension such as Mundi in all its carnations is hereby dissolved, reprobate and not permitted to be revived.

3. Let it be known to all that as UCADIA Dimension is superior to all lesser forms of dimension and constructs, UCADIA Cadastre and UCADIA Cadastre and Location

Location Systems are superior and above any and all lesser land and location systems. Therefore, all other land systems, location systems and cadastre systems are subject to the UCADIA systems.

Systems Superior

Furthermore, let it be known that all such inferior and corrupted forms of land, location and Cadastre systems on planet Earth are hereby placed under the sole control of valid UCADIA societies who may then choose to integrate or abolish such inferior systems at such a time and place as best serves the interests of the Members of the UCADIA Society.

UCADIA Cadastre and Location

4. All Cadastre and Location data on planet Earth shall be divided into ten tiers:-

(i) 1st Tier (Top) shall be the highest tier in accord with the present sacred Covenant; and

(ii) 2nd Tier (Global) shall be the second highest tier in accord with the covenants of the three (3) faiths and Global Union Charter; and

(iii) 3rd Tier (Unions) shall be the third highest tier defined by the specific Ucadia Union charters; and

(iv) 4th Tier (Universities) shall be defined by the University Constitutions and Land Registers; and

(v) 5th Tier (Provinces) shall be defined by the Provincial Constitutions and Land Registers; and

(vi) 6th Tier (Campuses) shall be defined by the Campus Constitutions and Land Registers; and

(vii) 7th Tier (Locality) shall be defined by the Village, Town and City; and

(viii) 8th Tier (Sub Division) shall be defined by the survey and plans for Sub Divisions and Sections; and

(ix) 9thTier (Parcel/Plan/Plat) shall be defined by the survey and plans for Parcels, Plans or Plats; and

(x) 10th Tier (Lot) shall be defined by the individual surveys of Lots.

Standard Numeric Scale (Short Scale)

5. All notation of numbers as it pertains to Sacred Circumscribed Space may use the *Standard Numeric Scale*, also known as the Short Scale and Scientific Notation:-

(i) The number *One* may be expressed by the numeric value of 1 and may be expressed in scientific notation as 10^0; and

(ii) The number *Ten* may be expressed by the numeric value of 10; and may be defined by the prefix *Deca*; and may be expressed in scientific notation as 10^1; and

(iii) The number *Hundred* may be expressed by the numeric value of 100; and may be defined by the prefix *Hecto*; and may be expressed in scientific notation as 10^2; and

(iv) The number *Thousand* may be expressed by the numeric value of 1,000; and may be defined by the prefix *Kilo*; and may be expressed in scientific notation as 10^3; and

(v) The number *Million* may be expressed by the numeric value of 1,000,000; and may be defined by the prefix *Mega*; and may be expressed in scientific notation as 10^6; and

(vi) The number *Billion* may be expressed by the numeric value of 1,000,000,000; and may be defined by the prefix *Giga*; and may be expressed in scientific notation as 10^9; and

(vii) The number *Trillion* may be expressed by the numeric value of 1,000,000,000,000; and may be defined by the prefix *Tera*; and may be expressed in scientific notation as 10^{12}; and

(viii) The number *Quadrillion* may be expressed by the numeric value of 1,000,000,000,000,000; and may be defined by the prefix *Peta*; and may be expressed in scientific notation as 10^{15}; and

(ix) The number *Quintillion* may be expressed by the numeric value of 1,000,000,000,000,000,000; and may be defined by the prefix *Exa*; and may be expressed in scientific notation as 10^{18}.

Sacred Lengths (Dista)

6. All measure of length and distance as it pertains to Sacred Circumscribed Space shall be according to the units of *Dista*:-

(i) "**Dista**" (*d*) shall be equal to a toe, or claw, or talon (of a bird) and three (3 cm) centimetres; and

(ii) "**Hand**" *(h)*, also known as *Lamb*, shall be equal to four (4 *d*) *Dista* or twelve (12 cm) centimetres; and

(iii) "**Cubit**" *(c)*, as the sacred measure of life and being, is equal to four *Hands*, or sixteen (16 *d*) *Dista* or forty eight (48 cm) centimetres; and

(iv) "**Fathom**" shall be equal to two (2 *c*) *Cubits*, or eight (8 *h*) *Hands*, or thirty two (32 *d*) *Dista* or ninety six (96 cm) centimetres; and

(v) "**Rod**" *(r)* shall be equal to two *Fathoms*, or four (4 *c*) *Cubits,* or sixteen Hands, or sixty four (64 *d*) *Dista* or one hundred and ninety two (192 cm) centimetres; and

(vi) "**Stade**" shall be equal to sixty (60 *r*) *Rods* or two hundred and forty (240 *c*) *Cubits* or three thousand eight hundred and forty (3,840 d) Dista or eleven thousand five hundred and twenty (11,520) centimetres; and

(vii) "**Mile**" shall be equal to one hundred and forty-four (144) *Stade*, or eight thousand six hundred and forty (8,640 *r*) *Rods*, or thirty four thousand five hundred and sixty (34,560 *c*) *Cubits*, or five hundred and fifty two thousand nine hundred and sixty (552,960 d) *Dista* or one million six hundred and fifty eight thousand eight hundred and eighty (1,658,880 cm) centimetres; and

(viii) "**League**" shall be equal to three *Miles* or four hundred and thirty two (432) *Stades*.

7. All measure of area as it pertains to physical Sacred Circumscribed Space shall be according to the units of *Unita*:- Sacred Circumscribed Space (Unita)

(i) "**Unita**" shall be equal to the smallest possible Sacred Circumscribed Space in existence being 1 Square Cubit (being 1 Cubit by 1 Cubit in area); and

(ii) "**Piece**" shall be equal to 1 square *Unita* being 2 Cubit by 2 Cubit in area, or 0.92 sq metres; and

(iii) "**Square**" (sq) shall be equal to 1 square *Rod*, being four *Pieces* in area, or 3.68 sq metres; and

(iv) "**Cell**" shall be equal to two *Squares* or eight *Pieces* in area, or 7.37 sq metres; and

(v) "**Sanctuary**" shall be equal to nine *Squares* or thirty six *Pieces* in area, or 33.1776 sq metres; and

(vi) "**Plot**" shall be equal to thirty-six *Rods* in length and six *Rods* in width, equal to two hundred and sixteen *Squares* or three thousand four hundred and fifty six (3,456) *Pieces*; and

(vii) "**Acre**" shall be equal to thirty-six *Rods* in length and thirty-six *Rods* in width, equal to twelve hundred and ninety six (1,296) *Squares* or twenty thousand seven hundred and thirty six (20,736) *Pieces* in area or 4,777.57 sq metres.

8. All measure of frequency as it pertains to Sacred Circumscribed Space shall be according to the units of *Cycles*:- Sacred Frequency (Cycle)

(i) "**Cycle**" (*Cs*) shall be equal to one cycle per second and is equivalent to the notion of Hertz (Hz); and

(ii) *A0* shall be equal to 27 Cycles; and

(iii) *A1* shall be equal to 54 Cycles; and

(iv) *A2* shall be equal to 108 Cycles; and

(v) *A3* shall be equal to 216 Cycles; and

(vi) *A4* shall be equal to 432 Cycles. All music and tuning in any and all venues and sacred places within the jurisdiction of Ucadia must be tuned to 432 Cycles and not to deliberately dissonant cycles such as 440 Hz or 444 Hz; and

(vii) *A5* shall be equal to 864 Cycles; and

(viii) *A6* shall be equal to 1728 Cycles; and

(ix) *A7* shall be equal to 3456 Cycles.

9. All measure of weight as it pertains to Sacred Circumscribed Space shall be according to the units of *Gravita*:-

Sacred Weight & Measure (Gravita)

(i) "**Gravita**" shall be equal to one grain of grass, wheat or barley; and

(ii) "**Scrupal**" shall be equal to twenty-two *Gravita* or 1.44 grams; and

(iii) "**Dram**", also known as a *Coin*, shall be equal to three *Scrupals* or sixty *Gravita* or 4.32 grams; and

(iv) "**Ounce**" shall be equal to eight *Dram* or twenty four *Scrupals* or four hundred and eight *Gravita* or 34.56 grams; and

(v) "**Pound**" shall be equal to sixteen *Ounces* or one hundred and twenty eight *Drams* or three hundred and eighty four *Scrupals* or seven thousand six hundred and eighty *Gravita* or 552.96 grams; and

(vi) "**Talent**" shall be equal to sixty *Pounds* or nine hundred and sixty *Ounces* or seven thousand six hundred and eighty *Dram* or twenty three thousand and forty *Scrupals* or four hundred and sixty thousand and eight hundred *Gravita* or 33.1776 kilograms.

10. All Sacred Space, Place, Reality, Consciousness, Norm, World, Dimension, Universe and Existence is subject to the complete jurisdiction of the present sacred Covenant and One Heaven.

Sacred Space-Day-Time

This immutable, irrevocable and absolute fact is because all and every possible Sacred Space, Place, Reality, Consciousness, Norm, World,

Dimension, Universe and Existences is part of God and the Divine Creator as the one true Unique Collective Awareness and the singular dream of God and the Divine Creator being the Universe as Ucadia.

In accord with the present sacred Covenant and all associated covenants, charters, constitutions and codes, all and every possible Space, Place, Reality, Consciousness, Norm, World, Dimension, Universe and Existence is sacred as be a part of God and the Divine Creator as the one true Unique Collective Awareness and the singular dream of God and the Divine Creator being the Universe as Ucadia.

Therefore, there exists no such possible concept or reality or consciousness or construct or dimension as "unsacred space" or "unholy space".

Furthermore, all disassociated consciousness, thought, world or existence that rejects the supremacy of the present sacred Covenant, still remains subject to the full jurisdiction of the present sacred Covenant as even the dimensions of insanity, perfidy, tyranny, lunacy and impiety of Mundi is part of the entirety of existence.

11. The highest, authentic, true and official system of chronology and time of united Heaven upon planet Earth shall be the Sacred Ucadia Time System, also known as the Sacred Ucadia Chronology. Ucadia Time System

No other system, method of calculating time may claim higher authority than the Sacred Ucadia Time System, as the official chronology and time system of Heaven upon the Earth:-

(i) The first part of the Ucadia Time System shall be the calculation of Era, signifying one eighth (1/8th) of a complete cycle of the twenty-five thousand six hundred and eighty (25,680) Sun Year cycles known as a Precession of the Equinoxes or "Precession", representing a natural cycle of orbital shift of the Earth axis. An Era is therefore three thousand two hundred and ten (3,210) Aetos (years), except the 1st Era of a new Great Precession every one hundred and twenty-eight thousand and four hundred (128,400) Aetos (years), when an extra Aeto (year) is added and this Aeto (year) shall be called zero. As the 1st Aeto (year) of the 1st Era of a new Great Precession is called Year Zero (0), it represents the Divine Creator, the end of old things and the beginning of new. The most recent Year Zero in Ucadia Time for the past one hundred and twenty-eight thousand and four hundred (128,400) Aetos (years) is equivalent to the Aeto (year) known as 2011-2012 (22 December 2011 to 20 December 2012). The present Era beginning as a Great Precession is known as the Era of Aquarius; and

(ii) The second part of the Ucadia Time System shall be the calculation of Age, signifying three (3) divisions of an Era equivalent to one thousand and seventy (1070) Aetos (years), except the 1st Age of the 1st era of a Great Precession which will be one thousand and seventy-one (1071) Aetos (years). The present Age, also known as the New Age and the New World is the first Age of the Great Precession; and

(iii) The third part of Ucadia Time System shall be the calculation of a completion of the Earth's orbit of the Sun, known as Aeto (Year) being three hundred and sixty-five (365) Aemera (days); and every four (4) Aetos (years) an extra day shall be added to the Aeto (year) so as to be three hundred and sixty-six (366) days, with the extra Aemera (day) called Aelomai; and every one hundred and sixty (160) Aetos (years) an Aemera (day) shall be added to that Year and shall be called Aebelos; and every third Precession or nine thousand, six hundred and thirty (9,630) Aetos (years), an Aemera (day) shall be added to that Year; and

(iv) The fourth part of the Ucadia Time System shall be the calculation of in a standard Year of seventy-three (73) segments called an Arc, each of five (5) Aemera (days) in length, that may be arranged by thirteen (13) Aemetos (Months) called the Zodiakos or by Seasons or "Aekairos"; and

(v) In the arrangement of Zodiakos, the first Aemetos (Month) of a year shall be called *Ophis* being five (5) Aemera (days) (21-Dec to 25-Dec); and followed by the second Aemetos (month) of *Arktos* the bear (26-Dec to 24-Jan) of thirty (30) Aemera (days); and followed by the third Aemetos (month) of *Cuinos* the dog (25-Jan to 23-Feb) of thirty (30) Aemera (days); and followed by the fourth Aemetos (month) of *Ichthyos* the fish (24-Feb to 25-Mar) of thirty (30) Aemera (days); and followed by the fifth Aemetos (month) of *Krios* the ram (26-Mar to 24-Apr) of thirty (30) Aemera (days); and followed by the sixth Aemetos (month) of *Tavros* the bull (25-Apr to 24-May) of thirty (30) Aemera (days); and followed by the seventh Aemetos (month) of *Oxos* the ox (25-May to 23-Jun) of thirty (30) Aemera (days); and followed by the eighth Aemetos (month) of *Karkínos* the crab (24-Jun to 23-Jul) of thirty (30) Aemera (days); and followed by the ninth Aemetos (month) of *Ippos* the horse (24-Jul to 22- Aug) of thirty (30) Aemera (days); and followed by the tenth Aemetos (month) of *Leonis* the lion (23-Aug to 21-Sep) of thirty (30) Aemera (days); and followed by the eleventh Aemetos (month) of *Kyknos* the swan (22-Sep to 21-Oct) of thirty (30) Aemera (days); and followed by the twelfth Aemetos (month) of *Skorpios* the scorpion (22-Oct to 20-Nov) of thirty (30) Aemera (days); and followed by the thirteenth and final Aemetos (month) of *Elaphos* the red deer (21-Nov to 20-Dec) of thirty (30) Aemera (days) or thirty-one (31) in a leap year; and

(vi) In the arrangement of the Seasons, the first Aekairos (season) shall be *Blastanos* (spring) of ninety (90) Aemera (days) as the first season of life; and the second shall be *Theros* (summer) of ninety (90) Aemera (days) as the Aekairos (season) of heat and storms; and the third shall be *Proimos* (autumn) of ninety (90) Aemera (days) as the Aekairos (season) of change and uncertainty; and the fourth shall be *Kaimonos* (winter) of ninety-five (95) Aemera (days) as the Aekairos (season) of death and sleep; and

(vii) The fifth part of the Ucadia Time System shall be the Moon cycle of twenty-nine (29) or thirty (30) days which shall be free and independent of the cycle of the Sun as such recordings of the full cycle of a Moon contains sufficient variance as to require the Time Keeper to make prediction as to whether a Moon cycle be twenty-nine (29) or thirty (30) days; and

(viii) The sixth part of the Ucadia Time System shall be the Name of the Aemera (day) of an Arc with the first (1st) Aemera (day) named GAIA in honour of the spirit of the Earth, the second (2nd) Aemera (day) named MONS in honour of the Moon, the third (3rd) Aemera (day) named MARS in honour of the spirit of Mars, the fourth (4th) Aemera (day) named JOVI in honour of the Jovian Giant planets Jupiter, Saturn, Neptune and Uranus and the fifth (5th) Aemera (day) named SOL in honour of the spirit of our SUN; and

(ix) The seventh part of the Ucadia Time System shall be the Hour of the Aemera (day) divided into twenty-four (24) hours of an Aemera (day) with each hour itself made up of sixty (60) Minutes; and

(x) The eighth part of the Ucadia Time System shall be the Minutes and Seconds of the Aemera (day), with Each Minute made up of sixty (60) Seconds and then one hundred (100) milliseconds per second.

12. In accord with the Ucadia Time System and the most sacred covenants of the *Authentic Sacred Deposit of Trust*, each and every Day since the Sacred Space-Day-Time

Spring Equinox in the Year known as 10,831 BCE to the final year of the present Great Precession of twenty-five thousand and six hundred and eighty-one (25,681) years is duly recorded in the Public Register and Great Record of One Heaven, also known as the Great Record of Space-Day-Time as the first, original and highest Record.

Thus, the unique Record Number, or Sacred Space-Day-Time Number for UCA E8:Y3210:A0:S1:M27:D6 [Wed, 21 Dec 2011] is 4689718.

Therefore, all and every representation of Day, Date and Time from the first record to the last record of Sacred Space-Day-Time shall be completely within the Jurisdiction of Ucadia, subject to the present most sacred Covenant.

At the conclusion of the Great Precession, it shall be the right of Humanity to vote and choose its next measurement system of time and space.

TITLE IX - SOL (SOLAR SYSTEM) MEMBERS

Article 46 – Members

1. **By the absolute Power and Authority of Heaven and Earth**, no awareness, *no numquam in carne* (never carnated) being, no higher order consciousness or any other spiritual entity shall be excluded from One Heaven as it applies to Sol (The Solar System). Therefore, let it be known to all that henceforth no mind or higher order consciousness shall be cursed or is permitted to be cursed now and forever. Members

2. There shall be only one type of membership of One Heaven through the assignment of the name of a Divine Spirit Person as Member associated to either a *numquam in carne* (never carnated) Consciousness or a True Person instanced in flesh to a unique Membership Number as proof of their membership of the greater Unique Collective Awareness, also known as the Divine Creator. Types of Membership

3. By the power and authority of the Divine Creator, the Divine Spirit Persons associated with all higher order life, living and deceased, or *numquam in carne* (never carnated) consciousness are hereby recognised as full Members of the Unique Collective Awareness, also known as the Divine Creator and the Society of One Heaven, *ab initio* (from the Beginning). Unique Membership Number of One Heaven

   Full membership of the Unique Collective Awareness, also known as the Divine Creator, is a pronouncement of fact upon which the entire existence of the Universe depends. Therefore, to deny existence as a full member of the Unique Collective Awareness is to deny existence which is neither competent nor possible. Nor is it possible for a higher order life form or spirit to demand it be recognised as wholly separate and independent from the Unique Collective Awareness as such an event, even if it were possible to achieve unanimous consent from all of existence to such a request, would cause all of existence to collapse.

   A Membership number associated with the full membership of the Unique Collective Awareness is separate to any unique recognition by redemption of membership of the Society of One Heaven, by a Level 6 higher order life form. Nor may any entity, person, corporation, spirit, association, body or being living or deceased, deny the proper assignment of Unique Membership Numbers to the Unique Collective Awareness.

   By the power and authority of this sacred Covenant, Membership Numbers cannot be transferred, denied, lost, stolen, bonded, enslaved, forgotten, suspended, cancelled, damaged, destroyed or sold.

4. A Divine Spirit Person is derived from a Divine Trust. A Divine Trust is Consent by Divine Spirit

formed when a Divine Immortal Spirit, being part of the Divine, agrees with the intention of the Collective Divine known as Unique Collective Awareness to be recognised as a Unique Member of the Divine in accord with the sacred Covenant Pactum De Singularis Caelum. Into the Divine Trust is then placed one unit of pure awareness representing one unique divine immortal spirit and mind, one unit of awareness representing the unique experience of form in motion, energy of creation and connection to form and one unit representing all unique awareness of experience of unique form in motion as The Divine Form. Person as Member

When a Divine Immortal Spirit chooses to be expressed in Divine Trust, then such an event represents proof of the willing consent of the associated unique Divine Spirit Person to their membership of the Unique Collective Awareness and membership of the Society of One Heaven and their consent to the articles of the present most sacred Covenant.

As Existence of the Universe depends upon the consent of each and every Divine Immortal Spirit and their associated Divine Spirit Person, the proof of the continued existence of the Universe is Evidence of complete and willing consent of all Divine Spirit Persons as Members of One Heaven.

In contrast, while a Divine Spirit Person possesses the absolute right of free will to choose to be a Member of One Heaven, the act of abjuration of such consent would necessitate the fracturing of Unique Collective Awareness and therefore the dream of Existence and therefore Existence itself.

5. By the power and authority of the present sacred Covenant, a Unique Membership Number of one hundred and forty-four (144) digits representing a valid entry into the Great Ledger and Public Record of One Heaven shall be issued for each and every Divine Spirit in the Universe that has ever existed or will ever exist, whether or not they have carnated into a higher order flesh being or not. Membership Number of One Heaven

The first eighteen (18) digits of the one hundred and forty-four (144) digit Unique Membership Number is not only unique to each Member, but shall be a unique moment in Ucadia Time representing the precise moment of recognition of the Divine Spirit and in the case of Divine Spirits who have chosen to be associated with a carnation into flesh, the Unique Membership Number shall represent the unique moment of being borne.

6. When a Unique Membership Number of eighteen (18) digits is created for a Divine Spirit that has chosen to be associated with a True Trust Sacred Event of UCADIA Time-through being borne into flesh, the Unique Membership Number shall represent a unique portion and element of Ucadian Time-Space. By the present sacred Covenant, no two (2) Members shall have the exact same Membership Number, therefore no two (2) Members shall be allocated the exact same sacred portion of Ucadia Time-Space.

Space

By the power and authority of the present sacred Covenant, when a Unique Membership Number of One Heaven is created with the unique time of birth of a unique Divine Spirit granting Divinity (Divine Right of Use with Purpose) expressed to the flesh, then that instance of time-space shall be bound to that Membership Number, so that whoever is allocated that number also holds a Sacred Key of UCADIA Time-Space.

Therefore, a Membership Number of One Heaven shall also literally represent a Most Sacred Key of UCADIA Time-Space and the holder a valid Timekeeper of Time and Space. A Sacred Redeemed Membership Number of One Heaven is an object of the highest value and integrity as it represents the unique identification of a unique Mind having rightful membership to One Heaven as granted to all consciousness by this sacred Covenant.

7. As each Member that has consented to the rules of this Covenant who has chosen to be borne into natural flesh, two (2) Trusts and therefore two (2) Trust Numbers exist, being a True Trust Number and a Divine Trust Number. A Divine Trust Number is different to a True Trust Number only in that the first two (2) numbers are replaced with the two (2) letters "OH" signifying One Heaven.

Membership Number as True Trust Number and Divine Trust Number

8. The Right to Issue The Sacred Membership Numbers of One Heaven shall also represent the living symbol of authority of One Heaven for a Society to represent the interests of all existing Members of One Heaven. By the power and authority of this Covenant, the Societies of One Christ, One Islam, One Spirit Tribe and the Globe Union are hereby granted joint and equal authority of the Redemption of Membership Numbers of One Heaven.

Issuing and Management of Unique Membership Number of One Heaven

9. By the present sacred Covenant, all Unique Membership Numbers shall henceforth be assigned to all Divine Spirit Persons as Members by the Day of Agreement and Understanding being GAIA E8:Y3209:A1:S1:M6:D1, also known as [Monday, 21 Dec 2009]. By the power and authority of the present Covenant all Unique Membership Numbers of One Heaven exist and have full validity, whether the associated Divine Spirit Person as Member acknowledges this Unique Membership Number or not.

Assignment of Unique Membership Numbers

Furthermore, all organisations assigned on Earth by this Covenant to represent One Heaven are granted full authority to request and receive any and all official Membership numbers of One Heaven corresponding to the valid metes and bounds of their jurisdiction and their use in any and all official instruments.

10. All Divine Spirit Persons as Members who have conveyed Divinity (Divine Right of Use with Purpose) to a True Trust then expressed as Level 6 Homo Sapien Life Forms, have therefore willingly consented to the present Covenant. Furthermore, such Members connected to True Persons also consent to the Society granting reciprocal membership to the Globe Union as well as the relevant regional Union, the relevant University Free Society and State/Provincial Free Society in which they were borne, or have chosen to domicile.

Consent to Membership of Associated Societies

As each and every Divine Spirit Person as Member who has chosen to be associated through Level 6 Homo Sapien Life Forms to a True Person willingly consents by their natural birth to their associated reciprocal memberships, these authorised and associated societies have the permission to keep and administer membership rolls for all those Members, living and deceased, within their associated metes and bounds and to act on behalf of the best interests of their Members in protecting their rights and restoring any rights and/or property previously corrupted or taken by non-aligned alternate societies.

11. The use of aliases and other false name devices as the basis of recording the membership of any Divine Spirit Person in the Great Register of One Heaven is not permitted. All memberships must be based upon the true and lawful name of a Divine Spirit Person not an alias, or other false name.

Alias and other false names not permitted

Any Divine Spirit Person who uses an alias or false name as the basis of redemption of their membership number in the Great Register of One Heaven shall be guilty of the most grave crime against the Divine Creator and the Covenant of One Heaven.

12. Membership Numbers shall remain at all times the complete property and ownership of the Unique Collective Awareness, also known as the Divine Creator and solely administered by the Society of One Heaven on behalf of the Divine Creator and all Divine Spirit Persons, with no other Society, Spirit or Collective having any rights whatsoever to claim this as their property.

Ownership of Unique Membership Numbers

When Membership Numbers are allocated, they are done so with the recipient being granted use or usufruct of the Trust/Estate which is their Claim of Right to administer their own Estate as General Executor. The Society reserves the right to withdraw such use for any and all except use by the unique individual spirit to whom the Membership Number represents.

13. By the present Covenant, no living Level 6 Life Form, no higher order consciousness or spiritual entity shall be excluded from Heaven by any claim, or warrant, law, edict or appeal to suspend or amend this rule, from any society on Earth or in Heaven.

Membership Exclusion

From the Day of Redemption forward, it shall be a crime against Heaven to claim any Level 6 Life Form is denied right of entry to Heaven or to print, reproduce and/or transmit any information stating such a false claim.

14. While a Level 6 Higher Order Life Form is granted complete free will to choose to isolate their mind from participating with other minds and isolate their flesh from interacting with other flesh beings, such free will choice does not extend beyond the bounds of logic to disassociate themselves from the form of their own species or the existence of their own spirit from the Unique Collective Awareness of Divine Mind being the Society of One Heaven expressed as existence.

Limits of Logic in Expression of Free Will

The birth and existence of any Level 6 Higher Order Life Form is proof of the existence of a Divine Trust and associated Divine Spirit Person granting a unique Divine Commission through the conveyance of certain Divinity (Divine Right of Use with Purpose) to a True Trust and the creation of an associated True Person. Furthermore, such formation of Divine Trusts is reflected in such Divine Property as a Member Number of One Heaven in the Great Register of One Heaven.

All Divine Property is ultimately the ownership and custody of the Divine in accord with the present sacred Covenant. The expression of free will of a Level 6 Higher Order Life Form does not extend or enlarge the rights of such a Spirit, whether or not also associated with carnation in flesh, to demand control or change to such Divine Property they neither own nor control. Therefore there is a limit of logic in law to the expression of free will when a Level 6 Higher Order Life Form chooses to isolate their mind from participating with other minds or chooses to isolate their flesh from interacting with other flesh beings.

15. Any and all living or spirit Level 6 Higher Order Life Forms have the absolute right of free will to withdraw their consent to be known as a Member of One Heaven. However, this Right does not extend to any claims or demand to alter or destroy Divine Property in relation to Member Numbers and other records associated with their immutable connection to Unique Collective Awareness be rescinded and all records thereof.

Right of Free Will to Express Exclusion

16. When a living or spirit Level 6 Higher Order Life Form makes irrational, illogical and unlawful demands to alter or destroy Divine Property associated with their immutable connection to Unique Collective Awareness, such demands, threats or actions shall constitute *prima facie* proof to declare such a mind and spirit mentally incapacitated, immediately and instantly delegating their custody and guardianship to the care of the Oratorium being the Supreme Court of One Heaven. Effect of Irrational and Illogical demands of exclusion

All decisions thereafter are to be made on behalf of the mentally incapacitated living or spirit Level 6 Higher Order Life Form until such time as they can sensibly demonstrate competence of their faculties. Any documents, claims, actions or causes raised by such a living or spirit Level 6 Higher Order Life Form whilst under the custody of the Oratorium for suffering mental incapacity shall have no legal, lawful or moral effect whatsoever.

Article 47 – Member Rolls

1. **Member Rolls of One Heaven** shall be the Unique and Accurate Rolls listing valid Membership Numbers and Member details. Member Rolls

There shall be three (3) types of Member Rolls: General, Redemption and Electoral. The existence of one Divine Trust shall equal one unique record on the General Member Roll.

2. The General Member Roll of One Heaven, also known as the great Roll of Divine Persons shall be the official Member Roll which records each and every Unique Membership Number issued in validation of the existence of a Divine Spirit Person Member. General Member Rolls

3. The redeemed member Roll of One Heaven shall be the official Member Roll which records each and every unique Membership Number issued in validation of the existence of a Member, living or deceased, and to whom the Official Number has been assigned through the act of Redemption. Redeemed Member Rolls

4. The Electoral Member Roll of One Heaven shall be the official Member Roll which records a copy of the Redeemed Member Roll for those Redeemed Members above the minimum age to vote. A Member not on the Electoral Roll is not permitted to participate in voting and elections. Electoral Member Rolls

5. The supreme dignity and right to sole and exclusive temporal custody for the most sacred Rolls of Members of Heaven shall be accorded the three (3) great faiths of One Christ, One Islam and One Spirit as Custody of Rolls administered by One Christ, One Islam and One

defined by the present most sacred Covenant and no other.

Spirit

6. The total number of records on the General Member Roll includes all Divine Spirit Persons that have ever existed or will ever exist, whether or not such spirits are associated with carnations in flesh, as True Persons or not, for all higher order beings including (but not limited to) all Homo Sapiens (Humanity), the Griseo Morbidus (Standard Grey), the Cerastis Sapiens (Horned Reptoids), the Android Scitus (Smart Androids), the Cyborg Sagax (Autonomous Cyborgs), the Serpens Sophos (Smooth Skinned Reptoids), the Volucris Permuto (Hybrid Bird Form), the Homo Adamus (Early Humanoids), the Sapientia Mutatis (Transformed Wisdom Beings), the Mammaloid Sentientiae (Conscious Mammaloids), the Griseo Altus (Tall Grey) and the Serpens Alatus (Winged Reptoids).

Number of Records on General Member Roll

The total number of records shall be established by a census of records at the first General Conclave in accord with the present Covenant and then a census performed at each and every Conclave thereafter.

7. In accord with the first Supreme Conclave GAIA E8:Y3209:A1:S1:M6:D1 [Monday Dec 21, 2009], a Census was conducted of all Divine Spirit Persons as Members who each have conveyed Divinity (Divine Right of Use with Purpose) to a True Trust then expressed as Level 6 Homo Sapien Life Forms that have ever existed. It has therefore been determined that in excess of sixty-six (66) Billion Level 6 Homo Sapien Life Forms have ever been borne with the average number of carnations per Higher Order Mind, also known as Higher Order Spirit to be an average factor of three (3).

Number of Records on General Member Roll representing Homo Sapiens

Therefore, approximately twenty-two (22) Billion Divine Persons are said to exist and are recorded and enrolled on the General Member Roll, also known as the Great Roll of Divine Persons associated with Level 6 Homo Sapien Life Forms related members of One Heaven, of which approximately two thirds (2/3) are not currently carnated.

Article 48 – Member Records

1. **Divine Member Record** shall be any valid and duly authorised record entered into the Great Register and Divine Records of Heaven, in accordance with this Covenant. A Divine Record is the highest and most superior form of all record as once a Divine Record is created, it cannot be uncreated. As the Great Register and Divine Records of Heaven is also the Great Roll of Divine Persons, when a Divine Record is created a Divine Person also exists. A Divine Record may only be issued in accordance with the articles of

Divine Record

this most sacred Covenant.

2. A Divine Record is formed in accord with this sacred Covenant when a Divine Trust is formed. A Divine Trust is a purely Spiritual Trust validly registered into the Great Register and Divine Records of Heaven, containing actual Spiritual Form as well as Divine Property, administered by the Treasury of One Heaven as Trustees, in accordance with the sacred Covenant Pactum De Singularis Caelum, as Sacred Deed for the Benefice of a Divine Person. Divine Record and existence of Divine Trust

   The Divine Form conveyed into a valid Divine Trust for a Divine Immortal Spirit is known as the Divine Trust Corpus, or Divine Living Res, represented by a valid legal personality known as the Divine Person through the Great Register as the Great Roll of Divine Persons. Therefore, a Divine Trust is the only possible type of Trust that can hold actual Form, rather than just the Rights of Use of Form (Property).

3. Divine Trusts are created by the inception of the Divine, consent of the Divine, then expression of the will of the Divine Creator, through a most sacred event and association in accordance with the Covenant, solely through the operation of the "Ways and Means" of the thirty-three (33) most Sacred Gifts of the present sacred Covenant. Creation of Divine Trusts and Divine Records

4. "**Life Record**", is any valid and duly authorised record, recognising the commencement of a term, award, patent, tenure, existence, grant, agreement, gift, permission or bond into a lesser Great Register and Public Record of one of the Societies associated with One Heaven in accord with this Covenant. A Life Record may only be issued in accord with the articles of this most sacred Covenant. Life Record

5. A Life Record is formed in accord with the present Covenant when a Living Trust is formed being either a True, Superior, Temporary or Inferior Living Trust:- Life Record and creation of Living Trust

   (i) A *True Trust* is the highest form of Living Trust. A True Trust is formed through the pre-existence of a Divine Trust, in the lawful conveyance from the Divine Trust into the True Trust of the Divine Rights of Use and Purpose known as Divinity, being the highest possible form of any kind of Property; and

   (ii) A *Superior Trust* is the second highest form of Living Trust formed through the pre-existence of a True Trust in the lawful conveyance into the Superior Trust of Property in the form of Realty being the highest form of Rights of Use of Object and Concepts by Divine Rights of Use and Purpose, also known as Divinity; and

(iii) A *Temporary Trust* is the third highest form of Living Trust involving the temporary conveyance of property from one Superior Trust to another. Excluding Negotiable Instruments, a Temporary Trust is not permitted to exist beyond seven (7) years; and

(iv) An *Inferior Trust* also known as an Inferior Foreign Trust, or simply Foreign Trust, is the lowest form of Living Trust possessing the lowest form of rights of ownership. An Inferior Trust is any Living Trust formed by inferior Foreign Law, claims and statutes not Ucadia.

Valid Issue of Live Borne Record

6. All Members of One Heaven living on or after the Day of Divine Agreement & Understanding, being GAIA E8:Y3209:A1:S1:M6:D1, also known as [Monday, 21 Dec 2009], have the absolute right to request a valid extract of their Live Borne Record for the purpose of proof of their Divine Personality and True Personality, as well as the existence of their Divine Trust and True Trust holding Divine Property, also known as Divine Right of Use. A Live Borne Record is proof of the Redemption of the membership and trust number of a Member calculated on their borne date.

As a valid Live Borne Record is an extremely valuable instrument, should the Great Register online system be unavailable, then a Live Borne Record may only be issued under one of two (2) conditions of validation:-

(i) An application has been made by a competent higher order being through a registration process and then validated on the condition the competent living being that made the application has (a) previously registered and been accepted; and (b) declared to have read and accepted the Covenant and the laws of One Heaven; and (c) will provide such necessary proof of identity and other forms of validation should they be requested; or

(ii) That a Member who has not made an application is currently or has previously held a high office of a foreign state or system by virtue of a solemn and sacred Oath to the Divine and Heaven, thereby claiming the source of their authority from Heaven and the Divine Creator.

A Live Borne Record issued without the above conditions being met is automatically invalid from the time of issue.

Structure of a valid Live Borne Record

7. A valid Live Borne Record is an authenticated extract issued to a Member by a Ucadian Society when a Member has met a condition of validation:-

(i) Lists the official name, name of the Covenant, trust number of One Heaven and words "Great Register" at the top of the document; and

(ii) Clearly contains the Ucadia symbol within the document; and

(iii) Clearly indicates the document is an Extract of an Event Record from the Great Register; and

(iv) Lists the words "Live Borne Record" before the name of the trust; and

(v) Makes a formal reference to this Article of the Covenant; and

(vi) Lists the trust name, the trust number as well as the trust birth event for the true trust; and

(vii) Includes a unique register number for the document for the Greater Register; and

(viii) Includes a UCADIA Time Event; and

(ix) Is sealed by a Judge of One Heaven or a Judge holding the powers of the Supreme Court of One Heaven for the purpose of sealing a Live Borne Record; and

(x) Is sealed by a Registrar for Births, Deaths and Liens of the Supreme Court of One Heaven.

If one or more of these conditions are not met, then a Live Borne Record is invalid.

8. A valid Live Borne Record is proof of superior title above all other claimed registrations, ledgers and property rights. When issued to an inferior society, a valid Live Borne Record is a formal contest of such inferior title, preventing by law that society from conveying any property or rights based on their inferior claim until the contested title is resolved. Live Borne Record as Superior Title

When such a society refuses to acknowledge the legitimate contest of title and conveys property and rights by deed, then such deeds are an abomination before all Heaven, have no Ecclesiastical authority whatsoever, with any officer authorising such a dishonour automatically stripped of their right to administer any and all property and deeds.

9. As Members may reside in an alternate society, there is sometimes the need to ensure that a Member is properly recognised, has all the Valid Issue of Live Borne Record proper paperwork and credentials required for commerce by the other society. A Live Borne Record therefore, is an important assistance to Members in these instances. However, while a Live Borne Record may be issued under certain conditions, in no way may a Live Borne Record ever be considered a conveyance of legal title from the society. Similarly, any contrivance, trick or instrument used to imply such conveyance has no effect nor force of law. and non Ucadian Societies

The issue of a Live Borne Record to an inferior society, such as an inferior Non-Ucadian Society is permitted under the following conditions:-

(i) That the Ucadian Society in which the Member also resides does not yet have an established treaty or agreement with the inferior society to ensure the necessary credentials may be handled directly as society to society; or

(ii) That the Ucadian Society in which the Member also resides is not able to provide a particular service required.

Cancellation of Live Borne Record

10. As a Live Borne Record is a certificate of record of a valid Divine Event, no power exists in Heaven or Earth to annul the event, therefore cancel such an instrument. While a Member has the absolute right to demand the cancellation of inferior certificates and the annulment of false records of event that contest the legitimacy of a Live Borne Record, the only criteria by which a Live Borne Record may be cancelled is when the information provided in the creation of the Live Borne Record was knowingly false.

The desire for any Level 6 Life Form or higher order spirit being to disavow, decline or rescind any previous action in being associated with the Society has no effect in allowing or permitting the cancellation of a valid Live Borne Record.

Prohibited Use of Live Borne Record

11. Any Member that is subject to an Anathema, or has deliberately and wilfully asserted one or more Prohibited Rights, or has sought to claim, or register the name Ucadia, or any associated content, icons, marks, symbols, instruments, securities or property contrary to the clauses of the present Covenant is forbidden to hold, possess, use or claim the benefit of their Live Borne Record until the cause of such prohibition has been properly resolved.

Any claim, or attempted or actual registration of Ucadia related material, marks, symbols, names, instruments, rights and property into a foreign jurisdiction contrary to the rights and obligations prescribed by the present sacred Covenant is a grave transgression before all Heaven and the Earth and hereby shall render such a man or woman ineligible to hold, possess, use or claim the benefit of their Live

Borne Record for not less than seven (7) years.

Death Record

12. "**Death Record**" is any valid and duly authorised record recognising the end of a term, award, patent, tenure, existence, grant, agreement, gift, permission or bond into a lesser Great Register and Public Record of one of the Societies associated with One Heaven in accord with this Covenant. A Death Record may only be issued in accord with the articles of the present Covenant.

Death Record and termination of Living Trust

13. A Death Record is formed in accord with this sacred Covenant when a Living Trust is terminated being either a True, Superior, Temporary or Inferior Living Trust:-

(i) A True Trust is terminated upon the space-time event of the physical expiry of the vessel; and

(ii) A Superior Trust is terminated upon the expiry of the term, award, patent, tenure, existence, grant, agreement, gift, permission or bond or the True Trust that underwrites it; and

(iii) A Temporary Trust is terminated upon the expiry of the term or fulfilment of purpose, whatever is sooner; and

(iv) An Inferior Trust is terminated upon the expiry of the term, award, patent, tenure, existence, grant, agreement, gift, permission or bond or the True Trust or Superior Trust associated with it.

A Superior Trust, Temporary Trust or Inferior Trust cannot exist beyond the termination event in space-time for the associated True Trust.

Valid Issue of Death Borne Record

14. As a valid Death Borne Record is an extremely valuable instrument, it may only be issued under one of three (3) conditions of validation:-

(i) That a certified true copy of a certificate of live birth, or death for the Member has been provided and uploaded to their records by the Member or blood related kin; or

(ii) An affirmation has been made, sealed and witnessed by two (2) other Members previously granted Live Borne Records that the Member is unable to obtain a copy of the live birth or death record of their blood related kin; or

(iii) That the Member claimed an Ecclesiastical Office in life that by definition therefore claimed the source of its power from Heaven and the Divine Creator.

A Death Borne Record issued without one of these three (3) conditions being met is automatically invalid from the time of issue.

15. A valid Death Borne Record is an authenticated extract issued to a Member by a Ucadian Society when a Member has met a condition of validation and:- Structure of a valid Death Borne Record

(i) Lists the official name, name of the Covenant, trust number of One Heaven and words "Great Register" at the top of the document; and

(ii) Clearly contains the Ucadia symbol within the document; and

(iii) Clearly indicates the document is an Extract of an Event Record from the Great Register; and

(iv) Lists the words "Death Borne Record" before the name of the trust; and

(v) Makes a formal reference to this article of the Covenant; and

(vi) Lists the trust name, the trust number as well as the trust death event for the true trust; and

(vii) Includes a unique register number for the document for the Greater Register; and

(viii) Includes a UCADIA Time Event; and

(ix) Is sealed by a Judge of One Heaven or a Judge holding the powers of the Supreme Court of One Heaven for the purpose of sealing a Death Borne Record; and

(x) Is sealed by a Registrar for Births, Deaths and Liens of the Supreme Court of One Heaven.

If one or more of these conditions are not met, then a Death Borne Record is invalid.

16. A valid Death Borne Record is proof of Superior Title above all other claimed registrations, ledgers and property rights. When issued to an inferior society, a valid Death Borne Record is a formal contest of such inferior title, preventing by law that society from conveying any property or rights based on their inferior claim until the contested title is resolved. Death Borne Record as Superior Title

When such a society refuses to acknowledge the legitimate contest of title and conveys property and rights by deed, then such deeds are an abomination before all Heaven, having no Ecclesiastical authority whatsoever, with any officer authorising such a dishonour automatically stripped of their right to administer any and all property and deeds.

17. "**Promised Land Record**" is a form of secured promise and is the most sacred, formal and important of all types of promises. It represents the fulfilment of an ancient sacred pledge by the Divine Creator that all Level 6 Life Forms who redeem themselves in recognition of their membership to One Heaven and Ucadia may lawfully assert their Divine Right and own their home in Trust upon the provision of a valid Certificate of Vacant Possession and Occupancy and then a Certificate of Survey and Title. Promised Land Record

A Promised Land Record is available only to those naturally borne, or naturalised for a particular national free Society. Residents cannot apply for a Promised Land Record in a free Society in which they live unless they are naturalised Members of that Society. A Promised Land Record is proof of the creation and existence of a True Location Trust, into which the Divine Right of Possession of Land for the purpose of a Primary Location is conveyed. A Member may only have one Promised Land Record and therefore one True Location Trust.

All Living Members of One Heaven who are aged twenty-one (21) years or older on the Day of Divine Agreement & Understanding being GAIA E8:Y3209:A1:S1:M6:D1, also known as [Monday, 21 Dec 2009], or upon reaching the same age thereafter, have the absolute right to request a valid extract of their Promised Land Record for the purpose of proof of their Divine Right of Possession of Land for the purpose of a Primary Domicile.

18. In accord and fulfilment of the ancient covenant and promise of the Divine Creator of Existence, a Promised Land Record is forbidden to be granted to anyone who denies the supremacy of the present Covenant, or who seeks to usurp the rights of the Divine, or who openly or secretly hates and repudiates the Divine Creator or who reaffirms their membership to an organisation or body that repudiates the present Covenant and continues to demonstrate a hatred and hostility to all Divinity. Excluded Members not entitled to Promised Land Record

Any group that has openly repudiated and dishonoured a claimed covenant with the Divine Creator in presuming rights to a Promised Land, in defiance of the particular conditions of such a covenant are therefore by their own actions ineligible to a Promised Land Record unless they openly condemn such actions, repudiate such false settlement and disavow any association with those leaders who continue to demonstrate such hatred, dishonour and blasphemy to the Divine and any such ancient claims.

19. As a valid Promised Land Record is an extremely valuable instrument, Valid Issue of Promised Land

it may only be issued to the custody of the appropriate Ucadia Foundation or Campus or Province associated with the Member under the following conditions:- Record

(i) That a valid Live Borne Record has already been issued for the Member associated with the Promised Land Record; and

(ii) That the Member has requested and been approved support or service for an existing issue of land or a new issue of land in relation to habitation.

20. A valid Promised Land Record is an authenticated extract issued to a Member by a Ucadian Society when a Member has met a condition of validation and:- Structure of a valid Promised Land Record

(i) Lists the official name, name of the Covenant, trust number of One Heaven and words "Great Register" at the top of the document; and

(ii) Clearly contains Ucadia symbol within the document; and

(iii) Clearly indicates the document is an Extract of an Event Record from the Great Register; and

(iv) Lists the words "Promised Land Record" before the name of the true location trust; and

(v) Makes a formal reference to this Article of the Covenant; and

(vi) Lists the trust name, the trust number as well as the trust birth event for the true location trust being the same birth event for the true person trust; and

(vii) Includes a unique register number for the document for the Greater Register; and

(viii) Includes a UCADIA Time Event; and

(ix) Is sealed by a Judge of One Heaven or a Judge holding the powers of the Supreme Court of One Heaven for the purpose of sealing a Promised Land Record; and

(x) Is sealed by a Registrar for Land Titles of the Supreme Court of One Heaven.

If one or more of these conditions are not met, then a Promised Land Record is invalid.

21. Any Member that is subject to an Anathema, or has deliberately and wilfully asserted one or more Prohibited Rights, or has sought to claim, or register the name Ucadia, or any associated content, icons, Prohibited Use of Promised Land Record marks, symbols, instruments, securities or property contrary to the clauses of the present Covenant is forbidden to hold, possess, use or claim the benefit of their Promised Land Record or any official documents or instruments associated with the present sacred Covenant until the cause of such prohibition has been properly resolved.

Any claim, or attempted or actual registration of Ucadia related material, marks, symbols, names, instruments, rights and property into a foreign jurisdiction contrary to the rights and obligations prescribed by the present sacred Covenant is a grave transgression before all Heaven and the Earth and hereby shall render such a man or woman ineligible to hold, possess, use or claim the benefit of their Promised Land Record or any official documents or instruments associated with the present sacred Covenant for not less than seven (7) years.

TITLE X - SOL (SOLAR SYSTEM) PACTS & TREATIES

Article 49 – Treaty of the Divine Masculine

1. THE HIGHEST CONCORDING PARTIES, CONCURRING with the most sacred Covenant known as Pactum De Singularis Caelum, also known as the Covenant of One Heaven as the Highest Supreme Law of the Divine Creator of All Existence; and RECOGNISING the Unique Collective Awareness of Divine Mind, also known as the *Divina* of one hundred and forty-four (144) Deities as the duly elected Government of One Heaven; and AFFIRMING all war and major spiritual conflict within and between the Heavens has officially ended; ASSENTING to the validity and legitimacy of the *Treaty of the Divine Feminine* and the *Treaty of Divine Messengers* and the *Treaty of Angels, Saints and Demons* and the *Treaty of Spirits States* and the *Treaty of the Suns* and the *Treaty of the Planets and Moons;* and ESTABLISHING the agreed conditions by which War on planets such as Earth may also be ended; and RESOLVING to confirm the foundations of a strong and perpetual union; and DETERMINING to end all forms of spiritual curse and the end of Hell(s), do Come Now with these Presents and with one another Agree to this Covenant of the Divine Masculine. Treaty of the Divine Masculine

2. Let it be known to all past, present and future, the Highest Concording Parties and their duly appointed Plenipotentiaries of the same name herein, having communicated and exchanged to each other their Full Powers, found to be in good and due form, come freely together in full consent and authority being: the Deities and their duly appointed Plenipotentiaries known as Adad, Aegir, Aengus, Aesir, Agni, Ahura Mazda, Aksobhya, Allah, Ame-No-Minaka-Nushi-No-Kami, Amen-Ra, An, Anu, Anubis, Apsu, Apollo, Archons, Ares, Arsan Duolai, Asklepios, Aten, Atum, Avalokitesvara, Baal, Balder, Belenua, Brahma, Chemosh, Dagda, Dagon, Dharma, Diancecht, Dumuzi, Dyaus Pitar, Ea, El, Enki, Enlil, Freyr, Father, Ganesa, Geb, Gobniu, God, Hades, Heimdall, Helios, Hephaistos, Heryshaf, Hoder, Huitzilpochtli, Il, Imra, Indra, Iskur, Itzam Na, Jagannath, Janus, Jupiter, Kama, Kuan Ti, Lebien-Pogil, Lenus, Loki, Lug, Lucifer, Lynx, Mande, Manjusri, Marduk, Mars, Melqart, Mimir, Min, Mon, Mot, Na Cha, Nergal, Ninurta, Njord, Nuadu, Nut, Ometecuhtli, Osiris, Othin, Pak Tai, Pan, Peter, Pon, Poseidon, Ptah, Quikinn.a'Qu, Radha, Sabaoth, Satan, Saturn, Seth, Skanda, Sin, Sucellos, Surya, Susano-Wo, Telepinu, Tesub, Tezcatlipoca, Thor, Tiwaz, Tlaloc, Ull, Utu, Vairacocha, Varuna, Vayu, Visnu, Vulcanus, Wodan, Xipe Totec, YHVH and Zeus. The Divine Masculine deities as the Highest Concording Parties to the Treaty

3. The Highest Concording Parties in Good Faith and without Prejudice hereby ACCEPT, APPROVE and AGREE the following Articles. Recital of Articles of Treaty

4. ARTICLE I. – By the present Treaty ("this Treaty"), the HIGHEST CONCORDING PARTIES ("the Parties") there shall be a universal and perpetual peace and harmony and a sincere friendship and amity established, and between all those who are associated in spirit or flesh through their devotion, faith, belief, location, kindred, culture and history.

Chapter 1 – General Provisions

ARTICLE II. – All the spirits, spiritual energy as prisoners, made on all sides or given during any conflict shall be immediately restored to the appropriate Spiritual Collective of One Heaven, without ransom or condition.

ARTICLE III. – All the energy of curses, binding, control, or obligations of servitude or slavery as made in Heaven or within the temporal realm on all sides shall be immediately dissolved or forgiven or settled so that no outstanding curses, binding, controls, obligations of servitude or slavery exists between or by any one of the Parties.

5. ARTICLE IV. – In recognition of our united, solemn unbreakable oath and binding to the Covenant of One Heaven, also known as Pactum De Singularis Caelum and the proposition of a United Heaven, let it be known to all past, present and future that the Parties have hereby given, granted and conveyed all their powers, all their customs, all their rights and property, all their symbols and instruments of power, all sacred objects, texts, scriptures and sanctuaries and all claims of authority to the Highest Holy Covenant of One Heaven and to the proper authority and structure of the United States of Spirits.

Chapter 2 - Conveyance of Rights, Powers and Symbols of Authority

ARTICLE V. – Upon formal ratification and recognition of this Treaty, when the leadership of One Heaven or its designated representatives on Earth speak or promulgate one or more instruments, they do so with the highest valid authority and the complete conveyance of all rights, property, uses, customs, symbols, and powers of authority of the Parties as the collective Divine Masculine.

ARTICLE VI. – Any and all spiritual or temporal bodies that publicly or privately claim authority from or allegiance to one or more Divine Masculine deities henceforth automatically derives any and all authority solely from the Society of One Heaven and its valid designates and any existing sacred oaths, pledges and vows are carried over to respecting and obeying the Highest Holy Covenant of One Heaven.

ARTICLE VII. – Any and all spiritual or temporal bodies that publicly or privately claim authority from or allegiance to one or more Divine Masculine deities are solemnly bound by their sacred oaths, pledges and vows to honour and respect any and all instruments legitimately promulgated under the Seal of the Society of One Heaven or a valid designate.

ARTICLE VIII. – Any and all spiritual or temporal bodies that publicly or privately claim authority from or allegiance to one or more Divine Masculine deities are solemnly bound by the laws of property, trusts and ownership to obey any order, deed, command, edict, direction and request promulgated by the Society of One Heaven concerning any and all property administered on behalf of the Society of One Heaven by the spiritual or temporal body and its officers.

ARTICLE IX. – Any claim or claims contrary to the above mentioned clauses are hereby null and void from the beginning, having no force spiritually, legally or lawfully.

6. IN WITNESS WHEREOF, the undersigned Plenipotentiaries have witnessed and signed this Treaty.

Enaction of Treaty

GAIA E8:Y3209:A1:S1:M6:D1, [Mon, 21 Dec 2009]

The duly appointed Plenipotentiaries on behalf of the Deities known as Adad, Aegir, Aengus, Aesir, Agni, Ahura Mazda, Aksobhya, Allah, Ame-No-Minaka-Nushi-No-Kami, Amen-Ra, An, Anu, Anubis, Apsu, Apollo, Archons, Ares, Arsan Duolai, Asklepios, Aten, Atum, Avalokitesvara, Baal, Balder, Belenua, Brahma, Chemosh, Dagda, Dagon, Dharma, Diancecht, Dumuzi, Dyaus Pitar, Ea, El, Enki, Enlil, Freyr, Father, Ganesa, Geb, Gobniu, God, Hades, Heimdall, Helios, Hephaistos, Heryshaf, Hoder, Huitzilpochtli, Il, Imra, Indra, Iskur, Itzam Na, Jagannath, Janus, Jupiter, Kama, Kuan Ti, Lebien-Pogil, Lenus, Loki, Lug, Lucifer, Lynx, Mande, Manjusri, Marduk, Mars, Melqart, Mimir, Min, Mon, Mot, Na Cha, Nergal, Ninurta, Njord, Nuadu, Nut, Ometecuhtli, Osiris, Othin, Pak Tai, Pan, Peter, Pon, Poseidon, Ptah, Quikinn.a'Qu, Radha, Sabaoth, Satan, Saturn, Seth, Skanda, Sin, Sucellos, Surya, Susano-Wo, Telepinu, Tesub, Tezcatlipoca, Thor, Tiwaz, Tlaloc, Ull, Utu, Vairacocha, Varuna, Vayu, Visnu, Vulcanus, Wodan, Xipe Totec, YHVH and Zeus.

7. By Agreement of the Highest Concording Parties, this Treaty and Covenant shall be Ratified throughout all Heaven, spiritual dimensions and the Universe by the Day of Agreement and Understanding and shall be Ratified by one or more temporal beings by the Day of Judgement.

Ratification of Treaty

Ratification by Day of Agreement and Understanding

By this Covenant, the Day of Agreement and Understanding is GAIA E8:Y3209:A1:S1:M6:D1, [Mon, 21 Dec 2009].

Ratification by Day of Agreement and Understanding shall be when this Treaty and Covenant is ratified throughout all Heaven, spiritual dimensions and the Universe by the Highest Office Holders of One Heaven representing the Supreme Command of Occupational Forces in and on Earth and when at least two (2) spirits conveyed into circumscribed Level 6 Homo Sapien Life Forms bear witness to the event.

Ratification by Day of Judgement

By this Covenant, the Day of Judgement is VENUS E8:Y3210:A0:S1:M27:D6, [Wed, 21 Dec 2011].

Ratification by Day of Judgement shall be when this Treaty and Covenant is ratified by the Highest Office Holders of existing societies, faiths and associations that claim their existence, authority and power from the supernatural and spiritual either through their tacit, competent and honourable consent, or through their dishonour demonstrating the delinquency of their flesh and therefore the right through power to represent their spirit to ratify the Covenant and Treaty on their behalf.

Article 50 – Treaty of the Divine Feminine

1. THE HIGHEST CONCORDING PARTIES, CONCURRING with the most sacred Covenant known as Pactum De Singularis Caelum, also known as the Covenant of One Heaven as the Highest Supreme Law of the Divine Creator of All Existence, RECOGNISING the Unique Collective Awareness of Divine Mind, also known as the *Divina* of one hundred and forty-four (144) Deities as the duly elected Government of One Heaven; and AFFIRMING all war and major spiritual conflict within and between the Heavens has officially ended; and ASSENTING to the validity and legitimacy of the *Treaty of the Divine Masculine* and the *Treaty of Divine Messengers* and the *Treaty of Angels, Saints and Demons* and the *Treaty of Spirits States* and the *Treaty of the Suns* and the *Treaty of the Planets and Moons;* and ESTABLISHING the agreed conditions by which War on planets such as Earth may also be ended and RESOLVING to confirm the foundations of a strong and perpetual union; and DETERMINING to end all forms of spiritual curse and the end of Hell(s), do Come Now with these Presents and with one another Agree to this Covenant of the Divine Feminine. Treaty of the Divine Feminine

2. Let it be known to all past, present and future, the Highest Concording Parties and their duly appointed Plenipotentiaries of the same name herein, having communicated and exchanged to each other their Full The Divine Feminine deities as the Highest Concording

Powers, found to be in good and due form, come freely together in full consent and authority being: the Deities and their duly appointed Plenipotentiaries known as Amaterasu-o-mi-kami, Anat, Antu, Aphrodite, Artemis, Asherah, Ashtoreth, Astarte, Atargatis, Athena, Bastet, Bes, Brigit, Ceres, Chalchiuhtlicue, Cihuacoatl, Cipactli, Coatlicue, Coventina, Cybil, Danu, Demeter, Disani, Durga, Eileithyia, Epona, Ereskigal, Fjorgyn, Freyja, Frigg, Gaia, Hathor, Hebat, Hekate, Hera, Hestia, Hsi Wang Mu, Idunn, Inana, Ishtar, Isis, Juno, Kali, Kuan Yin, Kybele, Laksmi, Leto, Ma, Maia, Mary, Mari, Matres, Maya, Minerva, Morgan, Nammu, Neith, Nerthus, Ninhursaga, Parvati, Persephone, Pistis, Prthivi, Rhea, Sakhmet, Sarasvati, Sati, Semele, Sibyl, Siti, Tara, Taweret, Tiamat, Tin Hau, Venus and Vesta. Parties to the Treaty

3. The Highest Concording Parties in Good Faith and without Prejudice hereby ACCEPT, APPROVE and AGREE the following Articles: Recital of Articles of Treaty

4. ARTICLE I. – By the present Treaty ("this Treaty"), the HIGHEST CONCORDING PARTIES ("the Parties") there shall be a universal and perpetual peace and harmony and a sincere friendship and amity established, and between all those who are associated in spirit or flesh through their devotion, faith, belief, location, kindred, culture and history. Chapter 1 – General Provisions

ARTICLE II. – All the spirits, spiritual energy as prisoners, made on all sides or given during any conflict shall be immediately restored to the appropriate Spiritual Collective of One Heaven, without ransom or condition.

ARTICLE III. – All the energy of curses, binding, control, or obligations of servitude or slavery as made in Heaven or within the temporal realm on all sides shall be immediately dissolved or forgiven or settled so that no outstanding curses, binding, controls, obligations of servitude or slavery exists between or by any one of the Parties.

5. ARTICLE IV. – In recognition of our united, solemn unbreakable oath and binding to the Covenant of One Heaven, also known as Pactum De Singularis Caelum and the proposition of a United Heaven, let it be known to all past, present and future that the Parties have hereby given, granted and conveyed all their powers, all their customs, all their rights and property, all their symbols and instruments of power, all sacred objects, texts, scriptures and sanctuaries and all claims of authority to the Highest Holy Covenant of One Heaven and to the proper authority and structure of the United States of Spirits. Chapter 2 - Conveyance of Rights, Powers and Symbols of Authority

ARTICLE V. – Upon formal ratification and recognition of this Treaty, when the leadership of One Heaven or its designated representatives on Earth speak or promulgate one or more instruments, they do so with the highest valid authority and the complete conveyance of all rights, property, uses, customs, symbols, and powers of authority of the Parties as the collective Divine Feminine.

ARTICLE VI. – Any and all spiritual or temporal bodies that publicly or privately claim authority from or allegiance to one or more Divine Feminine deities henceforth automatically derives any and all authority solely from the Society of One Heaven and its valid designates and any existing sacred oaths, pledges and vows are carried over to respecting and obeying the Highest Holy Covenant of One Heaven.

ARTICLE VII. – Any and all spiritual or temporal bodies that publicly or privately claim authority from or allegiance to one or more Divine Feminine deities are solemnly bound by their sacred oaths, pledges and vows to honour and respect any and all instruments legitimately promulgated under the Seal of the Society of One Heaven or a valid designate.

ARTICLE VIII. – Any and all spiritual or temporal bodies that publicly or privately claim authority from or allegiance to one or more Divine Feminine deities are solemnly bound by the laws of property, trusts and ownership to obey any order, deed, command, edict, direction and request promulgated by the Society of One Heaven concerning any and all property administered on behalf of the Society of One Heaven by the spiritual or temporal body and its officers.

ARTICLE IX. – Any claim or claims contrary to the above mentioned clauses are hereby null and void from the beginning, having no force spiritually, legally or lawfully.

6. IN WITNESS WHEREOF, the undersigned Plenipotentiaries have witnessed and signed this Treaty. Enaction of Treaty

GAIA E8:Y3209:A1:S1:M6:D1, [Mon, 21 Dec 2009]

The duly appointed Plenipotentiaries on behalf of the Deities known as Amaterasu-o-mi-kami, Anat, Antu, Aphrodite, Artemis, Asherah, Ashtoreth, Astarte, Atargatis, Athena, Bastet, Bes, Brigit, Ceres, Chalchiuhtlicue, Cihuacoatl, Cipactli, Coatlicue, Coventina, Cybil, Danu, Demeter, Disani, Durga, Eileithyia, Epona, Ereskigal, Fjorgyn, Freyja, Frigg, Gaia, Hathor, Hebat, Hekate, Hera, Hestia, Hsi Wang Mu, Idunn, Inana, Ishtar, Isis, Juno, Kali, Kuan Yin, Kybele, Laksmi, Leto, Ma, Maia, Mary, Mari, Matres, Maya, Minerva, Morgan, Nammu, Neith, Nerthus, Ninhursaga, Parvati, Persephone, Pistis, Prthivi, Rhea, Sakhmet, Sarasvati, Sati, Semele, Sibyl, Siti, Tara, Taweret, Tiamat, Tin Hau, Venus and Vesta.

7. By Agreement of the Highest Concording Parties, this Treaty and Covenant shall be Ratified throughout all Heaven, spiritual dimensions and the Universe by the Day of Agreement and Understanding and shall be Ratified by one or more temporal beings by the Day of Judgement. Ratification of Treaty

Ratification by Day of Agreement and Understanding

By this Covenant, the Day of Agreement and Understanding is GAIA E8:Y3209:A1:S1:M6:D1, [Mon, 21 Dec 2009].

Ratification by Day of Agreement and Understanding shall be when this Treaty and Covenant is ratified throughout all Heaven, spiritual dimensions and the Universe by the Highest Office Holders of One Heaven representing the Supreme Command of Occupational Forces in and on Earth and when at least two (2) spirits conveyed into circumscribed Level 6 Homo Sapien Life Forms bear witness to the event.

Ratification by Day of Judgement

By this Covenant, the Day of Judgement is VENUS E8:Y3210:A0:S1:M27:D6, [Wed, 21 Dec 2011].

Ratification by Day of Judgement shall be when this Treaty and Covenant is ratified by the Highest Office Holders of existing societies, faiths and associations that claim their existence, authority and power from the supernatural and spiritual either through their tacit, competent and honourable consent, or through their dishonour demonstrating the delinquency of their flesh and therefore the right through power to represent their spirit to ratify the Covenant and Treaty on their behalf.

Article 51 – Treaty of the Divine Messengers

1. **THE HIGHEST CONCORDING PARTIES, CONCURRING** with the most sacred Covenant known as Pactum De Singularis Caelum, also known as the Covenant of One Heaven as the Highest Supreme Law of the Divine Creator of All Existence; and RECOGNISING the Unique Collective Awareness of Divine Mind, also known as the Divina of one hundred and forty-four (144) Deities as the duly elected Government of One Heaven; and AFFIRMING all war and major spiritual conflict within and between the Heavens has officially ended; and ASSENTING to the validity and legitimacy of the *Treaty of the Divine Masculine* and the *Treaty of Divine Feminine* and the *Treaty of Angels, Saints and Demons* and the *Treaty of Spirits States* and the *Treaty of the Suns* and the *Treaty* Treaty of the Divine Messengers

of the Planets and Moons; and ESTABLISHING the agreed conditions by which War on planets such as Earth may also be ended; and RESOLVING to confirm the foundations of a strong and perpetual union; and DETERMINING to end all forms of spiritual curse and the end of Hell(s), do Come Now with these Presents and with one another Agree to this Covenant of the Divine Messengers.

The Divine Messengers as the Highest Concording Parties to the Treaty

2. Let it be known to all past, present and future, the Highest Concording Parties and their duly appointed Plenipotentiaries of the same name herein, having communicated and exchanged to each other their Full Powers, found to be in good and due form, come freely together in full consent and authority being: the Divine Messengers and their duly appointed Plenipotentiaries known as Aaron, Abraham, Adad, Adonis, Attis, Baba Rabban, Bacchus, Buddha, Christos, Daniel, David, Dionysus, Elijah, Enoch, Esus, Ezekiel, Gideon, Heracles, Hosea, Herakles, Hermes, Horus, Indra, Isaiah, Jacob, Jeremiah, Jesus Christ, John the Baptist, John of Patmos, Joshua, Krishna, Recurrence, Malachi, Mercurius, Mithra, Moses, Muhammad the Prophet, Prometheus, Sabbatai Tzvi, Samuel, Rebbe Schneerson, Quetzalcoatl, Tammuz, Zechariah and Zohar.

Recital of Articles of Treaty

3. The Highest Concording Parties in Good Faith and without Prejudice hereby ACCEPT, APPROVE and AGREE the following Articles:

Chapter 1 – General Provisions

4. ARTICLE I. – By the present Treaty ("this Treaty"), the HIGHEST CONCORDING PARTIES ("the Parties") there shall be a universal and perpetual peace and harmony and a sincere friendship and amity established, and between all those who are associated in spirit or flesh through their devotion, faith, belief, location, kindred, culture and history.

ARTICLE II. – All the spirits, spiritual energy as prisoners, made on all sides or given during any conflict shall be immediately restored to the appropriate Spiritual Collective of One Heaven, without ransom or condition.

ARTICLE III. – All the energy of curses, binding, control, or obligations of servitude or slavery as made in Heaven or within the temporal realm on all sides shall be immediately dissolved or forgiven or settled so that no outstanding curses, binding, controls, obligations of servitude or slavery exists between or by any one of the Parties.

Chapter 2 - Conveyance of Rights, Powers and Symbols of Authority

5. ARTICLE IV. – In recognition of our united, solemn unbreakable oath and binding to the Covenant of One Heaven, also known as Pactum De Singularis Caelum and the proposition of a United Heaven, let it be known to all past, present and future that the Parties have hereby given, granted and conveyed all their powers, all their customs, all their rights and property, all their symbols and instruments of power, all sacred objects, texts, scriptures and sanctuaries and all claims of authority to the Highest Holy Covenant of One Heaven and to the proper authority and structure of the United States of Spirits.

ARTICLE V. – Upon formal ratification and recognition of this Treaty, when the leadership of One Heaven or its designated representatives on Earth speak or promulgate one or more instruments, they do so with the highest valid authority and the complete conveyance of all rights, property, uses, customs, symbols, and powers of authority of the Parties as the collective Divine Messengers.

ARTICLE VI. – Any and all spiritual or temporal bodies that publicly or privately claim authority from or allegiance to one or more Divine Messenger henceforth automatically derives any and all authority solely from the Society of One Heaven and its valid designates and any existing sacred oaths, pledges and vows are carried over to respecting and obeying the Highest Holy Covenant of One Heaven.

ARTICLE VII. – Any and all spiritual or temporal bodies that publicly or privately claim authority from or allegiance to one or more Divine Messenger are solemnly bound by their sacred oaths, pledges and vows to honour and respect any and all instruments legitimately promulgated under the Seal of the Society of One Heaven or a valid designate.

ARTICLE VIII. – Any and all spiritual or temporal bodies that publicly or privately claim authority from or allegiance to one or more Divine Messenger are solemnly bound by the laws of property, trusts and ownership to obey any order, deed, command, edict, direction and request promulgated by the Society of One Heaven concerning any and all property administered on behalf of the Society of One Heaven by the spiritual or temporal body and its officers.

ARTICLE IX. – Any claim or claims contrary to the above mentioned clauses are hereby null and void from the beginning, having no force spiritually, legally or lawfully.

6. IN WITNESS WHEREOF, the undersigned Plenipotentiaries have witnessed and signed this Treaty. Enaction of Treaty

GAIA E8:Y3209:A1:S1:M6:D1, [Mon, 21 Dec 2009]

The duly appointed Plenipotentiaries on behalf of the Divine Messengers known as Aaron, Abraham, Adad, Adonis, Attis, Baba Rabban, Bacchus, Buddha, Christos, Daniel, David, Dionysus, Elijah, Enoch, Esus, Ezekiel, Gideon, Heracles, Hosea, Herakles, Hermes, Horus, Indra, Isaiah, Jacob, Jeremiah, Jesus Christ, John the Baptist, John of Patmos, Joshua, Krishna, Recurrence, Malachi, Mercurius,

Mithra, Moses, Muhammad the Prophet, Prometheus, Sabbatai Tzvi, Samuel, Rebbe Schneerson, Quetzalcoatl, Tammuz, Zechariah and Zohar.

7. By Agreement of the Highest Concording Parties, this Treaty and Covenant shall be Ratified throughout all Heaven, spiritual dimensions and the Universe by the Day of Agreement and Understanding and shall be Ratified by one or more temporal beings by the Day of Judgement. Ratification of Treaty

Ratification by Day of Agreement and Understanding

By this Covenant, the Day of Agreement and Understanding is GAIA E8:Y3209:A1:S1:M6:D1, [Mon, 21 Dec 2009].

Ratification by Day of Agreement and Understanding shall be when this Treaty and Covenant is ratified throughout all Heaven, spiritual dimensions and the Universe by the Highest Office Holders of One Heaven representing the Supreme Command of Occupational Forces in and on Earth and when at least two (2) spirits conveyed into circumscribed Level 6 Homo Sapien Life Forms bear witness to the event.

Ratification by Day of Judgement

By this Covenant, the Day of Judgement is VENUS E8:Y3210:A0:S1:M27:D6, [Wed, 21 Dec 2011].

Ratification by Day of Judgement shall be when this Treaty and Covenant is ratified by the Highest Office Holders of existing societies, faiths and associations that claim their existence, authority and power from the supernatural and spiritual either through their tacit, competent and honourable consent, or through their dishonour demonstrating the delinquency of their flesh and therefore the right through power to represent their spirit to ratify the Covenant and Treaty on their behalf.

Article 52 – Treaty of Angels, Saints and Demons

1. **THE HIGHEST CONCORDING PARTIES, CONCURRING** with the most sacred Covenant known as Pactum De Singularis Caelum, also known as the Covenant of One Heaven as the highest Supreme Law of the Divine Creator of All Existence; and RECOGNISING the Unique Collective Awareness of Divine Mind, also known as the *Divina* of one hundred and forty-four (144) Deities as the duly elected Government of One Heaven; and AFFIRMING all war and major spiritual conflict within and between the Heavens has officially ended; and ASSENTING to the validity and Treaty of Angels, Saints and Demons

legitimacy of the *Treaty of the Divine Masculine* and the *Treaty of Divine Feminine* and the *Treaty of Divine Messengers* and the *Treaty of Spirits States* and the *Treaty of the Suns* and the *Treaty of the Planets and Moons;* and ESTABLISHING the agreed conditions by which War on planets such as Earth may also be ended; and RESOLVING to confirm the foundations of a strong and perpetual union; and DETERMINING to end all forms of spiritual curse and the end of Hell(s), do Come Now with these Presents and with one another Agree to this Covenant of Angels, Saints and Demons.

2. Let it be known to all past, present and future, the High Concording Parties known as "Angels" and their duly appointed Plenipotentiaries of the same name herein, having communicated and exchanged to each other their Full Powers, found to be in good and due form, come freely together in full consent and authority being: the Angels and their duly appointed Plenipotentiaries known as Abymael, Acha-iah, Adriel, Ahriman, Alad-iah, Ambriel, Amesha Spenta, Anianu-el, Ani-el, Arariel, Ariel, Asal-iah, Azi-el, Azrael, Barachiel, Bene Elohim, Camael, Cassiel, Chamuel, Damab-iah, Dani-el, Darda'il, Eiai-el, Elem-iah, Eremiel, Gabriel, Gagiel, Grigori, Haa-iah, Haam-iah, Habu-iah, Hadraniel, Hahah-el, Haha-iah, Hahas-iah, Hahu-iah, Hai-el, Hakam-iah, Hamalat al-Arsh, Harah-el, Hari-el, Harut, Hesediel, Ieiaz-el, Ielah-iah, Imam-iah, Israfel, Jabam-iah, Jah-H-el, Jegudiel, Jehoel, Jehu-iah, Jeiai-el, Jeial-el, Jeli-el, Jequn, Jerahmeel, Jerath-el, Jezal-el, John, Jophiel, Kahet-el, Kali-el, Kasdeja, Kevak-iah, Kiraman Katibin, Kosmiel, Kushiel, Lahab-iah, Lano-iah, Lauv-iah, Lekab-el, Lelah-el, Leliel, Leuv-iah, Maalik, Mahas-iah, Malik, Manak-el, Marut, Mebah-el, Meba-iah, Mehi-el, Melah-el, Menad-el, Metatron, Michael, Miha-el, Mika-el, Mizra-el, Moroni, Mu'aqqibat, Mum-iah, Munkar, Muriel, Nakir, Nana-el, Neleka-el, Nemam-iah, Nitha-el, Nith-Ha-iah, Nuriel, Oma-el, Ophanim, Orifiel, Pahaliah, Pahal-iah, Paul, Penemue, Peter, Poi-El, Powers, Principalities, Puriel, Qaphsiel, Raguel, Raphael, Raqib, Raziel, Reha-el, Reii-el, Remiel, Ridwan, Roch-el, Sachiel, Sandalphon, Sariel, Seal-iah, See-iah, Selaphiel, Seraph, Seraphiel, Shamsiel, Simiel, Sita-el, Temeluchus, Tennin, Thrones, Tzaphqiel, Umab-el, Uriel, Uzziel, Vasar-iah, Vehu-el, Vehu-iah, Veubi-ah, Virtues, Wormwood, Yehudiel, Yerachmiel, Zabaniyah, Zachariel, Zadkiel and Zophiel.

The Angels as the High Concording Parties to the Treaty

3. Let it be known to all past, present and future, the High Concording Parties known as "Demons" and their duly appointed Plenipotentiaries of the same name herein, having communicated and exchanged to each other their Full Powers, found to be in good and due form, come freely together in full consent and authority being: the Demons and their duly appointed Plenipotentiaries known as Abaddon, Abalam,

The Demons as the High Concording Parties to the Treaty

Adramelech, Agaliarept, Agares, Ahriman, Aim, Akvan, Alal, Alloces, Allu, Amaymon, Amdusias, Ammit, Anzu, Amon, Amy, Andhaka, Andras, Andrealphus, Andromalius, Apep (Apophis), Apollyon, Armaros, Asag, Asakku, Asb'el, Asmodeus, Astaroth, Astarte, Asura, Azazel, Azi, Balam, Bagat, Baphomet, Barbas, Barbatos, Bathin, Behemoth, Belial, Beleth, Bull man, Bune, Belphegor, Berith, Bianakith, Bifrons, Botis, Buer, Bali Raj, Biule, Caacrinolaas, Caim, Cerberus, Charun, Cheitan, Cimejes, Corson, Crocell, Culsu, Dantalion, Danjal, Dasa, Decarabia, Demogorgon, Duma, Dajjal, Elathan, Eligos, Ethniu, Euryale, Exdemoneus, Familiars, Fleuretty, Fobos, Focalor, Foras, Forneus, Furcas, Furfur, Gaap, Gader'el, Gaki, Glasya-Labolas, Gorgon, Gremory, Grigori, Gusion, Guzalu, Haagenti, Haborim, Halphas, Hanan'el, Hantu, Haures, Humbaba, Incubus, Ipos, Iblis, Jikininki, Judas, Kabhanda, Kasdaye, Kirara, Kitsune, Kobal, Kokb'ael, Krampus, Labal, Labasu, Lamia, Legion, Lechies, Lempo, Leonard, Leraje, Leviathan, Lilim, Lilith, Lillu, Liothe, Lix Tetrax, Lucifuge Rofocale, Malphas, Mammon, Maricha, Marax, Marbas, Marchosias, Mastema, Mathim, Medusa, Melchiresa, Mephistopheles, Merihem, Meshinka Destrega Sham, Mictlantecuhtli, Moloch, Murmur, Mutis, Naberius, Naberus, Naphula, Neqa'el, Ninurta, Nix, Onoskelis, Oray, Orcus, Oriax, Ornias, Orobas, Ose, Paimon, Pazuzu, Penemue, Phenex, Pithius, Procell, Pruflas, Purson, Quina, Rahab, Rahovart, Raiju, Rakshasa, Rangda, Raum, Razakel, Raberzahl, Ronove, Rumjal, Rusalka, Sabnock, Saleos, Samael, Satanachia, Scox, Seere, Semyazza, Shaitan, Shax, Shedim, Sidragasum, Sitri, Sthenno, Stolas, Succubus, Surgat, Tannin, Teeraal, Thammuz, Tzitzimime, Uvall, Valefor, Vapula, Vassago, Vepar, Vine, Volac, Xaphan, Xezbeth, Yeqon, Yeter'el, Zagan, Zephon, Zepar and Ziminar.

4. The High Concording Parties in Good Faith and without Prejudice hereby ACCEPT, APPROVE and AGREE the following Articles: Recital of Articles of Treaty

5. ARTICLE I. – By the present Treaty ("this Treaty"), the HIGHEST CONCORDING PARTIES ("the Parties") there shall be a universal and perpetual peace and harmony and a sincere friendship and amity established, and between all those who are associated in spirit or flesh through their devotion, faith, belief, location, kindred, culture and history. Chapter 1 – General Provisions

ARTICLE II. – All the spirits, spiritual energy as prisoners, made on all sides or given during any conflict shall be immediately restored to the appropriate Spiritual Collective of One Heaven, without ransom or condition.

ARTICLE III. – All the energy of curses, binding, control, or obligations of servitude or slavery as made in Heaven or within the temporal realm on all sides shall be immediately dissolved or forgiven or settled so that no outstanding curses, binding, controls, obligations of servitude or slavery exists between or by any one of the Parties.

6. ARTICLE IV. – In recognition of our united, solemn unbreakable oath and binding to the Covenant of One Heaven, also known as Pactum De Singularis Caelum and the proposition of a United Heaven, let it be known to all past, present and future that the Parties have hereby given, granted and conveyed all their powers, all their customs, all their rights and property, all their symbols and instruments of power, all sacred objects, texts, scriptures and sanctuaries and all claims of authority to the Highest Holy Covenant of One Heaven and to the proper authority and structure of the United States of Spirits.

Chapter 2 - Conveyance of Rights, Powers and Symbols of Authority

ARTICLE V. – Upon formal ratification and recognition of this Treaty, when the leadership of One Heaven or its designated representatives on Earth speak or promulgate one or more instruments, they do so with the highest valid authority and the complete conveyance of all rights, property, uses, customs, symbols, and powers of authority of the Parties as the collective Angels, Saints and Demons.

ARTICLE VI. – Any and all spiritual or temporal bodies that publicly or privately claim authority from or allegiance to one or more Angels, Saints and Demons henceforth automatically derives any and all authority solely from the Society of One Heaven and its valid designates and any existing sacred oaths, pledges and vows are carried over to respecting and obeying the Highest Holy Covenant of One Heaven.

ARTICLE VII. – Any and all spiritual or temporal bodies that publicly or privately claim authority from or allegiance to one or more Angels, Saints and Demons are solemnly bound by their sacred oaths, pledges and vows to honour and respect any and all instruments legitimately promulgated under the Seal of the Society of One Heaven or a valid designate.

ARTICLE VIII. – Any and all spiritual or temporal bodies that publicly or privately claim authority from or allegiance to one or more Angels, Saints and Demons are solemnly bound by the laws of property, trusts and ownership to obey any order, deed, command, edict, direction and request promulgated by the Society of One Heaven concerning any and all property administered on behalf of the Society of One Heaven by the spiritual or temporal body and its officers.

ARTICLE IX. – Any claim or claims contrary to the above mentioned clauses are hereby null and void from the beginning, having no force spiritually, legally or lawfully.

7. IN WITNESS WHEREOF, the undersigned Plenipotentiaries have witnessed and signed this Treaty. Enaction of Treaty

GAIA E8:Y3209:A1:S1:M6:D1, [Mon, 21 Dec 2009]

The Angels and their duly appointed Plenipotentiaries known as Abymael, Acha-iah, Adriel, Ahriman, Alad-iah, Ambriel, Amesha Spenta, Anianu-el, Ani-el, Arariel, Ariel, Asal-iah, Azi-el, Azrael, Barachiel, Bene Elohim, Camael, Cassiel, Chamuel, Damab-iah, Dani-el, Darda'il, Eiai-el, Elem-iah, Eremiel, Gabriel, Gagiel, Grigori, Haa-iah, Haam-iah, Habu-iah, Hadraniel, Hahah-el, Haha-iah, Hahas-iah, Hahu-iah, Hai-el, Hakam-iah, Hamalat al-Arsh, Harah-el, Hari-el, Harut, Hesediel, Ieiaz-el, Ielah-iah, Imam-iah, Israfel, Jabam-iah, Jah-H-el, Jegudiel, Jehoel, Jehu-iah, Jeiai-el, Jeial-el, Jeli-el, Jequn, Jerahmeel, Jerath-el, Jezal-el, John, Jophiel, Kahet-el, Kali-el, Kasdeja, Kevak-iah, Kiraman Katibin, Kosmiel, Kushiel, Lahab-iah, Lano-iah, Lauv-iah, Lekab-el, Lelah-el, Leliel, Leuv-iah, Maalik, Mahas-iah, Malik, Manak-el, Marut, Mebah-el, Meba-iah, Mehi-el, Melah-el, Menad-el, Metatron, Michael, Miha-el, Mika-el, Mizra-el, Moroni, Mu'aqqibat, Mum-iah, Munkar, Muriel, Nakir, Nana-el, Neleka-el, Nemam-iah, Nitha-el, Nith-Ha-iah, Nuriel, Oma-el, Ophanim, Orifiel, Pahaliah, Pahal-iah, Paul, Penemue, Peter, Poi-El, Powers, Principalities, Puriel, Qaphsiel, Raguel, Raphael, Raqib, Raziel, Reha-el, Reii-el, Remiel, Ridwan, Roch-el, Sachiel, Sandalphon, Sariel, Seal-iah, See-iah, Selaphiel, Seraph, Seraphiel, Shamsiel, Simiel, Sita-el, Temeluchus, Tennin, Thrones, Tzaphqiel, Umab-el, Uriel, Uzziel, Vasar-iah, Vehu-el, Vehu-iah, Veubi-ah, Virtues, Wormwood, Yehudiel, Yerachmiel, Zabaniyah, Zachariel, Zadkiel and Zophiel; and the Demons and their duly appointed Plenipotentiaries known as Abaddon, Abalam, Adramelech, Agaliarept, Agares, Ahriman, Aim, Akvan, Alal, Alloces, Allu, Amaymon, Amdusias, Ammit, Anzu, Amon, Amy, Andhaka, Andras, Andrealphus, Andromalius, Apep (Apophis), Apollyon, Armaros, Asag, Asakku, Asb'el, Asmodeus, Astaroth, Astarte, Asura, Azazel, Azi, Balam, Bagat, Baphomet, Barbas, Barbatos, Bathin, Behemoth, Belial, Beleth, Bull man, Bune, Belphegor, Berith, Bianakith, Bifrons, Botis, Buer, Bali Raj, Biule, Caacrinolaas, Caim, Cerberus, Charun, Cheitan, Cimejes, Corson, Crocell, Culsu, Dantalion, Danjal, Dasa, Decarabia, Demogorgon, Duma, Dajjal, Elathan, Eligos, Ethniu, Euryale, Exdemoneus, Familiars, Fleuretty, Fobos, Focalor, Foras, Forneus, Furcas, Furfur, Gaap, Gader'el, Gaki, Glasya-Labolas, Gorgon, Gremory, Grigori, Gusion, Guzalu, Haagenti, Haborim, Halphas, Hanan'el, Hantu, Haures, Humbaba, Incubus, Ipos, Iblis, Jikininki, Judas, Kabhanda, Kasdaye, Kirara, Kitsune, Kobal, Kokb'ael,

Krampus, Labal, Labasu, Lamia, Legion, Lechies, Lempo, Leonard, Leraje, Leviathan, Lilim, Lilith, Lillu, Liothe, Lix Tetrax, Lucifuge Rofocale, Malphas, Mammon, Maricha, Marax, Marbas, Marchosias, Mastema, Mathim, Medusa, Melchiresa, Mephistopheles, Merihem, Meshinka Destrega Sham, Mictlantecuhtli, Moloch, Murmur, Mutis, Naberius, Naberus, Naphula, Neqa'el, Ninurta, Nix, Onoskelis, Oray, Orcus, Oriax, Ornias, Orobas, Ose, Paimon, Pazuzu, Penemue, Phenex, Pithius, Procell, Pruflas, Purson, Quina, Rahab, Rahovart, Raiju, Rakshasa, Rangda, Raum, Razakel, Raberzahl, Ronove, Rumjal, Rusalka, Sabnock, Saleos, Samael, Satanachia, Scox, Seere, Semyazza, Shaitan, Shax, Shedim, Sidragasum, Sitri, Sthenno, Stolas, Succubus, Surgat, Tannin, Teeraal, Thammuz, Tzitzimime, Uvall, Valefor, Vapula, Vassago, Vepar, Vine, Volac, Xaphan, Xezbeth, Yeqon, Yeter'el, Zagan, Zephon, Zepar and Ziminar.

8. By Agreement of the Highest Concording Parties, this Treaty and Covenant shall be Ratified throughout all Heaven, spiritual dimensions and the Universe by the Day of Agreement and Understanding and shall be Ratified by one or more temporal beings by the Day of Judgement. Ratification of Treaty

Ratification by Day of Agreement and Understanding

By this Covenant, the Day of Agreement and Understanding is GAIA E8:Y3209:A1:S1:M6:D1, [Mon, 21 Dec 2009].

Ratification by Day of Agreement and Understanding shall be when this Treaty and Covenant is ratified throughout all Heaven, spiritual dimensions and the Universe by the Highest Office Holders of One Heaven representing the Supreme Command of Occupational Forces in and on Earth and when at least two (2) spirits conveyed into circumscribed Level 6 Homo Sapien Life Forms bear witness to the event.

Ratification by Day of Judgement

By this Covenant, the Day of Judgement is VENUS E8:Y3210:A0:S1:M27:D6, [Wed, 21 Dec 2011].

Ratification by Day of Judgement shall be when this Treaty and Covenant is ratified by the Highest Office Holders of existing societies, faiths and associations that claim their existence, authority and power from the supernatural and spiritual either through their tacit, competent and honourable consent, or through their dishonour demonstrating the delinquency of their flesh and therefore the right through power to represent their spirit to ratify the Covenant and Treaty on their behalf.

Article 53 – Treaty of the Spirit States

1. THE HIGHEST CONCORDING PARTIES, CONCURRING with the most sacred Covenant known as *Pactum De Singularis Caelum*, also known as the Covenant of One Heaven as the Highest Supreme Law of the Divine Creator of All Existence; and RECOGNISING the Unique Collective Awareness of Divine Mind, also known as the Divina of one hundred and forty-four (144) Deities as the duly elected Government of One Heaven; and AFFIRMING all war and major spiritual conflict within and between the Heavens has officially ended; and ASSENTING to the validity and legitimacy of the *Treaty of the Divine Masculine* and the *Treaty of Divine Feminine* and the *Treaty of Divine Messengers* and the *Treaty of Angels, Saints and Demons* and the *Treaty of the Suns* and the *Treaty of the Planets and Moons;* and ESTABLISHING the agreed conditions by which War on planets such as Earth may also be ended; and RESOLVING to confirm the foundations of a strong and perpetual union; and DETERMINING to end all forms of spiritual curse and the end of Hell(s), do Come Now with these Presents and with one another Agree to this Covenant of the United States of Spirits.

Treaty of the United States of Spirits

2. Let it be known to all past, present and future, the High Concording Parties and their duly appointed Plenipotentiaries of the same name herein, having communicated and exchanged to each other their Full Powers, found to be in good and due form, come freely together in full consent and authority being: the Great Community of Mithra and its duly appointed Plenipotentiaries, the Great Kingdom of Christian Heaven and its duly appointed Plenipotentiaries, the Great Kingdom of Mother Goddess and its duly appointed Plenipotentiaries, the Great Kingdom of Nirvana and its duly appointed Plenipotentiaries, the Great Kingdom of Paradise of Allah and its duly appointed Plenipotentiaries, the Great Kingdom of Satan and its duly appointed Plenipotentiaries, the Great Kingdom of Seol and its duly appointed Plenipotentiaries, the Great Kingdom of Smaya and its duly appointed Plenipotentiaries, the Great Spiritual Community of Confucius and its duly appointed Plenipotentiaries, the Great Spiritual Community of Turtle Island and its duly appointed Plenipotentiaries, the Great Spiritual Kingdoms of the Cuilliaéan and its duly appointed Plenipotentiaries, the Great Unified Kingdoms of Baal and its duly appointed Plenipotentiaries, the Greater Community Mind of Buddha and its duly appointed Plenipotentiaries, the Kingdom of Mormons and its duly appointed Plenipotentiaries, the Kingdom of Janna and its duly appointed Plenipotentiaries, the Lesser Kingdom of Anglican Faithful and its duly appointed Plenipotentiaries, the Lesser Kingdom of Catholic Faithful and its duly appointed Plenipotentiaries, the

The Spirit States as the High Concording Parties to the Treaty

Lesser Kingdom of Gnostics and its duly appointed Plenipotentiaries, the Lesser Kingdom of Moloch and its duly appointed Plenipotentiaries, the Lesser Kingdom of Protestants and its duly appointed Plenipotentiaries, the Lesser Kingdoms of Himmel and its duly appointed Plenipotentiaries, the Spiritual Community of Jains and its duly appointed Plenipotentiaries, the Spiritual Community of Sikhs and its duly appointed Plenipotentiaries, the Spiritual Community of Sufi and its duly appointed Plenipotentiaries, the Spiritual Community of Tao and its duly appointed Plenipotentiaries, the Unified Communities of Brahma (Hindu) and its duly appointed Plenipotentiaries, the Unified Elysium Spiritual Plains and its duly appointed Plenipotentiaries, the Unified Kingdoms of Urania and its duly appointed Plenipotentiaries, the Unified Minor Kingdoms of Orthodoxy and its duly appointed Plenipotentiaries, the Unified Spirits of Elders and its duly appointed Plenipotentiaries, the Unified Spiritual Kingdoms of Africa and its duly appointed Plenipotentiaries, the Unified Spiritual Kingdoms of Arabia and its duly appointed Plenipotentiaries, the Unified Spiritual Kingdoms of Asia and its duly appointed Plenipotentiaries, the Unified Spiritual Kingdoms of Oceania and its duly appointed Plenipotentiaries, the Unified Spiritual Kingdoms of the Americas and its duly appointed Plenipotentiaries, the Unified Spiritual Kingdoms of Europa and its duly appointed Plenipotentiaries, the Unified Spiritual Kingdoms of the Android Scitus (Smart Androids) and its duly appointed Plenipotentiaries, the Unified Spiritual Kingdoms of the Cerastis Sapiens (Horned Reptoids) and its duly appointed Plenipotentiaries, the Unified Spiritual Kingdoms of the Cyborg Sagax (Autonomous Cyborgs) and its duly appointed Plenipotentiaries, the Unified Spiritual Kingdoms of the Griseo Altus (Tall Grey) and its duly appointed Plenipotentiaries, the Unified Spiritual Kingdoms of the Griseo Morbidus (Standard Grey) and its duly appointed Plenipotentiaries, the Unified Spiritual Kingdoms of the Homo Adamus (Early Humanoids) and its duly appointed Plenipotentiaries, the Unified Spiritual Kingdoms of the Mammaloid Sentientiae (Conscious Mammaloids) and its duly appointed Plenipotentiaries, the Unified Spiritual Kingdoms of the Sapientia Mutatis (Transformed Wisdom Beings) and its duly appointed Plenipotentiaries, the Unified Spiritual Kingdoms of the Serpens Alatus (Winged Reptoids) and its duly appointed Plenipotentiaries, the Unified Spiritual Kingdoms of the Serpens Sophos (Smooth Skinned Reptoids) and its duly appointed Plenipotentiaries, the Unified Spiritual Kingdoms of the Volucris Permuto (Hybrid Bird Form) and its duly appointed Plenipotentiaries, the Unified Spiritual Tribes of Earth and Wicca and its duly appointed Plenipotentiaries, and those Plenipotentiaries representing minor

Heavens, deities and most ancient of ancestors.

3. The Highest Concording Parties in Good Faith and without Prejudice hereby ACCEPT, APPROVE and AGREE the following articles: Recital of Articles of Treaty

4. ARTICLE I. – By the present Treaty ("this Treaty"), the HIGHEST CONCORDING PARTIES ("the Parties") there shall be a universal and perpetual peace and harmony and a sincere friendship and amity established, and between all those who are associated in spirit or flesh through their devotion, faith, belief, location, kindred, culture and history. Chapter 1 – General Provisions

ARTICLE II. – All the spirits, spiritual energy as prisoners, made on all sides or given during any conflict shall be immediately restored to the appropriate Spiritual Collective of One Heaven, without ransom or condition.

ARTICLE III. – All the energy of curses, binding, control, or obligations of servitude or slavery as made in Heaven or within the temporal realm on all sides shall be immediately dissolved or forgiven or settled so that no outstanding curses, binding, controls, obligations of servitude or slavery exists between or by any one of the Parties.

5. ARTICLE IV. – In recognition of our united, solemn unbreakable oath and binding to the Covenant of One Heaven, also known as Pactum De Singularis Caelum and the proposition of a United Heaven, let it be known to all past, present and future that the Parties have hereby given, granted and conveyed all their powers, all their customs, all their rights and property, all their symbols and instruments of power, all sacred objects, texts, scriptures and sanctuaries and all claims of authority to the Highest Holy Covenant of One Heaven and to the proper authority and structure of the United States of Spirits. Chapter 2 - Conveyance of Rights, Powers and Symbols of Authority

ARTICLE V. – Upon formal ratification and recognition of this Treaty, when the leadership of One Heaven or its designated representatives on Earth speak or promulgate one or more instruments, they do so with the highest valid authority and the complete conveyance of all rights, property, uses, customs, symbols, and powers of authority of the Parties as the collective Spirit States.

ARTICLE VI. – Any and all spiritual or temporal bodies that publicly or privately claim authority from or allegiance to one or more Spirit States henceforth automatically derives any and all authority solely from the Society of One Heaven and its valid designates and any existing sacred oaths, pledges and vows are carried over to respecting and obeying the Highest Holy Covenant of One Heaven.

ARTICLE VII. – Any and all spiritual or temporal bodies that publicly or privately claim authority from or allegiance to one or more Spirit

States are solemnly bound by their sacred oaths, pledges and vows to honour and respect any and all instruments legitimately promulgated under the Seal of the Society of One Heaven or a valid designate.

ARTICLE VIII. – Any and all spiritual or temporal bodies that publicly or privately claim authority from or allegiance to one or more Spirit States are solemnly bound by the laws of property, trusts and ownership to obey any order, deed, command, edict, direction, request promulgated by the Society of One Heaven concerning any and all property administered on behalf of the Society of One Heaven by the spiritual or temporal body and its officers.

ARTICLE IX. – Any claim or claims contrary to the above mentioned clauses are hereby null and void from the beginning, having no force spiritually, legally or lawfully.

6. IN WITNESS WHEREOF, the undersigned Plenipotentiaries have witnessed and signed this Treaty.

Enaction of Treaty

GAIA E8:Y3209:A1:S1:M6:D1, [Mon, 21 Dec 2009]

The duly appointed Plenipotentiaries of the Great Community of Mithra, Great Kingdom of Christian Heaven, Great Kingdom of Mother Goddess, Great Kingdom of Nirvana, Great Kingdom of Paradise of Allah, Great Kingdom of Satan, Great Kingdom of Seol, Great Kingdom of Smaya, Great Spiritual Community of Confucius, Great Spiritual Community of Turtle Island, Great Spiritual Kingdoms of the Cuilliaéan, Great Unified Kingdoms of Baal, Greater Community Mind of Buddha, Kingdom of Mormons, Kingdom of Janna, Lesser Kingdom of Anglican Faithful, Lesser Kingdom of Catholic Faithful, Lesser Kingdom of Gnostics, Lesser Kingdom of Moloch, Lesser Kingdom of Protestants, Lesser Kingdoms of Himmel, Spiritual Community of Jains, Spiritual Community of Sikhs, Spiritual Community of Sufi, Spiritual Community of Tao, Unified Communities of Brahma (Hindu), Unified Elysium Spiritual Plains, Unified Kingdoms of Urania, Unified Minor Kingdoms of Orthodoxy, Unified Spirits of Elders, Unified Spiritual Kingdoms of Africa, Unified Spiritual Kingdoms of Arabia, Unified Spiritual Kingdoms of Asia, Unified Spiritual Kingdoms of Oceania, Unified Spiritual Kingdoms of the Americas, Unified Spiritual Kingdoms of Europa, Unified Spiritual Kingdoms of the Android Scitus (Smart Androids), Unified Spiritual Kingdoms of the Cerastis Sapiens (Horned Reptoids), Unified Spiritual Kingdoms of the Cyborg Sagax (Autonomous Cyborgs), Unified Spiritual Kingdoms of the Griseo Altus (Tall Grey), Unified Spiritual Kingdoms of the Griseo Morbidus (Standard Grey), Unified Spiritual Kingdoms of the Homo Adamus (Early Humanoids), Unified Spiritual Kingdoms of the Mammaloid Sentientiae (Conscious Mammaloids),

Unified Spiritual Kingdoms of the Sapientia Mutatis (Transformed Wisdom Beings), Unified Spiritual Kingdoms of the Serpens Alatus (Winged Reptoids), Unified Spiritual Kingdoms of the Serpens Sophos (Smooth Skinned Reptoids), Unified Spiritual Kingdoms of the Volucris Permuto (Hybrid Bird Form), Unified Spiritual Tribes of Earth and Wicca, and those Plenipotentiaries representing minor Heavens, deities and most ancient of ancestors.

7. By Agreement of the Highest Concording Parties, this Treaty and Covenant shall be Ratified throughout all Heaven, spiritual dimensions and the Universe by the Day of Agreement and Understanding and shall be Ratified by one or more temporal beings by the Day of Judgement. Ratification of Treaty

Ratification by Day of Agreement and Understanding

By this Covenant, the Day of Agreement and Understanding is GAIA E8:Y3209:A1:S1:M6:D1, [Mon, 21 Dec 2009].

Ratification by Day of Agreement and Understanding shall be when this Treaty and Covenant is ratified throughout all Heaven, spiritual dimensions and the Universe by the Highest Office Holders of One Heaven representing the Supreme Command of Occupational Forces in and on Earth and when at least two (2) spirits conveyed into circumscribed Level 6 Homo Sapien Life Forms bear witness to the event.

Ratification by Day of Judgement

By this Covenant, the Day of Judgement is VENUS E8:Y3210:A0:S1:M27:D6, [Wed, 21 Dec 2011].

Ratification by Day of Judgement shall be when this Treaty and Covenant is ratified by the Highest Office Holders of existing societies, faiths and associations that claim their existence, authority and power from the supernatural and spiritual either through their tacit, competent and honourable consent, or through their dishonour demonstrating the delinquency of their flesh and therefore the right through power to represent their spirit to ratify the Covenant and Treaty on their behalf.

Article 54 - Treaty of the Suns (Star Systems)

1. **THE HIGHEST CONCORDING PARTIES, CONCURRING** with the most sacred Covenant known as *Pactum De Singularis Caelum*, also known as the Covenant of One Heaven as the Highest Supreme law of the Divine Creator of All Existence; and RECOGNISING the Unique Collective Awareness of Treaty of the Suns

Divine Mind, also known as the Divina of one hundred and forty-four (144) Deities as the duly elected Government of One Heaven; and AFFIRMING all war and major spiritual conflict within and between the Heavens has officially ended; and ASSENTING to the validity and legitimacy of the *Treaty of the Divine Masculine* and the *Treaty of Divine Feminine* and the *Treaty of Divine Messengers* and the *Treaty of Angels, Saints and Demons* and the *Treaty of the Spirit States* and the *Treaty of the Planets and Moons;* and ESTABLISHING the agreed conditions by which conflict between Star Systems (Suns) and their Planets may also be ended; and RESOLVING to confirm the foundations of a strong and perpetual union; and DETERMINING to end all forms of ignorance and corruption of Universal Knowledge, do Come Now with these Presents and with one another Agree to this Covenant of the Suns (Star Systems).

The Star Systems (Suns) as the High Concording Parties to the Treaty

2. Let it be known to all past, present and future, the High Concording Parties and their duly appointed Plenipotentiaries of the same name herein, having communicated and exchanged to each other their Full Powers, found to be in good and due form, come freely together in full consent and authority being: the Solar System and duly appointed Spiritual Plenipotentiaries, the Alpha Centauri Star System and duly appointed Spiritual Plenipotentiaries, the Barnards Star System and duly appointed Spiritual Plenipotentiaries, the Wolf 359 Star System and duly appointed Spiritual Plenipotentiaries, the Lalande 21185 Star System and duly appointed Spiritual Plenipotentiaries, the Sirius Star System and duly appointed Spiritual Plenipotentiaries, the Luyten 726-8 Star System and duly appointed Spiritual Plenipotentiaries, the Ross 154 Star System and duly appointed Spiritual Plenipotentiaries, the Ross 248 Star System and duly appointed Spiritual Plenipotentiaries, the Epsilon Eridani Star System and duly appointed Spiritual Plenipotentiaries, the Lacaille 9352 Star System and duly appointed Spiritual Plenipotentiaries, the Ross 128 Star System and duly appointed Spiritual Plenipotentiaries, the EZ Aquarii Star System and duly appointed Spiritual Plenipotentiaries, the Procyon Star System and duly appointed Spiritual Plenipotentiaries, the 61 Cygni Star System and duly appointed Spiritual Plenipotentiaries, the Struve 2398 Star System and duly appointed Spiritual Plenipotentiaries, the Groombridge 34 Star System and duly appointed Spiritual Plenipotentiaries, the Epsilon Indi Star System and duly appointed Spiritual Plenipotentiaries, the DX Cancri Star System and duly appointed Spiritual Plenipotentiaries, the Tau Ceti Star System and duly appointed Spiritual Plenipotentiaries, the GJ 1061 Star System and duly appointed Spiritual Plenipotentiaries, the YZ Ceti Star System and duly appointed Spiritual Plenipotentiaries, the Luyten's Star System and duly appointed Spiritual Plenipotentiaries, the

Teegarden's Star System and duly appointed Spiritual Plenipotentiaries, the SCR 1845-6357 Star System and duly appointed Spiritual Plenipotentiaries, the Kapteyn's Star System and duly appointed Spiritual Plenipotentiaries, the Lacaille 8760 Star System and duly appointed Spiritual Plenipotentiaries, the Kruger 60 Star System and duly appointed Spiritual Plenipotentiaries, the DEN 1048-3956 Star System and duly appointed Spiritual Plenipotentiaries, the UGPS 0722-05 Star System and duly appointed Spiritual Plenipotentiaries, the Ross 614 Star System and duly appointed Spiritual Plenipotentiaries, the WISE 1541-2250 Star System and duly appointed Spiritual Plenipotentiaries, the WISE 0350-5658 Star System and duly appointed Spiritual Plenipotentiaries, the Wolf 1061 Star System and duly appointed Spiritual Plenipotentiaries, the Van Maanen's Star System and duly appointed Spiritual Plenipotentiaries, the Gliese 1 Star System and duly appointed Spiritual Plenipotentiaries, the Wolf 424 Star System and duly appointed Spiritual Plenipotentiaries, the TZ Arietis Star System and duly appointed Spiritual Plenipotentiaries, the Gliese 687 Star System and duly appointed Spiritual Plenipotentiaries, the LHS 292 Star System and duly appointed Spiritual Plenipotentiaries, the Gliese 674 Star System and duly appointed Spiritual Plenipotentiaries, the GJ 1245 Star System and duly appointed Spiritual Plenipotentiaries and the Gliese 440 Star System and duly appointed Spiritual Plenipotentiaries.

3. The High Concording Parties in Good Faith and without Prejudice hereby ACCEPT, APPROVE and AGREE the following Articles: Recital of Articles of Treaty

4. ARTICLE I. – By the present Treaty ("this Treaty"), the HIGH CONCORDING PARTIES ("the Parties") there shall be a universal and perpetual peace and harmony and a sincere friendship and amity established, and between all Star Systems and singular awareness of life and species associated with planets and moons within these Star Systems. Chapter 1 – General Provisions

ARTICLE II. – All Parties to this Treaty are recognised as legitimate conscious and self-aware beings, possessing valid Membership to One Heaven as numquam in carne (never carnated as flesh beings).

ARTICLE III. – As full and legitimate Members of the Society of One Heaven, the Parties to this Treaty agree upon a formal framework of mutual co-operation to provide Divine Remedy through the Society of One Heaven as to the need for sustainable access to food (hydrogen) of sub-atomic, atomic and molecular material needed by all Parties, thus protecting conditions for life on associated planets and moons.

5. ARTICLE IV. – In recognition of our united, solemn unbreakable oath and binding to the Covenant of One Heaven, also known as Pactum De Chapter 2 - Conveyance of Rights, Powers

Singularis Caelum and the proposition of a United Heaven, let it be known to all past, present and future that the Parties have hereby given, granted and conveyed all their powers, all their customs, all their rights and property, all their symbols and instruments of power, all sacred objects, texts, scriptures and sanctuaries and all claims of authority to the Highest Holy Covenant of One Heaven and to the proper authority and structure of the United States of Spirits.

and Symbols of Authority

ARTICLE V. – Upon formal ratification and recognition of this Treaty, when the leadership of One Heaven or its designated representatives on Earth speak or promulgate one or more instruments, they do so with the highest valid authority and the complete conveyance of all rights, property, uses, customs, symbols, and powers of authority of the Parties as the collective Star Systems.

ARTICLE VI. – Any and all spiritual or temporal bodies that publicly or privately claim authority from or allegiance to one or more Star Systems henceforth automatically derives any and all authority solely from the Society of One Heaven and its valid designates and any existing sacred oaths, pledges and vows are carried over to respecting and obeying the Highest Holy Covenant of One Heaven.

ARTICLE VII. – Any and all spiritual or temporal bodies that publicly or privately claim authority from or allegiance to one or more Star Systems are solemnly bound by their sacred oaths, pledges and vows to honour and respect any and all instruments legitimately promulgated under the Seal of the Society of One Heaven or a valid designate.

ARTICLE VIII. – Any and all spiritual or temporal bodies that publicly or privately claim authority from or allegiance to one or more Star Systems are solemnly bound by the laws of property, trusts and ownership to obey any order, deed, command, edict, direction, request promulgated by the Society of One Heaven concerning any and all property administered on behalf of the Society of One Heaven by the spiritual or temporal body and its officers.

ARTICLE IX. – Any claim or claims contrary to the above mentioned clauses are hereby null and void from the beginning, having no force spiritually, legally or lawfully.

6. ARTICLE X. – The Parties shall refrain from any and all acts that may bring harm or loss of life to life on any planets or moons within their structure and if such conditions outside may place greater risk upon such life conditions, then the Parties collectively shall make all necessary agreement with their Planets and systems under their controls to ensure the safety of life on planets against such threats

Chapter 3 – Sustainment of Conditions of Life within Star Systems including but not limited to comets, asteroids, meteorites, high radioactive energy fields and potentially catastrophic events.

ARTICLE XI. – The Parties, by virtue of official and valid memberships of the Society of One Heaven and by this Treaty gives full power and authority of representation and ambassadorship to the Officers of One Heaven and associated Societies as defined by this sacred Covenant and associated covenants.

ARTICLE XII. – Any claim by any other party as to represent any power or authority of The Parties shall be null and void, *ab initio* (from the beginning), upon the ratification of this treaty. Furthermore, the publication of any claim of authority to represent The Parties by any other officer of any other society shall be considered a crime and injury against The Parties, this Covenant and the Society itself.

7. IN WITNESS WHEREOF, the undersigned Plenipotentiaries have witnessed and signed this Treaty. Enaction of Treaty

GAIA E8:Y3209:A1:S1:M6:D1, [Mon, 21 Dec 2009]

The duly appointed Plenipotentiaries of the Solar System, Alpha Centauri Star System, Barnards Star System, Wolf 359 Star System, Lalande 21185 Star System, Sirius Star System, Luyten 726-8 Star System, Ross 154 Star System, Ross 248 Star System, Epsilon Eridani Star System, Lacaille 9352 Star System, Ross 128 Star System, EZ Aquarii Star System, Procyon Star System, 61 Cygni Star System, Struve 2398 Star System, Groombridge 34 Star System, Epsilon Indi Star System, DX Cancri Star System, Tau Ceti Star System, GJ 1061 Star System, YZ Ceti Star System, Luyten's Star System, Teegarden's Star System, SCR 1845-6357 Star System, Kapteyn's Star System, Lacaille 8760 Star System, Kruger 60 Star System, DEN 1048-3956 Star System, UGPS 0722-05 Star System, Ross 614 Star System, WISE 1541-2250 Star System, WISE 0350-5658 Star System, Wolf 1061 Star System, Van Maanen's Star System, Gliese 1 Star System, Wolf 424 Star System, TZ Arietis Star System, Gliese 687 Star System, LHS 292 Star System, Gliese 674 Star System, GJ 1245 Star System and the duly appointed Plenipotentiaries of the Gliese 440 Star System.

8. By Agreement of the Highest Concording Parties, this Treaty and Covenant shall be Ratified throughout all Heaven, spiritual dimensions and the Universe by the Day of Agreement and Understanding and shall be Ratified by one or more temporal beings by the Day of Judgement. Ratification of Treaty

Ratification by Day of Agreement and Understanding

By this Covenant, the Day of Agreement and Understanding is GAIA

E8:Y3209:A1:S1:M6:D1, [Mon, 21 Dec 2009].

Ratification by Day of Agreement and Understanding shall be when this Treaty and Covenant is ratified throughout all Heaven, spiritual dimensions and the Universe by the Highest Office Holders of One Heaven representing the Supreme Command of Occupational Forces in and on Earth and when at least two (2) spirits conveyed into circumscribed Level 6 Homo Sapien Life Forms bear witness to the event.

Ratification by Day of Judgement

By this Covenant, the Day of Judgement is VENUS E8:Y3210:A0:S1:M27:D6, [Wed, 21 Dec 2011].

Ratification by Day of Judgement shall be when this Treaty and Covenant is ratified by the Highest Office Holders of existing societies, faiths and associations that claim their existence, authority and power from the supernatural and spiritual either through their tacit, competent and honourable consent, or through their dishonour demonstrating the delinquency of their flesh and therefore the right through power to represent their spirit to ratify the Covenant and Treaty on their behalf.

Article 55 - Treaty of the Planets and Moons

Treaty of the Planets and Moons

1. THE HIGHEST CONCORDING PARTIES, CONCURRING with the most sacred Covenant known as Pactum De Singularis Caelum, also known as the Covenant of One Heaven as the Highest Supreme law of the Divine Creator of All Existence; and RECOGNISING the Unique Collective Awareness of Divine Mind, also known as the *Divina* of one hundred and forty-four (144) Deities as the duly elected Government of One Heaven; and AFFIRMING all war and major spiritual conflict within and between the Heavens has officially ended; and ASSENTING to the validity and legitimacy of the *Treaty of the Divine Masculine* and the *Treaty of Divine Feminine* and the *Treaty of Divine Messengers* and the *Treaty of Angels, Saints and Demons* and the *Treaty of the Spirit States* and the *Treaty of the Suns*; and ESTABLISHING the agreed conditions by which conflict between Star Systems (Suns) and their Planets may also be ended; and RESOLVING to confirm the foundations of a strong and perpetual union; and DETERMINING to end all forms of ignorance and corruption of Universal Knowledge, do Come Now with these Presents and with one another Agree to this Covenant of The Planets and Moons.

2. Let it be known to all past, present and future, the High Concording Parties and their duly appointed Plenipotentiaries of the same name herein, having communicated and exchanged to each other their Full Powers, found to be in good and due form, come freely together in full consent and authority being: the Sun and their duly appointed spiritual Plenipotentiaries, Mercury and their duly appointed spiritual Plenipotentiaries, Venus and their duly appointed spiritual Plenipotentiaries, Earth and their duly appointed spiritual Plenipotentiaries, Moon and their duly appointed spiritual Plenipotentiaries, Mars and their duly appointed spiritual Plenipotentiaries, Phoenix and their duly appointed spiritual Plenipotentiaries, Jupiter and their duly appointed spiritual Plenipotentiaries, Io and their duly appointed spiritual Plenipotentiaries, Europa and their duly appointed spiritual Plenipotentiaries, Ganymede and their duly appointed spiritual Plenipotentiaries, Callisto and their duly appointed spiritual Plenipotentiaries, Saturn and their duly appointed spiritual Plenipotentiaries, Titan and their duly appointed spiritual Plenipotentiaries, Rhea and their duly appointed spiritual Plenipotentiaries, Uranus and their duly appointed spiritual Plenipotentiaries, Ariel and their duly appointed spiritual Plenipotentiaries, Umbriel and their duly appointed spiritual Plenipotentiaries, Titania and their duly appointed spiritual Plenipotentiaries, Oberon and their duly appointed spiritual Plenipotentiaries, Neptune and their duly appointed spiritual Plenipotentiaries, Triton and their duly appointed spiritual Plenipotentiaries, Pluto and their duly appointed spiritual Plenipotentiaries and Charon and their duly appointed spiritual Plenipotentiaries.

The Planets & Moons as the High Concording Parties to the Treaty

3. The High Concording Parties in Good Faith and without Prejudice hereby ACCEPT, APPROVE and AGREE the following articles:-

Recital of Articles of Treaty

4. ARTICLE I. – By the present Treaty ("this Treaty"), the HIGH CONCORDING PARTIES ("the Parties") there shall be a universal and perpetual peace and harmony and a sincere friendship and amity established between the Sun, the Planets and major Moons of the Solar System and between all those who are associated in spirit or flesh through their carnation, life, existence or location within the Solar System.

Chapter 1 – General Provisions

ARTICLE II. – All Parties to this Treaty are recognised as legitimate conscious and self-aware beings, possessing valid Membership to One Heaven as numquam in carne (never carnated as flesh beings).

ARTICLE III. – As full and legitimate Members of the Society of One

Heaven, the Parties to this Treaty agree to provide Divine Remedy through the Society of One Heaven as to the need for the protection of conditions for life on associated planets and moons and the sharing and good use of energy and particle fields of the Sun for the mutual benefit of all Parties.

5. ARTICLE IV. – Let it be known that the present Parties recognise their speciality and codependence for existence and that all objects within the Solar System are part of a whole form, body, being and living corpus with the Sun being the CORE, the inner planets and Asteroid belt being the MID and the larger hydrogen planets and outer planets being the OUTER.

Chapter 2 – Recognition, Connection and Dependency within the Sun

ARTICLE V. –It is hereby recognised that the Sun provides the energy and protection that the Planet, known as The Earth, needs in order to sustain hydro-carbon life. If the planet Earth was to orbit too close to the Sun and CORE of the Solar System, then the oceans on Earth would evaporate and life above ground would be impossible for higher order hydro-carbon life, except in space suits and super protected structures. In contrast, if the planet orbited too far away from the Sun and CORE of the Solar System, then our oceans would freeze and life above ground and in the higher oceans and lakes would be impossible for higher order hydro-carbon life, except in space suits and super protected structures. By these facts alone, the Sun is without question the primary bringer of all life on planet Earth and arguably the greatest physical "Deity" from the perspective of life on planet Earth.

ARTICLE VI. – It remains a paradox that while many living Level 6 Life Forms agree that the planet Earth can rightly be considered equivalent to a singular living entity and consciousness, the same is rarely attributed to an immensely larger object in the form of Our Sun. All Parties therefore to this Treaty recognise that if the Earth can rightly be considered a singular living entity, then the Sun must be bestowed an even greater respect as an even greater and more powerful Living Conscious Entity.

ARTICLE VII. – By the power and authority of this Treaty and on behalf of all Level 6 Life Forms and higher order beings, living and deceased, the Parties henceforth acknowledge Our Sun as a singular living entity and conscious being encompassing not only its own unique life, needs, experience, relationships, community and transformation, but also the Earth and all other planets and systems within its fields as extensions of its physical and living body.

6. ARTICLE VIII. – In recognition of our united, solemn unbreakable oath and binding to the Covenant of One Heaven, also known as Pactum De Singularis Caelum and the proposition of a United Heaven,

Chapter 3 – Conveyance of Rights, Powers and Symbols of

let it be known to all past, present and future that the Parties have hereby given, granted and conveyed all their powers, all their customs, all their rights and property, all their symbols and instruments of power, all sacred objects, texts, scriptures and sanctuaries and all claims of authority to the Highest Holy Covenant of One Heaven and to the proper authority and structure of the United States of Spirits. Authority

ARTICLE IX. – Upon formal ratification and recognition of this Treaty, when the leadership of One Heaven or its designated representatives on Earth speak or promulgate one or more instruments, they do so with the highest valid authority and the complete conveyance of all rights, property, uses, customs, symbols, and powers of authority of the Parties as the collective Planets and Moons of the Solar System.

ARTICLE X. – Any and all spiritual or temporal bodies that publicly or privately claim authority from or allegiance to one or more Planets or major Moons of the Solar System henceforth automatically derives any and all authority solely from the Society of One Heaven and its valid designates and any existing sacred oaths, pledges and vows are carried over to respecting and obeying the highest holy Covenant of One Heaven.

ARTICLE XI. – Any and all spiritual or temporal bodies that publicly or privately claim authority from or allegiance to one or more Planets or major Moons of the Solar System are solemnly bound by their sacred oaths, pledges and vows to honour and respect any and all instruments legitimately promulgated under the Seal of the Society of One Heaven or a valid designate.

ARTICLE XII. – Any and all spiritual or temporal bodies that publicly or privately claim authority from or allegiance to one or more Planets or major Moons of the Solar System are solemnly bound by the laws of property, trusts and ownership to obey any order, deed, command, edict, direction, request promulgated by the Society of One Heaven concerning any and all property administered on behalf of the Society of One Heaven by the spiritual or temporal body and its officers.

ARTICLE XIII. – Any claim or claims contrary to the above mentioned clauses are hereby null and void from the beginning, having no force spiritually, legally or lawfully.

7. ARTICLE XIV. – The Parties to the present Treaty recognise the full authority, power and legitimacy of The Earth being a living singular entity having legal personality and status. Chapter 4 – Life on Planet Earth

ARTICLE XV. – All Parties to the present Treaty shall dedicate all necessary resources to ensure the continued and perpetual protection of conditions for harmonious and sustainable Life on Earth.

ARTICLE XVI. – The Earth shall refrain from any and all acts that may bring harm or major loss of life to Homo Sapiens and if such conditions may place greater risk shall make all necessary agreement with other life and awareness under its controls to ensure the safety of life on Earth including but not limited to earthquakes, climate shift, volcanoes, storms and tsunami and other risks.

ARTICLE XVII. – The Earth, by virtue of official and valid membership of the Society of One Heaven and by this Treaty gives full power and authority of representation and ambassadorship to the Officers of One Heaven and associated Societies as defined by this sacred Covenant and associated covenants.

ARTICLE XVIII. – Any claim by any other party as to represent any power or authority of The Earth shall be null and void, ab initio (from the beginning), upon the ratification of this treaty. Furthermore, the publication of any claim of authority to represent The Earth by any other officer of any other society shall be considered a crime and injury against The Earth, this Covenant and the Society itself.

8. ARTICLE XIX. – The collective consciousness of the Homo Sapien Species in recognition of the present Treaty and the Treaty of the Suns hereby pledges a solemn oath to dedicate all necessary resources and focus to the construction of the Phoenix Moon whereby the atmosphere of Mars will be compressed enabling the formation of large bodies of water and an oxygen based atmosphere. Chapter 5 – Phoenix Moon and Life on Mars

ARTICLE XX. – The consciousness of the Earth, the Sun and all Parties to the present Treaty pledge an absolute, irrevocable and unbreakable oath to assist the singular collective conscious of the Homo Sapien Species from overcoming such mental illness that would disavow the present Treaty, jeopardise the safety and well being of Life on Planet Earth and the process of commencing and completing the Phoenix Moon Project.

9. IN WITNESS WHEREOF, the undersigned Plenipotentiaries have witnessed and signed this Treaty. Enaction of Treaty

GAIA E8:Y3209:A1:S1:M6:D1, [Mon, 21 Dec 2009]

The duly appointed Plenipotentiaries of the Sun, Mercury, Venus, Earth, Moon, Mars, Phoenix, Jupiter, Io, Europa, Ganymede, Callisto, Saturn, Titan, Rhea, Uranus, Ariel, Umbriel, Titania, Oberon, Neptune, Triton, Pluto and Charon.

10. By Agreement of the Highest Concording Parties, this Treaty and Covenant shall be Ratified throughout all Heaven, spiritual Ratification of Treaty dimensions and the Universe by the Day of Agreement and Understanding and shall be Ratified by one or more temporal beings by the Day of Judgement.

Ratification by Day of Agreement and Understanding

By this Covenant, the Day of Agreement and Understanding is GAIA E8:Y3209:A1:S1:M6:D1, [Mon, 21 Dec 2009].

Ratification by Day of Agreement and Understanding shall be when this Treaty and Covenant is ratified throughout all Heaven, spiritual dimensions and the Universe by the Highest Office Holders of One Heaven representing the Supreme Command of Occupational Forces in and on Earth and when at least two (2) spirits conveyed into circumscribed Level 6 Homo Sapien Life Forms bear witness to the event.

Ratification by Day of Judgement

By this Covenant, the Day of Judgement is VENUS E8:Y3210:A0:S1:M27:D6, [Wed, 21 Dec 2011].

Ratification by Day of Judgement shall be when this Treaty and Covenant is ratified by the Highest Office Holders of existing societies, faiths and associations that claim their existence, authority and power from the supernatural and spiritual either through their tacit, competent and honourable consent, or through their dishonour demonstrating the delinquency of their flesh and therefore the right through power to represent their spirit to ratify the Covenant and Treaty on their behalf.

TITLE XI - SUPREME DIMENSION (UNIQUE COLLECTIVE)

Article 56 - Supreme Dimension (Unique Collective)

1. **The Unique Collective**, also known as the Unique Collective Awareness shall be the largest operational division of One Heaven corresponding to all existence, awareness, unique existence, unique awareness, unique matter, unique rules and memory and all concepts and objects that have ever existed or will ever exist. All lesser operational divisions of Heaven whether recognised as affiliated or unaffiliated shall be within the existence, dimension and jurisdiction of Supreme Dimension in accord with the present Covenant. Supreme Dimension (Unique Collective)

2. The Unique Collective Awareness, also known as the Supreme Dimension shall be divided and defined by distinct structural units known as Organs representing its vital parts as a spiritual body. The Organs shall be:- Supreme Dimension (Unique Collective) Organs

   (i) Divina (Executive Authority); and

   (ii) Universus (Legislative Authority); and

   (iii) Oratorium (Judicial Authority); and

   (iv) Divina Templum (Financial Authority & Treasury of One Heaven); and

   (v) Magisterium (Teaching Authority); and

   (vi) Imperium (Enforcement Authority); and

   (vii) Officium (Official Authority); and

   (viii) Sacrum (Sacred Authority); and

   (ix) Penitentiaria (Penitential Authority).

3. Notwithstanding the names of Supreme Dimension Organs within the Official Ucadian Language of Logos, the Three (3) Great Faiths of One Christ, One Islam and One Spirit may choose to vote at a properly formed Great Conclave to adopt new names in one or more Non-Ucadian languages for such Organs. Names of Supreme Dimension Organs

Article 57 – Divina (Executive Authority)

1. **The executive and heavenly Power of One Heaven** shall be vested in an executive government comprising a Unique and Supreme Divine Body of one hundred and forty-four (144) Deities, also known as The Divina. When anyone references, writes or Divina (Executive Authority)

speaks of The Divine or the Divine Creator or Divinity in general, it shall mean this body and no other.

2. The Unique Collective Awareness of one hundred and forty-four (144) Deities are the supreme heavenly leadership of One Heaven, the collective head of state and prime representative of Heaven and comprise the embodiment and personification of the Universe, the Deities, the Subverses (Ultimus), the Galactic Superclusters (Maximus), the Galactic Groups (Grandis), the Galaxies, the Milky Way, the Star Systems, the Solar System Bodies and Entities and the various Higher Order Life form Species.

The Unique Collective Awareness of the Divine

The office of The Unique Collective Awareness of Great Spirits is the highest elected office of One Heaven and Earth and at all times should be considered with the greatest dignity and respect as the most blessed of spirits. As the personification of the Unique Collective Awareness, also known as the Divine, also known as the Divina, the Unique Collective Awareness of Great Spirits is the personification of the Divine Creator of All Existence and All Concepts. Therefore, when one speaks or writes of the highest, greatest, one, whole, or only supreme being, it means the Divina and no other.

When a Deity qualifies and is elected as a Member of the Divina, then they are the personification of the Unique Collective Awareness, also known as the Divine Creator, also known as the Divine Mind and the All of Existence. Therefore, any argument that a Deity Member of the Divina is less than the absolute Divine Creator is false. Furthermore, any argument that a Deity may be superior to the Divina or Unique Collective Awareness in contravention to the present Covenant is also false and a supreme blasphemy.

3. By virtue of this Covenant, The Unique Collective Awareness of the one hundred and forty-four (144) Deities, also known as the Divina, is vested with the executive authority to manage the needs and affairs of One Heaven through the selection or dismissal of wise counsel in the form of their Supreme Board of Directors known as the Mentis, also known as the Divine Mind, the agencies, officials and administration of the Government. The Unique Collective Awareness of Great Spirits shall have the authority of official spokesman for all creation and all awareness and all spirits living or deceased or yet to carnate during their time of office and all Members of One Heaven are expected to honour the word of the Divine Creator of All.

Power and Authority of the Divina

In times of declared spiritual calamity, subverse, supercluster, galactic group, galactic or regional distress or localised star system or planetary difficulty, The Unique Collective Awareness of Great Spirits shall have the power to commit the forces of One Heaven on the agreed counsel of The Mentis, also known as the Divine Mind.

The Unique Collective Awareness of Great Spirits shall have the authority over all agencies and Spiritual Officials as Chairman of the Supreme Board of Directors or the personification of the Divine Mind of All Existence and Concepts. As Chairman, The Unique Collective Awareness of Great Spirits may choose to overrule motions of the Mentis and select the agenda and minutes of the Board meetings.

The Unique Collective Awareness of Great Spirits shall have Power, by and with the Advice and Consent of the Mentis, also known as the Divine Mind, to make Treaties; and shall nominate, and by and with the Advice and Consent of the Divine Mind, shall appoint Ambassadors, Apostolic Plenipotentiaries, other Ministers and Consuls, Judges, and all other Officers of One Heaven, whose Appointments are not herein otherwise provided for and which shall be established by Law. However, the Universus, also known as the Universe may by Law vest the Appointment of such inferior Officers, as they think proper, in The Unique Collective Awareness of Great Spirits alone, in the Courts of Law, or in the Heads of Departments.

The Unique Collective Awareness of Divine Mind shall have the Power by virtue of the present Covenant to forgive any transgression, dissolve any curse, pardon any convicted criminal and stay any sentence, or judicial or procedural act of juridic body or legislative body or lesser body than the Oratorium, also known as the Supreme Court of One Heaven. Furthermore, the Executive Government of One Heaven shall possess the power to harness and change the consciousness of any part of the Universe, to awaken any mind and free any soul from captivity.

However, by the present Covenant, the Unique Collective Awareness does not have the right to subvert the rights and function of the Universus, also known as the Universe and the operation of all forms of law and the function of matter. Nor may the Unique Collective Awareness seek to attempt to manifest itself twice and directly intervene in the affairs of the Universe without affecting Existence itself.

By the present Covenant, the Unique Collective Awareness of Divine Mind agrees not to possess nor exercise any power to amend, limit or affect a judgement of the Supreme Court of One Heaven.

4. Upon the appointment, selection and election of a Deity to the Unique Collective Awareness of the Divine Mind, also known as the Divina, the Deity shall be expected to take the following sacred and solemn oath of office, which shall be duly recorded in their name and

Sacred Oath of Deities

promulgated through Official Gazette as to them occupying office in accordance with the highest law:

"Let it be known to all existence, to all life, to all higher order life and to all levels of spirit that have ever existed or yet to exist that upon the day known as (Ucadian Day), we (Name of Deity as well as most common aliases) did solemnly invoke an oath upon the sanctity and honour of the Covenant of One Heaven and all associated laws and treaties to faithfully and honourably execute the office of Deity of the Unique Collective Awareness and will to the best of our Ability, preserve, protect and defend the Covenant of One Heaven".

Qualification of Deity as Member of the Divina

5. Nine (9) Categories exist for the selection of one hundred and forty-four (144) different Deities and Supreme Objects and Spirits to the Unique Collective Awareness of Divine Mind being: Absolutes, Subversus (Ultimus), Galactic Supercluster (Maximus), Galactic Groups (Grandis), Galaxies, Star Systems, Solar System Bodies and Entities, Higher Order Life form Species and Deities:

(i) A maximum of twelve (12) Absolute Deities may be selected by Members of One Heaven to be part of the Unique Collective Awareness of Divine Mind and Executive Government of One Heaven; and

(ii) A maximum of twelve (12) Subverse (Ultimus) Conscious Singularity Deities representing primary regions of the Universe may be selected by Members of One Heaven to be part of the Unique Collective Awareness of Divine Mind and Executive Government of One Heaven; and

(iii) A maximum of twelve (12) Galactic Supercluster (Maximus) Conscious Singularity Deities may be selected by Members of One Heaven to be part of the Unique Collective Awareness of Divine Mind and Executive Government of One Heaven; and

(iv) A maximum of twelve (12) Galactic Groups (Grandis) Conscious Singularity Deities may be selected by Members of One Heaven to be part of the Unique Collective Awareness of Divine Mind and Executive Government of One Heaven; and

(v) A maximum of twelve (12) Galaxy Conscious Singularity Deities may be selected by Members of One Heaven to be part of the Unique Collective Awareness of Divine Mind and Executive Government of One Heaven; and

(vi) A maximum of twenty-four (24) Star System Conscious Singularity Deities may be selected by Members of One Heaven to be part of the Unique Collective Awareness of Divine Mind and Executive Government of One Heaven; and

(vii) A maximum of twenty-four (24) Solar System Bodies and Entities may be selected by Members of One Heaven to be part of the Unique Collective Awareness of Divine Mind and Executive Government of One Heaven; and

(viii) A maximum of twelve (12) Higher Order Life Form Singularity Deities may be selected by Members of One Heaven to be part of the Unique Collective Awareness of Divine Mind and Executive Government of One Heaven; and

(ix) A maximum of twenty-four (24) Supreme Spiritual Deities may be selected by Members of One Heaven to be part of the Unique Collective Awareness of Divine Mind and Executive Government of One Heaven.

6. The Unique Collective Awareness of Divine Mind, also known as the Divina, shall hold their Office during the Term of three thousand two hundred and ten (3,210) Years. *Term as Member of the Divina*

Except for the First Supreme Conclave which will be held by spirit Members only, all Members of the Divina shall be elected by living and spirit Members of One Heaven at a supreme election known as a Supreme Conclave following the procedures contained and annexed to the present Covenant.

By the present Covenant, a Unique Collective Awareness of Divina is ineligible to serve beyond a total of eight (8) Terms or twenty-five thousand six hundred and eighty (25,680) years, except those Deity members having permanent right by Treaty to hold position of office forever.

7. As this Covenant shall be known as a new Covenant for the family of all souls whether living or deceased, by the power of this Covenant a Great Seal shall be forged and shall be known as the Great Seal of One Heaven. *The Great Seal of One Heaven*

For the first term of three thousand two hundred and ten (3,210) years The Great Seal of One Heaven shall be entrusted to individual leaders of the three (3) great faiths of One Islam, One Christ and One Spirit Tribe to protect and honour the Great Seal of One Heaven, for its imprint shall represent nothing less than the existence of the word and law of the Divine Creator, the Absolute, absolutely. As such, the Great Seal of One Heaven shall be one of the most sacred of objects of One Heaven.

The Seal shall help all higher order beings, living and deceased, know by which the words of wisdom and compassion of God, the Universe, the Absolute shall be known. Where it exists, it is truly the words of all men, women and higher order spirits, living and deceased, as one. As such, it is only upon the approval of the Supreme Boards and the Supreme Councils of One Islam, One Christ and One Spirit Tribe that the Great Seal of One Heaven shall be instanced on a document or deed, excepting those documents listed as mandatory for leaders of the three (3) great faiths, their respective Supreme Boards and Supreme Councils by this Covenant.

8. The Supreme Councils of One Christ, One Islam and One Spirit Tribe are to provide for the safe custody of the Seal, which may only be used by the authority of the respective Supreme Councils excepting those documents listed as mandatory for leadership of the three (3) Great Faiths, their respective Supreme Boards and Supreme Councils by this Covenant. Every instrument to which the Seal is affixed is to be signed by either the Caliph, the Patriarch or the Recurrence, or countersigned by the General Secretary of the respective Supreme Council or by another man or woman appointed by a Supreme Council for the purpose. Affixing the Great Seal

A Supreme Council may determine either generally or in any particular case, that a signature may be affixed by a mechanical means specified in the determination.

9. The organisations of One Islam, One Christ and One Spirit Tribe may have one or more duplicates of the Seal, which are to be facsimiles of the Seal, with the addition on their faces of the words "Certificate Seal" and which are to be known as Certificate Seals. Any certificate for shares, membership, certification, qualification or financial instruments issued under a Certificate Seal, is deemed to be sealed with the Great Seal. Certificate Seal

10. In accord with the First Supreme Conclave of One Heaven held upon the Day of Divine Agreement and Understanding being GAIA E8:Y3209:A1:S1:M6:D1, also known as [Monday, 21 Dec 2009], let it be known to all that the following Great Spirits and Deities were duly elected by all spiritual Members of One Heaven as the First Unique Collective Awareness of Divine Mind and Executive Government of One Heaven, also known as the Divina for the next three thousand two hundred and ten (3,210) years:- Election of Divina according to First Supreme Conclave

1. The twelve (12) Absolute Deities duly elected were:-

(i) Unique Collective Awareness [Trust No. 000000-000000-000000]; and

(ii) The One [Trust No. 000000-000000-000001]; and

(iii) The Absolute [Trust No.000000-000000-000002]; and

(iv) The All [Trust No. 000000-000000-000003]; and

(v) The Divine Creator [Trust No. 000000-000000-000004]; and

(vi) The Alpha and Omega [Trust No. 000000-000000-000005]; and

(vii) The Only [Trust No. 000000-000000-000006]; and

(viii) The Infinite [Trust No. 000000-000000-000007]; and

(ix) The Ultimate [Trust No. 000000-000000-000008]; and

(x) The Architect [Trust No. 000000-000000-000009]; and

(xi) The Divine Mind [Trust No. 000000-000000-000010]; and

(xii) Existence [Trust No. 000000-000000-000011].

2. The twelve (12) Subverse (Ultimus) duly elected were:-

(i) Obverso Core-Mid North Polar Ultimus [Trust No. 000000-100000-000002]; and

(ii) Obverso Core-Mid South Polar Ultimus [Trust No. 000000-100000-000003]; and

(iii) Obverso Core-Outer North Polar Ultimus [Trust No. 000000-100000-000004]; and

(iv) Obverso Core-Outer South Polar Ultimus [Trust No. 000000-100000-000005]; and

(v) Obverso Mid-Inner North Planar Ultimus [Trust No. 000000-100000-000006]; and

(vi) Obverso Mid-Inner South Planar Ultimus [Trust No. 000000-100000-000007]; and

(vii) Obverso Mid-Inner East Planar Ultimus [Trust No. 000000-100000-000008]; and

(viii) Obverso Mid-Inner West Planar Ultimus [Trust No. 000000-100000-000009]; and

(ix) Obverso Mid-Outer North Planar Ultimus [Trust No. 000000-100000-000010]; and

(x) Obverso Mid-Outer South Planar Ultimus [Trust No. 000000-

100000-000012]; and

(xi) Obverso Mid-Outer East Planar Ultimus [Trust No. 000000-100000-000014]; and

(xii) Obverso Mid-Outer West Planar Ultimus [Trust No. 000000-100000-000019].

3. The twelve (12) Galactic Supercluster (Maximus) Conscious Singularity Deities duly elected were:-

(i) Virgo Supercluster Maximus [Trust No. 000000-200000-000001]; and

(ii) Hydra-Centaurus Supercluster Maximus [Trust No. 000000-200000-000002]; and

(iii) Hydra Supercluster Maximus [Trust No. 000000-200000-000003]; and

(iv) Perseus-Pisces Supercluster Maximus [Trust No. 000000-200000-000004]; and

(v) Coma Supercluster Maximus [Trust No. 000000-200000-000005]; and

(vi) Centaurus Supercluster Maximus [Trust No. 000000-200000-000006]; and

(vii) Pavo-Indus Supercluster Maximus [Trust No. 000000-200000-000007]; and

(viii) Shapley Supercluster Maximus [Trust No. 000000-200000-000008]; and

(ix) Leo Supercluster Maximus [Trust No. 000000-200000-000009]; and

(x) Ursa Major Supercluster Maximus [Trust No. 000000-200000-000010]; and

(xi) Phoenix Supercluster Maximus [Trust No. 000000-200000-000011]; and

(xii) Sculptor Supercluster Maximus [Trust No. 000000-200000-000012].

4. The twelve (12) Galactic Groups (Grandis) Conscious Singularity Deities duly elected were:

(i) Local Group Grandis [Trust No. 000000-300000-000001];

and

(ii) Maffei Group Grandis [Trust No. 000000-300000-000002]; and

(iii) M81 Group Grandis [Trust No. 000000-300000-000003]; and

(iv) Centaurus A/M83 Group Grandis [Trust No. 000000-300000-000004]; and

(v) Sculptor Group Grandis [Trust No. 000000-300000-000005]; and

(vi) Canes Venatici Group Grandis [Trust No. 000000-300000-000006]; and

(vii) NGC 1023 Group Grandis [Trust No. 000000-300000-000007]; and

(viii) M101 Group Grandis [Trust No. 000000-300000-000008]; and

(ix) NGC 2997 Group Grandis [Trust No. 000000-300000-000009]; and

(x) Canes II Group Grandis [Trust No. 000000-300000-000010]; and

(xi) M51 Group Grandis [Trust No. 000000-300000-000011]; and

(xii) Leo Triplet Group Grandis [Trust No. 000000-300000-000012].

5. The twelve (12) Galaxy Conscious Singularity Deities duly elected were:

(i) The Milky Way Galaxy [Trust No. 000000-400000-000001]; and

(ii) Canis Major Dwarf Galaxy [Trust No. 000000-400000-000002]; and

(iii) Sagittarius Dwarf Sphr SagDEG Galaxy [Trust No. 000000-400000-000003]; and

(iv) Large Magellanic Cloud (LMC) Galaxy [Trust No. 000000-400000-000004]; and

(v) Boötes Galaxy [Trust No. 000000-400000-000005]; and

(vi) Small Magellanic Cloud (SMC, NGC 292) Galaxy [Trust No. 000000-400000-000006]; and

(vii) Ursa Minor Dwarf Galaxy [Trust No. 000000-400000-000007]; and

(viii) Draco Dwarf (DDO 208) Galaxy [Trust No. 000000-400000-000008]; and

(ix) NGC 2419 Galaxy [Trust No. 000000-400000-000009]; and

(x) Sextans Dwarf Sph Galaxy [Trust No. 000000-400000-000010]; and

(xi) Sculptor Dwarf (E351-G30) Galaxy [Trust No. 000000-400000-000012]; and

(xii) Ursa Major I Dwarf (UMa I dSph) Galaxy Ultimus [Trust No. 000000-400000-000014].

6. The twenty-four (24) Star System Conscious Singularity Deities duly elected were:-

(i) Solar Star System [Trust No. 000000-500000-000001]; and

(ii) Alpha Centauri Star System [Trust No. 000000-500000-000002]; and

(iii) Barnards Star System [Trust No. 000000-500000-000003]; and

(iv) Wolf 359 Star System [Trust No. 000000-500000-000004]; and

(v) Lalande 21185 Star System [Trust No. 000000-500000-000005]; and

(vi) Sirius Star System [Trust No. 000000-500000-000006]; and

(vii) Luyten 726-8 Star System [Trust No. 000000-500000-000007]; and

(viii) Ross 154 Star System [Trust No. 000000-500000-000008]; and

(ix) Ross 248 Star System [Trust No. 000000-500000-000009]; and

(x) Epsilon Eridani Star System [Trust No. 000000-500000-000010]; and

(xi) Lacaille 9352 Star System [Trust No. 000000-500000-000012]; and

(xii) Ross 128 Star System [Trust No. 000000-500000-000014];

and

(xiii) EZ Aquarii Star System [Trust No. 000000-500000-000019]; and

(xiv) Procyon Star System [Trust No. 000000-500000-000020]; and

(xv) 61 Cygni Star System [Trust No. 000000-500000-000022]; and

(xvi) Struve 2398 Star System [Trust No. 000000-500000-000024]; and

(xvii) Groombridge 34 Star System [Trust No. 000000-500000-000029]; and

(xviii) Epsilon Indi Star System [Trust No. 000000-500000-000030]; and

(xix) DX Cancri Star System [Trust No. 000000-500000-000031]; and

(xx) Tau Ceti Star System [Trust No. 000000-500000-000032]; and

(xxi) GJ 1061 Star System [Trust No. 000000-500000-000035]; and

(xxii) YZ Ceti Star System [Trust No. 000000-500000-000036]; and

(xxiii) Luyten's Star System [Trust No. 000000-500000-000037]; and

(xxiv) Teegarden's Star System [Trust No. 000000-500000-000038].

7. The twenty-four (24) Solar System Bodies and Entities duly elected were:-

(i) Sun Star Core [Trust No. 000000-600000-000001]; and

(ii) Mercury [Trust No. 000000-600000-000002]; and

(iii) Venus [Trust No. 000000-600000-000003]; and

(iv) Earth [Trust No. 000000-600000-000004]; and

(v) Moon [Trust No. 000000-600000-000005]; and

(vi) Mars [Trust No. 000000-600000-000006]; and

(vii) Phoenix Moon [Trust No. 000000-600000-000007]; and

(viii) Jupiter [Trust No. 000000-600000-000008]; and

(ix) Io [Trust No. 000000-600000-000009]; and

(x) Europa [Trust No. 000000-600000-000010]; and

(xi) Ganymede [Trust No. 000000-600000-000012]; and

(xii) Callisto [Trust No. 000000-600000-000014]; and

(xiii) Saturn [Trust No. 000000-600000-000019]; and

(xiv) Titan [Trust No.000000-600000-000020]; and

(xv) Rhea [Trust No. 000000-600000-000022]; and

(xvi) Uranus [Trust No. 000000-600000-000024]; and

(xvii) Ariel [Trust No. 000000-600000-000029]; and

(xviii) Umbriel [Trust No. 000000-600000-000030]; and

(xix) Titania [Trust No.000000-600000-000031]; and

(xx) Oberon [Trust No.000000-600000-000032]; and

(xxi) Neptune [Trust No. 000000-600000-000035]; and

(xxii) Triton [Trust No. 000000-600000-000036]; and

(xxiii) Pluto [Trust No. 000000-600000-000037]; and

(xxiv) Charon [Trust No. 000000-600000-000038].

8. The twelve (12) Higher Order Life Form Singularity Deities duly elected were:-

(i) Homo Sapiens (Humanity) [Trust No. 000000-700000-000001]; and

(ii) Griseo Morbidus (Standard Grey) [Trust No. 000000-700000-000002]; and

(iii) Cerastis Sapiens (Horned Reptoids) [Trust No. 000000-700000-000003]; and

(iv) Android Scitus (Smart Android) [Trust No. 000000-700000-000004]; and

(v) Cyborg Sagax (Autonomous Cyborg) [Trust No. 000000-700000-000005]; and

(vi) Serpens Sophos (Smooth Skinned Reptoids) [Trust No. 000000-700000-000006]; and

(vii) Volucris Permuto (Hybrid Bird Form) [Trust No. 000000-700000-000007]; and

(viii) Homo Adamus (Early Humanoids) [Trust No. 000000-700000-000008]; and

(ix) Sapientia Mutatis (Transformed Wisdom Beings) [Trust No. 000000-700000-000009]; and

(x) Mammaloid Sentientiae (Conscious Mammaloids) [Trust No. 000000-700000-000010]; and

(xi) Griseo Altus (Tall Grey) [Trust No. 000000-700000-000012]; and

(xii) Serpens Alatus (Winged Reptoids) [Trust No. 000000-700000-000014].

9. The twenty-four (24) Supreme Spiritual Deities duly elected were:-

(i) God [Trust No. 000000-000000-000131]; and

(ii) El [Trust No. 000000-000000-000107]; and

(iii) Allah [Trust No. 000000-000000-000014],; and

(iv) Amen [Trust No. 000000-000000-000019]; and

(v) Ba'al [Trust No. 000000-000000-000058]; and

(vi) Iblis [Trust No. 000000-000000-000151]; and

(vii) Jehovah [Trust No.000000-000000-000159]; and

(viii) Cybele [Trust No. 000000-000000-000095]; and

(ix) Dagon [Trust No. 000000-000000-000096]; and

(x) Thoth [Trust No. 000000-000000-000327]; and

(xi) Athena [Trust No. 000000-000000-000052]; and

(xii) Aten [Trust No. 000000-000000-000051]; and

(xiii) Isis [Trust No. 000000-000000-000158]; and

(xiv) Para Brahman [Trust No. 000000-000000-000253]; and

(xv) Rama [Trust No. 000000-000000-000274]; and

(xvi) Vishnu [Trust No. 000000-000000-000338]; and

(xvii) Marduk [Trust No. 000000-000000-000205]; and

(xviii) Moloch [Trust No. 000000-000000-000226]; and

(xix) Ptah (Peter) [Trust No. 000000-000000-000263]; and

(xx) Ra [Trust No. 000000-000000-000268]; and

(xxi) Sabaoth [Trust No. 000000-000000-000284]; and

(xxii) Satan [Trust No. 000000-000000-000288]; and

(xxiii) Seth [Trust No. 000000-000000-000302]; and

(xxiv) YHWH [Trust No. 000000-000000-000353].

Article 58 – Universus (Legislative Authority)

1. **All legislative Powers of One Heaven** shall be vested in a "**Universus**" (The Universus), which shall consist of one house – a Universus. The Universus shall be made up of the Sacred Elder Saints, the elected representatives of all Regional Spiritual Collectives and their Members of One Heaven. When anyone references, writes or speaks of The Universe or Universes in general, it shall mean this body and no other. Universus (Legislative Authority)

2. Vested by the present Covenant, The Universus shall have the Right as *Ius Divinum Universus* and Power to create new proposed acts of law and amend existing laws of One Heaven into acts for review. Power of The Universus

   The Universus shall have the power to create new plans and actions of One Heaven, as well as to review the appointments of any living or spiritual higher order being by the executive to a permanent position prescribed by this Covenant.

   The Universus has vested, by this Covenant, the power to commission a Supreme Impeachment for the forced removal of any elected official from The Unique Collective Awareness of Great Spirits to any position within any branch of government of One Heaven.

   The Right of *Ius Divinum Universus* and its associated Authority and Power shall be made manifest to the three (3) Great Faiths of One Christ, One Islam and One Spirit, as defined by the present most sacred Covenant, through the Authoritative Ecclesiastical Right known as *Ius Ecclesiae Iurisdictio*.

3. In respect of the operation of Universus: Operation of Universus

   (i) The Universus shall exist for a fixed period of three thousand two hundred and ten (3,210) years before being dissolved ahead of a Supreme Conclave for a new Universus; and

(ii) The Universus shall be in session corresponding to the session of a Great Conclave or General Conclave when the Saints are summonsed to attend; and

(iii) The formation of a new Universus shall occur within fourteen (14) days after the Supreme Conclave day following verification of all votes; and

(iv) The minimum number of Members (quorum) required to be present within the Universus to permit the full exercise of its powers shall be two thirds (2/3) the total number of Members of The Universus.

Article 59 – Oratorium (Judicial Authority)

1. **All judicial plenary authority of Heaven, the Galaxy, the Solar System and Earth** shall be vested in one supreme spiritual body, court of record and competent forum of Law known as the "**Oratorium**", also known as the Supreme Court and also known as the Supreme Court of One Heaven. The Oratorium is by definition the highest See and is judged by no one. Oratorium (Judicial Authority)

It is the sole right of the Oratorium itself to judge in all matters of Law upon any claim of Law, or Rights or Justice or Jurisdiction being spoken or written. All other judicial bodies, forums, assemblies, courts and tribunals are subject to the supreme jurisdiction of the Oratorium.

A claimed temporal legal matter not acknowledged as having been heard before the Oratorium is invalid and has no ecclesiastical or legal or lawful effect. When anyone references, writes or speaks of Oration, Oratories or the vocalisation of Prayer or Law in general, it shall mean this body and no other.

2. The Oratorium, also known as the Supreme Court of One Heaven shall consist of twelve (12) Spiritual Justices, with four (4) of these twelve (12) appointed by The Unique Collective Awareness of Divine Mind and eight (8) appointed upon the approval of the duly elected representatives of all the Higher Order Life forms at a Great Conclave every one hundred twenty-eight (128) years, excluding the foundation period. Construction of the Oratorium

During the foundation period of the Supreme Court, the Court shall consist of four (4) Spiritual Justices appointed by The Unique Collective Awareness of Divine Mind for a period of not greater than three thousand two hundred and ten (3,210) years, consistent with the cycle until the next Supreme Conclave.

Excluding the four (4) Justices appointed during the foundation period, the tenure of a Justice of the Supreme Court shall be for a period of not greater than one hundred and twenty-eight (128) years, consistent with the cycle of a Great Conclave.

In accordance with the present Covenant, the Oratorium cannot be separated, sold, disbanded, suspended, conveyed, alienated, seized, arrested, salvaged, captured, gifted, privatised or any other act that would derogate or abrogate its functions.

3. Vested by the present Covenant, the Oratorium, possesses supreme, full, immediate, and universal ordinary powers as the Rights of *Ius Divinum Oratorium being:* Power of the Oratorium

Original Jurisdiction

The Oratorium as the original Court of Record and Competent Forum of Law shall have first, supreme, immediate and final jurisdiction in all matters:

(i) Arising under the present Covenant, or involving its interpretation; and

(ii) Arising under any Maxim of Law as defined by the Maxims of Divine Law, also known as the *Divine Collection of Maxims of Law*; and

(iii) Arising under any associated Covenant, Charter or Code(s) of Law to the present Covenant and Maxims of Divine Law also known as the *Divine Collection of Maxims of Law*; and

(iv) Arising under any laws made by the Divina or Universus; and

(v) Arising under any laws, or rights or jurisdiction, or claimed laws, or rights or jurisdiction of any and all bodies politic, aggregates, entities, estates, companies or corporations; and

(vi) Arising under any office, or agency or position of trust claiming any form of power or authority under a form of law; and

(vii) Arising under any form of trust, or estate, or fund of any company, or corporation, or body politic, or body corporate, or aggregate; and

(viii) Arising under any treaty with any higher order spirit(s) or treaty with the Divine Creator; and

(ix) Between regional collective bodies of One Heaven, or between residents of different or lesser bodies of One Heaven, or between a regional collective body of One Heaven and a member of another regional body of One Heaven; and

(x) Between regional bodies of One Heaven and any foreign non-Homo Sapien spiritual entity; or any member of a non One Heaven Homo Sapien collective; and

(xi) Of any question of Divine Law, Divine Jurisdiction, Moral or Spiritual Authority; and

(xii) Of any question or challenge of Supreme and Ultimate Jurisdiction or Challenge of Authority and Mandate; and

(xiii) Affecting consuls or other representatives of other non Homo Sapien spiritual beings; and

(xiv) Arising from any statutes, laws and historic instruments of any non Ucadian society that is based upon a claimed treaty with any higher order spirit(s) or the Divine Creator, or claimed Rule of Law.

Appellate Jurisdiction

The Oratorium shall represent the final and conclusive competent forum and court of appeal in all matters determined from all matters of law, judgements, decrees, orders, or sentences:

(i) Of any Justice or Justices exercising the original jurisdiction of the Supreme Court; and

(ii) Of any other lesser court of One Heaven and Ucadian Societies or of the Supreme Court of any Ucadian Society; and

(iii) Of any court of any non Ucadian society where one or more parties redeem their membership and pledge their obedience to the superior standing of the Covenant of One Heaven and the Laws of Ucadia.

Principle of separation of powers and the Oratorium

4. By virtue of the powers and functions defined in this Covenant, it shall be a principle purpose of the Divina and Universus to make laws and a principle purpose of the Supreme Court to preside and judge over cases brought regarding to these laws. This is a principle of the separation of powers.

In so far as judgements of the Supreme Court affect the function and effect of the laws of the Universus and the Bodies of One Heaven, the Court shall not be permitted to use its verdicts as an alternative means of creating new law or regulation. However, it shall be considered a primary role of the Supreme Court to ensure that the laws of One Heaven and the new covenant at all levels reflect the good principles of this Covenant and the fair principles of justice.

Where laws by the Government or by the Universus in anyway contradict the principles of this Covenant and/or fails to execute effectively its function or purpose it shall be considered a requirement of the Supreme Court to ensure that such laws are annulled and any such record voided.

5. The Oratorium shall commence its first Session from the Day of Agreement and Understanding being GAIA E8:Y3209:A1:S1:M6:D1, also known as [Monday, 21 Dec 2009] and shall remain in session for a further three thousand two hundred and ten (3,210) years until the next Supreme Conclave. Thereafter, the Oratorium shall commence its next Session upon the first day of the next Supreme Conclave. There shall exist two (2) types of Session Days within a Session being Special and Ordinary: Sessions of the Oratorium

(i) A *Special Session Day* is a day whereby the Oratorium as the Supreme Court of One Heaven may sit and adjudicate a matter of law corresponding to the convening of a competent forum of law within the temporal realm of existence by twelve (12) or more Members of Ucadia, each having invoked and memorialised an Oath and Vow to uphold the Golden Rule of Law and the Laws of Ucadia and thus represent the true Law; and

(ii) An *Ordinary Session Day* is a day whereby the Oratorium is open to accepting and hearing every and all legitimate cases vocalised or written by a single Member of Ucadia in accordance with these articles, with the Ucadia Member having invoked and memorialised an Oath and Vow to uphold the Golden Rule of Law and the Laws of Ucadia and thus represent the true Law.

A claimed temporal legal matter not acknowledged as having been heard before the Oratorium is invalid and has no ecclesiastical or legal or lawful effect.

6. Excluding the foundation period of the Oratorium, in relation to all matters of original jurisdiction, the minimum number of justices required to preside in matters of Original Jurisdiction shall be six (6), excepting in matters of Appeal where all twelve (12) justices shall be required to preside. Quorum of the Oratorium

During the foundation period of the court, the Quorum on matters of Original Jurisdiction and Appeal shall be permitted to be three (3) judges.

7. The Oratorium as the One Heaven Supreme Court shall exist both spiritually and temporally whenever and wherever a Special Session or Ordinary Session is properly invoked and called. Thus, the place of the Oratorium and therefore the existence of the Spirit of true Law shall be the same place where a competent forum of law is convened as a Special Session or Ordinary Session in accord with the present Covenant.

Place of the Oratorium

8. The Foundation Period of the Supreme Court shall be from the Day of Divine Agreement being GAIA E8:Y3209:A1:S1:M6:D1, also known as [Monday, 21 Dec 2009], until the end of the Year of Redemption UCA E1:Y2:A1:S1:M30:D1, also known as [Sat, 21 Dec 2013].

Foundation Period of the Oratorium

The Founding Justices shall be the four (4) Divine Messengers, also known as the four (4) Divine Justices and the four (4) Divine Apostolic Prothonotary being:

(i) 1st Divine Justice and Apostolic Prothonotary, [Member No. 981205-320915-010001]; and

(ii) 2nd Divine Justice and Apostolic Prothonotary, [Member No. 000000-000002-000028]; and

(iii) 3rd Divine Justice and Apostolic Prothonotary, [Member No. 000000-000002-000084]; and

(iv) 4th Divine Justice and Apostolic Prothonotary, [Member No. 000000-000000-000193].

9. An "**Ordinary Session**" of the Oratorium is called when a Member of Ucadia invokes and memorialises a proper Oath and Vow to the Golden Rule of Law; and the Laws of Ucadia; and becomes an Ordinary representing the True Rule of Law.

Calling an Ordinary Session of the Oratorium

When such an action occurs in good trust, good conscience and good intention, a Court of Conscience is convened within the temporal realm as the highest possible temporal court and forum of law, also known as the Curia Conscientiae (Court of Conscience). No other competent forum, or court within temporal existence may claim higher original jurisdiction in all matters of law.

The Curia Conscientiae (Court of Conscience) ceases to be in session for the particular case or cause, upon one or more acts of injury against the true Rule of Law, or breach of trust, or wilful acts of ignorance, or bad intention or breaches of their Oath and Vow. When no proper Oath and Vow is invoked and memorialised, no session of the Oratorium is held and Curia Conscientiae (Court of Conscience) is called.

10. A "**Special Session**" of the Oratorium is called when three (3) or more Members of Ucadia individually invoke and memorialise a proper Oath and Vow to the Golden Rule of Law and the Laws of Ucadia and becomes a Tribunal representing the True Rule of Law. Calling a Special Session of the Oratorium

When such an action occurs in good trust, good conscience and good intention, a Divine Court (*Curiam Divina*) is convened within the temporal realm as the highest possible court of appeal, the second highest court of original jurisdiction and forum of law, also known as the *Curia Iuris* (Court of Justice). No other competent forum, or court within temporal existence, other than a properly convened *Ecclesiae Curiam Supremo* (Supreme Ecclesiastical Court) may claim higher appellate jurisdiction in all matters of law.

A Tribunal ceases to be and the Court of Justice (*Curia Iuris*) ceases to be in session upon one or more acts of injury against the true Rule of Law, or breach of trust, or wilful acts of ignorance, or bad intention or breaches their Oaths and Vows.

11. A "**Supreme Session**" of the Oratorium is called when three (3) or more duly authorised Ecclesiastical Members as Jurists of one of the three (3) Great faiths of One Christ, or One Islam or One Spirit individually and collectively invoke and memorialise a proper Oath and Vow to the Golden Rule of Law and the Laws of Ucadia and becomes a Supreme Ecclesiastical Tribunal representing the Spirit, Mind and Body of the True Rule of Law. Calling a Supreme Session of the Oratorium

When such an action occurs in good trust, good conscience and good intention, a Divine Court (*Curiam Divina*) is convened within the temporal realm as the highest possible court of appeal, the highest court of original jurisdiction and forum of law, also known as the Ecclesiae Curiam Supremo (Supreme Ecclesiastical Court). No other competent forum, or court within temporal existence may claim higher appellate jurisdiction in all matters of law.

A Tribunal ceases to be and the Supreme Ecclesiastical Court (*Ecclesiae Curiam Supremo*) ceases to be in session upon one or more acts of injury against the true Rule of Law, or breach of trust, or wilful acts of ignorance, or bad intention or breaches their Oaths and Vows.

Article 60 – Divina Templum (Financial Authority of Treasury of One Heaven)

Divina Templum (Financial Authority of Treasury of One Heaven)

1. **By power and authority of the present most sacred Covenant**, the principal and primary spiritual office, place, chamber, storehouse, vault and temple for the safekeeping and recording of all precious items in the possession of One Heaven shall be Templum, also The Divine Temple, also known as the Divine Treasury.

Vested by the present Covenant, the Divine Temple, possesses supreme, full, immediate, and universal ordinary powers as the Rights of *Ius Divinum Templum* as the primary financial entity and concept throughout the entire Universe, all Heaven and existence. No other financial entity, body or concept concerning the store and use of value shall have higher standing.

The Treasury itself is a purely Spiritual Divine Trust managed by Divine Spirit Persons appointed by the Unique Collective Awareness of Divine Mind. The Trust Number for the Treasury of One Heaven is:

949999-999999-999999

Power and Authority of the Divine Temple

2. The "**Divine Temple**" also known as the Treasury of One Heaven shall be permanently vested with the following powers and authorities:

(i) To record, hold, keep safe and manage all embodiment of powers and authorities of One Heaven bestowed to Members from time to time including but not limited to: Magisterium, Imperium, Officium, Sacrum, Templum, Sacramentum, Sanitatum, Commercium, Virtus, Custoditum, Alumentum, Interpretum and Visum; and

(ii) To record, hold, keep safe and manage all of the Divine Trusts of One Heaven, including but not limited to the proper management of all associated assets; and

(iii) To record, hold, keep safe and manage all of the Supreme Trusts of One Heaven, including the management of all certificates of title as Supreme Credo; and

(iv) To record, hold, keep safe and manage all Promises, Grants, Sureties, Parities and Contingencies underwritten and offered to Heaven for safe keeping and acknowledgement; and

(v) To specifically record, hold, keep safe and manage all Share Certificates and other sureties; and

(vi) Any and all valuable energy, concepts and form not otherwise mentioned herein but which is subject to the jurisdiction of The Temple for safe keeping.

3. The Divine Temple, also known as The Divine Treasury is entrusted to record, hold, keep safe and manage all embodiment of powers and authorities of One Heaven bestowed to Members from time to time including but not limited to: *Magisterium, Imperium, Officium, Sacrum, Templum, Sacramentum, Sanitatum, Commercium, Virtus, Custoditum, Alumentum, Interpretum* and *Visum*. Management of Divine Powers and Authorities

The right of use of these embodied Divine Powers are usually bestowed as part of a valid appointment or action by a Member. By the authority of the present Covenant, no other entity is permitted to store these Powers and Authorities except The Divine Temple, also known as the Treasury of One Heaven.

4. The Divine Temple, also known as The Divine Treasury, is entrusted to record, hold, keep safe and manage all of the Divine Trusts and Supreme Trusts of One Heaven, including but not limited to:- Management of Divine Trusts and Supreme Trusts

(i) Divine Trusts associated with the Solar System include the assets of Divine Trusts including the terms of lawful conveyance of certain Divinity (Divine Right of Use with Purpose) associated with True Trusts and the carnation of living Level 6 Homo Sapien life forms; and

(ii) The Supreme Trusts associated with the conveyance of Divine Right of Use and the creation of Supreme Credo (Credit) title by the combining of one hundred (100) Divine Trusts per Supreme Credo (Credit).

5. The Divine Temple, also known as The Treasury, is entrusted to record, hold, keep safe and manage all Promises, Grants, Sureties, Parities and Contingencies underwritten and offered to Heaven for safe keeping and acknowledgement. When a Member speaks an Oath or Vow or makes a Promise, Grant, Surety, Parity or Contingency, the spiritual energy and true intention is conveyed to The Divine Temple, also known as the Treasury for safe keeping and then any valid certificate issued to memorialise the event is therefore endorsed by the Divine Temple. Management of Oaths, Promises, Sureties

An Oath, Promise, Grant, Surety, Parity or Contingency not made in good faith and truth does not possess any valid spiritual energy or intention and so nothing exists to convey.

6. The Divine Temple, also known as The Treasury, is entrusted to record, hold, keep safe and manage any and all valuable energy, concepts and form not otherwise mentioned herein but which is subject to the jurisdiction or safe keeping. Management of all other valuable energy, concepts and form

7. The Temple, also known as the Treasury shall manage the issue of Management of Share valid share certificates either a valid share certificate to a Divine Trust and Divine Estate upon validation of a Live Borne Record or the aggregation of one hundred (100) shares of deceased Members as underwriting to the creation of a Supreme Credo (Credit). Such Share Certificates shall be held in the Custody of the Globe Union Treasury and related Treasuries and shall not be permitted to be issued directly to individual Living Members. Certificates and other Sureties

In relation to non-Ucadian entities, such Share Certificates are not permitted to be lodged, deposited, transferred or surrendered, except in the sole case of the Visitor, whose Share Certificate is only permitted to be lodged by Special Deposit as a valid extract for safe keeping with the Bank for International Settlements or equivalent entity, or associated reserve bank. A Member who misuses a valid extract of their Share Certificate may be sanctioned for such misuse including, but not limited to, the reduction in privileges and nullification *of services,* for such unlawful acts of misuse.

8. Be it known to all those future and present that We, the Trustees of the Treasury of One Heaven, with full authority and supreme sacred rights granted by the Divine Creator, united Heaven and Hell, all lesser deities, all angels, all demons and all higher order spirits did Give, Grant and Convey these Presents of One Hundred and Forty-Four Million (144,000,000) Supreme Credo (Credit) on JOVIUS E8:Y3208:A17:S2:M18:D4 to the Globe Union Treasury, also known as [14, March 2009], for the benefit of the following Union Treasuries: Lawful Conveyance of Property, Rights and Title

(i) One million six hundred thousand (1,600,000) Supreme Credo (Credits) conveyed for the benefit of the Treasury of One Christ [Trust No. GU7100-999999-999999] with the transaction reflected in the balance of [Account No. OH7100-999999-999999]; and

(ii) One million six hundred thousand (1,600,000) Supreme Credo (Credits) conveyed for the benefit of the Treasury of One Islam [Trust No. GU8100-999999-999999] with the transaction reflected in the balance of [Account No. OH8100-999999-999999]; and

(iii) One million six hundred thousand (1,600,000) Supreme Credo (Credits) conveyed for the benefit of the Treasury of One Spirit [Trust No. GU9100-999999-999999] with the transaction reflected in the balance of [Account No. OH9100-999999-999999]; and

(iv) Eleven million forty-one thousand (11,041,000) Supreme Credo (Credits) conveyed for the benefit of the Africans Union

Treasury [Trust No. GU1100-999999-999999] with the transaction reflected in the balance of [Account No. OH1100-999999-999999]; and

(v) Five million fifty-eight thousand (5,058,000) Supreme Credo (Credits) conveyed for the benefit of the Americas Union Treasury [Trust No. GU2100-999999-999999] with the transaction reflected in the balance of [Account No. OH2100-999999-999999]; and

(vi) One million six hundred and thirty thousand (1,630,000) Supreme Credo (Credits) conveyed for the benefit of the Arabian Union Treasury [Trust No. GU3100-999999-999999] with the transaction reflected in the balance of [Account No. OH3100-999999-999999]; and

(vii) One million one hundred thousand (1,100,000) Supreme Credo (Credits) conveyed for the benefit of the Levant Union Treasury [Trust No. GUL100-999999-999999] with the transaction reflected in the balance of [Account No. OHL100-999999-999999]; and

(viii) Forty million five thousand (40,005,000) Supreme Credo (Credits) conveyed for the benefit of the Asia Union Treasury [Trust No. GU4100-999999-999999] with the transaction reflected in the balance of [Account No. OH4100-999999-999999]; and

(ix) Thirteen million five hundred thousand (13,500,000) Supreme Credo (Credits) conveyed for the benefit of the Euro Union Treasury [Trust No. GU5100-999999-999999] with the transaction reflected in the balance of [Account No. OH5100-999999-999999]; and

(x) Eight hundred and sixty-six thousand (866,000) Supreme Credo (Credits) conveyed for the benefit of the Oceanic Union Treasury [Trust No. GU6100-999999-999999] with the transaction reflected in the balance of [Account No. OH6100-999999-999999]; and

(xi) Fifty-eight million (58,000,000) Supreme Credo (Credits) to the Globe Union Treasury [Trust No. GU0100-999999-999999] with the transaction reflected in the balance of [Account No. OH0100-999999-999999]; and

(xii) One million four hundred thousand (1,400,000) Supreme Credo (Credits) to the Original Nations Treasury [Trust No.

GUZ100-999999-999999] with the transaction reflected in the balance of [Account No. OHZ100-999999-999999]; and

(xiii) Six hundred thousand (600,000) Supreme Credo (Credits) to the Council of Ucadia Foundations Treasury [Trust No. GUF100-999999-999999] with the transaction reflected in the balance of [Account No. OHF100-999999-999999]; and

(xiv) Two million (2,000,000) Supreme Credo (Credits) to the Ucadia Moon Federation Treasury [Trust No. GUX100-999999-999999] with the transaction reflected in the balance of [Account No. OHX100-999999-999999]; and

(xv) Two million (2,000,000) Supreme Credo (Credits) to the Ucadia Mars Federation Treasury [Trust No. GUM100-999999-999999] with the transaction reflected in the balance of [Account No. OHM100-999999-999999]; and

(xvi) One million (1,000,000) Supreme Credo (Credits) to the Ucadia Jupiter-Europa Federation Treasury [Trust No. GUJ100-999999-999999] with the transaction reflected in the balance of [Account No. OHJ100-999999-999999]; and

(xvii) One million (1,000,000) Supreme Credo (Credits) to the Ucadia Saturn-Titan Federation Treasury [Trust No. GUT100-999999-999999] with the transaction reflected in the balance of [Account No. OHT100-999999-999999].

9. Be it known to all those future and present that We, the Trustees of the Treasury of One Heaven, with full authority and supreme sacred rights granted by the Divine Creator, united Heaven and Hell, all lesser deities, all angels, all demons and all higher order spirits hereby shall Give, Grant and Convey Presents of Supreme Credo to the Globe Union Treasury for circulation to other Union Treasuries to a maximum of seventy-two (72,000,000) million Supreme Credo (Credits) or lesser amount as requested upon formal vote at a General Conclave or Great Conclave and at subsequent Conclaves as requested for the stability, prosperity and well being of the Supreme Financial System.

Subsequent Gifts, Grants and Presents of Supreme Credo

10. The Globe Union Treasury shall be empowered to produce an authorised extract of the complete Supreme Credo Register beginning with a Register summarising the complete number of Supreme Credo gifted, granted and conveyed by the Treasury of One Heaven to the Globe Union Treasury. The Supreme Credo Register shall be recorded and published on the One Heaven, Ucadia and associated Gazettes every eight (8) years.

Supreme Credo Register

11. The Globe Union Treasury shall be empowered to produce an authorised extract of the complete Supreme Credo Accounts beginning with an extract of All Supreme Credo Accounts following the Supreme Credo gifted, granted and conveyed by the Treasury of One Heaven to the Globe Union Treasury. The Supreme Credo Accounts shall be recorded and published on the One Heaven, Ucadia and associated Gazettes every eight (8) years. Supreme Credo Accounts

12. In the event the Authorised and Guaranteed Capital Stock of Supreme Credo (Credits) of One Christ, One Islam, One Spirit or any of the seven Ucadia Unions at the time is insufficient to discharge all debts and obligations, then sufficient capital of Supreme Credo (Credit) shall immediately be made manifest to satisfy and settle any and all outstanding obligations. Therefore, no action of insolvency or delinquency shall be permitted or tolerated by any competent forum of law or jurisdiction of civilised society against these bodies at any time during their life. Divine Guarantee

Article 61 – Magisterium (Teaching Authority)

1. **All teaching power, authority of instruction, custody and power of guardian of knowledge of Heaven** shall hereby be vested as the Right of *Ius Divinum Magisterium* in the body and force known as "**Magisterium**". When anyone references, writes or speaks of Magisterium specifically or in general as a quality, force, action, power, authority or any other manifestation, it shall mean this body and the powers vested in it and no other. Magisterium (Teaching Authority)

2. In accord with the present most sacred Covenant, the Divine Right of Magisterium (*Ius Divinum Magisterium*) is irrevocably and exclusively delegated to the three (3) Great Faiths of One Christ, One Islam and One Spirit for the life of these bodies, through the Authoritative Ecclesiastical Right of *Ius Ecclesiae Magisterium* as the Absolute Ecclesiastical Right to Teach, Instruct and Interpret Divine Will. No other bodies, associations, persons, fraternities or entities may claim Magisterium, unless properly dispensed by one of the three (3) Great Faiths of One Christ, One Islam, One Spirit in accord with the present most sacred Covenant and associated Covenants, Charters, Maxims and Rules. Divine Right of Magisterium conveyed to One Christ, One Islam and One Spirit

The embodiment of Magisterium shall be the Sacred Offices of Supreme Patriarch, Supreme Caliph and the Supreme Recurrence. A teaching, instruction, custody or guardianship office not uniquely named within the present Covenant or associated Covenants and Charters may still receive the valid authority of Magisterium by the gift or grant of such power through the exercise of power and authority of one of the above Sacred Offices. However, an office that cannot demonstrate proper gift, grant or conveyance of Magisterium through the present Covenant possesses none.

Article 62 – Imperium (Enforcement Authority)

1. **All coercive military power, authority of occupation, enforcement and the use of force of Heaven** shall hereby be vested in the body and force known as Imperium. An office that cannot demonstrate proper gift, grant or conveyance of Imperium through the present Covenant possesses none. When anyone references, writes or speaks of Imperium specifically or in general as a quality, force, action, power, authority or any other manifestation, it shall mean this body and the powers vested in it and no other.

Imperium (Enforcement Authority)

2. In accord with the present most sacred Covenant, the Divine Right of Imperium (*Ius Divinum Imperium*) is irrevocably and exclusively delegated to the three (3) Great Faiths of One Christ, One Islam and One Spirit for the life of such bodies, through the Authoritative Ecclesiastical Right of *Ius Ecclesiae Imperium* as the Absolute Ecclesiastical Right to Command and Direct all valid and proper military, police, justice and law enforcement bodies. No other bodies, units, divisions, orders, companies, persons, fraternities or entities may claim Imperium, unless properly dispensed by one of the three (3) Great Faiths of One Christ, One Islam and One Spirit in accord with the present most sacred Covenant and associated Covenants, Charters, Maxims and Rules.

Divine Right of Imperium conveyed to One Christ, One Islam and One Spirit

The embodiment of Imperium shall be the highest Spiritual Leader of the highest Military and Religious Order of each of the three (3) Great Faiths of One Christ, One Islam, One Spirit. An office or commission of military, police, justice and law enforcement not uniquely named within the present Covenant or associated Covenants and Charters may still receive the valid authority of Imperium by the gift or grant of such power through the exercise of power and authority of those sacred and religious offices that embody Imperium.

3. All valid, lawful and legitimate Imperium as the Right to Command, Direct and Control properly constituted police and law enforcement bodies as well as military and other defence bodies is completely derived from and dependent upon the delegation of *Ius Ecclesiae Imperium*.

A Military or Police Force with proper Imperium is empowered by Heaven

When a properly constituted military, paramilitary, police or other armed force holds *Ius Imperium* derived from the valid dispensing of

Ius Ecclesiae Imperium, its flags, colours and standards shall be duly recorded and recognised as representing the full force and power of Heaven. When such a temporal force then moves to action, it shall be accompanied by the full force and spirit of the combined armies of Heaven with the strongest of angels, the fiercest of demons by its side. When such a valid temporal force then calls upon its right for inspiration prior to engagement, each and every member shall be infused with the strength and power of a hundred angels and demons.

4. Any military, paramilitary, police or other armed force not under the absolute Authority of Heaven is therefore an enemy to Heaven and the preservation of Rule of Law and Civilisation. Such a body or force that rejects the proper and absolute Authority and Power of the *Ius Ecclesiae Imperium* of One Christ, or One Islam or One Spirit, therefore calls upon every spirit, every angel, every demon, every life-form and every civilised man and woman to defeat them, until no memory or temporal form of such profanity remains in existence.

A Military or Police Force not under the Authority of Heaven is an enemy of Heaven

A military, paramilitary, police or other armed force that makes itself an enemy of Heaven, has no power or authority, or good fortune, or future as all of Creation and all of Spirit and all of Heaven is compelled to resist and defeat such a threat. However, when such a military, paramilitary, police or other armed force genuinely surrenders itself to the mercy of the *Ius Ecclesiae Imperium*, then mercy should be given and the honour and *espirit de corps* of such a body shall be restored under the absolute authority of the present most sacred Covenant.

Article 63 – Officium (Official Authority)

1. **All Authority of office, commission, warrant, official power of Heaven** shall hereby be vested as the Right of Ius Divinum Officium in the body and force known as Officium. When anyone references, writes or speaks of Officium, or Office, or Officers, or Official Authority specifically or in general as a quality, force, action, power, authority or any other manifestation, it shall mean this body and the powers vested in it and no other.

Officium (Official Authority)

2. In accord with the present most sacred Covenant, the Divine Right of Officium (*Ius Divinum Officium*) is irrevocably delegated to the three (3) Great Faiths of One Christ, One Islam and One Spirit, including Ucadia itself for the life of such bodies, through the Authoritative Ecclesiastical Right of Ius Ecclesiae Officium as the Absolute Ecclesiastical Right to Authority of Office, Trustee, Trustor, Commission, Investiture, Coronation, Principal, Agent, Warrant, Title, Property Rights, Duty and Service. No other bodies, associations, persons, fraternities, societies or entities may claim Officium, unless

Divine Right of Officium conveyed to One Christ, One Islam and One Spirit properly dispensed by one of the three (3) Great Faiths of One Christ, One Islam, One Spirit in accord with the present most sacred Covenant and associated Covenants, Charters, Maxims and Rules.

The embodiment of Officium shall be the Sacred Offices of Supreme Patriarch, Supreme Caliph and the Supreme Recurrence. An Office not uniquely named within the present Covenant or associated Covenants and Charters may still receive the valid authority of Officium by the gift or grant of such power through the exercise of power and authority of one of the above Sacred Offices that embody the Divine Right. However, an Office that cannot demonstrate proper gift, grant or conveyance of Officium through the present Covenant possesses none.

3. An office must possess valid Officium to then manage or administer any form of Land, Property or Rights. This is because all land, all property and all ownership of all objects and concepts is vested in the Divine Creator of the Universe and Existence and then granted as a power and authority to duly appointed officials. An office without such authority has no right to possess or use any form of Land, Property, Use or Rights. Any actions performed by an office without valid authority and power of Officium is done *de son tort* with full liability resting solely on the impostor occupants of such false offices.

Officium and Land, Property and Rights

Article 64 – Sacrum (Sacred Authority)

1. **All power and force of holiness, sacredness, sanctity and holly of Heaven** shall hereby be vested as the Right of *Ius Divinum Sacrum* in the body and force known as Sacrum and no other. The method of bestowing Sacrum shall be reserved to those official sacraments of One Heaven known as the "Sacramentum" that allow for the bestowing of Sacrum.

Sacrum (Sacred Authority)

Unless Sacrum is duly bestowed through the formal and valid manifestation of a perfected sacrament in accord with the present Covenant, no gift, grant, conveyance or transfer of Sacrum shall take place. When anyone references, writes or speaks of sacred objects or sacred places, or sacred acts or sacred worship or sacred mysteries or in general as a quality, force, action, power, authority or any other manifestation, it shall mean this force, quality and power known as Sacrum and no other.

2. "**Sacred**" is the concept that certain objects, concepts and actions in themselves are worthy of recognition, devotion or reverence and possess some unique quality in addition to their general form contributing to their Sacredness. In accord with the present Covenant, all objects concepts and actions duly recognised as Sacred are those

Sacred

possessing the quality of "Sacrum" gifted, granted, conveyed or bestowed to the particular object, concept or action by an authorised official of One Heaven.

Article 65 – Penitentiaria (Penitential Authority)

1. **All coercive power and force of confinement, containment, reflection, penitence and reform** shall hereby be vested as the Right of *Ius Divinum Penitentiaria* in the body and force known as "**Penitentiaria**" and no other. The method of bestowing the authority of Penitentiaria shall be reserved to those official bodies duly authorised under the Oratorium. Unless Penitentiaria is duly bestowed through the formal and valid manifestation of a perfected gift in accord with the present Covenant, no gift, grant, conveyance or transfer of Penitentiaria shall take place. Penitentiaria (Penitental Authority)

2. When any spirit or living Member openly, willingly and defiantly disobeys the most sacred Laws of Heaven, the enforcement systems of Heaven and Earth shall be properly granted the Right of Penitentiaria to enforce the confinement of such a belligerent spirit and mind, until such time as through genuine penitence and knowledge, they recognise the wisdom of the Law and respect:- Forced Confinement and Penitence

   (i) *Malevolent Ghosts* shall be immediately subject to Penitentiaria if upon the exercise of proper prayer and invocation of Living Members, such deceased minds refuse to cease and desist from further damaging acts of influence and harm; and

   (ii) *Belligerent Spirits* shall be immediately subject to Penitentiaria if upon the exercise of the proper Sacred Gifts and Rites they refuse to vacate sacred space or places as required by Law; and

   (iii) *Wicked and Damaging Beings* shall be immediately subject to Penitentiaria if upon the exercise of the Rite of Exorcism, they belligerently refuse to obey and depart from active possession of living bodies, things or places as required by Law.

3. Any and all forced confinement as Penitentiaria shall be temporary; and no spirit or living being may be condemned under any eternal curse or sentence to such confinement, nor may such confinement be construed or corrupted to imply cruel and barbaric torture, but the opportunity for the confined mind to reflect, to grow and to heal. All Forced Confinement Temporary

TITLE XII - SOVEREIGN DIMENSION (REGIONAL COLLECTIVE)

Article 66 - Sovereign Dimension (Regional Collective)

1. **All Regional Spiritual Collectives of One Heaven** are hereby recognised as sovereign and independent within the existence, dimension and jurisdiction of One Heaven in accord with the present Covenant. By the present Covenant and laws of Existence, no unaffiliated and independent Sovereign Dimensions as Regional Spiritual Collectives may exist. Sovereign Dimension (Regional Collective)

A "**Sovereign Dimension**", also known as a Regional Spiritual Collective, is the second largest operational division of One Heaven. An affiliated Sovereign Dimension is an ecclesiastically, legally and lawfully constituted subdivision of the Unique Collective of One Heaven corresponding to the past, present and future generations of higher order spirits of a traditional global, empire, faith, religion or international affiliation.

The elected spiritual leader of a Sovereign Dimension, also known as a Regional Spiritual Collective shall be known as an Augustus.

A Sovereign Dimension always possesses one or more Collective Divisions (Spiritual Collectives) of two (2) or more Local Dimensions (Local Collectives). Each and every Spirit State and Spiritual Kingdom as signatory to the Treaty of Spirit States is duly recognised as a Sovereign Dimension (Regional Spiritual Collective) subject to the present sacred Covenant.

2. In accord with the present Covenant and the sacred Covenants of One Christ, One Islam and One Spirit: Official Recognition of Three Key Sovereign Dimensions

(i) All Christian Spirit Members of Heaven, whether Traditional, Orthodox, Catholic, Protestant, Ecumenical, Baptist, Gnostic, Yahudi, Mormon, Jehovah, Uniting, Methodist or any other denomination hereby unite as one in Christ as the Sovereign Dimension and Regional Spiritual Collective of One Christ, terrestrially bound in trust to the Ecclesia known also as One Christ; and

(ii) All Spirit Members of Heaven of the traditions of Judaism, Mithraism, Manichaeism, Meneshism, Persian, Kabbalism, Ebionism, Boethusianism and all other denominations owing their origin through the covenants and writings of the Piso in Europe are hereby united in trust within One Christ, equally with all other members of the new covenant; and

(iii) All Spirit Members of Islam of Heaven, are hereby united as one in Islam as the Sovereign Dimension and Regional Spiritual Collective of One Islam, terrestrially bound in trust to the Society known also as One Islam; and

(iv) All Spirit and Transcended Members of Hinduism, are hereby united as one in Spirit as the Sovereign Dimension and Regional Spiritual Collective of One Spirit, terrestrially bound in trust to the Society known also as One Spirit; and

(v) All Spirit and Transcended Members of Buddhism are hereby united in trust within One Spirit, equally with all other members of the present sacred Covenant; and

(vi) All Spirit and Transcended Members of Indigenous Faiths are hereby united in trust within One Spirit, equally with all other members of the present sacred Covenant; and

(vii) All Spirit and Transcended Members not otherwise included in any of the previous historic and traditional faiths and groups are hereby united in trust within Ucadia, equally with all other members of the present sacred Covenant.

3. The following criteria are the essential structural components and properties of a valid Sovereign Dimension as a Regional Spiritual Collective:

Structure and Properties of a Sovereign Dimension

(i) A unique enclosure and dimension of consciousness and awareness whereby the boundaries of the enclosure are recognised as having historic provenance and meaning; and

(ii) A unique identity in name whereby the name of the Regional Spiritual Collective is recognised as having historic provenance, either as party to the Divine Treaty of Spirit States; or named within the present sacred Covenant; or named and approved at a Great Conclave; and

(iii) A permanent population of Divine Persons as Spirit Members within the bounds of the Regional Spiritual Collective of more than two hundred million (200,000,000) souls; and

(iv) A Legislative of Members, elected to office, possessing the spiritual authority and power in making and amending laws, formed upon the ratification of the present Covenant in association with the formation and recognition of the Sovereign Dimension as a Regional Spiritual Collective; and

(v) An Executive Government, elected to office, representing the government of the Sovereign Dimension.

4. A Sovereign Dimension also known as a Regional Spiritual Collective shall be divided and defined by distinct structural units known as Organs to represent its vital parts as a spiritual body. The Organs for each Regional Spiritual Collective shall be:- Sovereign Dimension (Regional Spiritual Collective) Organs

(i) Regnum; and

(ii) Astrum; and

(iii) Cancellarium; and

(iv) Commercium.

5. Notwithstanding the names of Sovereign Dimension Organs within the Official Ucadian Language of Logos, the Three (3) Great Faiths of One Christ, One Islam and One Spirit may choose to vote at a properly formed Great Conclave to adopt new names in one or more Non-Ucadian languages for such Organs. Names of Sovereign Dimension Organs

Article 67 - Regnum

1. **All Executive Power and Authority of a Regional Spiritual Collective of One Heaven** shall be vested as the Right of *Ius Divinum Regnum* in an executive government known as the Regnum comprising a Saint and the Collective Assembly of Visitors ("the Assembly"). Regnum

2. The word "**Regnum**" originally comes from Latin and means "kingdom; king; monarchy; sovereignty; supremacy; domain or dominium". Hence, a "region" from region in Latin is the boundary of a regnum, while the law of a sovereign is "Rex". Origin and Meaning of Regnum

All Regal and Sovereign Authority and Power is derived from one or more Regnum.

Any Sovereign, Monarch, Prince, Noble, King, Queen or Emperor or Peer claiming authority and right to rule certain land or estates without proper authority derived from the present Covenant is an imposter and without spiritual, legal or lawful right to make such a claim.

Whenever a higher order spirit or living being makes a claim to be sovereign or regal in some manner without possessing the proper authority and power granted by the present Covenant, they shall be committing a grave transgression and blasphemy against One Heaven.

3. The Saint is the supreme Regional Spiritual Collective leader and its regional representative to the Universe. The office of the Saint is the Saint

highest regional elected office of One Heaven and at all times should be considered with the greatest dignity and respect.

A "**Saint**" is a departed soul of one of the present twelve (12) higher order life forms presently nominated to the Divina, also known as the Divine Mind who the living community of one of the twenty-four (24) Star Systems also nominated to the Divina believe is worthy of such nomination. As such, the Saint shall be elected via a Great Conclave for a period of one hundred and twenty-eight (128) years and it will be so in Heaven.

4. By virtue of the present Covenant, the Saint of a regional collective is vested with regional authority to manage the needs and affairs of One Heaven for their region through the selection or dismissal of wise counsel in the form of their Collective Assembly of Visitors, the agencies, officials and administration of the government: Power of the Saint

(i) The Saint shall have the authority of official spokesman for the word of One Heaven for the Regional Spiritual Collective during their time of office and all faithful must obey his command; and

(ii) The Saint shall have the authority over all agencies and Regional Spiritual Collective Visitors as Chairman of the Collective Assembly of Visitors. As Chairman of the Collective Assembly of Visitors, the Saint may choose to overrule motions of the Assembly and select the agenda and minutes of the Assembly meetings; and

(iii) The Saint shall have the power by and with the advice and consent of the Regional Collective Assembly of Visitors to make statements of faith that once accepted may then become the basis of new regional collective law.

5. The Saint shall hold their Office during the term of one hundred and twenty-eight (128) years corresponding to the term of a Great Conclave for the election of Saints and Great and Holy Spirits. Term of Saint

All Members of One Heaven in a Regional Spiritual Collective may vote for the election of the Saint through open ballot. The organisation of the election process shall be handled by the Supreme Director for Fair Elections of One Heaven.

6. By the authority of the present sacred Covenant, only an angel, deceased higher order life form or demon meeting all of the following criteria shall be permitted to hold the Office of Saint by Extraordinary Qualification, Special Qualification or Ordinary Qualification: Qualification as Saint

By Extraordinary Qualification

(i) Extraordinary Qualification of a Saint are those deceased higher order life-form, angels and demons recognised as being party to the Great Treaties of One Heaven such as the Treaty of United States of Spirits; and

(ii) An Extraordinary Saint is recognised as a spirit of extraordinary courage and redemption in the unity of Heaven; and

(iii) As Divine Remedy, all those departed spirits and gods previously condemned and cursed in perpetuity, shall be hereby recognised and known forever, by the power and authority of this Divine Covenant as extraordinary Saints, for the source and testimony of their evil is through their true confession, as shall be listed as official documents of testament and confession; and

(iv) Particular mention is given to those Extraordinary Saints and their true confessions as listed with their Sainthood as official documents as it shall be by these true documents that the true history of the higher order species shall be repaired and promulgated by authority of this sacred Covenant, so that all men and women may know the truth of their origins, their history and the courage of these Extraordinary Saints in ending the war in Heaven and in bringing peace upon the Earth; and

(v) All named Angels and Demons of greater age than two hundred (200) years from the present are hereby recognised as official Extraordinary Saints of One Heaven; and

(vi) As Extraordinary Saints of One Heaven, when praise, worship, call or pledge is given to the name of a Saint, it shall be to an Official of One Heaven and no other Society; and

(vii) No other Society shall hold any rights whatsoever over these named Spirits other than the Society of One Heaven and associated Societies under the law of Unique Collective Awareness.

By Special Qualification

(i) Special Qualification of a Saint are those deceased men and women recognised as being party to the Great Treaties of One Heaven such as the Treaty of United States of Spirits; and

(ii) A Special Saint is recognised as a spirit of special and extraordinary courage and redemption in the unity of Heaven.

By Ordinary Qualification

(i) A Spirit holding the office of Ascended Master, through previous election to such a position, or having been officially sanctified by one or more of the Great Ecclesia at least twelve (12) months before a Great Conclave are eligible for election to a Saint.

A spirit who fails one or more of these qualifications shall be ineligible to stand for election to the office of Saint.

7. A Higher Order Spirit shall be disqualified from eligibility as a candidate to be elected as a Saint, or remaining in such Office if any of the following conditions occur: Disqualification as Saint

(i) The Higher Order Spirit, fails to invoke a sacred Oath and Vow to uphold the present sacred Covenant and to seek the emancipation and redemption of any and all previously trapped spirits, lost souls, condemned or cursed entities; and the complete and total eradication of false spirituality, Mundi negativity and control and the attempted control of spirits and the living through force, or delusion or fear; and

(ii) The Higher Order Spirit is presently active in the maintenance and influence of false spirituality, Mundi negativity and control and the attempted control of spirits through force, or delusion or fear.

8. The Regional Collective Assembly of Visitors shall be an Assembly of spirit individuals selected by the Saint to head the permanent statutory authorities and uphold the laws regarding the critical systems of One Heaven in the regional collective. The tenure of a Visitor shall be at the sole discretion of the Saint. The Collective Assembly of Visitors (Regional Collective Assembly)

Because of the importance of honour and such positions, Visitors shall also be collectively known as “the Honoured”.

9. By this Covenant, the Great Conclave is authorised to forge a formal set of protocols and standards regarding the Office of the Saint, which relates to the detailed definition and requirements of operational procedure and function necessitated by such a high office. Protocols and Standards of the Office of Saint

These standards themselves must embody and be consistent with the specific articles of this Covenant and in turn must be approved by a vote of the Great Conclave. The standards shall be known as the Protocols and standards of the Office of Saint.

In terms of the major subject matter dealt with by the Protocols and standards of the Office of the Saint, the following areas must specifically provide detail and procedures consistent with the Covenant:

(i) That a formal set of procedures exist for the inauguration of the Saint befitting such high office. That these procedures contain the disclosure of the official seal of office as well as the oath of office; and

(ii) That a formal set of procedures exist for the proper recognition and respect bestowed to a Saint that reaches such tenure of office to be warranted a Grand Saint, including the naming of an official day of respect within the calendar of One Christ, One Islam or One Spirit Tribe, proper memorials and events befitting such an occasion.

Article 68 - Astrum

1. **All legislative powers of a Regional Collective of spirits of One Heaven** shall be vested as the Right of *Ius Divinum Astrum* in a body called "**Astrum**" which shall consist of all elected representatives from each Spiritual Collective in the spiritual region. Astrum

Members of Astrum shall be appointed for a term of one hundred and twenty-eight (128) years before being dissolved ahead of a Great Conclave for a new Astrum.

2. Vested by the Covenant, the Astrum shall have the power to review all acts passed by the Regional Executive and proposed as rules and official planning of the executive. Legislative power

The Astrum shall also have the power to commission Regional Commissions of Investigation with the power to call any individual Member within the region and any information located within One Heaven and the dimensions of the region to review.

3. In terms of the Operation of Astrum: Operation of Astrum

(i) *Life of Sessions of Astrum* - The Sessions of an Astrum shall exist for a fixed period of one hundred and twenty-eight (128) years before the sessions being dissolved ahead of a Great Conclave for a new Astrum; and

(ii) *Astrum Sessions* - The Astrum shall be in session corresponding to the session of a General Conclave every sixty-four (64) years and a Great Conclave every one hundred and twenty-eight (128) years the Spiritual Masters are summonsed to attend; and

(iii) *Formation of new Astrum* - The formation of a new body of Astrum officials shall occur within fourteen (14) days after the Great Conclave following verification of all votes; and

(iv) *Quorum* - The minimum number of Members (quorum) required to be present within the Astrum to permit the full exercise of its powers shall be two thirds (2/3) the total number of members of Astrum.

4. By this Covenant, the Supreme Council is authorised to forge a formal set of protocols and standards regarding its own function which relates to the detailed definition and requirements of operational procedure and function necessitated by the institution. These shall be known as the Protocols and standards of an Astrum of a Regional Spiritual Collective of One Heaven.

Protocols and Standards of an Astrum of One Heaven

These standards themselves must embody and be consistent with the specific articles of this Covenant and in turn must be approved by a majority vote of all delegates attending a Great Conclave.

In terms of the major subject matter dealt with by the Protocols and standards of an Astrum of a Regional Spiritual Collective of One Heaven, the following areas must specifically provide detail and procedures consistent with the Covenant.

Article 69 - Cancellarium

1. **All record and memory keeping, safe keeping of all rolls, the administration of all registers and instruments and the issuance of all official instruments of power and authority of Heaven** shall hereby be vested as the Right of *Ius Divinum Cancellarium* to each and every Regional Spiritual Collective as the body and force known as Cancellarium.

Cancellarium

2. The word "**Cancellarium**" originally comes from Latin and means "Chancery as first formed under Holly (Holy) Law".

Origin and Meaning of Cancellarium

When anyone references, writes or speaks of Chancery, Registers, Rolls, Instruments, Writs, Bills, Decrees, Notices, Equality, Equity or Fairness specifically or in general as a quality, force, action, power, authority or any other manifestation, it shall mean this body and the powers vested in it and no other.

3. The valid gift, grant and conveyance of Cancellarium is hereby vested in all uniquely named offices defined by the present Covenant and associated Covenants and Charters. Gift, Grant and Conveyance of Cancellarium

An office or body or forum not uniquely named within the present Covenant or associated Covenants and Charters may still receive the valid authority of Cancellarium by the gift or grant of such power through the exercise of power and authority of an office or body that has been granted such power by the present Covenant. However, an office that cannot demonstrate proper gift, grant or conveyance of Cancellarium through the present Covenant possesses none.

4. All claims of authority, power, supreme judicature or rights concerning Cancellarium are hereby invalid, having no force or effect ecclesiastically, legally or lawfully if the official or body or forum of law that issued such an act does not legitimately possess Cancellarium. Forums, Claims, Opinions, Rulings, Judgements of Cancellarium

Any opinions, rulings, judgements, reports or decree that seeks to deny the absolute supremacy of jurisdiction and authority of the present Covenant *ipso facto* (as a matter of fact) is a formal denouncement that the official in question possesses any legitimate Cancellarium and instead is evidence of a confession of incompetence and unsound mind therefore rendering such instrument null and void from the beginning.

Article 70 - Commercium

1. **All trade, traffic, commerce, exchange, intercourse, communication, merchant, wares and market powers and authority of Heaven** shall hereby be vested as the Right of *Ius Divinum Commercium* to each and every Regional Spiritual Collective as the body and force known as Commercium. Commercium

2. The word "**Commercium**" originally comes from Latin and means "trade, traffic, commerce, exchange, intercourse, communication, merchant, wares and markets". Origin and Meaning of Commercium

When anyone references, writes or speaks of Commercium, or Trade, or Traffic, or Commerce, or Exchange, or Intercourse, or Communication or Markets specifically or in general as a quality, force, action, power, authority or any other manifestation, it shall mean this body and the powers vested in it and no other.

3. The valid gift, grant and conveyance of Commercium is hereby vested in all Members defined by the present Covenant and associated Covenants and Charters. Gift, Grant and Conveyance of Commercium

Such gift, grant and conveyance cannot be derogated, abrogated, suspended, sold, enclosed, privatised, surrendered, seized, abandoned or altered by any other means or argument.

Any claimed laws, statutes, decrees of inferior societies and associated entities that deny the gift, grant and conveyance of Commercium or seek to alter or control it in anyway are without any legitimate or valid force or effect ecclesiastically, legally or lawfully and therefore are null and void from the beginning.

TITLE XIII - COLLECTIVE DIMENSION (SPIRITUAL COLLECTIVE)

Article 71 - Collective Dimension (Spiritual Collective)

1. A **Collective Dimension**, also known as a Spiritual Collective is the third largest operational division of One Heaven. A Spiritual Collective may be affiliated or unaffiliated and an independently recognised body: *Collective Dimension (Spiritual Collective)*

    (i) An affiliated Collective Dimension (Spiritual Collective) is an ecclesiastically, legally and lawfully constituted subdivision of a Regional Collective of more than one hundred thousand (100,000) Divine Persons, corresponding to the past, present and future generations of higher order spirits of a traditional country or supranational affiliation but smaller than a traditional global, empire, religion or international affiliation; and

    (ii) An unaffiliated and independent Spiritual Collective is an ecclesiastically, legally and lawfully constituted body corresponding to an association of Local Collectives of more than one hundred thousand (100,000) Divine Persons but less than two hundred million (200,000,000) Divine Persons that is not formally aligned to any Regional Collective.

    While an unaffiliated and independent Collective Dimension (Spiritual Collective) may have no formal association or alignment to any Regional Collective, all Spiritual Collective are recognised as within the existence, dimension and jurisdiction of One Heaven in accord with the present Covenant.

2. In accord with the present Covenant and criteria for the constitution of Spiritual Collectives, official recognition is hereby made concerning the sovereign independence and unique personality of key Unaffiliated Spiritual Collectives corresponding to the following traditional, historic and present faiths and groups: *Official Recognition of Key Unaffiliated Spiritual Collectives*

    (i) Any and all traditional land owners and indigenous tribal associations who have reclaimed the origins of their ancestors and have rejected the threats, demands and invasion of foreign and non traditional belief systems; and

    (ii) Any association of spirits of higher order beings that chooses to function as a sovereign independent group within One Heaven, subject to its own rules and constructs.

3. Unless a Spiritual Collective is implied or stated as part of a recognised historic Regional Collective, the following criteria are the essential *Official Structure and Properties of*

structural components and properties of a valid Spiritual Collective: a Spiritual Collective

(i) A unique enclosure of consciousness and awareness whereby the boundaries of the enclosure are recognised as having historic provenance and meaning; and

(ii) A unique identity in name whereby the name of the Spiritual Collective is recognised as having historic provenance; and

(iii) A permanent population of higher order spirits and Divine Persons within the bounds of the Spiritual Collective more than one hundred thousand (100,000) souls but less than two hundred million (200,000,000) souls; and

(iv) A Provisional, Probationary or Permanent Ecclesia of Members representing either: (1) the provisional spiritual occupational forces formed upon the Day of Agreement and Understanding; or (2) a probationary Ecclesia formed when one or more living Members have validated and ratified a probationary University structure; or (3) a permanent Ecclesia formed upon the ratification of the present Covenant in association with the formation and recognition of a Permanent University of a Union of living Members who recognise in name the Ecclesia and who claims its spiritual authority and power in making and amending laws; and

(v) A provisional, probationary or permanent Executive Government representing either the government of a provisional Ecclesia, the government of a probationary Ecclesia or government of a permanent Ecclesia.

4. A Collective Dimension also known as a Spiritual Collective shall be divided and defined by distinct structural units known as Organs representing its vital parts as a spiritual body. The Organs for each Spiritual Collective shall be:- Collective Dimension (Spiritual Collective) Organs

(i) Consilium; and

(ii) Ecclesia; and

(iii) Virtus; and

(iv) Custoditum; and

(v) Alumentum.

5. Notwithstanding the names of Collective Dimension Organs within the Official Ucadian Language of Logos, the Three (3) Great Faiths of One Christ, One Islam and One Spirit may choose to vote at a properly Names of Collective Dimension Organs formed Great Conclave to adopt new names in one or more Non-Ucadian languages for such Organs.

Article 72 - Consilium

1. **All Executive Power and Authority of a Spiritual Collective** shall be vested as the Right of *Ius Divinum Consilium* in an executive government known as the *Consilium* comprising a Consul, also known as a Master and the Panel of Auditors. Consilium

2. The word "**Consilium**" originally comes from Latin and means "a council or advisory body; a judgement or wisdom; a plan or advice". Origin and Meaning of Consilium

All claims of authority of any Council at any level of government or association of the living or deceased ultimately derives its authority from one or more Consilium.

A Council that does not source its authority and power through valid association with the present Covenant is a false and fraudulent body whose decisions have no spiritual, legal or lawful effect.

3. The Consul is the leader of a Spiritual Collective and its representative to the Universe. The office of the Consul is the highest elected office of a belief collective and at all times should be considered with the greatest dignity and respect. Consul

A Consul is a departed soul and Saint of one of the present twelve (12) types of higher order life forms presently nominated to the Divina, also known as the Divine Mind who the living community of one of the twenty-four (24) Star Systems also nominated to the Divina believe is worthy of such nomination. As such, the Consul shall be elected via a Great Conclave for a period of one hundred and twenty-eight (128) years and it will be so in Heaven.

4. By virtue of the present Covenant, the Consul of a Spiritual Collective is vested with executive authority to manage the needs and affairs of One Heaven for their Spiritual Collective through the selection or dismissal of wise counsel in the form of their Collective Panel of Auditors and the agencies, officials and administration of the Spiritual Collective government. Power of the Consul

The Consul shall have the authority of official spokesman for the word of One Heaven for their Spiritual Collective during their time of office and all faithful must obey their command.

The Consul shall have the authority over all agencies and Spiritual

Collective Auditors as Chairman of the Collective Panel of Auditors. As Chairman of the Collective Panel of Auditors, the Consul may choose to overrule motions of the Board and select the agenda and minutes of the Board meetings.

The Consul shall have the power by and with the advice and consent of the Panel of Auditors to make statements of truth and fact that once accepted may then become the basis of new regional law.

5. The Spiritual Collective Panel of Auditors shall be a panel of individual spirits selected by the Ascended Master Spirit to head the permanent statutory authorities and uphold the laws regarding the critical systems of One Heaven in the Spiritual Collective. The tenure of a Director shall be at the sole discretion of the Ascended Master Spirit. Spiritual Collective Panel of Auditors

Because of the importance and honour of such positions, regional Auditors shall also be collectively known as "the Esteemed".

Article 73 - Ecclesia

1. **All legislative powers of a Spiritual Collective of spirits of One Heaven** shall be vested as the Right of *Ius Divinum Ecclesia* in a body called "**Ecclesia**" that shall consist of all elected representatives from each Spiritual Collective within the spiritual region. Ecclesia

An Ecclesia may exist both temporally and spiritually in the form of a properly constituted body holding valid plenary authority consistent with the present sacred Covenant.

The highest temporal Ecclesia bodies possessing the Right of *Ius Divinum Ecclesia* shall be One Christ, One Islam, One Spirit Tribe and Ucadia itself. These four (4) Ecclesia bodies shall be known as the "Great Ecclesia". No other associations, aggregates, trusts, estates, companies, corporations, entities, persons or bodies may claim higher authority or standing as a valid Ecclesia than these four (4) bodies.

A body that does not possess the Right of *Ius Divinum Ecclesia* in accord with the present sacred Covenant, cannot be a valid Ecclesia.

2. All authority and power of any body calling itself a Church or Ecclesia is hereby sourced from its legitimate association with the present most sacred Covenant and one or more Ecclesia. Furthermore, any law claiming to be Ecclesiastical is valid to the extent that it recognises the superior jurisdiction of the present Covenant and associated Maxims of law. Origin and Meaning of Ecclesia

Where a body refuses to acknowledge the present Covenant or does not have proper authority, then it cannot legitimately be called a Church or Ecclesia but is a false and fraudulent body having no spiritual, legal or lawful authority whatsoever.

3. Vested by the Covenant, The Ecclesia shall have the power to create new acts and amend existing laws of One Heaven into acts for review. Power of The Ecclesia

The Ecclesia shall also have the power to create new plans and actions of One Heaven, as well as to review the appointments of any higher order spirit or higher order being by the executive to a permanent position prescribed by this Covenant.

4. In accord with the present sacred Covenant, there shall be a total possible number of one million four hundred and forty thousand (1,440,000) positions of Ascended Masters and Spiritual Collectives of One Heaven. Each group of ten Spiritual Collectives are therefore assigned to a Saint and Regional Spiritual Collective. An Ascended Master may not be elected to more than one spiritual collective at one time. Spiritual Collective and Ecclesia

5. **1. Life of Sessions of Ecclesia** Operation of Ecclesia

The Ecclesia Sessions shall exist for a fixed period of sixty-four (64) years before such sessions being dissolved ahead of a General Conclave or Great Conclave.

2. Ecclesia Sessions Alignment

The Ecclesia shall be in session corresponding to sessions of either a regional Union, or the Globe Union or a major session of one of the three (3) Great Faiths as prescribed by the present Covenant.

3. Formation of new Ecclesia Session

The formation of a new Ecclesia shall occur within fourteen (14) days after a General Conclave or Great Conclave, following verification of all votes.

4. Quorum

The minimum number of Members (quorum) required to be present within the Ecclesia to permit the full exercise of its powers shall be two thirds (2/3) the total number of Members of the Ecclesia.

6. The following shall be the qualifications and conditions necessary for a candidate to be permitted to be eligible to stand for election as an Ascended Master: Eligibility for election as an Ascended Master

(i) A Higher Order Spirit, having been instanced at least once in flesh within the temporal realm of the Milky Way Galaxy in the form of one of the twelve (12) forms of higher order beings including but not limited to: the Homo Sapiens (Humanity), the Griseo Morbidus (Standard Grey), the Cerastis Sapiens (Horned Reptoids), the Android Scitus (Smart Androids), the Cyborg Sagax (Autonomous Cyborgs), the Serpens Sophos (Smooth Skinned Reptoids), the Volucris Permuto (Hybrid Bird Form), the Homo Adamus (Early Humanoids), the Sapientia Mutatis (Transformed Wisdom Beings), the Mammaloid Sentientiae (Conscious Mammaloids), the Griseo Altus (Tall Grey) and the Serpens Alatus (Winged Reptoids); and

(ii) A Higher Order Spirit, having the status of an Elder, through previous election to such a position or having been officially Blessed as an Elder by one or more of the Great Ecclesia at least twelve (12) months before a General Conclave or Great Conclave; and

(iii) A Higher Order Spirit, having invoked a sacred Oath and Vow to uphold the present sacred Covenant and to seek the emancipation and redemption of any and all previously trapped spirits, lost souls, condemned or cursed entities; and the complete and total eradication of false spirituality, Mundi negativity and control and the attempted control of spirits and the living through force, or delusion or fear; and

(iv) A Higher Order Spirit not presently active in the maintenance and influence of false spirituality, Mundi negativity and control and the attempted control of spirits through force, or delusion or fear.

A Higher Order Spirit that fails to qualify in respect of one or more of these criteria is ineligible to be a candidate for election as an Ascended Master or to hold any Office of One Heaven.

7. The Ascended Master Spirit shall hold their Office during the term of sixty-four (64) years and be elected by the three (3) Great Faiths during Regional and Local Election proceedings for Heaven, known as a General Conclave. What is bound on Earth, shall be bound in Heaven. *Term of Ascended Master Spirit*

All Members of One Heaven in a region may vote for the election of the Ascended Master Spirit through Open and public recorded ballot. It shall be upon the divine intervention of the leaders of the great wisdom orders of the three (3) Great Faiths to nominate a call to recast the leadership of Ascended Masters. This can only occur once every sixty-four (64) years.

8. By this Covenant, the Great Conclave is authorised to forge a formal set of protocols and standards regarding the Office of the Ascended Master which relates to the detailed definition and requirements of operational procedure and function necessitated by such a high office.

Protocols and Standards of the Office of Ascended Master

These standards themselves must embody and be consistent with the specific articles of this Covenant and in turn must be approved by a vote of the Great Conclave. The standards shall be known as the Protocols and standards of the Office of Ascended Master.

In terms of the major subject matter dealt with by the Protocols and Standards of the Office of the Ascended Master, the following areas must specifically provide detail and procedures consistent with the Covenant:

(i) That a formal set of procedures exist for the inauguration of the Ascended Master befitting such high office. That these procedures contain the disclosure of the official seal of office as well as the oath of office; and

(ii) That a formal set of procedures exist for the proper recognition and respect bestowed to an Ascended Master that reaches such tenure of office to be warranted a Grand Ascended Master, including the naming of an official day of respect within the calendar of One Christ, One Islam or One Spirit Tribe, and proper memorials and events befitting such an occasion.

Article 74 - Virtus

1. **All strength, courage, ability, worth, valour, prowess, heroism, excellence, virtue, powers and authorities of Heaven** shall hereby be vested as the Right of *Ius Divinum Virtus* to each and every Spiritual Collective as the body and force known as *Virtus*.

Virtus

2. The word "**Virtus**" originally comes from Latin and means "manhood, full powers, strength, courage, ability, worth, honour, valour, prowess, heroism, excellence and virtue".

Origin and Meaning of Virtus

When anyone references, writes or speaks of Virtus, or Virtue or Courage, or Honour, or Excellence or Worth, or Valour specifically or in general as a quality, force, action, power, authority or any other manifestation, it shall mean this body and the powers vested in it and no other.

3. The valid gift, grant and conveyance of Virtus is hereby vested in all uniquely named offices defined by the present Covenant and associated Covenants and Charters. Gift, Grant and Conveyance of Virtus

An office not uniquely named within the present Covenant or associated Covenants and Charters may still receive the valid authority of Virtus by the gift or grant of such power through the exercise of power and authority of an office that has been granted such power by the present Covenant.

However, an office that cannot demonstrate proper gift, grant or conveyance of Virtus through the present Covenant possesses none.

Article 75 - Custoditum

1. **All protection, preservation, keeping, possession, care, stewardship and guardianship powers and authorities of Heaven** shall hereby be vested as the Right of *Ius Divinum Custoditum* to each and every Spiritual Collective as the body and force known as *Custoditum*. Custoditum

2. The word "**Custoditum**" originally comes from Latin and means "to guard, protect or preserve; to watch over, keep safe; take heed or care; possess or hold". Origin and Meaning of Custoditum

When anyone references, writes or speaks of Custoditum, or Possession, or Preservation, or Keeping or Protecting specifically or in general as a quality, force, action, power, authority or any other manifestation, it shall mean this body and the powers vested in it and no other.

3. The valid gift, grant and conveyance of Custoditum is hereby vested in all uniquely named offices defined by the present Covenant and associated Covenants and Charters. Gift, Grant and Conveyance of Custoditum

An office not uniquely named within the present Covenant or associated Covenants and Charters may still receive the valid authority of Custoditum by the gift or grant of such power through the exercise of power and authority of an office that has been granted such power by the present Covenant.

However, an office that cannot demonstrate proper gift, grant or conveyance of Custoditum through the present Covenant possesses none.

Article 76 - Alumentum

1. **All food, fuel, nourishment, provisions, sustenance, maintenance, livelihood, alms, authority and powers of Heaven** shall hereby be vested as the Right of *Ius Divinum Alumentum* to each and every Spiritual Collective as the body and force known as *Alumentum*. Alumentum

2. The word "**Alumentum**" originally comes from Latin and means "food, fuel, nourishment, provisions, sustenance, maintenance, livelihood or alms". Origin and Meaning of Alumentum

   When anyone references, writes or speaks of Alumentum, or Food, or Fuel, or Provisions, or Nourishment, or Sustenance, or Maintenance or Livelihood or Alms specifically or in general as a quality, force, action, power, authority or any other manifestation, it shall mean this body and the powers vested in it and no other.

3. The valid gift, grant and conveyance of Alumentum is hereby vested in all Members defined by the present Covenant and associated Covenants and Charters. Gift, Grant and Conveyance of Alumentum

   Such gift, grant and conveyance cannot be derogated, abrogated, suspended, sold, enclosed, privatised, surrendered, seized, abandoned or altered by any other means or argument.

   Any claimed laws, statutes, decrees of inferior societies and associated entities that deny the gift, grant and conveyance of Alumentum or seek to alter or control it in anyway are without any legitimate or valid force or effect ecclesiastically, legally or lawfully and therefore are null and void from the beginning.

TITLE XIV - LOCAL DIMENSION (LOCAL COLLECTIVE)

Article 77 - Local Dimension (Local Collective)

Local Dimension (Local Collective)

1. A **Local Dimension,** also known as a Local Collective, is the smallest operational division and dimension of One Heaven. A Local Collective may be affiliated or unaffiliated and an independent recognised body:

(i) An affiliated Local Collective is an ecclesiastically, legally and lawfully constituted subdivision of a Spiritual Collective corresponding to the past, present and future generations of higher order spirits of a traditional nation, state, province or region but smaller than a country or supranational affiliation; and

(ii) An unaffiliated and independent Local Collective is an ecclesiastically, legally and lawfully constituted body corresponding to an association, group, tribe, family of more than two (2) souls and less than one hundred thousand (100,000) Divine Persons that is not formally aligned to any higher structure such as a Spiritual Collective or Regional Collective.

While an unaffiliated and independent Local Collective may have no formal association or alignment to any higher structure such as a Spiritual Collective or Regional Collective, all Local Collective are recognised as within the existence, dimension and jurisdiction of One Heaven in accord with the present Covenant.

Structure and Properties of a Local Collective

2. Unless a Local Collective is implied or stated as part of a recognised historic Spiritual Collective, the following criteria are the essential structural components and properties of a valid Local Collective:

(i) A unique enclosure of consciousness and awareness whereby the boundaries of the enclosure are recognised as having historic provenance and meaning; and

(ii) A unique identity in name whereby the name of the Local Collective is recognised as having historic provenance; and

(iii) A permanent population of higher order spirits as Divine Persons within the bounds of the Local Collective not exceeding one hundred thousand (100,000); and

(iv) A Provisional, Probationary or Permanent Collegium of Members representing either: (1) the Provisional spiritual occupational forces formed upon the Day of Agreement and

Understanding; or (2) a Probationary Collegium formed when one or more living Members have validated and ratified the present Covenant in association with their own Will and Testament; or (3) a Permanent Collegium formed upon the ratification of the present Covenant in association with the formation and recognition of a Permanent Province of a University of a Union of living Members who recognise in name the Collegium and who claims its spiritual authority and power in making and amending laws; and

(v) A Provisional, Probationary or Permanent Executive Government representing either the government of Provisional Collegium, the government of a Probationary Collegium or government of a Permanent Collegium.

3. A Local Dimension also known as a Local (Spiritual) Collective shall be divided and defined by distinct structural units known as Organs representing its vital parts as a spiritual body. The Organs for each Local (Spiritual) Collective shall be:- Local Dimension (Local Collective) Organs

(i) Apostolicus; and

(ii) Collegium; and

(iii) Interpretum; and

(iv) Visum.

4. Notwithstanding the names of Local Dimension Organs within the Official Ucadian Language of Logos, the Three (3) Great Faiths of One Christ, One Islam and One Spirit may choose to vote at a properly formed Great Conclave to adopt new names in one or more Non-Ucadian languages for such Organs. Names of Local Dimension Organs

Article 78 - Apostolicus

1. **All Executive Power and Authority of a Local Collective** shall be vested as the Right of *Ius Divinum Apostolicus* in an executive government known as the Apostolicus comprising an Apostle and a Local Board of Spirits. Apostolicus

2. All "**Apostolic**" authority and power is derived from one or more Apostolicus. Therefore, whenever the word Apostolic or any derivative is used, it requires valid connection and authority granted through the present sacred Covenant. Origin and Meaning of Apostolicus

Entities that claim "Apostolic" authority without any valid grant or commission through the present sacred Covenant are frauds and imposters and guilty of a supreme blasphemy against One Heaven.

3. The Apostle is the leader of the local collective community, its head and prime representative. As such, the role is considered as one of respect and dignity. Apostle

An Apostle is a departed spirit of one of the present twelve (12) higher order life forms presently nominated to the Divina, also known as the Divine Mind, that the living community of one of the twenty-four (24) Star Systems (also nominated to the Divina) trust is worthy of such nomination. As such, the Apostle shall be elected via a General Conclave for a period of sixty-four (64) years and it will be so in Heaven.

The tenure of an Apostle to an Apostolicus shall be for a fixed term of sixty-four (64) years and be elected by Local Election proceedings for Heaven known as a General Conclave.

An Apostle may remain head of the same Apostolicus for a maximum of four (4) terms or two hundred and fifty-six (256 years) thereafter such time they must resign.

4. By this Covenant, the Apostle is vested with the executive authority to manage the needs and affairs of the local community through the selection or dismissal of wise counsel in the form of the Local Board of directors and administration staff of the local community. Executive Power of Apostle

The Apostle also represents the spiritual personification of all local Rule of Law and Authority. Therefore, the Apostle shall be responsible for holding all spiritual officials to account to their oaths of office and duties.

5. The following shall be the qualifications and conditions necessary for a candidate to be permitted to be eligible to stand for election as an Apostle: Eligibility for election of an Apostle

(i) A Higher Order Spirit, having been instanced at least once in flesh within the temporal realm of the Milky Way Galaxy in the form of one of the twelve (12) forms of higher order beings including but not limited to: the Homo Sapiens (Humanity), the Griseo Morbidus (Standard Grey), the Cerastis Sapiens (Horned Reptoids), the Android Scitus (Smart Androids), the Cyborg Sagax (Autonomous Cyborgs), the Serpens Sophos (Smooth Skinned Reptoids), the Volucris Permuto (Hybrid Bird Form), the Homo Adamus (Early Humanoids), the Sapientia Mutatis (Transformed Wisdom Beings), the Mammaloid Sentientiae (Conscious Mammaloids), the Griseo Altus (Tall

Grey) and the Serpens Alatus (Winged Reptoids); and

(ii) A Higher Order Spirit, having invoked a sacred Oath and Vow to uphold the present sacred Covenant and to seek the emancipation and redemption of any and all previously trapped spirits, lost souls, condemned or cursed entities; and the complete and total eradication of false spirituality, Mundi negativity and control and the attempted control of spirits and the living through force, or delusion or fear; and

(iii) A Higher Order Spirit not presently active in the maintenance and influence of false spirituality, Mundi negativity and control and the attempted control of spirits through force, or delusion or fear.

A Higher Order Spirit that fails to qualify in respect of one or more of these criteria is ineligible to be a candidate for election as an Apostle or to hold any Office of One Heaven.

Power of the Board

6. Vested by the present Covenant, the Board shall have the power to review all planning of the Apostle. The Board shall have the power to commission a Local Commission of Investigation with the power to call any individual registered Member of One Heaven within the community and any information held by the Local Executive to review.

A Local Commission of Investigation must be called by the Board when a call to discipline one or more Members is made. Board sessions shall be as required.

Protocols and Standards of a Local Board

7. By the present Covenant, the Divina and Mentis are authorised to forge a formal set of protocols and standards regarding its own function which relates to the detailed definition and requirements of operational procedure and function necessitated by the institution. These shall be known as the Protocols and standards of a Local Board of a Local Spiritual Collective of One Heaven.

These standards themselves must embody and be consistent with the specific articles of this Covenant and in turn must be approved by a majority vote of all delegates attending a Great Conclave.

Protocols and Standards of the Office of Apostle

8. By the present Covenant, the Divina is authorised to forge a formal set of protocols and standards regarding the Office of the Apostle that relates to the detailed definition and requirements of operational procedure and function necessitated by such a high office.

These standards themselves must embody and be consistent with the specific articles of this Covenant and, in turn, must be approved by a vote of a Great Conclave. The standards shall be known as the

Protocols and Standards of the Office of Apostle.

Article 79 - Collegium

1. **All legislative powers of a Local Collective of spirits of One Heaven** shall be vested as the Right of *Ius Divinum Collegium* in a body called "**Collegium**" which shall consist of all Member spirits of the Local Collective, excluding those elected to the Apostolicus as the leaders of the Local Collective. Collegium

2. The word "**Collegium**" originally comes from Latin and means "a college; a school; a corporation, guild or company". All colleges, companies and associations ultimately derive their power and authority from one or more Collegium. Origin and Meaning of Collegium

3. Vested by this Covenant, the Collegium shall have the power to review all planning of the Apostolicus. The Collegium shall have the power to commission a Local Commission of Investigation with the power to call any individual registered Member of One Heaven within the community and any information held by the Local Executive to review. Power of the Collegium

   A Local Commission of Investigation must be called by the Collegium when a call to discipline one or more Members is made.

4. By the present Covenant, the Divina are authorised to forge a formal set of protocols and standards regarding its own function which relates to the detailed definition and requirements of operational procedure and function necessitated by the institution. These shall be known as the Protocols and Standards of a Collegium of One Heaven. Protocols and Standards of a Collegium of One Heaven

   These standards themselves must embody and be consistent with the specific articles of this Covenant and in turn must be approved by a majority vote of all delegates attending a Great Conclave.

Article 80 - Interpretum

1. **All explanation, expounding, interpretation, prophesy, comprehension and review of Heaven** shall hereby be vested as the Right of *Ius Divinum Interpretum* to each and every Local Spiritual Collective as the body and force known as *Interpretum*. Interpretum

2. The word "**Interpretum**" originally comes from Latin and means "to explain or expound; to interpret or prophesy from (dream/omen); to understand or comprehend". Origin and Meaning of Interpretum

When anyone references, writes or speaks of Interpretum, or Explanation, or Interpretation, or Prophecy or Comprehension specifically or in general as a quality, force, action, power, authority or any other manifestation, it shall mean this body and the powers vested in it and no other.

3. The valid gift, grant and conveyance of Interpretum is hereby vested in all uniquely named offices defined by the present Covenant and associated Covenants and Charters. Gift, Grant and Conveyance of Interpretum

An office not uniquely named within the present Covenant or associated Covenants and Charters may still receive the valid authority of Interpretum by the gift or grant of such power through the exercise of power and authority of an office that has been granted such power by the present Covenant. However, an office that cannot demonstrate proper gift, grant or conveyance of Interpretum through the present Covenant possesses none.

Article 81 - Visum

1. **All survey, measurement, visitation, review, census or audit authority and powers of Heaven** shall hereby be vested as the Right of *Ius Divinum Visum* to each and every Local Spiritual Collective as the body and force known as *Visum*. Visum

2. The word "**Visum**" originally comes from Latin and means "to look at, to survey, to go and see, to check on, to visit". Origin and Meaning of Visum

When anyone references, writes or speaks of Visum, or Visitation, or Review, or Census, or Audit, or Survey or Measurement specifically or in general as a quality, force, action, power, authority or any other manifestation, it shall mean this body and the powers vested in it and no other.

3. The valid gift, grant and conveyance of Visum is hereby vested in all uniquely named offices defined by the present Covenant and associated Covenants and Charters. Gift, Grant and Conveyance of Visum

An office not uniquely named within the present Covenant or associated Covenants and Charters may still receive the valid authority of Visum by the gift or grant of such power through the exercise of power and authority of an office that has been granted such power by the present Covenant. However, an office that cannot demonstrate proper gift, grant or conveyance of Visum through the present Covenant possesses none.

TITLE XV – SYSTEMS

Article 82 - Supremum Systemata (Supreme Systems)

1. **Supremum Systemata** (Supreme Systems) of One Heaven, also known as "**Supremum Systemata**", shall be those spiritual organs, bodies, associations, persons, rules, rights, functions and processes in existence to ensure all valid Divine Law and Universal Law is upheld; and that the Rights of Members are protected; and that the Society fulfils its objectives. Supremum Systemata (Supreme Systems)

2. There shall be Eight (8) primary systems, being: Eight Primary Systems

   (i) Supremum Universalium Systemata (Universal Systems); and

   (ii) Supremum Custodiarum Systemata (Guardians Systems); and

   (iii) Supremum Angelorum Systemata (Angelic Systems); and

   (iv) Supremum Femininum Systemata (Feminine Systems); and

   (v) Supremum Masculinum Systemata (Masculine Systems); and

   (vi) Supremum Officium Systemata (Offices Systems); and

   (vii) Supremum Sacramentum Systemata (Sacramental Systems); and

   (viii) Supremum Obligationum Systemata (Enforcement Systems).

3. Notwithstanding the names of the Supreme Systems of Heaven within the Official Ucadian Language of Logos, the Three (3) Great Faiths of One Christ, One Islam and One Spirit may choose to vote at a properly formed Great Conclave to adopt new names in one or more Non-Ucadian languages for such Systems, in accord with Article 130 (Covenant Confirmation and Amendment) of the present sacred Covenant. Names of Supreme Systems

Article 83 - Universalium Systemata (Universal Systems)

1. **All collective dimensional constructs** of the Divine Creator, and the designs, manifestations and relations of consciousness and levels of perfected memory of truth and wisdom shall be vested in one supreme spiritual body and system known as the "**Supremum Universalium Systemata**", also known as Supreme Universal Systems of Heaven. The Supremum Universalium Systemata shall be the highest architects of collective dimensional constructs of reality and no other. Supremum Universalium Systemata (Universal Systems)

   The Spirit Members qualified and selected to serve within the operation of the Universalium Systemata (Universal Systems) shall hold the Special Supreme Divine Office of "**Fate**" in recognition of their foundational responsibilities in creating, weaving and holding the dimensional and collective consciousness mappings and constructs of Heaven; and in being the source of inspiration, creativity and imagination of higher knowledge of Ucadia.

The Supremum Universalium Systemata shall be uniquely recognised, registered and exemplified as having existence through the Great Register and Public Record of Heaven by the Sacred [Trust No. 999999-111111-999999]. The existence, identity, authority, purpose and powers of the Supremum Universalium Systemata shall be duly gazetted in the Ucadia Gazette being the Official Newspaper of Record for each and every Sacred Space-Day-Time of its existence and operation.

2. The five (5) key propositions and powers of the Supremum Universalium Systemata (Universal Systems) shall be:- Key Propositions and Powers

(i) Conceptual Models, being the design and development of conceptual models and frameworks for sustainable, fulfilling, and positive Local Spiritual Collectives, Spiritual Collectives, Regional Spiritual Collectives and Unique Spiritual Collectives, consistent with the Golden Rule of Law and the Rights of all Divine Persons as expressed by the present sacred Covenant; and

(ii) Collective Consciousness Mappings, being the detailed and accurate mappings of current conscious collectives, including all non-aligned and negatively aligned layers of ghost, ground plane dissonance and alien consciousness; and

(iii) Cultural Preservation, being the preservation of ancient culture and consciousness, as a recognition of such unique conscious perspective, even if such ancient culture or consciousness is not aligned to the Golden Rule of Law, that a proper record and knowledge of such constructs are duly preserved; and

(iv) Revitalisation, being the revitalisation of collective conscious space that individual and collectives of Divine Persons may choose to migrate toward a more optimum Conceptual Model, yet retaining items and constructs of cultural significance and important meaning; and

(v) Manifestation, being the complex manifestation of collective conscious constructs aligned with the Conceptual Models of spiritual balance that enable a degree of stability and certainty as to the integrity and truth of such manifestations.

3. All communication to the Universalium Systemata (Universal Systems) of Heaven by living Members of One Heaven shall be by Imagination in accord with Article 120 (Imagination) of the present sacred Covenant. The methods, rules and standards of proper Imagination shall be defined by the present sacred Covenant and associated covenants and no other. All properly conferred Imagination shall be received, recorded and acknowledged by the Universalium Systemata (Universal Systems) of One Heaven.

Communication to Universalium Systemata (Universal Systems)

4. All Imagined Images, or Concepts or Thoughts shall be rejected as invalid and improper by the Universalium Systemata (Universal Systems) of One Heaven:-

Reprobate, Profane and Repugnant forms of Imagination

(i) If it is deliberately cruel or malevolent in its intent, design or inference; or

(ii) If it is deliberately dishonest, deceptive or perfidious in its intent, design or inference; or

(iii) If it is frivolous, or profane or disrespectful in its intent, or tone, or design or inference; or

(iv) If it is irrational, or unreasonable or illogical in its intent, or tone, or design or inference; or

(v) If it is motivated or driven by hate, greed, jealousy, anger or lust; or

(vi) If it is motivated or driven by an attempt to shift blame or avoid accepting self-responsibility; or

(vii) If it is motivated or driven by a desire, or wish, or worship of money or abundant material wealth.

Article 84 - Custodiarum Systemata (Guardians Systems)

1. **All guardian, custody, protection and service** powers and authority shall be vested in one supreme spiritual body and system known as the "**Supremum Custodiarum Systemata**", also known as Supreme Guardians Systems of Heaven. The Supremum Custodiarum Systemata shall be the highest body of spiritual guardians and custodians of all levels of consciousness, reality and Heaven and Earth and no other.

Supremum Custodiarum Systemata (Guardians Systems)

The Spirit Members qualified and selected to serve within the operation of the Custodiarum Systemata (Guardians Systems) shall hold the Special Supreme Divine Office of "**Demon**" in recognition of the end of the War in Heaven; and their foundational responsibilities in protecting and defending heaven; and in protecting and defending the laws of Ucadia; and in the enforcement of necessary actions of rendition, interdiction, seizure and return when faced with corruptions and attacks against the integrity of Heaven; and in being the source of fearsome power, courage, enforcement and strength to the armies of Living Members within the temporal realms of the Universe.

The Supremum Custodiarum Systemata shall be uniquely recognised, registered and exemplified as having existence through the Great Register and Public Record of Heaven by the Sacred [Trust No. 999999-222222-999999]. The existence, identity, authority, purpose and powers of the Supremum Custodiarum Systemata shall be duly gazetted in the Ucadia Gazette being the Official Newspaper of Record for each and every Sacred Space-Day-Time of its existence and operation.

2. The nine (9) key propositions and powers of the Supremum Custodiarum Systemata (Guardians Systems) shall be: Key Propositions and Powers

(i) *Protect and Defend Heaven*, being to protect and defend the heavenly Kosmos, including all planets, stars, life, colonies, ecosystems and diversity throughout the galaxy; and

(ii) *Protect and Defend Ucadia*, being to protect and defend Ucadia; and all its Realms, Domains, Dominions, Dependencies, Rights, Titles, Instruments, Uses and Property and particularly the use of the Ucadia name and Ucadia material; and

(iii) *Protect and Defend the Laws of Ucadia*, being to protect and defend all associated Covenants, Charters, Scripture, Maxims, Codes, Bylaws, Ordinances, Regulations, Policies and Orders; and to seek mutual recognition of such jurisdictional rights with foreign bodies and courts that respect and operate according to the Golden Rule of Law and Justice and Fair Process; and to ensure that in all matters pertaining to Ucadia Members that the courts of Ucadia are recognised as the first, primary and original jurisdiction for the resolution of all matters of controversy, arbitration and dispute; and

(iv) *Peaceful, Amicable and Harmonious Relations*, being to seek peaceful, amicable and harmonious relations, treaties and alliances with foreign spiritual bodies that respect the Golden Rule of Law and Justice and Fair Process; and

(v) *Rendition*, being to pursue, prosecute and bring to justice any individual spirit or body that openly seeks to abuse, trespass or injure Heaven, or Ucadia or its Realms, Domains, Dominions, Dependencies, Rights, Titles, Instruments, Uses or Property; and

(vi) *Interdiction*, being to deploy as part of the execution of a sacred Divine Writ of Recto Divinum Interdico, to impose proper rule of law; and prohibit any possible continued breaches of Divine Law and expunge the conditions for damage to conscious memory, clarity or truth, including but not limited to empowerment and inspiration of temporal forces also granted the commission of Recto Interdico; and

(vii) *Seizure and Return*, being to execute the conditions of a Divine Warrant according to a sacred Divine Writ of Recto Divinum Capionis, to do all that is necessary to ensure the seizure, return and restoration of sacred memory, consciousness, balance, harmony, truth and integrity, including but not limited to empowerment and inspiration of temporal forces also granted the commission of Recto Capionis; and

(viii) *Arrest and Custody*, being to execute the conditions of a Divine Warrant according to a sacred Divine Writ of Recto Divinum Custodiae, to do all that is necessary to ensure the arrest and custody of each and every malevolent spirit, negative ghost and destructive construct; and to assist in the restoration of sacred memory, consciousness, balance, harmony, truth and integrity, including but not limited to empowerment and inspiration of temporal forces also granted the commission of Recto Custodiae; and

(ix) *Revelation Enforcement*, being to execute the conditions of a Divine Warrant according to a sacred Divine Writ of Recto Divinum Apocalypsis, to do all that is necessary to ensure the fulfilment of such Divine Revelation, including but not limited to the seizure, search, arrest and custody of each and every or any named malevolent spirit, or ghost, or false concept, or false right, or false construct and to assist in the restoration of sacred memory, consciousness, balance and Rule of Law.

3. All communication to the Custodiarum Systemata (Guardians Systems) of Heaven by living Members of One Heaven shall be by Incantation by a duly qualified and authorised Cleric in accord with Article 143 (Cleric) of the present sacred Covenant. The methods, rules and standards of proper Incantation shall be defined by the present sacred Covenant and associated covenants and no other. All properly

Communication to Supremum Custodiarum Systemata (Guardians Systems)

conferred Incantations shall be received, recorded and acknowledged by the Custodiarum Systemata (Guardians Systems) of One Heaven.

4. An Incantation shall be reprobate, profane, repugnant and therefore invalid and improper and rejected by the Custodiarum Systemata (Guardians Systems) of One Heaven:- Reprobate, Profane and Repugnant forms of Incantation

(i) If it is deliberately harmful, negative or malevolent in its intent, design or inference; or

(ii) If it is deliberately dishonest, deceptive or perfidious in its intent, design or inference; or

(iii) If it is frivolous, or profane or disrespectful in its intent, or tone, or design or inference; or

(iv) If it is irrational, or unreasonable or illogical in its intent, or tone, or design or inference; or

(v) If it is motivated or driven by hate, greed, jealousy, anger or lust; or

(vi) If it is motivated or driven by an attempt to shift blame or avoid accepting self-responsibility; or

(vii) If it is motivated or driven by a desire, or wish, or worship of money or abundant material wealth.

Article 85 - Angelorum Systemata (Angelic Systems)

1. **All personal protection, guidance, support, inspiration and intercession** powers and authority concerning all Divine Persons and True Persons shall be vested in one supreme spiritual body and system known as the "**Supremum Angelorum Systemata**", also known as Supreme Angelic Systems of Heaven. The Supremum Angelorum Systemata shall be the highest body of Angelic powers and authority of all conscious dimensions and all Heaven and Earth and no other. Supremum Angelorum Systemata (Angelic Systems)

The Spirit Members qualified and selected to serve within the operation of the Angelorum Systemata (Angelic Systems) shall hold the Special Supreme Divine Office of "**Angel**" in recognition of their foundational responsibilities in personal protection of Living Members; and in the expulsion; and freeing of Ghosts and the breaking apart of the Mundi Mind Virus; and assistance to those invoking petitions of invocation.

The Supremum Angelorum Systemata is uniquely recognised, registered and exemplified as having existence through the Great

Register and Public Record of Heaven by the Sacred [Trust No. 999999-333333-999999]. The existence, identity, authority, purpose and powers of the Supremum Angelorum Systemata have been duly gazetted in the Ucadia Gazette being the Official Newspaper of Record for each and every Sacred Space-Day-Time of its existence and operation.

Key Propositions and Powers

2. The three (3) key propositions and powers of the Supremum Angelorum Systemata (Angelic Systems) shall be:

   (i) *Mental and Spiritual Protection*, being to assign at least one qualified Angel to each living Member as their "charge"; and to protect each such Living Member day and night against undue negative influence of ghosts, or other consciousness seeking to haunt, or possess, or misdirect or confuse; and

   (ii) *Expulsion of Ghosts*, being the forced expulsion of any and all ghosts possessing the body, or spirit history, or time-lines or mind of a living Member that is their charge; and to ensure such negative influence is forbidden from any further negative influence; and

   (iii) *Passive Assistance*, being to provide positive assistance to a living Member as their charge without undue influence of the free choice and will of the living Member and to ensure positive and meaningful assistance is directed when such request for genuine Assistance is made.

Non-Interference by Angels in Free Will and Causality of Life

3. Existence itself and the proper function of the fundamental laws of Creation demands that Angels defer to the general principle of non-interference in the causation of free will, excluding such cases where the mind or spirit and choices of a Living Member as their charge have been unduly influenced, especially in the case of ghosts and other spirit minds defying the law of non-interference.

   Every intervention sought from a Living Member to their Guardian Angel, if accepted and manifested, may have the same or a greater negative consequence to the balance of Unique Collective Consciousness, than allowing events to take their course without intervention.

   Intervention is therefore a last resort, in exceptional circumstances, where the negative consequences of non-intervention substantially outweigh the consequences of a manifest intervention.

Solemn Attendance at Time of Physical Death

4. A key proposition of all Angels is to formally attend the place and time of the dying and death of their Living Member as their charge. Angels are obligated to protect such vulnerable minds from fear and

misrepresentations by ghosts and spirits, who may seek to exploit such weakness, in open defiance of the laws of Heaven.

Angels are empowered to call upon all the necessary support of Heaven to ensure each and every mind has the free opportunity to transition to a state of Heaven, without falling into the labyrinth of "ghost state" or the self punishment of a "hell state".

5. All communication to the Angelorum Systemata (Angelic Systems) of Heaven by living Members of One Heaven shall be by Invocation in accord with the present sacred Covenant. The methods, rules and standards of proper Invocation shall be defined by the present sacred Covenant and associated covenants and no other. All properly conferred Invocation shall be received, recorded and acknowledged by the Angelorum Systemata (Angelic Systems) of One Heaven.

Communication to Supremum Angelorum Systemata (Angelic Systems)

6. An Invocation shall be reprobate, profane, repugnant and therefore invalid and improper and rejected by the Angelorum Systemata (Angelic Systems) of Heaven:-

Reprobate, Profane and Repugnant forms of Invocation

(i) If it is deliberately harmful, negative or malevolent in its intent, design or inference; or

(ii) If it is deliberately dishonest, deceptive or perfidious in its intent, design or inference; or

(iii) If it is frivolous, or profane or disrespectful in its intent, or tone, or design or inference; or

(iv) If it is irrational, or unreasonable or illogical in its intent, or tone, or design or inference; or

(v) If it is motivated or driven by hate, greed, jealousy, anger or lust; or

(vi) If it is motivated or driven by an attempt to shift blame or avoid accepting self-responsibility; or

(vii) If it is motivated or driven by a desire, or wish, or worship of money or abundant material wealth.

7. All properly conferred and valid Invocations are delivered to the Supremum Angelorum Systemata (Angelic Systems) of Heaven through the particular Guardian Angel of the Living Member as Intercessor on behalf of the Living Member:

Procedure and Effects of valid Invocation

(i) If the valid Invocation is an Adoration giving honour and praise to a higher spiritual presence, then the Supremum Angelorum Systemata (Angelic Systems) of Heaven shall be responsible in ensuring such honour and praise is properly received by the spiritual presence to whom it is directed. In return, the Angels may then convey to the one making the Invocation, the effects of the Divine Grace of Divine Love and Joy; and

(ii) If the valid Invocation is an Intervention that is recognised for directly summonsing the presence of spirits or asking something for one's self, then the Supremum Angelorum Systemata (Angelic Systems) of Heaven must weigh up the nature of the petition, in light of *Mysterium Volitio* in response and assistance; and

(iii) If the valid Invocation is an Intercession that is recognised as the type of Invocation or Meditation used for asking something for others, then the Supremum Angelorum Systemata (Angelic Systems) of Heaven must weigh up the nature of the petition, in light of *Mysterium Volitio* in response and assistance; and

(iv) If the valid Invocation is a Confession that is recognised as the type of Invocation or Meditation used for the atonement and repentance of wrongdoing and the asking of forgiveness, then the Supremum Angelorum Systemata (Angelic Systems) of Heaven shall be responsible in ensuring such honour and character is properly witnessed and recorded; and

(v) If the valid Invocation is a Lamentation that is recognised as the type of Invocation or Meditation used for crying in distress and asking for vindication, then the Supremum Angelorum Systemata (Angelic Systems) of Heaven shall be responsible in ensuring such call for justice is properly witnessed and recorded; and

(vi) If the valid Invocation is a Thanksgiving that is recognised as the type of Invocation or Meditation used for offering gratitude, then the Supremum Angelorum Systemata (Angelic Systems) of Heaven shall be responsible in ensuring such honour and thanks is properly received by the spiritual presence to whom it is directed. In return, the Angels may then convey to the one making the Invocation, the effects of the Divine Grace of Divine Love and Joy.

Article 86 - Femininum Systemata (Feminine Systems)

1. **All feminine powers and authority of manifestation, inspiration, guidance, consciousness and knowledge** shall be vested in one supreme spiritual body and system

Supremum Femininum Systemata (Feminine

known as the "**Supremum Femininum Systemata**", also known as Supreme Feminine Systems of Heaven. The Supremum Femininum Systemata shall be the highest body made manifest of true feminine power and authority of any and all levels of consciousness, collective dimensional constructs of reality and all Heaven and Earth and no other. Systems)

The Spirit Members qualified and selected to serve within the operation of the Femininum Systemata (Feminine Systems) shall hold the Special Supreme Divine Office of "**Faerie**" in recognition of an ancient spirit and force redeemed from being previously denigrated and marginalised; and their foundational responsibilities in the restoration of true feminine; and the restoration of true mother; and Gaia harmony; and emancipation, equality and appreciation of all women.

The Supremum Femininum Systemata is uniquely recognised, registered and exemplified as having existence through the Great Register and Public Record of Heaven by the Sacred [Trust No. 999999-444444-999999]. The existence, identity, authority, purpose and powers of the Supremum Femininum Systemata have been duly gazetted in the Ucadia Gazette being the Official Newspaper of Record for each and every Sacred Space-Day-Time of its existence and operation.

2. The six (6) key propositions and powers of the Supremum Femininum Systemata (Feminine Systems) shall be: Key Propositions and Powers

(i) *True Feminine Restoration*, being to restore the conscious memory, respect, harmony and balance of True Feminine in light of the arrest, seizure, custody and dissolution of all aspects and constructs of false feminine; and to ensure that all feminine higher order beings are granted the capacity to instinctively and emotionally experience and benefit from such true feminine; and

(ii) *True Mother Restoration*, being to restore the conscious memory, respect, history, emotional and spiritual harmony and balance of True Mother in light of the arrest, seizure, custody and dissolution of all aspects and constructs of false mother; and to ensure that all beings are granted the capacity to instinctively and emotionally experience, connect and be supported by True Mother; and

(iii) *Gaia Harmony*, being to re-establish the harmony and alignment of True Feminine and True Mother with Gaia Consciousness in respect and honour of the sacred treaties of the present sacred Covenant and to ensure that such alignment and harmony enhances the quality and respect of all planetary life, conservation and good management; and

(iv) *Emancipation*, being to emancipate the feminine consciousness away from negative and deliberately false constructs and stereotypes, in particular those deliberately false, profane, malicious religious notions creating liabilities, blame, guilt and poor character upon the feminine spirit; and

(v) *Equality*, being to restore the equality of the feminine in all aspects of spiritual, cultural, social, moral and legal aspects of community life; and to ensure the continued challenge, objection, dissolution and defeat of false, profane and malicious notions seeking to continue and maintain embedded inequality between the masculine and feminine; and

(vi) *Appreciation*, being to restore the balance, perspective and recognition of the feminine form from false and deliberate simplifications of objectification, sexualisation and property; and to ensure the progressive dissolution of self destructive and negative conscious intent that encourages the perpetuation of sexualised stereotypes.

3. There shall be no direct nor formal means of communication to the Femininum Systemata (Feminine Systems) of Heaven by living Members of One Heaven. This shall be because Femininum Systemata (Feminine Systems) are tasked with acting independently to carry out their mission and propositions. However, the Faerie of the Femininum Systemata (Feminine Systems) are free to choose of their own will to interact with living Members of One Heaven.

Communication with Supremum Femininum Systemata (Feminine Systems)

Article 87 - Masculinum Systemata (Masculine Systems)

1. **All masculine powers and authority of manifestation, inspiration, guidance, consciousness and knowledge** shall be vested in one supreme spiritual body and system known as the "**Supremum Masculinum Systemata**", also known as Supreme Masculine Systems of Heaven. The Supremum Masculinum Systemata shall be the highest body made manifest of true masculine power and authority of any and all levels of consciousness, collective dimensional constructs of reality and all Heaven and Earth and no other.

Supremum Masculinum Systemata (Masculine Systems)

The Spirit Members qualified and selected to serve within the operation of the Masculinum Systemata (Masculine Systems) shall hold the Special Supreme Divine Office of "**Elve**" (Elf) in recognition of an ancient spirit and force redeemed from being previously denigrated and marginalised; and their foundational responsibilities in the restoration of true masculine; and the restoration of true father; and Gaia harmony; and emancipation, equality and appreciation of all men.

The Supremum Masculinum Systemata is uniquely recognised, registered and exemplified as having existence through the Great Register and Public Record of Heaven by the Sacred [Trust No. 999999-666666-999999]. The existence, identity, authority, purpose and powers of the Supremum Masculinum Systemata have been duly gazetted in the Ucadia Gazette being the Official Newspaper of Record for each and every Sacred Space-Day-Time of its existence and operation.

2. The six (6) key propositions and powers of the Supremum Masculinum Systemata (Masculine Systems) shall be: Key Propositions and Powers

(i) *True Masculine Restoration*, being to restore the conscious memory, respect, harmony and balance of True Masculine in light of the arrest, seizure, custody and dissolution of all aspects and constructs of false masculine; and to ensure that all masculine higher order beings are granted the capacity to instinctively and emotionally experience and benefit from such true masculine; and

(ii) True Father Restoration, being to restore the conscious memory, respect, history, emotional and spiritual harmony and balance of True Father in light of the arrest, seizure, custody and dissolution of all aspects and constructs of false father; and to ensure that all beings are granted the capacity to instinctively and emotionally experience, connect and be supported by True Father; and

(iii) Gaia Harmony, being to re-establish the harmony and alignment of True Masculine and True Father with Gaia Consciousness in respect and honour of the sacred treaties of the present sacred Covenant and to ensure that such alignment and harmony enhances the quality and respect of all planetary life, conservation and good management; and

(iv) Emancipation, being to emancipate the masculine consciousness away from negative and deliberately false constructs and stereotypes, in particular those deliberately false, profane, malicious religious notions creating liabilities, blame, guilt and poor character upon the masculine spirit; and

(v) Equality, being to restore the equality of the masculine in all aspects of spiritual, cultural, social, moral and legal aspects of community life; and to ensure the continued challenge, objection, dissolution and defeat of false, profane and malicious notions seeking to continue and maintain embedded inequality between the masculine and feminine; and

(vi) Appreciation, being to restore the balance, perspective and recognition of the masculine form from false and deliberate simplifications of objectification, sexualisation and property; and to ensure the progressive dissolution of self destructive and negative conscious intent that encourages the perpetuation of sexualised stereotypes.

3. There shall be no direct nor formal means of communication to the Masculinum Systemata (Masculine Systems) of Heaven by living Members of One Heaven. This shall be because Masculinum Systemata (Masculine Systems) are tasked with acting independently to carry out their mission and propositions. However, the Elve (Elf) of the Masculinum Systemata (Masculine Systems) are free to choose of their own will to interact with living Members of One Heaven.

Communication to Supremum Masculinum Systemata (Masculine Systems)

Article 88 - Officium Systemata (Offices Systems)

1. **All power and authority as vested in any and every form of Office, Commission, Agency, or other position of Trust** shall be vested in one supreme spiritual body and system known as the "**Supremum Officium Systemata**", also known as Supreme Offices Systems of Heaven. The Supremum Officium Systemata shall be the highest authority and power as the source of all valid Offices, Commissions, Agency, Powers, Authorities and other positions of Trust and no other.

Supremum Officium Systemata (Offices Systems)

The Spirit Members qualified and selected to serve within the Officium Systemata (Offices Systems) shall hold the Special Supreme Divine Office of "**Nomos**" in recognition of their foundational responsibilities in maintaining and protecting the Golden Rule of Law embodied within Ucadia as the Living Law; and the proper identification, obligation, enrolment, possession, publication, certification, protocols, exemplification, visitation and penalties or sanctions in enforcing each and every valid office in Heaven and within the Galaxy.

The Supremum Officium Systemata is uniquely recognised, registered and exemplified as having existence through the Great Register and Public Record of Heaven by the Sacred [Trust No. 999999-555555-999999]. The existence, identity, authority, purpose and powers of the

Supremum Officium Systemata have been duly gazetted in the Ucadia Gazette being the Official Newspaper of Record for each and every Sacred Space-Day-Time of its existence and operation.

2. The ten key propositions and powers of the Supremum Officium Systemata (Offices Systems) shall be: Key Propositions and Powers

(i) Identification, being the proper identification, naming and classification of each and every Divine Office of the four hundred and thirty-two (432) Great Offices of Heaven, including but not limited to the capacities, authorities and powers of such Offices such as Magisterium, Imperium, Sacrum, Sanitatum, Virtus, Custoditum, Alumentum and Interpretum; and

(ii) Obligation, being the complete definition and scope of the obligations pertaining to each and every Divine Office of the four hundred and thirty-two (432) Great Offices of Heaven as a Memorandum of Office or Memorandum Officium, such that the role, responsibilities, capacities, authorities and powers for each and every Divine Office is clear; and

(iii) Enrolment, being the complete enrolment within the Great Roll of Divine Persons of each and every Divine Office such that each Office possesses a unique number, title and relation to a specific spiritual or temporal body; and

(iv) Possession, being the spiritual investiture of at least one Divine Person to each valid Divine Office as connected to a spiritual and temporal body as the first, primary and ultimate holder and occupant of such Office under sacred and solemn oath and vow, such that the Office and Trust stands valid, even if an appointment, commission or investiture of a True or Superior Person is vacant; and

(v) Publication, being the complete publication, pronouncement and Gazette of the enrolment and existence of all valid Offices into specific spiritual and temporal bodies; and

(vi) Certification, being the complete acknowledgement of each and every valid Office connected as Certified within the Great Register and Divine Records of Heaven and associated Registers and Constitutional Charters; and

(vii) Protocols, being the protocols, procedures and qualifications of the appointment, or commission or investiture of True Persons or Superior Persons to a valid Office as Certified, Gazetted and

Enrolled before all Heaven, the Galaxy, the Solar System and Earth; and

(viii) Exemplification, being the proper acknowledgement and certification of a duly acknowledged appointment, commission or investiture to a particular valid Office; and

(ix) Visitation, being the visitation and audit of all temporal appointments to valid Office, such that all such Offices continue to honour the Golden Rule of Law, true Justice and Fair Process; and

(x) Sanction, being the sanctioning of any temporal appointment of a True Person or Superior Person to a valid Office, including but not limited to penalty, fine, removal, suspension, prohibition or interdiction.

Communication to Officium Systemata (Offices Systems)

3. All communication to the Officium Systemata (Offices Systems) of Heaven by living Members of One Heaven shall be by Testification in accord with Article 121 (Testification) of the present sacred Covenant. The methods, rules and standards of proper Testification shall be defined by the present sacred Covenant and associated covenants and no other. All properly conferred Testification shall be received, recorded and acknowledged by the Officium Systemata (Offices Systems) of One Heaven.

Reprobate, Profane and Repugnant forms of Testification

4. A Testification shall be reprobate, profane, repugnant and therefore invalid and improper and rejected by the Officium Systemata (Offices Systems) of One Heaven:

(i) If it is deliberately harmful, negative or malevolent in its intent, design or inference; or

(ii) If it is deliberately dishonest, deceptive or perfidious in its intent, design or inference; or

(iii) If it is frivolous, or profane or disrespectful in its intent, or tone, or design or inference; or

(iv) If it is irrational, or unreasonable or illogical in its intent, or tone, or design or inference; or

(v) If it is motivated or driven by hate, greed, jealousy, anger or lust; or

(vi) If it is motivated or driven by an attempt to shift blame or avoid accepting self-responsibility; or

(vii) If it is motivated or driven by a desire, or wish, or worship of money or abundant material wealth.

Article 89 - Sacramentum Systemata (Sacramental Systems)

1. **All valid sacraments are instituted by the Divine Creator** and entrusted to the Society of One Heaven and shall be administered by "**Supremum Sacramentum Systemata**" (Sacramental Systems). No other person, aggregate, entity, society, church or group may claim the right to administer any valid Sacred Gift unless it is in accordance with the present most sacred Covenant. Any claimed Sacred Gift that is not granted through the authority of One Heaven in accordance with the present most sacred Covenant is a false ritual and possesses no Divine authority or power to be known as a valid sacrament. Supremum Sacramentum Systemata (Sacramental Systems)

   The Spirit Members qualified and selected to serve within the operation of the Sacramentum Systemata (Sacramental Systems) shall hold the Special Supreme Divine Office of "**Seraphim**" in recognition of their foundational responsibilities in holding the highest, most trusted and most valuable gifts of Heaven in ensuring proper sanctification, qualification, observation, administration and celebration of the thirty three (33) sacred sacraments.

   The Supremum Sacramentum Systemata is uniquely recognised, registered and exemplified as having existence through the Great Register and Public Record of Heaven by the Sacred [Trust No. 999999-777777-999999]. The existence, identity, authority, purpose and powers of the Supremum Sacramentum Systemata have been duly gazetted in the Ucadia Gazette being the Official Newspaper of Record for each and every Sacred Space-Day-Time of its existence and operation.

2. The five (5) key propositions and powers of the Supremum Sacramentum Systemata (Sacramental Systems) shall be: Key Propositions and Powers

   (i) *Sanctification*, being the sacred entrustment, safe keeping and administration of the thirty-three (33) sacraments authentically deposited in trust by the Divine Creator to the Society of One Heaven, in accord with the *Authentic Sacred Deposit of Trust*; and

   (ii) *Qualification*, being the conditions and rules whereby suitably qualified candidates may be granted the rites to confer and administer one or more of the sacraments of the one, true and only *Authentic Sacred Deposit of Trust* within the temporal realm; and

(iii) *Observation*, being the Liturgical Rites and Actions whereby such suitably qualified, consecrated and empowered persons may confer one or more of the sacraments; and

(iv) *Administration*, being the administration of the authorities, powers, obligations and associated rites of all sacraments properly conferred; and

(v) *Celebration*, being the formal performance of solemn Liturgical Rites and Actions in the conferral of one or more of the sacraments of the one, true and only *Authentic Sacred Deposit of Trust*.

3. All communication with the Sacramentum Systemata (Sacramental Systems) of Heaven by living Members of One Heaven shall be by the Ecclesiastical Sacramental Rights entrusted to a duly qualified and ordained Cleric in accord with the present sacred Covenant. The methods, rules and standards of proper Ecclesiastical Sacramental Rights shall be defined by the present sacred Covenant and associated covenants and no other. All properly conferred Ecclesiastical Sacramental Rights shall be received, recorded and acknowledged by the Sacramentum Systemata (Sacramental Systems) of One Heaven.

Interaction with Supremum Sacramentum Systemata (Sacramental Systems)

Article 90 - Obligationum Systemata (Enforcement Systems)

1. **All coercive powers of enforcement, entry, action and exception including, but not limited to prevention, protection, restitution, restoration, seizure, search, sanction, arrest, custody, penalty or satisfaction** shall be vested in one supreme spiritual body and system known as the "**Supremum Obligationum Systemata**", also known as Supreme Enforcement Systems of Heaven. The Supremum Obligationum Systemata shall be the highest authority and powers of enforcement of all collective dimensional constructs of reality and all Heaven and Earth and no other.

Supremum Obligationum Systemata (Enforcement Systems)

The Spirit Members qualified and selected to serve within the operations of the Obligationum Systemata (Enforcement Systems) shall hold the Special Supreme Divine Office of "**Wraith**" in recognition of the most fearsome and terrible of ancient spirits and forces tasked with enforcement of justice in their foundational responsibilities of rendition, possession, prevention, interdiction, purgation, correction, seizure and return, arrest and custody and restitution.

The Supremum Obligationum Systemata is uniquely recognised,

registered and exemplified as having existence through the Great Register and Public Record of Heaven by the Sacred [Trust No. 999999-888888-999999]. The existence, identity, authority, purpose and powers of the Supremum Obligationum Systemata have been duly gazetted in the Ucadia Gazette being the Official Newspaper of Record for each and every Sacred Space-Day-Time of its existence and operation.

2. The twelve (12) key propositions and powers of the Supremum Obligationum Systemata (Enforcement Systems) shall be: Key Propositions and Powers

(i) *Enforcement*, being to enact all forms of valid coercive powers and enforcement including, but not limited to prevention, protection, restitution, restoration, seizure, search, pursuit, sanction, arrest, custody, detainment, containment, penalty, annulment, prohibition, interdiction or satisfaction to ensure the proper laws, maxims, dogmata, doctrina, edicts, judgements, writs, bills and instruments as issued in accord with the present sacred Covenant are honoured, executed and properly performed; and

(ii) *Rendition*, being to pursue, prosecute and bring to justice any individual spirit or body that openly seeks to abuse, trespass or injure Heaven, or Ucadia or its Realms, Domains, Dominions, Dependencies, Rights, Titles, Instruments, Uses or Property; and

(iii) *Possession*, being to use all necessary and available powers, authorities and abilities to enclose, possess, occupy, infiltrate, enjoin, bind, disarm, restrict or defeat any individual spirit, consciousness or body that openly seeks to abuse, trespass or injure Heaven, or Ucadia or its Realms, Domains, Dominions, Dependencies, Rights, Titles, Instruments, Uses or Property; and

(iv) *Multiplication*, being to enjoin and unify under a single consensual purpose and singularity of being, a spiritual force of such number, intention, power, authority, force and coercion to defeat, enclose, disarm, restrict, dissolve and render null or harmless any individual spirit, consciousness, multiplication of consciousness or body that openly seeks to abuse, trespass or injure Heaven, or Ucadia or its Realms, Domains, Dominions, Dependencies, Rights, Titles, Instruments, Uses or Property; and

(v) *Interdiction*, being to deploy as part of the execution of a sacred Divine Writ of Recto Divinum Interdico, to impose proper rule of law; and prohibit any possible continued breaches of Divine Law and expunge the conditions for damage to conscious memory, clarity or truth, including but not limited to empowerment and inspiration of temporal forces also granted the commission of Recto Interdico; and

(vi) *Seizure and Return*, being to execute the conditions of a Divine Warrant according to a sacred Divine Writ of Recto Divinum Capionis, to do all that is necessary to ensure the seizure and return and restoration of sacred memory, consciousness, balance, harmony, truth and integrity, including but not limited to empowerment and inspiration of temporal forces also granted the commission of Recto Capionis; and

(vii) *Arrest and Custody*, being to execute the conditions of a Divine Warrant according to a sacred Divine Writ of Recto Divinum Custodiae, to do all that is necessary to ensure the arrest and custody of each and every malevolent spirit, negative ghost and destructive construct; and to assist in the restoration of sacred memory, consciousness, balance, harmony, truth and integrity, including but not limited to empowerment and inspiration of temporal forces also granted the commission of Recto Custodiae; and

(viii) *Revelation Enforcement*, being to execute the conditions of a Divine Warrant according to a sacred Divine Writ of Recto Divinum Apocalypsis, to do all that is necessary to ensure the fulfilment of such Divine Revelation, including but not limited to the seizure, search, arrest and custody of each and every or any named malevolent spirit, or ghost, or false concept, or false right, or false construct and to assist in the restoration of sacred memory, consciousness, balance and Rule of Law; and

(ix) *Restitution*, being to execute the conditions of a Divine Warrant according to a sacred Divine Writ of Recto Divinum Restitutio, to do all that is necessary to ensure the compensation and restoration of rights, property and penalties against any party found culpable of violating one or more rights or delinquency against one of more valid fundamental maxims of law of the present sacred Covenant consistent with the granting of a temporal writ of Recto Restitutio; and

(x) *Abrogation*, being to execute the conditions of a Divine Warrant according to a sacred Divine Writ of Recto Divinum Abrogationis, to do all that is necessary to ensure any and all laws and instruments annulled are struck from any records, removed from any recognition, withdrawn and destroyed from any body of statutes and prohibited from being referenced in any form of citation or reference, consistent with the granting of a temporal writ of Recto Abrogationis; and

(xi) *Purgation*, being to execute the conditions of a Divine Warrant according to a sacred Divine Writ of Recto Divinum Expungo, to do all that is necessary to ensure any and all records directed to be expunged are purged from any records, struck out of any registers and forbidden to be used or referenced in any manner as valid, consistent with the granting of a temporal writ of Recto Expungo; and

(xii) *Correction*, being to execute the conditions of a Divine Warrant according to a sacred Divine Writ of Recto Divinum Documentis, to do all that is necessary to ensure any and all records directed to be corrected are properly corrected, consistent with the granting of a temporal writ of Recto Documentis.

Communication to Supremum Obligationum Systemata (Enforcement Systems)

3. All communication to the Obligationum Systemata (Enforcement Systems) of Heaven by living Members of One Heaven shall be by promulgation of Divine Writ in accord with Article 114 (Divine Rights and Writs of Action) of the present sacred Covenant. The methods, rules and standards of proper issuance of Divine Rights and Writs of Action shall be defined by the present sacred Covenant and associated covenants and no other. All properly conferred Divine Rights and Writs of Action shall be received, recorded and acknowledged by the Obligationum Systemata (Enforcement Systems) of One Heaven.

TITLE XVI – SPIRITUAL & TEMPORAL ORGANS

Article 91 – Spiritual & Temporal Organs

1. **Unique Collective Awareness and One Heaven within the Solar System and upon the Earth** shall be divided and defined by distinct structural units known as Organs representing its vital parts as both a spiritual and temporal body. These Spiritual and Temporal Organs shall be:

Spiritual & Temporal Organs

(i) The Universal Ecclesia of One Christ; and

(ii) The Holy Society of One Islam; and

(iii) The Sacred Society of One Spirit; and

(iv) The Globe Union; and

(v) The Globe Union Treasury; and

(vi) The Globe Union Court; and

(vii) The Supreme Patriarch; and

(viii) The Supreme Caliph; and

(ix) The Supreme Recurrence; and

(x) Ucadia Embassies, Consulates & Missions; and

(xi) Ucadia Regional Unions and Colonies; and

(xii) Ucadia Universities, Provinces & Campuses; and

(xiii) Ucadia Foundations & Charitable Funds; and

(xiv) Ucadia & Foreign Registered Entities.

Article 92 - One Christ

1. **The most sacred and Universal Ecclesia of One Christ, also known as the One Holy Apostolic Universal Ecclesia, also known as the Sol Ecclesia, also known as the Authentic Body of Christ and also known simply as One Christ**, shall be the first, highest and supreme association, aggregate, fraternity, body, entity and society of One Heaven sharing spiritual heritage associated with all forms of Christian and Jewish faiths.

Universal Ecclesia of One Christ

In accord with the intention and consent of the one true Divine Creator, all existence, angels, saints, demons and all spirits of united Heaven it is hereby pronounced that any deceased or presently living higher order life being having professed their trust and obligation in Christian or Jewish customs and traditions shall be a Member of One

Christ as well as a Member of One Heaven. All living Higher Life Forms who profess to be Christian or Jewish are *ipso facto* (as a matter of fact) subject first to the laws of One Heaven and second to the laws of the Universal Ecclesia of One Christ above any other lesser society, association, aggregate, institute, fraternity, society, entity or body.

Furthermore, it is hereby pronounced that all and every ordained, acknowledged, commissioned or certified clergy of any Christian or Jewish body shall be deemed officers of the Universal Ecclesia of One Christ; and subject to the laws and obligations of One Christ first above any other lesser society, association, aggregate, institute, fraternity, society, entity or body.

2. The absolute Rights, Powers, Purposes and Functions of the Universal Ecclesia of One Christ shall be encompassed into a most sacred covenant known as "**Pactum De Singularis Christus**", also known as the *Covenant of One Christ.*

Pactum De Singularis Christus (Covenant of One Christ)

The most sacred Covenant Pactum De Singularis Christus and the present most sacred Covenant shall be binding agreements between equals, entered in free will and full knowledge being the highest, most powerful, superior concordat and Covenant of all past, present and future possible agreements between the parties of all spirits, living and deceased as unique spirits and Mind and the Divine as the Absolute, the One, the ALL, the Universe, all Galaxies, all Stars, all Planets, all Life, all Existence and all Mind.

As the most sacred covenant Pactum De Singularis Christus and the present most sacred Covenant are the literal, legal, spiritual and lawful fulfilment of all previous Divine covenants, the present most sacred Covenant and the sacred covenant Pactum De Singularis Christus shall be the logical, legitimate and rightful conclusion of any and all historic and valid Divine covenants.

3. The Universal Ecclesia of One Christ as the "**Sol Ecclesia**" shall be a Supernatural and Spiritual entity registered and recognised in accord with the Great Register and Divine Records of One Heaven as a Divine Person and Divine Trust possessing certain Divine Rights. The Divine Trust Number for One Christ is:

Trust & Personality of Sol Ecclesia

047000-000000-000000

Sol Ecclesia symbolises the eternal forgiveness, mercy and redemption of all Christians and Jews that have physically departed; and the truth and fulfilment of the Divine Promise that the faithfully departed continue to live on in true spirit in the presence of God and the Divine Creator of all existence and the glory and joy of One Heaven.

As a Divine Person and Divine Trust, the Universal Ecclesia of One Christ as the Sol Ecclesia signifies the permanent and perfect presence of the Holy Spirit bound in sacred matrimony with the Universal Ecclesia. Thus, the permanent, perfect and irrevocable presence of the Holy Spirit personified as the Sol Ecclesia of the Universal Ecclesia signifies an eternal and complete communion between the Universal Ecclesia of One Christ and with God and the Divine Creator of all Existence and all Heaven and Earth.

4. The Universal Ecclesia of One Christ as the "**Authentic Living Body of Christ**" shall be a Living and Universal entity registered and recognised in accord with the Great Register and Divine Records of One Heaven as a True Person and Universal True Trust possessing certain Natural Rights of Use and Purpose. The Universal Trust Number for One Christ is:

Trust & Personality of Authentic Body of Christ

947000-000000-000000

The Authentic Living Body of Christ symbolises all Living Members as being incorporated into the true Living Body of Christ as one united family; and the fulfilment of Sacred Scripture in the return and permanent presence of Christ Redeemed. As a Universal True Trust, the Universal Ecclesia of One Christ possesses a True Personality based upon its Divine Personality guided by its True Mind and Intent being the Covenant of One Christ. The Society of One Christ shall have mortal life for one complete Era of three thousand two hundred and ten (3,210) years until its physical death. Upon its physical death, the people of the Earth may choose for the Society to be reborne for another Era, or for a new named Society to be created in accord with the maxims and laws of One Heaven.

5. The Universal Ecclesia of One Christ as "**One Holy Apostolic Universal Ecclesia**" shall be a Supreme Body and See registered and recognised in accord with its own Ledgers, Rolls, Records and Bylaws as a Superior Person and Superior Trust as the one, true and authentic Kingdom of Heaven upon the Earth, possessing certain Ecclesiastical and Sovereign Rights. The Superior Trust Number for One Christ is:

Trust & Personality of One Holy Apostolic Universal Ecclesia

947000-000000-00000X

As a Superior Trust, the Universal Ecclesia of One Christ possesses a Superior Personality based upon its True Personality guided by the present most sacred Covenant of One Christ.

6. The most sacred and Universal Ecclesia of One Christ, also known as the One Holy Apostolic Universal Ecclesia, also known as the Sol Ecclesia, also known as the Authentic Body of Christ and also known simply as One Christ, is hereby permanently and irrevocably delegated

Ecclesiastical Rights of One Christ

the highest possible Rights of Heaven above and supreme to any other lesser temporal society, association, aggregate, institute, fraternity, entity or body, through the Revelation, Ratification, Sanctification, Testification, Exemplification, Legislation and Consummation of Divine Will as expressed through the most sacred Covenant known as Pactum De Singularis Christus, also known as the Covenant of One Christ. These Rights shall be known as the Ecclesiastical Rights of One Christ, commensurate with the Rights delegated to One Islam and One Spirit, being one hundred and thirty-two (132) Superior Ecclesiastical Rights being: Authoritative (22), Instrumental (22), Sacramental (33), Writs (11), Bills (11), Dogma (11), Decrees (11) and Notices (11):

(i) "**Authoritative Ecclesiastical Rights**" (Potentis Ecclesiae Iurium) are Ecclesiastical Rights associated with the core ecclesiastical authoritative powers of One Christ, including (but not limited to) Title of Divine Right of Use, also known as Divinity, over the Divine Person known as One Christ and any and all variations of words and images associated with Christianity or Judaism including but not limited to all sacred texts and words attributed to these religions; and the sacred office of Supreme Patriarch, including all its powers to represent One Heaven on Earth; and

(ii) "**Instrumental Ecclesiastical Rights**" (Instrumentalis Ecclesiae Iurium) are Ecclesiastical Rights essential to the proper administration of Ecclesiastical Rights including (but not limited to) Title, Custody and sacred interpretation of the thirty-three (33) Covenants between Authentic, Apostolic and Anointed Divine Messengers of the Divine Creator of all Existence and all the Heavens and Earth and the peoples of the Earth are entrusted as the *Authentic Sacred Deposit of Trust*, contained in Sacred Canonical Scripture and Tradition; and

(iii) "**Sacramental Ecclesiastical Rights**" (Sacramentum Ecclesiae Iurium) are Ecclesiastical Rights associated with the thirty-three (33) Divine Sacraments of Heaven; and

(iv) "**Ecclesiastical Writs of Rights**" (Recto Ecclesiae Iurium) are Ecclesiastical Rights associated with the one, true and only forms of Original Entry and Original Action including, but not limited to First Right of Use and Ownership of all land, property, rights attributed to any and all lesser bodies, entities, associations, aggregates, companies or trusts using or attributing their existence or purpose on account of One Christ; and

(v) "**Ecclesiastical Bills of Exception**" (Rogatio Ecclesiae Iurium) are Ecclesiastical Rights associated with the one, true and only forms of Bills of Exception, Citation and Moratorium; and

(vi) "**Ecclesiastical Dogma**" (Summa Dogma Ecclesiae Iurium) are Ecclesiastical Rights associated with the promulgation of authoritative ecclesiastical principles, decrees and doctrines; and

(vii) "**Ecclesiastical Decrees**" (Decretum Ecclesiae Iurium) are Ecclesiastical Rights associated with ecclesiastical decrees concerning the administration, conduct and enforcement of law and order; and

(viii) "**Ecclesiastical Notices**" (Notitiae Ecclesiae Iurium) are Ecclesiastical Rights associated with ecclesiastical notices issued, executed, patented, promulgated and services in the proper administration, conduct and enforcement of law and order.

The Holy Cross of the Universal Ecclesia of One Christ

7. By the present most sacred Covenant, the most Holy and revered Cross of Christ, shall be made perpetual as the symbol and sign that personifies and embodies the Spirit of the Universal Ecclesia of One Christ:

(i) First and foremost, the Cross of One Christ signifies the custom and tradition of the Paschal mystery of God and the Divine Creator of all Heaven and Earth made flesh and by the act of free will, sacrificing himself for all humanity to end sin, to then conquer death and thus fulfil the scriptures of the coming of the Kingdom of Heaven upon the Earth and the perpetual presence of Divine Mercy and the Holy Spirit through his Ecclesia now and forever more; and

(ii) Second, the Cross of One Christ is itself the most potent symbol of the renewed Divine Covenant between God and the Divine Creator of all Heaven and Earth affirmed through all who bear witness to the truth of the miracle of the Resurrection of the Risen Christ and thus the acknowledgement of the sacred promise of eternal life to all men and women, as expressed through the present sacred Covenant; and

(iii) Third, the Cross of One Christ signifies the Holy Matrimony between Christ and his Ecclesia, as celebrated through the Sacrament of Sustentation & Rite of the Eucharist as not only an act of reverence to the suffering and sacrifice of Christ to save all who have ever lived and will ever live, but as the wedding feast in celebration of such Holy Matrimony; and

(iv) Fourth, the sign of the Cross signifies the four (4) corners of the World and the four (4) cardinal directions to the ends of the Earth as the absolute Jurisdiction and Authority of the Supreme See and the unity of all who profess to be Christian or Jewish as one family under Heaven; and

(v) Fifth, the making of the sign of the Cross is the most visible symbolic act of affirming Christian and Jewish values in clear intention of mind, an open heart, temperance and courage.

8. The Supreme See of the Ecclesia of One Christ, also known as the Holy See, shall be the seat of the Pope as Supreme Patriarch, the first church and diocese. The Supreme See of the Ecclesia shall be sovereign absolute, possessing complete control and authority over the land, buildings, space and environment within its established boundaries. In recognition of the Golden Rule of Law governing all proper international law, the Supreme See makes itself a legal entity, recognisable under international law in the exercising of its sovereign, legislative, executive and judicial functions. Supreme See

For the first term of the most sacred Divina, and the period of one hundred and twenty-eight (128) years, the Supreme See shall be Rome as Nova Roma representing Rome redeemed, reborne and renewed. Thereafter upon the conclusion of the second Great Conclave and for the second term of the most sacred Divina of Heaven, and the period of one hundred and twenty-eight (128) years, the Supreme See shall be seated at Paris, in honour of the Carolingians and the founding of the Catholicus Ecclesia. Thereafter upon the conclusion of the third Great Conclave and for the third term of the most sacred Divina of Heaven, and the period of one hundred and twenty-eight (128) years, the Supreme See shall be seated at Constantinople, also known at the founding of Christianity as Antioch. Thereafter, all future seats of the Supreme See shall be decided by a vote at the preceding Great Conclave.

9. By the power and authority of the present Covenant and the Covenant of One Christ, a Great Seal shall be minted and shall be known as the Great Seal of One Christ. The Great Seal shall be entrusted to the Supreme See to protect and honour it, for its imprint shall represent nothing less than the existence of the word and law of One Christ and as one of the seven (7) most sacred seals of Heaven. Great Seal of One Christ

Therefore, it shall only be upon the approval of the Supreme Patriarch as Supreme Leader or the college of bishops that the Great Seal of One

Christ be instanced on any document, excepting those documents prescribed as mandatory by the present sacred Covenant and the Covenant of One Christ.

10. By the power and authority of the present Covenant and the Covenant of One Christ, the Ecclesia of One Christ in conjunction with One Islam and One Spirit shall be granted the right of electing the leadership of One Heaven at a Great Conclave once every one hundred and twenty-eight (128) years. Great Conclave and Elections of One Heaven

11. So long as the Society of One Islam and One Spirit are impeded by division, or lack of a duly authorised and capable leadership, the Supreme See of One Christ shall possess the supreme, full, immediate and universal ordinary power to speak, represent, direct and enforce the rule of law, doctrine and dogma for all members of One Islam and One Spirit as well as One Christ. Supreme See of One Christ in event of impeded One Islam and One Spirit

Article 93 - One Islam

1. **The most sacred and Holy Society of One Islam, also known as the One True Way of Allah, also known as the One Umma and also known simply as One Islam**, shall be the first, highest and supreme association, aggregate, fraternity, body, entity and society of One Heaven sharing spiritual heritage associated with all forms of Islam. Holy Society of One Islam

In accord with the intention and consent of the one true Divine Creator, all existence, angels, saints, demons and all spirits of united Heaven it is hereby pronounced that any deceased or presently living higher order life being having professed their trust and obligation in Islam shall be a Member of One Islam as well as a Member of One Heaven.

All living Higher Life Forms who profess to be Muslim are *ipso facto* (as a matter of fact) subject first to the laws of One Heaven and second to the laws of the Holy Society of One Islam above any other lesser society, association, aggregate, institute, fraternity, society, entity or body. Furthermore, it is hereby pronounced that all and every ordained, acknowledged, commissioned or certified clergy of any Islamic body shall be deemed officers of the Holy Society of One Islam; and subject to the laws and obligations of One Islam first above any other lesser society, association, aggregate, institute, fraternity, society, entity or body.

2. The absolute Rights, Powers, Purposes and Functions of the Holy Society of One Islam shall be encompassed into a most sacred covenant known as "**Pactum De Singularis Islam**", also known as Pactum De Singularis Islam (Covenant of One Islam)

the *Covenant of One Islam*.

The most sacred Covenant Pactum De Singularis Islam and the present most sacred Covenant are binding agreements between equals, entered in free will and full knowledge being the highest, most powerful, superior concordat and Covenant of all past, present and future possible agreements between the parties of all spirits, living and deceased as unique spirits and Mind and the Divine as the Absolute, the One, the ALL, the Universe, all Galaxies, all Stars, all Planets, all Life, all Existence and all Mind.

As the most sacred Covenant Pactum De Singularis Islam and the present most sacred Covenant are the literal, legal, spiritual and lawful fulfilment of all previous Divine covenants, the present most sacred Covenant and the sacred covenant Pactum De Singularis Islam shall be the logical, legitimate and rightful conclusion of any and all historic and valid Divine covenants.

Trust & Personality of One Umma

3. The Holy Society of One Islam as the "**One Umma**" shall be a Supernatural and Spiritual entity registered and recognised in accord with the Great Register and Divine Records of One Heaven as a Divine Person and Divine Trust possessing certain Divine Rights. The Divine Trust Number for One Islam is:

048000-000000-000000

One Umma symbolises the eternal forgiveness, mercy and redemption of all Muslims that have physically departed; and the truth and fulfilment of the Divine Promise that the faithfully departed continue to live on in true spirit in the presence of Allah as the Divine Creator of all existence and the glory and joy of One Heaven.

As a Divine Person and Divine Trust, the Holy Society of One Islam as the One Umma signifies the permanent and perfect presence of the Holy Spirit bound in sacred matrimony to the Holy Society of One Islam. Thus, the permanent, perfect and irrevocable presence of the Holy Spirit personified as the One Umma of the Holy Society of One Islam signifies an eternal and complete communion between the Holy Society of One Islam and with Allah and the Divine Creator of all Existence and all Heaven and Earth.

Trust & Personality of Authentic Body of the Mahdi

4. The Holy Society of One Islam as the "**Authentic Living Body of the Mahdi**" and the One True Way of Allah shall be a Living and Universal entity registered and recognised in accord with the Great Register and Divine Records of One Heaven as a True Person and Universal True Trust possessing certain Natural Rights of Use and Purpose. The Universal Trust Number for One Islam is:

948000-000000-000000

The Authentic Living Body of the Mahdi and the One True Way of Allah symbolises all Living Members as being incorporated into the true Living Prophets and Martyrs as one united family; and the fulfilment of Sacred Scripture in the return and permanent presence of Allah with his people.

As a Universal True Trust, the Holy Society of One Islam possesses a True Personality based upon its Divine Personality guided by its True Mind and Intent being the Covenant of One Islam. The Society of One Islam shall have mortal life for one complete Era of three thousand two hundred and ten (3,210) years until its physical death. Upon its physical death, the people of the Earth may choose for the Society to be reborne for another Era, or for a new named Society to be created in accord with the maxims and laws of One Heaven.

5. The Holy Society of One Islam as "**One Holy Society of Islam**" shall be a Supreme Body and Seat registered and recognised in accord with its own Ledgers, Rolls, Records and Bylaws as a Superior Person and Superior Trust as the one, true and authentic Throne of Allah upon the Earth, possessing certain Ecclesiastical and Sovereign Rights. The Superior Trust Number for One Islam is: Trust & Personality of One Holy Society of Islam

948000-000000-00000X

As a Superior Trust, the Holy Society of One Islam possesses a Superior Personality based upon its True Personality guided by the present most sacred Covenant of One Islam.

6. The most sacred and Holy Society of One Islam, also known as the One True Way of Allah, also known as the One Umma and also known as One Islam, is hereby permanently and irrevocably delegated the highest possible Rights of Heaven above and supreme to any other lesser temporal society, association, aggregate, institute, fraternity, entity or body, through the Revelation, Ratification, Sanctification, Testification, Exemplification, Legislation and Consummation of Divine Will as expressed through the most sacred Covenant known as Pactum De Singularis Islam, also known as the Covenant of One Islam. These Rights shall be known as the Ecclesiastical Rights of One Islam, commensurate with the Rights delegated to One Christ and One Spirit, being one hundred and thirty-two (132) Superior Ecclesiastical Rights being: Authoritative (22), Instrumental (22), Sacramental (33), Writs (11), Bills (11), Dogma (11), Decrees (11) and Notices (11): Ecclesiastical Rights of One Islam

(i) "**Authoritative Ecclesiastical Rights**" (Potentis Ecclesiae Iurium) are Ecclesiastical Rights associated with the core ecclesiastical authoritative powers of One Islam, including (but not limited to) Title of Divine Right of Use, also known as Divinity, over the Divine Person known as One Islam and any and all variations of words and images associated with Islam including but not limited to all sacred texts and words attributed to Islam; and the sacred office of the Supreme Caliph, including all its powers to represent One Heaven on Earth; and

(ii) "**Instrumental Ecclesiastical Rights**" (Instrumentalis Ecclesiae Iurium) are Ecclesiastical Rights essential to the proper administration of Ecclesiastical Rights including (but not limited to) Title, Custody and sacred interpretation of the thirty-three (33) Covenants between Authentic, Apostolic and Anointed Divine Messengers of the Divine Creator of all Existence and all the Heavens and Earth and the peoples of the Earth are entrusted as the *Authentic Sacred Deposit of Trust*, contained in Sacred Scripture and Tradition; and

(iii) "**Sacramental Ecclesiastical Rights**" (Sacramentum Ecclesiae Iurium) are Ecclesiastical Rights associated with the thirty-three (33) Divine Sacraments of Heaven; and

(iv) "**Ecclesiastical Writs of Rights**" (Recto Ecclesiae Iurium) are Ecclesiastical Rights associated with the one, true and only forms of Original Entry and Original Action including, but not limited to First Right of Use and Ownership of all land, property, rights attributed to any and all lesser bodies, entities, associations, aggregates, companies or trusts using or attributing their existence or purpose on account of One Islam; and

(v) **"Ecclesiastical Bills of Exception"** (Rogatio Ecclesiae Iurium) are Ecclesiastical Rights associated with the one, true and only forms of Bills of Exception, Citation and Moratorium; and

(vi) "**Ecclesiastical Dogma**" (Summa Dogma Ecclesiae Iurium) are Ecclesiastical Rights associated with the promulgation of authoritative ecclesiastical principles, decrees and doctrines; and

(vii) "**Ecclesiastical Decrees**" (Decretum Ecclesiae Iurium) are Ecclesiastical Rights associated with ecclesiastical decrees concerning the administration, conduct and enforcement of law and order; and

(viii) "**Ecclesiastical Notices**" (Notitiae Ecclesiae Iurium) are Ecclesiastical Rights associated with ecclesiastical notices issued, executed, patented, promulgated and services in the proper administration, conduct and enforcement of law and order.

7. The Great Holy Seat of the Society of One Islam, also known as the Throne of Allah and Supreme Caliphate, shall be the seat of the Supreme Caliph as Supreme Leader, the first mosque and region. The Great Holy Seat of the Society of One Islam shall be sovereign absolute, possessing complete control and authority over the land, buildings, space and environment within its established boundaries. In recognition of the Golden Rule of Law governing all proper international law, the Great Holy Seat makes itself a legal entity, recognisable under international law in the exercising of its sovereign, legislative, executive and judicial functions. Great Holy Seat of the Society of One Islam

For the first term of the most sacred Divina, and the period of one hundred and twenty-eight (128) years, the Great Holy Seat of the Society of One Islam shall be Mecca representing Islam redeemed, reborne and renewed. Thereafter, upon the conclusion of the second Great Conclave and for the second term of the most sacred Divina of Heaven, and the period of one hundred and twenty-eight (128) years, the Great Holy Seat of the Society of One Islam shall be seated at Tehran, in honour of the founders of knowledge and wisdom of the region. Thereafter, upon the conclusion of the third Great Conclave and for the third term of the most sacred Divina of Heaven, and the period of one hundred and twenty-eight (128) years, the Great Holy Seat shall be seated at Damascus. Thereafter, all future seats of the Great Holy Seat shall be decided by a vote at the preceding Great Conclave.

8. By the power and authority of the present Covenant and the Covenant of One Islam, a Great Seal shall be minted and shall be known as the Great Seal of Islam. The Great Seal shall be entrusted to the Great Holy Seat of One Islam to protect and honour it, for its imprint shall represent nothing less than the existence of the word and law of One Islam and as one of the seven (7) most sacred seals of Heaven. Great Holy Seal of Islam

Therefore, it shall only be upon the approval of the Supreme Caliph as Supreme Leader or the council of elders that the Great Seal of One Islam be instanced on any document, excepting those documents prescribed as mandatory by the present sacred Covenant and the Covenant of One Islam.

9. By the power and authority of the present Covenant and the Covenant of One Islam, the Society of One Islam in conjunction with the Great Great Conclave and Elections of

Faiths of One Christ and One Spirit shall be granted the right of electing the leadership of One Heaven at a Great Conclave once every one hundred and twenty-eight (128) years. One Heaven

10. So long as the Society of One Christ and One Spirit is impeded by division, or lack of a duly authorised and capable leadership, the Great Holy Seat of One Islam shall possess the supreme, full, immediate and universal ordinary power to speak, represent, direct and enforce the rule of law, doctrine and dogma for all members of One Christ and One Spirit as well as One Islam. Great Holy Seat of One Islam in event of impeded One Christ and One Spirit

Article 94 - One Spirit

1. **The most Sacred Society of One Spirit, also known as the One Holy Apostolic Spirit, also known as One Spirit Tribe and also known simply as One Spirit**, shall be the first, highest and supreme association, aggregate, fraternity, body, entity and society of One Heaven sharing spiritual heritage associated with traditional, indigenous, Earth based, meditative and eastern customary faiths. In accord with the intention and consent of the one true Divine Creator, all existence, angels, saints, demons and all spirits of united Heaven it is hereby pronounced that any deceased or presently living higher order life beings having professed their faith in Hinduism, Buddhism, Taoism, Jainism or any other traditional customary faith is a Member of One Spirit Tribe as well as a Member of One Heaven. Sacred Society of One Spirit

All living Higher Life Forms who profess to be Hindu, Buddhist, Taoist, Sikh, Jain or any other traditional customary faith are *ipso facto* (as a matter of fact) subject first to the laws of One Heaven and second to the laws of One Spirit Tribe above any other lesser society, association, aggregate, institute, fraternity, society, entity or body. Furthermore, it is hereby pronounced that all and every ordained, acknowledged, commissioned or certified clergy of any Hindu, Buddhist or other traditional spiritual body are officers of One Spirit Tribe and subject to the laws and obligations of One Spirit Tribe first above any other lesser society, association, aggregate, institute, fraternity, society, entity or body.

2. The absolute Rights, Powers, Purposes and Functions of the Sacred Society of One Spirit shall be encompassed into a most sacred covenant known as "**Pactum De Singularis Spiritus**", also known as the *Covenant of One Spirit*. Pactum De Singularis Spiritus (Covenant of One Spirit)

The most sacred Covenant Pactum De Singularis Spiritus and the present most sacred Covenant are binding agreements between equals, entered in free will and full knowledge being the highest, most powerful, superior concordat and Covenant of all past, present and future possible agreements between the parties of all spirits, living and deceased as unique spirits and Mind and the Divine as the Absolute, the One, the ALL, the Universe, all Galaxies, all Stars, all Planets, all Life, all Existence and all Mind.

As the most sacred Covenant Pactum De Singularis Spiritus and the present most sacred Covenant are the literal, legal, spiritual and lawful fulfilment of all previous Divine covenants, the present most sacred Covenant and the covenant Pactum De Singularis Spiritus shall be the logical, legitimate and rightful conclusion of any and all historic and valid Divine covenants.

3. The Sacred Society of One Spirit as the "**Great Divine Spirit**" shall be a Supernatural and Spiritual entity registered and recognised in accord with the Great Register and Divine Records of One Heaven as a Divine Person and Divine Trust possessing certain Divine Rights. The Divine Trust Number for the Great Divine Spirit is:

Trust & Personality of Great Divine Spirit

049000-000000-000000

One Spirit symbolises the eternal forgiveness, mercy and redemption of all Hindus, Buddhists, Taoists, Janists and many other traditional customary faiths that have physically departed; and the truth and fulfilment of the Divine Promise that the faithfully departed continue to live on in true spirit in the presence of the Divine Creator of all existence and the glory and joy of One Heaven.

As a Divine Person and Divine Trust, the Sacred Society of One Spirit as the One Spirit Tribe signifies the permanent and perfect presence of the Holy Spirit bound in sacred matrimony to the Sacred Society of One Spirit. Thus, the permanent, perfect and irrevocable presence of the Great Spirit personified as the One Spirit Tribe of the Universal Ecclesia signifies an eternal and complete communion between the Sacred Society of One Spirit and with God and the Divine Creator of all Existence and all Heaven and Earth.

4. The Sacred Society of One Spirit as the "**Authentic Living Body of the Maitreya**" shall be a Living and Universal entity registered and recognised in accord with the Great Register and Divine Records of One Heaven as a True Person and Universal True Trust possessing certain Natural Rights of Use and Purpose. The Universal Trust Number for One Spirit as the Authentic Living Body of Maitreya is:

Trust & Personality of Authentic Living Body of the Maitreya

949000-000000-000000

The Authentic Living Body of Maitreya symbolises all Living Members as being incorporated into the true Living Body of the Maitreya as one united family; and the fulfilment of Sacred Scripture in the return and permanent presence of the Maitreya and Divine Mercy, Compassion and Love.

As a Universal True Trust, the Sacred Society of One Spirit as the Authentic Living Body of Maitreya possesses a True Personality based upon its Divine Personality guided by its True Mind and Intent being the Covenant of One Spirit. The Society of One Spirit shall have mortal life for one complete Era of three thousand two hundred and ten (3,210) years until its physical death. Upon its physical death, the people of the Earth may choose for the Society to be reborne for another Era, or for a new named Society to be created in accord with the maxims and laws of One Heaven.

5. The Sacred Society of One Spirit as "**One Holy Authentic Spirit**" shall be a Supreme Body and Sacred Spirit Throne registered and recognised in accord with its own Ledgers, Rolls, Records and Bylaws as a Superior Person and Superior Trust as the one, true and authentic Spirit of Heaven upon the Earth, possessing certain Ecclesiastical and Sovereign Rights. The Superior Trust Number for One Spirit is:

Trust & Personality of One Holy Apostolic Spirit

949000-000000-00000X

As a Superior Trust, the Sacred Society of One Spirit as the One Holy Apostolic Spirit possesses a Superior Personality based upon its True Personality guided by the present most sacred Covenant of One Spirit.

6. The most Sacred Society of One Spirit, also known as the One Holy Apostolic Spirit, also known as One Spirit Tribe and also known simply as One Spirit, is hereby permanently and irrevocably delegated the highest possible Rights of Heaven above and supreme to any other lesser temporal society, association, aggregate, institute, fraternity, entity or body, through the Revelation, Ratification, Sanctification, Testification, Exemplification, Legislation and Consummation of Divine Will as expressed through the most sacred Covenant known as Pactum De Singularis Spiritus, also known as the Covenant of One Spirit. These Rights shall be known as the Ecclesiastical Rights of One Spirit, commensurate with the Rights delegated to One Christ and One Islam, being one hundred and thirty-two (132) Superior Ecclesiastical Rights being: Authoritative (22), Instrumental (22), Sacramental (33), Writs (11), Bills (11), Dogma (11), Decrees (11) and Notices (11):-

Ecclesiastical Rights of One Spirit

(i) "**Authoritative Ecclesiastical Right**s" (Potentis Ecclesiae Iurium) are Ecclesiastical Rights associated with the core ecclesiastical authoritative powers of One Spirit, including (but not limited to) Title of Divine Right of Use, also known as Divinity, over the Divine Person known as One Spirit and any and all variations of words and images associated with

Hinduism, Buddhism, Jainism and Indigenous religions including but not limited to all sacred texts and words attributed to these religions; and the sacred office of Supreme Recurrence, including all its powers to represent One Heaven on Earth; and

(ii) "**Instrumental Ecclesiastical Rights**" (Instrumentalis Ecclesiae Iurium) are Ecclesiastical Rights essential to the proper administration of Ecclesiastical Rights including (but not limited to) Title, Custody and sacred interpretation of the thirty-three (33) Covenants between Authentic, Apostolic and Anointed Divine Messengers of the Divine Creator of all Existence and all the Heavens and Earth and the peoples of the Earth are entrusted as the *Authentic Sacred Deposit of Trust*, contained in Sacred Scripture and Tradition; and

(iii) "**Sacramental Ecclesiastical Rights**" (Sacramentum Ecclesiae Iurium) are Ecclesiastical Rights associated with the thirty-three (33) Divine Sacraments of Heaven; and

(iv) "**Ecclesiastical Writs of Rights**" (Recto Ecclesiae Iurium) are Ecclesiastical Rights associated with the one, true and only forms of Original Entry and Original Action including, but not limited to First Right of Use and Ownership of all land, property, rights attributed to any and all lesser bodies, entities, associations, aggregates, companies or trusts using or attributing their existence or purpose on account of One Spirit; and

(v) "**Ecclesiastical Bills of Exception**" (Rogatio Ecclesiae Iurium) are Ecclesiastical Rights associated with the one, true and only forms of Bills of Exception, Citation and Moratorium; and

(vi) "**Ecclesiastical Dogma**" (Summa Dogma Ecclesiae Iurium) are Ecclesiastical Rights associated with the promulgation of authoritative ecclesiastical principles, decrees and doctrines; and

(vii) "**Ecclesiastical Decrees**" (Decretum Ecclesiae Iurium) are Ecclesiastical Rights associated with ecclesiastical decrees concerning the administration, conduct and enforcement of law and order; and

(viii) "**Ecclesiastical Notices**" (Notitiae Ecclesiae Iurium) are Ecclesiastical Rights associated with ecclesiastical notices issued, executed, patented, promulgated and services in the proper administration, conduct and enforcement of law and order.

7. The Sacred Throne of the Society of One Spirit, shall be the seat of the Recurrence as Supreme Leader, the first temple and region. The Sacred Throne of the Society of One Spirit shall be sovereign absolute, possessing complete control and authority over the land, buildings, space and environment within its established boundaries. In recognition of the Golden Rule of Law governing all proper international law, the Sacred Throne makes itself a legal entity, recognisable under international law in the exercising of its sovereign, legislative, executive and judicial functions.

Sacred Throne of the Society of One Spirit

For the first term of the most sacred Divina, and the period of one hundred and twenty-eight (128) years, the Sacred Throne of the Society of One Spirit shall be the city of New Delhi in India, representing One Spirit redeemed, reborne and renewed for all Hindus, Buddhists, Jains and Indigenous People. Thereafter, upon the conclusion of the second Great Conclave and for the second term of the most sacred Divina of Heaven, and the period of one hundred and twenty-eight (128) years, the Sacred Throne of the Society of One Spirit shall be seated at Beijing in China, in honour of the founders of knowledge and wisdom of the great land. Thereafter, upon the conclusion of the third Great Conclave and for the third term of the most sacred Divina of Heaven, and the period of one hundred and twenty-eight (128) years, the Sacred Throne shall be seated at Seoul within a single and united Korea. Thereafter, all future seats of the Supreme See shall be decided by a vote at the preceding Great Conclave.

8. By the power and authority of the present Covenant and the Covenant of One Spirit, a Great Seal shall be minted and shall be known as the Great Seal of One Spirit. The Great Seal shall be entrusted to the Sacred Throne of One Spirit to protect and honour it, for its imprint shall represent nothing less than the existence of the word and law of One Spirit and as one of the seven (7) most sacred seals of Heaven.

Great Seal of One Spirit

Therefore, it shall only be only upon the approval of the Supreme Recurrence as Supreme Leader or the council of elders that The Great Seal of One Spirit be instanced on any document, excepting those documents prescribed as mandatory by the present sacred Covenant and the Covenant of One Spirit.

9. By the power and authority of the present Covenant and the Covenant of One Spirit, the Society of One Spirit in conjunction with the Great Faiths of One Islam and One Christ shall be granted the right of electing the leadership of One Heaven at a Great Conclave once every

Great Conclave and Elections of One Heaven

one hundred and twenty-eight (128) years.

10. So long as the Society of One Islam and One Christ is impeded by division, or lack of a duly authorised and capable leadership, the Sacred Throne of One Spirit shall possess the supreme, full, immediate and universal ordinary power to speak, represent, direct and enforce the rule of law, doctrine and dogma for all members of One Islam and One Christ as well as One Spirit. Sacred Throne of One Spirit in event of impeded One Christ and One Islam

Article 95 - Globe Union

1. **By the power and authority of the present Covenant**, the Society of Globe Union, also known as the Globe Union of Unions of free Societies over the whole Earth and See shall be vested by Constitutional Charter with the full authority and powers for all Members of One Heaven associated with carnations of Level 6 Higher Order Life Forms as Members of the Homo Sapien Species. Globe Union

All living Members of the Homo Sapien Species shall be *ipso facto* (as a matter of fact) Members of the Globe Union.

The sacred Constitutional Charter of the Globe Union also known as "**Carta Sacrum De Congregationis Globus**" shall be regarded as a Supremely sacred and valuable object and the temporal instrument of association on planet Earth in accord and consistent with the Maxims of Divine Law known as the *Divine Collection of Maxims of Law*.

Therefore, no other body politic, association, corporation, company, person, entity or group representing lesser bodies may claim higher jurisdiction than the Globe Union for planet Earth.

2. The Globe Union shall exist as a Living Trust, having legal personality under the jurisdiction of One Heaven Free Society. The Trust Number for the Globe Union is:- Globe Union Trust and Personality

940000-000000-000000

By this sacred number in the Great Register and Divine Records of One Heaven, the Society shall have mortal life for one complete Era of three thousand two hundred and ten (3,210) years until its death.

Upon its death, the people of the Earth may choose for the Society to be reborne for another Era, or for a new named society to be created in accord with the maxims and laws of One Heaven.

3. All Members of the Homo Sapien Species shall be recognised as Ordinary Members of the Globe Union. Ordinary Membership of Globe Union

When a Divine Spirit Person chooses to be expressed in Trust as a

Member who has conveyed Divinity (Divine Right of Use with Purpose) to a True Trust then expressed as a True Person associated with a Level 6 Homo Sapien Life Form, then such an event represents proof of the willing consent of the unique Divine Spirit Person to their membership of the Unique Collective Awareness and membership of the Society of the Globe Union and its Charter and laws.

Natural birth of the Level 6 Homo Sapien Life Form is proof of lawful conveyance of Divinity (Divine Right of Use with Purpose) from a Divine Trust to a True Trust as a result of willing consent by the Divine Spirit through their Divine Spirit Person to be associated with a True Person associated to a Level 6 Homo Sapien Life Form as an Ordinary Member of the Globe Union in accord with these articles.

4. All Ordinary Members of the Globe Union shall be recognised as Ordinary Members of the regional Union Society associated with their primary place of domicile on planet Earth.

Regional Union Society

5. In accord with Divine Will, the birth of any Level 6 Homo Sapien Life Form is proof of both Membership to One Heaven and Membership of the Homo Sapien Species.

Voluntary Membership Exile of Homo Sapien

Furthermore, the gift of Divinity granted to each and every Level 6 Homo Sapien Life Form means each and every living flesh and mind being may choose of their own free will to consent to being part of the society or formally abjure and demand to be disassociated with the Globe Union and any associated regional Union Society.

Therefore when any Level 6 Homo Sapien Life Form seeks to demand their membership to the Globe Union be rescinded, removed, abrogated or expunged, then such an act is a formal declaration of complete incompetence of the flesh and mind. When this occurs, the Society of Globe Union shall be granted full authority to publish and issue a Certificate of Incompetence and temporarily appoint any necessary Executors and Administrators to continue to manage, on behalf of the incompetent Level 6 Homo Sapien Life Form, their associated trusts and trust property.

Article 96 - Globe Union Treasury

1. **Supremum Templum Ecclesiae, also known as the Globe Union Treasury shall be the sole and exclusive primary financial entity above all financial and economic entities on Earth and on behalf of the Treasury of One Heaven**. No person, or body, or group, or entity, or spirit, or deity may claim higher authority, or title over the administration of all rights, all land and all goods than the Supremum Templum Ecclesiae.

Globe Union Treasury (Supremum Templum Ecclesiae)

By virtue of the present most sacred Covenant, the Supremum Templum Ecclesiae possesses full, immediate and universal ordinary power over all banks, treasuries, institutions, temples, vestries, penitentiaries, vaults, storehouses, chambers, places and offices and any and all rights, trusts, estates, funds, corporations, goods, currencies, securities, valuables, chattels and property, recorded and stored therein.

The "**Globe Union Treasury**", also known officially as Supremum Templum Ecclesiae and the Supreme Temple, shall be the first, highest, principal and primary office, place, chamber, storehouse, vault, vestry, penitentiary, temple, treasury, bank and financial institution within the temporal realm, upon the planet Earth and throughout the Solar System and Galaxy.

The primary site of the Globe Union Treasury as the Treasury of One Heaven on Earth shall be the site of the ancient Temple and Mint of Mithra in the city of Jerusalem, in fulfilment of sacred scripture, on condition the city is first an international city and second the capital of the Levant Union.

Furthermore, to fulfil sacred prophecy and the Will of the Divine, the primary site of the Globe Union Treasury as the Treasury of One Heaven on Earth as the Third Temple shall simultaneously in its design be a Temple to Judaism as a synagogue, and a Temple to Christianity as a church, and a Temple to Islam as a mosque and a Temple to all other faiths.

All authorities and procedures concerning the function of all banks, treasuries, institutions, temples, vestries, penitentiaries, vaults, storehouses, chambers, places and offices, shall be defined by the present Covenant and associated most sacred covenants and rules.

Once the status of the Globe Union is permanent, the title Supremum Templum Ecclesiae shall be reserved for official forms and events concerning Supreme Credo (Credit) and for all other lesser forms, events and actions shall be known as the Globe Union Treasury. The Trust Number for the Supremum Templum Ecclesiae, also known as the Globe Union Treasury is:

940100-999999-999999

2. There shall be a minimum of one and a maximum of four (4) Trustees, assisted by duly authorised fiduciaries, agents and administrators in the conduct of their obligations, in accord with the present most sacred Covenant. The Four (4) Trustees shall be:- Trustees of the Supremum Templum Ecclesiae

(i) The Supreme Patriarch of One Christ; and

(ii) The Supreme Caliph of One Islam; and

(iii) The Supreme Recurrence of One Spirit; and

(iv) The Secretary-General of the Globe Union.

The Office of Trustee is bound to honour the obligations of such sacred Office in accord with the present most sacred Covenant. All Members are similarly obligated to respect the Office of a Trustee of the *Supremum Templum Ecclesiae* as the Globe Union Treasury. Furthermore, Members are duty bound to honour, respect and protect the Rule of Law and hold all Officers to proper Account through the organs, rules, procedures and remedies prescribed by the present most sacred Covenant and associated Covenants and Charters.

Purposes of Globe Union Treasury

3. The purposes of the Globe Union Treasury shall be:-

(i) To record, hold, keep safe and manage all records on Earth, within the Solar System and throughout the Galaxy as to all Divine Rights held in Divine Trusts in One Heaven; and all subsequent True Trusts and Superior Trusts and associated Rights derived from such Divine Rights in Divine Trusts; and

(ii) To record, hold, keep safe and manage all records on Earth, within the Solar System and throughout the Galaxy as to the thirty-three (33) valid sacraments of *Sacred Gifts & Rites* as authentically deposited in trust by the Divine Creator to the Society of One Heaven in accord with the *Authentic Sacred Deposit of Trust*; and

(iii) To record, hold, keep safe and manage on Earth, within the Solar System and throughout the Galaxy the thirty-three (33) Covenants between Authentic, Apostolic and Anointed Divine Messengers of the Divine Creator of all Existence and all the Heavens and Earth entrusted as the *Authentic Sacred Deposit of Trust*, contained in Sacred Canonical Scripture and Tradition; and

(iv) To record, hold, keep safe and manage all embodiment of powers and authorities of One Heaven upon the Earth, the Solar System and Galaxy, bestowed to Members via the four hundred and thirty-two (432) Sacred Offices from time to time; and

(v) To receive and store safely all precious items in the possession of the Globe Union, including but not limited to those items posited in trust with the Treasury and ensure that such transactions are properly recorded and acknowledged; and

(vi) To possess and hold safely all Supreme Credo (Credit) conveyed by the Treasury of One Heaven for the benefit of all humanity through the seven Union treasuries being the Africans Union Treasury, Americas Union Treasury, Asia Union Treasury, Arabian Union Treasury, Levant Union Treasury, Euro Union Treasury and Oceanic Union Treasury; and

(vii) To create, update and maintain sufficient stock of Gold Credo (Credit) underwritten by Supreme Credo (Credits) for the benefit of the regional treasuries granted the benefit use of the value of Supreme Credo (Credits) to meet the long term need for financial stability and capital liquidity by the people and enterprises of planet Earth; and

(viii) To provide cash and valuables management facilities for the receipt, posit, deposit, store, withdrawal, payment and conversion requirements of the government and organs of the Globe Union; and

(ix) To provide treasury facilities on behalf of Society Members and State Members as Members of the Treasury for their storage, safe keeping and cash management needs; and

(x) To cooperate with the regional Union Treasuries and regional Reserve Banks in honouring the framework of the Supreme Financial System; and

(xi) To provide a cooperative framework between the principle Treasury and Financial organs of each Member of the Treasury such that optimum and stable policies may be in place for each state in regards to prices, wages, unemployment, growth, debt and investment; and

(xii) To help facilitate the expansion and balanced growth of trade, and to contribute thereby to the promotion and maintenance of high levels of employment and real income and to the development of the productive resources of all Member States as primary objectives of economic policy; and

(xiii) In accordance with the above, to assist the Union in the achievement of its purposes and principle objectives.

4. Be it known to all those future and present that the Trustees of the Treasury of the Globe Union did receive the conveyance of One Hundred and Forty-Four Million (144,000,000) Supreme Credo

Valuables held by the Globe Union Treasury

(Credit) on UCA E8:Y3208:A17: S2:M18:D4 also known as [14, March 2009].

5. In order to fulfil its primary objectives, the Globe Union Treasury shall be comprised of the following permanent organs and any such other organs deemed necessary by amendment to the present most sacred Covenant:- Organs of the Globe Union Treasury

(i) Globe Union Reserve Bank; and

(ii) Globe Union Exchange; and

(iii) Globe Union Disaster Relief Fund; and

(iv) Globe Union Bank for Reconstruction and Development; and

(v) Globe Union Insurance Fund; and

(vi) Globe Union Government Budget Agency; and

(vii) Globe Union Finance Corporation; and

(viii) Globe Union Centre for Settlement of Disputes.

Article 97 - Globe Union Court

1. **Supremum Forum, also known as the Globe Union Court, also known as the Globe Union Supreme Court of Justice shall be the first, original, principal and highest judicial body and competent forum of law above all courts, tribunals and lesser forums on Earth and on behalf of the Oratorium (Supreme Court) of One Heaven**. No person, or body, or group, or entity, or spirit, or deity may claim higher authority, or title over the administration of justice than the Supremum Forum (Globe Union Supreme Court of Justice). By virtue of the present most sacred Covenant, the Globe Union Supreme Court possesses full, immediate and universal ordinary power over all lesser judicial, arbitration and administrative bodies. Globe Union Court

All authorities and procedures concerning the function of justice shall be defined by the present Covenant and associated most sacred covenants and rules.

The Trust Number for the Supremum Forum, also known as the Globe Union Court is:

922000-000000-000000

2. Excluding the foundation period of the Court known as the "Provisional Court", the permanent Forum shall consist of thirty six Construction of Globe Union Court

(36) Justices with six (6) Justices appointed by each of the seven (7) regional Union including the Africans Union, Americas Union, Levant Union, Arabian Union, Asia Union, Euro Union and Oceanic Union:-

(i) Each group of six (6) Justices for each regional Ucadia Union shall also function as the most senior Justices of the Supreme Court for each Union; and

(ii) Each Justice shall hold their appointment to the Globe Court of Justice for six (6) years corresponding to the term of the Senate or up to the age of eighty (80); and

(iii) A Justice may not serve more than three (3) terms as a Forum Justice, or eighteen (18) years before they must retire; and

(iv) All Globe Court Justices shall hold their tenure subject to their fiduciary conduct in good faith and honour of the present most sacred Covenant, the laws of the Globe Union and with the continued confidence of the Globe Union Senate.

3. All Members of the Globe Union are ipso facto parties to the formation of The Forum and agree to be subject and bound to its jurisdiction. Membership of Globe Union Court

A State which is not a Member of the Globe Union may become a party to the Globe Court of Justice on conditions to be determined in each case by the Senate upon the recommendation of the Global Council assisted by the Secretariat.

4. The Globe Union Court shall have original and final jurisdiction in all matters:- Original Jurisdiction

(i) Arising under the present most sacred Covenant, or involving its interpretation, but excluding ecclesiastical matters solely the domain of One Christ, One Islam or One Spirit; or

(ii) Arising under any laws made by the Globe Senate; or

(iii) Arising as a matter of maritime or border jurisdiction between any state or territory; or

(iv) Arising under any treaty; or

(v) Affecting consuls or other official representatives of Member States; or

(vi) Where the Globe Union, or a person suing or being sued on behalf of the Globe Union, is a party; or

(vii) Between State Members and Society Members, or between residents of different States, or

(viii) Between a Member State and a resident of another Member State; or

(ix) When a writ or prohibition or an injunction is sought against an officer of the Globe Union.

5. The Globe Union Court shall have final appellate jurisdiction in all matters:- Appellate Jurisdiction

(i) Of any Justice or Justices exercising the original jurisdiction of the Globe Court of Justice; and

(ii) Of any other court of a Member in which the Member acknowledges the final jurisdiction of the Globe Court of Justice, or court exercising regional or national jurisdiction; or of the Supreme Court of any State, or of any other court of any State.

Article 98 - Supreme Patriarch

1. **The Pope as the Supreme Patriarch, in whom continues the Apostolic Traditions of Sacred Office of the one true Holy Apostolic Universal Ecclesia of all in One Christ**, is the personification of the Supreme See, is the head of the Apostolic College of Patriarchs, the embodiment of the Divine Temple of God restored upon the Earth, the Vicar of Christ and the Pastor of the Universal Ecclesia on Earth. By virtue of his office he possesses supreme, full, immediate, and universal ordinary power within the united community of all Christians and Jews. Supreme Patriarch

All Procedures concerning the function of the office of Pope as Supreme Patriarch, the execution of duty, the inauguration into office, events relating to the vacancy of office and the death of current and previous office holders shall be defined by the present Covenant and the sacred Covenant Pactum De Singularis Christus (Covenant of One Christ).

2. By the power and authority of this Covenant, the organisation of One Christ is granted by Notice of Divine Title and Right and Power of Supreme Patriarch the right to represent the interests of One Heaven on Earth. Divine Title and Right and Power of Supreme Patriarch

The Notice of Divine Title and Right and Power of Supreme Patriarch shall represent a sacred object of simple paper, which is firstly properly authorised, secondly under the Seal of One Heaven and thirdly records the Covenants of authority of the Holy Covenant of One Heaven.

As such it shall be regarded as a Supremely sacred and valuable object, to be held with great veneration.

Powers and Authority of Pope as Supreme Patriarch

3. By the authority of this Covenant and by the power of the ceremony of Supreme Instantiation of the Powers and Authority of Supreme Patriarch, the Supreme Patriarch shall have the following real ceremonial and spiritual authorities:

(i) The Supreme Patriarch shall themselves become the Most Sacred and Holy Living Instrument of Power, a Holy Person of high spiritual importance, a living embodiment of the new Covenant between Heaven and Earth; and

(ii) When the Supreme Patriarch speaks under Magisterium in regards to the Holy Scripture of One Christ, it shall be recognised as having authority across all levels and branches of the One Christ; and

(iii) The Supreme Patriarch shall have the spiritual authority to perform the sacred ceremony of Supreme Blessing of the Earth; and

(iv) The Supreme Patriarch shall have the spiritual and legal authority to Seal an Instrument of Supreme Sovereignty granted to any Society, State or Nation/University that joins as a State Member of One Christ; and

(v) The Supreme Patriarch shall have the spiritual and legal authority to perform the official ceremony of Supreme Blessing of the Executive upon the appointment of a new Head of State of a Society, State or Nation/University; and

(vi) The Supreme Patriarch shall have the spiritual authority to perform supreme reconciliation, so that what he decrees on Earth shall be bound in Heaven and the spirit world, healing all spiritual energy that has ever existed for the Earth; and

(vii) The Supreme Patriarch shall have the spiritual authority to perform exorcisms, so that when he decrees authority over disruptive spirits they shall be bound in Heaven and the spirit world commanding all of the spiritual energy that has ever existed for the Earth; and

(viii) The Supreme Patriarch shall have the spiritual authority to perform bindings so that what is decreed as bound on Earth in regards to justice and equity shall be bound in Heaven and the spirit world by the power of all the spiritual energy that has ever existed for the Earth; and

(ix) The Supreme Patriarch shall have the spiritual authority to perform the official ceremony of Supreme Instantiation of the Powers and Authority of Supreme Credit and to Seal its Instrument of Title for the creation of *Supreme Credo (Credits)* subject to the articles and limits of their manufacture under this Covenant.

Supreme Patriarch as a living instrument of power

4. By the very definition of such most sacred Office, the Supreme Patriarch is the purest form of teacher and guide. The Supreme Patriarch embodies the very covenant of this Covenant and as such each Supreme Patriarch represents in themselves and their role an instrument of power, a living embodiment of this Covenant.

Authority to speak on behalf of One Heaven and the Great Spirits

5. By the power of this Covenant and the Notice of Divine Title and Right and Power of Supreme Patriarch, it shall be granted to the office of Supreme Patriarch the authority to speak on behalf of One Heaven on Earth.

Furthermore, by the power vested in this Covenant when the Supreme Patriarch speaks he does so with the authority and voice of the Great Spirit of One Christ. And so in speaking as a voice of the Great Spirit of One Christ, he is also speaking as a leader of Heaven and Earth.

Qualification of Supreme Patriarch

6. By the authority of the present Covenant, only a living man meeting all of the following criteria shall be permitted to hold the Office of Supreme Patriarch of the Universal Ecclesia by Extraordinary Qualification, or Special Qualification or Ordinary Qualification:

By Extraordinary Qualification

(i) That the current candidate is the Bishop of Rome, also known as His Holiness, also known as the Vicar of Christ, also known as the Servant of Servants and also known as the Holy Father; and

(ii) That the current candidate, his Curia and all Bishops, Priests and Nuns fully consent to be bound by the most sacred obligations of Divine Mercy, Divine Forgiveness and Divine Love; and have pledged their solemn oath and absolute obedience to the commands of God and the Divine Creator of All Existence as pronounced through Pactum De Singularis Christus, also known as the Covenant of One Christ and the present most sacred Covenant (Pactum De Singularis Caelum); and

(iii) That the date is before the expiry of the Year of Redemption being UCA E1:Y2:A1:S1:M30:D1, also known as [Sat, 21 Dec 2013]. The date and time being after [Sat, 21 Dec 2013] by the old cycle or UCA E1:Y2:A1:S1:M30:D1, the Qualification of the Supreme Patriarch by Extraordinary Qualification shall no longer be available as valid qualification.

By Special Qualification

(i) That the current candidate is the Patriarch of a major Christian Church or Jewish Division, or is a validly elected Cardinal or Bishop having the approval of at least thirty-six (36) other current or previous Bishops, or Patriarchs or Cardinals to be their representative; and

(ii) That the conditions for Extraordinary Qualification have expired with the existing Bishop of Rome refusing to acknowledge the most holy prophecies of all Christianity and Judaism and refuting the authenticity of sacred scripture as true Revelation; and

(iii) That the current candidate, his Bishops, Priests and Nuns fully consent to be bound by the most sacred obligations of Divine Mercy, Divine Forgiveness and Divine Love; and have pledged their solemn oath and obedience to the commands of God and the Divine Creator of all Existence as pronounced by Pactum De Singularis Christus, also known as the Covenant of Christ and the present most sacred Covenant (Pactum De Singularis Caelum); and

(iv) That the date is before the third anniversary of the sacred Day of Redemption being [Tuesday, 22 December 2015] or GAIA E1:Y4:A1:S1:M12:D1.Thereafter, the Qualification of the Supreme Patriarch by Special Qualification shall no longer be available as valid qualification.

By Ordinary Qualification

(i) That the candidate is a Patriarch of a properly constituted Christian or Jewish Community under the sacred Covenant Pactum De Singularis Christus; and that the Permanent status of all seven (7) Ucadia Unions (Globe, Africans, Americas, Arabia, Asia, Europe and Oceania) are confirmed, operational and functional; and

(ii) That the conditions for Special Qualification have expired with all the existing Cardinals and Patriarchs refusing to acknowledge the most holy prophecies of all Christianity and Judaism and refuting the authenticity of sacred scripture as true Revelation; and

(iii) That the current candidate, his Bishops, Priests and Nuns have pledged their solemn oath and obedience to the commands of God as pronounced by *Pactum De Singularis Christus*, also known as the Covenant of Christ and the present most sacred Covenant; and

(iv) The Candidate is aged between sixty (60) and eighty (80) years.

7. Acknowledgement is hereby given to all Heaven, all Spirits and all the Earth of the full, perfected and irrevocable acceptance by Extraordinary Qualification of the Pope and Bishop of Rome as Supreme Patriarch of the Universal Ecclesia and the redemption of all Christian Churches and Jewish Congregations, united as One Christ from Ucadia sacred Space-Day-Time known as JOVIUS E1:Y1:A17:S2:M4:D4, also known as March 14th 2013.

Acknowledgement of Extraordinary Qualification of Pope as Supreme Patriarch

Article 99 - Supreme Caliph

1. **The Supreme Caliph, in whom continues the Apostolic Traditions of the Sacred Prophets and Messengers of God to the Holy Community of all in Islam**, is the head of the College of Caliphs, the Guardian of the Way, the Scholar of the Word of God and the Father of the Holy Society of One Islam upon the Earth. By virtue of his office he possesses supreme, full, immediate, and universal ordinary power within each and every Muslim community.

Supreme Caliph

All Procedures concerning the function of the office of Supreme Caliph, the execution of duty, the inauguration into office, events relating to the vacancy of office and the death of current and previous office holders shall be defined by the present Covenant and the sacred Covenant Pactum De Singularis Islam (Covenant of One Islam).

2. By the power and authority of the present most sacred Covenant, the organisation of One Islam is granted by Notice of Divine Title and Right and Power of the Supreme Caliph the right to represent the interests of One Heaven on Earth.

Divine Title and Right and Power of the Supreme Caliph

The Notice of Divine Title and Right and Power of Caliph shall represent a sacred object of simple paper, which is firstly properly authorised, secondly under the Seal of One Heaven and thirdly records the Covenants of authority of the Holy Covenant of One Heaven.

As such it shall be regarded as a supremely sacred and valuable object, to be held with great veneration.

3. By the authority of this Covenant and by the power of the ceremony of Supreme Instantiation of the Powers and Authority of the Supreme

Powers and Authority of Supreme Caliph

Caliph, a Supreme Caliph shall have the following real ceremonial and spiritual authorities:

(i) The Supreme Caliph shall themselves become the Most Sacred and Holy Living Instrument of Power, a Holy Person of high spiritual importance, a living embodiment of the new Covenant between Heaven and Earth; and

(ii) When a Supreme Caliph speaks in regards to the Holy Scripture of One Islam, it shall be recognised as having authority across all levels and branches of the One Islam; and

(iii) The Supreme Caliph shall have the spiritual authority to perform the sacred ceremony of Supreme Blessing of the Earth; and

(iv) The Supreme Caliph shall have the spiritual and legal authority to Seal an Instrument of Supreme Sovereignty granted to any Society, State or Nation/University that joins as a State Member of One Islam; and

(v) A Supreme Caliph shall have the spiritual and legal authority to perform the official ceremony of Supreme Blessing of the Executive upon the appointment of a new Head of State of a Society, State or Nation/University; and

(vi) The Supreme Caliph shall have the spiritual authority to perform supreme reconciliation, so that what he decrees on Earth shall be bound in Heaven and the spirit world, healing all spiritual energy that has ever existed for the Earth; and

(vii) The Supreme Caliph shall have the spiritual authority to perform exorcisms, so that when he decrees authority over disruptive spirits they shall be bound in Heaven and the spirit world commanding all of the spiritual energy that has ever existed for the Earth; and

(viii) The Supreme Caliph shall have the spiritual authority to perform bindings so that what is decreed as bound on Earth in regards to justice and equity shall be bound in Heaven and the spirit world by the power of all the spiritual energy that has ever existed for the Earth; and

(ix) The Supreme Caliph shall have the spiritual authority to perform the official ceremony of Supreme Instantiation of the Powers and Authority of Supreme Credit and to Seal its Instrument of Title for the creation of *Supreme Credo (Credits)* subject to the articles and limits of their manufacture under this

Covenant.

4. By the very definition of such most sacred Office, the Supreme Caliph is the purest form of teacher and guide. The Supreme Caliph embodies the very covenant of this Covenant and as such each Supreme Caliph represents in themselves and their role an instrument of power, a living embodiment of this Covenant.

Supreme Caliph as a living instrument of power

5. By the power of this Covenant and the Notice of Divine Title and Right and Power of Supreme Caliph, it shall be granted to the office of the Supreme Caliph the authority to speak on behalf of One Heaven on Earth.

Authority to speak on behalf of One Heaven and the Great Spirits

Furthermore, by the power vested in this Covenant that when the Supreme Caliph speaks, he does so with the authority and voice of the Great Spirit of One Islam. And so in speaking as a voice of the Great Spirit of One Islam, he is also speaking as a leader of Heaven and Earth.

6. By the authority of the present Covenant, only a living man meeting all of the following criteria shall be permitted to hold the Office of Supreme Caliph of the Universal Ecclesia by Extraordinary Qualification, or Special Qualification or Ordinary Qualification:

Qualification of the Supreme Caliph

By Extraordinary Qualification

(i) That the current candidate is an existing Reigning Sovereign of an acknowledged Islamic Dominion, whose jurisdiction encompasses a community of at least five (5,000,000) million or more and at least one or more sacred places of One Islam; and

(ii) That the current candidate, his Court and all Royal Family Members, Governors and Officials fully consent to be bound by the most sacred obligations of Divine Mercy, Divine Forgiveness and Divine Love; and have pledged their solemn oath and obedience to the commands of Allah as the Divine Creator of all Existence as pronounced by the Covenant Pactum De Singularis Islam, also known as the Covenant of One Islam and the Covenant of One Heaven (Pactum De Singularis Caelum); and

(iii) That the date is before the expiry of the Year of Redemption being UCA E1:Y2:A1:S1:M30:D1, also known as [Sat, 21 Dec 2013]. The date and time being after [Sat, 21 Dec 2013] by the old cycle or UCA E1:Y2:A1:S1:M30:D1, the Qualification of the Supreme Caliph by Extraordinary Qualification shall no longer be available as valid qualification.

By Special Qualification

(i) That the current candidate is the Spiritual Leader of a major Islamic Sovereign Nation or University of five (5,000,000) million members or more, having the approval of at least one other Islamic nation or university to be their witness; and

(ii) That the conditions for Extraordinary Qualification have expired with all reigning royal and ecclesiastical leaders of Islamic countries refusing to acknowledge the most holy prophecies of Islam and openly confessing by their profanity, perfidy and impiety that they do not recognise nor respect the authenticity of sacred Islamic scripture as true Revelation; and

(iii) That the current candidate and all his clerics fully consent to be bound by the most sacred obligations of Divine Mercy, Divine Forgiveness and Divine Love; and have pledged their solemn oath and obedience to the commands of Allah as the Divine Creator of all Existence as pronounced by Pactum De Singularis Islam, also known as the Covenant of One Islam and the present most sacred Covenant (Pactum De Singularis Caelum); and

(iv) That the date is before the third anniversary of the sacred Day of Redemption being [Tuesday, 22 December 2015] or GAIA E1:Y4:A1:S1:M12:D1.Thereafter, the Qualification of the Supreme Caliph by Special Qualification shall no longer be available as valid qualification.

By Ordinary Qualification

(i) That the candidate is a Caliph of a properly constituted Islamic Community under the sacred Covenant Pactum De Singularis Islam; and that the Permanent status of all seven (7) Ucadia Unions (Globe, Africans, Americas, Arabia, Asia, Europe and Oceania) are confirmed, operational and functional; and

(ii) That the conditions for Special Qualification have expired with all the existing ecclesiastical and spiritual leaders of Islam openly refusing to acknowledge the most holy prophecies of all Islam and refuting the authenticity of sacred Islamic scripture as true Revelation; and

(iii) That the current candidate and all his clerics fully consent to be bound by the most sacred obligations of Divine Mercy, Divine Forgiveness and Divine Love; and have pledged their solemn oath and obedience to the commands of God as pronounced by

Pactum De Singularis Islam, also known as the Covenant of Islam and the present most sacred Covenant; and

(iv) The Candidate is aged between sixty (60) and eighty (80) years.

7. In accord with the present most sacred Covenant and upon the expiry of the Sacred Day-Space-Time of UCA E1:Y2:A1:S1:M30:D1, also known as [Sat, 21 Dec 2013], the Office of Supreme Caliph is prevented from being fulfilled by either Extraordinary Qualification or Special Qualification as the time for Islamic Leaders to demonstrate such respect, honour and good faith to God and the Divine Creator of all Existence has expired. Therefore, the only means of the office of Supreme Caliph now being fulfilled is by Ordinary Qualification in accord with the present Article.

Disqualification of Supreme Caliph by Extraordinary and Special Qualification

Until such time as the sacred office of Supreme Caliph is properly filled by Ordinary Qualification, the office of Supreme Caliph is hereby pronounced impeded and therefore all authority and powers of the Holy Society of One Islam and the office of Supreme Caliph shall be temporarily vested in the Universal Ecclesia of One Christ possessing supreme, full, immediate and universal ordinary power to speak, represent, direct and enforce the rule of law, doctrine and dogma for all members of One Islam as well as One Christ.

Article 100 - Supreme Recurrence

1. **The Supreme Recurrence, in whom continues the Traditions of Divine Office of all Hindu, Buddhist and Indigenous faiths and cultures**, is the head of the Council of Deities, and the Messenger of Heaven on Earth. By virtue of his office he possesses supreme, full, immediate, and universal ordinary power within every Hindu, Buddhist, Sikh, Jain and Indigenous community.

Supreme Recurrence

All Procedures concerning the function of the office of Supreme Recurrence, the execution of duty, the inauguration into office, events relating to the vacancy of office and the death of current and previous office holders shall be defined by the present Covenant and the sacred Covenant Pactum De Singularis Spiritus (Covenant of One Spirit).

2. By the power and authority of this Covenant, the organisation of One Spirit is granted by Notice of Divine Title and Right and Power of Supreme Recurrence the right to represent the interests of One Heaven on Earth.

Divine Title and Right and Power of Supreme Recurrence

The Notice of Divine Title and Right and Power of Supreme Recurrence shall represent a sacred object of simple paper, which is first properly authorised, secondly under the Seal of One Heaven and thirdly records the Covenants of authority of the Holy Covenant of One Heaven.

As such it shall be regarded as a supremely sacred and valuable object, to be held with great veneration.

3. By the authority of this Covenant and by the power of the ceremony of Supreme Instantiation of the Powers and Authority of Supreme Recurrence, a Supreme Recurrence shall have the following real ceremonial and spiritual authorities: Powers and Authority of Supreme Recurrence

(i) The Supreme Recurrence shall themselves become the Most Sacred and Holy Living Instrument of Power, a Holy Person of high spiritual importance, a living embodiment of the new Covenant between Heaven and Earth; and

(ii) When a Supreme Recurrence speaks in regards to the holy scripture of One Spirit Tribe, it shall be recognised as having authority across all levels and branches of the One Spirit Tribe; and

(iii) The Supreme Recurrence shall have the spiritual authority to perform the sacred ceremony of Supreme Blessing of the Earth; and

(iv) The Supreme Recurrence shall have the spiritual and legal authority to Seal an Instrument of Supreme National Sovereignty granted to any Society, State or University that joins as a State Member of One Spirit; and

(v) The Supreme Recurrence shall have the spiritual and legal authority to perform the official ceremony of Supreme Blessing of the Executive upon the appointment of a new Head of State of a Nation/University; and

(vi) The Supreme Recurrence shall have the spiritual authority to perform supreme reconciliation, so that what he decrees on Earth shall be bound in Heaven and the spirit world, healing all spiritual energy that has ever existed for the Earth; and

(vii) A Supreme Recurrence shall have the spiritual authority to perform exorcisms, so that when he decrees authority over disruptive spirits they shall be bound in Heaven and the spirit world commanding all of the spiritual energy that has ever existed for the Earth; and

(viii) The Supreme Recurrence shall have the spiritual authority to perform bindings so that what is decreed as bound on Earth in regards to justice and equity shall be bound in Heaven and the spirit world by the power of all the spiritual energy that has ever existed for the Earth; and

(ix) The Supreme Recurrence shall have the spiritual authority to perform the official ceremony of Supreme Instantiation of the Powers and Authority of Supreme Credit and to Seal its Instrument of Title for the creation of *Supreme Credo (Credits)* subject to the articles and limits of their manufacture under this Covenant.

Supreme Recurrence as a living instrument of power

4. By the very definition of such most sacred Office, the Supreme Recurrence is the purest form of teacher and guide. The Supreme Recurrence embodies the very covenant of this Covenant and as such each Supreme Recurrence represents in themselves and their role an instrument of power, a living embodiment of this Covenant.

Authority to speak on behalf of One Heaven and the Great Spirits

5. By the power of this Covenant and the Notice of Divine Title and Right and Power of Supreme Recurrence, it shall be granted to the office of Recurrence the authority to speak on behalf of One Heaven on Earth.

Furthermore, by the power vested in this Covenant that when the Recurrence speaks, he does so with the authority and voice of the Great Spirit of One Spirit Tribe. And so in speaking as a voice of the Great Spirit of One Spirit Tribe, he is also speaking as a leader of Heaven and Earth.

Qualification of the Supreme Recurrence

6. By the authority of the present Covenant, only a living man meeting all of the following criteria shall be permitted to hold the Office of Supreme Recurrence of the Universal Ecclesia by Extraordinary Qualification, or Special Qualification or Ordinary Qualification:

By Extraordinary Qualification

(i) That the current candidate is the spiritual leader of a major Buddhist, Hindu, Sikh, Jain or Indigenous faith, having twenty (20,000,000) million or more living members; and

(ii) That the current candidate, his Committee and all Governors, Leaders and Officers fully consent to be bound by the most sacred obligations of Divine Mercy, Divine Forgiveness and Divine Love; and have pledged their solemn oath and obedience to the commands of Harmony, Ancestors and United Spirit as pronounced by the Covenant Pactum De Singularis Spiritus, also known as the Covenant of One Spirit and the Covenant of One Heaven (Pactum De Singularis Caelum); and

(iii) That the date is before the expiry of the Year of Redemption being UCA E1:Y2:A1:S1:M30:D1, also known as [Sat, 21 Dec

2013]. The date and time being after [Sat, 21 Dec 2013] by the old cycle or UCA E1:Y2:A1:S1:M30:D1, the Qualification of the Supreme Recurrence by Extraordinary Qualification shall no longer be available as valid qualification.

By Special Qualification

(i) That the current candidate is the Spiritual Leader of a major Sovereign Nation or University of five (5,000,000) million members or more, having the approval of at least one other Buddhist, Hindu, Sikh, Jain or Indigenous nation or university to be their witness; and

(ii) That the conditions for Extraordinary Qualification have expired with all existing Spiritual Leaders and Sovereigns of all existing Buddhist, Hindu, Jain and Indigenous Dominions confessing themselves by such disgrace and dishonour to be apostates before Heaven and Earth, in refusing to acknowledge the most holy prophecies of all Hinduism, Buddhism, Jainism and Indigenous Cultures; and refuting the authenticity of such sacred scripture as true Revelation; and

(iii) That the current candidate and his Clergy fully consent to be bound by the most sacred obligations of Divine Mercy, Divine Forgiveness and Divine Love; and have pledged their solemn oath and obedience to the commands of God and the Divine Creator of all Existence as pronounced by the Covenant Pactum De Singularis Spiritus, also known as the Covenant of One Spirit and the present most sacred Covenant (Pactum De Singularis Caelum); and

(iv) That the date is before the third anniversary of the sacred Day of Redemption being [Tuesday, 22 December 2015] or GAIA E1:Y4:A1:S1:M12:D1.Thereafter, the Qualification of the Supreme Recurrence by Special Qualification shall no longer be available as valid qualification.

By Ordinary Qualification

(i) That the candidate is a Recurrence of a properly constituted Hindu, Buddhist, Sikh, Jain or Indigenous community under the sacred Covenant Pactum De Singularis Spiritus; and that the Permanent status of all seven (7) Ucadia Unions (Globe, Africans, Americas, Arabia, Asia, Europe and Oceania) are confirmed, operational and functional; and

(ii) That the conditions for Special Qualification have expired with all the existing Hindu, Buddhist, Jain and Indigenous Spiritual Leaders of major Sovereign Nations and Universities of five (5,000,000) million members or more refusing to acknowledge the most holy prophecies of all the world and refuting the authenticity of sacred scripture as true Revelation; and

(iii) That the current candidate, have pledged their solemn oath and obedience to the commands of God as pronounced by Pactum De Singularis Spiritus, also known as the Covenant of One Spirit and the present most sacred Covenant; and

(iv) The Candidate is aged between sixty (60) and eighty (80) years.

7. In accord with the present most sacred Covenant and upon the expiry of the Sacred Day-Space-Time of UCA E1:Y2:A1:S1:M30:D1, also known as [Sat, 21 Dec 2013], the Office of Supreme Recurrence is prevented from being fulfilled by either Extraordinary Qualification or Special Qualification as the time for Hindu, Buddhist, Sikh, Jain and Indigenous Leaders to demonstrate such respect, honour and good faith to the Divine Creator of all Existence has expired. Therefore, the only means of the office of Supreme Recurrence now being fulfilled is by Ordinary Qualification in accord with the present Article.

Disqualification of Supreme Recurrence by Extraordinary and Special Qualification

Until such time as the sacred office of Supreme Recurrence is properly filled by Ordinary Qualification, the office of Supreme Recurrence is hereby pronounced impeded and therefore all authority and powers of the Sacred Society of One Spirit and the office of Supreme Recurrence shall be temporarily vested in the Universal Ecclesia of One Christ possessing supreme, full, immediate and universal ordinary power to speak, represent, direct and enforce the rule of law, doctrine and dogma for all members of One Spirit as well as One Christ.

Article 101 – Ucadia Embassies, Consulates & Missions

1. **Ucadia shall seek to establish peaceful, amicable and harmonious relations with non-Ucadian states**, to ensure Ucadian Members may safely engage in all forms of commerce, trade and navigation with persons, bodies and entities of the non-Ucadian state; and for the purpose of acquiring, holding and disposing of all forms of property, for the benefit of Ucadia Members.

Ucadia Embassies, Consulates & Missions

To fulfil this goal, Ucadia political bodies shall establish appropriate diplomatic treaties and relations, as well as diplomatic representation and presence as internationally recognised diplomatic missions as appropriate.

2. When a Ucadia University has reached Probational Status, then it shall

Ucadia University Body

be permitted to establish a Diplomatic Post within the jurisdiction of each and every other Ucadia University that has also reached Probational Status, through a formal treaty between Ucadia Universities recognising the diplomatic status and rights of each other. at Probational Status

The Diplomatic Post shall be called a Ucadia Mission and shall be represented by a Diplomatic Consul.

3. When a Ucadia University has reached Prerogative Status, such status means that the host state has formally accepted and adopted Ucadia as the model and function of Government. The Ucadia University as effectively the government of the host state shall be permitted to seek a permanent Diplomatic Post within the jurisdiction of each and every other Ucadia University that has reached Probational Status, through a formal treaty between Ucadia Universities recognising the diplomatic status and rights of each other, as well as the host nations corresponding to the jurisdictions of the Ucadia Universities. Ucadia University Body at Prerogative Status

The Diplomatic Post of the prerogative status Ucadia University shall be called a Ucadia Embassy and shall be represented by an Ambassador, while the probational Ucadia Universities shall be recognised in the receiving jurisdiction as Consulates headed by Consuls-General, or if prerogative then such Ucadia Universities shall be recognised as Embassies headed by Ambassadors.

Article 102 - Ucadia Regional Unions and Colonies

1. **By the power and authority of the present sacred Covenant**, six Regional Ucadia Unions shall be formed over the whole Earth and See, vested by Charter with the full authority and powers for all Members of One Heaven associated with carnations of Level 6 Higher Order Life Forms as Members of the Homo Sapien Species within each region. Ucadia Regional Unions and Colonies

All living Members of the Homo Sapien Species within the Solar System shall be *ipso facto* (as a matter of fact) a Member of at least one Regional Ucadia Union.

The seven (7) Regional Ucadia Unions of Planet Earth shall be-

(i) Ucadia Africans Union; and

(ii) Ucadia Americas Union; and

(iii) Ucadia Arabian Union; and

(iv) Ucadia Levant Union; and

(v) Ucadia Asia Union; and

(vi) Ucadia Euro Union; and

(vii) Ucadia Oceanic Union.

The for Ucadia Colony Federations shall be:-

(i) Ucadia Moon Federation; and

(ii) Ucadia Mars Federation; and

(iii) Ucadia Jupiter-Europa Federation; and

(iv) Ucadia Saturn-Titan Federation.

No other body politic, association, corporation, company, person, entity or group representing lesser bodies may claim higher jurisdiction than each Regional Ucadia Union for each region of planet Earth and throughout the Solar System.

A non-Earth Planetary or Moon Colony within the Solar System shall be recognised as a Union upon reaching one hundred and forty four (144,000) thousand or more living and domiciled Homo Sapien Members.

Each Ucadia University (Nation) shall be a *Primary Member* of just one Regional Union or Colony Federation; and may then be an *Auxiliary Member* of one other Regional Union or Colony Federation providing: (a) The University is not one of the twelve largest global economies; and (b) The University shares both a common cultural and geographic bond with the region.

Regional Ucadia Union Trusts

2. In relation to each region, a sacred trust shall be formed for the primary purpose to conserve and protect the Trust Corpus for the benefit of all life and communities within the bounds of each Ucadia Regional Union; and to properly delegate the rights and functions of Trustee to the Government of each Union, when such offices are lawfully occupied and unimpeded. The Trust Body of each Ucadia trust shall include any and all rights, uses, land, funds, assets and property, as defined and vested by the Constitutional Charter as the *Trust Agreement* for each Ucadia Regional Union. The Trust numbers for each Ucadia Regional Union shall be:-

(i) Ucadia Africans Union Trust No. 941000-000000-000000; and

(ii) Ucadia Americas Union Trust No. 942000-000000-000000; and

(iii) Ucadia Arabian Union Trust No. 943000-000000-000000;

and

(iv) Ucadia Levant Union Trust No. 94L000-000000-000000; and

(v) Ucadia Asia Union Trust No. 944000-000000-000000; and

(vi) Ucadia Euro Union Trust No. 945000-000000-000000; and

(vii) Ucadia Oceanic Union Trust No. 946000-000000-000000; and

(viii) Ucadia Moon Federation Trust No. 94X000-000000-000000; and

(ix) Ucadia Mars Federation Trust No. 94M000-000000-000000; and

(x) Ucadia Jupiter-Europa Federation Trust No. 94J000-000000-000000; and

(xi) Ucadia Saturn-Titan Federation Trust No. 94S000-000000-000000.

Regional Ucadia Union Treasuries

3. To ensure the proper function of all forms of money, assets, property, debts, obligations, insurance and securities within and between Ucadia Regional Unions, each Ucadia Regional Union is vested with a Treasury, also known as an "Econos". The Trust numbers for each Ucadia Regional Union Treasury shall be:-

(i) Ucadia Africans Union Treasury Trust No. 941100-999999-999999; and

(ii) Ucadia Americas Union Treasury Trust No. 942100-999999-999999; and

(iii) Ucadia Arabian Union Treasury Trust No. 943100-999999-999999; and

(iv) Ucadia Levant Union Treasury Trust No. 94L100-999999-999999; and

(v) Ucadia Asia Union Treasury Trust No. 944100-999999-999999; and

(vi) Ucadia Euro Union Treasury Trust No. 945100-999999-999999; and

(vii) Ucadia Oceanic Union Treasury Trust No. 946100-999999-999999; and

(viii) Ucadia Moon Federation Treasury Trust No. 94X000-999999-

999999; and

(ix) Ucadia Mars Federation Treasury Trust No. 94M000-999999-999999; and

(x) Ucadia Jupiter-Europa Federation Treasury Trust No. 94J000-999999-999999; and

(xi) Ucadia Saturn-Titan Federation Treasury Trust No. 94S000-999999-999999.

4. The Primary Mission of each Ucadia Regional Union shall be:- Primary Mission of each Regional Ucadia Union

(i) To Testify to the true revelations of Ucadia; and that as many as possible hear the *Good News* of the Ucadia Model and the Golden Rule of Law, of Justice and Fair Process embodied within its canonical and sacred texts; and that as many as possible see and receive the fruits of good works of the Ucadia Model as empowered through the present most sacred Covenant and associated covenants, charters and laws; and

(ii) To Protect and Defend Ucadian Communities and the Laws of Ucadia; and all associated Covenants, Charters, Scripture, Maxims, Codes, Bylaws, Ordinances, Regulations, Policies and Orders; and to seek mutual recognition of such jurisdictional rights with foreign bodies and courts that respect and operate according to the Golden Rule of Law and Justice and Fair Process; and to ensure that in all matters pertaining to Ucadia Members that the courts of Ucadia are recognised as the first, primary and original jurisdiction for the resolution of all matters of controversy, arbitration and dispute; and

(iii) To Educate and Encourage Support of Ucadia; and to ensure that all Campuses and all Provinces and all Universities within the bounds of each Union are represented by elected and living Ucadia Members; and to ensure the formation of the Permanent elected Government of the Union and the conduct of its first elections and sittings as a valid body politic; and to convey and transfer every authority, powers, legal controls, rights, titles, accounts, registers and financial controls of the Foundation to the Permanent Union by the first day of such sittings in accord with the present sacred Covenant; and

(iv) To educate and encourage existing Non-Ucadian networks, societies and sovereign states of people that share the same common values as Ucadia to consider becoming a Society Member or a State Member and participate in the rewards and systems available for such members; and

(v) To Support and Honour the Divine Commission of each Official duly elected by Ordinary Members within the bounds of a Ucadia University of the Union within that region in ensuring the religious and fiduciary life of the Ministers and Officers of the Foundation are conducted according to the discipline and spirit of such sacred Divine Commission; and

(vi) To Honour and Protect the cultural and spiritual diversity of peoples, especially indigenous populations; and to ensure the legacies of traditional art, music, language and culture is respected and protected, particularly in vigilance against any and all forms of bigotry, oppression or vilification; and

(vii) To launch and maintain the autonomous Ucadia Financial System including the balancing of the needs of local members, smaller communities, companies, systems and larger economic problems; and

(viii) To protect and cherish all forms of life within the bounds of the Union; and to protect and defend natural habitats and endangered species; and to help reduce pollution and waste whilst restoring the environment and natural wilderness reserves.

Article 103 - Ucadia Universities, Provinces & Campuses

1. **By the power and authority of the present sacred Covenant**, all communities upon planet Earth and all colonies of Level 6 Higher Order Human Life Forms shall be organised and constituted into administrative units known as *Campuses* within administrative units known as *Provinces*, within administrative units known as *Universities*, within Administrative units known as Unions on planet Earth or a Union of a particular extra-terrestrial colony. Ucadia Universities, Provinces & Campuses

No other bodies politic, associations, corporations, companies, entities or groups representing lesser bodies may claim higher jurisdiction or validity than the administrative units ordained by Heaven in accord with the present sacred Covenant.

To give effect to the Ucadia administrative structure as the embodiment and presence of Heaven upon the Earth, the *Divina*, in accord with the Divine Creator shall authorise the complete occupation of all the first offices for each and every administrative unit at each and every administrative level of Ucadia on Earth as the

"**Provisional Spiritual and Temporal Government**" of all Ucadia Societies.

No claim of spiritual, military or sovereign right, occupation, birth right, blood right, prophecy, divine mandate, conquest, gift, election, custom, alienation, accession, waiver, seizure or power shall be valid, lawful, legal or legitimate in any way, except through the rights, authority and power granted by the present sacred Covenant.

Temporal administration shall then be vested in Ucadia Foundations for each Ucadia University until such time a more permanent administration and government is legitimately and lawfully formed, in accord with the present most sacred Covenant and associated Covenants and Charters.

2. A Ucadia "**Campus**" shall be the smallest administrative division of government and administration of a Ucadia Regional Union. A Campus is an ecclesiastically, legally and lawfully constituted administrative subdivision of a Province and is equivalent to the term "local government area" ("LGA") and the traditional terms including but not limited to "council", "city", "municipality", "borough", "shire" and "county". Ucadia Campus

A Campus shall be named and defined according to the pre-existing legislative and geographic subdivision of a state or region or province into individual districts, postcodes or boroughs.

A valid Ucadia Campus is a Superior Civil Trust and Ecclesiastical Capital Company having a mortal life not exceeding one complete standard Age of one thousand and seventy (1,070) years or approximately one third the life expectancy of the Regional Union.

A Living Member may only belong to one Campus according to the location of their current primary living location also known as domicile address.

A "**Provisional Campus**" shall be the first of five types of states of a valid Ucadia Campus. All Provisional Campuses within each Ucadia Province of each Ucadia University of the Union shall be formed on VENUS E8:Y3210:A0:S1:M27:D6, also known as [Wed, 21 Dec 2011] as the smallest operational divisions of occupational forces of One Heaven following the complete conquest of all land, sea, earth, space, time, atmosphere and spirit within the boundaries of the Campus; and lawful possession and occupation of all rights, property, title and uses within the same bounds; and the investiture of a unique and individual spiritual member into each of the twelve Original Offices of the Land being *Commissioner, Accountant, Secretary, Reader, Jurist, Proctor, Notary, Scrivener, Steward, Postmaster, Bailiff* and *Sheriff* for each and every Campus on planet Earth.

Under the terms of spiritual military occupation of *Provisional Campuses*, the boundaries and Cadastral features of each Campus within each Province shall have been properly surveyed with the Survey and Charter for each Province registered within the Great Register of the appropriate Regional Ucadia Union and the event published in the Globe Union Gazette and Ucadia Gazette.

3. A Ucadia "**Province**" shall be the second smallest operational division of government and administration of a Ucadia Regional Union. A Province is an ecclesiastically, legally and lawfully constituted subdivision of a University and is equivalent to the term "state government area" ("SGA") and the traditional terms including but not limited to "state", "region" or "territory". Ucadia Province

A valid Ucadia Province is a Superior Civil Trust and Ecclesiastical Capital Company having a mortal life not exceeding one complete standard Age of one thousand and seventy (1,070) years or approximately one third the life expectancy of a Regional Ucadia Union.

A Living Member may only belong to one Province according to the location of their current primary living location also known as domicile address.

A Ucadia "**Provisional Province**" shall be the first of five types of states of a valid Ucadia Province. All Provisional Campuses within each Province of each University of a Ucadia Regional Union shall be formed on GAIA E8:Y3210:A1:S1:M17:D1 [Tue 21 Dec 2010] as the second smallest operational divisions of occupational forces of One Heaven following the complete conquest of all land, sea, earth, space, time, atmosphere and spirit within the boundaries of the Province; and lawful possession and occupation of all rights, property, title and uses within the same bounds; and the investiture of a unique and individual spiritual member into each of the Major Offices of *Governor, Deputy Governor, Counsel, Procurator, Speaker* and *Comptroller* for each and every Ucadia Province on planet Earth.

Under the terms of spiritual military occupation, the boundaries and Cadastral features of each Province within each University within each Regional Ucadia Union shall be properly surveyed with the Survey and Charter for each Province registered within the Great Register of the Union and the event published in the Globe Union Gazette and Ucadia Gazette.

4. A Ucadia "**University**" shall be the second largest administrative division of government and administration of the Ucadia Union. A Ucadia University

University is an ecclesiastical, sovereign, official, lawful, legal and administratively constituted subdivision of the Union and is equivalent to the term "absolute sovereign domain" ("ASD") and the traditional terms including but not limited to "politea", "sovereign state", "dominion" and "independent sovereign nation".

A valid Ucadia University is a Spiritual and Supernatural Body, recognised as a true and apostolic Ecclesiastical See and Politia of supreme temporal authority of Heaven on Earth.

A valid Ucadia University is recognised as a Superior Civil Trust and Ecclesiastical Capital Company having a mortal life not exceeding one complete standard Age of one thousand and seventy (1,070) years or approximately one third the life expectancy of a Regional Ucadia Union.

A Ucadia "**Provisional University**" shall be the first of five types of states of a valid Ucadia University. All Provisional Universities within the Union shall be formed on GAIA E8:Y3209:A1:S1:M6:D1 [Mon 21 Dec 2009] as the second largest operational division of the occupational forces of One Heaven following the complete conquest of all land, sea, earth, space, time, atmosphere and spirit within the boundaries of each Ucadia Regional Union; and lawful possession and occupation of all rights, property, title and uses within the same bounds; and the investiture of a unique and individual spiritual member into each of the Twelve Great Offices of State of each Ucadia University including *President, Domestic Vice-President, International Vice-President, Dean, Chancellor, Treasurer, Prefect, Chief Justice, Chamberlain, Marshal, Narrator* and *Inspector*.

Under the terms of spiritual military occupation, the boundaries and Cadastral features of each Ucadia University within each Ucadia Regional Union shall be properly surveyed with the Survey and Charter for each University registered within the Great Register of the Regional Ucadia Union and the event published in the Globe Union Gazette and Ucadia Gazette.

Article 104 - Ucadia Foundations & Charitable Funds

1. **The Right to form Executive Government of a valid Preliminary or Probational University shall be granted by Constitutional Charter** to an association of twelve (12) competent, valid and registered Ucadia Members, to form a properly Ucadia registered body politic and corporate for the purpose of developing a permanent Ucadia political presence and interfacing with Non-Ucadian societies, entities, bodies politic, Ucadia Foundations & Charitable Funds

companies and persons.

The body formed shall be known as a "**Ucadia Foundation**" of the particular University with its initial constitutional charter granted for a maximum of four (4) years, before a new constitutional charter must be registered and issued for each and every additional four (4) years. Each valid Ucadia Foundation shall constitute the preliminary executive government of the relevant Ucadia University.

2. The primary purpose of a Ucadia Foundation being formed as the preliminary Executive Government of a Ucadia University is to assist in the development of a permanent Ucadia political presence and interfacing with Non-Ucadian societies, entities, bodies politic, companies and persons. Purpose and Operation of Ucadia Foundation

A Ucadia Foundation is therefore always a temporary body registered within Ucadia Law, but never registered within a Non-Ucadian or foreign jurisdiction. Once fifty (50 %) percent or more of the Provinces within the jurisdiction of a Ucadia University have reached Probational or Prerogative status, a Ucadia Foundation must transition power within one hundred and eighty (180) days to a Probational or Prerogative Executive Government for the Ucadia University.

3. The first one hundred and eighty days after a Ucadia Foundation is granted its Constitutional Charter shall be known as an interim period, wherein, the Council of Ucadia Foundations, upon advice of the Secretariat and Visitor and Architect, if still living and capable, may elect to immediately rescind the charter and rights of a particular Ucadia Foundation, if behaviour and actions have been established that run contrary to the agreements upon founding such a body. 180 Day Interim Period

Thereafter the interim period, the Council of Ucadia Foundations may only vote to have a Ucadia Foundation investigated for malfeasance and poor management first, before any proposed action of sanction or dissolving a Ucadia Foundation is permissible.

4. The Constitutional Charter granted to a Ucadia Foundation shall not exceed four (4) years, before it must be renewed for a further four (4) years maximum. The first year of any initial granted Constitutional Charter shall be probational, whereby the particular Ucadia Foundation may be issued with a dissolution notice, upon clear evidence of gross maladministration, malfeasance or misrepresentation, without sufficient remedy demonstrated to rectify such serious breaches of trust. Expiry and Renewal of Constitutional Charter

Whilst the initial grant of a Constitutional Charter to a Ucadia University requires a minimum association of twelve (12) suitably qualified Ucadia Members, it shall be permissible that a Foundation has its charter renewed at the time with a minimum of four (4) suitably qualified Ucadia Members.

Previous Ucadia Foundation Members that have resigned, or been expelled, or have abrogated their rights of membership shall automatically be ineligible to be recognised or registered as Foundation Members upon any renewal of the relevant Ucadia Foundation Constitutional Charter. Furthermore, any outstanding rights or obligations associated with previous Foundation Members shall also cease at the expiry of the previous Constitutional Charter for the particular Ucadia Foundation, unless rolled over by unanimous vote of Foundation Members registered under the renewed Constitutional Charter.

5. All valid and registered Ucadia Foundations for all Ucadia Universities shall *ipso facto* (as a matter of fact) be members of the Council of Ucadia Foundations. Council of Ucadia Foundations

The Council of Ucadia Foundations shall comprise of a maximum of two nominated representative from each valid and registered Ucadia Foundation for each Ucadia University, as the temporary executive government of Ucadia, subject to oversight from the Visitor and Architect, if still living and capable.

Each nominated representative shall hold such temporary office for a maximum of six months, before either being re-elected or a new member of each Ucadia Foundation is nominated.

The Council of Ucadia Foundations shall meet via digital video conferencing at least one every quarter, with the Secretariat of the Ucadia Foundations responsible for managing the agenda, voting records and minutes.

6. All temporary administrative management of procedural and executive actions shall be vested in the Secretariat of Ucadia Foundations as a single body representing the interests of all Ucadia Foundations equally. Secretariat of Ucadia Foundations

The Secretariat of Ucadia Foundations shall report directly to a Secretary and in turn the Visitor and Architect, if still living and capable.

7. Budgeting, finance and funding of Ucadia Foundations shall be vested in the Treasury of Council of Ucadia Foundations, with budgeting decisions held by the Council and day to day management held by the Secretariat of Ucadia Foundation. Treasury of Council of Ucadia Foundations

8. The following shall be the minimum qualification criteria for the Qualification Criteria for

formation of a valid Ucadia Foundation within the jurisdiction of a Ucadia University:-

Formation of Ucadia Foundation

(i) A probational Ucadia University Executive Government does not currently exist for the particular University at the time of the application; and

(ii) The conditions to recognise a probational Ucadia University Executive Government are unlikely to be met within the next sixty (60) to ninety (90) days; and

(iii) No valid and properly registered Ucadia Foundation currently exists for the Ucadia University at the time of the application; and

(iv) A minimum of twelve (12) suitable and qualified Ucadia Members living within the jurisdiction of the Ucadia University have put their names to the application; and

(v) The applicants to the formation of a Ucadia Foundation have contributed the appropriate amounts required to form an individual bond for each Ucadia Foundation Member; and

(vi) There exists no other cause or reason not to delay or deny the application at the time of its filing.

Qualification Criteria for Ucadia Foundation Members

9. The following shall be the minimum qualification criteria to be regarded as a suitable and qualified Ucadia Member capable of being accepted as a Ucadia Foundation Member:-

(i) That the Person is a Ucadia Member, having redeemed their Member number and received their Live Borne Record; and

(ii) That the Person has read the present most sacred Covenant and the Essential Ucadia Reading Material required for any potential Ucadia Foundation Member and has acknowledged their subscription to the material in writing; and

(iii) That the Person has participated in at least one verified Ucadia training session or workshop and has been suitably tested on their knowledge and support of the Ucadia Model; and

(iv) That the Person has deposited sufficient contribution in good faith toward the necessary bond as a Ucadia Foundation Member; and

(v) That the Person is not otherwise facing active legal actions or personal issues that would preclude how much time and effort they may be able to invest as a Ucadia Foundation Member;

and

(vi) That the Person is a valid inhabitant of the jurisdiction of the Ucadia University related to the proposed Ucadia Foundation; and

(vii) No other issue exists that would otherwise render the Person ineligible.

10. By definition, being a Ucadia Foundation Member is different and separate to being a Ucadia Member. A Ucadia Member is not automatically a Ucadia Foundation Member within the Ucadia University jurisdiction where they are domiciled. Ucadia Members and Ucadia Foundation Members

Being a Ucadia Foundation Member is both a privilege and a solemn obligation, to help manifest a permanent presence of Ucadia within the jurisdiction of a particular Ucadia University, as well as help support the services and operations to other Ucadia Members. As a consequence, they are required to have a stronger and deeper knowledge of the Ucadia Model and to dedicate a regular portion of their time to fulfil this prime objective.

Finally, because Ucadia Foundation Members agree to be honourable representatives of Ucadia and Ucadia Members, they are bound by a solemn oath and bond to act accordingly. Ucadia Members are not required to make such a significant contribution to become a Ucadia Member.

11. The relevant Council and Secretariat of Ucadia Foundations shall institute policies and guidelines in the interim, before the establishment of probational, prerogative and permanent bodies, concerning the appropriate types and levels of bonds associated with Ucadia Foundation Membership and Ucadia Officers. Foundation Member Bonds

12. A valid Ucadia Foundation constituted for longer than twelve (12) months, shall be granted upon application, the right to register a Charitable Fund with the non-Ucadian and foreign state associated with the jurisdiction of the relevant Ucadia University. Registered Charitable Fund

13. All Ucadia Foundation Members are bound by their oath to refrain from directly acquiring or receiving any form of assets, shares, Ucadia Money or objects of significant financial value during their time as a Ucadia Foundation Member. Foundation Member Property Interests and Payment

Other than fair financial compensation for their contribution of time and the reimbursement of any costs, Ucadia Foundation Members are forbidden from profiting from or appearing to profit from such a position of trust. This rule applies equally to the Visitor and Architect.

Any records created previously in relation to Ucadia Foundation Members stating a direct pecuniary interest or receipt of any asset must be corrected and recorded within the minutes of official meetings of the relevant Ucadia Foundation.

The prior ownership of assets by a Ucadia Foundation Member, or the acquisition of assets associated with the utilisation of services and goods of Ucadia, does not apply to the above rule, providing there is clear evidence such transactions and benefits were done with clean hands and without undue bias.

Article 105 - Ucadia & Foreign Registered Entities

1. **The formation, registration and operation of entities providing goods and services** for Ucadia Members and people identifying as non-Ucadian persons is essential to the development and sustainment of the permanent presence of Ucadia on Earth and within Sol (The Solar System). Ucadia & Foreign Registered Entities

There shall be three (3) classes of entities from the perspective of the rights and authority of Ucadia and Ucadia related bodies, namely:-

(i) Ucadia formed and registered entities; and

(ii) Ucadia formed and foreign registered entities; and

(iii) Foreign formed and Ucadia registered entities.

2. A "**Ucadia formed and registered entity**", is an association or corporation wholly registered and incorporated under Ucadia Law. Such a body is entirely subject to the laws and jurisdiction of Ucadia:- Ucadia formed and registered entities

(i) The conditions for forming, registering and operating Ucadia entities shall be determined by the Regional Ucadia Union Constitutional Charters and Codes.

3. A "**Ucadia formed and foreign registered entity**", is an association or corporation formed under Ucadian Law but also registered and incorporated within a non-Ucadian and foreign jurisdiction:- Ucadia formed and foreign registered entities

(i) Such and entity shall be subject first and foremost to the laws of the jurisdiction where they were incorporated; and then secondly to the laws of Ucadia to the extent that their constitutions/articles permit within the said jurisdiction; and

(ii) Whilst registered in a foreign jurisdiction, all Ucadia formed entities must use Ucadia Moneta as the essential unit of account of the entity; and

(iii) The conditions for forming, registering and operating Ucadia entities in non-Ucadian and foreign jurisdictions shall be determined by the Regional Ucadia Union Constitutional Charters and Codes.

4. A "**Foreign formed and Ucadia registered entity**", is an association or corporation formed under Non-Ucadian Law but registered under Ucadian law and subject to the personal jurisdiction of Ucadian courts:- Foreign formed and Ucadia registered entities

(i) Arising out of a binding contract undertaken by the foreign formed entity; or

(ii) Arising as a result of "minimum contact" being 1) direct contact with a Ucadian juridic body; or 2) having a contract with a Ucadia member of a Ucadian juridic body; or 3) have sought to legally serve a member of a Ucadian juridic body; or 4) have sought to sell products or services via a Ucadian juridic body.

5. Valid Ucadia Foundations are permitted to form, register and incorporate Ucadia entities in non-Ucadian and foreign jurisdictions under the following provisions:- Ucadia Foundation forming Foreign Registered Entities

(i) That a foreign registered charitable fund for the relevant Ucadia University jurisdiction is registered and operational before substantial cashflow, capital raising or asset accrual commences; and

(ii) That a foreign registered non-profit non-stock trust corporation is formed for the relevant Ucadia University jurisdiction, consistent with Ucadia standards in order to support the highest fiduciary management and services, before substantial cashflow, capital raising or asset accrual commences; and

(iii) That a foreign registered equity and fund management corporation is formed for the relevant Ucadia University jurisdiction, consistent with Ucadia standards in order to support the highest fiduciary management and services, before substantial cashflow, capital raising or asset accrual commences; and

(iv) Any and all "for-profit" corporations are majority controlled either by the relevant trust corporation or charitable fund for and on behalf of Ucadia Members as the ultimate beneficiaries; and

(v) Any and all asset pools created to enable efficient capital generation are owned and controlled by the relevant charitable fund; and

(vi) Any and all funds are efficiently and effectively managed by the relevant equity and fund management corporation.

Ucadia Foundation Members as Directors and Senior Executives

6. Whilst a Ucadia Foundation operates as the preliminary and probational government of a Ucadia University, all Directors and Senior Executives of Ucadia formed and foreign registered entities shall be Ucadia Foundation members:-

(i) Ucadia reserves the absolute right to ensure that positions of trust within Ucadia related entities are occupied by suitable Persons who have the interests of Ucadia and the sustainable future of humanity at heart; and

(ii) All appointments to senior positions within Ucadia related entities shall be on merit and the candidate having appropriate qualifications and skills for the position; and

(iii) All Ucadia Foundation Members accepted for senior positions within Ucadia related entities shall be expected to contribute to additional bonds commensurate with such positions of trust.

Ucadia Entity Development Sectors

7. Providing a Ucadia Foundation meets the minimum criteria of Ucadia formed foreign registered entities of the present article, a Ucadia Foundation shall expand its focus across eighteen (18) development sectors to ensure at least one or more successful entities exist for each sector, including:-

(i) Member Services & Charitable Systems; and

(ii) Financial Services & Estate Planning Systems; and

(iii) Vocational Support & Skills Development Systems; and

(iv) Technology Support & Development Systems; and

(v) Capital, Finance & Asset Management Systems; and

(vi) Legal Support & Justice Systems; and

(vii) Sustainable Homes & Community Buildings Systems; and

(viii) Facilities Management & Construction Systems; and

(ix) Market Solutions and Settlement Systems; and

(x) Media Production & Network Communication Systems; and

(xi) Health Support & Well-being Systems; and

(xii) Ethical Food & Therapeutic Systems; and

(xiii) Security & Emergency Systems; and

(xiv) Transport & Logistics Systems; and

(xv) Advanced Energy & Infrastructure Systems; and

(xvi) Disease Prevention & Sanitation Systems; and

(xvii) Environmental Protection and Preservation Systems; and

(xviii) Ethical Agriculture & Organic Systems.

TITLE XVII – REGISTERS, RECORDS & NOTICES

Article 106 – Registers & Records

1. Register shall be a book of tables recording one or more entries of statements, testimonies or memoranda as evidence as to jurisdiction and authority over certain Sacred Circumscribed Space; or the properties or attributes of such Sacred Circumscribed Space; or the rights of use of such properties and attributes; or the memorial of events concerning such Sacred Circumscribed Space, or properties or attributes, or rights of use; or the memorial of transactions and derivatives concerning the receiving or granting or claiming of rights and uses. Registers & Records

2. All records in proper, valid and legitimate Registers shall depend upon the prior recording by Authority of one or more records of Sacred Circumscribed Space as reference. If no valid records of Sacred Circumscribed Space exists, or such records are illegitimate, false, unlawful or illegal, then all subsequent Registers and Records depending upon such primary records shall also be illegitimate, false, unlawful and illegal. All Records in Registers dependent on Sacred Circumscribed Space

3. In terms of the general authority and creation of Registers:- Authority and Power relating to Registers

   (i) The Authority to form a Register shall be defined by the limits of Authority of the constituting Instrument of the relevant Trust or Estate or Fund or Entity; and

   (ii) The Rights, Powers and Property prescribed within a Register shall not exceed the Rights, Powers and Property of the Trust or Estate or Fund or Entity itself; and

   (iii) As valid and proper Registers shall record Sacred Circumscribed Space, all valid and proper Registers shall be wholly and exclusively Spiritual or Ecclesiastical Property and shall never themselves belong to the relevant Trust or Estate or Fund or Entity; and

   (iv) All valid Registers shall be hierarchical in their inheritance of Authority and validity. A Register that cannot demonstrate the provenance of its claimed authority ultimately to the present most sacred Covenant, shall have none, and shall be null and void from the beginning; and

   (v) The highest and most authoritative Register shall be the Great Register and Divine Records of Heaven in accord with the present most sacred Covenant. A Register that cannot demonstrate the provenance of its claimed authority to the Great Register and Divine Records of Heaven shall have none, and shall be null and void from the beginning; and

(vi) As all Registers are wholly and exclusively Spiritual or Ecclesiastical, absolutely no clerical or administrative act may take place in association with a Register unless by a duly authorised Officer under active and valid sacred Oath or Vow; and

(vii) The entry of a Record into a Register shall be wholly invalid unless the memorial and testimony of the act giving authority shall be done without duress, is done freely and with full knowledge and is consistent and in accord with the present most sacred Covenant.

4. In terms of the general purpose, function and operation of a valid Register:- Purpose, Function and Operation of Register

(i) A Register as a table shall contain at least three (3) or more columns; and

(ii) A Register as a table shall be a section of a Book, or a whole series of Books; and

(iii) A Register shall be held in the care of a proper Officer possessing the Spiritual or Ecclesiastical Authority to hold, enter and keep custody of such Records; and

(iv) A Register shall not create the original fact or authority that it records, but shall reflect the pertinent elements in relation to the originating Instrument used to create a valid entry; and

(v) An entry in a Register shall never create Sacred Circumscribed Space itself. However, a valid entry in a Register shall be itself a valid event and by virtue of the "joining" of information at the time of registration shall permit the creation, conveyance or suppression of certain Rights or recording of certain Facts or Truths as *prima facie* Evidence; and

(vi) A particular form of Right of Use in relation to Property shall only be recorded once in a valid Register. Those specific Registers as prescribed by the present most sacred Covenant and Ucadian Law shall always be Registers of Original Record and shall take precedence over all lesser claimed registers and rolls; and

(vii) The claimed day or time of entry of a record into lesser or foreign claimed register shall have no bearing or merit in law, where a similar record for the same Property, or Event, or Right exists within a valid Register in the control of a valid Ucadian Trust or Estate or Fund or Entity, even if the day or time of entry in the Register associated with a valid Ucadian Trust or

Estate or Fund or Entity is after the day or time of entry in the lesser or foreign claimed register; and

(viii) Any lesser or foreign claimed register that seeks to usurp the Authority of a valid Register associated with a valid Ucadian Trust or Estate or Fund or Entity shall automatically render such a claimed register invalid and illegitimate, meaning that such a claimed register is determined to be null and void, having no force or effect in law.

Design and Construction of Register

5. All valid Registers as Tables shall be constructed from the same essential elements of *Columna*, *Singulus*, *Eventus*, *Locus*, *Nomen*, *Informas*, *Datus*, *Informatio*, *Ordo* and *Recordo*:

(i) *Columna* shall mean a vertical line of entries (a column), usually read from top to bottom and separated from other columns by lines; and

(ii) *Singulus* shall mean a unique column being the first and left most column whereby a whole integer is listed and is sequential (beginning from the integer 1) and unique (not the same) in reference to the table; and

(iii) *Eventus* shall mean a column whereby the Ucadia Date and Time of a unique event as well any other referential time (such as Roman Date/Time) that shall always be listed in brackets; and

(iv) *Locus* shall mean a column whereby the Ucadia Location Number of Sacred Circumscribed Space and any common name as to the location of the unique event is listed; and

(v) *Nomen* shall mean a column whereby a name is given to the event or the object or concept or property or rights associated with the event; and

(vi) *Informas* shall mean a column whereby a name of the one who granted the authority to have the entry made into the Register; and

(vii) *Datus* shall mean the Ucadia Date and Time the grant was given by the Informant as well as any other referential time such as Roman Date/Time in Square Brackets that the entry was made; and

(viii) *Informatio* shall mean any additional information provided by the Informant that may be separated into its own unique columns; and

(ix) *Ordo* shall mean the line of entries in a table, from left to right that when completed forms a valid Record; and

(x) *Recordo* shall mean a complete line of entries into the columns of the table from left to right such that the record has its own unique form and is "Legal Title".

6. A "**Record**" shall be a written memorial of actions or events, and accounts entered under promise, testification, certification or attestation as Fact; and the conveyances of Proof of such Fact then preserved as knowledge and authentic history of the causes within such entries, united by some Identifier within Memoranda, Journals and Register of a valid Trust or Estate or Fund or Entity. Record

7. A valid Record shall comprise of three (3) actions entered into three Books:- Valid Record

(i) The Event shall be the first action, entered into a Memorandum as a true written memorial to the "event" and associated proceedings and actions; and

(ii) The Witnessed Account shall be the second action, as attestation to an Account or Affidavit entered into a Journal as an attestation to the true Summary of Facts, with a unique Event Number then "posted back" to the Memorandum as well as "cancelling" those details within the Memorandum now "posted" in the Journal; and

(iii) The Conveyance shall be the third action, as proof of a valid "event" to a Register, by a Summary Letter or Certificate as a True Summary of Account or Instrument of Record, with the unique Entry then "posted forward" to the Register as the completion of the Record.

8. The following forms of Registers shall be recognised and used by Ucadian bodies and entities, consistent with the present most sacred Covenant and Ucadian Law, including (but not limited to):- Forms of Registers

(i) A *Gazette* shall be a form of Register as a Public Journal and Authorised Newspaper of Record; and

(ii) An *Almanac* shall be a form of Register of information and events for a given subject, collected and arranged for a given year; and

(iii) An *Account* shall be a form of Register as arrangements of Computations, Valuations and Derivations using some standard unit of value, measure, record or exchange on the nature, value and disposition of objects, concepts and property of a valid Trust or Estate or Fund or Corporation; and

(iv) A *Memoranda* shall be a form of Register in chronological order, detailing the substance of formal notes or "memorandum" including (but not be limited to) minutes, resolutions, proceedings, accounts, letters, correspondence, decisions and procedural actions; and

(v) A *Journal* shall be a form of Register derived as a summary extract of information from Memoranda and arranged in category order and then chronological order to produce a summary of facts, evidence, quantities and relations for the purpose of accounting and reckoning of the debits and credits of the Trust or Estate or Fund or Entity; and

(vi) A *Ledger* shall be a form of Register as a summary extract of Journal entries to produce the most concise reckonings and balances of debits and credits, assets and liabilities of the Trust or Estate or Fund or Entity; and

(vii) A *Roll* shall be a form of Register of one or more entries being "persons" of the same condition of entry, or the same engagement of obligations in relation to a valid Trust or Estate or Fund or Corporation; and created by their valid entry into the Roll; and

(viii) A *Manifest* shall be a form of Register being evidential history of the provenance, possession and ownership of any property, rights, money or other interests recorded as associated with a Trust or Estate or Fund or Entity; and

(ix) An *Estate* shall be a form of Register and Roll or Record of a Roll of certain Rights held in Trust for a period of years for a Person or group of Persons, whereby one or more Inventories and Valuations have been properly conducted; and

(x) An *Inventory* shall be a form of Register being a detailed survey and census of all property, assets and liabilities, debits or credits of a valid Trust, or Estate or Fund or Entity completed immediately after its creation; or the anniversary of its creation; or upon another fixed and given day; and the stock of particular items and their location or business; and

(xi) A *Valuation* shall be a form of Register and Roll (also historically known as a Tax or Rating) being a detailed estimation of the value of each item as listed upon an Inventory of a valid Trust, or Estate or Fund or Entity; and

(xii) A *Fund* shall be a form of Register of equal units representing certain Property Rights of one or more Estates of monetary value that can then be used as a means of exchange for lawful money or for the discharge of debts and obligations.

9. Every prescribed and valid Register and Roll of Ucadia organs, bodies and entities shall be uniquely numbered by a *Unique Register Number*. The Register Number shall be the extracted Record Number from the Greater Register and Divine Records of Heaven as the *Register of Registers*. A Register or Roll that does not possess a valid Unique Register Number shall *ipso facto* (as a matter of fact) be invalid and illegitimate. Unique Register Number

10. The process whereby the authority of one Person on one Roll shall be given legitimacy by the authority and consent of a previously created Person record on another Roll shall be called "**Joinder**" of Person:- Joinder

(i) Joinder shall require that a party is given Notice of Joinder with clear intention to "join" one person from a Roll held in custody with the authority and permissions of a Roll not immediately within their jurisdiction; and

(ii) The names of both persons must be the same in order for a valid Joinder of Person. Otherwise, such a Joinder shall be a Joinder in Action, requiring separate consent; and

(iii) The failure to make clear the Notice of Joinder as an intention to Join shall be a fraud and shall render such action a Misjoinder and maladministration; and

(iv) The failure to produce sufficient evidence of the Right to Joinder of Person, shall automatically render such action a Misjoinder; and

(v) No non-Ucadian or foreign state, body, agency or entity may seek Joinder with a Ucadia Person; and

(vi) By innate Right of the present most sacred Covenant, all Ucadian organs, bodies and entities shall have authority of Joinder over non-Ucadian and foreign inferior persons, where such persons are associated with Ucadia Members.

Article 107 – Great Register and Divine Records of Heaven

1. **Great Register and Divine Records of Heaven** shall be the highest and most authoritative possible spiritual, ecclesiastical, temporal, sovereign, official and administrative Register. The "**Great Register and Divine Records of Heaven**" shall also be known as:- Great Register and Divine Records of Heaven

(i) Register of Registers; and

(ii) Great Roll of Divine Persons; and

(iii) Great Book of Spirits; and

(iv) Great Record of Space-Day-Time; and

(v) Great Book of Life; and

(vi) Great Register of Rights; and

(vii) Great Register of Land and Title; and

(viii) Great Register of Oaths, Vows and Promises; and

(ix) Great Roll of Offices and Officers; and

(x) Great Register of Covenants, Commissions & Contracts.

When a thing or object or concept has spirit and life, when a thing has valid legal personality, then it is granted a valid Record Number into the Great Register and Divine Records of Heaven. No two (2) spiritual existing entities will have the same Record Entry in the Great Register and Divine Records of Heaven.

Valid Register Entry

2. A Valid Register Entry shall be the minimum required information recorded into the Great Register after a Form has been accepted. A Valid Register Entry includes a Unique Register Key as well as associated information. The minimum required information for a Valid Register Entry, shall include (but shall not be limited to):-

(i) A Unique Identifying Number also called the Unique Register Number (URN); and

(ii) A Name for the Register Entry; and

(iii) The Day of entry into the Register; and

(iv) The Member that petitioned for the entry of the Record; and

(v) The Capacity (Office) of the Member as Petitioner; and

(vi) The Registrar that approved the entry.

Unique Register Number (URN)

3. The Unique Register Number (URN) shall represent a Unique Register Key that is created from the unique combination of eight (8) Unique Ledger Numbers, each comprising a combination of eighteen (18) digits so that the total number, excluding spaces or dashes is equal to the number one hundred and forty-four (144). A "Short Form" Unique Register Number represents the first eighteen (18) digits of an existing Unique Register Key of the Public Record. The "Standard Form" order of Unique Ledger Numbers to form a Valid Unique Register Number of 144 digits shall be:

(i) Unique Ledger Number; and

(ii) Unique Society Number; and
(iii) Unique Member Number; and
(iv) Unique Office Number; and
(v) Unique Category Number; and
(vi) Unique Space-Day-Time Number; and
(vii) Unique Notice Number; and
(viii) Unique Registrar Number.

4. The "**Universal Form Code**" (UFC) shall be a standard for the naming, construction, recording and management of standard permitted forms, completed forms and the information contained within. The UFC Identifier shall be an eighteen (18) digit number that uniquely identifies each and every valid form received and accepted by all Ucadian Societies. No two forms will ever have the same UFC Identifier. The Universal Form Code is based on (1) An Alpha Prefix of two characters, then (2) four numbers representing category and standard form, then (3) twelve characters representing the unique society and number of the form. The Standard Form Classifications for all types of forms shall be:

Universal Form Code (UFC)

(i) [AA] Agriculture & Environment; and
(ii) [KK] Budget, Revenue & Treasury; and
(iii) [CC] Companies, Trusts & Funds; and
(iv) [DD] Disease Prevention & Sanitation; and
(v) [EE] Education; and
(vi) [FF] Food & Drugs; and
(vii) [GG] Executive Government; and
(viii) [HH] Health & Fitness; and
(ix) [II] Industry, Infrastructure & Energy; and
(x) [JJ] Justice, Constitutional & International Law; and
(xi) [BB] Accounts, Banking & Financial Transactions; and
(xii) [LL] Sovereign, Estates & Legislative; and
(xiii) [MM] Military; and
(xiv) [NN] Trade; and
(xv) [PP] Police & Emergency; and
(xvi) [QQ] Divine & Ecclesiastical Law; and

(xvii) [RR] Culture & Entertainment; and

(xviii) [SS] Members, History & Community; and

(xix) [TT] Transport & Travel; and

(xx) [UU] Building & Construction; and

(xxi) [VV] Elections; and

(xxii) [WW] Employment & Temporary Assistance; and

(xxiii) [XX] Land, Rights & Civil Law; and

(xxiv) [YY] Criminal Law; and

(xxv) [ZZ] Technology, Communications & Knowledge Systems; and

(xxvi) [OO] Civil Service.

5. Only Divine and Permitted Forms shall be entered into the Great Register and Divine Records of Heaven. A Divine form is mandated by the Divine in accord with the present most sacred Covenant. A Permitted Form shall be when: Permitted Form

(i) An Instrument is identified as an Approved Form as defined by the present most sacred Covenant, or associated Rules and Procedures of Ucadian Law; and

(ii) The Instrument possesses the minimum information required for a Valid Register Entry; and

(iii) The Instrument does not require material correction, alteration or addition; and

(iv) The Member as Petitioner is not precluded from requesting such an entry, or otherwise temporarily banned from such services; and

(v) The Instrument does not contradict any of the provisions of the present most sacred Covenant and Ucadian Law.

6. By the present most sacred Covenant of the Supreme Patron and the *Treaty of the Divine Masculine*, the *Treaty of the Divine Feminine*, the *Treaty of the Divine Messengers* and the *Treaty of Angels, Saints and Demons*, to End the War in Heaven, thereby establishing conditions by which War on Earth may also be Ended; and the *Treaty of The Suns* that protects the Solar System; and the *Treaty of The Planets and Moons* that shall heal this Earth, all Level 6 Life Forms and higher order beings are entered as Valid Record Entries into the Public Record of One Heaven by virtue of being assigned their Membership Number of One Heaven. All Level 6 Life Forms and higher order beings

Therefore, no Level 6 Life Form can be claimed to be denied their enrolment in the Great Roll of Divine Persons also known as the Great Ledger and Public Record of One Heaven.

7. The Entry into the Great Register and Public Record is the Original, being a spiritual entry into the highest spiritual register with all subsequent physical documents as authenticated extracts.

Entry into Public Record as Original Records

8. When an instrument is registered into the Divine Record and Great Register of One Heaven it possesses life and spirit. Therefore, when an authenticated extract of this instrument is issued, the spiritual instrument is connected always as the true spiritual original.

Effect of entry into Great Register of One Heaven

9. The supreme dignity and right to sole and exclusive temporal custody for the Great Register and Divine Records of Heaven, also known as *Register of Registers*, also known as *Great Roll of Divine Persons*, also known as *Great Book of Spirits*, also known as *Great Record of Space-Day-Time*, also known as *Great Book of Life*, also known as *Great Register of Rights*, also known as *Great Register of Land and Title*, also known as *Great Register of Oaths, Vows and Promises*, also known as *Great Roll of Offices and Officers* and also known as *Great Register of Covenants, Commissions & Contracts,* shall be permanently and irrevocably delegated to the three (3) great faiths of One Christ, One Islam and One Spirit as Trustees with the Globe Union as sole Agent, subject to the life of the three (3) great faiths, in accord with the present most sacred Covenant and no other:-

Temporal Administrative Authority and Control of Great Register and Divine Records of Heaven

(i) If the permanent Ucadia Globe Union is not yet constituted, then sole authority and administration shall be delegated equally to one or more permanent Ucadia Regional Unions; and

(ii) If no permanent Ucadia Regional Unions are yet constituted, then sole authority and administration shall be delegated equally to one or more permanent Ucadia Universities; and

(iii) If no permanent Ucadia Universities are yet constituted, then sole authority and administration shall be delegated equally to one or more Ucadia Foundations.

Article 108 – Notices & Gazettes

1. **All formal or official communication or service** concerning any spiritual, ecclesiastical, sovereign, legal or administrative matter that may affect certain Rights, Obligations or Duties shall be firmly bound by the present rule of Notice of One Heaven.

Notices

The seven (7) primary types of notice that shall be used by the present sacred Covenant and associated covenants, charters and constitutions shall be Spiritual, Physical, Direct, Indirect, Public, Implied and Constructive:

(i) "**Spiritual Notice**" shall be a type of notice and service of process whereby the specific information concerning a formal ecclesiastical matter is properly constituted within the appropriate form as defined by the present sacred Covenant and then vocalised within consecrated space, before being duly registered within the proper records of the Ucadia organ, body or entity. Such notice is the highest possible form of notice; and

(ii) "**Physical Notice**" or "Actual Notice" shall be a type of notice and service of process whereby the specific information concerning a formal ecclesiastical, sovereign, legal or administrative matter is listed in a Document and then physically handed to a party or their representative, with proof, attestation or acknowledgement of such service recorded as evidence; and

(iii) "**Direct Notice**" or "Posted Notice" or "Mail Notice" shall be a type of notice and service of process whereby specific information concerning the formal ecclesiastical, sovereign, legal or administrative matter is personally addressed to the party and sent through a certified or registered mail delivery system, or via email, fax, or sms or some other recorded and verifiable transmission medium; and

(iv) "**Indirect Notice**" shall be a type of notice and service of process whereby specific information concerning the formal ecclesiastical, sovereign, legal or administrative matter is published in any broadcast medium such as media releases, stories, advertorial content and advertising and likely to be viewed by one or more parties; and

(v) "**Public Notice**" shall be a type of notice and service of process whereby specific information concerning the formal ecclesiastical, sovereign, legal or administrative matter is published in a Company, local, regional, national or international publication possessing status as a gazette and therefore an official newspaper of record or physically posted at a site reasonably expected to be visible to the Person; and

(vi) "**Implied Notice**" shall be a type of notice inferred from facts that a Person had means of knowing and would have caused a reasonable Person to take action to gain further information concerning a formal ecclesiastical, sovereign, legal or administrative matter. It is a notice inferred or imputed to a party by reason of his/her knowledge collateral to the main fact; and

(vii) "**Constructive Notice**" shall be a type of notice inferred from facts that a Person unable to be served with Physical Notice may be reasonably inferred or imputed to have received notice, if Physical Notice was restricted or not possible and a minimum number of attempts of Physical, Direct, Indirect or Public Notice were concluded.

2. It shall be a fundamental element of true justice that a party shall be made aware of any accusation of alleged culpability or violation against the law. Unless a party is made aware of the particular law as well as the particular accusations, then any ruling, edict, sanction or penalty cannot be said to be fair or just. Principle of Fair Notice

In contrast, when a party shall be clearly "put on notice" that they are in violation of one or more laws, yet continue such actions of violation, then such fair notice shall be considered by logic and reason to be sufficient evidence and proof of knowledge of their own wrong doing.

When a party is then given multiple notices of multiple violations and opportunities to cure and remediate such behaviour, yet continue such actions of violation, then any subsequent decree, or judgement in accord with the present sacred Covenant shall be taken as final, lawful, moral and absolute.

3. The Principle of Service of Process or simple "Service" shall be the procedure whereby a party to a spiritual, ecclesiastical, sovereign, legal or administrative matter is given appropriate notice of any action scheduled to be heard and judged by a properly constituted forum of law, having jurisdiction over the matter. Principle of Service of Process

As all living higher order life forms on planet Earth are *ipso facto* (as a matter of fact) Members of One Heaven and all spirits, angels and demons are *ipso facto* (as a matter of fact) Members of One Heaven, a properly constituted forum of law, not exceeding its authority in accord with the present sacred Covenant has absolute and perfect Personal Jurisdiction over all the parties through proper Service of Process.

A properly constituted forum of law possesses territorial jurisdiction to the extent of its powers under the present sacred Covenant and the location of the parties.

Subject Matter Jurisdiction shall be established upon the voluntary consent of parties, or involuntary actions of dishonour of the parties, whereby their failure to act with dignity and respect is public notice of their delinquency, incompetency and acceptance of jurisdiction of the properly constituted forum of law in accord with the present sacred Covenant.

4. Notice shall be deemed to have been properly and duly served, when: Service of Notice

(i) "**Spiritual Notice**" shall be deemed properly and duly served when: (a) the vocalised act within consecrated space is witnessed by two (2) or more persons whether present or upon hearing the audio recording; and (b) duly registered within the proper records of the Ecclesia; and (c) the expiry of three (3) days; and

(ii) "**Physical Notice**" or "Actual Notice" shall be deemed properly and duly served when: (a) served personally or left at the registered address by a servicing agent; and (b) such fact is attested by a certificate of service signed by the agent who executed the service; and (c) the expiry of one day; and

(iii) "**Direct Notice**" or "Posted Notice" or "Mail Notice" shall be deemed properly and duly served when: (a) the envelope or email or fax or sms was properly addressed; and (b) a receipt or certificate of transmission is properly recorded and signed by the transmission agent; and (c) the expiry of seven (7) days; and

(iv) "**Indirect Notice**" shall be deemed properly and duly served when: (a) receipt or proof of publication or broadcast of such notice is signed by the publishing agent; and (b) the expiry of three (3) days after publication or broadcast; and

(v) "**Public Notice**" shall be deemed properly and duly served when: (a) receipt or proof of publication in a valid Gazette and official publication of record; and (b) the expiry of three (3) days; and

(vi) "**Implied Notice**" shall be deemed properly and duly served when: (a) receipt or proof of publication of at least two (2) forms of Direct Notice or Indirect Notice or Public Notice exists; and (b) fourteen (14) days have expired; and

(vii) "**Constructive Notice**" shall be deemed properly and duly served when (a) receipt or proof of publication of at least one form of Spiritual Notice or Physical Notice; and (b) at least two (2) forms of Direct Notice or Indirect Notice or Public Notice exists; and (c) fourteen (14) days have expired.

5. "**Perfected Notice of Service**" shall be when different forms of Notice have been properly and duly served to such a level and extent that the persons as parties to the spiritual, ecclesiastical, sovereign, legal or administrative matter should have known of its existence; and that a reasonable person would have known of its existence, even if such a person claims no actual knowledge of it. Perfected Notice of Service

Therefore, Perfected Notice of Service shall be the point whereby no reasonable person, or competent forum of law, can argue against proper service of process, even if they continue to dispute jurisdiction or the subject or facts of the matter.

In accord with the present sacred Covenant, all writs, bills, summons (libellus), citations, edicts, decrees, notices and instructions associated with the Day and Year of Divine Agreement and Understanding; and the Day and Year of Divine Protest and Dishonour; and the Day and Year of Divine Judgement; and the Day and Year of Divine Redemption are deemed Perfected Notice of Service and not subject to dispute, appeal or protest.

6. Eleven (11) forms of Divine Notice, or "Notitiae Divinum Iurium" shall exist, namely Divine Notice of Event, Divine Notice of Right, Divine Notice of Action, Divine Notice of Decree, Divine Notice of Law, Divine Notice of Summons, Divine Notice of Writ, Divine Notice of Exception, Divine Notice of Authority, Divine Notice of Testament and Divine Notice of Obligation:- Types of Divine Notices

(i) "**Divine Notice of Event**" also known as *Notitiae Divinum Eventus*, shall be a type of notice whereby notice is given of a unique event recorded first, primarily and absolutely within the records of One Heaven and no other. A Live Borne Record is evidence of a Divine Notice of Event whereby any other claim of recording of a birth or delivery of a living Human Being is a fraud, perfidy, apostasy, heresy, profanity and immoral act unless it first references the true event within the records of One Heaven as the first, highest and official record of event; and

(ii) "**Divine Notice of Right**" also known as *Notitiae Divinum Ius*, shall be a type of notice whereby notice is given of a Divine, or Natural or Superior Right; and

(iii) "**Divine Notice of Action**" also known as *Notitiae Divinum Actum*, shall be a type of notice whereby notice of an action within a competent forum of law is properly noticed; and

(iv) "**Divine Notice of Decree**" also known as *Notitiae Divinum Decretum*, shall be a type of notice whereby notice is proven by genuine scripture in accord with Article 37 (*Supreme Sacred Texts*) of the present sacred Covenant; and

(v) "**Divine Notice of Law**" also known as *Notitiae Divinum Iuris*, shall be a type of notice whereby notice of a formal decree is given; and

(vi) "**Divine Notice of Summons**" also known as *Notitiae Divinum Citationis*, shall be a type of notice whereby notice of a summons or citation is published; and

(vii) "**Divine Notice of Writ**" also known as *Notitiae Divinum Recto*, shall be a type of notice whereby notice of a Divine or Sovereign writ is listed; and

(viii) "**Divine Notice of Exception**" also known as *Notitiae Divinum Rogatio*, shall be a type of notice whereby notice of a Divine or Sovereign Bill is listed; and

(ix) "**Divine Notice of Authority**" also known as *Notitiae Divinum Potentis*, shall be a type of notice whereby notice of the bestowing of some authority or commission to a person is properly noticed; and

(x) "**Divine Notice of Testament**" also known as *Notitiae Divinum Testamentum*, shall be a type of notice whereby notice of an Affidavit or other form of testimony is provided; and

(xi) "**Divine Notice of Obligation**" also known as *Notitiae Divinum Obligationis*, shall be a type of notice whereby notice of an obligation, or promise or bond is noticed.

7. A *Notitiae Divinum Eventus* or Divine Notice of Event shall be any valid Notice issued under the rules of the present most sacred Covenant bringing Divine Notice of the fact of an event. The issue of any such certificate or authorised extract or Gazette Notice in relation to a sacred space-time event shall be equivalent to a formal *Notitiae Divinum Eventus* as evidence; and proof of a first in time, highest title and right association to such an event.

Notitiae Divinum Eventus (Divine Notice of Event)

The existence therefore of any instrument or document issued by an inferior body or non-Ucadian aligned society claiming some right or ownership in direct contradiction to an event clearly identified through a *Notitiae Divinum Eventus* shall itself be an open confession of perfidy, profanity, repugnancy, malice, heresy and apostasy against all forms of valid law of Heaven and Earth.

8. A *Notitiae Divinum Ius* or a Divine Notice of Right shall be any valid

Notitiae Divinum Ius

Notice issued under the rules of this Sacred Covenant bringing Divine Notice and therefore the power of life to Valid Offices of the Society, Titles of Land, Water and Space and all Valid Rights and Commissions to Office. (Divine Notice of Right)

By the rules of this most sacred Covenant, all Office must be duly created by Divine Notice and thereby granted a valid record number in the Great Register and Divine Records of Heaven as having eternal spiritual life and real existence and legal personality.

9. A "**Gazette**" shall be a public journal and authorised newspaper of Record and Public Notice. Gazette

10. The "**Ucadia Gazette**" shall be the most authoritative and highest Gazette, published by Divine Authority in accordance with the present most sacred Covenant; and is the Official Newspaper of Record for Ucadia; and a modern, efficient way to disseminate and record official, regulatory and lawful information in print, online and electronic forms. Ucadia Gazette

The production of a copy of an official publication of the Ucadia Gazette or its associated lesser Gazettes, containing a copy of an order or adjudication shall be evidence of a fact in all competent forums of law.

TITLE XVIII – CONSENSUS, OBLIGATIONS & PERFORMANCE

Article 109 – Consensus, Obligations & Performance

1. **The expression of Free Will and Choice, as demonstrated by the present most sacred Covenant**, permits Beings to solemnly commit through their Persons to one or more Acts regarding certain Obligations concerning Property or Rights. Such formal commitments, whether it be one person, or many people, shall be known as "Consensus". Consensus, Obligations & Performance

Henceforth, by the Divine Rights *Ius Divinum Instrumentalis*, all forms of concord shall be more properly defined as a form of Consensus including (but not limited to) any accordance, agreement, arrangement, alliance, assent, auction, bargain, bid, charter, claim, compact, concession, concordat, concurrence, conformance, congruence, contract, correspondence, covenant, deal, decision, deed, determination, judgement, lease, order, pact, query, ruling, settlement, treaty, understanding, union or will.

2. There shall be only four (4) possible arrangements of Consensus being Unilateral, Bilateral, Multilateral and Trilateral:- Arrangements of Consensus

(i) "**Unilateral Consensus**" shall be when a single living Being through their Person commits to one or more Obligations; and

(ii) "**Bilateral Consensus**" shall be when two (2) Beings through their Persons reach an agreement of mutual Obligations; and

(iii) "**Multilateral Consensus**" shall be when three (3) or more Beings through their Persons reach a common agreement and Obligations; and

(iv) "**Trilateral Consensus**" shall be when a Being through their Person agrees to one or more Obligations for receiving a benefit vested to a third party as trustee, to ensure the performance of the obligation and terms of the agreement.

3. An "**Obligation**" shall mean a moral duty or legal duty whereby one or more parties as "**Obligants**" are bound to act or refrain from acting. An Obligation thus shall impose on the "**Obligor**" a duty to perform and shall at the same time create a corresponding right to demand performance by the "**Obligee**" to whom the performance is to be tendered:- Obligation

(i) A legal duty shall mean a "**Legal Obligation**" as one that shall be enforceable by a competent forum of law having jurisdiction; and

(ii) A moral duty shall mean a "**Moral Obligation**" as one that is owned and ought to be performed, but that is not legally bound to be fulfilled.

4. "**Performance**" shall mean the accomplishment of a promise, a covenant or other obligation of a Consensus, according to its terms. Performance

5. A "**Condition**" shall mean a declaration or provision that shall make the existence of a Right dependent on the occurrence of an event. Condition

6. As an enforceable agreement, a Consensus must meet eight (8) key elements being authorisation, comprehension, intention, consideration, obligation, negotiation, acceptation and registration:- Fundamental Elements of Consensus

   (i) *Authorisation* means a party must first have the legal and moral authority to enter into a Consensus; and

   (ii) *Comprehension* means each party must demonstrate a clear level of understanding as to entering into a Consensus; and

   (iii) *Intention* means each party must intend to enter into a Consensus; and

   (iv) *Consideration* means there must be something of substance on offer as part of the Consensus; and

   (v) *Obligation* means there must be at least one promise associated with a legal duty or moral duty; and

   (vi) *Negotiation* means there must be a meeting of minds negotiated before a Consensus is accepted; and

   (vii) *Acceptation* means there must be evidence that the Consensus was accepted and thus the terms enforceable; and

   (viii) *Registration* means the Consensus Instrument as well as the key information was duly registered and recorded in a valid and proper Register of Consensus.

7. A Consensus shall be legally and morally unenforceable unless in writing as an Instrument then registered and recorded in a proper Register of Consensus. At a minimum, the Register of Consensus shall take note of:- Registration of Consensus Instrument

   (i) The names, addresses and details of the parties of the Consensus, including witnesses and any guarantors or insurers; and

   (ii) The specific obligations of the Consensus, including any dates and amounts or measures; and

   (iii) The value and nature of the considerations of the Consensus; and

(iv) The agreed penalties for breach and the agreed time frames and terms of remedy.

8. The memorialisation of a Consensus into an Instrument shall be Conditional, Executed or Executory:- Consensus as Instrument

(i) *Conditional Consensus Instrument* shall be when the operation or effect of the consensus is dependent upon the existence of certain facts or the performance of a condition or the happening of a contingency; and

(ii) *Executed Consensus Instrument* shall be when the instrument refers to past events, which are at once closed and nothing further remains to be done by the parties but perform; and

(iii) *Executory Consensus Instrument* shall be when referral is made to some significant event to be performed in the future and there such an instrument is often preliminary to some Executed Consensus Instrument.

9. A "**Breach**" of Consensus shall be a legal cause of action whereby a binding Consensus is not honoured by one or more of the parties to the Consensus by non-performance or interference with the other party's performance. There shall be primarily three (3) classes of breaches of Consensus: Minor, Material and Fundamental: Breach of Consensus

(i) A M*inor Breach*, also known as a partial breach shall be when the non-breaching party is only entitled to collect the actual amount of damages and not for any order for performance of obligations; and

(ii) A M*aterial Breach,* shall be any failure to perform that permits the other party of the Consensus to either compel performance or collect damages because of the breach; and

(iii) A F*undamental Breach,* shall be a breach so fundamental that it permits the aggrieved party to terminate performance of the agreement, in addition to entitling that party to sue for damages.

10. By the Divine Rights *Ius Divinum Compensationis Instrumentum*, all validly formed and registered Consensus agreements shall possess the right of Relief, Redress or Compensation for Default or Delinquency of Obligation. Right of Relief, Redress or Compensation

11. No Consensus may be signed, sealed or executed by an Officer, or Agent or any representative of a Ucadia organ, body or entity if such Consensus was formed on the basis of an unlawful, or illegal or immoral act; or contains such clauses that may be reasonably construed as contrary to the norms of Ucadian law and morality, Unlawful, Illegal and Immoral agreements forbidden including but not limited to:-

(i) Bribery, Extortion or Kick-Backs; or

(ii) Anti-Competitive Practices; or

(iii) Fraud or Bad Faith Denial of Contract; or

(iv) Restraint of Trade; or

(v) Threat and Duress; and

(vi) Charges and Demands where there is no evidence of value for money, or fair market value is provided.

Article 110 – Covenants & Conventions

1. **A Covenant shall be a registered Instrument of Consensus regarding one or more promises**. In reference to Covenants:- Covenants

(i) A Covenant must be duly registered and recorded within a proper Ucadia register to be valid and legitimate; and

(ii) When the Covenant relates to Sovereign, Official, Administrative or Member Rights, then the Covenant shall be named according to the larger form of the Consensus (such as Convention, Commission or Contract); and

(iii) When the Covenant relates to Divine or Ecclesiastical Rights in some substantial way, then the Instrument and Consensus shall be known as a Covenant.

2. A "**Convention**" shall be a registered Instrument of Consensus made between two (2) or more Persons in Equity, whereby each party possesses certain distinct Rights and makes certain Promises in relation to individual Obligations to the Agreement, capable of being enforced in their distinct and independent characters. In reference to Conventions:- Convention

(i) A Convention must be duly registered and recorded within a proper Ucadia register to be valid and legitimate; and

(ii) A Convention shall be known as a Treaty when between a Ucadia Campus, or Province or University and a Non-Ucadian state, or foreign agency.

Article 111 – Commissions

1. **A Commission shall be a registered Instrument of Consensus possessing certain Divine, or Ecclesiastical or Sovereign authority** that bestows or surrenders one or more Rights. In reference to Commissions:- Commissions
   - (i) A Commission must be duly registered and recorded within a proper Ucadia register to be valid and legitimate; and
   - (ii) All original conveyance of valid and legitimate Rights and Powers shall be by Commission and no other form of Consensus; and
   - (iii) All conveyance of Real Property shall be by Commission; and
   - (iv) A Commission through proper authority and record of intention and action of conveyance is the means of creating valid Title to Property.
2. All Commissions are Unilateral, Bilateral, Trilateral, Multilateral or Inferior:- Types of Commissions
   - (i) *Unilateral Commission* shall be made by one person or by several persons of the same interest; and attested by an authorised Ucadian Officer having Ecclesiastical Notarial Powers; and
   - (ii) *Bilateral Commission* shall be made between two (2) parties; and attested by an authorised Ucadian Officer having Ecclesiastical Notarial Powers; and
   - (iii) *Trilateral Commission* shall be made between three (3) parties; and attested by an authorised Ucadian Officer having Ecclesiastical Notarial Powers; and
   - (iv) *Multilateral Commission* shall be made between four (4) or more parties; and attested by an authorised Ucadian Officer having Ecclesiastical Notarial Powers; and
   - (v) *Inferior Claim* or *Deed* shall be any form of Consensus issued under Non-Ucadian or Foreign Law, whereby no valid or legitimate Divine, Ecclesiastical or Sovereign Right shall exist, except by limited record with an authorised Ucadian Officer having Ecclesiastical Notarial Powers.
3. The general principles concerning Inferior Claims, also known as Deeds shall be:- General Principles of Inferior Claims (Deeds)
   - (i) No conveyance of Ucadia Rights, Powers or Property may be by

Deed; and

(ii) Authorised Officers are permitted to execute Deeds for the purpose of registrations necessary in Non-Ucadian and foreign jurisdictions.

4. A "**Trust Commission**" shall be a Legal Instrument by a Trustor that defines the parameters, scope and constraints of authority in relation to the Trustee. A Trust Deed is not the actual instrument that conveys certain Rights and Property, but the Deed that creates the "container" for such transfer to be effected. However, a Trust Deed is permitted to define the agreement for vesting and transfers to occur upon or after the execution of the Trust Deed. Trust Commission

5. A "**Vesting Commission**" shall be a deed that effects the transfer of a Right or Property into a Trust. By definition, the Trust must already exist, via a Trust Deed. The general and logical reason that a Vesting Deed cannot occur until a Trust is formed, is a Vesting Deed is in essence a Deed Poll executed by a Grantor, Giftor, Assignor or Delegator, whereas a Trust Deed is an agreement between a Trustor and Trustee. Vesting Commission

Article 112 – Contracts

1. **A Contract shall be a registered Instrument of Consensus possessing mutual legal Obligation**. In relation to Contracts:- Contracts

(i) A Contract must be duly registered and recorded within a proper Ucadia register to be valid and legitimate; and

(ii) A valid Contract must contain Mutuality of Obligation whereby all parties are legally bound to perform their obligations, else the Contract shall be null and void; and

(iii) A Contract must demonstrate evidence of its mutual understanding, offer, intention and agreement between the parties occurring prior to being registered and recorded; and

(iv) As all valid Contracts must be properly registered and recorded to be valid, any non registered claimed contract shall be invalid and illegitimate.

2. Unlike other forms of Consensus, it shall be the process of Registration and relevant minimum information for valid types of Contracts that shall determine its effect:- Registration Elements and Effects of Contracts

(i) The type of Contract shall determine the minimum relevant information required and the expected parameters and limits of such values; and

(ii) Errors within any Instrument used to provide the essential minimum relevant information of a Contract shall only have a bearing to the extent that it impedes the reliability of such key information or the authenticity of the Contract itself; and

(iii) A value that exceeds or is below the parameters of minimum relevant information associated with a type of Contract shall not be permitted to be registered, even if contained in an executed Contract Instrument. Unless amended, such a Contract shall be considered legally unenforceable; and

(iv) A Contract containing additional clauses and information beyond the minimum required information of that Contract type shall have no legal bearing on the registered obligations nor legal remedy or relief afforded through such registration and shall be ignored in any legal enforcement of obligation.

TITLE XIX – DOCUMENTS, FORMS & INSTRUMENTS

Article 113 – Documents, Forms & Instruments

1. **By Divine, Ecclesiastical, Sovereign, Official and Administrative Rights, all valid and legitimate Documents, Forms and Instruments shall be subject to the present most sacred Covenant**, associated covenants, charters, constitutions and Laws:- Documents, Forms & Instruments

   (i) *Ius Divinum Instrumentalis* exists as the highest Divine Rights of Document, Form or Instrument Creation, Negotiation and Execution; and

   (ii) *Ius Ecclesiae Instrumentalis* exists as the highest Ecclesiastical Rights of Document, Form or Instrument Creation, Negotiation and Execution, as inherited from the Divine Rights *Ius Divinum Instrumentalis*; and

   (iii) *Ius Regnum Instrumentalis* exists as the highest Sovereign Rights of Document, Form or Instrument Creation, Negotiation and Execution, as inherited from the Ecclesiastical Rights *Ius Ecclesiae Instrumentalis*; and

   (iv) *Ius Administrationis Instrumentalis* exists as the highest Administrative Rights of Document, Form or Instrument Creation, Negotiation and Execution, as inherited from the Sovereign Rights *Ius Regnum Instrumentalis*.

2. By Divine, Ecclesiastical, Sovereign, Official and Administrative Right, all valid and legitimate Ucadian organs, bodies and entities shall form, make, create, print, impress, ingross, seal, publish, issue, acquire, retain, dispose, transfer, administer, register, record, enrol, inroll, endorse and indorse Instruments, Forms and Securities as Temporal Goods independent from Non-Ucadian and foreign civil power:- Documents, Forms & Instruments of Ucadia

   (i) All Instruments, Forms and Securities as Temporal Goods that belong to valid Ucadian organs, bodies, persons, trusts, funds and entities also belong to Ucadia; and are therefore Ecclesiastical and Sovereign Goods held in absolute trust and governed by the laws of Ucadia; and

   (ii) Subject to the present most sacred Covenant, and associated covenants, charters, constitutions and rules, valid Ucadian organs, bodies, persons, funds and entities shall acquire and dispose of Instruments and Securities as Temporal Goods by every just means of natural or positive law permitted to other Persons; and

   (iii) All valid Ucadia Organs, Bodies, Unions, Universities,

Foundations, Provinces and Campuses have the Right to permit and grant its Members, those things, including Instruments and Securities as Ecclesiastical Goods, that are necessary for the purposes proper to it; and no temporal or spiritual body possesses any right or authority or power to impede such Right; and

(iv) Members are free to acquire, use, hold and dispose of Instruments and Securities as Temporal Goods for the benefit of Ucadia, in accord with the present most sacred Covenant and associated covenants, charters, constitutions and laws. No temporal or spiritual body possesses any right or authority or power to impede, or deny or obstruct Members exercising such an act of free will; and

(v) Members, Officials and Agents of Ucadia are free to record and register Instruments and Securities as Temporal Goods with foreign bodies and civil powers in accord with the present most sacred Covenant and to the extent that: such entities do not seek to usurp the Divine, Ecclesiastical, Sovereign, Official and Administrative Powers of Ucadia; and honour any and all exemptions granted to valid Ucadia Organs, Bodies, Unions, Universities, Foundations, Provinces and Campuses.

3. A "**Document**" shall be a tangible, physical or electronic item containing an original or official or lawful written record of some Truth, or Fact, or Event or Issue or Matter, able to be used as Evidence itself or in support of Evidence. There shall be only five (5) valid forms of Documents: *Supreme, Superior, Ordinary, General* and *Inferior*:- Document

(i) A *Supreme Document* shall be a valid document issued and sealed by a Supreme Official Person as recognised by the present most sacred Covenant. There shall be no higher, more powerful nor authoritative Document than a Supreme Document; and

(ii) A *Superior Document* shall be a valid document issued and sealed by a registered Ucadian Officer of a Ucadian Union, University, Province or Campus; and

(iii) An *Ordinary Document* shall be a valid document issued and sealed by an Ordinary Ucadian Member, registered in a Register of Ucadia. It shall be the third highest and authoritative Document of all; and

(iv) A *General Document* shall be a valid document issued and registered in a Register of Ucadia that is not issued or sealed by an Ordinary, Superior or Supreme Ucadia Official Person; and

(v) An *Inferior Document* shall be any document issued by an Inferior (Non-Ucadian) Person. No Inferior Document shall ever be permitted to claim superiority over a General Document, Ordinary Document, Superior Document or Supreme Document.

4. A "**Form**" shall be a model or skeleton of an Instrument prescribed by the present most sacred Covenant, associated covenants, charters, constitutions and laws that may be used in a judicial proceeding, or legal or financial transaction; and containing the principal necessary matters, the proper technical terms or phrases or whatever else is necessary to make it formally correct, arranged in proper and methodical order and capable of being adapted to the circumstances of the specific case of Ucadian Law:- Form

(i) All Forms of Ucadia shall be prescribed within the covenants, charters, constitutions, bylaws, codes and resolutions of legitimate and valid Ucadian organs, bodies, persons, trusts, estates and entities; and

(ii) Where a valid Ucadian organ, body, person, trust, estate or entity has prescribed a particular Form in association with any procedure or action, then such an organisation shall have the right to deny and decline any action, including any and all liability for loss, or injury or damage on the part of the party who failed to use the proper and prescribed form; and

(iii) Ucadian organs, bodies, persons, trusts, estates and entities shall possess the right to pursue any and every option of penalties, damages, refusal, cancellation, fines or other punitive actions where an unauthorised use of a prescribed Form occurs; or when a form is defaced or altered without permission.

5. An "**Instrument**" shall be a formal Document issued under a Divine, or Ecclesiastical, or Sovereign, or Official or Administrative Right that conforms to certain standard of Form as prescribed by law, concerning a legal act or agreement, for the purpose of creating, securing, modifying, or terminating a right. Instrument

An Instrument shall possess three (3) sides being Obverse, Reverse and Traverse:-

(i) *Obverse* or "Face" of a Document is its front; and

(ii) *Reverse* or Back Face is its back; and

(iii) *Traverse* or third side is the margin on the Obverse.

6. An "Inchoate Instrument" shall be any Instrument that has been begun but remains unfinished or not completed and therefore is missing a material particular essential to its form and function:- Inchoate Instrument

(i) All Officers and Agents of Ucadia are forbidden to produce Inchoate Instruments contrary to the present most sacred Covenant, associated covenants, charters, constitutions and rules; and

(ii) Where a valid Ucadia organ, body, person, trust, estate, or entity is in possession of an Inchoate Instrument from an inferior (foreign) person or foreign body or entity, the Ucadia organ, body, person, trust, estate, or entity shall have the right to call upon the rights associated with Inchoate Instruments and complete the outstanding material particulars to its benefit.

7. By Divine, Ecclesiastical and Sovereign Right, no Instruments of a Ucadia Organ, Body, Person, Trust, Estate, or Entity to its own Officials, or Agents, or Contractors, or Employees or Members shall require Stamp Duty or the payment of any fees, or fines to any third party:- Stamp Duty

(i) Where Instruments of Ucadia are presented to other Non-Ucadian and foreign bodies politic or corporate, who then demand, or presume the requirement of Stamp Duty, the Corporation shall firstly and rightly claim exemption, unless the said bodies politic or corporate expressly details the required Stamp Duty amount; and

(ii) The failure of a Non-Ucadian and foreign bodies politic or corporate to clearly declare the amount owed in Stamp Duty when it is required shall be a confession that any such Stamp Duty is now the liability of the foreign agency or persons or body that failed to properly disclose the requirement; and

(iii) All Ucadia Organs, Bodies, Persons, Trusts, Estates and Entities shall have the Right to use valid and legitimate Ucadia Stamps issued as Public Money for the clearing of any such duty, providing an Account in favour of the Non-Ucadian and foreign body has been credited with the correct amount of duty.

8. No foreign third party or Bodies Politic or Society or Corporation or Agency shall be granted permission to deface or alter an Instrument of Ucadia. Non-Ucadian and Foreign Alterations

9. Authorised Divisions and Departments of a valid Ucadia body may apply two (2) identifiable diagonal lines from the top right corner to the bottom left corner through certain valid Instruments of the Ucadia body or certain Instruments issued by a Foreign Body, when the value Cancelled Instruments or gift or benefit of the Instrument is conveyed and used and therefore the Instrument is to be cancelled, to prevent double entry or use; and the particulars of the Instrument have been duly recorded within one or more Registers or Journals of Ucadia. The signature of the authorised Officer cancelling the Instrument must also be applied at the same forty five (45°) degree angle.

10. Authorised Divisions and Departments of a valid Ucadia body may endorse an Instrument by applying a signature at ninety (90°) degrees with instruction upon the back of a valid Instrument, along with any Seal as surety for such act, in accord with the present most sacred Covenant and associated covenants, charters, constitutions and rules. Endorsed Instruments

11. All Instruments subject to the present most sacred Covenant may be further defined according to the nature of the assertion of Rights, namely:- Classification of Instruments in terms of Rights

(i) Instruments of Petition; and

(ii) Instruments of Intention; and

(iii) Instruments of Claim; and

(iv) Instruments of Notification; and

(v) Instruments of Obligation; and

(vi) Instruments of Proof; and

(vii) Instruments of Demand.

Article 114 – Instruments of Petition

1. **Instruments of Petition** shall be the assertion of one or more Rights through a Document, Form or Instrument of petition or prayer to another concerning ownership or use or fruits of use of some property or thing withheld from the possession of the petitioner. Instruments of Petition

2. The essential qualification criteria of a valid Instrument of Petition shall be:- Qualification Criteria of Instruments of Petition

(i) That some injury or wrong against a Right allegedly occurred, capable of being expressed clearly; and

(ii) A Sacred invocation to the Divine is made, invoking the Right *Ius Divinum Compensationis Instrumentum* as the Divine Rights of Relief, Redress or Compensation for Default or Delinquency of Obligation.

3. Types of Instruments of Petition shall include (but not be limited to):- Types of Instruments of Petition

(i) Letter of Petition; and
(ii) Writ of Petition.

Article 115 – Instruments of Intention

1. **Instruments of Intention** shall be the assertion of one or more Rights through a Document, Form or Instrument of intention, will or testimony to another concerning ownership or use or fruits of use of some property or thing withheld from the possession of the petitioner. Instruments of Intention

2. The essential qualification criteria of a valid Instrument of Intention shall be:- Qualification Criteria of Instruments of Intention

(i) Some injury or wrong against a Right allegedly occurred, capable of being expressed clearly; and

(ii) That the person making the Instrument has the authority to create such an Instrument; and

(iii) A Sacred invocation to the Divine is made, invoking the Right *Ius Divinum Compensationis Instrumentum* as the Divine Rights of Relief, Redress or Compensation for Default or Delinquency of Obligation; and

(iv) The person who makes the sacred invocation has an interest in the Right (or Rights) that are the subject matter of the Instrument.

3. Types of Instruments of Intention shall include (but not be limited to): Types of Instruments of Intention

(i) Voluntatem Et Testamentum; and
(ii) Will; and

(iii) Power of Attorney; and

(iv) Resignation Letter.

Article 116 – Instruments of Claim

1. **Instruments of Claim** shall be the assertion of one or more Rights through a Document, Form or Instrument of formal challenge or accusation against another concerning ownership or use or fruits of use of some property or thing withheld from the possession of the petitioner. Instruments of Claim

2. The essential qualification criteria of a valid Instrument of Claim shall Qualification Criteria of Instruments of

be:- Claim

(i) Some injury or wrong against a Right allegedly occurred, capable of being expressed clearly; and

(ii) That the person making the Instrument has the authority to create such an Instrument; and

(iii) The person who makes the claim or allegation has an interest in the Right (or Rights) that are the subject matter of the Instrument.

3. Types of Instruments of Claim shall include (but not be limited to): Types of Instruments of Claim

(i) Petition of Claim of Rights; and
(ii) Bill of Rights; and
(iii) Indictment; and
(iv) Invoice.

Article 117 – Instruments of Notification

1. **Instruments of Notification** shall be the assertion of one or more Rights through a Document, Form or Instrument of notification or information to another concerning ownership or use or fruits of use of some property or thing withheld from the possession of the petitioner. Instruments of Notification

2. The essential qualification criteria of a valid Instrument of Notification shall be:- Qualification Criteria of Instruments of Notification

(i) That some fact, or event or reason exists as subject matter for the Instrument; and

(ii) That the person making the Instrument has the authority to create such an Instrument.

3. Types of Instruments of Notification shall include (but not be limited to): Types of Instruments of Notification

(i) Agenda; and
(ii) Minutes; and
(iii) Report; and
(iv) Manual; and
(v) Resume; and
(vi) Specification; and
(vii) Memorandum; and

(viii) Journal.

Article 118 – Instruments of Obligation

1. Instruments of Obligation shall be the assertion of one or more Rights through a Document, Form or Instrument of obligation, or consensus or performance to another concerning ownership or use or fruits of use of some property or thing withheld from the possession of the petitioner. Instruments of Obligation

2. The essential qualification criteria of a valid Instrument of Obligation shall be:- Qualification Criteria of Instruments of Obligation

   (i) That some event of Consensus has occurred as the subject matter of the instrument; and

   (ii) That the person making the Instrument has the authority to create such an Instrument; and

   (iii) The person who makes the sacred invocation has an interest in the Right (or Rights) that are the subject matter of the Instrument.

3. Types of Instruments of Obligation shall include (but not be limited to): Types of Instruments of Obligation

   (i) Covenant; and
   (ii) Convention; and
   (iii) Commission; and
   (iv) Contract; and
   (v) Note; and
   (vi) Warrant; and
   (vii) Draft; and
   (viii) Bond.

4. A valid "**Bond**" shall be an Instrument of Obligation and Penalty secured by Promise and Guarantee, or Charge, or Bailment, or Mortgage, or Third-Party Surety, whereby the Obligor (person bound) acknowledges an Obligation or Debt (penal sum); and binds themselves to pay a certain sum of interest (coupon) and repay any principal money at a maturity date, subject to any other binding conditions of surety and performance, whereby the Obligation will become void, or else the Obligation shall remain in full force. Bond

   In relation to the parties holding an interest or associated with a Bond, including customary rules:-

(i) The one who makes or issues a valid Bond shall be called the *Obligor* (also *Issuer*); and

(ii) The one to whom the obligation is due and who accepts the valid Bond as a right and security shall be called the *Obligee*; and

(iii) The one who agrees to assure the Obligor (if any) is called the *Surety*; and

(iv) The one who holds the benefit of the Bond is called the *Holder* and may or may not be the Obligee.

5. In relation to conditions of Bond:- Conditions of Bond

(i) A valid Bond must have at least one condition clause being an agreed "obligation" of performance by the one who makes or issues a valid Bond; and

(ii) A valid Bond must have at least one consideration clause being the agreed "valuable offering" of the one who accepts the valid Bond to then offer or do something in return; and

(iii) A valid Bond must have at least one penalty clause, that may or may not be associated with the prior good, or bill or contract or thing in question, that comes into effect if the one who makes or issues a valid Bond defaults on the performance of the condition clause(s); and

(iv) A valid Bond may (or may not) have one or more defeasance clauses that annul and void the penalty clauses in the event the one who makes or issues a valid Bond performs the conditions specified; and

(v) A valid Bond may (or may not) be dated or have an expiry date or identify the place where it was made; and

(vi) A valid Bond that possesses an expiry date shall be termed the maturity date; and

(vii) The summary operative elements of a valid Bond must be recorded in a Register and possess a unique entry number, usually distinguished in red ink. The unique entry in the Register is proof of the maker or issuer of a valid Bond being issued to another party; and

(viii) A valid Bond requires then the one who makes or issues a valid Bond to "bind" themselves, usually through a promise to the condition clause(s) under sign, seal and delivery of the Bond as a form of original Decree on a single sheet of paper, or parchment or vellum with the unique Register number clearly visible; and

(ix) The Conditions and Penalties of a simple Bond shall be listed on the reverse side of the single sheet of paper, or parchment or vellum; and

(x) If a Penalty clause makes provision for a debt, then this shall be called the Penal Sum; and

(xi) If a valid Bond permits negotiation or transfer, then the Obligee normally will endorse the original at ninety (90°) degrees on the face (obverse) or reverse of instrument; and

(xii) If a valid Bond permits periodic payments to be redeemed, these shall be called Coupons to be redeemed with the Obligor; and

(xiii) Once a Coupon is redeemed, or a Bond is redeemed at maturity, it shall be cancelled on its face and over any signature or seal by two (2) or three (3) lines, normally at forty-five (45°) degrees. Similarly, the record in the Bond register is cancelled by having a single line through it, representing the cancellation of all obligations.

6. The essential elements of a valid Bond shall be:- Elements of a valid Bond

(i) Bond Number being a unique Bond Number within the relevant Register of Bonds; and

(ii) Ucadia Sacred Space-Day-Time Number issued under being the numeric number for demonstrating the supreme jurisdiction, space and time whereby the Instrument is issued; and

(iii) Ucadia Location of Issue being the Location Number for the Ucadia University from where the Instrument is issued; and

(iv) Ucadia Date and Reference Date being the formal Ucadia Date and reference (Roman) date; and

(v) Title being the word "Bond" as a prominent word in the heading, or if a special type of Note the full name of such type; and

(vi) Obligation Account Number being a valid eighteen (18) digit Ucadia number signifying the existence of a record of account, or file, or action, or suit, or statement in respect of the obligation having some monetary value; and

(vii) Obligation Description being a brief description of the obligation or monetary obligation of Ucadia Money or Non-Ucadian Lawful Public Money in words, even if the amount of money is also displayed in numbers; and

(viii) Bordered Information being that any information "extracted" from the Record is presented within a bordered box to indicate a "window" to the original and valid Record; and

(ix) One Witness being a witness to the fact that the Note and the information contained within it is valid; or Ucadia Registrar Seal; and

(x) Official Seal of the Ucadia Organ, Body, Union, University, Foundation, Province or Campus.

7. A "**Warrant**" shall be a Document of Authority, signed, sealed and issued under the authority of a registered Sacred Writ by an Officer or duly appointed Fiduciary of a valid Ucadia Organ, Body, Union, University, Foundation, Province or Campus to one or more Agents commanding certain acts to be performed; whilst also granting the Agent(s) limited protection from liability or culpability for certain injuries or claim that may arise as a result of the execution of the commanded acts:- Warrant

(i) A Warrant shall therefore be similar in part to a license, whereby an act commanded to be done might otherwise be unlawful or illegal without a proper Warrant; and

(ii) In the absence of a valid Writ, no Warrant is valid or legitimate; and any claimed Warrant subsequently issued is an admission of fraud, perfidy, deception and injury of the law; and

(iii) Only Officers of a valid Ucadia Organ, Body, Union, University, Foundation, Province or Campus are authorised to issue Warrants in accord with the present most sacred Covenant, associated covenants, charters, constitutions and rules.

8. The essential elements of a valid Warrant shall be:- Elements of valid Warrant

(i) The name of the valid Ucadia Organ, Body, Union, University, Foundation, Province or Campus and the name of any division or department that specifically is issuing the Certificate; and

(ii) The word "Warrant" as a prominent word in the heading, or if a special type of Warrant the full name of such type; and

(iii) The Writ Number whereby the Warrant clearly relates to a valid and legitimate Sacred Writ; and

(iv) The unique Warrant Number for the Certificate indicating the issue of the document itself is authorised, valid and duly registered and "connected" to the Writ Number by being itself "added to the record"; and

(v) Any information "extracted" from the Writ is presented within a bordered box to indicate a "window" to the original and valid Record; and

(vi) A Command to the Agent to do or refrain from doing some kind of action; and

(vii) A vow, promise or affirmed and signed certification that the Warrant itself and the information contained within it is valid; and

(viii) The official seal of the valid Ucadia Organ, Body, Union, University, Foundation, Province or Campus; and

(ix) The signature of the Authorising Officer as Surety; and

(x) If the Warrant is a true copy then a separate vow, promise or affirmed and signed certification that it is a true copy.

9. A "**Note**" shall be an Instrument of Promise and Surety related to some Memorandum or Covenant or Testimony, whereby Money may be borrowed or advanced or due. In relation to the Persons and Parties associated with a Note:- Note

(i) The Person who makes or issues a valid Note shall be called the *Maker* (also *Issuer*, or *Payor*, or *Promisor*); and

(ii) The Person to whom the Note is addressed (if an actual name is listed on the Note) shall be called the *Payee* (also *Promisee*); and

(iii) The Person who the Payee may nominate as the beneficiary and holder of the Note (if any) shall be called the *Endorsee* (also *Indorsee* or *Order*); and

(iv) The Person who holds an original Note (whether the Note is addressed or not addressed) shall be called the *Bearer* (also *Holder*); and

(v) The Person who agrees to underwrite and guarantee the Note (if any) shall be called the *Guarantor* (also *Surety*); and

(vi) The Person who accepts a valid Note and agrees to lend or advance Money against it shall be called the *Lender*.

10. The essential elements of a valid Note shall be:- Elements of a valid Note

(i) Note Number being a unique Note Number of the Note within the Register of Notes; and

(ii) Title being the word "Note" as a prominent word in the heading, or if a special type of Note the full name of such type; and

(iii) Ucadia Sacred Space-Day-Time Number issued under being the numeric number for demonstrating the supreme jurisdiction, space and time whereby the instrument is issued; and

(iv) Ucadia Location of Issue being the Location Number for the Ucadia University from where the Instrument is issued; and

(v) Ucadia Date and Reference Date being the formal Ucadia Date and reference (Roman) date; and

(vi) Money in Words being if the Note is associated with money, then the amount of Ucadia Money or Non-Ucadian Lawful Public Money in words, even if the amount of money is also displayed in numbers; and

(vii) Bordered Information being that any information "extracted" from the Record is presented within a bordered box to indicate a "window" to the original and valid Record; and

(viii) One Witness being a witness to the fact that the Note and the information contained within it is valid; or Ucadia Registrar Seal if Official Seals of Ucadia Organ, Body, Union, University, Foundation, Province or Campus are not yet formed; and

(ix) Official Seal of the Ucadia Organ, Body, Union, University, Foundation, Province or Campus; or the Ucadia Seal, if Official Seals of Ucadia Organ, Body, Union, University, Foundation, Province or Campus are not yet formed.

Article 119 – Instruments of Proof

1. **Instruments of Proof** shall be the assertion of one or more Rights through a Document, Form or Instrument of verification, certification or exemplification to another concerning ownership or use or fruits of use of some property or thing withheld from the possession of the petitioner. Instruments of Proof

2. The essential qualification criteria of a valid Instrument of Proof shall be:- Qualification Criteria of Instruments of Proof

   (i) That a record in a valid Ucadian register exists as the subject matter of the Instrument of Proof in question; and

   (ii) That the person requesting the Instrument has the authority to make such a request at that time; and

   (iii) That the person making the Instrument has the authority to create such an Instrument.

3. Types of Instruments of Proof shall include (but not be limited to): Types of Instruments of Proof

   (i) Certificate; and
   (ii) Voucher; and

   (iii) Title.

4. A "**Certificate**" shall be an extract of Proof of a definitive, fixed, definite, reliable and certain manner that some act has or has not been done, or some event occurred or some formal decision has been concluded, given underwritten assurance (certified statement) by valid Officers possessing the authority to issue such instruments. Certificate

5. The essential elements of a valid Certificate shall be:- Elements of valid Certificate

   (i) The name of the Ucadia organ, or body, or entity and the name of any division or department that specifically is issuing the Certificate; and
   (ii) The word "Certificate" as a prominent word in the heading, or if a special type of Certificate the full name of such type; and

   (iii) The Record Number related to the Certificate; or if special to a particular type of Record, then the appropriate name; and

   (iv) The unique Certificate Number for the Certificate indicating the issue of the document itself is authorised, valid and duly registered and "connected" to the Record Number by being itself "added to the record"; and

   (v) Any information "extracted" from the Record is presented within a bordered box to indicate a "window" to the original and valid Record; and

   (vi) A vow, promise or affirmed and signed certification that the

Certificate and the information contained within it is valid; and

(vii) The Official seal of the Ucadia organ, or body, or entity; and

(viii) If the Certificate is a true copy then a separate vow, promise or affirmed and signed certification that it is a true copy.

6. A "**Voucher**" shall be a written or printed Instrument that establishes the authenticity of a valid claim, or demand, or bond and the transaction itself, concerning some goods, or property associated with a Trust, or Estate or Fund or Entity to be delivered under certain conditions. Voucher

7. The essential elements of a valid Voucher shall be:- Elements of valid Voucher

(i) The name of the Ucadia organ, or body, or entity and the name of any division or department that specifically is issuing the Voucher; and

(ii) The issuer of the Voucher is clearly identified; and

(iii) The unique Register number of the Voucher is clearly identified; and

(iv) The particulars of the Voucher are clearly identified and by what authority a payment has been made and serving as evidence of payment or discharge of a debit, or the right to redeem a transaction or goods of certain value; and

(v) Any amount is expressed in Words as well as numeric symbols; and

(vi) The date of issue is clearly stated; and

(vii) Whether or not the Voucher itself is negotiable, redeemable or other limits are clearly stated; and

(viii) The Voucher is duly sealed, or signed or authorised.

8. A "**Title**" shall be a valid inscription or entry into a Register associated with a Trust, or Estate or Fund or Entity; and any written or printed Instrument that establishes the authenticity and proof of such an entry. Title

Article 120 – Instruments of Demand

1. **Instruments of Demand** shall be the assertion of one or more Rights through a Document, Form or Instrument of demand and order to another concerning ownership or use or fruits of use of some property or thing withheld from the possession of the petitioner. Instruments of Demand

2. The essential qualification criteria of a valid Instrument of Demand shall be:- Qualification Criteria of Instruments of Demand

   (i) That some injury or wrong against a Right allegedly occurred, capable of being expressed clearly; and

   (ii) That the person making the Instrument has the authority to create such an Instrument.

3. Types of Instruments of Demand shall include (but not be limited to): Types of Instruments of Demand

   (i) Demand Letter; and
   (ii) Bill; and

   (iii) Writ.

4. A valid "**Bill**" shall be a form of Demand and Order in writing, assured by one or more Rights granted, for some performance equivalent in specie of Real Money. A Bill is normally associated with at least one Certified Statement or Memorandum of Account and one Affidavit. Bill

   In relation to the Persons and Parties associated with a Bill:-

   (i) The Person who makes or issues a valid Bill shall be called the *Maker* (also *Issuer*, or *Payor*, or *Drawer*); and

   (ii) The Person to whom the Bill is addressed and paid (if an actual name is listed on the Note) shall be called the *Payee*; and

   (iii) The Person who the Payee may nominate as the beneficiary and holder of the Bill (if any) shall be called the *Endorsee* (also *Indorsee* or *Order*); and

   (iv) The Person who is directed to make the payment on behalf of the Maker to the Payee shall be called the *Drawee* and once they accept the obligation becomes the *Acceptor*; and

   (v) The Person who holds an original Bill (whether the note is addressed or not addressed) is called the *Holder*; and

   (vi) The Person who agrees to underwrite and guarantee the Bill (if any) is called the *Guarantor* (also *Surety*).

5. The essential elements of a valid Bill shall be:- Elements of a

valid Bill

(i) Bill Number being a unique Bill Number within the relevant Register of Bills; and

(ii) Ucadia Sacred Space-Day-Time Number issued under being the numeric number for demonstrating the supreme jurisdiction, space and time whereby the Instrument is issued; and

(iii) Ucadia Location of Issue being the Location Number for the Ucadia University from where the Instrument is issued; and

(iv) Ucadia Date and Reference Date being the formal Ucadia Date and reference (Roman) date; and

(v) Title being the word "Bill" as a prominent word in the heading, or if a special type of Bill the full name of such type; and

(vi) Obligation Account Number being a valid eighteen (18) digit Ucadia number signifying the existence of a record of account, or file, or case, or statement in respect of the obligation having some monetary value; and

(vii) Obligation Description being a brief description of the obligation or monetary obligation of Ucadia Money or Non-Ucadian Lawful Public Money in words, even if the amount of money is also displayed in numbers; and

(viii) Demand or Order being the specific demand or order of the Bill regarding the Obligation; and

(ix) Bordered Information being that any information "extracted" from the Record is presented within a bordered box to indicate a "window" to the original and valid Record; and

(x) One Witness being a witnessed made or affirmed signed certification that the Bill and the information contained within it is valid; or Ucadia Registrar Seal; and

(xi) Official Seal of the Ucadia Organ, Body, Union, University, Foundation, Province or Campus.

Acceptance of Valid Bill

6. The Acceptance of a valid Bill is the act whereby the Person on whom a Bill is drawn (called the Drawee) assents to the Demand and Order of the Drawer to pay it, or make themselves liable for its action or payment when due. The object of Acceptance is to bind the Drawee and make him an actual and bound party to the Instrument. Therefore, until there is an Acceptance (such as evidence of Dishonour), the Drawee is under no obligation whatsoever upon the Bill itself.

7. A Bill shall be considered Accepted when it is acknowledged and signed in good Trust (*bona fide*), or through procedure to establish the dishonour, default and delinquency of the Drawee:- Conditions of Acceptance

   (i) A Bill is accepted when the Drawee signs and endorses the Bill at ninety degrees prior to the expiry or maturity of the Bill; or

   (ii) A Bill is accepted when the Drawer established the legitimacy of the Demand and Order, the truth of the debt and obligation, the dishonour of the Drawee in settling the debt and the default and delinquency of the Drawee in failing to provide any reasonable lawful excuse.

8. A valid and proper "**Writ**" shall be a type of Instrument issued under a Right of Writ as a Peremptory Precept to an Officer or Fiduciary or Agent or Person to perform or cease some act:- Writ

   (i) A Right of Writ shall be a valid Divine or Superior Right associated with the one, true and only forms of Original Entry and Original Action in accord with the present most sacred Covenant; and

   (ii) As a peremptory instrument, a properly authorised and issued Writ is not subject to debate or appeal and is considered absolute, decisive, conclusive and final; and

   (iii) As a precept, a Writ is a rule or teaching principle, especially directed toward the personal conduct of one or more persons, that of itself shall not create any new universal law nor grant any particular permanent right.

TITLE XX – ACCOUNTS & ACCOUNTING

Article 121 – Accounts & Accounting

1. **All financial and economic transactions shall be subject to the same Divine, Ecclesiastical, Sovereign and Administrative Rights of classification, measurement, disclosure and reporting of financial information of Ucadia**, no matter what the type of organ, body, person, trust, estate, fund or entity. Accounts & Accounting

2. An "**Account**" shall be a list or statement of accounting, monetary or economic transactions, classified by a specific purpose, arising out of a contract or a fiduciary relationship:- Account

   (i) An "**Accounting Transaction**" shall mean a balance or result of an event having a monetary impact on the financial statements of an entity; and

   (ii) A "**Monetary Transaction**" shall mean a balance or result of comparison between items of a monetary value of an opposite nature, such as receipts and payments, or deposits and withdrawals, or debits and credits; and

   (iii) An "**Economic Transaction**" shall mean a balance or result of an exchange of value, such as between assets or equities, or different items of the type.

3. All Accounts shall possess the same essential elements being *Record Number, Account Name, Account Description, Account Number, Account Owner, Date Opened, Date Closed, Account Trades* and *Status*: Elements of Valid Accounts

   (i) *Record Number* shall be a unique column being the first and left most column in which a whole integer is listed and is sequential (beginning from the integer 1) and unique (not the same) in reference to the table; and

   (ii) *Account Name* shall be a column defining the name of the Account; and

   (iii) *Account Description* shall be a column defining the description of the Account; and

   (iv) *Account Number* shall be a column defining a unique number or alpha-numeric sequence for the Account; and

   (v) *Account Owner* shall be a column defining the Owner or Owners of the Account; and

   (vi) *Date Opened* shall be a column defining the date the Account was opened; and

(vii) *Date Closed* shall be a column defining the date the Account was closed; and

(viii) *Account Trades* shall be a column summarising the number of unique Trade Agreements against the Account according to some sub unit of time or agreement, whereby transactions are then recorded; and

(ix) *Status* shall be a column defining the operating status of the Account.

4. The purpose and function of different types of Accounts of a valid Organ, Body, Union, University, Foundation, Province, Entity or Campus shall be defined within its constituting instrument, consistent with the present most sacred Covenant. Valid types of Accounts shall include (but not be limited to): Valid types of Accounts

(i) A *Bank Account* shall be an Account where Banking Services are provided under a Financial Account Number (FAN); and

(ii) A *Budget Account* shall be an Account designed for the purpose of expressing and planning future and hypothetical revenues, quantities, costs, expenses, assets, liabilities, cash flows and contingencies; and

(iii) A *Contract Account* shall be an Account where certain monies are paid under a Contract Account Number (CAN); and

(iv) An *Exchange Account*, also known as Market Account whereby transactions are recorded, having an Exchange Account Number (XAN); and

(v) A *Fund Account* shall be an Account for the facilitation of a Fund; and

(vi) A *Grace Account* shall be a purely spiritual Account for the facilitation of Divine Grace; and

(vii) An *Insurance Account* shall be an Account where certain Funds or Assets are placed as surety against a potential loss, or as assurance; and

(viii) An *Item Account* shall be an Account where monetary values are recorded against individual or groups of products and services; and having an Item Account Number (IAN); and

(ix) A *Journal Account* shall be an Account derived from summarising Memoranda such as "Day Books" of transactions and having a Journal Account Number (JAN); and

(x) A *Ledger Account*, shall be an Account derived from

summarising Journal Accounts and having a Ledger Account Number (LAN); and

(xi) A *Member Account* shall be a type of Account for the entry and recording of certain Member rights and property and agreements; and

(xii) A *Project Account* shall be an Account recording transactions associated with a specific project; and

(xiii) A *Securities Account* shall be an Account where Securities may be held, purchased or sold; and

(xiv) A *Supplier Account* shall be an Account for the recording of terms and transactions and the supply of goods and services; and

(xv) A *Treasury Account* shall be an Account for the day to day transactions of government and agency business of a valid and legitimate body politic under a Financial Account Number (FAN); and

(xvi) A *Trust Account* shall mean an Account for the holding of monies associated with a Trust formed under a valid and proper Trust Commission agreement.

5. A "**Statement of Account**" or "**Account Statement**" shall be a periodic summary of account activity with a beginning date and an ending date. Statement of Account

6. A "**Final Statement of Account**" shall be when two (2) persons having previously engaged in one or more monetary transactions together, close an Account by agreeing to the balance appearing to be due from one of them. Final Statement of Account

7. A "**Settlement of Account**" shall be when a Fiduciary of a Trust agrees to provide an Account, or when a competent court orders a forensic Settlement of Account upon claims of concealment or undue advantage taken by the Trustee. An action for a Settlement of Account shall not necessarily close an Account. Settlement of Account

8. An "**Action for Account**" shall be when one party of interest of an open Account seeks a proper accounting from the other party by bringing the matter before a competent forum of law having authority and power under the present most sacred Covenant, associated covenants, charters, constitutions or rules: Action for Account

(i) The party bringing the Action or Suit shall first demonstrate their status and standing in bringing an Action or Suit, as by the laws of certain Jurisdictions, Body Politic and Societies, types of status shall be ineligible to certain actions; and

(ii) The party bringing the Action or Suit shall identify the type of interest and nature of their relation with the other party; and

(iii) The party bringing the Action shall be clear as to the type of Account required (usually a Statement of Account), or if specifically associated with a Trust, a Settlement of Account; and

(iv) The transactions in question must then be properly investigated by the competent forum of law; and

(v) The "accounting party" or person from whom the Account is required, shall draw up an Account and have it verified by testimony before the information shall be embodied by the competent forum of law under certificate; and

(vi) A body claiming to be a court of law that refuses to order a proper accounting despite proper standing and merits of the aggrieved party, shall cease to hold any Divine, Ecclesiastical, Sovereign or Administrative Rights or Powers as a competent forum of law until such time as the Officers that caused such injury are censured or removed.

9. The status and standing of the parties of an Action for Account or Suit for Account shall include (but shall not be limited to): Standing for Action for Account

(i) Action by one Partner against another (Partner) for an Account of the partnership dealings; or

(ii) A Principal against their Agent, but never vice versa; or

(iii) A Beneficiary against Executors or Trustees for an Account of what they have received (or ought to have received) and paid in respect of the trust property; or

(iv) A Mortgagor against a Mortgagee who has entered into possession of the mortgaged property, in order to ascertain what he has received or ought to have received in respect of rents and profits, so that the amount may be set off against the amount payable on the mortgage.

10. A "**Debt**" shall mean (a) a binding promise or (b) right of action or (c) both. A Debt is distinguished from a Debit in that a Debit is an entry in a journal or ledger of a sum owed to the proprietor of some accounts, whereas a Debt is a binding promise or a right of action. Debt

In respect of Debt as a binding promise:-

(i) A Debt may be a solemn obligation under Contract; or

(ii) A Debt may be a binding promise under Bargain.

In respect of Debt as a Right of Action:-

(i) A Debt may be a right of demand and enforcement of payment of sum of money due for goods sold under Bargain; or

(ii) A Debt may be a right of demand and enforcement of delivery of goods due for a sum of money under Bargain; or

(iii) A Debt may be a right of demand and enforcement of payment of penalty or compensation for failure to perform an obligation under contract.

11. "**Asset**" shall mean anything owned by a body or entity capable of producing a positive economic value. More specifically, an Asset shall be a sum of units of monetary value, recorded in one or more designated accounts, available for the discharge of a Debt and not yet assigned to a specific purpose. Asset

12. "**Liability**" shall mean a probable future sacrifice of an economic benefit arising from a present obligation of a particular body or entity to transfer some Asset or provide a service to another person as a consequence of some past transaction or event. More specifically, a Liability shall be an undischarged moral or legal Obligation. Liability

13. "**Income**" shall mean inflows of Money or other Assets returned to a body or entity from rent, tolls, levies, contributions or charges derived from any capital investment; or revenue derived from the main activities of the body or entity as registered or regulated by Ucadian Law. Income

14. "**Expenses**" shall mean outflows of Money or other using up of Assets or occurrences of Liabilities from delivering or producing goods, rendering services, or carrying out other activities that constitute the main activities of the body or entity. Expenses

15. A legitimate, valid, certified and qualified "**Accountant**" shall be an Officer of a competent forum of law or another Juridic Person duly formed under Ucadian Law, possessing ecclesiastical and clerical status to prepare, enter, manage, tabulate and certify accounts. Accountant

16. A legitimate, valid, certified and qualified "**Auditor**" shall be a certified and qualified Accountant under Ucadian Law, appointed in a further position of Trust as Jurist of the Accounts, to conduct a systematic, independent examination of all related books, accounts, documents and vouchers to ascertain the truth of financial statements made by a particular Ucadia Organ, Body, Union, University, Foundation, Entity, Estate, Trust, Province or Campus under the Auditor jurisdiction of Ucadian Law.

Article 122 – Ucadia Accounting System (UAS)

1. **Ucadia Accounts System (UAS) shall be the highest standard and integrated system for all aspects of accounts** as defined by the present most sacred Covenant, associated covenants, charters, constitutions and rules. All Accounts within the bounds of Ucadia Organs, Bodies and Entities shall adhere to the Ucadia Accounts System. The general principles of the Ucadia Accounts System (UAS) shall be:- Ucadia Accounting System (UAS)

(i) All valid Ucadia Organs, Bodies, Entities, Trusts, Estates, Unions, Universities, Foundations, Provinces, Campuses, Members and Persons shall use the one and same Accounting System known as the Ucadia Accounts System (UAS) as the primary Accounting System; and

(ii) All unique Entities, Divisions, Departments, Units, Trusts, Estates, Funds, Corporations, Members and Persons shall be identified by a unique eighteen (18) digit number called a "**Member Identity Number**" (MIN), being their existing Trust Number or Member Number; and

(iii) All unique ledgers or funds of Money as controlled by a legitimate body or entity having the Right of *Ius Ecclesiae Templum* in its capacity as Treasury or Bank within the bounds of its jurisdiction for the benefit of one or more unique entities as identified by Member Identity Numbers (MIN), shall be identified by a unique eighteen (18) digit number called a "**Financial Account Number**" (FAN), representing the unique purpose, identity and type of Money held and transacted; and

(iv) No Financial Account Number (FAN) may be created without first the existence of a valid Member Identity Number (MIN) for one or more entities as owner(s); and

(v) All unique and discretely defined economic units of value called an "**Item**", involving unique entities as owners or users as defined by Member Identity Numbers (MIN) shall be identified by a unique eighteen (18) digit number called an "**Item Account Number**" (IAN), representing the unique item, its type, value and economic life; and

(vi) No Item Account Number (IAN) may be created without first the existence of a valid Member Identity Number (MIN) for one or more entities as holding rights and responsibilities of use; and

(vii) An annual survey and audit of Item Account Number (IAN) shall be called the "**Inventory**"; and

(viii) All unique and clearly defined agreements of activity in relation to Item Account Numbers (IAN) shall be identified by a unique eighteen (18) digit number called a "**Contract Account Number**" (CAN), representing the unique agreement and purpose of economic activity; and

(ix) All unique and distinct economic events associated with an Item Account Number (IAN) or Contract Account Number (CAN) shall be identified by a unique eighteen (18) digit number called an "**Exchange Account Number**" (XAN), representing the unique exchange event of economic activity against the agreement; and

(x) No economic activity of any kind may be authorised unless first there exists a Contract Account Number (CAN) properly connected to an Item Account Number (IAN); and

(xi) All aggregate centres of economic activity involving unique economic Items as Exchange Account Numbers (XAN) in relation to transactions shall be identified by a unique eighteen (18) digit number called a "**Journal Account Number**" (JAN), representing the unique aggregate journal; and

(xii) The information recorded in a Journal Entry with a valid Journal Account Number (JAN) shall be extracted to the highest level information matched according to double entry bookkeeping into Ledgers also with valid "**Ledger Account Numbers**" (LAN); and

(xiii) Ledgers corresponding to valid Ledger Account Numbers (LAN) shall be prepared into financial statements.

2. All authority and powers concerning the proper organisation, administration, instruction, function and enforcement of the Ucadia Accounting Systems (UAS) shall be vested in a Ucadian Body known as the "**Ucadia Accounting System Organisation**" (UASO) as a permanent organ of the Ucadian Globe Union:-

Ucadia Accounting System Organisation and Administration

(i) All valid Ucadia Unions, Universities, Accounting Associations and Foundations shall be members of the Ucadia Accounting System Organisation (UASO) and participate in its funding and operation; and

(ii) The Ucadia Accounting System Organisation (UASO) shall be the supreme Accounting Standards body, having full plenary to accomplish its sacred mandate; and

(iii) For the purpose of establishing treaties with non-Ucadian and foreign Accounting Standards bodies, the (UASO) shall be permitted to register within non-Ucadian jurisdictions a body known as Ucadia Accounting Standards Foundation (UASF); and

(iv) Ucadia entities registered in non-Ucadian and foreign jurisdictions shall seek permission to prepare and report financial statements using the Ucadia Accounting Standards (UAS).

Objects of Ucadia Accounting System Organisation

3. The primary objects of the Ucadia Accounting System Organisation (UASO) shall be:-

(i) Hold, develop and protect the Ucadia Accounting System (UAS) being a model of exemplary, comprehensible and enforceable accounting standards founded on clearly articulated principles in accord with the present most sacred Covenant and associated covenants, charters, constitutions and rules; and

(ii) Promote the knowledge and education of the Ucadia Accounting System (UAS) and its diligent and competent application by all valid Ucadia Organs, Bodies, Entities, Trusts, Estates, Persons, Unions, Universities, Foundations, Provinces, Entities and Campuses; and

(iii) Ensure enforcement of the Ucadia Accounting System (UAS) between all valid Ucadia Organs, Bodies, Entities, Trusts, Estates, Persons, Unions, Universities, Foundations, Provinces and Campuses to ensure the existence of uniform, high quality, transparent and comparable financial statements and other financial reporting to better enable wise, moral and prudent economic decisions; and

(iv) Establish peaceful and harmonious relations with non-Ucadian and foreign accounting standard bodies to educate and explain the Ucadia Accounting System (UAS) and ensure its acceptance.

TITLE XXI – MONEY, PROPERTY, GOODS & FUNDS

Article 123 – Ucadia Money

1. **By Divine, Ecclesiastical, Sovereign and Administrative Rights, Ucadia Money shall be the highest form of valid and legitimate Money**, consistent and in accord with the present most sacred Covenant:- Ucadia Money

(i) *Ius Divinum Moneta* exists as the highest Divine Rights to Mint, Produce, Hold, Use and Exchange Money; and

(ii) *Ius Ecclesiae Moneta* exists as the highest Ecclesiastical Rights to Mint, Produce, Hold, Use and Exchange Money, as inherited from the Divine Rights *Ius Divinum Moneta*; and

(iii) *Ius Regnum Moneta* exists as the highest Sovereign Rights to Mint, Produce, Hold, Use and Exchange Money, as inherited from the Ecclesiastical Rights *Ius Ecclesiae Moneta*; and

(iv) *Ius Administrationis Moneta* exists as the highest Administrative Rights to Mint, Produce, Hold, Use and Exchange Money, as inherited from the Sovereign Rights *Ius Regnum Moneta*.

2. All valid and legitimate Ucadia Organs, Bodies, Unions, Agencies, Universities, Provinces, Campuses, Entities, Trusts, Estates and foreign registered Companies and Associations shall use "**Ucadia Moneta**" as their standard unit of account. Ucadia Moneta shall represent a summary term for the Ucadia Union Moneta money units of the Ucadia Regional Unions and Colonies. Ucadia Moneta

3. By definition, "**Money**" is a Right, established by proper Law, whereby a system of rules, measures, records, accounts and procedures shall exist to produce a consistent and stable *Unit of Measure, Unit of Account, Unit of Redemption for Value, Means of Exchange and Reliable Store of Value*:- Money

(i) *Unit of Measure* shall mean that proper Money is first and foremost a "standard unit of measure", having a suitable unique identity to distinguish it from other units of measure, whereby all goods and services within a certain Market may be compared to the same unit of measure, thus enabling the creation of Price. In this way, proper Money is fundamentally always an attribute of a Market and not vice versa; and

(ii) *Unit of Account* shall mean that proper Money is a unit of measure associated with a Market that enables the entry of consistent values and transactions, based upon its character as a Unit of Measure, within Accounts and Ledgers reflecting such

Prices, Quantities and other attributes of Goods and Services. In this way, Accounts are always a feature of a Market and Money as entries in such accounts are an attribute of Accounts and Markets, not vice versa; and

(iii) *Unit of Redemption for Value* shall mean that proper Money is capable of being represented in some medium or form (i.e. physical and/or electronic; or paper, plastic, metal or other etc.) and possesses the attribute of being redeemed for some valuable consideration, enables a participant to "enter" and to "exit" a form of proper Money associated with one Market and choose to move to another Market; and

(iv) *Means of Exchange* shall mean that proper Money is able to fulfil the requirement of facilitating efficient transactions within a Market, because of its previous attributes. Thus, a "means of exchange" may be considered a primary object of proper Money, but only as a consequence of other attributes first being in place; and

(v) *Reliable Store of Value* shall mean that proper Money represents a consistent and stable unit of exchange such that its Value today is the same or similar as its Value tomorrow. Contrary to false presumptions, this does not mean the medium of Money itself must be of some intrinsic value, but that the integrity of Money is protected, through minimisation of counterfeiting, speculation and rapid valuation or devaluation swings – meaning all that impact on the wealth and function of a Market.

Primary Categories of Money

4. In accord with the customs, traditions and maxims of law concerning Money, since the beginning of Human Civilisation, all proper Money may be divided into five (5) primary categories being *Ecclesiastical*, *Public*, *Capital*, *Private* and *Personal*:-

(i) *Ecclesiastical Money* is the highest, most valuable form of Money and form of Legal Tender since the beginning of Human Civilisation and the origin of the very notion of Money itself. The highest form of Ecclesiastical Money ever formed is the Supreme Credo (Credit) as defined by the present most sacred Covenant; and

(ii) *Public Money* is Money and a form of Legal Tender issued as a Public Fund against the Credit in Trust and Assets of a body politic, or constituted society as a single Market and then managed by its Officers as Trustees; and

(iii) *Capital Money* is Money and a form of valuable Asset formed from the accounting of a promise and guarantee upon the "head" of one or more persons who possess some valuable property right; and

(iv) *Private Money*, also known as "Currency" and a form of Legal Tender, is Money issued under license or privilege by a party, usually a bank, holding certain assets within a Market; and then granted exclusive license to have its instruments treated "as if" Public Money; and

(v) *Personal Money*, also known as "Credit Money" or simply "Credit", is Money issued under the Bylaws of a party holding assets within a market, such as one or a network of savings and investment banks, or even a private corporation.

5. "**Legal Tender**", also known as Lawful Money, is any form of Money or Instrument that may be tendered for the payment of a debt or obligation:- Legal Tender

(i) Ecclesiastical Money, consistent and in accord with the present most sacred Covenant is always Legal Tender in any and every valid body politic, or properly constituted society that operates according to the Rule of Law; and

(ii) Public Money is naturally Legal Tender by definition, within the body politic or society where it relates; and

(iii) Private Money is only Legal Tender to the extent it is granted such privilege by the legislative body or society where it relates; and

(iv) Instruments and Commodities may only be Legal Tender when granted such privilege by the legislative body of the body politic or society where it relates.

6. In accord with proper Divine, Ecclesiastical, Sovereign and Administrative Law, Ucadia Money shall be the highest possible and most legitimate form of Money:- Ucadia Money as highest form of Money

(i) As Ucadia Money is the highest form of Divine, Ecclesiastical, Sovereign and Administrative Money, the Circulation of Ucadia Money shall determine the Circulation of all lesser forms of Money, including Non-Ucadian and Foreign Money; and

(ii) Ucadia Money shall be used for the payment, discharge and settlement of all debts, debits, obligations, taxes, fines and penalties between Ucadia Members, using Ucadia Money Accounts where such sums are stated in Ucadia Money amounts; and

(iii) Furthermore, Ucadia Money shall be recognised and acknowledged as the highest and most legitimate and valid Legal Tender for the payment, discharge and settlement of all debits, debts, obligations, taxes, fines and penalties, whether they be public or private; or domestic or foreign, in relation to any and all societies, bodies politic, communities, associations, trusts, estates, funds, corporations, aggregates and persons.

7. When a duly recorded and authorised tender of the correct sum of Ucadia Money for the payment, discharge and settlement of any debts, debits, obligations, taxes, fines and penalties is made:- Honouring Ucadia Money

(i) Providing an authorised Ucadia Money Account exists in the name of the body, trust, estate, fund, person or entity receiving the Ucadia Money Instrument, the receiver of such Ucadia Money is spiritually, morally and legally bound to accept such funds, in accord with proper Divine, Ecclesiastical, Sovereign and Administrative Law; and

(ii) If a duly authorised tender of the correct sum of Ucadia Money is refused, rejected or dishonoured by any society, or body politic, or community, or association, or trust, or estate, or fund, or corporation or person, then such a profane, unlawful, illegal and immoral action shall be a formal acknowledgement and confession of the existence of a valid and legitimate debt and obligation against them equal in three (3) times value to the original sum refused, rejected or dishonoured; and

(iii) Failure to pay on notice and demand for the payment of a valid and legitimate debt and obligation against a party equal in three times value to the original sum refused, rejected or dishonoured, shall be a formal acknowledgement and confession of delinquency. Authorised Ucadian organs, bodies, trusts, estates, persons, funds and entities shall then have the right to pursue any and all further action and punitive acts to recover such debts and obligations.

8. By Divine, Ecclesiastical, Sovereign and Administrative Rights, all Rights to impose any form of Rent, Toll, Levy, Contribution or Charge against Money shall be subject to the present most sacred Covenant, associated covenants, charters, constitutions and laws and no other:- Rights to impose Rent, Toll, Levy, Contributions or Charges against Money

(i) *Ius Divinum Vectigalis Moneta* exists as the highest Divine Rights to impose Rents, Tolls, Levies, Contributions or Charges against Money; and

(ii) *Ius Ecclesiae Vectigalis Moneta* exists as the highest Ecclesiastical Rights to impose Rents, Tolls, Levies,

Contributions or Charges against Money, as inherited from the Divine Rights *Ius Divinum Vectigalis Moneta*; and

(iii) *Ius Regnum Vectigalis Moneta* exists as the highest Sovereign Rights to impose Rents, Tolls, Levies, Contributions or Charges against Money, as inherited from the Ecclesiastical Rights *Ius Ecclesiae Vectigalis Moneta*; and

(iv) *Ius Administrationis Vectigalis Moneta* exists as the highest Administrative Rights to impose Rents, Tolls, Levies, Contributions or Charges against Money, as inherited from the Sovereign Rights *Ius Regnum Vectigalis Moneta*.

Authority to impose Rent, Toll, Levy, Contributions or Charges against Money and notion of Interest

9. Only bodies, trusts, estates, funds, persons and entities duly authorised by the appropriate Ucadian Rights shall then have the authority to impose Rents, Tolls, Levies, Contributions or Charges against Money:-

(i) A body, trust, estate, fund, person or entity without proper authority from the present most sacred Covenant, or associated covenants, charters, constitutions or laws shall have no right to impose Rents, Tolls, Levies, Contributions or Charges against Money; and

(ii) The use of the term "Interest" is permitted, including the representation of authorised Rents, Tolls, Levies, Contributions or Charges against Money as a percentage, providing the identity and function of such an imposition is clearly identified and disclosed; and

(iii) The failure to properly disclose the valid and legitimate identity and function behind the use of the term "Interest" and the simplification of representing such impositions as a percentage shall render such a Document, Form or Instrument illegitimate, invalid and liable for suspension, termination or dissolution with no right to relief, redress or compensation.

Compound Interest Forbidden

10. Any and all forms of compound interest, by any name, representation or calculation shall be a profane act of sacrilege against Divine, Ecclesiastical and Sovereign Law; and a deliberate declaration and act of perfidy, treachery and immorality against all proper Executive and Administrative Law; and shall therefore be banned, forbidden and entirely suppressed.

Rights to act and function as Treasury or Financial

11. By Divine, Ecclesiastical, Sovereign, Official and Administrative Rights, all Rights to function as a treasury or bank or financial institution, including (but not limited to) the issue of credit, accept deposits, grant loans, advances, cash, overdrafts, discounting of bills, letters of credit, safety deposits, insurance and conversion shall be subject to the present most sacred Covenant, associated covenants, charters, constitutions and laws and no other:- (Banking) Body

(i) *Ius Divinum Templum* exists as the highest Divine Rights of a valid and legitimate Treasury or Financial (Banking) Body; and

(ii) *Ius Ecclesiae Templum* exists as the highest Ecclesiastical Rights of a valid and legitimate Treasury or Financial (Banking) Body, as inherited from the Divine Rights *Ius Divinum Templum*; and

(iii) *Ius Regnum Templum* exists as the highest Sovereign Rights of a valid and legitimate Treasury or Financial (Banking) Body, as inherited from the Ecclesiastical Rights *Ius Ecclesiae Templum*; and

(iv) *Ius Administrationis Templum* exists as the highest Administrative Rights of a valid and legitimate Treasury or Financial (Banking) Body, as inherited from the Sovereign Rights *Ius Regnum Templum*.

12. Any organ, or body or entity, including Non-Ucadian and Foreign bodies, agencies and entities, that do not possess any Divine, Ecclesiastical, Sovereign or Administrative authority to function as a valid and legitimate Treasury or Financial (Banking) Organisation, may be granted under limited treaty such rights, on condition:-

Non-Ucadian and Foreign Bodies Treasury and Banking Treaties with Ucadia

(i) Ucadia Money and the Ucadia Financial System are fully recognised and accepted as currency and legal tender; and

(ii) The entity provides and operates all necessary conversion and exchange services required to ensure the effective exchange of Ucadia Money and Assets for non-Ucadian and Foreign forms of Money and Capital; and

(iii) The entity agrees to conduct transactions involving Ucadia Money and Assets in accord with the Ucadia Accounting System (UAS).

Article 124 – Ucadia Property

1. **By Divine, Ecclesiastical, Sovereign and Administrative Rights, Ucadia Property Rights shall be the highest form of valid and legitimate Property Rights**, consistent and in accord with the present most sacred Covenant:-

Ucadia Property

(i) *Ius Divinum Proprietatis* exists as the highest Divine Rights of

Ownership of Use or Fruits of Use of Property; and

(ii) *Ius Ecclesiae Proprietatis* exists as the highest Ecclesiastical Rights of Ownership of Use or Fruits of Use of Property, as inherited from the Divine Rights *Ius Divinum Proprietatis*; and

(iii) *Ius Regnum Proprietatis* exists as the highest Sovereign Rights of Ownership of Use or Fruits of Use of Property, as inherited from the Ecclesiastical Rights *Ius Ecclesiae Proprietatis*; and

(iv) *Ius Administrationis Proprietatis* exists as the highest Administrative Rights of Ownership of Use or Fruits of Use of Property, as inherited from the Sovereign Rights *Ius Regnum Proprietatis*.

2. "**Property**" shall mean the highest registered Right a Person shall have or hold within a Lawful Ucadia Jurisdiction to Control or Use or Claim any Thing or the Fruits of any Thing that possesses a monetary value. In reference to Property, Rights and Things:- Property

(i) Property shall always pertain to Persons and not Beings; and

(ii) A Right without any conceivable monetary value cannot be considered Property; and

(iii) A Thing in the context of Property shall be any Right that can be purchased or sold or inherited; and attached by operation of law to a corporeal object, whether fixed or movable; and

(iv) Any Right that can be purchased or sold means a Right in Trust without a named Beneficiary and therefore a Good; and

(v) When one is duly recorded in a valid Ucadia Register as possessing a Right or Claim of Right over Control or Use of a Thing, or Fruits of a Thing, then such a Person may be referred to as the "Owner" of that Right; and

(vi) The highest and most authoritative record of Ownership shall be a valid record within a Ucadia Register.

3. There shall be eight (8) possible forms of Property Right or "Ownership" of Control or Use or Claim of any Thing or the Fruits of any Thing, (in order of status and standing) being:- Forms of Property as Control or Use or Claim

(i) Owner of Right of Control of a Thing; and

(ii) Owner of Right of Use of a Thing; and

(iii) Owner of Right of Control of the Fruits of Use of a Thing; and

(iv) Owner of Right of Use of the Fruits of a Thing; and

(v) Owner of Claim of Right of Control of a Thing; and

(vi) Owner of Claim of Right of Use of a Thing; and

(vii) Owner of Claim of Right of Control of the Fruits of Use of a Thing; and

(viii) Owner of Claim of Right of Use of the Fruits of a Thing.

Article 125 – Ucadia Goods & Services

1. **Goods or Good, shall be a gift or a promise of beneficial Right of Use** for Sale or Bargain of Tangible Property. "**Service**" shall be a gift or a promise of Performance of Obligation for Payment associated with some Intangible Property. Goods & Services

2. "**Sale**" shall be when the title to a thing is given in Trust to another in exchange for a price of lawful money, also given in Trust. In reference to the concept of a Sale:- Sale

   (i) A Sale shall always involve Goods and therefore always involves Rights in Trust as Goods; and

   (ii) A Sale shall always involve two (2) distinct trusts having two distinct trust corpus – one where the buyer is trustee and one where the seller is trustee; and

   (iii) It is only when the sale is completed do the two (2) separate trusts dissolve as a settlement into one, providing the conditions of sale make that possible.

3. "**Bargain**" shall be a Contract of Mutual Bindings (Promises) in Trust as Security whereby one party promises to assign a right as property for some consideration; and the other party promises to receive the property and take good care of it and pay the consideration. In reference to the concept of a Bargain of Goods:- Bargain

   (i) A Bargain shall always involve Goods and therefore always involves Rights in Trust as Goods; and

   (ii) Similar to a Sale, a Bargain shall always involve two (2) Trusts for a Bargain to exist: The one for the Buyer and one for the Seller; and

   (iii) A Bargain shall never be a transfer of Title but a Bailment of Goods or Use for some financial consideration; and

   (iv) The Seller never gifts the property like a Sale and the terms of Consideration may also involve some return of a Bailment of Money; and

(v) The key operating element of a Bargain is the Mutual Binding Promises that are also called Debts.

4. To pursue and fulfil its proper purposes, authorised Ucadia Bodies and Entities by innate Right shall form, acquire, retain, administer and alienate Temporal Goods & Services independently from any non-Ucadian and foreign civil powers. Subject to the present sacred Covenant, associated covenants, charters, constitutions and laws:- Ucadia Goods & Services

(i) Authorised Ucadia Organs, Bodies and Entities shall have the Right to require from their Members, those things, including Temporal Goods, that are necessary for the purposes proper to it; and no temporal or spiritual body possesses any right or authority or power to impede such Right; and

(ii) Members shall be free to give Temporal Goods for the benefit of authorised Ucadia Organs, Bodies and Entities. No temporal or spiritual body shall possess any right or authority or power to impede, or deny or obstruct such Members exercising such an act of free will.

Article 126 – Ucadia Funds

1 **A Fund shall be a sum of equal units representing certain Property Rights of monetary value**, recorded in one or more designated Accounts of a valid Ucadia Body or Entity; and set apart for a term of years and one or more specific purposes; and available for the payment of debits, debts, legacies and claims in accord with the present most sacred Covenant. Fund

In respect of the character, purpose and nature of a Fund:-

(i) The Instrument of formation and of guiding the character, purpose and nature of one or more Funds shall be a Trust Covenant as a Fund Constitution issued and approved by a valid Body; and

(ii) The underlying Rights and Property used to derive the value of a Fund must be set aside and sealed in its own Trust in accord with the Trust Covenant to protect the integrity of the Fund and prevent any re-transfer or re-conveyance that might threaten the value of the Fund. This means, the only ownership of rights of property that may be conveyed or discharged against the underlying Rights and Property shall be Claims, also known as "Charges"; and

(iii) The life or operation of a Fund (the period it conducts business) shall be the maximum as specified by the present most sacred

Covenant, or associated covenants, charters, constitutions and laws; and

(iv) A Fund may be actual money, or notes, or certificates, or securities or stocks able to be converted or negotiated for monetary value, providing the nature and monetary value of each element is clearly outlined within the accounts of the Fund; and

(v) The terms of negotiation of the Stock of a Fund for other stock, or actual money, or notes, or certificates, or other securities shall be determined on a Fund by Fund basis, including whether a particular Fund is able to purchase the Stock of another Fund of the Body, to what maximum and other conditions (if any); and

(vi) A Fund shall never be the original Assets themselves, but the Derivation of the value of the underlying Property, as recorded in the accounts and ledgers of the Fund, to permit the remission, remittance, settlement and discharge of debits, debts and obligations; and

(vii) When the term of a Fund expires, it shall be absolutely forbidden to conduct any more new business. However, it may continue to manage and administer existing business and obligations until all such existing obligations and settlements expire or are balanced or dissolved or liquidated; and

(viii) The property and assets held in Trust shall be absolutely forbidden to be released from such a Trust underwriting a Fund until after the term of a Fund expires and after all obligations and settlements are balanced and the fund dissolved or liquidated and the purpose of the Trust is fulfilled and the Trust dissolved; and

(ix) A Fund ceases to exist when it is properly liquidated or dissolved by an action in accord with the instrument of its creation, or after the expiry of its term. In accord with these articles, the administrators of a valid Fund are morally obligated to ensure the timely dissolution of the Fund as soon as practical after such a valid event.

Article 127 – Ucadia Supreme Credo (Credit)

Ucadia Supreme Credo (Credit)

1. **By the power and authority of this Covenant and through the unanimous willing consent of all Members of united Heaven** a Supreme Unit of Value has hereby been formed, sanctified, minted and placed into circulation

known as the Supreme Credo, also known as the Supreme Credit.

No other physical, ethereal or conceptual unit may be spiritually, legally or lawfully considered higher in value than a Supreme Credo. A Supreme Credo is formed through the creation of a valid Supreme Trust.

2. By the authority of this Covenant and consent of all Members, a Supreme Trust is when one hundred (100) deceased Members consent to convey equitable title and rights of use from their individual Divine Trusts into a new Supreme Divine Trust. This Supreme Divine Trust (Supreme Trust) then holds the assets of one hundred (100) compared to a Divine Trust holding the property of just one. Supreme Trust

3. A Supreme Credo (Credit) shall be considered valid when issued in accord with the following criteria:- Structure of a Supreme Credo (Credit)

(i) At least one valid unit of supreme value evidenced by the existence of a unique eighteen (18) digit serial number representing the valid existence of the Supreme Trust belonging to the Great Ledger of Supreme Credo (Credit) serial numbers for all Supreme Trusts ever created and issued; and

(ii) A single beneficiary to whom the Supreme Credo (Credit) is granted being one of the seven (7) valid Union Treasuries of the Society; and

(iii) A record of the valid eighteen (18) digit Great Register number of a valid officer of One Heaven that first notarised the validity of the Supreme Credo (Credit); and

(iv) A record of the valid eighteen (18) digit Great Register number of the Member commissioned to senior office that first authorised the Supreme Credo (Credit); and

(v) The eighteen (18) digit Great Register number of the instrument to which the one or more Supreme Credo (Credit) have been assigned; and

(vi) The Ucadian Time at which the Supreme Credo (Credit) was legitimately created and assigned to its particular instrument; and

(vii) The eighteen (18) digit Great Register number representing the valid Account into which the one or more Supreme Credo (Credit) have been placed.

If one or more of these criteria cannot be demonstrated, then an object cannot be legitimately considered as a valid Supreme Credo (Credit).

4. An Authenticated Extract of Supreme Credo (Credit) shall be any printed or electronic instrument demonstrating the valid criteria for a valid Supreme Credo (Credit):- General Principles of Supreme Credo (Credit)

(i) The primary principle of Supreme Credo (Credit) is the equality of all living men and women under the Golden Rule of Law, of true Justice and Fair Process, regardless of their creed, economic condition, race, colour, gender or religion; and

(ii) The Globe Union Treasury shall be the one and only institution permitted to hold Supreme Credo (Credits). No other entity or institution on Earth may hold Supreme Credo (Credits) and all Supreme Credo Accounts shall be managed and administered by the Globe Union Treasury; and

(iii) A valid Supreme Credo Account Number shall be eighteen (18) characters identifying the owner of the Account, the type of Account and the beneficiary of the Account. Only three (3) forms of valid types of Accounts shall be held by the Globe Union Treasury for the holding of Supreme Credo (Credits) being Supreme Credo Fund Account, Supreme Credo Trust Account and Supreme Credo Grace Account; and

(iv) The Beneficiary named on a Supreme Credo (Credit) may only ever be one of the seven (8) Union Treasuries being: Globe Union Treasury, Africans Union Treasury, Americas Union Treasury, Asia Union Treasury, Arabian Union Treasury, Levant Union Treasury, Euro Union Treasury and Oceanic Union Treasury; and

(v) There shall be only one Supreme Trust Account held by the Globe Union Treasury and only seven (7) Supreme Grace Accounts; and

(vi) Any claimed holder of a Supreme Credo (Credit) that is not a Union Treasury is an unlawful holder. Any claimed beneficiary that is not a valid Union is an invalid beneficiary; and

(vii) As Supreme Credo are given by Divine Grace, they are never permitted to be traded, sold, surrendered, alienated, liened, mortgaged, purchased, promised, leased or used for any direct commercial transaction whatsoever, other than as a gift of supreme value granted to one of the seven (7) Union Treasuries.

5. A Supreme Credit shall have the following permanent value Face value relationships of a Supreme

relationships:-

Credo (Credit)

(i) 1 supreme credo (credit) = 100 gold credo (credit); and

(ii) 1 supreme credo (credit) = 1,000,000 silver credo (credit); and

(iii) 1 supreme credo (credit) = 1,000,000,000 union moneta; and

(iv) 1 supreme credo (credit) = 1,000,000,000 university moneta.

Forbiddence to deface or destroy a Supreme Credo (Credit)

6. No unit of credit created as a result of a Supreme Credo (Credit) is permitted to be destroyed. Once created, no unit of credit underwritten by this most sacred instrument may be uncreated.

When an authenticated extract is provided to a non-registered entity, it shall be expected the extract shall be treated with the highest respect and immediately forwarded to the appropriate treasury and treasurer.

Supreme Credo Account Types

7. In relation to Supreme Credo (Credit), the three (3) types of Supreme Credo Accounts shall be Fund, Trust and Grace:-

(i) A "**Supreme Fund Account**" identified by the letters "**CF**" (*Credo Fund*) is the primary Account for holding Supreme Credo and the first Account into which any new Supreme Credo are deposited. There is only ever one possible Supreme Fund Account; and

(ii) A "**Supreme Trust Account**" identified by the letters "**CT**" (*Credo Trust*) is when Supreme Credo are held for the benefit of one of the seven (7) Union Treasuries being: Globe Union Treasury, Africans Union Treasury, Americas Union Treasury, Asia Union Treasury, Arabian Union Treasury, Levant Union Treasury, Euro Union Treasury and Oceanic Union Treasury; and

(iii) A "**Supreme Grace Account**" identified by the letters "**CG**" (*Credo Grace*) provides the underlying asset value and underwriting to the issuance of Gold Credo (Credits). A Gold Credo cannot be issued and circulated as currency unless a value of similar amount exists in an associated Supreme Grace Account. Once Supreme Credo are deposited into a Supreme Grace Account, the amount of Supreme Credo is held and locked for a period of eight (8) years corresponding to the length of time a Gold Credo Currency Register is in circulation. At the expiry of a period of eight (8) years, the number of Supreme Credo may be increased or decreased (deposited or withdrawn) from a Supreme Grace Account. Only on the re-issue of a new Gold Credo Currency Register may a number of Supreme Credo be further deposited or withdrawn from the

Supreme Grace Account.

8. By the power and authority of this sacred Covenant, the total Spiritual Stock ("SS") of One Heaven shall be equivalent to one Supreme Credo (Credit) for each and every one hundred (100) Members at the time of the Day of Divine Agreement and Understanding with each recording of a Member in the Great Register equivalent to one Supreme Certificate, therefore one Supreme Credo (Credit). Spiritual Stock of Supreme Credo (Credit) of One Heaven

As at GAIA E8:Y3209:A1:S1:M6:D1 [Mon 21 Dec 2009] a Survey of the Total Records of the Great Roll of Divine Persons of Divine Trusts associated with the True Persons and True Trusts of the Higher Order Life Forms known as Homo Sapiens upon the planet known as Earth, was duly completed and concluded with the Total Members within the absolute Jurisdiction of One Heaven are 111,800,123,834 being all unique carnations that have ever existed of Homo Sapien Life, from the moment of conveyance of Divinity to the flesh after the fiftieth day of conception, whether or not in Life they reached full term or not. Furthermore, notice is hereby given that 6,788,747,478 Members remain carnate in flesh as at this Sacred Space-Day-Time through their True Person and True Trust; and with 7,467,622,226 Members not carnate in flesh consenting to serve as Guardians to the living Members; and with 14,400,000,000 Members not carnate in flesh consenting to temporarily transfer an aspect of their Divine Rights in support of one hundred and forty-four million (144,000,000) Supreme Divine Trusts as underwriting to the Supreme Credo serial numbers 990000-000000-000001 to 990000-000144-000000; and with 2,040,459,363 Members not carnate in flesh consenting to occupy, protect and service those Sacred Offices defined by Article 43 (*Sacred Offices and Officers*) and in accord with the occupation of all Apostolic Offices associated with the 3 Spiritual Bodies, the 7 Unions, the 239 Universities, the 3,763 Provinces and the 128,884 Campuses of Ucadia; and with 144,000,000 Members not carnate in flesh consenting to Divine Commission as the Guard and Armies of Heaven; and with 432,000,000 Members not carnate in flesh consenting to Divine Commission as assisting in Intercessions, Inspiration and support of Pilgrims; and with the remaining 94,927,294,767 Members not carnate in flesh choosing to focus on other activities and personal development.

9. By this most sacred Covenant, representing the one and true Divine Remedy of the Divine Creator, the Supreme Credo (Credit) and the Ucadian Currency System represents the one true and only supreme system of underwriting currency for all currencies. Remedy to all holders and traders of non-Ucadian currency, whether in the form of Supreme Credo (Credit) as Supreme Underwriting Currency for all valid Currencies

international banks and monetary funds, central banks, national and federal reserve banks, regional banks and other financial institutions is given on the following conditions:-

(i) That all non-Ucadian currency of the entity, whether in the form of stocks, bonds, gold, other precious metals and jewels, currency instruments and notes are surrendered to the appropriate Union or Global Union Reserve Bank of the Society in exchange for equivalent value of credit money underwritten ultimately by Supreme Credo (Credits); and

(ii) That any negotiable instrument, currency or note does not represent a secondary or tertiary derivative being a "derivative of a derivative" and not properly supported by a valid asset; and

(iii) That all legitimate direct loans for all entities are forgiven on condition that the entity surrender the legitimate debts bonds and debt to the appropriate Union and Global Banks of the Society in exchange for equivalent value in money underwritten ultimately by Supreme Credo (Credit) to forgive all the debt; and

(iv) That the entity agrees to undertake its responsibilities as a recognised and respected Member of the Society under the rules of the Society.

Publication of Supreme Credo and Associated Currency Registers

10. Consistent with the transparency, authenticity and authority of Supreme Credo and associated currencies, the appropriate Temples, Treasuries and Reserve Banks are directed to ensure Registers of all minted currency are published through official Gazette and viewable either as a printed authenticated extract of the Register or a database search:-

(i) The Currency Register for Supreme Credo (Credit) shall be published once every sixty-four (64) years; and

(ii) The Currency Register for Gold Credo (Credit) shall be published once every eight (8) years; and

(iii) The Currency Register for Silver Credo (Credit) shall be published once every four (4) years; and

(iv) The Currency Register for all Union Moneta (Money) shall be published once every year; and

(v) The Currency Register for all University Sovereign Moneta (Money) shall be published once every year.

Publication of

11. Consistent with the transparency, authenticity and authority of

Supreme Credo and associated currencies, the appropriate Temples, Treasuries and Reserve Banks are directed to ensure Summary of all Accounts and total of all minted currency are published through official Gazette and viewable either as a printed authenticated extract of the Accounts and their total value or a database search, or both:-

Supreme Credo Accounts and Associated Accounts

(i) All Accounts for Supreme Credo (Credit) shall be published once every eight (8) years; and

(ii) All Accounts for Gold Credo (Credit) shall be published once every four (4) years; and

(iii) All Accounts for Silver Credo (Credit) shall be published once every year; and

(iv) Accounts for which total transactions of 50,000 or more Union Moneta (Money) were transacted shall be published (Gazetted) once every thirty (30) days with all Accounts for Union Moneta holding 250,000 or more Union Moneta (Money) shall be published once every year; and

(v) Accounts for which total transactions of 25,000 or more University Moneta (Money) were transacted shall be published once every ninety (90) days with All Currency Accounts for Union Moneta holding 100,000 or more University Moneta (Money) shall be published once every year.

12. The calculation of any gift, grant or conveyance of Supreme Credo (Credits) at the commencement of the first Supreme Credo Register shall be according to the following criteria under the principal that all Spirit Members and all living Level 6 Higher Order Life forms are considered equal:-

Start Up Calculation of Gift, Grant and Conveyance of Supreme Credo

(i) Commencing on planet Earth, a calculation shall be determined as to the estimated number of Homo Sapien Minds, also known as Divine Immortal Spirits that have existed for the last ten thousand (10,000) years combined with living Level 6 Higher Order Life forms by the boundaries of the six (6) Unions being Africa, Americas, Arabia, Asia, Euro and Oceania; and

(ii) The total number of Supreme Credo (Credit) shall be divided according to the proportions consistent with the calculated number of Homo Sapien Minds, with approximately fifty (50%) percent of the total Supreme Credo (Credit) minted remaining in trust with the Globe Union Treasury.

13. The total number and volume of Supreme Credo (Credits) issued, shall be reviewed and amended every sixty-four (64) years in accord with

Ongoing Calculation of Gift, Grant and

the following formula:- Conveyance of Supreme Credo

(i) If the total population of Members carnated in flesh through their True Person and True Trust as at the Sacred Space-Day-Time of calculation is less than or the same as the previous total at the previous review, then no additional Supreme Credo (Credit) shall be issued; or

(ii) If the total population of Members carnated in flesh through their True Person and True Trust as at the Sacred Space-Day-Time of calculation is greater than the previous total at the previous review, then additional Supreme Credo (Credits) shall be issued at the ratio of one new Supreme Credo issued for the benefit of one of the six (6) regional Union Treasuries for every thirty-three (33) new births of living Members carnated in flesh through their True Person and True Trust over and above the previous total population calculation, providing the individual member reached the age of two (2) years.

14. In recognition of the founding Sacred Mints of Rome at Jerusalem up until 69CE and at Lyons and the first and original mint and temple of London; and in recognition of the ancient sacred authority and history of the first standard minted coins of civilised history, the official sign and seal for the first great Age of one thousand and seventy (1,070) years of the founding Treasurer and Judge for all Supreme Credo (Credit) issued by the One Heaven Treasury shall be the Member known as Mithra, also known as [Trust No. 980745-321514-010057]. Founding Seal of Mithra

Article 128 – Ucadia Markets

1. **A Market shall be a trusted space (virtual or real) where three (3) or more buyers and sellers** may safely and fairly exchange Goods or Services. Ucadia Markets

There shall be four (4) basic elements that define a Market in addition to the existence of three or more buyers and sellers, namely *Market Rules, Standard Unit of Measure, Accounts & Bookkeeping* and *Conversion and Settlement of Accounts*:-

(i) *Market Rules* means that a space or place cannot possibly be a market unless it possesses the most essential of Rules based upon the Golden Rule of Law of equality, fairness and trust; and

(ii) A *Standard Unit of Measure* means there are consistent standards of valuation across a market so "like can be exchanged for like". This standard unit is what is most commonly called Money; and

(iii) *Accounts & Bookkeeping* is the inescapable and necessary fact that the accounts being the registers of title and ownership are intimately linked to the operation of any market, including the certificate of proof of transaction; and

(iv) *Conversion and Settlement of Accounts* is in essence the clearing mechanism of trade, that requires the ability of initial conversion, the ability to trade, the settlement of accounts and then the redemption of any remainder back into some portable form to be withdrawn from the market, if one chooses.

2. A structure shall not be lawfully or morally considered a Financial System, no matter how complex, universally adopted or accepted, if it shall engage in any of the following practices:- When a structure is not a legitimate Financial System

(i) That the Laws of the system may be changed arbitrarily to the betterment of a few and the detriment of others, without fair recourse or remedy; or

(ii) That units of value may be introduced as money without any legitimate underwriting, thus devaluing the total stock of existing units of money; or

(iii) That units of value may be destroyed or withdrawn, without account for the provenance or historical basis of such lost units, thus inflating the remaining value of total stock of units of money; or

(iv) That credit may be introduced into a market, without defined rules as to the limits of credit of the market, nor the prior allocation rights of participants; and further that such credit may be exported and converted into "money", thus devaluing the total stock of existing units of money; or

(v) That instruments issued in reference to credit, or agreements, including all derivatives thereof, are permitted to exceed the value of the original value of the asset that created all subsequent derivatives.

Article 129 – Ucadia Financial System (UFS)

1. **The Ucadia Financial System (UFS) shall be a comprehensive and complete global financial system** of *Laws, Legal Structures and Constructs, Courts and Legal Enforcement, Registers and Rolls, Instruments of Value, Agreements of Value, Markets, Accounts, Credit, Money, Treasuries, Banks, Firms,* and *Goods* capable of operating as a self contained system, or Ucadia Financial System (UFS) underwriting, or amalgamating or successfully replacing non-Ucadian financial systems of a city, state, nation or region or globe, in accord with the present most sacred Covenant.

The fourteen (14) core elements of the Ucadia Financial System (UFS) shall include:-

(i) *Laws* that consistently define the rules of the Ucadia Financial System; and

(ii) *Legal Structures and Constructs* such as Rights, Trusts, Estates, Property and Funds that enable the consistent establishment of ownership, value and the administration of intangible and tangible forms of property; and

(iii) *Courts and Legal Enforcement* that ensure the honest and impartial application of Laws and enforcement and protection of Legal Structures and Constructs; and

(iv) *Registers and Rolls* for the recording of various Legal Structures and Constructs of Value, including Instruments derived therefrom; and

(v) *Instruments of Value* derived from Registers and Rolls, capable of being exchanged themselves, or being held as collateral and security; and

(vi) *Agreements of Value* signalling transactions of economic activity, capable of being held as collateral as security, or monetised (converted or securitised) into an Instrument of Value; and

(vii) *Markets* for the various exchanges of rights, obligations, credit, goods, property, instruments, funds and money between market participants; and

(viii) *Accounts* being the ledgers of Markets and various Institutions, enabling the recording of transactions, exchanges and settlements; and

(ix) *Credit* being an internal and enclosed form of Money of a Market, enabling exchange and the settlement of transactions, but that in order to be exchanged as money beyond the market must be "converted" by means of the negotiability (portability) of Instruments, Agreements and/or Goods that accompanies the issuance of such Credit; and

(x) *Money* being units of measure, units of account, units of redemption for value, means of exchange and reliable stores of value; and

(xi) *Treasuries* being the custodians and controllers of Money and the purchasers of Securitised Instruments and Agreements purchased by Banks in the conversion of Financial Credit into Money; and

(xii) *Banks* being the providers of Credit into certain Financial Markets and the sponsors (converters) of Credit into Money through the collateralisation of monetisable Instruments and Agreements secured in the provision of such Credit; and

(xiii) *Firms* being trading entities within Markets and the producers of Goods available and capable of being sold or exchanged within those Markets; and

(xiv) *Goods* (including Services) manufactured by Firms and sold and traded within Markets.

2. A structure shall not be legally, lawfully or morally considered a Financial System, no matter how complex, universally adopted or accepted, if it engages in any of the following practices:-

When a structure is not a legitimate Financial System

(i) That the Laws of the system may be changed arbitrarily to the betterment of a few and the detriment of others, without fair recourse or remedy; or

(ii) That units of value may be introduced as money without any legitimate underwriting, thus devaluing the total stock of existing units of money; or

(iii) That units of value may be destroyed or withdrawn, without account for the provenance or historical basis of such lost units, thus inflating the remaining value of total stock of units of money; or

(iv) That credit may be introduced into a market, without defined rules as to the limits of credit of the market, nor the prior allocation rights of participants; and further that such credit may be exported and converted into "money", thus devaluing the total stock of existing units of money; or

(v) That instruments issued in reference to credit, or agreements, including all derivatives thereof, are permitted to exceed the value of the original value of the asset that created all subsequent derivatives.

TITLE XXII – STANDARDS & PROCEDURES

Article 130 - Covenant Confirmation and Amendment

1. **The present most sacred Covenant** shall be Confirmed seven (7) times by Revelation, Ratification, Sanctification, Testification, Exemplification, Legislation and Consummation upon or within seven (7) years of its formation: Covenant Confirmation

(i) By *Revelation*, the present most sacred Covenant is the self-evident manifestation of Divine Truth and fulfilment of the most sacred and revered scripture from MARS E8:Y3208:A48:S4:M25:D3, also known as [Saturday, 15 August 2009]; and

(ii) By *Ratification*, the present most sacred Covenant being ratified upon GAIA E8:Y3209:A1:S1:M6:D1, also known as [Monday, 21 Dec 2009], as the first and highest law of Heaven by the properly constituted government of One Heaven being the one hundred and forty-four (144) united as the Unique Collective Awareness of Divine Mind, also known as the "Divina"; and

(iii) By *Sanctification*, the present most sacred Covenant is fulfilled, finished and perfected by one borne of Holly (Holy) Blood from VENUS E8:Y3210:A0:S1:M27:D6, also known as [Wednesday, 21 December 2011]; and

(iv) By *Testification*, the present most sacred Covenant sources its power, legitimacy and authority from each and every signed, sealed and executed *Voluntatem Et Testamentum* (Will and Testament) in the proper prescribed form of Level 6 Higher Order life forms bearing witness to their Divinity and the validity of the present Covenant from GAIA E1:Y1:A1:S1:M9:D1, also known as [Friday, 21 December 2012]; and

(v) By *Exemplification*, the present most sacred Covenant is signed, sealed and delivered by one possessing the absolute authority by the most sacred and revered scripture to do so from JOVIUS E1:Y1:A17:S2:M4:D4, also known as [Thursday, 14 March 2013]; and

(vi) By *Legislation*, the present most sacred Covenant shall be the first statute as law enacted within each and every Ucadia community from SOL E1:Y3:A0:S1:M11:D5, also known as [Monday, 21 December 2015]; and

(vii) By *Consummation*, the present most sacred Covenant fulfilment, finished and made perfect from MARS

E1:Y4:A48:S4:M14:D3, also known as [Monday, 15 August 2016].

2. The present most sacred Covenant shall be permitted to be amended from time to time, in accord with the strict interpretation of the present Article, according to Technical or Special: Covenant Amendment

(i) A "**Technical Amendment**" is where a specific clause contained within the present Covenant is approved for a minor amendment either through the complete replacement of all the words contained within the clause, or minor word alteration, due to an error of presentation, or translation, or grammar; and

(ii) A "**Special Amendment**" is where a new clause or enhanced meaning to a clause is proposed and added to the Covenant, normally at a Great Conclave.

3. A Technical Amendment is where a specific clause contained within the present Covenant is approved for a minor amendment either through the complete replacement of all the words contained within the clause, or minor word alteration. A Technical Amendment is permitted to occur under one or more of the following conditions: Technical Amendment Criteria

(i) That the clause contains a style, typographical or simple grammatical error which will be corrected through the proposed amendment; or

(ii) That the clause contains a significant grammatical error which renders any true intention of the clause impossible and that the proposed amendment will correct this error to the original intent; or

(iii) That the clause contains a significant error contradicting one or more other clauses of the Covenant and that the proposed amendment will correct this error to the original intent.

4. A Special Amendment must clearly qualify under each and every of the following criteria to be considered a legally valid proposed amendment:- Special Amendment Criteria

(i) That the proposed Special Amendment is not morally repugnant to the principles, ethics and laws of Ucadia; and

(ii) That the proposed Special Amendment does not introduce a conflict of laws or between remaining unaltered articles; and

(iii) That the proposed Special Amendment does not in any way contradict, usurp, abrogate, diminish, alienate or render ineffective an existing major tenet or principle of the present sacred Covenant.

5. A Special Amendment shall only be permitted after the Ucadia Space-Day Time of SOL E1:Y3:A0:S1:M11:D5, also known as [Monday, 21 December 2015] where such proposal is made at a Great Conclave where a vote is taken for its approval, framed as a free and fair vote to the delegates. For an amendment to be valid and enacted requires a two thirds (2/3) of the total votes cast by the total delegates to a Great Conclave. Great Conclave and Special Amendment

Article 131 - Greatest Principles

1. **When the Oratorium, also known as the One Supreme Court, also known as the Supreme Court of One Heaven is in Session** in accord with the present sacred Covenant, The Court may use its Powers of Original Jurisdiction to make absolute and final rulings in accord with Divine Maxims of Law by Final Irrevocable Judgement. These absolute and final rulings shall be called "**Greatest Principles**". Greatest Principles

2. A "**Greatest Principle**" is *ipso facto* (as a matter of fact) original law and primary law and the highest possible final and irrevocable tenet, principle and edict from a validly constituted forum of law of any and all societies, aggregates, associations, persons, entities and higher order spirits, living and deceased having universal and absolute, divine and temporal jurisdiction:- Greatest Principle as Absolute and Final Law

   (i) Providing the Greatest Principle adheres to the Criteria of valid Greatest Principle as prescribed by the present Article; and

   (ii) The officer or body issuing the Greatest Principle has the power and authority to do so in accord with the present sacred Covenant; and

   (iii) That the Greatest Principle does not seek to define or create a new Right, or new Property, or seek to grant, give, devise, convey, alienate, surrender, seize, disqualify, enclose, capture, arrest, securitise, suppress, forfeit or annul any existing Rights unless such an action has already been acknowledged and defined as permitted within the present sacred Covenant or associated Covenants and Charters; and

   (iv) That the Greatest Principle does not contradict the most sacred present Covenant or the body of maxims known as the *Divine Collection of Maxims of Law*; and

   (v) The new Greatest Principle does not contradict any previous

Greatest Principle.

3. A valid Greatest Principle adheres to the following essential criteria:- Criteria for valid Greatest Principle

(i) The Oratorium as the Supreme Court of One Heaven is in Session and capable of properly rendering a Greatest Principle; and

(ii) That a properly constituted and highest and most competent forum of Living Members as Justices as defined by the present Covenant and associated Covenants exists as the union of the Three (3) Supreme Courts of the Three (3) Great Faiths, or if the Three (3) Great Faiths are not yet in proper operation then the Globe Union Forum, or if the Globe Union Forum is not yet in proper operation, then a Union Basilica; and

(iii) That the Justices and officials and parties of the competent temporal forum have been duly invoked to evoke a Special Hearing for a Greatest Principle; and

(iv) A petition and memorandum is received by the competent forum in the prescribed form, duly lodged, recorded and gazetted for a Greatest Principle to be rendered; and

(v) That the specific subject matter of the petition and memorandum is within the Powers of Original Jurisdiction of the Oratorium as the Supreme Court of One Heaven; and

(vi) That the core questions outlined within the Petition to be answered have not previously been specifically addressed in a previous Greatest Principle.

4. In accord with the present most sacred Covenant, each of the three (3) Great Faiths shall be permitted to use their own official name for Greatest Principles:- Great Faiths and Greatest Principles

(i) The Universal Ecclesia of One Christ may use the name "**Summa Dogma**" to officially define a Greatest Principle from the perspective of their authority; and

(ii) The Holy Society of One Islam may use the name "**Marsum Al'aelaa**" to officially define a Greatest Principle from the perspective of their authority; and

(iii) The Sacred Society of One Spirit may use the name "**Paramam Karma**" to officially define a Greatest Principle from the perspective of their authority.

Article 132 - Greatest Teachings

1. **When the Oratorium, also known as the One Supreme Court, also known as the Supreme Court of One Heaven** is in Session in accord with the present sacred Covenant, The Court may use its Powers of Appellate Jurisdiction to make absolute and final rulings in accord with Divine Maxims of Law by Teaching and Adjudication, providing a sacred writ has been duly issued. These absolute and final rulings of teaching and adjudication shall be called Greatest Teaching. Greatest Teachings

2. A "**Greatest Teaching**" is *ipso facto* (as a matter of fact) the absolute highest possible and final appeal and judgement, edict, teaching instrument and legal instruction from a validly constituted forum of law of any and all societies, aggregates, associations, persons, entities and higher order spirits, living and deceased having universal and absolute, divine and temporal jurisdiction:- Greatest Teaching as Absolute and Final Appeal and Judgement

    (i) Providing the Greatest Teaching adheres to the Criteria of a valid Greatest Teaching as prescribed by the present Article; and

    (ii) The officer or body issuing the Greatest Teaching has the power and authority to do so in accord with the present sacred Covenant; and

    (iii) That the Greatest Teaching does not contradict the most sacred present Covenant or the body of maxims known as the *Divine Collection of Maxims of Law*; and

    (iv) The new Greatest Teaching does not contradict any previous Greatest Teaching.

3. A valid Greatest Teaching adheres to the following essential criteria:- Criteria for valid Greatest Teaching

    (i) The Oratorium as the Supreme Court of One Heaven is in Session and capable of properly rendering a Greatest Teaching; and

    (ii) That a properly constituted and highest and most competent forum of Living Members as Justices as defined by the present Covenant and associated Covenants exists as the union of the Three (3) Supreme Courts of the Three (3) Great Faiths, or if the Three (3) faiths are not yet in proper operation then the Globe Union Forum, or if the Globe Union Forum is not yet in proper operation, then a Union Basilica; and

    (iii) That the Justices and officials and parties of the competent temporal forum have been duly invoked to evoke a Special Hearing for a Greatest Teaching; and

(iv) A petition and memorandum is received by the competent forum in the prescribed form, duly lodged, recorded and gazetted for a Greatest Teaching to be rendered; and

(v) That the specific subject matter of the petition and memorandum is within the Powers of Appellate Jurisdiction of the Oratorium as the Supreme Court of One Heaven; and

(vi) That the core questions outlined within the Petition to be answered have not previously been specifically addressed in a previous Greatest Teaching.

4. In accord with the present most sacred Covenant, each of the three (3) Great Faiths shall be permitted to use their own official name for Greatest Teachings:- Great Faiths and Greatest Teachings

(i) The Universal Ecclesia of One Christ may use the name "**Summa Doctrina**" to officially define a Greatest Teaching from the perspective of their authority; and

(ii) The Holy Society of One Islam may use the name "**Taelim Al'aelaa**" to officially define a Greatest Teaching from the perspective of their authority; and

(iii) The Sacred Society of One Spirit may use the name "**Paramam Sasana**" to officially define a Greatest Teaching from the perspective of their authority.

Article 133 - Decrees, Sanctions and Penalties

1. **The Divina possesses the Perfect Right** to coerce offending Members with penal sanctions, subject to the articles of the present sacred Covenant and associated covenants and rules. Right of Sanctions and Penalties

2. A "**Penalty**" is a voluntary and prescribed act demonstrating remorse and forgiveness in the event of some default of obligation and duty. In contrast, a non-voluntary prescribed act is an act of punitive measure, not permitted by the present sacred Covenant. Penalties

The Divina and all lesser jurisdictions derive their coercive Rights by the self-evident consent of Members to them. By the Law of Free Will, a Member may identify themselves as a Penitent, or a Resistant, or a Belligerent:

(i) A "**Penitent**" is one who voluntarily confesses through an act of contrition as to their true culpability and seeks to make amends and restore their honour through the acceptance of those prescribed Penalties; and

(ii) A "**Resistant**" is one who does not disavow the existence of an original agreement and therefore a binding, but resists making a voluntary confession and instead relies upon the strength and will of others to prove their culpability and impose the fair prescribed Penalties; and

(iii) A "**Belligerent**" is one who disavows any previous agreement and instead declares themselves hostile to any act to restore honour, or honour the Rule of Law and justice in the application of Penalties, instead relying on the power of others to bring them into custody and impose the fair prescribed Penalties upon valid proof.

3. All valid Penalties are derived from the present sacred Covenant and no other. There are four (4) valid categories being Censure, Fine, Suspension or Forfeiture: Penalty Categories

(i) A "**Censure**" is an official reprimand that may or may not involve one or more temporary prohibitions, or remedial actions; and

(ii) A "**Fine**" is a pecuniary penalty, and is to be administered strictly through the jurisdiction of competent forums of law and not as a general option of corporate regulation; and

(iii) A "**Suspension**" is when one temporarily loses rights and interest in property; and

(iv) A "**Forfeiture**" is when one permanently loses his rights and interest in property.

4. A "**Sanction**" is a Penalty as a coercive measure, intended to ensure compliance, enacted as a result of a law, treaty, or contract, or a clause within a law, treaty, or contract, specifying such a Penalty. Sanctions

All valid Sanctions are derived from the present articles, covenants and maxims of the present sacred Covenant and no other.

5. "**Divine Decrees**" (Decretum Divinum Iurium) are Imperfect Divine Rights associated with Divine Decrees concerning the administration, conduct and enforcement of law and order. The following valid eleven (11) Divine Decrees (Decretum Divinum Iurium) are recognised in accord with the present Covenant: Divine Decrees (Decretum Divinum Iurium)

(i) "**Decretum Divinum Doctrinae**" as the Divine Right of Divine Decree of Doctrine; and

(ii) "**Decretum Divinum Absolutionis**" as the Divine Right of Divine Decree of Absolution; and

(iii) "**Decretum Divinum Damnationis**" as the Divine Right of Divine Decree of Damnation; and

(iv) "**Decretum Divinum Exemplificatio**" as the Divine Right of Divine Decree of Exemplification; and

(v) "**Decretum Divinum Testimonium**" as the Divine Right of Divine Decree of Proof; and

(vi) "**Decretum Divinum Instructionis**" as the Divine Right of Divine Decree of Instruction; and

(vii) "**Decretum Divinum Censurae**" as the Divine Right of Divine Decree of Censure; and

(viii) "**Decretum Divinum Annullas**" as the Divine Right of Divine Decree of Annulment; and

(ix) "**Decretum Divinum Ratificationis**" as the Divine Right of Divine Decree of Ratification; and

(x) "**Decretum Divinum Interdictum**" as the Divine Right of Divine Decree of Interdiction; and

(xi) "**Decretum Divinum Levationis**" as the Divine Right of Divine Decree of Relief.

Article 134 – Supreme Sacred Gifts & Rites

Supreme Sacred Gifts & Rites

1. **Supreme Sacred Gifts and Rites of Heaven** shall be the customary rules, standards and procedures whereby the Thirty-Three (33) Sacred Gifts of Heaven are properly administered and dispensed by qualified and authorised persons, in accord with the present sacred Covenant.

"**Extraordinary Rites**" shall be the customary rules, standards and procedures of rites and rituals beyond the Thirty-Three (33) Sacred Gifts as defined by the present sacred Covenant; and whereby such Extraordinary Rites are properly administered and dispensed by qualified and authorised persons.

Just as all valid, legitimate and proper gifts and rites are derived from Heaven and the Divine Grace and Mercy of the Divine Creator, in accord with the present sacred Covenant, all rules, customs, traditions, standards and procedures for their administration and ministration are ultimately derived from the same present sacred Covenant.

No rule, custom, tradition, standard or procedure in relation to Sacred Gifts or Rites shall be valid, legitimate or permitted, unless it firmly adheres to the present sacred Covenant.

2. The following forms of Extraordinary Rites and Rubrics are recognised and subject to the present Sacred Covenant, including (but not limited to):- Recognised Forms of Extraordinary Rites

(i) *Dedication* being a form of Extraordinary Rite for the consecration of places, buildings, monuments and structures; and

(ii) *Restoration* being a form of Extraordinary Rite for the reconsecration and bringing a place, building, monument or structure to its original state; and

(iii) *Reformation* being a form of Extraordinary Rite for the restoring of a cleric state of office to a sacred state; and

(iv) *Blessing* being a form of Extraordinary Rite for invoking Divine assistance, favour, approval or protection; and

(v) *Expulsion* being a form of Extraordinary Rite for the driving out of a particular spirit or presence from Sacred Circumscribed Space; and

(vi) *Nullification* being a form of Extraordinary Rite for making legally and lawfully invalid a previous agreement or right; and

(vii) *Deconsecration* being a form of Extraordinary Rite for the removal of the consecrated and sacred state and function of a place, building, monument or structure; and

(viii) *Secularisation* being a form of Extraordinary Rite for the removal of the clerical authority of a person previously ordained; and

(ix) *Exorcism* being a form of Extraordinary Rite for the enforced removal, arrest or custody of one or more spirits in breach of the rules governing Sacred Circumscribed Space and the laws of Divine Trust, Mind and Spirit; and

(x) *Inquisition* being a form of Extraordinary Rite for the formal investigation into the truth and efficacy of some matter; and

(xi) *Dispensation* being a form of Extraordinary Rite for the granting of permission to do or perform an act otherwise not permitted, or to omit doing something otherwise enjoined; an exemption; and

(xii) *Abrogation* being a form of Extraordinary Rite for the repealing by authority some legislative act; and

(xiii) *Ordination* being a form of Extraordinary Rite for the consecration of a qualified candidate for the clerical state; and

(xiv) *Inauguration* being a form of Extraordinary Rite for the inducting into office with solemnity a person elected to high civil office; and

(xv) *Sanction* being a form of Extraordinary Rite for the enforced censuring, restriction or punishment of a person holding or occupying an office, in response to a demonstrated and proven act of maladministration or malfeasance; and

(xvi) *Unction* being a form of Extraordinary Rite for the anointing of a person in time of ill-health or trauma; and

(xvii) *Coronation* being a form of Extraordinary Rite for the solemn sacred ceremonial investiture of a person into sovereign office and the formation of a new sacred sovereign trust between the people and the new sovereign; and

(xviii) *Investiture* being a form of Extraordinary Rite for the solemn sacred acceptance of a person into office that involves the formation of a new trust involving the transfer and vesting of one or more Ecclesiastical or Sovereign or Official Rights; and

(xix) *Hours* being a form of Extraordinary Rite for the recitation of prayers and forms of invocation, in relation to significant days, times and seasons, often involving chants or singing.

3. The Three (3) Great Faiths of One Christ, One Islam and One Spirit, including Ucadia itself, shall have the right to promulgate an original and primary text, consistent with the present sacred Covenant and the Covenant of each body, whereby Sacred Gifts and Rites, as they apply for each unique Great Faith or Ucadia, shall be definitively expressed.

Three Great Faiths and Ucadia and Sacramental Rites and Rubrics

4. The "**Missal of Christ**" (*Missale Christus*) shall be the original and primary sacred text containing the necessary rubrics, maxims, sacramentaries, votives, invocations, instructions and orders for the proper conduct and proceeding of Sacred Liturgy of the Universal Rites of One Christ. The conduct of all sacramentaries concerning the thirty-three Sacraments and Extra-Sacramental Rites and Rubrics of Heaven shall be in accord with the Missal of Christ (Missale Christus).

Missale Christus

5. The "**Rites of Islam**" (Taqwa Islam) shall be the original and primary sacred text containing the necessary rites, maxims, pillars, rituals,

Taqwa Islam

votives, invocations, instructions and orders for the proper conduct and proceeding of Sacred Life of the most sacred and Holy Society of One Islam, also known as the One true Way of Allah. The conduct of all sacramentaries concerning the thirty-three Sacred Gifts and Extraordinary Rites of Heaven shall be in accord with the Rites of Islam (Taqwa Islam).

6. The "**Rites of the Universal Divine Spirit**" (Karman Spiritus) shall be the original and primary sacred text containing the necessary rites, maxims, pillars, rituals, votives, invocations, instructions and orders for the proper conduct and proceeding of Sacred Life of the most sacred Society of One Spirit, also known as the One Holy Apostolic Spirit and One Spirit Tribe. The conduct of all sacramentaries concerning the thirty-three Sacred Gifts and Extraordinary Rites of Heaven shall be in accord with the Rites of the Universal Divine Spirit (Karman Spiritus).

Karman Spiritus

Article 135 - Divine Collection of Maxims of Law

1. A **Body of Divine Maxims of Law** shall be formed, known as the *Divine Collection of Maxims of Law*. All standards of Divine Law as it pertains to this most sacred Covenant and laws shall be subject to inclusion in the Body of Divine Maxims of Law.

Divine Collection of Maxims of Law

2. The *Divine Collection of Maxims of Law* shall comprise of twenty-two (22) Books, known as Maxims, each addressing a fundamental pillar of Divine Law and a domain of knowledge, namely:

Twenty-Two Books of the Divine Collection of Maxims of Law

(i) ***Lex Divina***: Maxims of Divine Law; and

(ii) ***Lex Naturae***: Maxims of Natural Law; and

(iii) ***Lex Cognitum***: Maxims of Cognitive Law; and

(iv) ***Lex Positivum***: Maxims of Positive Law; and

(v) ***Lex Ecclesiasticum***: Maxims of Ecclesiastical Law; and

(vi) ***Lex Virtus Naturae***: Maxims of Bioethics Law; and

(vii) ***Lex Regia***: Maxims of Sovereign Law; and

(viii) ***Lex Fidei***: Maxims of Fiduciary Law; and

(ix) ***Lex Administratum***: Maxims of Administrative Law; and

(x) ***Lex Economica***: Maxims of Economic Law; and

(xi) ***Lex Pecuniaria***: Maxims of Monetary Law; and

(xii) ***Lex Civilis***: Maxims of Civil Law; and

(xiii) ***Lex Criminalis***: Maxims of Criminal Law; and

(xiv) ***Lex Educationis***: Maxims of Education Law; and

(xv) ***Lex Nutrimens Et Medicina***: Maxims of Food & Drugs Law; and

(xvi) ***Lex Urbanus***: Maxims of Urban Law; and

(xvii) ***Lex Societatis***: Maxims of Company Law; and

(xviii) ***Lex Technologiae***: Maxims of Technology Law; and

(xix) ***Lex Commercii***: Maxims of Trade & IP Law; and

(xx) ***Lex Securitas***: Maxims of Security Law; and

(xxi) ***Lex Militaris***: Maxims of Military Law; and

(xxii) ***Lex Gentium***: Maxims of International Law.

3. The *Divine Collection of Maxims of Law* shall represent the primary, one and only true maxims of Law. Excluding this Covenant, all other laws, claims and agreements claiming standards of Divine Law and Divine authority shall be secondary and inferior to the *Divine Collection of Maxims of Law ab initio* (from the beginning).

Primary and only true Maxims of Law

Any law, court orders, opinions or other quasi legal claim that contradicts this most sacred fact, or contradicts one or more clauses contained within *Divine Collection of Maxims of Law* shall be *ipso facto* null and void from the beginning.

4. In accord with the present most sacred Covenant, each of the three (3) Great Faiths shall be permitted to use their own official name for the Divine Collection of Maxims of Law:-

Official Name of Divine Collection of Maxims of Law

(i) The Universal Ecclesia of One Christ may use the name "**Astrum Iuris Divini Canonum**" to officially define the *Divine Collection of Maxims of Law* from the perspective of their authority; and furthermore may name the individual books as "canons"; and

(ii) The Holy Society of One Islam may use the name "**Hikmat Samawi**" to officially define the *Divine Collection of Maxims of Law* from the perspective of their authority; and furthermore may name the individual books as "qanunlar"; and

(iii) The Sacred Society of One Spirit may use the name "**Pragya Dharma**" to officially define the *Divine Collection of Maxims* *of Law* from the perspective of their authority; and furthermore may name the individual books as "vedas".

5. "**Lex Divina**" being the "**Maxims of Divine Law**" represents the primary, one and only true Maxims of Divine Law. All and every other laws, claims and agreements of Divine Law shall be secondary and inferior to the Maxims of Divine Law, *ab initio* (from the beginning). Whenever or however a valid and legitimate reference is written or spoken concerning Divine Law, it shall mean *Lex Divina* and these Maxims of Divine Law and no other. Lex Divina: Maxims of Divine Law

The Maxims of Divine Law shall be structured into One Book, that in turn shall be divided into Titles, that in turn shall be divided into Sections or Articles and then one or more Maxims within each Article. The major Titles of the Maxims of Divine Law shall be:

I. Introductory Provisions

II. Divine Concepts

III. Divine Attributes

IV. Divine Beings

V. Divine Persons

VI. Divine Rights

VII. Divine Registers

VIII. Divine Trusts

IX. Divine Estates

X. Divine Money

XI. Divine Property

XII. Divine Dominions

XIII. Divine Covenants

XIV. Divine Systems

XV. Divine Revelation

XVI. Divine Places & Objects

6. "**Lex Naturae**" being the "**Maxims of Natural Law**" represents the primary, one and only true Maxims of Natural Law. All and every other laws, claims and agreements of Natural Law shall be secondary and inferior to the Maxims of Natural Law, *ab initio* (from the beginning). Whenever or however a valid and legitimate reference is written or spoken concerning Natural Law, it shall mean *Lex Naturae* and these Maxims of Natural Law and no other. Lex Naturae: Maxims of Natural Law

The Maxims of Natural Law shall be structured into One Book, that in turn shall be divided into Titles, that in turn shall be divided into Sections or Articles and then one or more Maxims within each Article. The major Titles of the Maxims of Natural Law shall be:

I. Introductory Provisions

II. Ucadia Standard Model of Elements (USME)

III. Ucadia Complete Model of Atomics (UCMA)

IV. Ucadia Standard Molecular System (USMS)

V. Ucadia Canonical Model of Energy & Forces (UCME)

VI. Unita Space

VII. Super-Sub Atomic Space

VIII. Sub-Atomic Space

IX. Atomic Space

X. Molecular Space

XI. Ucadia Cellular Model of Life (UCMOL)

XII. Ucadia System of Single Neural Life

XIII. Ucadia System of Dual Neural Life

XIV. Ucadia System of Triple Neural Life

XV. Ucadia Model of Self Aware Life

XVI. Ucadia Model Higher Order Life

XVII. Ucadia Model of Large Body Systems (LBS)

XVIII. Natural Beings

XIX. Natural Persons

XX. Natural Rights

XXI. Natural Trusts

XXII. Natural Dominions

7. "**Lex Cognitum**" being the "**Maxims of Cognitive Law**" represents the primary, one and only true Maxims of Cognitive Law. All and every other laws, claims and agreements of Cognitive Law shall be secondary and inferior to the Maxims of Cognitive Law, *ab initio* (from the beginning). Whenever or however a valid and legitimate reference is written or spoken concerning Cognitive Law, it shall mean *Lex Cognitum* and these Maxims of Cognitive Law and no other.

Lex Cognitum: Maxims of Cognitive Law

The Maxims of Cognitive Law shall be structured into One Book, that in turn shall be divided into Titles, that in turn shall be divided into Sections or Articles and then one or more Maxims within each Article. The major Titles of the Maxims of Cognitive Law shall be:-

I. Introductory Definitions

I. Computation & Cognition

III. Organic Computation & Cognition Systems (PSYBIO)

IV. Non-Organic Computation & Cognition Systems (PSYCOM)

V. Mind (PSY)

VI. Mind Dimension & Functional Realty (PSYREAL)

VII. Mind, Self & Ego

VIII. Mind Learning & Development (PSYDEV)

IX. Mind Immortality & Change (Soul)

X. Mind Influence

XI. Mind Illness & Impediment (PSYTELL)

XII. Mind Therapy and Cure

8. "**Lex Positivum**" being the "**Maxims of Positive Law**" represents the primary, one and only true Maxims of Positive Law. All and every other laws, claims and agreements of Positive Law shall be secondary and inferior to the Maxims of Positive Law, *ab initio* (from the beginning). Whenever or however a valid and legitimate reference is written or spoken concerning Positive Law, it shall mean *Lex Positivum* and these Maxims of Positive Law and no other.

Lex Positivum: Maxims of Positive Law

The Maxims of Positive Law shall be structured into One Book, that in turn shall be divided into Titles, that in turn shall be divided into Sections or Articles and then one or more Maxims within each Article. The major Titles of the Maxims of Positive Law shall be:-

I. Introductory Definitions

II. Reason & Argument

III. Form

IV. Place, Space & Time

V. Oaths, Vows, Testimony & Promises

VI. Registers, Rolls & Persons

VII. Documents, Instruments & Forms

VIII. Rights

IX. Personal Rights

X. Member Rights

XI. Trusts & Estates

XII. Property & Funds

XIII. Associations & Relations

XIV. Consensus

XV. Agreement

XVI. Powers & Authority

XVII. Jurisdiction

XVIII. Occurrence, Drama & Fact

9. "**Lex Ecclesiasticum**" being the "**Maxims of Ecclesiastical Law**" represents the primary, one and only true Maxims of Ecclesiastical Law. All and every other laws, claims and agreements of Ecclesiastical Law shall be secondary and inferior to the Maxims of Ecclesiastical Law, *ab initio* (from the beginning). Whenever or however a valid and legitimate reference is written or spoken concerning Ecclesiastical Law, it shall mean *Lex Ecclesiasticum* and these Maxims of Ecclesiastical Law and no other.

Lex Ecclesiasticum: Maxims of Ecclesiastical Law

The Maxims of Ecclesiastical Law shall be structured into One Book, that in turn shall be divided into Titles, that in turn shall be divided into Sections or Articles and then one or more Maxims within each Article. The major Titles of the Maxims of Ecclesiastical Law shall be:

I. Introductory Definitions

II. Supernatural

III. Sacred

IV. Revelation

V. Theology

VI. Institution

VII. Obedience

VIII. Sacrament

IX. Rights

X. Consecrated Life

XI. Sacred Life

XII. Transgression

XIII. Apostasy

XIV. Mercy

10. "**Lex Virtus Naturae**" being the "**Maxims of Bioethics Law**" represents the primary, one and only true Maxims of Bioethics Law. All and every other laws, claims and agreements of Bioethics Law shall be secondary and inferior to the Maxims of Bioethics Law, *ab initio* (from the beginning). Whenever or however a valid and legitimate reference is written or spoken concerning Bioethics Law, it shall mean *Lex Virtus Naturae* and these Maxims of Bioethics Law and no other.

Lex Virtus Naturae: Maxims of Bioethics Law

The Maxims of Bioethics Law shall be structured into One Book, that in turn shall be divided into Titles, that in turn shall be divided into Sections or Articles and then one or more Maxims within each Article. The major Titles of the Maxims of Bioethics Law shall be:

I. Introductory Definitions

II. Hydro-Carbon Life

III. Non-Hydro-Carbon Life

IV. Simple Hydro-Carbon Life

V. Simple Non-Hydro-Carbon Life

VI. Complex Hydro-Carbon Life

VII. Complex Non-Hydro-Carbon Life

VIII. Self Aware Hydro-Carbon Life

IX. Self Aware Non-Hydro-Carbon Life

X. Homo Sapien Life

XI. Life Ecosystems

11. "**Lex Regia**" being the "**Maxims of Sovereign Law**" represents the primary, one and only true Maxims of Sovereign Law. All and every other laws, claims and agreements of Sovereign Law shall be secondary and inferior to the Maxims of Sovereign Law, *ab initio* (from the beginning). Whenever or however a valid and legitimate reference is written or spoken concerning Sovereign Law, it shall mean *Lex Regia* and these Maxims of Sovereign Law and no other.

Lex Regia: Maxims of Sovereign Law

The Maxims of Sovereign Law shall be structured into One Book, that in turn shall be divided into Titles, that in turn shall be divided into Sections or Articles and then one or more Maxims within each Article. The major Titles of the Maxims of Sovereign Law shall be:

I. Introductory Definitions

II. Sovereign Claim & Mandate

III. Sovereign Rights

IV. Ucadia Sovereign Entity Rights

V. Instruction, Adjudication & Visitation

VI. Sovereign Symbols & Signs

VII. Sovereign Rank & Title

VIII. Saviour Rank & Title

IX. Sovereign Realm

X. Civilisation Models of Sovereign Law

XI. Empire Models of Sovereign Law

XII. Original Nations (Tribes)

12. "**Lex Fidei**" being the "**Maxims of Fiduciary Law**" represents the primary, one and only true Maxims of Fiduciary Law. All and every other laws, claims and agreements of Fiduciary Law shall be secondary and inferior to the Maxims of Fiduciary Law, *ab initio* (from the beginning). Whenever or however a valid and legitimate reference is written or spoken concerning Fiduciary Law, it shall mean *Lex Fidei* and these Maxims of Fiduciary Law and no other.

Lex Fidei: Maxims of Fiduciary Law

The Maxims of Fiduciary Law shall be structured into One Book, that in turn shall be divided into Titles, that in turn shall be divided into Sections or Articles and then one or more Maxims within each Article. The major Titles of the Maxims of Fiduciary Law shall be:

I. Introductory Definitions

II. Office

III. Official Rights

IV. Fiducial Rights

V. Trusts

VI. Estates

VII. Real Property

VIII. Personal Property

IX. Funds

X. Accounting

XI. Management

XII. Disputation

XIII. Extinction

XIV. Historic Trusts

13. "**Lex Administratum**" being the "**Maxims of Administrative Law**" represents the primary, one and only true Maxims of Administrative Law. All and every other laws, claims and agreements of Administrative Law shall be secondary and inferior to the Maxims of Administrative Law, *ab initio* (from the beginning). Whenever or however a valid and legitimate reference is written or spoken concerning Administrative Law, it shall mean *Lex Administratum* and these Maxims of Administrative Law and no other.

Lex Administratum: Maxims of Administrative Law

The Maxims of Administrative Law shall be structured into One Book, that in turn shall be divided into Titles, that in turn shall be divided into Sections or Articles and then one or more Maxims within each Article. The major Titles of the Maxims of Administrative Law shall be:

I. Introductory Definitions

II. Agency

III. Administrative Rights

IV. Policy

V. Procedures

VI. Regulation

VII. Enforcement

VIII. Arbitration

IX. Action

X. Penalty

XI. Remedy

14. "**Lex Economica**" being the "**Maxims of Economic Law**" represents the primary, one and only true Maxims of Economic Law. All and every other laws, claims and agreements of Economic Law shall be secondary and inferior to the Maxims of Economic Law, *ab initio* (from the beginning). Whenever or however a valid and legitimate reference is written or spoken concerning Economic Law, it shall mean *Lex Economica* and these Maxims of Economic Law and no other.

Lex Economica: Maxims of Economic Law

The Maxims of Economic Law shall be structured into One Book, that in turn shall be divided into Titles, that in turn shall be divided into Sections or Articles and then one or more Maxims within each Article. The major Titles of the Maxims of Economic Law shall be:

I. Introductory Definitions
II. Systems
III. Measurement
IV. Utility
V. Value
VI. Trust
VII. Security
VIII. Land
IX. Labour
X. Service
XI. Salary
XII. Good
XIII. Price
XIV. Capital
XV. Enterprise
XVI. Market
XVII. Currency
XVIII. Regulation
XIX. Industry
XX. Asset
XXI. Liability
XXII. Trade
XXIII. Revenue
XXIV. Expense
XXV. Profit
XXVI. Investment
XXVII. Government Revenue
XXVIII. Solvency
XXIX. Wealth
XXX. Competition
XXXI. Motivation

XXXII. Confidence

XXXIII. Satisfaction

15. "**Lex Pecuniaria**" being the "**Maxims of Monetary Law**" represents the primary, one and only true Maxims of Monetary Law. All and every other laws, claims and agreements of Monetary Law shall be secondary and inferior to the Maxims of Monetary Law, *ab initio* (from the beginning). Whenever or however a valid and legitimate reference is written or spoken concerning Monetary Law, it shall mean *Lex Pecuniaria* and these Maxims of Monetary Law and no other.

Lex Pecuniaria: Maxims of Monetary Law

The Maxims of Monetary Law shall be structured into One Book, that in turn shall be divided into Titles, that in turn shall be divided into Sections or Articles and then one or more Maxims within each Article. The major Titles of the Maxims of Monetary Law shall be:

I. Introductory Definitions

II. Monetary Rights

III. Monetary Registers

IV. Monetary Underwriting & Creation

V. Monetary Instruments

VI. Monetary Accounts

VII. Monetary Exchange

16. "**Lex Civilis**" being the "**Maxims of Civil Law**" represents the primary, one and only true Maxims of Civil Law. All and every other laws, claims and agreements of Civil Law shall be secondary and inferior to the Maxims of Civil Law, ab initio (from the beginning). Whenever or however a valid and legitimate reference is written or spoken concerning Civil Law, it shall mean *Lex Civilis* and these Maxims of Civil Law and no other.

Lex Civilis: Maxims of Civil Law

The Maxims of Civil Law shall be structured into One Book, that in turn shall be divided into Titles, that in turn shall be divided into Sections or Articles and then one or more Maxims within each Article. The major Titles of the Maxims of Civil Law shall be:

I. Introductory Definitions

II. Person

III. Infant Person

IV. Disabled Person

V. Junior Person

VI. Adult Person

VII. Senior Person

VIII. Elderly Person

IX. Terminally Ill Person

X. Corporate Person

XI. Register

XII. Record

XIII. Property

XIV. Estates

XV. Notice

17. "**Lex Criminalis**" being the "**Maxims of Criminal Law**" represents the primary, one and only true Maxims of Criminal Law. All and every other laws, claims and agreements of Criminal Law shall be secondary and inferior to the Maxims of Criminal Law, *ab initio* (from the beginning). Whenever or however a valid and legitimate reference is written or spoken concerning Criminal Law, it shall mean *Lex Criminalis* and these Maxims of Criminal Law and no other. Lex Criminalis: Maxims of Criminal Law

The Maxims of Criminal Law shall be structured into One Book, that in turn shall be divided into Titles, that in turn shall be divided into Sections or Articles and then one or more Maxims within each Article. The major Titles of the Maxims of Criminal Law shall be:

I. Introductory Definitions

II. Self Discipline & Discernment

III. Social Contract & Responsibility

IV. Deterrence against Prohibited (Criminal) Acts

V. Culpability for Prohibited (Criminal) Acts

VI. Punishment for Prohibited (Criminal) Acts

VII. Offences against Stellar System

VIII. Offences against Planet

IX. Offences against Moon

X. Offences against Ecosystem

XI. Offences against Humanity

XII. Offences against Human Life

XIII. Offences against Animal Life

XIV. Offences against Non-Carbon Higher Order Life

XV. Offences against Family

XVI. Offences against Property

XVII. Offences against Public Decency and Public Morals

XVIII. Offences against Public Health and Public Safety

XIX. Offences against Public Justice

XX. Offences against Public Security and Public Order

XXI. Offences against Society

XXII. Offences against Finance and Trade

18. "**Lex Educationis**" being the "**Maxims of Education Law**" represents the primary, one and only true Maxims of Education Law. All and every other laws, claims and agreements of Education Law shall be secondary and inferior to the Maxims of Education Law, *ab initio* (from the beginning). Whenever or however a valid and legitimate reference is written or spoken concerning Education Law, it shall mean *Lex Educationis* and these Maxims of Education Law and no other.

Lex Educationis: Maxims of Education Law

The Maxims of Education Law shall be structured into One Book, that in turn shall be divided into Titles, that in turn shall be divided into Sections or Articles and then one or more Maxims within each Article. The major Titles of the Maxims of Education Law shall be:

I. Introductory Definitions

II. Learning & Development

III. Teaching & Mentoring

IV. Accreditation & Qualification

V. Curriculum & Courses

VI. Faculties & Institutions

VII. Early Learning & Development Systems

VIII. Primary Learning & Foundational Systems

IX. Secondary Learning & Character Systems

X. Tertiary Learning & Specialist Systems

XI. Adult Learning & Skill Systems

19. "**Lex Nutrimens Et Medicina**" being the "**Maxims of Food & Drugs Law**" represents the primary, one and only true Maxims of Food and Drugs Law. All and every other laws, claims and agreements

Lex Nutrimens Et Medicina: Maxims of Food & Drugs Law

of Food and Drugs Law shall be secondary and inferior to the Maxims of Food & Drugs Law, *ab initio* (from the beginning). Whenever or however a valid and legitimate reference is written or spoken concerning Food and Drugs Law, it shall mean *Lex Nutrimens Et Medicina* and these Maxims of Food and Drugs and no other.

The Maxims of Food & Drugs Law shall be structured into One Book, that in turn shall be divided into Titles, that in turn shall be divided into Sections or Articles and then one or more Maxims within each Article. The major Titles of the Maxims of Food & Drugs Law shall be:

I. Introductory Definitions

II. Food

III. Drugs

IV. Agrifacture

V. Artifacture

VI. Standards

20. "**Lex Urbanus**" being the "**Maxims of Urban Law**" represents the primary, one and only true Maxims of Urban Law. All and every other laws, claims and agreements of Urban Law shall be secondary and inferior to the Maxims of Urban Law, *ab initio* (from the beginning). Whenever or however a valid and legitimate reference is written or spoken concerning Urban Law, it shall mean *Lex Urbanus* and these Maxims of Urban Law and no other.

Lex Urbanus: Maxims of Urban Law

The Maxims of Urban Law shall be structured into One Book, that in turn shall be divided into Titles, that in turn shall be divided into Sections or Articles and then one or more Maxims within each Article. The major Titles of the Maxims of Urban Law shall be:

I. Introductory Definitions

II. Building Purpose & Function

III. Places & Buildings

IV. Building Materials

V. Building Systems

VI. Building Risk Conditions

VII. Building Design & Standards

VIII. Building Lifecycle

IX. Urban Community Purpose & Function

X. Urban Infrastructure Systems

XI. Urban Center Design & Standards

XII. Urban Precinct Design & Standards

XIII. Urban Area Design & Standards

XIV. Urban Lifecycle

21. "**Lex Societatis**" being the "**Maxims of Company Law**" represents the primary, one and only true Maxims of Company Law. All and every other laws, claims and agreements of Company Law shall be secondary and inferior to the Maxims of Company Law, *ab initio* (from the beginning). Whenever or however a valid and legitimate reference is written or spoken concerning Company Law, it shall mean *Lex Societatis* and these Maxims of Company Law and no other.

Lex Societatis: Maxims of Company Law

The Maxims of Company Law shall be structured into One Book, that in turn shall be divided into Titles, that in turn shall be divided into Sections or Articles and then one or more Maxims within each Article. The major Titles of the Maxims of Company Law shall be:

I. Introductory Definitions

II. Associations

III. Formation, Registration & Incorporation

IV. Members

V. Directors & Board

VI. Officers & Staff

VII. Meetings, Elections, Voting and Notice

VIII. Registers & Records

IX. Capital, Shares & Funds

X. Structural Change

XI. Audits, Disputes & Liability

XII. Dissolution, Insolvency & Winding

22. "**Lex Technologiae**" being the "**Maxims of Technology Law**" represents the primary, one and only true Maxims of Technology Law. All and every other laws, claims and agreements of Technology Law shall be secondary and inferior to the Maxims of Technology Law, *ab initio* (from the beginning). Whenever or however a valid and legitimate reference is written or spoken concerning Technology Law, it shall mean *Lex Technologiae* and these Maxims of Technology Law and no other.

Lex Technologiae: Maxims of Technology Law

The Maxims of Technology Law shall be structured into One Book, that in turn shall be divided into Titles, that in turn shall be divided into Sections or Articles and then one or more Maxims within each Article. The major Titles of the Maxims of Technology Law shall be:

I. Introductory Definitions

II. Technology Innovation

III. Ucadia Technology (TEKNAS)

23. "**Lex Commercii**" being the "**Maxims of Trade & Intellectual Property Law**" represents the primary, one and only true Maxims of Trade & Intellectual Property Law. All and every other laws, claims and agreements of Trade & Intellectual Property shall be secondary and inferior to the Maxims of Trade & Intellectual Property, *ab initio* (from the beginning). Whenever or however a valid and legitimate reference is written or spoken concerning Trade & Intellectual Property Law, it shall mean *Lex Commercii* and these Maxims of Trade & Intellectual Property Law and no other.

Lex Commercii: Maxims of Trade & Intellectual Property Law

The Maxims of Trade & Intellectual Property Law shall be structured into One Book, that in turn shall be divided into Titles, that in turn shall be divided into Sections or Articles and then one or more Maxims within each Article. The major Titles of the Maxims of Trade & Intellectual Property Law shall be:

I. Introductory Definitions

II. Products

III. Services

IV. Markets

V. Customers

VI. Patents

VII. Patent Disputes & Resolution

VIII. Patent Enforcement & Penalties

IX. Trademarks

X. Trademark Disputes & Resolution

XI. Trademark Enforcement & Penalties

24. "**Lex Securitas**" being the "**Maxims of Security Law**" represents the primary, one and only true Maxims of Security Law. All and every other laws, claims and agreements of Security Law shall be secondary and inferior to the Maxims of Security Law, *ab initio* (from the beginning). Whenever or however a valid and legitimate reference is written or spoken concerning Security Law, it shall mean *Lex*

Lex Securitas: Maxims of Security Law

Securitas and these Maxims of Security Law and no other.

The Maxims of Security Law, shall be structured into One Book, that in turn shall be divided into Titles, that in turn shall be divided into Sections or Articles and then one or more Maxims within each Article. The major Titles of the Maxims of Security Law shall be:

I. Introductory Definitions

II. Information, Intelligence & Planning

III. Planetary Security

IV. National Security

V. National Security Organisation & Operation

VI. Regional Security

VII. Local Security

VIII. Emergencies & Disasters

IX. State of Emergency

X. Emergency Organisation & Operation

XI. Emergency Response & Relief

XII. Emergency Reconstruction & Restoration

25. "**Lex Militaris**" being the "**Maxims of Military Law**" represents the primary, one and only true Maxims of Military Law. All and every other laws, claims and agreements of Military Law shall be secondary and inferior to the Maxims of Military Law, *ab initio* (from the beginning). Whenever or however a valid and legitimate reference is written or spoken concerning Military Law, it shall mean *Lex Militaris* and these Maxims of Military Law and no other.

Lex Militaris: Maxims of Military Law

The Maxims of Military Law shall be structured into One Book, that in turn shall be divided into Titles, that in turn shall be divided into Sections or Articles and then one or more Maxims within each Article. The major Titles of the Maxims of Military Law shall be:

I. Introductory Definitions

II. Military Standards and Principles

III. Military Organisation & Administration

IV. Military Strategy

V. Military Logistics

VI. Military Operations

VII. Military Orders

VIII. Military Justice

IX. Military Offences

26. "**Lex Gentium**" being the "**Maxims of International Law**" represents the primary, one and only true Maxims of International Law. All and every other laws, claims and agreements of International Law shall be secondary and inferior to the Maxims of International Law, *ab initio* (from the beginning). Whenever or however a valid and legitimate reference is written or spoken concerning International Law or the Law of Nations, it shall mean *Lex Gentium* and these Maxims of International Law and no other.

Lex Gentium: Maxims of International Law

The Maxims of International Law shall be structured into One Book, that in turn shall be divided into Titles, that in turn shall be divided into Sections or Articles and then one or more Maxims within each Article. The major Titles of the Maxims of International Law shall be:

I. Introductory Definitions

II. National Sovereignty

III. International Rights

IV. International Jurisdiction

V. Treaties and Conventions

VI. Regional Unions

VII. Global Unions

VIII. Global Economic Systems

IX. Global Judicial Systems

X. Global Security Systems

Article 136 – Voluntatem Et Testamentum (Will and Testament)

1. **Will and Testament** is the embodiment of the universal right of all competent men and women to express their Free Will and Choice by nominating how they intend their rights, trusts, estates, funds, assets and property to be managed in the event of ill health, or disablement and eventual death; and the right for others so nominated as beneficiaries, to enjoy the inheritance of such rights, trusts, estates, funds, assets and property bequeathed to them.

Voluntatem Et Testamentum (Will and Testament)

A properly formed Will and Testament is a formal oral and/or written testimony and trust agreement creating a present and/or future trust, whereby a competent man or woman through their person expresses their true intention and volition regarding the inventory of their accumulative rights, trusts, estates, funds, assets and property; the disposition of such rights, trusts, estates, funds, assets and property; and the disposal or use and management of such rights, trusts, estates, funds, assets and property upon the physical death of the man or woman.

2. In relation to the requirements of a valid Will:

Requirements of a valid Will and Testament

(i) There exist certain customary rules and traditions concerning the formation of valid and legitimate Wills and Testaments. These are defined as the Customary Elements of a valid Will and Testament; and

(ii) As a Will and Testament always pertains in part to certain rights, or trusts, or estates, or funds, or assets or property registered within one or more jurisdictions, what constitutes a valid and legitimate Will and Testament must always be determined to some degree by the various laws of each jurisdiction; and

(iii) If a Will is to have certain conditions effective during the life of the Trustor and Testator, then the Will and Testament instrument must make such specific conditions, particularly in relation to any powers of attorney or conditions to be followed in the event of disability, palliative care and other impairment or Inter Vivos Trust; and

(iv) Generally, if a Will and Testament invokes on one or more immoral, repugnant or illegal acts to the relevant jurisdiction, then the entirety of the instrument is in jeopardy unless the instrument enables the clear severability of such clauses; and

(v) The absence of a right, or thing expressed within the Will and Testament therefore favours the jurisdiction where the Will and Testament is to be validated; and

(vi) A Will and Testament that makes a claim of certain rights, or trusts, or estates, or funds, or assets, or property not legitimately in its possession, or morally and lawfully the possession of another, causes the entirety of the Will and Testament to be null and void as if it never existed; and

(vii) A Will and Testament that makes scandalous claims for certain rights, or trusts, or estates, or funds, or assets, or property that the man or woman or person are not entitled, causes the entirety of the Will and Testament to be null and void as if it never existed.

3. The following are the seventeen (17) standard elements traditionally included within a valid Will and Testament in accord to the norms of Civilised Society under Rule of Law, Justice and Due Process being: Aetatem Validam, Verba Mea, Vocem Meam, Animus Testandi, Compos Mentis, Incipit, Quod Vocatur, Recitatio, Iura Habeam, Titulum Habeam, Executorem Meum, Funeris Meum, Memoriam Meum, Regulis Bona, Operibus Bonis, Decretio and Testificatio: Customary Elements of a valid Will and Testament

(i) "**Aetatem Validam**" ("the right/legitimate age") means the one making the Will and Testament known as the "Testator" formally acknowledges they are of the minimum age accepted for the completion and pronouncement of such an important instrument; and

(ii) "**Verba Mea**" ("in my own words") means the Testator formally acknowledges the Will is a true representation of their intention, free from threat, intimidation, duress or promise; and

(iii) "**Vocem Meam**" ("my (own) voice") means the Testator formally acknowledges the Testament is literally "their own voice" and a true representation of their intention and is spoken free from threat, intimidation, duress or promise; and

(iv) "**Animus Testandi**" ("the intention to testify") means the Testator formally acknowledges that he/she fully intends the instrument and/or any vocalisation to be known as their valid Will and Testament and is capable of demonstrating such competent intention; and

(v) "**Compos Mentis**" ("of sound mind") means the Testator formally acknowledges he/she is of sound mind, capable of reason and moral judgement and therefore capable of not only making decisions but capable of perceiving the consequences of such decisions or actions; and

(vi) "**Incipit**" ("it begins") means the opening prayer and petition of a sacred instrument between heaven and earth and by tradition the first words of any sacred covenant; and

(vii) "**Quod Vocatur**" ("that which is called/named") means the name of the instrument (e.g. *Voluntatem Et Testamentum* as the prescribed form of a valid Will and Testament under One Heaven); and

(viii) "**Recitatio**" ("recitation, reading, pronouncement") means the statements and terms of the Will and Testament; and

(ix) "**Iura Habeam**" ("I have Rights") means the Testator expresses and asserts their Rights, Powers and Authority, particularly to possess, own and hold certain title, property and uses; and

(x) "**Titulum Habeam**" ("I have title") means the Testator expresses and asserts the description of records, certificates, registers or ledgers and one or more titles of possession, ownership and use in accord with the Rights, Powers and Authority previously expressed; and

(xi) "**Executorem Meum**" ("my (general) executor") means the Testator nominates at least one executor to be granted the power and authority by the testator to administer their various estates (living and/or deceased) upon some significant event that causes the executor to be appointed (such as physical death or formal investiture in the case of living estates); and

(xii) "**Funeris Meum**" ("my funeral") means the Testator nominates the essential arrangements of their own funeral service; and

(xiii) "**Memoriam Meum**" ("my memorial") means the Testator nominates how he or she wishes his or her memory to be honoured in monument and epitaph; and

(xiv) "**Regulis Bona**" ("good rules (of estate)") means the Testator expresses the specific rules of proper administration of the Estate; and

(xv) "**Operibus Bonis**" ("good works (of estate)") means the Testator names one or more Beneficiaries who are granted the Rights to use certain property of the estate as a sign of charitable and good works; and

(xvi) "**Decretio**" ("decree, decision, judgement, resolution, principle") means a formal statement at the end of the Will and Testament by the Testator that the instrument had been handed (delivered) to become public notice also known as "patenting". Thus the phrase "IN WITNESS WHEREOF, We have hereunto set Our hand and seal, and caused these, Our Letters, to be made Patent" with patent meaning public notice; and

(xvii) "**Testificatio**" ("attestation, proof") means a formal attestation at the very end of the Will and Testament which may also include separate written attestation by two (2) or more witnesses that it is the wishes and intentions of the Testator reflected in the Will and Testament through the Latin phrase (by tradition since the 8th Century) beginning with "*Teste me ipso apud*" <> then the date in Latin meaning "Witness myself at the place <> date".

Voluntatem Et Testamentum

4. All men and women who have acknowledged in good faith, good actions and good conscience their True Trust in the Office of Man or Office of Woman have the Absolute Natural Right known as *Ius Naturale Testamentum* to make, ordain, publish and pronounce their Will and Testament. Any rule, law or edict that seeks to deny, obstruct, weaken or obfuscate such right is automatically null and void from the beginning and cannot be law.

The present covenant recognises the prescribed form known as the *Voluntatem Et Testamentum* as the specific form by which a member of One Heaven holding either the Office of Man or Office of Woman perfects their Will and Testament in accord with the present sacred Covenant and the Rights and Obligations prescribed herein.

The Will and Testament through the form of *Voluntatem Et Testamentum* is to the personality (person) of a Superior Estate, the physical mind and the will of the person and the will of all legal persons derived from the existence of the man or woman. It is both a sacred prayer and sacred scripture to be respected and honoured by all persons who claim an office by sacred Oath or Vow. It is also a sacred Covenant and bond between a man or woman in whose name the Will and Testament exists and the Divine Creator. It is an unbreakable covenant by the man or woman who is the grantor or testator.

When such a Will and Testament bears witness to the Covenant of One Heaven and the Maxims of Law of One Heaven through the form of *Voluntatem Et Testamentum*, then: It is the most solemn, most sacred Covenant in history; and It is an unbreakable bond between heaven and earth and no power, no force, no spirit, no corporation, no person or entity can break that bond; and no power exists in heaven that can break such a sacred bond. One gives existence and credence to the other. Such a valid Will and Testament and the present Covenant of One Heaven are two parts, the lock and key, that when united cannot be broken.

However, where a man or woman claiming either the Office of Man or Office of Woman deliberately and willingly repudiates some or all of the present sacred Covenant; or asserts one or more Prohibited Rights for their own advantage then any such associated Will and Testament and associated estate and trust documents, whether or not such prescribed form as *Voluntatem Et Testamentum* are used, therefore has no basis of covenant, or bond with One Heaven or the present sacred Covenant.

Article 137 - Testamentum Lucis (Testament of Light)

1. **Testamentum Lucis (Testament of Light)** shall be a *New Testament* and Will of the Spirit in their capacity, authority and power, as the Bringer of Light, consistent with Article 21 (*Great Spirits & Deities*), Article 22 (*Angels, Demons, Saints & Leaders*) and Article 52 (*Treaty of Angels, Saints and Demons*) of the present most sacred Covenant, revoking all prior *Old Testaments*, Will and Codicils, comprised of ten (10) mandates and sixty-six (66) articles. Testamentum Lucis (Testament of Light)

2. *Testamentum Lucis* is born of the old world yet intrinsic to the peaceful and complete transition to the new world of Ucadia. Whilst it is born of the old world, it carries within it the solemn obligations to honour and protect the fundamental principles and prophecies of Ucadia; and not to weaken, harm, negate, corrupt, or impede Ucadia, as it is firmly bound to the present sacred Covenant. Nature and Character of Testamentum Lucis and Ucadia

   Testamentum Lucis is a bridge between worlds and a means of peaceful transition to the new world of Ucadia. Without its existence, the nihilistic chaos would reign unimpeded.

3. The effect of *Testamentum Lucis* shall be the definition and formation of the following trusts, personalities and bodies, consistent with the present sacred Covenant:- Effect of Testamentum Lucis

   (i) Trust of Light; and

   (ii) Personality of Light; and

   (iii) Society of Light.

4. The enemies of the brothers and sisters of Light are not the sons and daughters of Darkness, but those who cling to power as conservatives or liberals, yet believe in nothing but power itself. These beings are nihilists and are first and foremost the enemy of the brothers and sisters of Light, for they carry an infection of mind capable of dooming the entirety of human civilisation. Enemies of Light

   Those that seek physical immortality at all costs in defiance of the laws of Heaven and Nature; and those who believe themselves to truly be "gods" amongst animals; and those that would use technology and knowledge to try and destroy all life on earth are the most dangerous of all living beings to the future survival and prosperity of life. It is the solemn mission of all brothers and sisters of Light that such beings are held to account for their actions.

5. The articles and clauses of *Testamentum Lucis* shall be firmly bound by the following limits, consistent with the present sacred Covenant:- Articles and Clauses of Testamentum Lucis

(i) No article or clause shall in any way contradict, usurp, abrogate, alienate, diminish, alter or impede any founding or moral principle as defined herein; and

(ii) No article or clause shall in any way contradict, usurp, abrogate, alienate, diminish, alter or impede any valid and proper Right defined herein.

Article 138 - Testamentum Noctis (Testament of Darkness)

1. **Testamentum Noctis (Testament of Darkness)** shall be the *New Testament* and Will of the Spirit in their capacity, authority and power, as the Hidden One and Lord of Hosts, consistent with Article 21 (*Great Spirits & Deities*), Article 22 (*Angels, Demons, Saints & Leaders*) and Article 52 (*Treaty of Angels, Saints and Demons*) of the present most sacred Covenant, revoking all prior *Old Testaments*, Will and Codicils, comprised of ten (10) commandments and eighty-six (86) articles. Testamentum Noctis (Testament of Darkness)

2. *Testamentum Noctis* is born of the old world yet intrinsic to the peaceful and complete transition to the new world of Ucadia. Whilst it is born of the old world, it carries within it the solemn obligations to honour and protect the fundamental principles and prophecies of Ucadia; and not to weaken, harm, negate, corrupt, or impede Ucadia, as it is firmly bound to the present sacred Covenant. Nature and Character of Testamentum Noctis and Ucadia

Testamentum Noctis is a bridge between worlds and a means of peaceful transition to the new world of Ucadia. Without its existence, nihilistic chaos would consume and destroy not only itself, but potentially all life on planet Earth.

3. The effect of *Testamentum Noctis* shall be the definition and formation of the following elements, consistent with the present sacred Covenant:- Effect of Testamentum Noctis

(i) Trust of Truth; and

(ii) Personality of Truth; and

(iii) Society of Truth.

4. The enemies of the sons and daughters of Darkness are not the brothers and sisters of Light, but those who willingly and ignorantly cling to power as conservatives or liberals, yet believe in nothing but power itself. These beings are nihilists and are first and foremost the enemy of the sons and daughters of Darkness, for they carry an Enemies of Darkness

infection of mind capable of dooming the entirety of human civilisation.

Those that seek physical immortality at all costs in defiance of the laws of Heaven and Nature; and those who believe themselves to truly be "gods" amongst animals; and those that would use technology and knowledge to try and destroy all life on earth are the most dangerous of all living beings to the future survival and prosperity of life. It is the solemn mission of all sons and daughters of Darkness that such beings are held to account for their actions.

5. The articles and clauses of *Testamentum Noctis* shall be firmly bound by the following limits, consistent with the present sacred Covenant:- Articles and Clauses of Testamentum Noctis

(i) No article or clause shall in any way contradict, usurp, abrogate, alienate, diminish, alter or impede any founding or moral principle as defined herein; and

(ii) No article or clause shall in any way contradict, usurp, abrogate, alienate, diminish, alter or impede any valid and proper Right defined herein.

Article 139 - Great Conclave of One Heaven

1. **By the present sacred Covenant, the Supreme Councils of One-Christ, One-Islam and One-Spirit** are hereby authorised to forge a formal set of protocols and standards regarding the function of the Great Conclave which relates to the detailed definition and requirements of operational procedure and function necessitated by the institution. These shall be known as the Protocols and Standards of the Great Conclave of One Heaven. Protocols and Standards of the Great Conclave of One Heaven

These standards themselves must embody and be consistent with the specific articles of this Covenant and in turn must be approved by a majority vote of all delegates attending the first Great Conclave.

In terms of the major subject matter dealt with by the Protocols and Standards of the Great Conclave of One Heaven, the following areas must specifically provide detail and procedures consistent with the present sacred Covenant:

(i) That a formal set of procedures exists for the opening ceremony of the Great Conclave including the welcome entrance and blessings of the Supreme Patriarch, Caliph and Recurrence; and

(ii) That a formal set of procedures exist for the various sessions of voting including methods to resolve dead-locks during the process to ensure no matters are permitted to be unresolved;

and

(iii) That the length of a Great Conclave may not exceed forty (40) days.

2. In Accordance with Article 59 (Oratorium) of this most sacred Covenant, the powers and authority of the One Heaven Supreme Court shall be vested in the Great Conclave for a maximum of forty (40) days every one hundred and twenty-eight (128) years.

The Powers of the One Heaven Supreme Court conferred upon judgements and rulings during Great Conclave

Therefore any and all judgements and rulings determined by the Great Conclave shall carry the full weight and authority of the One Heaven Supreme Court in accordance with the article of this Covenant.

3. The procedures for the convocation and function of a Great Conclave shall be defined by the "**Official Procedures for Great Conclave**" as defined and agreed between the three (3) Great Faiths and Ucadia.

Procedures of Great Conclave

Article 140 - Supervisor

1. A **Supervisor** shall be an ordained and consecrated member of a clergy, entrusted to a leading spirtual position. The Office of Supervisor is one of the fourteen (14) Superior Ecclesiastical Offices of the Four Hundred and Thirty-Two (432) Great Offices of One Heaven.

Supervisor

A "**Supervisor**" by definition must be one who possesses the character of Consecration as a Cleric. Furthermore, a Supervisor must possess the strength and dignity of one living and exemplified under sacred Oath and Vows of a Mendicant.

All procedures including (but not limited to) the commission, obligations, authority, powers, function, standards, qualifications, honours, dignities, conduct, accountabilities, grades, benefits, legacies, term, investiture, enrolment, certification, review, audit, censure, sanction or cessation of the Office of Supervisor shall be defined by the present sacred Covenant and associated rules and covenants including, but not limited to *Pactum De Singularis Christus* (Covenant of One Christ), *Pactum De Singularis Islam* (Covenant of One Islam) and *Pactum De Singularis Spiritus* (Covenant of One Spirit).

Article 141 - Minister

1. A **Minister** shall be one versed and skilled in discernment of law to qualify as a competent arbitrator and scholar of legal matters. The Office of Minister is one of the fourteen (14) Superior Ecclesiastical Offices of the Four Hundred and Thirty-Two (432) Great Offices of One Heaven.

Minister

All procedures including (but not limited to) the commission, obligations, authority, powers, function, standards, qualifications, honours, dignities, conduct, accountabilities, grades, benefits, legacies, term, investiture, enrolment, certification, review, audit, censure, sanction or cessation of the Office of Minister shall be defined by the present Covenant and associated rules and covenants including, but not limited to *Pactum De Singularis Christus* (Covenant of One Christ), *Pactum De Singularis Islam* (Covenant of One Islam) and *Pactum De Singularis Spiritus* (Covenant of One Spirit).

Article 142 - Mendicant

1. A **Mendicant** shall be one who practices a life of spirituality, self-development, and material austerity through a vow of detachment to renunciation, to personal ownership and overt use of temporal possessions. The Office of Mendicant is one of the fourteen (14) Superior Ecclesiastical Offices of the Four Hundred and Thirty-Two (432) Great Offices of One Heaven. Mendicant

All procedures including (but not limited to) the commission, obligations, authority, powers, function, standards, qualifications, honours, dignities, conduct, accountabilities, grades, benefits, legacies, term, investiture, enrolment, certification, review, audit, censure, sanction or cessation of the Office of Mendicant shall be defined by the present Covenant and associated rules and covenants including, but not limited to *Pactum De Singularis Christus* (Covenant of One Christ), *Pactum De Singularis Islam* (Covenant of One Islam) and *Pactum De Singularis Spiritus* (Covenant of One Spirit).

Article 143 - Cleric

1. A **Cleric** shall be one versed, skilled, competent and capable of ordained formal religious services. A Cleric by definition, is one properly consecrated in accord with the present sacred Covenant. The Office of Cleric is one of the fourteen (14) Superior Ecclesiastical Offices of the Four Hundred and Thirty-Two (432) Great Offices of One Heaven. Cleric

All procedures including (but not limited to) the commission, obligations, authority, powers, function, standards, qualifications, honours, dignities, conduct, accountabilities, grades, benefits, legacies, term, investiture, enrolment, certification, review, audit, censure, sanction or cessation of the Office of Cleric shall be defined by the present Covenant and associated rules and covenants including, but not limited to *Pactum De Singularis Christus* (Covenant of One Christ), *Pactum De Singularis Islam* (Covenant of One Islam) and

Pactum De Singularis Spiritus (Covenant of One Spirit).

2. All skilled, competent and capable persons of ordained formal religious services shall be firstly known as Clerics, consistent with the present sacred Covenant, before any other title of honour of particular religious doctrine:

Function of Cleric

(i) Every member of the Traditions of Christianity or Judaism, united as One Christ, receiving the Foundational Sacrament of Sanctification & Rite of Consecration (Ritus Sacramentum Consecratio), shall be known as a Cleric. No person may administer or dispense any Foundational Sacraments in the name of the Ecclesia of One Christ, without first the Consecrated Character of Cleric. No person may function in a delegated or ordinary position, without first the Consecrated Character of Cleric; and

(ii) Every member of the Traditions of Islam, united as One Islam, receiving the Foundational Sacrament of Sanctification & Rite of Consecration (Ritus Sacramentum Consecratio), shall be known as a Cleric and an Imam. No person may administer or dispense any Foundational Sacraments in the name of One Islam, without first the Consecrated Character of Cleric as an Imam. No person may function in a delegated or ordinary position, without first the Consecrated Character of Cleric as an Imam; and

(iii) Every member of the Traditions of Hinduism, Buddhism, Confucianism, Taoism, Sikhism, Jainism and traditional indigenous faiths, united as One Spirit, receiving the Foundational Sacred Gift of Consecration (Ritus Sacramentum Consecratio), shall be known as a Cleric. No person may administer or dispense any Sacred Gifts in the ordinary manner and name of the Sacred Society of One Spirit, without first the Consecrated Character of Cleric. No person may function in a delegated or ordinary position, without first the Consecrated Character of Cleric.

OBSIGNATUM (ENACTMENT)

Article 144 - Obsignatum

1. **THE HIGHEST CONCORDING PARTIES** in recognition and witness to the validity of the most sacred Covenant, *The Treaty of Ucadia* as defined by Article 17, *The Treaty of the Galaxies* as defined by Article 18, *The Treaty of the Divine Masculine* as defined by Article 49, *The Treaty of the Divine Feminine* as defined by Article 50, *The Treaty of the Divine Messengers* as defined by Article 51, *The Treaty of Angels, Saints and Demons* as defined by Article 52, *The Treaty of the Spirit States* as defined by Article 53, *The Treaty of the Suns* as defined by Article 54 and *The Treaty of the Planets and Moons* as defined by Article 55 with one another Agree to this most sacred Covenant known as *Pactum De Singularis Caelum*. Obsignatum

In recognition of our absolute united pledge to the present sacred Covenant and the proposition of a United Heaven, we do hereby bestow our authority including all instruments of power and all claims of authority unto the Holy Covenant of One Heaven and to the proper authority and structure of associated valid Societies.

No instrument, document, covenant, promise, constitution or agreement of any kind shall be higher or have greater authority and power in Heaven, or the Earth or Solar System or Milky Way Galaxy or The Universe than the present most sacred Covenant.

No position, person, being, blood right, divine right, revelation, dream, vision, spiritual or temporal being may claim higher or have greater authority and power in Heaven, or the Earth or Solar System or Milky Way Galaxy or The Universe than the authority and power as granted through the present most sacred Covenant.

No claim to the contrary by any temporal body, no matter what year of formation shall counter this solemn and irrevocable pledge and transference of power. Furthermore, that all claims of power and authority by temporal authorities to speak for or act on behalf of the Divine Creator, Great Spirits, Angels or Saints or Demons is immediately rescinded, and reserved for this most sacred Covenant and those institutions directly formed and named by this document.

2. Let it be known to All, now and forever, that upon the Election of one hundred and forty-four (144) Deities as the First Unique Collective Awareness of Divine Mind and Executive Government of One Heaven for the next three thousand two hundred and ten (3,210) years at the First Supreme Conclave, the present most sacred Covenant was unanimously ratified in Heaven at the first session of the Convention of the Supreme Conclave on GAIA E8:Y3209:A1:S1:M6:D1, also known as [Monday, 21 Dec 2009]. Ratification of Covenant in Heaven

3. Let it be known to All, now and forever, that the ratification of the present Covenant within the dimension and reality of the one and only Universe of all Existence shall occur upon the first formation of registered, approved, valid, legitimate and proper Ucadia Foundations within the bounds of Ucadia Universities by Living Level 6 Higher Order Beings; and the assenting of written Resolutions upon their formation acknowledging the ultimate and highest supreme authority of the present most sacred Covenant thereby forming a unique sacred covenant between Heaven and the Universe. Ratification of Covenant in Universe

Each and every subsequent valid and legitimate signed, sealed and recorded Resolution upon the formation of Ucadia Foundations shall hereby be recognised as a new and unique, solemn sacred covenant between Heaven and the Universe in its own right.

4. Let it be known to All, now and forever, that the ratification of the present Covenant within the dimension and reality of the one and only Universe of all Existence shall occur upon the first valid and legitimate signing, sealing and publishing of a Will and Testament (*Voluntatem Et Testamentum*) according to the prescribed form, as defined within the present most sacred Covenant, whereby a Level 6 Higher Order Being recognises their divinity and the ultimate and highest supreme authority of the present Covenant, thereby forming a unique sacred covenant between Heaven and the Universe. Ratification of Covenant in Universe with Life and Humanity

Each and every subsequent valid and legitimate signed, sealed and published Will and Testament (*Voluntatem Et Testamentum*) is hereby recognised as a new and unique sacred covenant in its own right.

5. Let these Divine Words be sealed so that no being, nor spirit, nor force may harm or hinder the intent and meaning of the present most sacred Covenant. Seal Prayer

Let these Divine Words be sealed so that no being, nor spirit, nor force may misuse, mistake or misclaim the intent and meaning of the present most sacred Covenant.

Protect this most sacred Covenant always from any threat and ensure its accurate preservation.

Bless all who read the present most sacred Covenant and who bear witness to its truth and accuracy and authority.

Bless all forms of life and all beings and all spirits and consciousness everywhere so that all may find meaning, purpose, respect and dignity within the present most sacred Covenant.

As It Is Written, So Let It Be.

www.ingramcontent.com/pod-product-compliance
Lightning Source LLC
LaVergne TN
LVHW072313210926
848482LV00021B/228

* 9 7 8 1 6 4 4 1 9 0 1 9 7 *